Thomas Warren Field

An Essay towards an Indian Bibliography

Thomas Warren Field

An Essay towards an Indian Bibliography

ISBN/EAN: 9783741197789

Manufactured in Europe, USA, Canada, Australia, Japa

Cover: Foto ©Thomas Meinert / pixelio.de

Manufactured and distributed by brebook publishing software
(www.brebook.com)

Thomas Warren Field

An Essay towards an Indian Bibliography

AN ESSAY

TOWARDS AN

INDIAN BIBLIOGRAPHY.

BEING A

CATALOGUE OF BOOKS,

RELATING TO THE

HISTORY, ANTIQUITIES, LANGUAGES, CUSTOMS, RELIGION, WARS, LITERATURE, AND ORIGIN OF THE

AMERICAN INDIANS,

IN THE LIBRARY OF

THOMAS W. FIELD.

WITH BIBLIOGRAPHICAL AND HISTORICAL NOTES, AND SYNOPSES OF THE CONTENTS OF SOME OF THE WORKS LEAST KNOWN.

NEW YORK:
SCRIBNER, ARMSTRONG, AND CO.
1873.

PREFACE.

EVERY book is more or less a confession of egotism, but when the work contains little beside a schedule of the author's personal property, it needs something more than the usual prefatory apology, for his exculpation. Few readers will be interested in his plea for condonement of his offense, and fewer still will care to learn, that his work had its origin, in motives more honorable than ostentatious display.

A general catalogue of works illustrative of the history, literature, and archæology of the Aborigines of both Americas, had been in progress of composition for several years, as a guide to the author's collection of that class of books. As it grew in proportions, by the slow accretions which study and experience furnished, the author's vanity was easily flattered into the design of producing a work of more general utility. The material collected at length covered so wide a range, that it embraced not only transcripts of the titles of such printed works as were personally examined, or were to be found in catalogues of public and private libraries, with a collation of their pages, and synopses of their contents, but also the titles of articles upon the same subjects, printed in reviews, historical collections, magazines, and other ephemera. More than two thousand five hundred separate works, and twelve hundred essays, had been catalogued, with their topical range noted, before the vast extent of the unexplored territory to be examined, began to exhibit some of its formidable proportions. It was plainly demonstrated, that the projected task must be either abandoned or greatly abridged. That portion of the task which could be most readily detached and wrought into unity, was the catalogue of works on the American Aborigines, in the author's possession. To determine the selection of works which should be included in that category, they have been subjected to a few simple rules of classification.

All works which purported in their titles to contain historic, narrative, or literary material, relating to the American Indians.

Books in which any distinct portion, chapter, or appendix claimed by its heading, or table of contents to be devoted to that subject.

Works containing engravings, illustrative of the manners and peculiarities of the aborigines, when derived from actual observation.

All treatises, or essays, upon their origin, or the pre-Columbian discovery of America, as affecting the source of its population.

Those works of fiction or poetry founded on Indian life, to which were appended historical notes, incidents of personal experience, or traditions and legends, of the Indians.

All works containing grammatical analyses, or vocabularies of their language, as well as translations, into or from them, would of course form a part of the collection.

In a limited number of cases, marked with a star (*), books not actually in the author's collection have been admitted to the catalogue. This exceptional adoption has been made to complete the bibliographical history of those series of works of which the library contained only a portion, and thus afford the collector a full view of such treatises as complete any section of the subject.

In a few cases, the titles have been much abbreviated, but only when they formed a complete table of contents to the work, or a feeble prolixity of matters foreign to the subject of the catalogue.

Indian Bibliography.

ABBILDUNG.
Nordamericanischer. Lander und Eingebohrner Wilden dabey die Erd-Beschreybung und Natur Seltenheiten der dortigen Gegenden, auch die son derbahren Gebrauche des Landes Einwohner, die Handlung, Policey and Regiments. Verfassung .... Erfurt. *Folding plate, pp.* xii + 360. *J. H. Nonnens.* 1787. 1

[A picture of North America and the Aboriginal Savages inhabiting it.] The viiith Atheilung is entitled: "Of the North American Wildmen" (Indians), and occupies pp. 220–262. The folding plate has in the foreground a view of a battle between two tribes of savages.

ABBOTT (John S. C.)
History of King Philip (Sovereign Chief of the Wampanoags). Including the early history of the Settlers of New England. *With engravings.* 12° 410 *pp.* *New York*, 1857. 2

Frontispiece, Engraved Title, Full Title, Contents, Table of Illustrations, each 1 leaf; pages 13 to 410 including eleven engravings with reverse of each blank.

ABBOTT (Jacob).
American History, by Jacob Abbott, illustrated with numerous maps and engravings. Vol. I. Aboriginal America. 12° *New York*, n. d. (1860.) 3

ABERT (J. W.)
Report of the Secretary of War communicating in answer to a resolution of the Senate, a Report and Map of the Examination of New Mexico, made by Lieutenant J. W. Abert. 8° 132 *pp. Map and 23 plates. Washington*, 1848. 4

The accounts of the author's visits to the Pueblos or fortified Indian villages of Northern Mexico, with several portraits of the chiefs and their families, form the principal interest of this volume.

ABSARAKA.
See Carrington, M. J. 5

ACCOUNT
Of the proceedings of the Illinois and Ouabache Land Companies. See Smith, William. 6

ACCOUNTS
Of Two Attempts towards the Civilization of Some Indian Natives. 8° *London*, n. d. (1806.) 7

ACOSTA (Joseph).

The | Natural and | Morall Historie of the East | and | West Indies. | Intreating of the remarkable things of Heaven; of the Elements, Mettalls, Plants and Beasts which are pro | per to that Country. Together with the Manners, | Ceremonies, Lawes, Governments and Warres of | the Indians. | Written in Spanish by Ioseph Acosta and translated | into English by E. G. | 4° 3 *prel. pp.* + 590 + (xiv.) *London, Printed by Val: Sims for Edward Blount and William Aspley*, 1604. 8

Father Acosta, a native of Medina del Campo, entered the Society of Jesus at the age of fourteen, and in 1571 when thirty-one years old, became the deputy provincial of Peru. He died at Salamanca in 1600, having passed the greater part of the intervening years in America. His work has been justly esteemed for its intrinsic merit, indubitable evidence of which is found in the fact that it has been translated into almost every language of Europe having a literature. Books V., VI., and VII. pp. 327 to 590, are entirely devoted to a relation of the history, customs and *warres* of the Indians. This portion of the work is replete with the most curious details of the Aborigines, before their peculiar customs had become modified by contact with the whites. Although he was one of the earliest, yet he was one of the most curious and accurate observers of the customs and peculiarities of the Aborigines who have attempted to describe them. Scarcely a trait which has excited the attention of the historian or the narrator in the three centuries which have elapsed, has escaped his observation and description. Perfect copies of the English edition are quite rare, but the others are often sold at very low rates.

ACOSTA (Joseph de).

Iosephi | Acosta | societatis | Iesv | de Natvra Novi Orbis | libri duo | . Et | De Promvlgatione | evangelii apud | Barbaros | sine | de pro cvranda Indorvm | salute Libri Sex. | Coloniae Agrippinae, In officiana Birckmannica, Sumptibus Arnoldi Mylii 1596. Cum gratia, & Priuilegio S. Cas Maiest. 12° xvi. *prelim. pp.* + 581. 9

["Joseph Acosta of the Society of Jesus. Natural History of the New World, in two books, And of the Promulgation of the Gospel among the Savages; with the method of securing the salvation of the Indians; In Six Books."]

This is an entirely distinct work from the *Historia Natural* printed at Sevilla in 1590, and translated into almost every language of Europe. Books one and two were subsequently enlarged to the *Natural History*, but at page 99 the title "De Procuranda Salute Indorum" announces another work which has never been printed in English. All the remainder of the volume is devoted to a description of the methods by which the Indians of the New World were to be brought into the dominion of the Christian Church. All the difficulties are investigated. Their idolatries, their superstitions, their rites, their customs, their love of warfare, and the chase, their licentiousness, and their savage habits, are all described, and the various means by which the rites of the Christian discipline can be made to control them discussed. Pinelo claims that this portion of Acosta's work was taken from the MSS. of a Dominican monk named Diego Duran. This is the second edition, the first having been printed at Salamanca the year previous. The six books relating to the Indians are divided into 130 chapters with subject headings.

ACUGNA (C. de'.)

Voyages and Discoveries in South-America. The First up the River of Amazons to Quito in Peru, and back again to Brazil, perform'd at the Command of the King of Spain. By Christopher D'Acugna. The Second up the River of Plata, and thence by Land to the Mines of Potosi. By Mons. Acarete. The Third from Cayenne into Guiana, in Search of the Lake of Parima; reputed the richest Place in the World. By M. Grillet and Bechamel. Done into English from the Originals, being the only Accounts of those Parts hitherto extant. *The whole illustrated with Notes and Maps.* 8° *pp.* viii. + 190 + *2d title and pp.* 79 + *3d title and pp.* ii. + 68 + 2 *maps. London*, 1698. 10

Chapters xxvi. to xliii. of Acugna's Relation, and almost all of that of Fathers Grillet and Bechamel are devoted to descriptions of the peculiarities of the Indian tribes they encountered. Their narratives possess a greater interest from being made by the first Europeans who traversed these regions, and penetrated to the territories of the Indian nations, the Arragoues and Nouragones.

ADAIR (James).

The History of the American Indians; particularly those nations adjoining to the Mississippi, East and West Florida, Georgia, South and North Carolina, and Virginia. Containing an account of their Origin, Language, Manners, Religious and Civil Customs, Laws, Form of Government, Punishments, Conduct in War and Domestic Life, their Habits, Diet, Agriculture, Manufactures, Diseases, and Method of Cure, and other Particulars sufficient to render it A Complete Indian System [*etc.* 10 *lines.*] By James Adair, a Trader with the Indians, and resident of their country for forty years. 4° *pp.* x. + 464. *Map. London*, 1775. 11

Although it cannot be claimed for this author that he ranked first in priority of time, his name is first on our alphabetical register of a great number of writers whose imagination has been struck by the astonishing coincidence of many particulars of the customs and religious rites of some of the American Nations with those of the Jews. The relations of an intelligent observer (as this Indian trader seems to have been), for so long a period as forty years, of the peculiarities of the Southern Indians, among whom he resided for that period, is not without great value; although we should have reason to hold it in still greater esteem, had the author cherished no favorite dogma to establish, or detested any which he wished to destroy.

ADAMS (   ).

Speech of Mr. Adams of Mississippi, on the Bill to remove the Indians West of the Mississippi. Delivered in the Senate of the United States, April, 1830. 8° *pp.* 31. *Washington, printed by Duff Green*, 1830. 12

ADAMS (Amos).

A Concise, Historical View of the Difficulties, Hardships, and Perils which attended the Planting and progressive Improvements of New-England, with A particular Account of its Long and Destructive Wars, Expensive Expeditions, &c. By Amos Adams, A. M. Pastor of the First Church of Roxbury. [*Motto 6 lines.*] *Boston, printed. London, reprinted for Edward and Charles Dilly, in the Poultry,* 1770. 8° *Half title and title 2 leaves + pp.* 1 to 68. 13

ADELUNG (J. C. and VATER, J. S).

Mithradetes oder allgemeine Sprach enkunde mit dem Vater Unser als Sprachprobe in beynahe funfhundert Sprachen und Mundarten von Johann Christoph Adelung Hofrath und Ober-Bibliothekar zu Dresden. Mit Benützung einiger Papieredesselben fortgesetzt, und aus zum Theil ganz neuen oder wenig bekannten Hulfsmitteln bearbeitet von Dr. Johann Severin Vater. *Dritter Theil. Erste Abtheilung. Berlin,* 1812. *5 vols numbered 4 — Vol. III. in two parts.* 8°. 14

[Mithridates, or general Linguistics, with the Lord's Prayer as Proof in nearly 500 Languages and Dialects by J. C. Adelung, Aulic Counsellor and Chief Librarian at Dresden. Continued with the Use of his Papers and some quite unknown Sources by J. S. Vater.]

This work is the result of such a vast amount of research and learning as to perfectly appall the mind of any person who in forming a fair acquaintance with the literature of two or three languages, has felt that he had accomplished something. It has Grammatical Analyses or at least Vocabularies of most of the languages of the world. More than one fourth of the work is devoted to the Aboriginal languages of America. Pages 399 to 708 of Vol. III. Part I., and the whole of Part II. pp. 474, are occupied with the examination of the languages spoken by the Indians of North and South America. The dialects of more than two hundred nations are represented by some fragments of vocabularies.

ADVENTURES

Of Hunters and Travellers and Narratives of Border Warfare. By an Old Hunter. 12° *pp.* 308. *Philadelphia, Theodore Bliss & Co.,* n. d. (1852.) 15

This is the most meagre collection of commonplace tales, and perfectly worthless, for all purposes except a child's story-book.

AFFAIRS

At Fort Chartres, 1768, 1781. 4° *pp.* 12. *Albany, J. Munsell, 78 State Street,* 1864. 16

The letters of which this work consists, were written by an English officer at Fort Chartres on the Mississippi, just after the close of Pontiac's War, and owe their principal interest to their portrayal of the condition of the country when that wonderful chieftain's heroic effort had failed, and he himself had perished under the assassin's knife.

ALASCO.

An Indian Tale. Two Cantos, with other Poems. *Published for the author by J. B. Lippincott & Co., Philadelphia,* 1857. 17

141 pp. of verse without a note.

ALBACH (James R.)

Annals of the West, embracing a Concise Account of Principal Events which have occurred in the Western States and Territories from the Discovery of the Mississippi Valley to the Year

Eighteen Hundred and Fifty. Compiled from the most authentic sources, and *published by James R. Albach.* 8° *pp.* 818. *St. Louis,* 1852. 18

Two previous editions of this collection of incidents in Western warfare, were assigned on the title-pages to different authors. The first was accredited to J. M. Peck, and the second to J. H. Perkins. Albach was the publisher of both. The taste of the public for the work seems to have survived the editors, as the publisher and legal proprietor of the work published a third edition as revised and corrected. Upon the title-page of this he left no other name than his own. It is a great collection of details of frontier warfare; but contains little material that is new, or indeed not published in a hundred forms, yet it is much esteemed as a history of Western Settlement.

ALDAMA (D. Joseph Augustin).

Arte de la Lengua Mexicana. Dispuesto por D. Joseph Augustin de Aldáma y Guevara, Presbytero de el Arzobispado de Mexico [*engraved ornament*]. En La Imprenta nueva de la Bibliotheca Me-xicana. En frente de el Convento de San Augustin. *Ano de* 1754. 16° *pp. Engraved folding sheet, with verses in Mexican.* 19

[Art of the Mexican Tongue. Arranged by Don Joseph Augustin de Aldama y Guevara, Presbyter of the Archbishoprick of Mexico. In the new printing-office of the Biblioteca Mexicana. In front of the Convent of San Augustin, year 1754.]

ALDEN (Rev. Timothy).

An Account of Sundry Missions performed among the Senecas and Munsees; in a Series of Letters. With an Appendix. By Rev. Timothy Alden, President of Alleghany College. 24° *Half title, portrait, and pp.* 180. *New York, printed by J. Seymour,* 1827. 20

Although purporting to be only a narration of the pious labors of an Indian Missionary, yet this little volume contains many valuable historical and biographical sketches, particularly one of Cornplanter. From this eminent Chief and Warrior the author derived some very interesting particulars of Indian History, more especially of the Seneca Tribe. A short vocabulary of the dialect of that nation is given in the Appendix.

ALLEN (A. J.)

Ten Years in Oregon. Travels and Adventures of Doctor E. White and Lady, West of the Rocky Mountains, with Incidents of Two Sea Voyages via Sandwich Islands around Cape Horn. Containing also a brief History of the Missions and Settlement of the Provisional Government, Number and Customs of the Indians. Incidents Witnessed whilst Traversing and Residing in the Territory. Description of the Soil, Production, and Climate. Compiled by Miss A. J. Allen. 12° *pp.* 430. *Ithaca,* 1850. 21

ALLEN (A. J.)

Thrilling Adventures, Travels and Explorations of Doctor Elijah White among the Rocky Mountains and in the Far West. [*etc.* 3 *lines.*] Containing also a Brief History of the Missions and Settlement of the Country, Origin of the Provisional Governments of the Western Territories, Number and Customs of the Indians, Incidents Witnessed while Traversing and Residing in the Territories, Description of the Soil, Production, and Climate. Compiled by Miss A. J. Allen. 8° *pp.* 430. *New York*, 1859. 22

This and the preceding work entitled *Ten Years in Oregon* are identical. They purport to be and doubtless are the veritable relations of an extraordinary mission, partaking of both a religious and a political character. Dr. White was a Presbyterian Missionary to the wilds of Oregon, who developed a remarkable aptitude for organization of border communities into regular civic bodies. These traits were not less notably exhibited by his dealings with the Indians; among whom some of his adventures are little less than marvelous.

ALLEN (Charles).
Report on the Stockbridge Indians, in answer to a "Memorial of Darius Charles and others of the Stockbridge Tribe of Indians." Made to the Legislature of Massachusetts, January 18, 1870. 8° *pp.* 23. *Boston*, 1870. 23

This Report contains a statement of the various sales of land made by the Stockbridge tribe of Indians, under the authority of the State, the consideration for the conveyance, and some interesting historical information not hitherto known. Some particulars relating to the Dutch traders among them, who opposed their conversion to Christianity; and of the Missions of Sargent, Williams, and Edwards are related. The Report has a more considerable interest as a historical treatise than most of those of its kind.

ALLEN (L. L.)
A Thrilling Sketch of the Life of the distinguished Chief Okah Tubbee, alias William Chubbee, son of the Head Chief Mosholeh Tubbee, of the Choctaw Nation of Indians. By Rev. R. L. Allen. 12° *pp.* 43. *New York*, 1843. 24

This is the first part of a narrative which was intended to be completed in several numbers, but which is not known to have survived the first. Another edition of the same date was printed at Springfield in the same year with additional particulars. See Tubbee.

ALLEN (Paul).
See Lewis and Clarke. 25

ALLEN (Wilkes).
The History of Chelmsford, from its origin in 1653, to the year 1820, together with an Historical Sketch of the Church and Biographical Notices of the Four First Pastors. To which is added A Memoir of the Pawtucket Tribe of Indians, with a large Appendix. By Wilkes Allen, A. M., Pastor of the Church and Society in Chelmsford. *Boards, uncut.* 8° *pp.* 192. *Haverhill, printed by P. N. Green*, 1820. 26

ALLEN (William).
The History of Norridgewock, Comprising Memorials of the Aboriginal Inhabitants and Jesuit Missionaries, Hardships of the Pioneers, Biographical Notices of the Early Settlers, and Ecclesiastical Sketches, by William Allen, Norridgewock. 12° 252 *pp.* *Published by Edward J. Peet*, 1849. 27

ALSOP (George).

A Character of the Province of Maryland Described in four distinct parts. Also a small Treatise on the wild and naked Indians (or Susquehanokes) of Maryland, their Customs, Manners, Absurdities, and Religion; together with a Collection of Historical Letters. By George Alsop. A New Edition, with an Introduction and Copious Historical Notes. By John Gilmary Shea. 8° *pp.* 125. *Portrait and Map. New York, Wm. Gowans,* 1869. 28

This volume is a reprint of the very rare work printed in London 1666, with the same Title. The description of the Susquehanock Indians although meagre, is not without value, as a monument of their existence. It occupies pp. 71 to 81 of the Volume. The notes, however, form a very important part of its real value as they are the product of one of the most learned scholars on the subject of Indian history. They bestow upon the reprint a much greater intrinsic value than even the rare original possesses.

AMERICAN PIONEER (The).

A Monthly Periodical devoted to the objects of the Logan Historical Society; or to collecting and publishing Sketches relative to the Early Settlement and Successive Improvement of the Country. 2 *vols.* 8° *Cincinnati, O.; edited and published by John S. Williams,* 1844. *R. P. Burks, printer.* 29

This judicious collection of documents and material relating to the Border Settlements of the West, was published in twenty-two numbers, commencing in January 1842, and terminating with October 1843. The title-page of Vol. I. bears date 1844, while that of the second is dated 1843.

Vol. I. consists of twelve monthly numbers having a total of 448 pp. with 24 illustrations, of which ten are full pages with reverse blank. Vol. II. consists of ten monthly numbers having a total of 480 pp. with nineteen illustrations, eleven of which are full paged with reverse blank. The great mass of historic material in these two volumes is composed of Journals of Campaigns against the Indians, Narratives of Captivity, Incidents of Border Warfare, Biographical Sketches of Frontiersmen, Indian Warriors, and White Scouts. Everything relating to the Aborigines finds in these volumes a place which are in effect, a great storehouse of incidents, and historical data regarding them.

AMERICAN STATE PAPERS.

(Class II. Indian Affairs.) [*Half Title.*] Documents Legislative and Executive of the Congress of the United States, from the First Session of the First to the Third Session of the Thirteenth Congress inclusive, commencing March 3, 1789, and ending March 3, 1815. Selected and edited under the authority of Congress. By Walter Lourie and Mathew St. Clair Clarke. *Folio. Two vols. pp.* 864 *each and Index lxxxiv. Washington,* 1832. 30

Vols. —— of the State Papers contain an immense mass of details of the official relations of the U. S. Government with the Indians, and are of great value in their history.

ANDERSON (Mr.)

The History of the Life and Adventures of Mr. Anderson, containing his Strange Varieties of Fortune in Europe and

America. Compiled from his own Papers. 18° *pp.* 243. *Berwick,* 1782. 31

One of a numerous class of fictitious works of little merit, which aimed to attract attention by assuming a title giving an air of veracity to the narrative.

ANDERSON (Rufus).

Memoir of Catharine Brown, a Christian Indian of the Cherokee Nation. By Rufus Anderson, A. M. Second edition, 24° *pp.* 144. *Boston and New York,* 1825. 32

The work has been many times reprinted in varying sizes and forms.

ANECDOTES OF THE AMERICAN INDIANS.

Illustrating their Eccentricities of Character. **By the Author of Evenings in Boston, Ramon the Rover, etc. 18° *pp.* 252.** *Hartford,* 1852. 33

ANNUAL REPORT

Of the Select Committee of the Society for Propagating the Gospel among the Indians and others in North America. Presented November 4, 1845. 8° *pp.* 32. *Boston,* 1845. 34

THE SAME. 8° *pp.* 31. *Boston,* 1847. 35

THE SAME. 8° *pp.* 36. *Boston,* 1850. 36

THE SAME. 8° *pp.* 67. *Boston,* 1862. 37

THE SAME. 8° *pp.* 135. *Boston,* 1856. 38

ANTIQUITATES MEXICAINES (Du Capitaine Dupaix).

Antiquitates Mexicaines. Relation des Trois Expeditions du Capitaine Dupaix, Ordonnees en 1805–1806, et 1807; pour la Recherche des Antiquites du pays, notamment celles de Mitla et de Palenque; Accompagnee des dessins de Casteñada et d'une Carte du pays explore. Suivie d'un parallele de ces monuments avec ceux de l'Egypte, de l'Indostan, et du reste de l'ancien Monde par M. Alexandre Lenoir. D'une dissertation sur l'origine de l'ancienne population des deux Ameriques, et sur les diversees Antiquites de ce continent, par M. Warden, avec un discours preliminaire par M. Charles Farcy, et des explicatives et autres documents par MM. Baradire de St. Priest et plusieurs Voyageurs qui ont parcourir l'Amerique. 2 *vols. folio.* Vol. I. *Text* 224 *pp. and contents* 4 *pp.* Vol. II. 164 *pp. of plates, and* 3 *pp. contents.* *Paris,* 1834. 39

[Mexican Antiquities. Relations of three Expeditions of Captain Dupaix, undertaken for the purpose of researches among the Antiquities of Mexico; more particularly those of Mitla and Palenque. Accompanied by designs from Casteñada, and a map of the country explored, followed by a parallel drawn between these monuments, and those of Egypt, and of the rest of the Ancient World, by M. Alex. Lenoir. Also a dissertation on the Origin of the Aboriginal population of the Two Americas, and of the various antiquities of that Continent, by M. Warden, with a preliminary dissertation, by M. Charles Farcy, and explanation of other documents, by Messrs. Baradire de St. Priest, and many other travellers who have visited America.]

These noble volumes contain a vast amount of information regarding the ruins of Palenque and Mitla, of which also they present one hundred and sixty-five splendid views. The last are seldom found complete in the few copies offered for sale, as the work was published and distributed in fragments.

APES (William).

The Increase of the Kingdom of Christ. A Sermon. By William Apes, a Missionary of the Pequod tribe of Indians. 12° pp. 24. *New York, printed for the author by G. F. Bunce,* 1831. 40

This tract, written by the Indian William Apes, contains on the last four pages a treatise entitled "The Indians, the Ten Lost Tribes."

APES (William).

Indian Nullification of the Unconstitutional Laws of Massachusetts, relative to the Marshpee Tribe; or, The Pretended Riot Explained. By William Apes, an Indian, and Preacher of the Gospel. *Cloth.* 12° *pp.* 168. *Boston,* 1835. *Press of Jonathan Howe.* 41

If all the statements of the author, who claims to be a lineal descendant of the tribe, which suffered such murderous slaughter at the hands of Captains Church and Underhill, are true, there is a long score of wrongs to be settled with the State of Massachusetts. According to this author, the descendants of the men who sold the son of King Philip, and more than two hundred of his subjects into the cruel slavery of the Spanish Islands, still held the feeble remnants of her aboriginal population in a species of slavery. The thrifty selectmen of any town in Massachusetts could, if adroit and unscrupulous, pay the whole annual tax of the town by seizing upon the proceeds of the labor of two or three Indians. Apes declared that if any active whaleman of aboriginal blood (as many of the most expert of the Gayhead and Nantucket harpooners were) should be entitled to a share of five or six hundred dollars, the selectmen could seize upon, and convert it to defray any expenses for indigent Indians. I have seen no other evidence to corroborate his statements.

APES (William).

Eulogy on King Philip, as pronounced at the Odeon, in Federal Street, Boston. By the Rev. William Apes, an Indian, January 8, 1836. Second Edition. 8° *pp.* 48. *Boston, published by the author,* 1837. 42

APES (William, a Son of the Forest).

The Experience of William Apes, a Native of the Forest. Comprising a notice of the Pequod Tribe of Indians; written by himself. *Published by the Author.* 18° *half roan. New York,* 1829. 43

APESS (William).

Experience of Five Christian Indians of the Pequod Tribe. Published by William Apess, Missionary of that Tribe and author of The Son of the Forest. Second Edition. 8° *pp.* 47. *Boston, printed for the publisher,* 1837. 44

APPLETON (Nathaniel).

Gospel Ministers Must be fit for the Masters Use and Prepared to every Good Work if they would be Vessels unto Honour: Illustrated in A Sermon Preached at Deerfield, August 31, 1735. At the ordination of Mr. John Sargent, to the Evangelical Ministry, with a Special Reference to the Indians of Housatonnoc, who have lately manifested their desires to receive the Gospel. By Nathaniel Appleton, M. A., Pastor of the Church of Christ in Cambridge. [*Motto 4 lines.*] 8° *pp.* xiv. + 33. *Boston, printed and sold by S. Kneeland and T. Green, in Queen Street*, 1735. 45

The Preface, pp. xiv. is a Historical Narration of Missions among the Housatonic Indians; pages 1 to 33 Sermon.

ARCHÆOLOGIA AMERICANA.

Transactions and Collections of the American Antiquarian Society. Published by Direction of the Society. Vol. I. *Worcester, Massachusetts. Printed for the American Antiquarian Society, by William Manning*, 1832. Vol. II. *Cambridge*, 1836. Vol. III., *n. p.*, 1857. Vol. IV., *n. p.*, 1860. *Large* 8° 46

This Collection is largely composed of treatises upon and histories of the Aborigines of America; volumes I. and II. being wholly devoted to them. The most valuable essay on the languages of America, is only to be found printed in the second volume of this collection.

Contents of Volume I.:—

1. HENNEPIN (Father Lewis). A New Discovery of a Large Country in the Northern America, extending above four thousand miles, pages 61 to 104.
2. ATWATER (Caleb). Description of the Antiquities discovered in the State of Ohio, and other Western States. Illustrated by Engravings of Ancient Fortifications, Mounds, etc., from Actual Survey, pp. 105 to 267, 10 maps, 1 plate, and many cuts in the text.
3. JOHNSTON (John). Account of the Present State of the Indian Tribes Inhabiting Ohio, with a Vocabulary of the Shawanese Language, pp. 269 to 299.
4. FISKE (Moses). Conjectures respecting the Ancient Inhabitants of North America, pp. 300 to 307.
5. ALDEN (Timothy). Antiquities and Curiosities of Western Pennsylvania, pp. 308 to 313.
6. MITCHEL (Samuel L.) Seven Letters and Addresses descriptive of Indian Poetry, Antiquities, and Origin, pp. 313 to 355.
7. Two Letters from J. Farnham and Charles Wilkins upon the Same.
8. SHELDON (W.) Brief Account of the Caribs, pp. 365 to 433.

Contents of Vol. II.:—

9. GALLATIN (Albert). Synopsis of the Indian Tribes in North America (north of Mexico), pp. 1 to 422. Tables of comparative vocabularies, and verbal forms, occupy the last 155 pages of this noble work, of one of the most accurate and learned men of America.
10. GOOKIN (Daniel). An Historical Account of the doings and Sufferings of the Christian Indians in New England, in the years 1695 to 1697, pp. 423 to 564.
11. NEWPORT'S (Capt. James) Discoveries, Virginia, 1607, pp. 40 to 65 of Vol IV.

ARENAS (Pedro de).

Vocubvlario | de las Lengvas | Castellana y Mexicana | en qve se contienen | las palabras, preguntas, y respuestas mas co | munes, y ordinarias que se suelen offre | cer en el trato, y communicacion | entre Espanoles, e Indios. | Compuesto por Pedro | de Arenas. | Impresso con licencia, y approbacion. | En Mexico. | En la emprenta | de Henrico Martinez. (1611). *Small*

4°. 8 *prelim. leaves, namely, Title*, 1 *leaf, License*, 1 *leaf, Prologo*, 1 *leaf, Tabla* 5 *leaves. pp.* 1–160. 47

[Vocabulary, or Manual of the Spanish and Mexican Languages; in which are contained the words, questions, and answers most ordinarily used in communications between the Spaniards and Indians. Composed by Pedro de Arenas. Printed with license and approbation in Mexico, 1611.]

The date of the Petition is found at the end of the Privilege. The note to the title of this edition in *Sabin's Dictionary*, says, "A volume of great rarity. A complete copy is scarcely known." Ternaux, "A small and very rare volume."

Boturini, in his *Catalogo del Museo Indio*, places the *Vocabulario* under the date of 1583; but as it is not uncommon to antedate works printed without the year being named, I am inclined to believe the edition of 1611 to be the first. An instance of this is seen in White Kennett, who places the English edition of Peter Martyr without date under 1597; while the first with a date is 1612. The *Manual of Arenas* was reprinted in 1690, 1700, 1728, 1793, 1831, and with the addition of French phrases in 1862.

ARICKAREE INDIANS.

Correspondence Relative to Hostilities of the Arickaree Indians. *Washington*, 1823. 48

Pages 55 to 109 of Government Documents containing the testimony, etc., official reports and narratives of Military Expeditions against the Arickarees.

ARROYO DE LA CUESTA (Rev. F. Felipe).

A Vocabulary or Phrase Book of the Mutsun language of Alta California. By the Rev. F. Felipe Arroyo de la Cuesta, of the Order of St. Francis. *Large* 8° *Two titles, English and Latin, pp.* 96. *New York, Cramoisy Press*, 1862. 49

No. VIII. Shea's *Library of American Linguistics*. The vocabulary in Mutsun and Latin.

ARROYO DE LA CUESTA (Father Felipe).

Grammar of the Mutsun Language spoken at the Mission of San Juan Bautista Alta California, by Father Felipe Arroyo de la Cuesta. *Large* 8° *English and Spanish titles each* 1 *leaf, pp.* 48. 50

No. IV. Shea's *American Linguistics*.

The Mutsuns were a tribe of Indians occupying a valley in California about forty miles northwest of Monterey, and were the most northerly tribe of whose language the Spanish missionaries compiled a grammar.

The San Juan Bautista Mission was established among the Mutsun Indians, in 1799. The work was printed from the original MSS. forwarded to the Smithsonian Institute by the President of Santa Inez College. Their language closely resembles that of the Indians Diegeno, a savage people living near the Mission Soledad on the River Salinas, and also that of the Indians of the Mission of San Carlos near Monterey. Father Felipo Arroyo de la Cuesta came to California in 1810, and died at Santa Inez Mission in 1842.

ASHER (G. M.)

Henry Hudson the Navigator. The original documents in which his career is recorded, collected, partly translated, and annotated, with an Introduction, by G. M. Asher. 8° *Prel. pp.* (10), *Introduction*, ccxviii. *Divers Voyages, pp.* 1 to 292. *London, printed for the Hakluyt Society*, 1860. 51

The relations of his three voyages to the coast of America by the eminent and unfortunate discoverer, afford us the first authentic information regarding the Indians of New York, and of the Esquimaux of Labrador. The editor asserts what we do not recollect to have seen elsewhere stated: "Verrazano seems to have been the pilot [of the *Samson* and *Mary*] and to have lost his life in an encounter with the North American Indians." p. xcv. of *Introduction*.

ATHERTON (William).

Narrative of the Sufferings and Defeat of the Northwestern Army, under General Winchester; Massacre of the Prisoners; Sixteen Months Imprisonment of the Author and others with the Indians and British. 12° *Frankfort, Ky.* 1842. 52

ATWATER (Caleb).

The writings of Caleb Atwater. *Columbus*, 1833. [*2d Title.*] A Description of the Antiquities discovered in the Western Country; originally communicated to the American Antiquarian Society, by Caleb Atwater. 8° *pp.* 408. 53

The third title, at p. 167, is, "Remarks made on a Tour to Prairie Du Chien; thence to Washington City in 1829." The first work, "A Description of Antiquities" has never been printed in a separate form, its first publication having been in the first volume of *Archæologia Americana*. In this the plans and maps were much better executed, some even having been omitted in the Cincinnati edition.

The Tour is a reprint of the greater portion of that published in 12°, pp. 296, at Columbus in 1831. In this however the rudiments of the Sioux Grammar are omitted. The antiquarian portion is a well written description, apparently conscientiously accurate, of the mounds, fortifications, mortuary remains, implements, and weapons of the ancient Aborigines of Ohio. The zeal and industry of the author, stimulated by a thirst for the acquisition of knowledge regarding the mysterious people of whom these were the relics, have produced a work not much less valuable, because the author had little scientific training, to teach him what to search for. Ethnology indeed, at the period of Mr. Atwater's researches, had not crystallized its facts into a science. The work is accompanied by eleven plans, mostly folding, besides several cuts printed in the text, illustrative of subjects mentioned.

ATWATER (Caleb).

Remarks made on a Tour to Prairie Du'Chien: thence to Washington City in 1829, by Caleb Atwater, late Commissioner employed by the United States to negotiate with the Indians of the Upper Mississippi, for the purchase of mineral country, and author of Western Antiquities. 12° *pp.* 296. *Columbus, O., published by Isaac N. Whiting*, 1831. 54

Some very curious particulars relating to Customs of the Winnebagoes are related by Atwater. Although nothing indicating the mission of Atwater appears on the title, yet the real object of his tour was to procure as Commissioner of the government, a cession of the title of the Winnebago, Pottawatomie, Chippewa, and Ottawa Indians, in the rich mineral lands, now forming the State of Wisconsin and part of Illinois.

Much the greater part of the work is devoted therefore to a narration of the peculiarities of those tribes which he visited, biography of some of their chiefs, Indian poetry, specimens of their language, and incidents of his associations with them.

On pages 149 to 172 the author has given "Rudiments of the Grammar of the Sioux Language," all of which is omitted in the edition of 1833. On pp. 75 to 84 he offers an analysis of the Winnebago dialect, as amplifying some theories regarding the origin of the Chippewa tribes.

ATWATER (Caleb).

A History of the State of Ohio, Natural and Civil, by Caleb Atwater, A. M. Second edition. 8° *pp.* 407. *Cincinnati* (1838). 55

That portion of the History which is included between pp. 107 and 160 is devoted to the narration of "Lord Dunmore's War on the Ohio" Indians — Harmar's and St. Clair's Campaign in 1790 and 1791, and "Wayne's War." On pp. 197 to 238 are narrated the principal incidents of "Gen. Tupper's Expedition," Mississinaway Expedition, "The Siege of Fort Meigs," and Croghan's Defense of Fort Stephenson.

AUCHINLECK (G.)

A History of the War between Great Britain and the United States of America, during the years 1812, 1813, and 1814, by G. Auchinleck. 8° *pp.* vii. + 408 + iii. *Toronto, Published by Maclear & Co.*, 1855. 56

This book, written by a Canadian, contains many particulars of the employment of Indians by the British Government, and educes evidence to disprove the charge of the barbarous cruelty in the treatment of prisoners by the savages.

AURACANIAN INDIANS.

Rambles in Chili and life among the Auracanian Indians in 1836, by "Will the Rover." 8° *pp.* 88. *Thomaston (Me.)*, 1851. 57

The book bears the very legible marks of romance, though certified on the title-page by the publisher to be veritable.

AUSS AMERICA

das ist auss der Newen Welt. Vnderschildticher Schreiben Extract von den Jaren 1616, 1617, 1618. Was gestalt Acht Patres Societatis vnd zwo andere Ordens personen Von dess Christlichen Glaubens wegen Ihr Blut vergossen. Was auch sonst die Patres Societatis Gott zu Ehrons unnd zu auk breitlung. 4° *Two prel. leaves* + *pp.* 1 to 91. *Getruckt zu Augsburg*, 1620. 58

[From America, that is, from the New World. Extracts of Letters of the years 1616, 1617, 1618. How eight Fathers of the Society of Jesus and two other Members of that Society shed their blood for the Christian Belief. Also what the said Society did more for the Glory of God and the Promulgation (of the Gospel). *Printed at Augsburg*, 1620.]

AUTHENTIC MEMOIRS

Of William Augustus Bowles, Esquire, Ambassador From the United Nations of Creeks and Cherokees to the Court of London. 8° *Title; To the Public, pp.* vi.; *text*, 79. *London, R. Faulder*, 1791. 59*

The subject of this biographical sketch attracted much attention to himself in England, whither he went to enlist the interposition of the crown in favor of the Creek Indians, over whom he had acquired a sort of chieftainship. He claimed for them the rights of an independent and sovereign nation. Several treatises were printed regarding him and his lucubrations, among others, one attempting to establish from his testimony the existence of a tribe of Indians speaking the Welsh language. The work whose title is above given, is ranked among the rarest works relating to American Aborigines. Colonel Force once said that he had attempted for twenty years to procure a copy without success. Some particulars in the life of Bowles can be found in Haywood's *Aboriginal and Civil Histories of Tennessee* and White's *Historical Collections of Georgia.*

AUTHENTIC NARRATIVE OF THE SEMINOLE WAR.
Its Cause, Rise and Progress, and a Minute Detail of the Horrid Massacres of the Whites by the Indians and Negroes in Florida, in the months of December, January, and February, communicated for the press by a gentleman who has spent eleven weeks in Florida near the scene of the Indian depredations and in a situation to collect every important fact relating thereto. 8° *pp.* 21. *Folding Plate. Providence,* 1836. 60

AVILA (P. F. Francisco de).
Arte de Lengua Mexicana, y breves platicas de los Mysterios de N. Santa Fee Catholica, y otras para exortacion de su obligacion a los Indios. Compuesta por el P. F. Francisco de Avila, Predicador, Cura Ministro por Su Magestad del Pueblo de la Melpan, y Lector del Idioma Mexicana, del Orden de los Menores de N. P. San Francesco. Dedicado al M. R. P. F. Joseph Pedrasa. [*Official Titles, 9 lines, etc.*] Con Licencia de los Superiores. En Mexico, por los Herederos de la Viuda de Miguel de Ribera Caldero en el Empedradillo, Ano de 1717. *Small* 4° 12 *prel. leaves* + 37 *numbered leaves.* 61

[Art of the Mexican tongue, and short exercises in the mysteries of our Holy Catholic Faith, and others for the exhortation of its duties to the Indians. Composed by the Father Friar Francisco de Avila, preacher, serving curate for his Majesty of the town of M——, and Reader of the Mexican Idiom, of the Order of Minors of our Father San Francisco. Dedicated to the very Rev. Father Friar, Joseph Pedrasa.]

AZARA (Felix de).
Voyages dans L'Amerique Meridionale, par Don Felix de Azara, Commissaire et Commandant des limites Espagnoles dans le Paraguay, depuis 1781 jusq'en 1801. Contenant la description geographique, politique et civile du Paraguay et de la riviere de La Plata; l'histoire de la decouverte et de la conquete de ces contrees; des details nombreux sur leur histoire naturelle, et sur les peuples sauvages qui les habitent; le recit des moyens employes par les Jesuites pour assujetir et civiliser les indigines, etc., publies d'apres les manuscrits de l'auteur avec une notice sur sa vie et ses ecrits; par C. A. Walckenaer, etc. Accompagnes d'un Atlas de vigt-cinq planches. *Paris: Dentu, imprimeur-libraire,* 1809. 4 *vols.* 8°, *and* 1 *vol. atlas,* 4°, *containing* 13 *maps and plans, and* 12 *plates.* 62

[Travels in South America, by Don Felix de Azara, from 1781-1801; containing a geographic, political, and civil description of Paraguay and of the River de la Plata. The history of the conquest of these countries; numerous details of their natural history; and of the savage people who inhabit them. With a narration of the means employed by the Jesuits to subject and civilise the Indians, etc.]

Of Vol. II., the author devotes chapters x. to xviii., pp. 1–391, to "The Indian Savages." "Means employed by the conquerors and the Jesuits of America to subject the Indians, and the manner in which they governed them." "Notice of all the Tribes, Villages, etc., of the Indians in Paraguay and in Buenos Ayres." "History of the Discovery and Conquest of La Plata and of Paraguay." Don Félix de Azara was born at Barbunales, in 1746. He received the appointment of Colonel of Engineers in 1780, and embarked in 1781 as a commissioner on the part of Spain to settle the boundary between the Spanish possessions in Paraguay and the Portuguese territory of Brazil. In this employment he remained for twenty-two years. He was recalled by the King of Spain in 1803; and honored with the appointment of Councillor of the Indies.

Back (Captain).
Narrative of the Arctic Land Expedition to the Mouth of the Great Fish River, and along the Shores of the Arctic Ocean, in the years 1833, 1834, and 1835; by Captain Back, R. N., Commander of the Expedition. Illustrated by a Map and Plates. 4° *pp.* xl. + 663 + *map and* 14 *plates* + 3 *plates fish. London, John Murray, Albemarle Street*, 1836. 63

This very beautiful edition of Captain Back's Journey, is exactly a counterpart, page by page, of the octavo size. It is in fact an impression of the octavo on a quarto page of thick paper, and is therefore a large paper size, of which a few copies were probably taken for presentation. The impressions of the plates are on India paper, and having as well as the text been taken with great care, the whole work is a splendid specimen of typographic art. Captain Back's Narrative is crowded with details of his intercourse with the Crees, Chippewyans, Dog Rib, and Coppermine Indians, upon whom he, as well as Captain Franklin, was obliged to depend in great measure for subsistence during the terrible privations of an Arctic winter. No intelligent comprehension of the character of the savage tribes of the frozen regions of North America can be obtained without reading the narratives of Captains Franklin and Back; both of whose Journals of their overland expeditions are very largely occupied with descriptions of Indian life and peculiarities.

Back (Captain).
Narrative of the Arctic Land Expedition to the Mouth of the Great Fish River, and along the Shores of the Arctic Ocean, in the years 1833, 1834, and 1835, by Capt. Back, R. N., Commander of the Expedition. Illustrated by a Map and Plates. 8° *pp.* 663 + 16 *plates and Map. London, John Murray*, 1836. 64

Back (Captain).
Narrative of the Arctic Land Expedition to the Mouth of the Great Fish River, and along the Shores of the Arctic Ocean, in the years 1833, 1834, and 1835, by Capt. Back, R. N., Commander of the Expedition. Illustrated by a Map. 8° *Philadelphia*, 1836. 65

Bacqueville (de la Potherie).
Histoire | de | L'Amerique | Septentrionale | Divisee en quatre Tomes | Tome Premier | Contenant | le Voyage du Fort de Nelson, dans | la Baye d' Hudson, a l'extremite de l Ame- | rique. Le premier etablissement des Francois | dans ce vaste pays, la prise dudit Fort | de Nelson, la Description du Fleure

de Saint | Laurent, le gouvernement de Quebec, des | trois Rivieres & de Montreal, depuis 1534 | jusqu' a 1701. | Par M. de Bacqueville de la Potherie | né a la Guadaloupe, dans l' Amerique Me | ridionale Aide Major de la dite Isle. | Enriche des Figures. 4 *vols.* 16° Vol. I. *Pref. pp.* (xii) + 1 *to* 370 + *table pp.* (4) + 2 *maps and* 16 *plates.* Vol. II. *Title and pp.* 356 + *table* 7 *pp.* + 1 *map and* 4 *plates.* Vol. III. *Title, preface, and Terms of the Savages pp.* (12) + 310 + *table pp.* (6) + 5 *plates.* Vol. IV. *Title and pp.* 271 + *table pp.* (iv) + 2 *plates. A Paris,* 1753. 66

[History of North America, divided into four volumes. Vol. I., containing the Voyage to Fort Nelson in Hudson's Bay on the northern extremity of America. The first establishment of the French in this vaste country, the capture of the said Fort Nelson, Description of the River St. Lawrence, the Government of Quebec, of the Three Rivers and of Montreal from 1534 to 1701.]

The subject of the work is very imperfectly described in the title to the first volume. Each one of the four composing it has a distinct title, as much descriptive of a different purpose as a separate work. To afford a full comprehension of its scope I append a translation of the title of each volume: —

Vol. II. "History of the Native Allies of New France, their Manners and their Maxims, their Religion, and their Interests with all the Nations of the upper Lakes, among which are the Hurons and the Illinois, the alliance made with the French and these people, and all which occurred the most remarkable under Messieurs de Traci de Frontenac, de la Barre and of Denonville."

Vol. III. "History of the Irroquois, their Manners, their Maxims, their Customs, their Government, their Interests, with the English their Allies, all the transactions of the war with them from the years 1689 to 1701; their Negotiations, their Embassies for a general Peace with the French, and with the Native Allies of New France."

Vol. IV. "History of the Abenaquis Indians, the general Peace in all North America, under the government of the Count Frontenac and the Chevalier de Callieres, during which the Indian Nations residing six hundred leagues from Quebec assembled at Montreal."

De la Potherie's work, it will be seen, is a history of the Indian nations of Canada, being entirely devoted to that subject and the relations of the French with the natives. Much of his work is written from his own observation, and the remainder seems to have been derived from authentic sources. A comparison of De la Potherie's volumes with unquestioned authorities, like Le Clercq and Sagard, does not sustain the criticism of Father Charlevoix copied by Mr. Rich. Most of the twenty-seven plates are illustrative of scenes or peculiarities in Indian life.

Balboa (Miguel Carello).

History du Perou par Miguel Carello Balboa. Inedite. *Volume XVII. of Ternaux-Compans, Voyages et Relations. Paris,* 1840. 67

This History of Peru, never before printed, was written by a gentleman who went to Bogota in 1566, where he resided ten years; then removed to Quito, where he finished his history in 1586, twenty years after he arrived in America. The Manuscript, as found by M. Ternaux, was divided in three books, of which the first two make no mention of America, except some worthless speculations about its being the land of Ophir.

In his third book, however, he gives the results of his communications from a learned monk named Juan de Oruzco, of Bogota, who had written many treatises on the origin and antiquities of the Indians.

The volume is entirely occupied with the history of the Incas, and other

Indian nations, prior to the invasion of Pizarro, and closes with the murder, by this tyrant, of Atahualipa. Its value to us is greatly enhanced in its being an independent chronicle, according so often with, and differing so often from, that of Garcilaso de la Vega. Both their agreements and their differences establish the fact of a common source of historic data.

BALDWIN (Thomas).

Narrative of the Massacre by the Savages of the Wife and Children of Thomas Baldwin, who since the melancholy period of the destruction of his unfortunate family, has dwelt entirely alone, in a hut of his own construction, in the extreme Western part of Kentucky. *New York*, 1835. 68

Very little of this fugitive chapbook relates to the subject of the massacre by the savages, and that little is worthless; the rest is mere rhapsody and bombast.

BALLANTYNE (Robert Michael).

Hudson's Bay; or, Every-Day Life in the Wilds of North America, during Six Years' Residence in the Territories of the Hon. Hudson's Bay Company. 12° *pp.* 298. *Boston*, 1859. 69

No part of the American Continent has had so many intelligent and well educated observers of Indian traits as the Hudson's Bay Territory. The great Company encouraged the occasional presence and association of a superior employé. Among the considerable number of writers who have served that company, none have produced a more complete, interesting, and evidently faithful narration of the various phases of a Fur Trader's life among the Indians, than Mr. Ballantyne. Crowded as his book is in details of their life, habits, and peculiarities, we feel an unchecked confidence in their truthfulness as we progress in its perusal.

BANCROFT (Edward).

An Essay on the Natural History of Guiana, in South America. Containing a Description of many Curious Productions in the Animal and Vegetable Systems of that Country. Together with an Account of the Religion, Manners, and Customs of Several Tribes of its Indian Inhabitants [*etc.* 6 *lines*]. 8° *London*, 1769. 70

The especial subject of the author's inquiries regarding the Indians, is the nature and use of the Wourali Poison, with which their weapons are charged. Although a work of some merit, written as it was by an English-man of learning, it has little value as a narration of personal experience. It is probable, from the entire absence of personal details, that the book was written in England, perhaps by one who had no more than a short visit to Guiana to qualify him for the task.

Much the best portion of the work is Chap. iii. occupying 100 pp. of description of the peculiarities of the natives of the country. The subject has however been much better performed by the Missionary, Brett.

BARAGA (Rev. F.)

A Theoretical and Practical Grammar of the Otchipwe Language, the language spoken by the Chippewa Indians; which is also spoken by the Algonquin, Otawa, and Potawatami Indians, with little difference. For the use of Missionaries and other persons living among the Indians of the above named tribes. By the Rev. Frederick Baraga, Missionary at L'Anse Lake

Superior. *Square*, 12° pp. 576. *Detroit, Jabez Fox, printer*, 1850. 71

BARAGA (F.)
Jésus Obimaisiwin oma aking gwaiakossing anamiewin ejitwatjig mi sa Catholique enamiadjig gewabandangig. *Map*, 18° *Paris*, 1837. 72*

BARAGA (F.)
Otchipwe anamie masinaigan. Gwaiakossing anamiewin ejigwatjig mi si Catholique enamiadjig gewabandangig. 18° *Paris*, 1837. 73*

BARAGA (F.)
Abrege de l'Histoire des Indiens de L'Amerique Septentrionale. Traduit de L'Allemand. 12° pp. 296. *Paris*, 1845. 74*

BARAGA (F.)
A Dictionary of the Otchipwe Language, explained in English. This language is spoken by the Chippewa Indians, as also by the Otawas, Potawatamies, and Algonquins, with little difference. For the use of Missionaries and other persons living among the above mentioned Indians. By the Rev. Frederick Baraga. 12° pp. vii. + 662. *Cincinnati*, 1853. 75*

BARBARITIES OF THE ENEMY
Exposed in a Report of the Committee of the House of Representatives of the United States, appointed to enquire into the spirit and manner in which the war has been waged by the enemy, and the Documents accompanying said Report. 16° pp. 192. *Printed at Worcester, by Isaac Sturtevant, for Remark Dunnell*, 1814. 76

Pages 123 to 162 are occupied with the testimony criminating the British military officers in the horrible massacres perpetrated by the Indians after the surrender of the Americans as prisoners of war on various occasions.

BARBER (Mrs.)
Narrative of the Tragical Death of Mr. Darius Barber and his Seven Children, who were inhumanly butchered by the Indians in Camden County, Georgia, January 26, 1816. (*Wood cut of 8 Coffins.*) To which is added an account of the Captivity and Sufferings of Mrs. Barber, who was carried away a Captive by the Savages, and from whom she fortunately made her escape six weeks afterwards. It may be a gratification to the reader to learn that the said tribe of Savages have been since exterminated by the Brave and Intrepid Gen. Jackson, and the Troops under his Command. 12° pp. 24. *Boston, Printed for David Hazen. Price 9d.* 77

BARBER (John Warner).
The History and Antiquities of New England, New York, New Jersey, and Pennsylvania, embracing the following Subjects, viz.: Discoveries and Settlements; Indian History; Indian, French,

and Revolutionary Wars; religious history; Biographical Sketches; Anecdotes, Traditions, Remarkable and Unaccountable Occurrences; with a great variety of Curious and Interesting Relics of Antiquity. Illustrated by numerous Engravings, collected and arranged by John Warner Barber. Third edition. 8° pp. 624. *Hartford, Allen S. Stillman & Son*, 1856. 78

At page 69 commences, "An Account of the Indians of N. E., N. Y., N. J." which with Discoveries and Settlements and Indian Wars, extends to page 304.

Barcia (D. Andres Gonzales).

Historiadores Primitivos de las Indias Occidentales que junto traduxo en parte, y saco a luz, ilustrados con eruditas Notas, y copias Indices, el Illustrissimo Señor D. Andres Gonzales Barcia, del Consejo, y Camara de S. M. Dividos en tres tomos, cuyo contenido se vera en el folio figuiente. 3 *vols. folio. Madrid*, año MDCCXLIX. 79

[Original Historical Memoirs of the West Indies, collected, and partly translated, for the formation of a clearer history; illustrated with learned Notes and copious Indices by the celebrated gentleman, Don Andreas Gonzales Barcia.]

This collection of histories is rarely complete, the pieces having been printed separately and at different periods, and having each an independent pagination, were looked upon as complete in themselves. Many of them having been destroyed, it is believed that not more than one hundred complete copies now exist. The parts were not collected until after the death of the author, which took place while they were passing through the press. Mr. Stevens says that it is difficult now to pronounce what constitutes a complete set, or in what order the parts should be arranged, as the printing occupied a period of more than twenty years. The copies sold by himself and in Leclerc's Sale contained only the following parts: —

Vol. I. No. 1. Life of Columbus. By his Son Ferdinand. 128 pp.
2. Second, Third, and Fourth Relations of Cortez. 158 pp.
3. Three Relations of Alvarado and Godoy. — Sent to Cortez. 157-173 pp.
4. Oviedo's Natural History of the Index. 57+8 pp.
5. Marquis Loretto's Examination of Cabeca de Vaca's Narrative. 50 pp
6. Cabeca de Vaca's Relation. 43+9 pp.
Commentaries of Cabeca de Vaca. 70+2 pp.

Vol. II. No. 1. Gomara, General History of West Indies and Conquest of Peru, 226+60 pp.
2. Chronica de la Nueva Espana. 214+46 pp.

Vol. III. No. 1. Zarate, Conquest of Peru. (10)+176+28 pp.
2. Xeres, Conquest of Peru. 179-237+7 pp. In all 66 in number; but there is an error in pagination by which the Nos. from 210 to 228 are omitted. So that in fact the true number of pages is only 48.
3. Schmeidel, History and Discovery of Rio de la Plata. 31+9 pp.
4. Don Martin del Barco Centenera Argentina and the Conquest of Rio de la Plata, Peru, etc. A Poem. 107+17 pp. A Poem in 28 Cantos.
5. Torre's Voyage around the World. 45 pp.
6. Abstract of a Relation of a Voyage of Merchants, from Moka in Arabia. pp. 45 to 48.

Barcia (Don Andreas Gonzales).

Ensayo Chronologico para la Historia general de la Florida. Contiene los descubrimientos, y principales sucesos, acaecidos en este Gran Reino, a los Españoles, Franceses, Suecos, Dinemarqueses, Ingleses, y otras Naciones, entre si, y con los Indios: cuias Costumbres, Genios, Idolatria, Governio, Batallas, y Astucias, se refieren: y los Viages de algunos Capitanes y Pilotos por el Mar de el Norte, a buscar Paso a Oriente, o union de aquella Tierra con Asia. Desde el ano de 1512 que descubrio la Florida Juan Ponce de Leon, hasta el de 1722. Escrito por Don Gabriel de Cardenas Z Cano Dedicado al Principe Nuestro Senor. *En Madrid,* 1723. *Folio,* 20 *prel. leaves, pp.* 366+28 *leaves Tabla.* 60

[Memoirs, Chronological, for a General History of Florida; containing the Discoveries, and the principal events which happened in that Great Kingdom, to the Spaniards, French, Swedes, Danes, English, and other Nations, not only among themselves, but with the Indians. The Customs, Genius, Idolatries, Government, Wars and Strategies of the Indians, as related by themselves. Of the Voyages of some Captains and Pilots, in search of a Passage from the North Sea to the East, or a junction of the land with Asia: from the year 1512, when Florida was discovered by Juan Ponce de Leon to that of 1722, written by Don Gabriel de Cardenas a Cano, Madrid, 1723.]

Under this pseudonym, an anagram of his name, the learned Barcia, who edited the work, concealed his association with it. It is filled with the most valuable material relating to the Indians who once inhabited the vast territory claimed by the Spaniards under the title of Florida, reaching from the northern lakes to the Gulf of Mexico and covering nearly all the States united under the Federal Government. Almost all that we know of the character of some of the tribes which once inhabited this territory, and were swept from existence by the conquest of the Spaniards, is derived from Cabeza de Vaca, and Garcilaso de la Vega. In this work their relations of Florida are continued; among which the Narrative of the Sufferings of Father Jogues, a Jesuit Missionary to the Iroquois in the present State of New York, and the painful incidents of his final martyrdom will most interest those who examine them. Pages 203 to 217 are principally occupied with the relation of the Missions among the Hurons and Iroquois, and of the captivity and martyrdom of Fathers Jogues, Lalemande, Garnier, and Chabanel. Some particulars of the wars of the Iroquois are given on pages 227 to 244, and throughout the work are found many details of Missions and visits to the Northern tribes, and of the long series of conflicts with them. The Chronological History of Florida is a continuation of *La Florida del Inca.*

The learned and zealous historian Barcia was not only the author of the works attributed to him under his name, *Historiadores Primitivos de las Indias Occidentales* (Primitive History of the West Indies, South America), and *Ensayo Chronologico para la Historia de la Florida* (Chronological Essays towards the History of Florida) but he was the editor of a vast mass of historical works, which had become rare even in his day. They consisted of the following books, which will be found under their authors' names in this Catalogue.

TORQUEMADA. *Monarchia Indiana,* in three folio volumes printed at Madrid in 1723.

GARCILASO DE LA VEGA. *Primera parte de los Commentarios, Reales Origen de los Incas,* and Garcilaso's *Historia general del Peru,* and *La Florida del Inca.* The three works printed uniform in folio. Madrid, 1723.

GARCIA. *Origen de los Indios.* One vol. folio. Madrid, 1729.

HERRERA. *Historia General.* Eight decades, in four folio vols. Madrid, 1726.

PINELO. *Bibliotheca Oriental y Occidental.* Three folio vols. in 1737.

ERCILLA. *La Araucana.* In one volume folio, in 1633.

Barcia's works, original and edited, therefore fill 19 volumes.

Rich says that copies of all these works were printed on fine paper with large margins, which are very rarely reunited in complete sets. Barcia's zeal in historical labors, was not exhausted in the reprinting and perpetuating rare works, for he collected a vast mass of books and manuscripts upon the history of America, which at his death met the usual melancholy fate of such repositories. He was to a great extent the author of his edition of the *Bibliotheca Oriental y Occidental* of Pinelo, which was originally printed in one small quarto, but by Barcia's additions grew to three folios, of which the third is devoted to the titles of books and manuscripts relating to American history. Barcia's works did not escape sharp criticism in his own day. Salazar, the author of some dull volumes on the *History of Spain and the Indies*, printed a work entitled *Crisis del Ensayo a la Historia de la Florida*, which evinced more jealousy than merit.

BARD (Samuel A.)

Waikna, or Adventures on the Mosquito Shore. 12° *New York*, 1855.

See Squier. 81

BARKER (Rev. James W.)

Narrative of the perilous adventures, miraculous escapes, and sufferings of Rev. James W. Barker during a frontier residence in Texas of fifteen years, with an impartial description of the climate, soil, timber, water, etc. of Texas, written by himself. To which is appended a Narrative of the Capture and Subsequent Sufferings of Mrs. Rachel Plummer (his daughter) during a captivity of twenty-one months among the Cumanche Indians, with a sketch of their manners, customs, laws, etc. with a short description of the country over which she travelled whilst with the Indians, written by herself. 12° *pp.* 1 *to* 95 *of First Narrative and Title*, + *pp.* 1 *to* 36 *of Second Narrative. Printed at the Morning Courier Office, Fourth Street, Louisville, Kentucky*, 1844. 82

BARLAEUS (Caspar).

Casparis Barlaei rerum per octennium in Brasilia. Et alibi nuper gestarum, Sub Praefectura Illustrissimi Comitis I. Mavritii, Nassoviae, &c. Comitis, Nunc Vesaliae Gubernatoris & Equitatus Foederatorum Belgii Ordd. sub Avrioco Ductoris, Historia. *Folio. Engraved title, title and pref. l.* 5 + *pp.* 1 *to* 340 + (viii.) + *portrait and fifty-six double-page plates. Amstelodami*, 1647. 83

[History of what happened during eighty years in Brazil under the command of the illustrious Count J. Mauritious of Nassau, and other commanders of the United Provinces.]

Notwithstanding the great number of large and beautifully executed plates, which this costly volume contains, the principal value to us is to be found in the vocabulary of the language of the Indians of Chili on pp. 283 to 289, with some account of the natives.

The work is a splendid specimen of typography and engraving.

BARNARD (Thomas).

A Discourse before the Society for Propogating the Gospel among the Indians and others in North America, delivered November 6, 1806, by Thomas Barnard. 8° *pp.* 47. *Charlestown*, 1806. Including an Appendix of historical matter relating to the Indians. *pp.* 10. 84

BARR (Capt. James).

A correct and authentic Narrative of the Indian War in Florida, with a description of Maj. Dade's Massacre and an account of the extreme suffering, for want of provisions, of the army, having been obliged to eat horses' and dogs' flesh, by Capt. James Barr. 16° *pp.* 32. *New York,* 1836. 85

Barratt (Joseph).

The Indian of New England and the North-Eastern Provinces. A sketch of the Life of an Indian Hunter, Ancient Traditions relating to the Etchemin Tribe, their modes of life, fishing, hunting, etc. with vocabularies in the Indian and English, giving the names of the Animals, Birds, and Fish. The most complete that has been given for New England in the languages of the Etchemin and Micmacs [*etc.* 3 *lines*], derived from Nicola Tenesles, by a citizen of Middleton, Conn. (5 *lines*) 12° *pp.* 24. *Middletown, Conn.* 1851. 86

Some of the copies have a slip with the printed words: "By Joseph Barratt, M. D., Member of several Learned Societies," pasted over the name of Nicola Tenesles. A sketch of the life of this Indian, with some traditions of his tribe, occupy the first eleven pages, the remaining thirteen pages are devoted to a Vocabulary and Grammatical Analysis of the language spoken by the Etchemins and Micmacs.

Barrere (Pierre).

Nouvelle relation de la France Equinoxiale contenant la Description des Cotes de la Guiane de l'Isle de Cayenne; le Commerce de cette Colonie; les divers changemens arrives dans le Pays; & les Moeurs & Coutumes des differens Peuples Sauvages qui l'habitent. Avec des Figures dessinees sur les lieux. Par Pierre Barrere. 12° *Title, half title, and prel. pp.* iv. + 250, 16 *folding plates,* 3 *maps. Paris,* 1743. 87

[New Relation of France Equinoxial, containing the Description of the Coasts of Guiana; of the Island of Cayenne; the Commerce of this Colony; the different changes happening in the country; and the Manners and Customs of the different savage peoples, who inhabit it.]

The minute descriptions of savage life, and numerous illustrations thereof, afford to the reader a very accurate picture of the Carib manners and customs.

Almost the whole of the text as well as most of the sixteen plates are descriptive of the natives of Guiana, where the author resided. He gives us many new particulars regarding the Indians.

Bartlett (John Russell).

The Progress of Ethnology, an Account of recent Archaeological, Philological, and Geographical Researches in various parts of the Globe tending to elucidate the Physical History of Man. 8° *pp.* 151. *New York,* 1847. 88

Barton (Benj. Smith).

New Views of the Origin of the Tribes and Nations of America. By Benjamin Smith Barton. 8° *pp.* xii. + cix. + 86. *Philadelphia, printed for the author,* 1797. 89

Of this treatise, pp. cix. are entitled, "A Preliminary Discourse," in which the author maintains that in the comparative vocabularies he cites, there is such an affinity that the various Indian nations of America must have had a common origin; and from some synonymic works of Indian and Asiatic languages, he decides that all the people of the two continents were derived from the same parent stock. Pages 1 to 81, succeeding the Preliminary Discourse, are entirely occupied with vocabularies of forty Indian tongues; to which are compared some of the primitive words of several languages of Europe. The names of objects there presented, Mr. Barton declares he obtained from the Indians of the several tribes, or from interpreters.

THE SAME. 8° *pp.* cix. + 133, *and Appendix* 32. *Philadelphia*, 1798. 90

BARTON (Benj. Smith).

Observations on some Parts of Natural History, to which is prefixed an Account of several Remarkable Vestiges of an Ancient Date, which have been discovered in different parts of North America. Part I. By Benjamin Smith Barton. 8° *pp.* 76. *London* (1787). 91

BARTRAM (John).

Observations on the Inhabitants, Climate, Soil, Rivers, Productions, Animals, and other matters worthy of notice, made by Mr. John Bartram, in his Travels from Pensilvania to Onondago, Oswego, and the Lake Ontario, in Canada. To which is annexed a Curious Account of the Cataracts at Niagara, by Mr. Peter Kalm, a Sweedish Gentleman, who travelled there. 8° *Title*, 1 *leaf* + *pp.* viii., *and* 9 *to* 94, *and plate. London*. 1751. 92

This visit of the father of the naturalist, William Bartram, to the central council fire of the Six Nations, is especially interesting, not only as having been made at so early a period, but for affording us in this work a plan and view of the Long-House, peculiar to the tribes of that confederacy. As the greater portion of the work is a copious daily journal of incidents of travel, we are indulged by many intimate associations with scenes of aboriginal life.

BARTRAM (John).

An Account of East Florida, with a Journal kept by John Bartram, of Philadelphia, Botanist to His Majesty for the Floridas, upon a Journey from St. Augustine up the River St. Johns. 8° *London*, *n. d.* *Title* 1 *leaf*; *Dedication*, 2 *leaves*; *Introduction*, *pp.* i. *to* xxii.; *Account*, *pp.* 23 *to* 90; *Title and Dedication to Journal*, *pp.* viii.; *Journal*, *pp.* 1 *to* 70. 93

BARTRAM (Wm.)

Travels through North and South Carolina, East and West Florida, the Cherokee Country, the Extensive Territories of the Muscogulges, or Creek Confederacy, and the Country of the Choctaws. Containing an Account of the Soil and Natural Productions of these Regions, together with Observations on the Manners of the Indians. Embellished with Copper Plates. 8° *Map and seven plates*, *pp.* xxxiv. + 522. *Philadelphia*, 1791. 94

The Philadelphia Edition has a second full title to Book iv. page 481, reverse blank, as follows: —

"An Account of the Persons, Manners, Customs, and Government of the Muscogulges or Creeks, Cherokees, Choctaws, etc., Aborigines of the Continent of North America. By William Bartram. Philadelphia, 1791," pp. 433 to 522. All other editions have only half titles with the same description of contents without date or place.

It has been customary to repeat in most of the Catalogues containing Bartram's Travels, the comment found in Coleridge's *Table Talk*, that it is "*The latest book of Travels I know, written in the spirit of the Old Travellers.*"

This I suppose to mean that Bartram wrote with all the enthusiasm and interest with which the fervent old Spanish friars and missionaries narrated the wonders of the new found world. Bartram, however, has much the advantage of these chroniclers, who often became mere rhapsodists, as he was a man of scientific training, with a mind too well disciplined in logical fidelity to be deluded by his own fancies.

Although more especially a naturalist, he neglected nothing which would add to the common stock of human knowledge. He not only offers us pictures of Indian life, and sketches of the striking peculiarities of the tribes he visited, but he gives us tables of the names and localities of the numerous towns of the populous nations of the Creeks and Cherokees. Fifty-three villages of the first, and forty-five of the latter are enumerated and named.

BARTRAM (W.)

Travels, etc. *Title, Size, Pagination, Plates and Index identical with the first London edition, but evidently a reprint. Dublin,* 1793. 95

BARTRAM (W.)

Travels through North and South Carolina, Georgia, East and West Florida, the Cherokee Country, the extensive Territories of the Muscogulges or Creek Confederacy, and the Country of the Choctaws, containing an Account of the Soil, and Natural Productions of those Regions; together with Observations on the Manners of the Indians. Embellished with Copper-plates. The Second Edition in London. 8° *pp.* xxiv. + 520 + (vii.). *Map. Frontispiece, a Creek Chief, and 7 plates. Philadelphia, printed by James & Johnson,* 1791; *London, reprinted for J. Johnson,* 1794. 96

BASANIERRE (M.)

L'Histoire Notable de la Floride situe es Indes Occidentales. Contenant les Trois Voyages faits en icelle par certains Capitaines et Pilotes Francois, descrits par le Capitaine Laudonierre, qui y a commande l'espace d'un au trois moys: a laquelle a este adjouste un quatriesme voyage fait par le Capitaine Gourgues. Mise en lumire par M. Basaniere. *A Paris,* 1853. 16° *pp.* xvi. + 228. 97

[History Notable of Florida. Containing the three Voyages made to it by certain Captains and Pilots described by Captain Laudonierre, who commanded in them for three months. To which is added a fourth voyage made by Captain Gourgues.]

The narratives of the three voyages of Jean Ribaut, first published in 1586, contain the earliest accounts of the Indians of Florida, except such as are found in the Relacion of Cabeca de Vaca. In one respect, at least, it relieves the ferocity charged upon the savages by most writers, by its narration of the horrible massacre perpetrated on the French, by the fiend Menendez, whose name be consigned to infamy, as his soul is to perdition.

BATES (Joshua).

A Sermon delivered before the Society for Propagating the Gospel among the Indians in North America, at their Anniversary, November 4, 1813. By Joshua Bates. 8° *pp.* 44. *Boston,* 1813. 98

The Historical Notes in the Appendix fill the last fifteen pages.

B(audry de) L(ozieres).
Voyage a La Louisiane, et sur le Continent de l'Amerique Septentrionale, fait dans les annees, 1794 a 1798; Contenant un Tableau Historique de la Louisiane, des Observations sur son Climat ses Riches, Productions, le Caractere et le Nom des Sauvages [*etc. 4 lines*], par B** D** orne de une Belle Carte. 8° *Map, pref. pp.* viii. + 382. *Paris, An XI* (1802). 99

[Travels in Louisiana and on the Continent of North America, made in the years 1794 to 1798; containing a Historic Tableau of Louisiana, with Observations on its Climate, its most valuable Productions, the Character of the Indians, etc.]

Like most of the works called Voyages, written by Frenchmen, this is principally occupied with a *resumé* of the history of the country purported to be visited, with scarcely nothing of personal observation. The character, manners, and wars of the native savages of course occupy his attention largely; but his work is principally notable for "Two Vocabularies of the Savages," the Naoudouessis and the Chipouais, covering pp. 348 to 362.

Baxter (Rev. Joseph).
Journal of several Visits to the Indians on the Kennebec, by the Rev. Joseph Baxter, of Medfield, Mass., 1717. with Notes, by the Rev. Elias Nason. Reprinted from the N. E. Hist. and Genealogical Register, for January, 1867. 8° *pp.* 18. *Boston,* 1867. 100

A short vocabulary terminates the Journal.

Beamish (N. L.).
The Discovery of America by the Northmen, in the Tenth Century, with Notices of the Early Settlements of the Irish in the Western Hemisphere, by Nath' Ludlow Beamish. 8° *Two maps and pp.* (xvi.) + 340 + *folding table* + (x.) *London,* 1841. 101

The book is principally occupied with translations of the Sagas, from Prof. Rafn's Danish work, entitled *Antiquitates Americanæ.* The author attempts to prove that as Irish ecclesiastics were constantly passing between Iceland and Ireland, that it is more than probable that America was first discovered by men of Hibernian birth.

Beatty (Charles).
The Journal of a Two-Months' Tour; with a View of Promoting Religion among the Frontier Inhabitants of Pennsylvania, and of Introducing Christianity among the Indians to the Westward of the Allegh-geny Mountains. To which are added Remarks on the Language and Customs of some particular Tribes among the Indians; with a brief Account of the various Attempts that have been made to civilize and convert them, from the first Settlement of New-England to this Day. By Charles Beatty, A. M. 8° *pp.* 110. *London,* 1768. 102

The tour of this zealous and intelligent observer to the Indian towns in Pennsylvania and Ohio, lying far beyond the frontiers, was made at a period of great interest in their history. The warriors of the Delaware and Shawnese had ravaged them with the tomahawk and firebrand for twenty years, and the Journal of the missionary is filled with notes of their awful massa-cites. It is very full and minute in its details of interviews with Indian chiefs, and the various phases of aboriginal life which attracted his attention.

BEATTY (Charles).

The Journal of a Two Months' Tour; with a view of Promoting Religion among the Frontier Inhabitants of Pennsylvania, and of Introducing Christianity among the Indians to the Westward of the Allegany Mountains, to which are added Remarks on the Language and Customs of some particular Tribes among the Indians; with a brief Account of the various Attempts that have been made to civilize and convert them, from the first Settlement of New England to this day. By Charles Beatty, A. M. *pp.* 50. *Edinburgh*, 1798. 103

This is the second edition, printed as the Appendix to the Edinburgh edition of Brainard's *Journal of a Mission among the Indians.* Some copies seem to have been printed separately. The first edition is quite difficult to procure complete.

BEAUFOY (Mark).

Mexican Illustrations founded upon Facts; indicative of the Present Condition of Society, Manners, Religion, and Morals among the Spanish and Native Inhabitants of Mexico; with Observations upon the Government and Resources of the Republic of Mexico, as they appeared during part of the years 1825, 1826, and 1827, interspersed with occasional remarks upon the Climate, Produce, and Antiquities of the Country, mode of working the Mines, etc. By Mark Beaufoy, late of the Coldstream Guards. 8° *pp.* xiv. + 310 + *map and six plates. London, Carpenter and Son*, 1828. 104

Chap. xiii., pp. 189 to 224, is entitled "Antiquities and Origin of the Mexicans." Chapter xv., "The Indians and Mode of Working the Mines," occupies pp. 256 to 274. Seven wood-cuts, illustrative of Indian modes of labor, are printed with the text.

BEECHEY (F. W. Captain).

Narrative of a Voyage to the Pacific and Beerhing's Strait, to co-operate with the Polar Expeditions: performed in His Majesty's Ship Blossom, under the command of Captain F. W. Beechey. Published by authority of the Lords' Commissioners of the Admiralty. In two parts. *London, Henry Colburn and Richard Bentley*, 1831. 4° Part I. — *pp.* xxi. + 1 *to* 392. Part II. — *pp.* viii. + 393 *to* 742 + 25 *plates and maps.* 105

BEECHEY (Captain F. W.)

Narrative of a Voyage to the Pacific and Beering's Strait, to co-operate with the Polar Expeditions; performed in His Majesty's Ship Blossom, under the command of Captain F. B. Beechey, R. N., in the years 1825, 1826, 1827, 1828. Published by authority of the Lords' Commissioners of the Admiralty. *Large* 8° *pp.* 493. *Philadelphia, Carey and Lea*, 1832. 106

Chapters xiii. and xiv., pp. 292 to 344, are devoted to a description of the

Missions and Indians of California; and Chapter xix., pp. 458 to 481, contains a relation of personal adventures among the Esquimaux, with descriptions of their peculiar habits and customs.

Beside the natural interest which attaches to the narrative of a visit to the Indian Missions of California, and a description of those petty yet wonderful hierarchs, just on the verge of extinction, we are afforded in Captain Beechey's book an insight into the secret history of these important institutions, which increases that interest greatly. The Mission Fathers, long isolated from the civilized world, had become as severe tyrants in their little monarchies as any of the secular class, and regularly recruited their subjects from the wild tribes of savages, by expeditions against them, in which fire and sword had more victims than the cord and the prison.

BEESON (John).

A Plea for the Indians; with Facts and Features of the late War in Oregon. 12° *pp.* 144, *paper.* 1858. 107

On the cover of this earnest statement of the needs and wrongs of the natives of Oregon, was printed an announcement of the immediate publication of *A Further Plea for the Indians*, which it is believed never appeared.

BELKNAP (Jeremy).

Discourse intended to commemorate the Discovery of America by Christopher Columbus [*etc.* 5 *lines*], to which are added Four Dissertations connected with the various parts of the discourse, namely: I. On the circumnavigation of Africa by the ancients. II. An examination of the pretensions of Martin Behaim to a discovery of America prior to that of Columbus, with a Chronological detail of all the Discoveries made in the 15th Century. III. On the question whether the honey-bee is a native of America. IV. On the color of the native Americans, and the recent population of this Continent. By Jeremy Belknap. 8° *pp.* 113. *Boston*, 1792. 108

BELL (W. A.)

New Tracks in North America. A Journal of Travel and Adventure whilst engaged in the Survey for a Southern Railroad to the Pacific Ocean during 1867–8. By William A. Bell, M. A.; with contributions by General W. J. Palmer, Major A. R. Calhoun, C. C. Perry, and Captain W. F. Colton. In two volumes. 8° Vol. I. *pp.* lxiv. + 236 + 10 *colored plates and* 13 *wood-cuts in the text.* Vol. II. *pp.* viii. + 322 + 13 *colored plates and* 9 *wood-cuts, with three maps. London, Chapman and Hall; New York, Scribner, Welford, and Co.*, 1869. 109

Part II., pp. 153 to 231 of Vol. I., is entitled, "The Native Races of New Mexico," and is something more than a recital of the Spanish narrations from Venegas to Bascana, with their much less than credible theories of the origin of the aborigines of Northwestern Mexico. He traces the migration northward of the Aztec race, driven by Spanish cruelty, with much ingenuity, by the ruins of their peculiar architecture.

BELTRAMI (J. C.)

La Decouverte des Sources du Mississippi et de la Riviere Sanglante. Description entier du Mississippi [*etc.* 6 *lines*]; Observations Critico Philosophiques, sur les Moeurs, la Religion, les

Superstitions, les Costumes, les Armes, les Chasses, la Guerre, la Paix, le Denombrement, l'Origine etc. etc. of de Plusiers Nations Indiennes. Parallele de ces Peuples avec ceux de l'Antiquite [*etc. 7 lines*], par J. C. Beltrami. 8° *Nouvelle-Orleans*, 1824. 110

BELTRAMI (J. C.).

A Pilgrimage in Europe and America leading to the Discovery of the Sources of the Mississippi and Bloody River; with a Description of the whole course of the former, and of the Ohio. By J. C. Beltrami, Esq. In two volumes. 8° Vol. I. *pp.* 76 + 472. *Portrait of the author in his dress when among the Indians. 2 maps.* Vol. II. *pp.* 545 + 6, *and 3 plates and plan. London, printed for Hunt and Clarke*, 1828. 111

Vol. II. is almost entirely devoted to the author's travels among the Northwestern Indians, of whom he gives some novel particulars. The narrations of what he witnessed are tinged with the peculiar glow of the author's temperament. Beltrami must have moved in a gigantic world, if he saw external objects through the same media with which he viewed his own person and accomplishments.

This volume is a translation, or perhaps more nearly a paraphrase, of that noticed above.

BENEZET (Anthony).

Observations on the Situation, Disposition, and Character of the Indian Natives of this Continent. 16° *pp.* 59. *Philadelphia, printed and sold by Joseph Cruikshank*, 1784. 112

Anthony Benezet, born in 1713, of a French family of St. Quentin, was driven from France by the revocation of the Edict of Nantes. Having fixed his residence in Philadelphia, he adopted the doctrine of the Quakers. His humanity impelled him to attempt an amelioration of the condition of both the Indians and negroes, by publishing treatises exhibiting the unhappy state to which each had been reduced, by the cupidity and neglect of the whites. He died in 1784.

BENSON (Henry C.).

Life among the Choctaw Indians, and Sketches of the Southwest. By Henry C. Benson, with an Introduction by Rev. T. A. Morris. 12° *pp.* 314. *Cincinnati*, 1860. 113

This is evidently a veritable relation of personal experience during three years' service as teacher and missionary among the Choctaws; and is the work of a man of sense, who does not fill his pages with the emotional religious exercises of his converts, but narrates the every-day story of incidents and character, grave or ludicrous, which presented themselves.

BENSON (Egbert).

Memoir read before the Historical Society of the State of New York, 31st December, 1816. By Egbert Benson. *pp.* 72. *New York*, 1817. 114

First edition of Benson's Memoirs of the Indian, Dutch, and English names of localities in the vicinity of New York.

BENSON (Egbert).

Memoir read before the Historical Society of the State of New York, December 31, 1816. By Egbert Benson. Second

Edition with Notes. 12° *pp.* 127. *Jamaica, Henry C. Sleight, Printer*, 1825. 115

An essay on the Indian and Dutch names of New York, first printed in 1817, by the author. The peculiarly abrupt, and not very perspicuous style of the work, excited the criticisms of the directors of the Society, who required some verbal changes before publication, which the author's pride induced him to reject with indignation. A controversy arose of much acrimony, and Mr. Benson determined to vindicate his style by printing his essay. He does not however seem to have been entirely satisfied with it himself, as several copies exist with numerous manuscript additions and corrections.

The second edition printed in Jamaica includes some of these, and is quite difficult to procure. The Society in 1848, after the death of the author, printed the address, in their seventh volume of Collections. Of this a few copies were issued in a separate form bearing on the title "Reprinted from a copy with the Author's last Corrections."

BENTON (Nathaniel S.).

The History of Herkimer County and the Upper Mohawk Valley, from the Earliest Period to the Present Time, with a Brief Notice of the Iroquois Indians, the Early German Tribes, the Palatine Immigrations into the Colony of New York, and Biographical Sketches of the Palatine Families, the Patentees of Burnetsfield in the year 1725; also Biographical Notices of the most Prominent Public Men of the County, with Important Statistical Information. 8° *pp.* 497, *maps, etc. Albany*, 1856. 116

BENZONI (Giralamo).

La Historia del Mondo Nuovo. Di M Giralamo Benzoni Milanese. Laqual tratta dell' isole & Mari nuoua mente ritrouati & delle nuove citta da lui proprio redute, per acqua & per terra in quattordeci anni. Venitia Per anni xv. (Colophon). *In Venitia Appresso Francesco Rampazetto*, MDLXV. 24° *Portrait of the Author. Title and* 3 *prel. leaves* + 1 *to* 175, *numbered leaves.* 117

This rare book is the work of an old Italian traveller who, incited by the wonderful stories of the world discovered by his countryman fifty years before, adventured in 1541 to gain personal knowledge of it. The Aborigines of the countries he visited always seemed first to attract his attention; and he has accordingly afforded us some of the rarest pictures of their condition and habits at that early day, of which the rude wood-cuts printed in the text are quaint but spirited illustrations. It is the first book of Travels of which America has been so fruitful, as Benzoni seems to have been the first who travelled merely to gratify his curiosity and recorded his observations.

BENZONI (Giralamo).

History of the New World, by Giralamo Benzoni of Milan, showing his Travels in America from A. D. 1541 to 1556; with some particulars of the Island of Canary. Now first translated and edited by Rear Admiral W. H. Smyth. 8° *pp.* iv. + (vi.) + 280. *London, printed for the Hakluyt Society*, 1857. 118

The narrative of Giralamo Benzoni is one of the most interesting of all the early travellers in America, not only for the minute details of the life and habits of the Aborigines more than three centuries ago, but for the evident fidelity to truth, and the consequent reliance we may feel that we are viewing the common life of the natives before what we term civilization had corrupted them. Eighteen fac-similes of the curious wood-cuts of the period are inserted in the text, most of which are illustrative of some phases in the customs of the Indians. They were reproduced by De Bry. Born at Milan in 1519, he abandoned his country to seek for adventures in the New World at the age of twenty-two. After fourteen years of travels he returned in 1556 and published his *Historia del Mondo*, which has been esteemed a great success, and translated into several languages.

BENZONI (H.).

Novae Novi Orbis Historiae Id est Rerum ab Hispanis in India Occidentali hactenus gestarum, & acerbo illorum in eas gentes dominatu, Libri tres. Urbani Calvetonis opera industriasque ex Italicus Hieronymi Benzonis Mediolanensis, qui eas terras xiiii. annorum peregrinatione obyt commentariis descripti Latini facta ac perpetuis notis, argumentis & locu pleti memorabilium rerum acessione illustrati. Hic ab eodem adjuncta est De Gallorum in Floridam expeditione & insigni Hispanorum in eos saeuitiae-exemplo Brevis Historia Apud Eustathium Vignon, 1578. 12° *Title and pref. pp.* (xxii.) + 480 + *Index*, xii. + *Errata*, 1 *leaf.* 119

[New History of the New World containing a summary of all that the Spaniards have done to the present time in the West Indies, and of the cruel treatment they have given the unfortunate natives. Translated from the Italian of Jerome Benzoni, the Milanois, who travelled in that country fourteen years. Enriched with many observations and facts worthy of being preserved. By Urban Chauveton, together with a short history of a massacre committed by the Spaniards upon some Frenchmen in Florida. With an Index of the most remarkable events.]

This is the first Latin edition of Benzoni, and is chiefly valuable for the addition by Chauveton of the narration of Laudonierre, which is found commencing at page 427, with the title in Latin, "Brief History of the Expedition of the French to Florida, and of the Massacre so barbarously executed upon them by the Spaniards in 1565." Charlevoix supposes this portion of the work to have been taken from that of La Challeux, printed in 1556. In the next year the first French translation of Benzoni was printed, to which this account of the Massacre was also added.

It was this translation of Benzoni's work which was printed by De Bry as Parts IV., V., and VI. of his Great Voyages, with 78 plates.

BERENDT (C. Hermann).

Analytical Alphabet for the Mexican and Central American Languages, by C. Hermann Berendt, M. D.; published by the American Ethnological Society. 8° *pp.* 6 + 8. *New York. Reproduced in fac-simile, by the American Photo-Lithographic Company*, 1869. 120

The gentleman whose name is attached to this ingenious analysis of the elementary sounds of the Maya and other dialects, has devoted twelve years of his life to their study, most of which time he has resided in Yucatan. His zeal is only equaled by his scholarship; and to the ethnological results of his grammatical comparison of the eighteen dialects of which he is preparing a Dictionary and Grammar, many scholars in this country and in Europe are directing the most profound regard.

BERTONIO (L.).

Libro | de la Vida y | Milagros de Nvestro Senor | Jesu Christo en dos Lenguas Aymara y Romance | traducido de el que recopilo el Licenciado Alon | so de Villegas quitadas y anadidas algunas | cosas y acomodado alo capacidad de los Indios | Por el Padre Lucovico Bertonio Ita | liano de la Compania de Jesus en la Provincia de el Piru natural | de Rocca Contrado de la Marca de Ancona. Dedicado al illustrissimo y reverendissimo Senor don Alonso de Peralta primer Arcobispo de los Charcas. Impresso en la Casa de la Compania de Jesus de Juli Pueblo en la Provincia de Chucuyto por Francisco del Canto 1612. Esta tassado este libro a Real cada pliego en papal. 4° *Title*, 1 *leaf*. *Erratas*, 1 *leaf*. *Approbacion and Licencia*, 1 *leaf*. 2d *Approbacion*, 1 *leaf*. 2d *Licencia with Approbacion*, 2 *leaves*. *Dedicatoria*, 2 *leaves*. *Total prelim. leaves* 8 + *pp*. 560, *numbered erroneously* 660 *pp*. + *tabla* viii. 121

[Book of the Life and Miracles of our Lord Jesus Christ, in two languages, Aymara and Spanish, translated from the compilation of the Licentiate Alonso de Villegas, together with some other things adapted to the comprehension of the Indians, by the Father Lodovico Bertonio. Printed at the House of the Society of Jesus, in the Village of Juli, Province of Chuquitos (Peru), 1612.]

Father Bertonio entered the Society in 1575, and passed his life in Peru as a missionary to the Indians. He died at Lima in 1628 at the age of seventy-three years.

The other works of Bertonio in the Indian languages are: *Arte de la Lengua Aymara*, Rome, 1603, 8°, and 1608; *Arte de la Lengua Aymara*, Juli, 1612, 8°, and 1614; *Confessionario de las Lenguas Aymara y Romance*, 1612, 8°; *Vocabulario de la Lengua Aymara*, Juli, 1612, 4°; also, a MS. *Historia de los Quatro Evangelios en Aymara*. Other works of Bertonio are known to have been printed, but we have lost even the titles. All of these works are excessively rare, and considered very valuable for the history of typography in Peru.

Ferdinand del Canto was a celebrated printer of Peru, who was also the director of the press of the Jesuits at Juli.

(Beverly) (Robert).

History of Virginia in Four Parts. 1st. The History of the First Settlement of Virginia, and the Government thereof, to the year 1706. 2d. The Natural Productions and Conveniences of the Country, suited to Trade and Improvement. 3d. The Native Indians, their Religion, Laws and Customs, in War and Peace. 4th. The Present State of the Country, etc. By a Native and Inhabitant of the Place. Second Edition Revised and Enlarged by the Author. 8° *Engraved title, title and 5 prel. leaves* + *pp*. 104 + 40 + 64 + 83 + 16 *and* 4 *unnumbered pp*. *London*, 1722. 122

The work appeared anonymously in two English and one French edition, but is known to have been written by Robert Beverly. The plates are reduced copies of those in Harriott's *Virginia*, drawn and engraved by the brothers De Bry.

Beyard (Col. Nicholas).

Journal of the Late Actions of the French at Canada, by Col. Nicholas Beyard and Lieut. Col. Charles Lodowick. *New York: Reprinted for Joseph Sabin*, 1868. 123

The title-page of the first edition of 1693 announces the other subjects of the book, which are: I. Account of two Dutch Men Prisoners in Canada. II. Examination of a French Prisoner. III. Governor Fletcher's Speech to the Indians, The Reply of the Chiefs of the Five Nations, and The Proposals of four Chiefs to Gov. Fletcher.

BIBAUD (F. M. Maximillien).

Biographie des Sagamos Illustres de l'Amerique Septentrionale. Precede d' un Index de l'Historique fabuleuse de ce Continent. Par F. M. Maximillien Bibaud. 8° *pp.* 309. *Montreal de l'Imprimerie de Lovell et Gibson rue St. Nicolas*, 1848. 124

[Biography of Illustrious Indian Chiefs of North America, preceded by an Index of the Mythical History of that Continent. By F. M. Maximilian Bibaud.]

This work attempts something more than biographical sketches of famous Indians, as it gives a *resumé* of discovery, and wars with the natives, as a frame in which to hang his portraits of them. It is a very good compilation of the quite well known facts of aboriginal history, and, although containing little that is not already stored in the common stock of knowledge, it does not include much, if anything, of his own composition which is fallacious or speculative.

BIBLE BOY

Taken Captive by the Indians. Written for the American Sunday-School Union, and revised by the Committee of Publication. 18° *pp.* 35. *Philadelphia, n. d.* 125

BICKLEY (George W. L.).

History of the Settlement and Indian Wars of Tazewell County, Virginia. 8° *Cincinnati*, 1852. 126*

BIERCE (Gen. L. V.).

Historical Reminiscences of Summit County (Ohio). By Gen. L. V. Bierce. *Square* 12° *pp.* 157. *Akron, Ohio, T. & H. C. Canfield, publishers*, 1854.

Many new incidents of Indian life and warfare are recorded in this little volume.

BIET (Antoine).

Voyage de la France Equinoxiale en l'isle de Cayenne, entrepris par les Francois en l'annee M.DC.LII. Divise en trois Livres. *Le Premier*, contient l'establissement de la Colonie, son embarquement, & sa route iusques a son arrivee en l'isle de Cayenne. *Le Second*, ce qui s'est passe pendant quinze mois que l'on a demeure dans le pais. *Le Troiseme* traitte du temperament du pais, de la fertilite de la terre & des Moeurs, & facons de faire des Sauvages de cette contree. Avec un Dictionaire de la Langue du mesme Paya. Par Mr. Antoine Biet, Prestre, etc. *A Paris*, 1664. 4° *prel. pp.* (24) + 432. 127

[Voyage to France Equinoxial, in the island of Cayenne; undertaken by the French in 1652. Divided into three Books. The First containing the establishment of the Colony, etc. The Second, a narrative of what took place during five months, etc. The Third, treating of the climate and fertility of the country, and of the manners and habits of life of the savages of the country. With a dictionary of the language.]

That portion of the third part treating of the savages and the language occupies pp. 339 to 432, the last ninety-three pages of the work.

BIGLOW (William).

History of the Town of Natick, Mass., from the days of the Apostle Eliot, MDCL., to the present time. MDCCCXXX. By William Biglow. 8° pp. 87. *Boston, published by Marsh, Capen, & Lyon*, 1830. 128

This local history contains many notices of the Aborigines, and incidents of their life and manners.

BIGOT (Vincent Pere).

Relation De ce Qui s'est passe de plus remarqvable dans la Mission des Abnaquis a l'Acadie, l'annee 1701. Par le Pere Vincent Bigot de la Compagnie de Jesus. 4° *A Manate de la Presse Cramoisy de Jean-Marie Shea*, 1858. 129

Relation of the most remarkable events which transpired in the Abnaquis Mission of Acadia, in the year 1701. By the Rev. Father Vincent Bigot of the Company of Jesus.]

Father Vincent Bigot, a Frenchman of the Society of Jesus, was a missionary among the Indians of Canada. This letter is dated as having been written from a village of the Abnaquis in Acadie. He is not noticed in the Bibliotheque of the Fathers Backer, which only cites the name and relations of Father Jacques Bigot, who sent relations of the Missions of the Abnaquis to his Superior at Quebec, in 1681, 1685, and 1709, showing that he served as a missionary at least eighteen years. He is the author of the three following *Relations*.

Mr. John Gilmary Shea, of New York, to whom we owe these excellent contributions to our literature, has printed a series extending to twenty-three *Relations*. The edition of each work was limited to one hundred copies, which have been so much sought after that it is very difficult to obtain a complete set. In Europe the estimation of the *Relations*, and of Mr. Shea's series of *Indian Linguistics*, is much greater than in this country.

No. 4, Shea's *Jesuit Relations*.

BIGOT (Jacques R. P.)

Relation De Ce Qui s'est passe de plvs remarkable dans la Mission Abnaquise de Saint Joseph de Sillery et dans l'Establissement de la Nouvelle Mission de Saint Francois de Sales l'annee 1684. Par le R. P. Jacques Bigot de la Compagnie de Jesus. 4° pp. 61. *A Manate de la Presse Cramoisy de Jean-Marie Shea.* 1857, 130

[Relation of the most remarkable events which transpired in the Abnaquis Mission of Saint Joseph of Sillery and in the Establishment of the New Mission of Saint Francis of Sales, in the year 1701. By the Rev. Father Vincent Bigot, of the Company of Jesus.]

No. 7, Shea's *Jesuit Relations*.

BIGOT (Jacques R. Pere).

Relation de ce qui s'est passe de plus remarquable Dans La Mission Abnaquise de Saint Joseph de Sillery et de Saint François de Sales l'année, 1685. Par le R. Pere Jacques Bigot de la Compagnie de Jesus. 4° *A Manate de la Presse Cramoisy de Jean-Marie Shea*, 1858. 131

[Relation of the most remarkable events which took place in the Abnaquis Mission of Saint Joseph of Sillery, and of Saint Francis of Sales, in the year 1685. By the Rev. Father Jacques Bigot, of the Society of Jesus.]

No. 6, Shea's *Jesuit Relations*.

Bigot (Pere Jacques).

Relation de la Mission Abnaquisse de St. François de Sales l'année 1702. Par le Pere Jacquise Bigot De la Compagnie de Jesus. *pp.* 26 (8°) *Nouvelle-York. Presse Cramoisy de Jean-Marie Shea*, 1865. 132

[Relation of the Abnaquis Mission of Saint Francis de Sales in the year 1702. By the Father Jacques Bigot, of the Society of Jesus.]

No. 23, Shea's *Jesuit Relations.*

Bigsby (John J.).

The Shoe and Canoe, or pictures of travel in the Canadas, illustrative of their scenery and of colonial life with facts and opinions on emigration, state policy, and other points of public interest. With numerous Plates and Maps. By John J. Bigsby, M. D. *In two volumes. pp.* 352, 346. *London*, 1850. 133

The second volume contains the narrative of a tour through the wilds of Canada which border the upper Great Lakes, and affords us some accounts of the recent condition of the Aborigines inhabiting them. Some of the plates (which are fine steel engravings) are illustrative of scenes he witnessed in Indian life.

Billaine (Louis).

Receuil de divers Voyages faits en Afrique et l'Amerique qui n'ont esti encore publiez: Contenant L'Origine Les Moeurs, les Coutumes & les Commerce des Habitans de ces deux Parties du Monde. Avec des Traitez curieux touchant la Haute Ethyopie, le debordment du Nil, la mer Rouge, et le Pretd-Jean. Le tout enrichi de Figures & de Cartes Geographiques qui servent a l'Intelligence des choses contennes en ce volume. 4° *A Paris*, 1674. 16 *prel. pp.* + *Histoire des Barbades, pp.* — + *Relation du Nil, pp.* 262 + 9 *maps and plates. Description de l'Empire du Pretre-Jean, pp.* 1 *to* 35. *Relation d' Afrique, pp.* 1 *to* 23. *Relation de l' Origine, Moeurs, Coustumes, Religion, Guerres, et Voyages des Caraibes, Sauvages des isles Antilles de l'Amerique Faite par le Sieur de la Borde Employe a la Conversion des Caraibes, estant avec le R. P. Simon, Jesuite; Et tiree du Cabinet de Monsieur Blondel. Three plates in* 12 *compartments, pp.* 1 *to* 40. *Relation de la Guiane*, 41 *to* 49. *Des* *de la Jamaique, map and* 1 *to* 27. *Rel des Barbades*, 29 *to* 45. *Colonies Angloises, Map* + 47 *to* 81. 134

[Collection of several Voyages made to Africa and America which have never before been published. Containing the Origin, the Manners, the Customs, and the Commerce of the Natives of these two parts of the World. With curious treatises concerning Upper Ethiopia, the Mouth of the Nile, the Red Sea, and Prester John. The whole embellished with Plates and Maps. *Fifth Relation*,— Relation of the Origin, Manners, Customs, Religion, Wars, and Travels of the Caribs, native Savages of the Antilles in America, made by Father de la Borde, a Missionary to the Caribs with the Jesuit Father Simon. With Plates from drawings of the cabinet of Mons. Blondel.]

These Plates are each divided into four compartments, representing some of the manufactures, weapons, utensils, or habitations of the Caribs. Father La Borde's *Relation* is valuable as the narration of an intelligent observer of the habits and peculiarities of a people who have long since passed away. He was careful, he says, to record nothing which he had not himself observed, or which the character and intelligence of his savage informant did not entitle to perfect credence. His *Relation* has never been published, as far as my investigation has reached, in any other form.

BILSON (R.)

The Hunters of Kentucky; or the Trials and Toils of Traders and Trappers during an Expedition to the Rocky Mountains, New Mexico, and California. 8° *pp.* 100. *New York, W. H. Graham*, 1847. 135

This work is a reproduction of Pattie's narrative, which the penury of the thieving writer's imagination has not empowered him to clothe with new language, or interleave with new incidents. The air of veracity, which every page of Pattie's interesting narrative possesses was in consequence transferred to the stolen sheets of Bilson, and long perplexed me by the clearness of statement, and the unmistakable flavor of truthfulness which pervaded a work that brought no voucher for its reality.

BISHOP (Harriet E.).

Floral Home; or First Years of Minnesota. Early Sketches, Later Settlements, and Further Developments. By Harriet E. Bishop. 12° *pp.* 342. *New York and Chicago*, 1857. 136

Under this romantic and unpromising title the author has given her personal experiences of aboriginal life.

BLACKBIRD (A. J.).

Education of Indian Youth. Letter of Rev. Samuel Bissel, and appeal of A. J. Blackbird, a Chippewa Chief. 16° *pp.* 15. *Philadelphia, William F. Geddes, printer*, 1856. 137

BLACK HAWK.

Life of Ma-ka-tai-me-she-kia-kia or Black Hawk embracing the Tradition of his nation — Indian Wars in which he has been engaged — Cause of joining the British in their late war with America and its history. Description of the Rock River Village.— Manners and Customs — Encroachments by the Whites contrary to treaty. Removal from his village in 1831, With an Account of the Cause and general History of the Late War, his Surrender and Confinement at Jefferson Barracks and Travels Through the United States, Dictated by Himself. J. B. Patterson of Rock Island Editor and Proprietor. *Portrait.* 16° *pp.* 155. *Boston*, 1845. 138

BLAKE (Alex. V.).

Anecdotes of the American Indians. 16° *pp.* 252. *Hartford*, 1850. 139

BLATCHFORD (Samuel).

An Address delivered to the Oneida Indians, September 24, 1810. By Samuel Blatchford, D. D., together with the Reply by Christian, a Chief of said Nation. 8° *pp.* 11. *Albany*, 1810. 140

BLEEKER (Capt. Leonard).

The Order Book of Capt. Leonard Bleeker, Major of Brigade in the early part of the Expedition under James Clinton, against the Indian Settlements of Western New York, in the Campaign of 1779. Edited by Franklin B. Hough. 4° *New York, Jos. Sabin*, 1865. 141

BLEECKER. The Same. *Foolscap 4° pp.* 138. *New York, Jos. Sabin*, 1865. 142

Two hundred copies printed.

BLUNT (Joseph).

Historical Sketch of the Formation of the Confederacy, particularly with reference to the provincial Limits and the Jurisdiction of the General Government over Indian Tribes and the public Territory. 8° *pp.* 116. *New York* 1852. 143

This is a very careful consideration of the tenure by which the United States acquired a title to the lands once occupied or claimed by the Indians. Mr. Blunt analyses in a most judicious and impartial manner, the complex rights of the savage and the civilized claimants; more especially of those by which the State of New York assumes proprietorship of the lands once held by the Six Nations, and of the States of Georgia, Alabama, and Mississippi, in those of the Creeks, Choctaws, and Cherokees.

BOGART (W. H.).

Daniel Boone and the Hunters of Kentucky. 12° *pp.* 464. *New York*, 1854. 144

A popular collection of the often repeated stories of frontier life and Indian warfare, veritable enough, but neither better or worse told than in a hundred other forms.

BOISTHIBAULT (M. Doublet de).

Les Voeux des Hurons et des Abnaquis, A Notre-Dame de Chartres. Publies pour la premiere fois' d'Apres les manuscripts des archives d'Eure-et-Loire. Avec les lettres des missionaires catholiques au Canada, une introduction et des notes, par M. Doublet de Boisthibault. *Chartres, Noury-Cognard, libraire.* 12° *pp.* 83, *and folding plate. Philadelphia, John Pennington & Son.* 1857. 145

[The Vows of the Hurons and the Abnaquis to Our Lady of Chartres. Published for the first time from the MS. in the Archives of d'Eure-et-Loire, with the letters of the Catholic Missionaries in Canada, an introduction and notes, by M. Doublet de Boisthibault.]

The Vows of the Indians are reproduced only in Latin and French, although they were written and registered in Abnaquis. The neglect to preserve this fragment of the language of the Abnaquis, renders this document comparatively valueless. The relations of the Jesuit Missionaries accompanying it are interesting, and add to our stock of historical data.

BOLLAERT (William).

Antiquarian, Ethnological and other Researches in New Granada, Equador, Peru, and Chile, with Observations on the Pre-Incarial, Incarial and other Monuments of Peruvian Nations. By William Bollaert; with plates. 8° *pp.* 279+17 *full page plates. London*, 1860. 146

Mr. Bollaert is the author of several treatises on ethnological subjects, printed in the Anthropological Transactions of Europe, and brings to the consideration of his subject a rare combination of learning, ability, and zeal. He twice visited and personally examined the monuments of Incarial grandeur in Para, and, besides the facts obtained during his tours in that country, his book is a cyclopedia of the records of South American Antiquities. Vocabularies of several Indian dialects are given on pp. 61 to 70 and 103 to 111. Most of the plates are illustrations of the ornaments, utensils, buildings, or idols of the natives.

BOLLER (Henry A.)

Among the Indians. Eight Years in the Far West, 1858–1866. Embracing Sketches of Montana and Salt Lake. 12° *pp.* 428. *Philadelphia*, 1868. 147

No words can give a fairer description of the purpose, scope, and narration of this work, than the author's language in his preface: "The following pages have been written from a Journal and Notes kept during my residence of eight years in the Far West. I have endeavored to narrate truthfully, and without exaggeration, only such incidents as fall under my *personal observation*, and also to portray faithfully Indian life in its home aspect. At the present time when the Indian is being held up before the world as an incarnate fiend, it is but fair that his redeeming qualities should likewise be recorded." The author whose position as a fur trader among the savage tribes of the great plains on the upper Missouri for eight years, enabled him to form his judgment on solid experience, has clearly redeemed his pledges in the Preface.

BONNELL (George W.)

Topographical Description of Texas, to which is added an Account of the Indian Tribes, by George W. Bonnell. 24° *Austin*, 1840. 148

BONNER (T. D.)

The Life and Adventures of James P. Beckworth, Mountaineer, Scout, and Pioneer; Chief of Crow Nation of Indians. Written from his own dictation. By T. D. Bonner. 12° *pp.* 357. *New York*, 1856. 149

This narrative, said to have been dictated to Mr. Bonner long after the period of these marvelous adventures, bears the marks of that talent for exaggeration for which the border men are so remarkable. Beckworth at this time had retired from the hazardous chieftainships he had attained, of several hostile tribes in succession, to a hut, where he was dispensing fire-water to the emigrants, who thronged the trail near his groggery.

Although he speaks in rather sounding terms of his Revolutionary sire, he neglects to state that his mother was a mulatto slave; and Mr. Bonner is equally silent upon the tokens he must have seen of slight regard to truthfulness. Jim Beckworth was known for many years on the frontier as a daring adventurer, and an unscrupulous savage, not less brutal and bloodthirsty than his Indian allies; but no frontiersman ever made the mistake of believing all he said.

BONNYCASTLE (Sir Richard Henry).

Newfoundland in 1842. A Sequel to the Canadas in 1841. By Sir Richard Henry Bonnycastle, Knt. In Two Volumes. Vol. I. *pp.* xi. + 367. Vol. II. *pp.* 331 + *map* + 5 *plates*. *London, Henry Colburn, publisher*, 1842. 150

A very interesting account of the fierce tribe of Red Indians, of Newfoundland, their unrelenting hatred of the whites, their merciless persecution by the latter, and the frequent expeditions undertaken to secure peaceful relations with them, is given by the author on pages 251 to 278.

BOOK (The)

Of American Indians, containing Comprehensive Details of Indian Battles, Massacres, Border Warfare, Biographical Sketches of Distinguished Indians, etc. New Edition. 12° *pp.* 384, *including* 40 *engravings. Dayton, Ohio. Published by B. F. Ellis,* 1854. 151

Hunters' narrative of captivity forms the first half of the volume, and anecdotes of Indians the remainder, both reprints of very common books, without addition.

BOON (Colonel Daniel).

Life and Adventures of Colonel Daniel Boon, The first white settler of the State of Kentucky. Comprising An Account of his first excursion to Kentucky in 1769, then a wild Wilderness inhabited by no other human beings but Savages, his remove there with his family, in 1773, and of his various encounters with the Indians, from the years 1769 to 1782. Written by himself. To which is added a narration of the most important incidents of his life [*etc.,* 9 *lines*]. 12° *Portrait, and* 36 *pages. Brooklyn,* 1824. 152

BOQUET (Col. Henry).

See Smith, Wm., and Parkman, Francis. 153

BORRENSTEIN (D. A.)

Mengwe, a Tale of the Frontier. A Poem. 12° *pp.* 76. *Princeton Press, printed for D. A. Borrenstein,* 1825. 154

Pages 4 to 10, and 57 to 76, are occupied with an Introduction and Notes of incidents and historical data relating to the American Indians.

BOSCANA (Geronimo).

Chinigchinich: a Historical Account of the Origin, Customs, and Traditions of the Indians at the Missionary Establishment of St. Juan Capistrano, Alta California, called The Acagchemem Nation; collected with the greatest care from the most intelligent and best instructed in the matter. By the Reverend Father Friar Geronimo Boscana, of the Order of Saint Francisco, Apostolic Missionary at said Mission. Translated from the original Spanish manuscript, by one who has been many years a resident of Alta California. *New York: published by Wiley & Putnam,* 1846. 12° *Title and pp.* 231 *to* 341 *of*

Life in California during a residence of several years in that Territory, comprising a description of the Country and the Missionary Establishments, with incidents, observations, etc., etc., illustrated with numerous engravings, by an American; To which is annexed "A Historical Account" [*etc., as in the title first given*]. *New York,* 1846. 155

Father Boscana's Manuscript Account was found in possession of the Spanish Syndic of Missions, and by him presented to the translator, who wrote the narrative entitled "Life in California," as an Introduction to Boscana's valuable history.

BOSSU (M.)

Noveaux Voyages aux Indes Occidentales; Contenant une Relation des differens Peuples qui habitent les environs du grand

Fleuve Saint-Louis, appelé vulgairement le Missisipi; leur Religion; leur gouvernement; leurs moeurs; leurs guerres & leur commerce. Par M. Bossu, Capitaine dans les Troupes de la Marine. *A Paris*, 1768. 12° 2 *vols.* Vol. I. *pp.* xx. + 244 *and plate.* Vol. II. *pp.* 264 + 2 *plates.* 156

Bossu (Mr.)

Travels through that part of North America formerly called Louisiana; by Mr. Bossu, Captain in the French Marines. Translated from the French by John Rheinhold Forster. Illustrated with Notes, relative chiefly to Natural History; to which is added by the Translator, a Flora Americae [*etc.*, 10 *lines*]. 2 vols. 8° *pp.* 407, 432. *London*, 1771. 157

A translation of the French edition of 1768, entitled *Nouveaux Voyages.* The first volume is almost entirely filled with historical and personal sketches of the Southern Indian Tribes of the present United States.

Bossu (M.)

Nouveaux Voyages dans l'Amerique Septentrionale, contenant une collection de lettres ecrites sur les lieux par l'auteur a son ami, M. Douin, chevalier, capitaine dans les troupes du roi, ci-devant son camarade dans le Nouveau Monde. Par M. Bossu, chevalier, **etc.** 8° *pp.* 392 + 4 *plates.* *Amsterdam* (*Paris*), 1778. 158

Bossu's account of his first two voyages to Louisiana, was printed in 1768, after which he made a third voyage, the account of which is given in this volume; which not having been reprinted, or translated into any other language, is a much scarcer work than the former. There are copies with the date of 1778, and with "nouvelle edition" on the title-page, but it is the same. —*Rich.*

This work, like the former of Captain Bossu, is very largely devoted to the narration of his personal intercourse with the natives of that portion of New France called Louisiana. Chapters iv., v., vi., vii., and viii., pp. 133 to 268, are entirely occupied with descriptions of the various tribes he encountered, and their peculiarities.

Botturini (Benaduci).

Idea de Una Nueva Historia General de la America Septentrional, fundada sobre material copioso de figuras, Symbolos, Caracteres, y Geroglificos, Cantares, y Manuscritos de Autores Indios, ultimamente descubiertos. Dedicala al Rey N^{tro} Señor en su real y supremo consejo de las Indias el Cavallero Lorenzo Boturini Benaduci, Señor de la Torre, y de Pono. Con licencia. 4° 2 *plates, prel. leaves* (xx.) + *pp.* 167. *En Madrid: En la Imprenta de Juan de Zuñiga.* Año MDCCXLVI.

Catalogo del Museo Historico Indiano del Cavallero Lorenzo Boturini Benaduci . . . e Imperias antiquos de los Indios . . . fundada en Monumentes indisputables de los mismos Indios. 4 *prel. leaves* + *pp.* 1 *to* 96. 159

[Plan of a New General History of North America, founded upon copious materials, composed of Figures, Symbols, Characters, and Hieroglyphics, Songs and MSS. of ancient Indian writers, lately discovered. Dedicated to the King, etc.

Catalogue of the Indian Historical Museum of L. B. Boturini, of the ancient emperors of the Indians, discovered in the monuments of the same Indians.]

This plan of a new general history of North America, to be founded upon a large amount of material, composed of figures, symbols, hieroglyphics, songs, and MSS. of Indian authors, is a favorite idea of the more ardent of Mexican archæologists. These documents of the varied character described, the author declares on the title-page to be then newly discovered.

The Catalogue of his Indian Historical Collection of MSS., Maps, and Dictionaries, and Grammars of the Mexican languages, occupies four leaves after p. 167 of the "Idea," and the succeeding pp. 1 to 96. Most of these valuable relics of the golden age of the American Aborigines disappeared during the one hundred and twenty-five years which have since elapsed. This wonderful collection included historic material relating to each of the six great Mexican nations. Although so great a length of time has elapsed since its dispersal, M. Aubin, an amateur collector at Paris, has had the good fortune to recover many of them.

"Lorenzo Boturini Benaduci was a Milanese gentleman, who, after much trouble in obtaining copies of the best manuscripts and paintings, printed his outline of a grand work, which I have been informed did not appear in consequence of his death." — *Dr. Cabrera.*

This great museum of Mexican antiquities and MSS., copies of the equally wonderful histories of the Indian nations, written by learned Indians, was seized by the jealous and vindictive authorities of Mexico; and although for many years preserved among the archives of the Viceroy, yet the learned and industrious antiquarian was most wantonly deprived of the results of his labors. Clavigero saw some of this precious store before 1770, in which year was printed a work in Mexico, containing copies of thirty-two of the paintings.

The author resided eight years in Mexico, and not only studied and copied the ancient MSS. and paintings, preserved in monasteries, churches, and colleges, but he formed an intimate acquaintance with the customs and habits of the living Indians.

BOURNE (Benjamin Franklin).

The Captive in Patagonia, or Life among the Giants. A Personal Narrative. By Benjamin Franklin Bourne. With Illustrations. 12° *pp.* 233 + 4 *plates. Boston*, 1858. 160

There is every internal evidence that this is a veritable relation of experience among the Aborigines of Patagonia, a race which has afforded the greatest range for conjecture and controversy. The author narrates the story of his captivity with a plain, yet interesting fidelity to the occurrences of the hideous life he endured. While he does not confirm the traditions of the early travellers, regarding the vast size of the Patagonians, his narrative shows that there was more than an ordinary basis for such tales in the superior height of these people.

BOUTON (Nathaniel).

The History of Concord from its first grant in 1725, to the organization of the City government in 1853. With a history of the Ancient Penacooks; the whole interspersed with numerous interesting incidents and anecdotes down to the present period, 1855. Embellished with maps, with portraits of distinguished Citizens, and views of Ancient and modern residences. By Nathaniel Bouton. 8° *pp.* 786. *Concord*, 1856. 161

BOUTWELL (Governor).

Address of Governor Boutwell at the Dedication of the Monument to the Memory of Capt. Wadsworth, at Sudbury, Mass., November 23, 1852. n. d. s. l. 8° *pp.* 8, *double columns.* 162

BOWNAS (Samuel).

An Account of the Captivity of Elizabeth Hanson, now, or late of Kuchecky, in New England, who, with Four of her Children and Servant Maid, were taken Captive by the Indians, and carried into Canada. Setting forth their Sore Trials, Wonderful Deliverance, &c. Taken in Substance, from her own mouth, by Samuel Bownas. Second edition. 8° *pp.* 28. *London*, MDCCLX. 163

BOYER (Lieut.).

A Journal of Wayne's Campaign. Being an Authentic Daily Record of the most important occurrences during the Campaign of Major General Anthony Wayne, against the North Western Indians; commencing on the 28th day of July, and ending on the 2d day of November, 1794; including an account of the Great Battle of August 20th. By Lieutenant Boyer. 4° *pp.* 23. *Cincinnati, O.* 1866. 164

Appended to Jacob's *Life of Captain Cresap.*

BOZMAN (John Leeds).

The History of Maryland, from its first Settlement, in 1633, to the Restoration in 1660, with a copious introduction and notes and illustrations. By John Leeds Bozman. 2 *Vols.* 8°. Vol. I. *pp.* xii. + 9 *to* 314. Vol. II. *pp.* 728. *Baltimore, James Lucas and E. K. Deaver.* 1837. 165

After a *resumé* of the aboriginal history of the State derived from the relations of all the voyagers and travellers from Verrazano to John Smith, the author gives on pages 103 to 181 of Vol. I.: "A general Sketch of the tribes of Indians then inhabiting Virginia and Maryland." The names of the various tribes, and the localities they occupied, together with the origin and signification of the Indian names of rivers and places, receive great attention from the author, whose numerous and lengthy notes attest the labor he bestowed upon the aboriginal history of his State.

BRACKENRIDGE (H. M.).

Journal of a Voyage up the River Missouri performed in Eighteen Hundred and Eleven, by H. M. Brackenridge, Esq. Second Edition, Revised and Enlarged by the Author. 12° *pp.* 246. *Baltimore.* 1816. 166

The work of a man who examined carefully into the habits and character of the Indians of the Upper Missouri; wrote with a punctilious sensitiveness to his obligation to narrate nothing but the truth; and who told the story of his sojourn among the savages and traders in a manner to attract and preserve the reader's interest. Mr. Brackenridge, being the first traveller after Captains Lewis and Clark to visit these distant tribes, his "Relation" has a more than ordinary value to the ethnologist and the historian.

BRACKENRIDGE (H. M.).

Views of Louisiana; containing Geographical, Statistical, and Historical Notices of that vast and important portion of America. By H. M. Brackenridge, Esq. 12° *pp.* 323. *Baltimore, printed by Schaeffer & Maund*, 1817. 167

Chap. ii. is entitled "War with the Chickasaws." Chap. viii. is devoted to "Indian nations; trade; general enumeration;" and Chap. X. to "Antiquities of the Valley of the Mississippi." Although a careful examination of the subjects, but little new of thought or facts is added to our knowledge.

BRADAEN (Louis).

The Aztec City of Sumal, and Discovery of America before the Time of Columbus. By Louis Bradaen. 12° *pp.* 48. *New York, Thomas Husted & Co.,* 97 *Nassau Street,* 1847. 168

BRADFORD (Alexander W.)

American Antiquities and Researches into the Origin and History of the Red Race, by Alexander W. Bradford. 8° *pp.* 435. *New York, Dayton & Saxton,* 1841. 169

Part I. pp. 15 to 161, is occupied with a *resumé* of the discoveries of American antiquities, with a description of their size, character, and location, and is a very excellent collection of the material facts relating to them. In this part of the work the author entirely avoids any discussion, or speculation regarding their origin, or age. Part II. pp. 163 to 435, is entitled "Researches into the Origin and History of the Red Race;" and the several divisions into chapters embrace such subjects as: Comparison of the Ancient Monuments; Ancient Civilization; Aboriginal Monuments; Aboriginal Migrations; Routes of Migration; Drifting of Vessels; Origin of the Aborigines and the Pyramids. In these chapters the author gives free indulgence to the hypothetical, sustained, however by a close adhesion to logical conclusion and scientific analysis. Mr. Bradford was peculiarly fitted for such a treatment of this subject, which will forever be the debatable ground of the ethnologist and the philosopher. He was for many years surrogate of the city of New York; and so able was he deemed by lawyers that his decisions in his court are recognized as fixing the limits of law and precedent in that line of practice. He died in 1867.

BRADMAN (Arthur).

A Narrative of the Extraordinary Sufferings of Mr. Robert Forbes, his Wife and five Children, during an unfortunate Journey through the Wilderness from Canada to the Kennebeck River, in the year 1784. In which three of their Children were Starved to Death. Taken partly from their own mouths and partly from an imperfect journal, and published at their request. By Arthur Bradman. 8° *pp.* 16. *Price Six Pence. Philadelphia. Printed for M. Carey,* 1794. 170

With a Narrative of the Captivity and Escape of Mrs. Frances Scott.

BRADSTREET (Lieut. Col.).

An Impartial Account of Lieut. Col. Bradstreet's Expedition to Fort Frontenac, to which are added a few Reflections on the Conduct of that Enterprise, and the Advantages resulting from its success. By a Volunteer on the Expedition. 12° *pp.* 60. *London,* 1759. 171

The narrative of Colonel Bradstreet's expedition, although purporting to be written by another hand, bears internal evidence of having been at least dictated by himself. His conduct in the expedition against the Ohio Indians needed exculpation, and had this work been published earlier we might have supposed it was intended to divert public attention towards a real service he had performed for the Colonies. He was impatient of the subordinate rank he held in the campaign; and while in command of the northern division of the army moving against the Ohio Indians in 1764, he disobeyed the orders of Colonel Boquet, and made a separate treaty of peace, which would have been productive of most disastrous circumstances had it not been promptly disavowed by Boquet.

BRAINERD (Rev. David).

Memoirs of the Rev. David Brainerd Missionary to the Indians, on the Borders of New York, New Jersey, and Penn., chiefly taken from his own Diary. By Rev. Johnathan Edwards of Northampton including his own Journal, now for the first time incorporated with the rest of his Diary, in regular Chronological Series by Sereno Edwards Dwight. 8° *pp.* 507. *New Haven*, 1822. 172

The same with Beatty's Journal. *Edinburgh*, 1798. 173

BRASSEUR (de Bourbourg, Abbe).

Histoire des Nations Civilisees du Mexique et de l'Amerique-Centrale, durant les siecles Anterieurs a Christophe Colomb, ecrite sur des documents originaux et entierement inedits puises aux anciennes Archives des Indigines, par M. L'Abbe Brasseur de Bourbourg, ancien aumonier de la legation de France au Mexique, et Administrateur ecclesiastique des Indiens de Rabinal (Guatemala). Comprenant les temps Heroiques et l'histoire de l'empire des Tolteques. Paris, Arthus Bertrand, editeur libraire de la societe de geographie, 1857. *Large* 8° 4 *vols.* Vol. I. *pp.* xcii. + 440 *and Map.* Vol. II. *pp.* 616. Vol. III. *pp.* 692. Vol. IV. *pp.* vi. + 851. 174

[History of the Civilized Nations of Mexico and Central America, during the ages prior to Christopher Columbus; written from original documents and entirely unedited: taken from the ancient archives of the Aborigines by the Abbe Brasseur de Bourbourg, formerly almoner of the French legation in Mexico, and ecclesiastic Administrator of the Indians of Rabinal, in Guatemala. Containing records of the heroic period in the history of the Toltec Empire.]

BRASSEUR DE BOURBOURG.

Collection de documents dans les langues indigines pour servir a l'etude de l' histoire et de la philologie de l'Amerique ancienne. 4 *vols.* 175

[Collection of documents upon the native languages, to aid in the study of the history and of the philology of ancient America.]

This is the general title of four volumes of which the separate titles are as follows: —

Vol. I. of the Collection: —

* Popol Vuh. Le livre sacre et les mythes de l' antiquite Americaine, avec les livres heroiques et historiques des Quiches. Ouvrage original des indigines de Guatemala, texte Quiche et traduction francaise en regard, accompagnee de notes philologiques et d'un commentaire sur la mythologie et les migrations des peuples anciens de l'Amerique, etc., compose sur des documents originaux et inedits, par l'Abbe Brasseur de Bourbourg. 8° *Title, pp.* cclxxix. + 367 + (1) 2 *maps and lithograph.* *Paris*, 1861.

[Popol Vuh. The Sacred Book, and the Myths of American Antiquity, with the heroic and historic annals of the Quichuas. An original work of the Indians of Guatemala, with the text in Quichua, and French translation, accompanied by philologic notes and a commentary on the mythology and migrations of the ancient people of America, composed from original and unedited documents.]

Vol. II. of the Collection: —

Grammaire de la Lengua Quiche. Grammaire de la Langue Quichee. Espagnole-Francaise mise en parallele avec ses deux dialectes Cakchiquel et Tzutubil. Tiree des manuscrits des meilleurs auteurs Guatemaliens. Ouvrage accompagne de Notes philologiques. Avec un Vocabulaire comprenant les sources principales du Quiche comparees aux langues Germaniques et suivi d'un essai sur la poesie, la musique, la danse et l'art dramatique, chez les Mexicains et les Guatemaliques avant la conquete; servant d'introduction au Rabinal-Achi drame indigine avec la musique original, texte Quiche et traduction Francaise en regard. Recueille par L'Abbe Brasseur de Bourbourg. Paris, Arthur Bertrand, éditeur, 1862. 8° *pp.* xvii. + 246 + 132 + 12.

[Grammar of the Quichua Language. Grammar of the Quichua Language, written in Spanish and French, and compared with the two dialects, Cachiquel and Tzutohil. Taken from ancient Manuscripts of the best Guatemalian authors. The work accompanied by philological notes, and with a Vocabulary comprising the principal elements of the Quichua compared with the German language, and followed by an essay on the poetry, music, dance and dramatic art as found among the ancient Mexicans and Guatemalians before the conquest, to serve as an introduction to the Rabinal-Achi, an Aboriginal drama, with the original music. The text in Quichua, translated literally into French, collected by the Abbe Brasseur de Bourbourg.]

Vol. III. of the Collection :—

Relation des choses de Yucatan de Diego de Landa. Texte espagnol et traduction francaise en regard comprenant les signes du calendrier et de l'alphabet hieroglyphique de la langue Maya, avec une grammaire et un vocabulaire abreges francais Maya. 8° *pp.* cxii. + 516. *Paris, Arthus Bertrand.*

[Relation of events in the history of Yucatan by Diego de Landa. The text in Spanish with a French translation, both containing the signs of the calendar, and the hieroglyphic alphabet of the Maya language, with a grammar and a short vocabulary of Maya and French words.]

Pages cxii. are occupied with an introduction by Brasseur de Bourbourg. Landa's Relation of Yucatan fill pages 1 to 429. A treatise on the Indians of Hayti by Father Romaine Paul, which formed part of the lost biography of Columbus written by his son. The grammar and vocabulary of the Maya tongue occupy pp. 459 to 516.

Vol. IV. of the Collection :—

Quatre lettres sur le Mexique. Exposition absolue du systeme hieroglyphique Mexicain la fin de l'age pierre, epoque glaciare temporaire commencement de l'age de bronze, origines de la civilization et des religions de l'antiquite d'apres le Teo-amoxtli et autres documents Mexicains, etc. Par M. Brasseur de Bourbourg. 8° *pp.* xx. + 463. *Paris*, 1868.

[Four letters on Mexico. Correct statement of the Mexican hieroglyphic system, the end of the age of stone, glacial epoch, commencement of the age of bronze. Origin of the civilization and the religions of antiquity from the Teo-amoxtli and other Mexican documents.]

BRASSEUR (de Bourbourg).

Lettre A. M. Leon de Rosny sur la decouverte de documents relatifs a la haute antiquite Americaine, et sur le dechiffrement et l' interpretation de l' ecriture phonetique et figurative de la langue Maya, par Brasseur de Bourbourg. 8° *pp.* 20 *and folding plate.* *Paris*, 1869. 176

[Letter to M. Leon de Rosny on the discovery of documents relative to the ancient period of America, and on the deciphering and translation of the phonetic and figurative writing of the Maya's. By Brasseur de Bourbourg.]

It is very difficult to assign the place which this extraordinary man will occupy in the annals of science, for his works are to-day nearly as great mysteries as the hieroglyphs his labors have illustrated. His industry in his researches into the history of the Aztec races is something not less than mar-vicious. Following his vocation as a priest and a missionary, his literary appetite could only be allayed by writing a history of Canada, and perhaps the most unfortunate event for his fame which could possibly have happened was that it was printed. It did not escape the notice of historical students that the Abbe had accepted so much which was apocryphal, that his history was little better than a romance. When, therefore, he had, with heroic sacrifice of all personal ease, accepted the life of self-immolation of a missionary to the Indians of Mexico; had studied for years the relics of Aztec picture-writing; had learned and systematized in great treatises their modern dialects; the immense works which he then printed upon the history of the pre-Cortesian races, made scarcely a ripple on the quiet of the scientific world. He stands alone in the vast temple of learning which he has restored, if he did not erect. No human being can contest his solution of Aztec pictographs, nor does there exist one who can prove it to be true. His numerous volumes have at least this merit,—they have done much to perpetuate the memory of a wonderful race. Besides those already noted he has printed,—

Antiquites Mexicains. Apropos d'un Memoire. 8° Paris, 1852.
Apercu d'un Voyage de Guatemala. 8° Paris, 1857.
Archives des Indigines. 8° pp. 604. Paris, 1857.
Cartas' a la His' Primitiva Naciones Am'. 8° pp. 75. Mexico, 1851.
Coup d' Œil sur la Nation Wapis-Roncio Orientale. Paris, 1864.
Histoire de M'gr de Laval premier eveque de Quebec. 8° Quebec, 1845.
Histoire du Canada et de ses Missions. 2 vols. 8° Paris, 1852.
Histoire du Commerce et de l'Industrie Nations Azteques (published in "Nouveau Annales des Voyages").
Monuments anciens du Mexique Palenque, etc. 4° Paris, 1860.
Monuments anciens du Mexique, etc. folio, pp. 115, with Maps and Plates. pp. 56. Paris, 1866.
Voyage sur l'Isthme de Tehuantepec, en 1860. 8° pp. 209. Paris, 1861.

Numerous articles upon Mexican Antiquities, from the pen of this prolific author, have appeared in the European Reviews, principally excerpts from his printed works. Some copies of these have been separated and distributed in the magazine sheets.

The industry, zeal, and learning which the Abbe Brasseur de Bourbourg brought to the investigation of the Aztec and other Central American literature, have produced scarcely any other result than the accumulation of so vast an amount of printed matter as to appal the stoutest-hearted ethnologist. In the world of conjecture he is without a rival. He has however, with his national perversity of egotism, destroyed the value of his own labors, by interpolating so much of his own baseless conjectures. He has invented as much as he has discovered; and the difficulty of separating his assumptions from material fact, has not been considered a sufficient compensation for the labor of analysis.

Brett (W. H.)

The Indian Tribes of Guiana; their Condition and Habits, with researches into their past history, superstitions, legends, antiquities, languages, &c. By the Rev. W. H. Brett, Missionary in connection with the Society for the propagation of the gospel in foreign parts, and rector of Trinity parish, Essequibo. 8° *pp.* xxi. + 500. 8 *colored and* 13 *plain plates, and folding map. London, Bell and Daldy, York Street. Covent Garden,* 1868. 177

Neither the horrors of a forest Savannah stretching hundreds of miles without sufficient dry ground to build a camp upon; the danger of receiving a flight of arrows freighted with the deadly ouarri poison, from the tameless savages of the hills, or the equally subtle and less avoidable pestilence which pervades every breath of the malaria saturated atmosphere, could appal the missionaries of the Cross to the Caribs and other wild savages of Guiana.

The forest is twined with gigantic serpents above, and roamed by ferocious beasts below, the paths are barred by the webs of monstrous and poisonous spiders, and every rotten trunk houses a hundred centipedes. On the shores hides the loathsome cayman, or basks the rattlesnake; and in the water millions of ferocious little fish, whose mouths are armed with steel-traps, fasten with resistless voracity on the intruding stranger. All we know of the Aborigines who inhabit these deadly climes, is communicated by such fearless missionaries as Brett and Bernau.

Brett (Rev. W. H.). The Indian Tribes of Guiana. 12° *pp.* 352. *New York, Carter & Brother*, 1852. 178

Brewerton (G. Douglass).
Wars of the Western Border, or New Homes and a Strange People. By G. Douglass Brewerton. 12° *pp.* 400. *New York*, 1860. 179

Brice (James R.).
History of the Revolutionary War with England A. D. 1776. Brief Account of the Captivity and Cruel Sufferings of Captain Dietz and John and Robert Brice [*etc.*, 2 *lines*] who were taken Prisoners of War by the British Indians and Tories. Now first Published over said Robert Brice's own Signature, the Horrible Massacre of the Dietz Family in Bern Albany Co., Seventy-one years ago. [*etc.*, 18 *lines.*] 8° *pp.* 48. *Albany*, 1851. 180

Brice (Wallace A.).
History of Fort Wayne from the earliest known accounts of this point to the present period. Embracing an extended view of the Aboriginal Tribes of the Northwest including more especially the Miamies of this locality — their habits, customs — etc. together with a comprehensive summary of the general relations of the Northwest from the latter part of the Seventeenth Century to the Struggles of 1812–14, with a Sketch of the Life of General Anthony Wayne. Including also a lengthy biography of the late Hon. Samuel Hanna together with short sketches of several of the early Pioneer Settlers of Fort Wayne. Also an account of the manufacturing Mercantile and Railroad Interests of Fort Wayne and Vicinity. By Wallace A. Brice, with Illustrations. 8° *pp.* xvi. + 324 + 33 + 7 *plates. Fort Wayne, Ind., D. W. Jones and Son*, 1868. 181

Brickell (John).
The Natural History of North Carolina. With an Account of the Trade Manners and Customs of the Christian and Indian Inhabitants Illustrated with Copper-Plates whereon are Curiously Engraved the Map of the Country, Several strange Beasts, Birds, Fishes, Snakes, Insects, Trees and Plants &c. By John Brickell M. D. [*Motto*] 8° *Title, reverse blank, pref.* 2 *leaves, Subscribers* 1 *leaf (total pp.* viii.), *map and pp.* 408, *and two folding leaves of finely executed copperplate cuts of birds, beasts, and reptiles of N. C. Dublin*, 1737. 182

The material for this work was stolen from Lawson with scarcely the disguise of change of form. All that portion of the work, from pages 277 to 408, is devoted to "An Account of the Indians of North Carolina," which is, such a mutilated, interpolated, and unscrupulous appropriation of the unfortunate John Lawson's work of the same sub-title, that the transcription is scarcely more than a parody.

BRIEF ACCOUNT (A).

Of the Proceedings of the Committee appointed in the year 1795, by the yearly Meeting of Friends, of Pennsylvania, New Jersey, etc., for promoting the Improvement and gradual Civilization of the Indian Natives. 8° pp. 45. *Philadelphia, printed by Kimber, Conrad, and Co.,* 1805. 183

BRIEF ACCOUNT (A).

Of the Proceedings of the Committee appointed in the year 1795, by the yearly Meeting of Friends, of Pennsylvania, New Jersey, etc., for promoting the improvement and gradual civilization of the Indian Nations. 12° pp. 50. *Philadelphia. Reprinted, London,* 1806. 184

BRIEF ACCOUNT

Of the Society for propagating the Gospel among the Indians and others in North America. 8° pp. 7. *Boston,* 1798. 185

The tract contains a "Historical Sketch of the Society," and a list of the names of the officers and members.

BRIEF SKETCH (A)

Of the efforts of Philadelphia yearly meeting of the Religious Society of Friends, to promote the Civilization and Improvement of the Indians; also of the Present Condition of the Tribes in the State of New York. 8° pp. 56. *Philadelphia, Friends' Book Store,* 1866. 186

This is a very interesting report of a deputation of Friends who visited every Indian Reservation and Tribe in the State of New York, and the details of their observation are among the latest, as they are certainly the most trustworthy which have been made public regarding these Indians. At pp. 49 to 52, are recorded their statements regarding the Shinnecock Indians on Long Island, the last of the Montauks. The devices of white sharpers, by which these Indians have been deprived of their lands, are not more or less atrocious than usual; but the fact which most surprises us is that these Indians have not succumbed to their disheartening ill-fortunes, but have steadily risen, and are temperate, cleanly, and thriving. They are skillful and experienced fishermen and whalemen, and from the proceeds of their labor have built a neat village and support a school and two churches.

BRINTON (Daniel G.).

The Myths of the New World. A Treatise on the Symbolism and Mythology of the Red Race of America. By Daniel G. Brinton. 12° pp. 337. *New York,* 1868. 187

This is one of the most thoughtful and philosophical of all the mere speculative treatises on the American Aborigines. From the incompetency of their languages to express abstract ideas, he determines that they could never have originated or entertained any ideas of a purely spiritual Deity, and that in consequence, they must have derived all the notions they possess of a Great Spirit from European sources, subsequent to the Columbian discovery. That there is a unity of origin in all the varieties of the Red Race, he derives, — 1st. From the discovery of verbal similarities running through all their languages. 2d. From the universality of their agricultural products: corn, cotton, and tobacco; and 3d. From "the mental condition of all in which humanity mirrors itself; to wit: their religious and moral consciousness; being at one uniform level, in all the tribes and nations, however diverse the natural influences under which they lived." While he scouts the notion of tracing their descent from the Jews (that fatal stumbling-block of all theorists, from Torquemada and Thorowgood to Mrs. Simon and Joe Smith), there is one formidable historic weapon against it he does not use: That the Indian of America had a more pronounced and established idea of the immortality of the human existence than the most pious of Jews. There was a deeper conviction of the truth of some sort of resurrection among the most debased of the Aborigines than existed among the Jews at the period of the separation of their tribes. Mr. Brinton treats at length, and with masterly clearness in grouping, the vast mass of traditions, symbols, rites, and superstitions which governed the life of the savages of America as affecting their common origin.

BRINTON (D. G.).
The National Legend of the Chata-Muskokee Tribes. By D. G. Brinton, M. D. 8° *pp.* 13, *double columns. Morrisania, N. Y.* 1870. 188

With the thoroughness which characterizes all of Mr. Brinton's literary labors, he has exhausted all the reservoirs of information relating to his subject. He takes no less pains to finish and illustrate it, when only a magazine article, than when it assumes the proportions of a volume.

BRINTON (Daniel G.).
Notes on the Floridian Peninsula, its Literary History, Indian Tribes, and Antiquities. By Daniel G. Brinton, A. B. 12° *pp.* 202. *Philadelphia,* 1859. 189

BRINTON (D. G.).
The Ancient Phonetic Alphabet of Yucatan. By D. G. Brinton. 8° *pp.* 8 + *printed covers. New York, J. Sabin & Sons,* 1870. 190

BRINTON (D. G.).
Contributions to a Grammar of the Muskokee Language. By D. G. Brinton, M. D. From the Proceedings of the American Philosophical Society. 8° *Title, and pp.* 9. *Philadelphia, McCalla & Stavely, printers,* 1870. 191

BRINTON (D. G.).
The Arawack Language of Guiana in its Linguistic and Ethnological Relations. By D. G. Brinton, M. D. *Large* 4° *Title, and* 18 *pp. Philadelphia, McCalla & Stavely,* 1871. 192

The object announced by the author, as the province of this work, is the tracing of the ancient course of empire and migration of this interesting tribe. Though now dwindled to the small number of two thousand souls, it is probable, from linguistic and social characteristics, that they are the representatives of a once great people, affiliating with now distant nations.

BROMLEY (Walter).
An Address delivered at the Freemason's Hall, Halifax, August 3d, 1813, by Walter Bromley, Late Paymaster of the 23d Regiment Welsh Fusiliers. On the deplorable State of the Indians. 8° *pp.* 16. *Halifax, Anthony H. Holland, printer,* 1813. 193

BROWN (J. M.).
Origin of the American Indians, or How the New World Became Inhabited. A Lecture, by Hon. J. Madison Brown, before the Society of Historical Research, at Julian College. Delivered February 9, 1854, and Published by Request of the Society. *Small* 4° *pp.* 38 + 9 *leaves, Adver. and two printed cover leaves.* (*Jackson*) *Mich.* (1860). 194

The author adduces most of the arguments, brought by the advocates of the descent of the American Aborigines from the lost Hebrew tribes, to fortify their hypothesis. He adds nothing to strengthen their position.

BROWN (C. D.).
Memoir of the late Rev. Lemuel Covell, Missionary to the Tuscarora Indians, and the Province of Upper Canada. Comprising a history of the origin and progress of Missionary operations in the Shaftesbury Baptist Association, up to the time of Mr. Covell's decease, in 1806. Also a Memoir of Rev. Alanson L. Covell, son of the former, and late a pastor of the First Baptist Church in the City of Albany, N. Y. By Mrs. C. D. Brown, daughter and sister of the deceased. Two volumes in one. 12° *pp.* 174 + 226. *Brandon Telegraph Office,* 1839. 195

BROWN (Samuel R.).
Views of the Campaigns of the Northwestern Army, comprising sketches of the campaigns of generals Hull and Harrison. A minute and interesting account of the naval conflict on Lake Erie, Military Anecdotes, Abuses in the Army, etc. 12° *pp.* 156. *Philadelphia,* 1815. 196

BROWNE (J. Ross).
Adventures in the Apache Country. A tour through Arizona and Sonora; with notes on the Silver Regions of Nevada. By J. Ross Browne. Illustrated by the Author. 12° *pp.* 535, *with* 155 *wood-cuts printed with the text,* 26 *of which are illustrative of aboriginal life. New York, Harper and Brothers,* 1869. 197

Notwithstanding the air of mocking raillery with which this author envelopes most of the scenes he describes, his work has one great value, as it is a truthful portraiture of the terrors which attend border life in Arizona, where one twentieth part of the population had been swept away by the incursions of the Apaches in three years.

BROWNELL (Charles de Wolf).
The Indian Races of North and South America; comprising An Account of the principal Aboriginal Races; a description of their national customs, mythology and religious ceremonies; the history of their most powerful tribes, and of their most celebrated Chiefs and Warriors; their intercourse and wars with the European Settlers; and a great variety of anecdote and description, illustrative of personal and national character. By Charles De Wolf Brownell. With numerous and diversified colored illustrations, entirely new, many of which are from original designs, executed in the best style of the art, by the

first artists in America. Published by subscription only. 8° *pp.* 720 + 40 *full-page plates. New York, published at the American Subscription House and branches,* 1857. 198

The last half of the title-page must have been written by the publisher, and the illustrations drawn by his infant son, as the Preface and Text indicate too respectable a mind to have concocted such a farrago, involving at least half a dozen falsehoods regarding the plates, which are the most tawdry and offensive daubs.

The work is fairly executed, and contains much condensed information, which had, however, been better presented in the collection of Mr. Drake.

BRYAN (Daniel).

The Mountain Muse: comprising The Adventures of Daniel Boone, and the power of Virtuous and refined Beauty. By Daniel Bryan, of Rockingham County, Virginia. 12° *pp.* 252. *Harrisonburg, printed for the Author, by Davidson & Bourne.* 1813. 199

"The Adventures of Daniel Boone" having been versified by Lord Byron, the "Mountain Muse" essays the task through seven thousand lines, in which he beats the aristocratic poet by more than six thousand nine hundred and fifty.

BRYANT (Charles S.).

A History of the Great Massacre by the Sioux Indians in Minnesota, including the personal narratives of many who escaped. By Charles S. Bryant and Abel B. Murch. 12° *pp.* 504. *Cincinnati,* 1864. 200

BRUYAS (Rev. James).

Radical Words of the Mohawk Language, with their derivatives. By Rev. James Bruyas, S. J., missionary on the Mohawk. *Large* 8° *pp.* 123. *New York, Cramoisy Press,* 1862. 201

No. 10, Shea's *American Linguistics.*

Mr. Shea says in his Preface, "This volume contains undoubtedly the oldest grammatical or lexicogriphal treatise on the language of the Mohawks." It was probably written on the banks of the Mohawk River, in the latter part of the seventeenth century. The closely written manuscrips of 146 pp., from which this work is printed, is almost the only monument remaining of the warlike and formidable nation who once inhabited the State of New York. The wonderful men who defied even the fierceness of this savage race, and for the first time subdued that ferocity, were the Jesuit Missionaries, "who, from the days of the devoted Jogues to the close of the seventeenth century, when the cruel act of Bellomont prohibited any farther attempts to Christianize them, labored among the tribes, studied the various dialects with the care and ability of educated men. Chaumonot wrote a Huron Grammar, and works in Onondaga, Carhiel in Cayuga, and Bruyas in Mohawk."

BRUYAS (Rev. James).

Radical Words of the Mohawk Language, with their derivatives. By Rev. James Bruyas. Published from the Original Manuscript. Senate Documents of New York. 8° *pp.* 1 *to* 123. *Albany,* 1863. 202

The same, page for page, as published by Mr. J. G. Shea, in his series of *American Linguistics.*

"The work was printed from the closely written MS., preserved for many years in the Mission House at Caughnanaga, on the Sault St. Louis of the St. Lawrence, near Montreal, thus adding interest to the room where Charlevoix and Lafitau wrote. The author, a missionary of the Jesuit Order, was born in Lyons, and arrived in Canada in 1666. One year after, he set out for the Mohawk Valley, and until his death, in 1700, at the Mission where his manuscript was found, he was arduously engaged in his missionary labors among the Indians of the Five Nations. He spoke the Mohawk language with as much facility as his native French, and must have been equally familiar with all the dialects of the Confederacy, as he resided for considerable periods of time with each of the tribes." — *Shea.*

BUCHANAN (James).

Sketches of the History, Manners, and Customs of the North American Indians. By James Buchanan, Esq., his Majesty's Consul for the State of New York. 8° *Map and pp.* xi. + 371. *London, printed for Black and Young,* 1824. 203

The author's curiosity led him to examine the character and condition of some Indians with whom he was casually brought into contact. A much more respectable sentiment, his humanity, was soon aroused, and he at once commenced the collection of material, to form a treatise which should attract the notice of the governments of the United States and Great Britain to the wrongs and sufferings of the aborigines. The appearance of Heckwelder's *Historical Account of the Indian Nations,* deterred him from completing his work. He has therefore given us a short *resume* of relations of "Cruel Conduct exercised towards the Indians," with traits of character and anecdotes, on pp 1 to 209. While the remainder is devoted to a reproduction of Dr. Jarvis' Address "On the Religion of the Indian Tribes," Duponceau's paper on "Language of the Indians," Governor Clinton's "Address on the Indian Tribes of New York," with extracts from Blome and Colden.

BUCHANAN (James).

Sketches of the History, Manners, and Customs of the North American Indians, with a Plan for their Melioration. By James Buchanan, Esq., His Britannic Majesty's Consul for the State of New York. In Two Volumes. 12° *pp.* 182 *and* 156. *New York, published by William Borradaile,* 1824. 204

In this edition is printed Mr. Buchanan's Plan, occupying the last 18 pp., which is not found in the 8° London edition.

BULFINCH (Thomas).

Oregon and Eldorado; or Romance of the Rivers. By Thomas Bulfinch. 12° *pp.* 464. *Boston, J. E. Tilton and Company,* 1866. 205

This work is a *resumé* of books of travel along the great rivers of America, and contains much relating to Indian life, which perhaps is not common, but certainly easily attainable.

BURKE (Edmund).

An Account of the European Settlements in America. In Six Parts: I. A Short History of the Discovery of that Part of the World. II. The Manners and Customs of the Original Inhabitants. III. Of the Spanish Settlements. IV. Of the Portugese. V. Of the French, Dutch, and Danish. VI. Of the English [*etc.,* 7 *lines*]. In Two Volumes. The Fourth Edition with Improvements. 8° *pp.* xii. + 1 *to* 324, *and pp.* xii. + 1–308. *London, printed for J. Dodsley,* 1765. 206

Part II. pp. 167 to 202, Volume I., are devoted to a description of the Manners of the Aborigines. Part I., pp. 1 to 166, on the reduction of Mexico and Peru, also contain a synopsis of the history of the Aztec and Incarial governments during the Spanish invasion.

BURNET (Jacob).

Notes on the Early Settlement of the Northwestern Territory. 8° *pp.* 501. *New York, D. Appleton. Cincinnati, Derby and Bradly*, 1847. 207

A truthful history of the Northwest could not fail to be a record of Indian wars, treaties, and border difficulties; and such the greater portion of this work is. A portion of it had its first appearance in volume I., part second, of the Ohio Historical Society's Collections.

BUSCHMAN (Joh Carl Ed).

Uber die Aztekischen Ortsnamen von Joh Carl Ed Buschman, Erbste Abtheilung. 4° *pp.* 205. *Berlin*, 1858. 208

[Upon the Aztec Names of Places. First part.]

BUSCHMAN.

Die sprachen Kizh und Netella von Neu Californien. 4° *Berlin*, 1856. 209*

[The languages of the Kizh and Netella Indians of California.]

BUSCHMAN.

Der Athapaskische. Sprachstamm. *pp.* 171. *Berlin*, 1856. 210*

[Of the Athapasken Language.]

BUSCHMAN.

Die Pima-Sprache—und die Sprache der Koloschen, dargelstellt. 4° *pp.* 132. *Berlin*, 1857. 211*

[The Pima language, and the language of the Koloschens, explained.]

BUSCHMAN.

Die Lautveranderungen Aztekischer Worter in den Sonorischen Sprachen und die Sonorische Endung. A M E dargestellt. 4° *pp.* 118. *Berlin*, 1857. 212*

[The change of pronunciation in the Aztec words in Sonora, and in the Sonora words ending in A M E, explained.]

BUSCHMAN (Joh Carl Ed).

Die Volker und Sprachen Neu-Mexico's und der Westseite der Britischen Nordamerika's Dartrestellt von Joh Carl Ed Buschman. *Large* 4° *pp.* 209 *to* 414. *Berlin*, 1858. 213

[The People and Languages of New Mexico, and the West Coast of British North America.]

BUSCHMAN.

Die Spuren der aztekischen Sprache im nordlichen Mexico und hoheren Amerikanischen Norden. Zugleich eine Musterung der Volker und Sprachen des nordlichen Meziko's und der Westseite Nordamerika's von Guadalaxara an bis zum Eismeer. 2 *vols.* 4° *Berlin*, 1859. 214*

[The traces of the Aztec language in Northern Mexico and North America. Together with a comparison of the people and language of Northern Mexico and the west coast of North America from Guadalaxara to the Arctic Ocean.]

BUSCHMAN.
Systematische Worttafel des Athapaskischen, Sprachstamms, aufgestellt und erlautert, von C. E. Bushman Dritte Abtheilung des Apache. 4° *pp.* 88. *Berlin*, 1860. 215*

[Systematic Dictionary of the Athapasken language, arranged and illustrated by C. E. Buschman. Third part. Of the Apache.]

BUSCHMAN (J. C. E.).
Das Apache als eine Athapaskische Sprach erwiesen; in Verbindung, mit einer Systematischen Worttafel des athapaskischen Sprachstammes. 4° *pp.* 69. *Berlin*, 1860. 216*

[The Apache and the Athapaskan languages proved to be the same. With a systematic table of Athapaskan roots.]

BUSCHMAN.
Die Vrwandtschafts Verhältnisse der Athapaskischen Sprachen. Zeweite Abtheilung. Des Apache. 4° *pp.* 60. *Berlin*, 1863. 217*

[The relationship of the Athapaskan language. Second part. Of the Apache.]

BUSCHMANN (Joh. Carl Ed.).
Grammatik der Sonorischen Sprachen; vorzüglich der Tarahumara, Tepeguana, Cora und Cahita; als IX^ter Abschnitt der Spuren, der Aztekischen Sprache. Ausgearbeitet. 4° *pp.* 85. *Berlin*, 1864. 218*

[Grammar of the language of Indians of Sonora, especially of the Tarahumara, Tepeguana, Cora, and Cahita tribes.]

Mr. Buschman is the author of eleven very considerable works, treating of the nations and languages of various parts of America. They are very highly esteemed by ethnologists, who have been able to peruse them in the German language, in which only they have been printed.

BUSTAMENTE (Don Calixto Carlos).
El Lazarillo de Ciegos, Caminantes desde Buenos Ayres, hasta Lima con ſus Itinerarios segun la mas puntual observacion, con algunas noticias utiles a los Nuevos Comerciantes que tratan en Mulas, y otras historias [*etc.*, 7 *lines*] por Don Calixto Bustamente Carlos Inca, alias Concolorcorvo, Natural del Cuzco, que acompaño al referido Comisionado en dicho Viage, y escribio sus Extractos. Con Licencia. *En Gigon, en la Emprenta de la Rorada Ano de* 1773. 255 *numbered leaves, and a folding table.* 219

[The Blind Man's Guide for Travelers from Buenos Ayres to Lima, with a journal of the tour, from the most accurate observation, with many remarks useful to New Traders in Mules; with some historical notes by Don Carlos Bustamente, otherwise Concolorcorvo, a native Inca of Cuzco.]

This curious volume, written by an Indian of the race of the Peruvian Incas, was probably printed in Lima, notwithstanding it bears on its title the announcement of its place of publication, being a small village in Old Spain. The author accompanied Venders, the superintendent appointed by the King of Spain to establish posts, resting-places, and couriers, from Buenos Ayres to Peru. His work, although incidentally treating of the Indians along the route described, has little interest for us beside the fact of its being the work of one of that race.

BUTLER (Mann).

A History of the Commonwealth of Kentucky, from the Exploration and Settlement by the Whites, to the Close of the Northwestern Campaign in 1813. With an Introduction, exhibiting the Settlement of Western Virginia, &c. By Mann Butler. Second edition, revised and enlarged by the Author. 12° *pp.* 396 + *Portrait. Louisville*, 1834. 220

BUTTERFIELD (Consul W.)

History of Seneca County (Ohio), containing A Detailed Narrative of the principal events that have occurred since its first settlement down to the present time; A History of the Indians that formerly resided within its limits; Geographical descriptions, early customs, Biographical sketches, etc. 8° *pp.* 251. *Sandusky*, 1848. 221

BYINGTON (Cyrus).

Grammar of the Choctaw Language, by the Rev. Cyrus Byington. Edited from the original MSS. in the Library of the American Philosophical Society, by D. G. Brinton. 8° *pp.* 56 + *printed cover. Philadelphia*, 1870. *McCalla & Stavely, printers*, 1870. 222

BYINGTON (Rev. Cyrus).

The Acts of the Apostles translated into the Choctaw Language. Chlaus hlalat im Anupeshi Vhliba Vmmona kvt nana akaniohmi tok puta isht annoa chata anumpa isht atapho hoke. 12° *pp.* 165. *Boston*, 1839. 223

BYRON (John).

The Narrative of the Honourable John Byron (Commodore in a Late Expedition round the World), containing An Account of the great distresses Suffered by Himself and his Companions on the Coast of Patagonia, from the Year 1740, till their Arrival in England, 1746, with a Description of St. Jago de Chili, and the Manners and Customs of the Inhabitants. Also a Relation of the Loss of the Wager, Man of War, one of Admiral Anson's Squadron. Written by Himself. The Second Edition. 8° *Frontispiece, title and pp.* viii. + 237. *London*, 1768. 224

The grandfather of Lord Byron, the poet, in suffering shipwreck upon the shores of Patagonia, was afforded the opportunity of writing some of the most interesting particulars regarding the tall natives of that country. His work abounds in information, more novel, perhaps, than strictly accurate; at least, it was the fashion a century since to deride his account.

BYRON (Commodore).

A Voyage round the World in His Majesty's Ship The Dolphin, Commanded by the Honourable Commodore Byron. In which is contained A faithful Account of the several Places, People, Plants, Animals, etc., seen on the Voyage; and among other particulars, A minute and exact Description of the Streights of Magellan, and of the Gigantic People called Patagonians; together with An accurate Account of Seven Islands lately discovered in the South Seas by an Officer on Board the said Ship. 8° *Title 1 leaf. Pref. 1 leaf. pp. 1 to 186 + 3 plates. London, printed by J. Newberry, 1767.* 225

[BERENDT (C. H.).]

Cartilla en Lengua Maya, para la enseñanza de los Niños Indigenas, por C. H. B. 12° *pp.* 14. *Merida*, 1871. 226

[Primer in the Maya Language, for the instruction of the Indian children, by C. H. B[erendt].]

In this little work are given the principles of pronunciation, and elementary sounds of the Maya language, spoken by the Indians of Yucatan.

CABEÇA DE VACA.

Relation et Naufrages d'Alvar Nunez Cabeça de Vaca. Vallodolid, 1555. 8° *pp.* 302. *Paris, Arthus Bertrand*, 1837. 227

Published as the Seventh Number of Ternaux-Compans' Series of *Voyages, Relations, et Memoires.*

CABEÇA DE VACA (Alvar Nunez).

The Narrative of Alvar Nuñez Cabeca de Vaca. Translated by Buckingham Smith. *Large* 4° *pp.* 138 + 8 *maps. Washington*, 1851. 228

One hundred copies of the Narrative were privately printed for Mr. G. W. Riggs of Washington, entirely for presentation to societies and personal friends. It is the earliest relation of Florida, and the territory from the Atlantic coast across the Mississippi to the Pacific which we possess.

The narration of the unfortunate expedition of Cabeça de Vaca across the territory now occupied by the Southern States from Florida to Texas in the year 1527, nearly three and a half centuries ago, is full of the most melancholy yet absorbing interest. Nine years of wanderings and captivity among the Indians elapsed before this ill-fated member of a still more unfortunate band escaped almost alone of all who set out so joyously with him. His narration has been received by all historians and antiquaries as veracious. It is certainly most valuable to us in one particular: that as it is the earliest historic memoir of the Indian races of that portion of America, it is also the most minute and full in its narrations of their national traits.

CABEÇA DE VACA (A. N.)

Relation of Alvar Nunez Cabeca de Vaca. Translated from the Spanish by Buckingham Smith. 8° *pp.* 300. *New York*, 1871. 229

The "Relation" occupies pp. 11 to 205, with the notes at the foot of the page instead of as in the former quarto edition being appended to the Narrative. An Appendix, pp. 206 to 232, contains additional papers. A Memoir of Cabeça de Vaca by T. W. Field, occupies pp. 233 to 254. A Preface by Hon. H. C. Murphy, precedes the Relation. A Memoir of the translator, written by Mr. J. G. Shea, fills pp. 255 to 263. The sadden death of the talented translator, occurring while these sheets were passing through the press, filled the hearts of many bibliophiles with sadness.

The work was brought out under the patronage and personal care of the Hon. H. C. Murphy, and formed a fitting monument to the earnest scholar and gentleman who first made the valuable Relations of Cabeca available to those who could not read it in the original.

CABEÇA DE VACA (Alvar Nunez).

Commentaires d'Alvar Nunez Cabeça de Vaca, Adelantade et Gouverneur du Rio de la Plata, rediges par Pero Hernandez,

Notaire et Secretaire de la Province. Valladolid 1555. 8° *pp.* 507. *Paris, Arthus Bertrand, libraire-editeur*, 1837. 230

[Commentaries of Cabeça de Vaca, Governor of the Province of Rio de la Plata. Arranged by Pedro Hernandez, Notary and Secretary of the Province.]

Published as the Sixth Number of Ternaux-Compan's collection of *Voyages, Relations, et Memoires.* The Commentaries have never been translated into English.

The first edition of Cabeça's *Relacion* was printed at Sevilla in 1542, 4° 66 leaves; the second at Valladolid in 1555. This is divided into two parts, of which the first only is attributed to Cabeça de Vaca himself, entitled *Naufragios de Alvar Nunez de Cabeca de Vaca* (also in the Collection of Barcia); the second, *Commentarios de Alvar Nunez Cabeca de Vaca*, a work which is supposed to have been written by his Secretary, Pierre Fernandez, while Nunez was in prison. "These two works," says M. Ternaux, "were composed for the justification of Cabeça de Vaca, but did not prevent the disappointment of his being condemned to exile in Africa on account of the *cruelties* perpetrated by him in America." During his long wanderings among the Indians, with whom he became a sort of divinity or prophet, he traversed the entire breadth of the continent from Florida to the Pacific, leading the tribes of devotees, whose superstitious reverence he had excited. The first of these works has been many times reprinted: by Barcia in 1749; by Ternaux in 1837; by Buckingham Smith in 1851, and a new edition by the latter in 1871.

The story of his arrest and imprisonment is told by Ulrich Schmidel in his *Vera Historia Admirandæ*, chapters xxxix. and xl. Having been appointed governor of Buenos Ayres in 1540, he a few months after organized an expedition against a tribe of Indians known as the Surucusis. On arriving near their territory he was seized with a disease which seems to have rendered him incapable of command, perhaps partially insane. His camp was fixed for nearly three months in one of the most pestilential spots of the whole country, and no entreaties could induce his withdrawal or advance.

Schmidel says the governor exercised his authority with so rigorous a hand that his soldiers equally detested and feared him. At length, determined no longer to endure the governor's harshness and inactivity, they seized him in his tent, and kept him a prisoner for more than a year, when he was sent under guard to Spain. Mr. Harrisse asserts that Cabeça de Vaca was born at Xeres, and that he has seen it stated somewhere that he died at a ripe old age at Seville in 1564. This fact is stated by Techo in his *Historia Provinciæ Paraguariæ. Leodii*, 1673. Both editions of his work are rare, the first exceedingly so.

The *Relacion* aroused the ire of Caspar Plautus, who under the cognomen of Philoponus wrote the *Nova-Typis*. At page 91 he arraigns Cabeça for presuming to perform miracles through his intercessions with the Deity; Philoponus claiming such prerogatives as solely belonging to the priestly orders and not to the "Milicia Christiana." The answers to his prayers, exhibited in the falling of showers of rain, the healing of the sick, and the raising of the dead, were not considered by Philoponus as conclusive evidence on that point. So important was the arraignment of Philoponus deemed in that day, that a treatise was written by Don Antonio Arduino, to refute the calumnies of the monk. This was printed by Barcia in the first volume of his *Historiadores Primitivos* under the title of *Examen Apologetico de la Historica Narracion de los Naufragios, Peregrinaciones, i Milagros de Alvar Nuñez Cabeza de Vaca.* [Apologetical Examination of the Historical Narrative of the Shipwrecks, Travels, and Miracles of Cabeza de Vaca.] The treatise is ponderous with learning, and canvasses every possible phase of the conditions of possible miracles.

CABRERA (Paul Felix).

Description of the Ruins of an Ancient City discovered near

Palenque in the Kingdom of Guatemala in Spanish America: Translated from the Original Manuscript Report of Captain Don Antonio del Rio: Followed by Teatro Critico Americano, or a Critical Investigation and Research into the History of the Americans. By Doctor Felix Cabrera, of the City of New Guatemala. 4° *pp.* xiii. + 128 + 17 *plates.* *London, published by Henry Berthoud,* 1822. 231

Captain Del Rio discovered and examined the now famous ruins of Palenque in 1787, but his manuscript report remained in the provincial archives of Guatemala until a short time prior to their translation and publication in the present form. The translator gave so literal a version that he did not change the references in the body of the work which referred to drawings that had been irrecoverably lost. Captain Del Rio's Report occupies pp. 1 to 21, and in the remainder of the work Dr. Cabrera attempts to establish the theory that the figures upon the monuments of Palenque prove a connection between the Egyptians and the Aboriginal race which constructed them. All this is very ingeniously argued, and the comparison, on the whole, more fairly and learnedly stated than the weavers of hypotheses usually do. From the occurrence of an eclipse recorded 291 years before Christ, corresponding with the same date in the Mexican calendar, he constructs a table of the Mexican years.

CAMPANIUS (Thomas).

Lutheri | Catechismus | Ofwersatt | pa | American-Virginiske | Spraket. | 24° *pp.* 160. Engraved Title. + Rubricated Title + *pp.* (xiv) + 160. *Stockholm,* | *Anno* MDCXCVI. | 232

[Luther's Catechism translated into the American-Virginia (Indian) Language. *Stockholm,* 1696.]

This translation of Luther's Catechism into the language of the Virginia (or more correctly the Delaware) Indians was made by Thomas Campanius, of Stockholm. He was for many years the resident pastor of the colony, and a learned and zealous man, not only in the exercise of his religious functions but in literary pursuits. This book was printed for distribution in America, among the people into whose tongue it was translated, and has in consequence become very rare. The last six pages are devoted to an analysis and Vocabulary of the Mohawk dialect of the Iroquois. The author styled himself John Campanius Holmensis, or Campanius of Stockholm, and in consequence in some catalogues the book is found credited to Holme.

CAMPANIUS (T.).

Kort Beskrifning | om | Provincien | Nya Swerige | uti | America, | some nu förtiden af the Engelske kallas | Pensylvania. Aflarde och trowardige Mans skriften och berattelser ihopale | ted och sammanskrefwen, samt med åthskillige Figurer | utzirad af | Thomas Campanius Holm. | 4° *pp.* xvi. + 190. 4 *maps and* 3 *plates.* *Stockholm Tryckt uti kongl. Boktr hos. Sal. Wankijfs* | *Antiamed egen bekostnad, af J. H. Werner Abr* MDCCII. 233

CAMPANIUS (Thos.)

A Short Description of the Province of New Sweden, now called by the English Pennsylvania in America. Compiled from the relations and writings of persons worthy of credit and adorned with maps and plates, by Thomas Campanius Holm. Translated from the Swedish, for the Historical Society of Pennsylvania, with

Notes by Peter S. du Ponceau. 8° *pp.* 165 + 2 *maps and* 3 *plans. Philadelphia, McCarty & Davis*, 1834. 234

This was the work of a grandson of the Swedish missionary, who translated Luther's Catechism into the language of the Virginia Indians. Book iii. pp. 112 to 143, is entitled "Of the American Indians in the Province," and Book iv. pp. 144 to 160, has the heading, "Vocabulary and Phrases in the American Language of New Sweden." The descriptions of the characteristics of the Indians of Pennsylvania as given by Campanius, have not a little value, as statements made probably from the narrations of an actual observer. Pastor Campanius, his grandfather, must have had a very intimate acquaintance with the aborigines, as his translation of the Catechism in the Indian tongue fully attests.

CAMPBELL (A.).

The Sequel to Bulkley and Cummins Voyage to the South Seas, or the Adventures of Capt. Cheap the Hon. Mr. Byron, etc. of the Wager, containing A faithful Narrative of the unparalleled Sufferings of these gentlemen [*etc.*, 4 *lines*] till they fell into the Hands of the Indians who carried them into New Spain, etc. The whole Interspersed with descriptions of . . . . the American Indians and Spaniards, and of their Treatment of the Author and his Companions, by Alexander Campbell, Late Midshipman of The Wager. 8° *pp.* 108 + *title* 1 *leaf. London*, 1747. 235

CAMPBELL (Robert).

(Memorial of Robert Campbell of Savannah to the Senate of Georgia) on (the present situation of the Cherokee Indians). 8° *pp.* 20. *Savannah, January*, 1829. 236

This statement of the wrongs of the Cherokee Indians by this eminent humanitarian, was refused a reading before the Georgia Senate on the ground of being disrespectful.

CAMPBELL (William W.).

Annals of Tryon County; or, the Border Warfare of New York, during the Revolution. *Map.* 8° *New York*, 1831. 237

CAMPBELL (William W.).

The Border Warfare of New York, during the Revolution, or the Annals of Tryon County. 12° *pp.* 396. *New York*, 1849. 238

The same as above, with the addition of an Appendix from pp. 233 to 396.

CAMPBELL (Maria) and CLARKE (James Freeman).

Revolutionary Services, and Civil Life of General William Hull, prepared from his Manuscripts by his daughter, Mrs. Maria Campbell, together with the History of the Campaign of 1812 and Surrender of the Post of Detroit by his grandson James Freeman Clarke. 8° *pp.* 482. *New York*, 1848. 239

CANADA INDIANS.

Report on the Indians of Upper Canada. By a Sub-Committee of the Aborigines Protection Society. 8° *pp.* 52. *London*, 1839. 240

CAPTIVE (The) CHILDREN.

New York General Protestant Episcopal Sunday School Union and Church Book Society. 16° 35 *pp.* n. d. 241

A child's book, narrating the conduct of some Christian children, captives among the Indians.

CARDENAS (C. C.).

Breve practica, y regimen del confesionario de Yndios, en Mexicana y Castellano, para instruccion del confesor principiente, dispuesto por el Br Don Carlos Celedonio de Cardenas y Leon en (   ) 1761. (See Velasquez.) 242

[Short practice and rules for the confession of Indians, in Mexican and Castilian, for the instruction of the newly beginning confessor. Arranged by the Br Don Carlos Celedonio of Cardenas and Leon in (   ) 1761.]

CARLI (J. R.).

Lettres Americaines, dans lequelles on examine l'Origine l' Etat Civil Politique, etc., des Anciens Habitans de l'Amerique; les grandes Epoques de la Nature, etc., par M. le Compte J. R. Carli, President du Conseil Supreme, etc. *Two vols. A Boston et ce troure de Paris*, 1788. 243

[American Letters, in which are discussed the Origin, and the Civil and Political State of the Ancient Inhabitants of America; the great Epochs of Nature, etc., by Count Carli.]

[CARRINGTON (Mrs. M. J.).]

Absaraka, Home of the Crows (Indians), being the Experience of an Officer's Wife on the Plains [1 *line*] during the occupation of the new route to Virginia City, Montana, 1866–7, and the Indian hostility thereto. [5 *lines.*] 12° *pp.* 284. *Philadelphia*, 1868. 244

The lady who wrote this pleasing, but not very valuable work, had little personal experience among the Indians, and therefore fills its pages with incidents and speculations derived from the gossip of the camp. The most valuable portion of the book is that in which she gives the personal narrations of some restored captives, scarcely to be deemed happy in surviving the awful massacres of their families. They were all married women, who, having witnessed the slaughter of their husbands and children, were reserved by the savages for a worse fate. It is now well known, that although the Algonquin and Iroquois tribes never violated their female captives, the Indians of the Plains almost as invariably subject them to the most horrible personal outrages.

CARTWRIGHT (George).

A Journal of Transactions and Events during a Residence of nearly Sixteen Years on the Coast of Labrador; containing many interesting Particulars, both of the Country and its Inhabitants, not hitherto known. Illustrated with proper Charts. By George Cartwright, Esq., in Three Volumes. *Large* 4° Vol. I. *Frontispiece* + *map* + *pp.* (xxiv.) + 287. Vol. II. *Map* + *pp.* x. + 505. Vol. III. *Map* + *pp.* x. + 248 + 15. *Newark, Eng., printed and sold by Allin and Ridge*, 1792. 245

Among the great mass of details of a fur-hunter's life, which these immense quartos afford us, some particulars of the Aborigines of the Peninsula of Labrador may be gleaned which are not elsewhere obtainable. It is much to be regretted that the author had not made use of his long intervals of inaction, to record more of his observations of Indian life in that region, and to abbreviate his journal. Every fox and bear's cub which fell a victim to his skill, is immortalized by a paragraph; but ethnology has little to thank him for in the records of aboriginal traits and incidents.

CARSON (Christopher).

The Life and Times of Christopher Carson, the Rocky Mountain Scout and Guide; with Reminiscences of Fremont's Exploring Expedition and Notes in New Mexico. 12° *pp.* 94. *New York and London. Beadle and Co., publishers.* 246

No person ever lived who knew the character of the Indian better than this famous frontiersman; and he seems to have had a fair critic for a biographer. His book is crowded with the incidents of border warfare, and encounters with the savage tribes of the Great Plains and the Rocky Mountains.

CARTIER (J.).

Breve et Succincta Narratione Della nauigation fatta por ordine de la Maesta Christianissima all Isole de Canada, Hochelaga Saguenai & altre, al presente, dette la nuova Francia con particolari costumi & cerimonie de gli habitanti. *Folio, leaves* 441 *to* 453, *of Vol. III. of Ramusio, Navigatione et Viaggi* (3 *vols. Venetia*, 1554 *to* 1565). 247

[Brief Narrative of the navigation made to the islands of Canada, Hochelaga, Saguenay, and others, and particularly of the manners, language, and ceremonies of their inhabitants, by Jacques Cartier.]

Folio 447 is a folding plan of Hochelaga, with sections of the fortifications and figures of the native Indians. A general map of America occupies folio 456. A vocabulary of the language of the natives forms a portion of pp. 453 and 454.

CARTIER (Jacques).

Prima Relatione di Jacques Cartier della Terra Nuova detta nuova Francia, trouata nell' anno M.D.XXXIIII. *Leaves* 435 *to* 440 *of the 3d vol. of Ramusio. Venitia*, 1565. 248

[First Relation of Jacques Cartier of the New World called New France, discovered in the year 1533.]

Page 441 contains a vocabulary of the language of the Canadian Indians.

The first edition of Cartier's *Relations* printed at Paris in 1545, has proved hitherto to be of such extreme rarity as that but a single copy has been known to exist for nearly three hundred years. The editor of the third, printed at Rouen in 1598, announces that he had translated it from a foreign language, which was, doubtless, the Italian of this second edition of Ramusio, a fact which proves that even at a date so early as only fifty years after its publication, the first edition was unknown. Cartier's *Relations* afford us the first positive information regarding the Indians of Canada, and contain the first vocabularies ever printed of the languages of any nation of American aborigines. Mr. Fross has reproduced Cartier's Relations in two very handsome volumes, together with a third consisting of documents hitherto unpublished. The second, contains a fac-simile of the large folding plate; noticed in No. 247, and of the map accompanying it.

CARVALHO (S. N.).

Incidents of Travel and Adventure in the Far West with Colonel Fremont's last Expedition, across the Rocky Mountains; including Three Month's Residence in Utah; and a perilous trip across the Great American Desert to the Pacific. By S. N.

Carvalho, Artist to the Expedition. 12° *pp.* 250, *and also pp.* 1 *to* 130 *Mormonism. New York, Derby and Jackson,* 1860. 249

The adventures of Colonel Fremont among the Indian tribes of the mountains and the plains, are more minutely narrated in this volume than in either of the many narratives, journals, or reports of the explorer himself.

Carver (Jonathan).

Three Years' Travels through the Interior Parts of North America for more than 5,000 Miles; containing an Account of the Great Lakes, &c. [4 *lines*]. With a Description of the Birds, Beasts, Insects, and Fishes, peculiar to the Country. Together with a concise History of the Genius, Manners, and Customs of the Indians [*etc.*, 7 *lines*]. By Captain Jonathan Carver, of the Provincial Troops in America. 8° *Philadelphia, Key and Simpson,* 1796. 250

Carver (John).

Travels through the Interior Parts of North America in the years 1766, 1767 and 1768. By J. Carver, Esq., Capt. of a Company of Provincial Troops during the late war with France. Illustrated with Coloured Copper Plates. The Third Edition. To which is added some account of the Author, and a Copious Index. 8° *Portrait. London, C. Dilley,* 1781. 251

Title and Advertisement 2 leaves + some account of Captain J. Carver, pp. 1 to 22. Dedication and Contents, pp. (xxii.) + Introduction, pp. xvi. + Journal, etc., pp. 1 to 544 + Index, pp. (xx.). Portrait, two folding maps, and five plates; three of which are pictures of Indian costumes, chiefs, women, and utensils. The journal of Capt. Carver's travels among the tribes of Indians around the upper great lakes, occupies pp. 1 to 180. Chapters i. to xvii. pp. 181 to 448, are entitled, Of the Origin, Manners, Customs, Religion and Language of the Indians, of which the last twenty are devoted to a Vocabulary of the Chippeway language. In this division he gives the results of his personal experiences among the Indians he visited, or warred with. Not the least interesting is the author's account of the dreadful massacre at Fort William Henry; and of his narrow escape from the Indians at the time.

Case of the Seneca Indians.

The Case of the Seneca Indians in the State of New York. Illustrated by Facts. Printed for the Information of the Society of Friends, etc. 8° *Philadelphia,* 1840. 252

The Senecas having, at the suggestion of the Society of Friends, consented to sell their lands, a controversy arose regarding the transaction which became on the part of their opponents somewhat acrimonious. To justify themselves the committee of the society having the matter in charge, printed this pamphlet. A sharp answer written by N. T. Strong, one of the Seneca chiefs, appeared in the succeeding year, and this met with several rejoinders and replies.

Cass (Gen. Lewis).

Life of General Lewis Cass; comprising an account of his Military Services in the North West, during the War with Great Britain, his diplomatic career and civil history, to which is appended a Sketch of the public and private history of Major General W. O. Butler, of the Volunteer Service of the United States. With two portraits. 12° *pp.* 210. *Philadelphia, G. B. Zieber and Co.,* 1848. 253

CASTENEDA DE NAGERA.

Relation du Voyage de Cibola, entrepris en 1540; ou l'on traite de toutes les peuplades qui habitent cettee contree, de leurs moeurs et coutumes, par Pedro de Casteneda de Nagera, inedit. 8° *pp.* 392. *Paris, Arthus Bertrand, editeur.* 1838. 254

[Narrative of the journey to Cibola (New Mexico), undertaken in 1540, which treats of all the people who inhabit that country, of their manners and customs.]

This volume forms No. 10 of Ternaux-Compans' collection of *Voyages, Relations, et Memoires*, never before printed. Although this relation is declared to be superior to most of the narratives of the period, and its author without doubt a gentleman at least by education, it is probable that he served as a private soldier in the memorable expedition. The famed Cibola ranked in attraction to the Spanish Adventurers, with the El Dorado of South America, and Norumbega, the great city thought to exist on the peninsula, now occupied by the New England States and the two most eastern British Colonies. The Seven Cities, of whose marvels so much had been told, were the destination of the expedition; and it remained for the government of the United States to prove their existence, more than three hundred years after the exploration of Coronado. In the State of New Mexico still exists the many storied structures of Zuni and other cities of the Aztec, or pre-Aztec race. The work is one of the highest interest, not only as a relation of the first visit to the territories of New Mexico, Arizona, and Colorado, but more particularly to the subject of this bibliography, in presenting a view by such an intelligent observer, of the Indian nations three hundred years ago.

The work is divided into three parts, of which the second is entitled, "Description of the Provinces, Mountains, and of the Villages and their Inhabitants, Of the Religion and of the Manners of the Natives." At pages 8 to 14 will be found an account of the return of Cabeça de Vaca and his three companions; of the impostor Estevan, the negro, who accompanied Cabeça; of his engagement to act as the avant courier of Vasquez, of his royal progress through the country with his constantly increasing harem of beautiful Indian girls; and finally his condemnation to death by the Caciques of Cibola, on the charge of absurd deceit, in announcing that he, a black man, was the ambassador of those who were white as the snow.

CASTLENAU (Francis de).

Expedition dans les parties centrales de l'Amerique du Sud, de Rio de Janeiro a Lima et de Lima au Para, executee par ordre du Gouvernment Francais pendant les annees 1843 a 1847, sous la direction de Francis de Castlenau, etc. Troiseme Partie. Antiquities des Incas et autres peuples anciens. Les Planches Lithographees par Champin. 4° 6 *parts containing 7 pp. text + 60 large quarto plates. Paris, Chez P. Bertrand,* 1852. 255

[Expedition in the central parts of South America, from Rio Janeiro to Lima, and from Lima to Para, performed by order of the French Government during the years 1843 to 1847, under the direction of Francis de Castlenau. The Third Part (containing the) Antiquities of the Incas and other Ancient People.]

This portion of Castlenau's great work is complete by itself; and contains sixty plates illustrative of almost every form of Incarial antiquities, which have been preserved. The temples, idols, and domestic utensils of this wonderful people, as well as portraits of some of their princesses, preserved by their own art, are excellently portrayed in these engravings.

CATLIN (George).

Catlin's Notes of eight years travels and residence in Europe with his North American Indian Collection with anecdotes and incidents of the travels and adventures of three different parties of American Indians whom he introduced to the Courts of England, France and Belgium. In two volumes octavo, with numerous illustrations. Vol. I. *pp.* xvi. + 296 + 8 *plates. New York*, 1848. Vol. II. *pp.* xii. + 336 + 16 *plates. London*, 1848. 256

The same as the London edition of the work, with title commencing "Adventures, etc."

Catalogue of Collection of Paintings of Indian Subjects, occupies pp. 253 to 296 of vol. i.

CATLIN (Geo.).

Catalogue of Catlin's Indian Gallery of Portraits, Landscapes, Manners, and Customs, Costumes, &c. &c., collected during seven years travel amongst thirty-eight different tribes, speaking different languages. 12° *pp.* 40. *New York*, 1838. 257

This is a catalogue of the celebrated Indian Museum collected by Catlin, and exhibited for many years in this country and in Europe.

CATLIN (George).

Catlin's North American Indian Portfolio Hunting Scenes and Amusements of the Rocky Mountains and Prairies of America. From Drawings and Notes of the Author, made during eight Years' travel amongst forty-eight of the Wildest and most remote Tribes of Savages in North America. *Imperial folio, case containing twenty-five plates, colored in imitation of drawings, with twenty pages of text, also in folio. George Catlin, London.* 1844. 258

These beautiful views of scenes in Indian life are probably the most truthful ever presented to the public. Their great size (two feet by twenty inches) allows the figures to be distinct and life-like; and as no one was ever better fitted by experience and facility of power to secure upon the canvas all that would interest us in aboriginal life, these prints will remain, probably as long as their fabric lasts, the best delineations of its scenes.

CATLIN (George).

Fourteen Ioway Indians. Key to their Various Dances, Games, Ceremonies, Songs, Religion, Superstitions, Costumes, Weapons, etc. etc. By George Catlin. *Second title:* Unparalleled Exhibition — The Fourteen Ioway Indians and their Interpreter, just arrived from the Rocky Mountains [*etc.*, 12 *lines*]. 16° *pp* 28. *London*, 1844. 259

CATLIN (George).

Illustrations of the Manners and Customs and Condition of the North American Indians, with Letters and Notes written during eight years of Travel and Adventure among the wildest and most remarkable Tribes now existing. With three hundred and sixty Engravings from the Author's original Paintings, by George Catlin. *Two vols. large* 8° *pp.* 264 + 266 + 179 *colored plates. London*, 1841. (*Tenth Edition*) 1866. 260

A number of copies (often announced to have been but twelve) have the etchings colored. The first which were offered to the public were sold at a high price on account of the supposed rarity, but it is said that a large number of copies with colored etchings were found by Mr. Bohn in an out-house, and they have consequently become somewhat more common. They are still, however, held at nearly ten times the price of the plain copies.

CATLIN (George).

Letters and Notes of the Manners, Customs, and Condition of the North American Indians, written during eight years travel amongst the wildest tribes of Indians in North America. By George Catlin. *Two vols.* 8° *With one hundred and fifty illustrations on steel and wood.* *pp.* 792 + 41 *plates.* *Philadelphia*, 1857. 261

This is a reprint of the large work of Catlin, the title of which commences *Illustrations*. The plates of this are not so numerous as in the London edition, and are shaded instead of etched.

CATLIN (George).

O kee-pa, A Religious Ceremony and other Customs of the Mandans, by George Catlin. With Thirteen Colored Illustrations. *Large* 8° *pp.* 52 + 13 *plates.* *Lippincott, Philadelphia*, 1867. 262

In the latter part of 1866 one of the numbers of Truebner's monthly catalogue contained a notice of a pamphlet purporting to be written by Mr. Catlin upon the secret customs of the Mandans, said to be indescribably lascivious. This excited the indignant denial by Mr. Catlin, of his authorship of the essay, of which, as only fifty copies were printed, little was known. The next year, as a more effectual disproval of his association with what he deemed a disreputable performance, Mr. Catlin produced *O-kee-pa*. It was as much a defense of his early friends the Mandans as of himself. The terrible religious and civil rite, here pictured with such horrible fidelity, is no longer practiced, as the interesting people who described it are totally extinct as a nation.

CATLIN (George).

Life amongst the Indians; A Book for Youth. By George Catlin. 12° *pp.* xii. + 339. *Fourteen plates of scenes in Indian Life.* *New York, D. Appleton & Co.* 1867. 263

CATLIN (George).

Last Rambles amongst the Indians of the Rocky Mountains and the Andes, by George Catlin. 12° *pp.* x. + 361 + *eight plates and sixteen wood cuts of Indian portraits, life, and scenery.* *New York, D. Appleton and Company*, 1867. 264

CATON (J. D.).

The Last of the Illinois, and a Sketch of the Pottawatomies. Read before the Chicago Historical Society, December 13, 1870. By John Dean Caton. 8° *pp.* 36, *and printed cover.* *Chicago, Rand, McNally, and Co.* 1870. 265

CAVELIER (M.).

Relation Du Voyage Entrepris parfeu M. Robert Cavelier Sieur de la Salle pour decouvrir dans le golfe du *Mexique* l'embouchure du Fleuve de Missiaspy. Par son Frere M. Cavelier prêtre de St. Sulpice l'un des compagnons de ce Voyage. *Small* 4° *pp.* 54. *A Manate de la Presse Cramoisy de Jean-Marie Shea*, 1858. 266

[Relation of the Voyage undertaken by M. Robert Cavelier de la Salle for the discovery in the Gulf of Mexico of the Mouth of the River Mississippi. By his brother M. Cavelier, friar of St. Sulpice, one of his companions in the Voyage.]

No. 3 of Shea's *Jesuit Relations*.

Mr. Shea printed this Relation from the MSS. in the possession of Mr. Parkman, as a necessary supplement to the Journal of M. Joutel, and that of Father Anastase, Recollet, printed by Father Chretien Le Clercq, in his work *l'Establissement de la Foy*. The Relation is principally occupied with descriptions of the tribes of Indians whose territories the hardy explorer visited.

CHAHTA

Uba isht taloa holisso; or, Choctaw Hymn-book. *Second edition, revised and much enlarged.* 16° *Boston*, 1833. 267

CHAMPLAIN (S^r.).

Les | Voyages | de la | Nouvelle France | Occidentales dicte | Canada, | faits par le Sr de Champlain | Xainctongeois Capitaine pour le Roy en la Marine du | Ponant, & toutes les Decouuertes qu'il a faites en | ce pais depuis l'an 1603, iusques en l'an 1629. | Ou se voit comme ce pays a este premierrement decouuerte par les François | Sous l'authorite de nos Roys tres Chretiennes iusques au regne | de Sa Maieste a present regnante Lovis XIII. | Roy de France & de Navarre. | Auec vn traitte [*etc.*, 7 *lines*]. Ensemble vne Carte generalle de la description dudit faicte en Son Meridien selon la | declinacion de la guide Aymant & vn Catechisme ou Instruction traduicte du | Francois au langage des peuples Sauuages, de quelque Contree, auec ce | qui s'est passe en ladite Nouvelle France en l'annee 1631. A Monseignevr Le Cardinal Dvc de Richeliev. A Paris. Chez Lovis Sevestre Imprimeur. — Libraire rue du Meurier, pres la porte S Victor, & en sa Boutique dans la Cour du Palais. MDCXXXII. Auec Priuilege du Roy. 4° *pp.* 16 + 308. *Seconde Partie, pp.* 310 + 2 *blanks* + *table pp.* 8 + *Traite* 54 + 2 *blanks*. *Doctrienne Chretienne, pp.* 20. *Map*, 2 *sheets*, 33 × 21 *inches*. 8 *plates in the text*. 268

[Voyages made in New France called Canada, by the Sieur Champlain, Captain of the Marine for the King, and (Accounts) of all the discoveries which he made in that Country from 1603 to 1629, in which it will be seen that this Country was first discovered by the French, etc. Together with a Map, and a Catechism or Book of Instruction, translated from the French into the language of the Sauvages, the people of that Country, with a Narration of all which transpired in New France to the year 1631.]

An imperfect fac-simile of the large map made for Mr. Tross is usually substituted for the rare original.

This edition is the only complete one of Champlain's Voyages. The first part of the volume is an almost literal reproduction of all the other voyages, excepting some minuter relations of the same events in the edition of 1613, with most of the plates printed in the text instead of on separate sheets. The second part is wholly new matter never before printed; being a relation of what transpired in New France from 1619, the date of his latest work, to 1632. The great map is also printed here for the first time. A second edition of this complete Work of Champlain bears the date of 1640, differing in only one or two verbal particulars. A third edition was printed by the government of France in 1830, in 2 vols. 8°, and a fourth in 1870, in quarto, at Quebec.

Beside these, some copies of the edition of 1632 have two variations in the imprint of the publisher: one being *Chez Claude Collet*, and the other *Chez Pierre le Mer*. Mr. Stevens asserts also that two leaves, bearing the signatures Dij and Diij, were canceled in most copies and reprinted to escape the censure of a reflection upon Cardinal Richelieu. The first paragraph on p. 27, Sig. Dij of the amended copies ends with "telles decouvertes." The rejected passage was the mildest possible assertion in five lines, that great princes might know well how to conduct the government of a kingdom, and yet not know how to sail a ship. The map with the imprint of *Collet* is slightly smaller than in the others, which both contain the additional words, "Faict l'an 1632 par le Sieur de Champlain." This work gives us the first accurate accounts we have of the Indians of the interior of the present State of New York. It is very largely devoted to descriptions of their habits, modes of life and warfare; and of personal observations and experiences among the Algonquins and Iroquois. The most remarkable event in Indian history was caused by Champlain's first visit to the shores of the lake bearing his name. In a conflict between the two named races of savages, he gave the victory to his friends the Abnaquis, by the use of his musket. The Iroquois never forgave the injury, and thousands of Frenchmen were slaughtered to avenge it. The Six Nations always fought with the English against their enemies, and twice nearly destroyed the French colonies with their own warriors alone.

Champlain (Samuel).

Narrative of a Voyage to the West Indies and Mexico in the years 1599–1602. With Maps and Illustrations. By Samuel Champlain. Translated from the original and unpublished Narrative, with a biographical notice and notes by Alice Wilmere, edited by Norton Shaw. 8° *Rep^t, pp. 4. Title, half title, 3 leaves. Intro.* vi. *Biog.* xcix. *Narrative, pp.* 48 + 12 *plates. London, printed for the Hakluyt Society,* 1859. 269

This "Narrative of Champlain's First Voyage to the New World," is of great value to us in establishing, by an unimpeachable authority, the story of the awful cruelties which were inflicted upon the Indians of the West Indies by the Spaniards. Fac-simile lithographs of Champlain's drawings are given; among which are representations of Indian feasts, flogging Indians to church, and burning groups of the natives at the stake. The biography gives an interesting narration of Champlain's dealings with the Indians of New France.

Champlain (S.)

Oeuvres de Champlain publiees sous les patronage de l'Universitie Laval. Par L'Abbe C. H. Laverdiere. Seconde Edition. 4° *Quebec, Imprimirie au Seminaire par Geo. E. Desbarats,* 1870. 270

This beautiful edition of the Works of Champlain in six volumes, is worthy of all praise, except for the scant justice done the fine plates of the originals, in the feeble lithograph reproductions. Vol. I. contains, Title and Preface by the editor, pp. viii. A Biographical Notice of Champlain (pp. lxxvi.), Preface of first edition, lv. A Brief Discourse of the most remarkable events which Samuel Champlain experienced in the West Indies, pp. 48 + 62 Plates, on 46 separate sheets. This work is a reprint of the preceding first printed by the Hakluyt Society. This edition comprises six quarto volumes, the titles of the remaining five being given in the next following four numbers.

Champlain (Samuel).

Des Savvages, ov Voyage de Samvel Champlain de Brovage, fait en la France Novvelle, l'an mil six cens trois: Contenant Les Moeurs, façon de viure, mariages, guerres & habitation des Sauuages de Canadas. De la descouuerte de plus de quatre cens cinquante lieues dans les pais des Sauuages. Quels peuples y habitent: des animaux qui s'y trouuent; des riuieres, lacs, isles, & terres, & quels arbres & fruicts elles produisent. De la Coste d'Arcadie, des terres que l'on y a descouuertes, & de plusieurs mines qui y sont, selon le rapport des sauuages. A Paris, Chez Claude de Monstroeil tenant sa boutique en la Cour du Palais au nom de Iésus. Auec priuilege du Roy. *Small* 8° *Prel. leaves,* 3. *Text,* 36 *leaves* (1603). *Reprinted, Quebec* 1870. 4° *prel. pp.* 4 + viii. + 63. 271

[The Savages or Voyage of Samuel Champlain of Brovage, made in 1603. Containing The Manners, mode of life, marriages, wars and dwellings of the Savages of Canada. Of the Discovery of more than 450 leagues of the Country of the Savages. What peoples inhabit it, of the animals which are found there, of the rivers, lakes, islands, and lands, and what trees and fruits are produced. Of the Coast of Acadie, lands which have been discovered there, and what mines there are according to the report of the Savages.]

This is the first of Champlain's printed works, the original edition of which is the rarest of all of them. It needs no more than the title to show that its subject is almost wholly the Aborigines of New France.

CHAMPLAIN (Sieur de).

Les Voyages dv Sievr de Champlain Xaintongeois Capitaine ordinaire pour le Roy en la marine. Divisez en deux livres, ou Journal tres-fidele des observations faites es descouuertures de la nouuelle France: tant en la descriptio des terres, costes, riuieres, ports, haures, leurs hauteurs & plusieurs declinaisons de la guide-aymant; qu'en la creance des peuples, leurs superstitions, facon de viure & de guerroyer, enrichi de quantite de figures. Ensemble deux cartes [*etc.,* 7 *lines*]. A Paris. Chez Jean Berjon rue S Iean de Beauuais, au Cheval Volant & en sa boutique au Palais, a la gallerie des prisonniers. 1613. Avec privilege dv Roy. 4° 10 *leaves* + *pp.* 325 + 5 + *Fourth Voyage made in* 1613, *pp.* 1 *to* 52. 8 *maps and* 4 *plates* + *plates in the text. Reprinted, Quebec* 1870. 4° *pp.* iv. + xvi. + 327 + 24 *maps and plates on separate sheets.* 272

[The Voyages of the Sieur de Champlain Xaintongeois, divided into two books, or a very faithful Journal of observations made of the discoveries in New France, with descriptions of the lands, etc; what is known of the Peoples, their Superstitions, manner of Living, and of Warfare, embellished with many engravings.]

This Journal of the second, third, and fourth voyages of Champlain, is a relation of the events recorded consecutively in the order, and with the date of their occurrence. Although almost wholly reprinted in the edition of 1632, yet the minuteness and chronological order of the diary not being observed therein, this edition is much esteemed.

CHAMPLAIN (Le Sieur de).

Voyages et descovvertvres faites en la Novvelle France, depuis l'année 1615, iusques à la fin de l'année 1618. Par le Sieur de Champlain Capitaine ordinaire pour le Roy en la Mer du Ponant. Où sont descrits les moeurs, coustumes, habits, façons de guerroyer, chasses, dances, festins, et enterrements de dieurs peuples Sauuages, et de plusieurs choses remarquables qui luy sont arriuées audit païs, auec vne description de la beauté, fertilité, et temperature d'iceluy. Paris, Claude Collet, au Palais en la gallerie des Prisonniers 1619. *Small* 8° *Engraved title and six plates, four of which are in the text,* 8 *prel. leaves* + 158 *leaves. Reprinted, Quebec* 1870. 4° *prel. pp.* (iv.) + viii. + 143 + 6 *plates on separate sheets.* 273

[Voyages and discoveries made in New France from the year 1615 to the end of the year 1618. In which are portrayed the manners, customs, habits, modes of warfare, of hunting feasts, and burials of various Savage tribes; and of many other remarkable things which occurred in that country; with a description of its beauty, fertility, and climate.]

This volume, printed twelve years before Champlain's collected voyages, was incorporated therein, with the omission of several plates. It is a continuation of the voyages printed in 1613, and was reprinted, or at least issued, as a second edition in 1620 and another in 1627. The plates, illustrative of scenes in Indian life, are beautiful specimens of the engraving of the period.

CHAMPLAIN (S.).

Les Voyages de la Nouvelle France [*etc., as in the edition of* 1632, *No.* 268.] Two Vols. *Prel. pp.* viii. + 16 + 328. *Seconde Partie* 1 *to* 343 + *Traite* 1 *to* 55 + *Table* 8 + *Doctrienne Chretienne translated into the Montagnais language pp.* 20 + *Pieces Justicative* 86 + *Table,* 31. *Total, pp.* 846. 4° *Quebec,* 1870. 274

Very enthusiastic and wealthy collectors are not satisfied with anything less than perfect copies of all the editions of Champlain's Works. They are also exceedingly scrupulous in obtaining them with large margins, and all the maps and plates in fine condition. A fastidious collector, with only ordinary greed of acquisition, may, however, rest well satisfied with a fair sound copy of Champlain's Voyages of the edition of 1632 with the original map. He has therein all which the great discoverer wrote relating to New France, as it finally left his own hands perfected. If, however, unsatisfied longings still haunt his brain, he may add the edition of 1613 with its beautiful plates and plans; but let him beware of setting his heart on *The Sauvages* of 1603, as he will most probably pass a lifetime without even seeing a copy. Copies of any of the editions of Champlain in perfect condition are exceedingly rare, and have, within a few years, risen to almost fabulous prices. $150 each has been paid for the editions of 1613, 1615, 1620, 1627, and 1632.

CHAMPLAIN (Le Sieur de).

Voyage du Sieur de Champlain, ou Journal des Decouvertes de la Nouvelle France. 2 *vols.* 8° *Paris,* 1830. 275*

"Only 250 copies of this edition were printed, and at the expense of the government, to furnish employment to the printers rendered destitute by the Revolution." — *Rich.*

CHABERT (X.).

An Historical Account of the Manners and Customs of the Savage Inhabitants of Brazil, together with a sketch of the life of the Botecudo Chieftain and family. By X. Chabert, printed for and sold by the author, price one shilling. 8° *pp.* 24 + *printed cover. Birmingham,* 1822. 276

This is a very meagre account of one of the savage tribes of South America, purporting to be derived from personal experience, but largely quoted from Maximilian's travels.

CHANNING (William Henry).
The Memoir and Writings of James H. Perkins, edited by William Henry Channing, in Two Volumes. 12° *Portrait* + *pp.* vi. + 527 + 502. *Boston, Wm. Crosby and H. P. Nichols; Cincinnati, Trueman and Spofford*, 1851. 277

Chapters v. to x. pp. 126 to 426 of Vol. II. are devoted to the "Early French Travellers in the West," "English Discoveries in the Ohio Valley," "The Pioneers of Kentucky, "Border Warfare of the Revolution," "Settlement of the Northwestern Territory," "Fifty Years of Ohio," in which there are many details of frontier life and Indian warfare, presented in an interesting and scholarly manner.

CHAPIN (Alonzo).
Glastenbury for Two Hundred Years, a Centennial Discourse May 18, A. D. 1853. With an Appendix containing historical and statistical papers of interest. By Rev. Alonzo B. Chapin. 8° *pp.* 252. *Hartford*, 1853. 278

"Indian History and Sale" is the title of a subdivision of the work extending from pp. 9 to 25, in which the etymology and significance of the Indian names is discussed, and an enumeration of the tribes which inhabited the town, together with a transcript of the Indian title, and a narration of some incidents of the association of the first settlers with the savages.

CHAPIN (Walter).
The Missionary Gazetteer, comprising a view of the Inhabitants, and a Geographical Description of the Countries and Places, where Protestant Missionaries have labored; alphabetically arranged and so constructed as to give a particular and general History of Missions Throughout the World, etc. By Walter Chapin. 12° *pp.* 420. *Woodstock, printed by David Watson*, 1825. 279

Seventy-nine articles descriptive of Missions among the American Indians, with statistics of their number, etc., are contained in this volume.

CHAPMAN (Isaac A.).
A Sketch of the History of Wyoming, by the late Isaac A. Chapman, Esq. To which is added an Appendix containing a Statistical Account of the Valley and adjacent Country, by a Gentleman of Wilkesbarre. 12° *pp.* 209. *Wilkesbarre, Penn., printed and published by Sharp D. Lewis*, 1830. 280

This is the first of the histories of Wyoming, and is principally occupied with the narration of its settlement, wars with the Indians, and the sad story of the massacre of its inhabitants by them.

CHAPPELL (Lieut. Edward).
Voyage of His Majesty's Ship Rosamond to Newfoundland and the southern coast of Labrador, of which countries no account has been published by any British traveller since the reign of Queen Elizabeth. By Lieut. Edward Chappell, R. N., author of A Voyage to Hudson's Bay. 8° *pp.* 270 + 17 *plates. London, printed for J. Mawmen, Ludgate Street*, 1818. 281

A minute description of the Esquimaux, Montaineer, and Micmacs of Labrador, and the Red Indians of Newfoundland, with three plates of aboriginal life and physiognomy, fairly entitle this book to a place in this Catalogue.

CHARLEVOIX (P. de).

Histoire et description generale de la Nouvelle France avec Le Journal Historique d'un Voyage fait par ordre du Roi dans l'Amerique Septentrionale. Par le P. De Charlevoix de la Compagnie de Jesus. 4° 3 *vols.* Vol. I. *Half title* + *title* + *pp.* xxvi. + lxl. + 664 + 9 *maps.* Vol. II. *Half title, title, pp.* xvi. + 582 *and Des. of Plantes pp.* 1 *to* 64 + 8 *maps and* 22 *plates of plantes.* Vol. III. *Half title, title* + *pp.* xiv. + 543 + 10 *maps. A Paris, Chez Nyon Fils Libraire, Quai des Augustins a l'Occasion,* 1744. 282

[General History and Description of New France, with the Historical Journal of a Tour made by order of the King in North America.]

Vol. III. contains the "Journal of a Voyage," which has been translated into English, and published in London and Dublin in two volumes.

The extraordinary man who was the author of these volumes left no subject relating to the history of the affairs of his wonderful order in America untouched, and as the missions of the Company of Jesus among the Indians were the principal purpose of the fathers in both of the Americas, the curiosity of Charlevoix permeated every accessible square mile of their surface to learn the habits, the customs, and the secrets of the life of the strange people his brethren sought to subdue to the influence of the cross. Father Charlevoix accomplished results in his investigations which seem marvelous to us in the vast accumulation of facts which his pen has illustrated. Of his numerous works, the *Nouvelle France* is the greatest achievement.

Father Charlevoix depended very largely for his authorities, upon the documents found in the Archives of the French Marine, but as these only covered the period subsequent to the establishment of that department under the Minister Colbert, he has left the events prior to that era in some darkness. The historical portion of his work therefore, partakes more of the nature of a biographical narrative of the affairs of the Viceroys or Governors of Canada, but is not the less interesting on that account. It is doubtless the most truthful, as, being the work of a learned man, it is certainly the most valuable treatise upon the affairs of New France. Father Charlevoix however shared the prejudices of his order, against the missionaries of other branches of the Catholic Church, and accordingly the works of those eminent Recollects, Fathers Sagard and Hennepin, who preceded him, are much decried by him. The works of Father LeClercq, although somewhat superciliously treated in his "Histoire" have evidently aided him in his researches.

It is doing no more than justice to the merit of Charlevoix to say that in all the high qualities requisite for a great historian he had no superior. His learning, his research, and his opportunities, were only equaled by his zeal, his intelligence, and we had nearly said his impartiality. In only a very limited number of instances can he be impeached on the charge of unfairness. His partisanship for his own order most unjustly deprived of the privileges won by the noblest self-sacrifices, inclined him to render at least only scant justice to the Recollects, who anticipated the Jesuits in missions to the Indians of Canada. The Introduction has a most valuable criticism of the authors who had written treatises upon the origin of the American Indians. It is so copious as to extend over fifty-nine pages.

An almost endless variety exists in the editions and changes of position of the parts in Charlevoix's three volumes. The Part [lxl.] is often wanting, but is necessary to form a complete copy. Another edition was printed in Paris in 1744 in 6 vols. 12°.

CHARLEVOIX (P. de).

Journal of a Voyage to North-America. Undertaken by Order of the French King, containing The Geographical Description and Natural History of that Country, particularly Canada, together with An Account of the Customs, Characters, Religion, Manners, and Traditions of the original Inhabitants. In a Series of Letters to the Duchess of Lesdiguierres. Translated from the French of P. de Charlevoix. In two volumes. Vol. I. *Half title, title and table, pp.* viii. + *map* + *pp.* 382. Vol. II. *Half title, title, and table, pp.* viii. + 380 + (xxvi.). *London, printed for R. and J. Dodsley in Pall Mall,* 1761. 283

This is a translation of the third volume of the *Histoire de la Nouvelle France.* Another edition, and an entirely independent translation of Charlevoix's work, was printed in one volume, London, 1763, entitled *Letters to the Duchess of Lesdiguieres.* It is printed in a much inferior manner, and somewhat less complete. The accounts of the Indians of Canada, as written by this eminent historian, are among the most authentic which have ever been given us. He was himself a missionary among them; conversant with other learned priests who had spent their lives among the natives, and he had access to a great mass of documents of most unsuspected veracity. His work teems with the most vivid relations of their customs, religious rites, and other peculiarities.

CHARLEVOIX (P. Francois-Zavier).

The History of Paraguay. Containing amongst many other New, Curious, and Interesting Particulars of that Country a full and Authentic Account of the establishment formed there by the Jesuits from among the Savage Natives, in the very Centre of Barbarism. Establishments allowed to have realised the Sublime Ideas of Fenelon, Sir Thomas More, and Plato. Written originally in French, by the celebrated Father Charlevoix. 2 *vols.* 8° *London,* 1769. 284

CHARLEVOIX (P. F. X. de).

History and General Description of New France. By the Rev. P. F. X. de Charlevoix. Translated with Notes by John Gilmary Shea. *In six volumes. Imperial* 8° Vol. I. *pp.* 286 + 5 *plates and map.* Vol. II. *pp.* 284 + 6 *plates and* 2 *maps.* Vol. III. *pp.* 312 + *portrait and* 4 *maps.* Vol. IV. *pp.* 308 + *map and* 8 *plates.* Vol. V. *pp.* 311 + 9 *maps and plates. New York, John Gilmary Shea.* 1866 *to* 1872. 285

These five volumes are all hitherto published; the other it is asserted is already in press. Of the quarto, twenty-five copies only were printed. The accurate scholarship, and the fastidious taste of Dr. Shea, are sufficient guarantees that the work is a faithful translation, in graceful English, of Father Charlevoix's great work.

CHASE (G. W.).

The History of Haverhill, Massachusetts. From its first Settlement in 1640, to the year 1860. By George Wingate Chase. 8° *pp.* 603 + xx. *maps and plates. Haverhill, published by the author,* 1861. 286

Chapters xli. to xvi., pp. 148 to 264, are devoted to the Narration of the Indian troubles in which the town was involved from 1688 to 1720. The numerous incidents which fill these pages are derived partly from printed histories and partly from tradition, and but slightly from documents not hitherto known.

CHATEAUBRIAND (Viscount de).

Travels in America and Italy, by Viscount de Chateaubriand. In two volumes. 8° *pp.* 356 *and* 429. *London, Henry Colburn, New Burlington Street,* 1828. 287

All of the first volume, from p. 196 to p. 356, and all of Vol. II. from p. 1 to p. 142, are devoted to the relation of the history and customs of the Aborigines, or an examination of their antiquities.

CHAUMONOT (Pierre Joseph Marie).

La Vie du R. P. Pierre Joseph Marie Chaumonot, De la Compagnie de Jesus Missionnaire dans la Nouvelle France. Ecrite par lui-meme, par ordre de Son Superieur l'an 1688. 4° *pp.* 108. *Nouvelle York, Isle de Manate A la Presse Cramoisy de Jean-Marie Shea,* 1858. 288

[The Life of the Rev. Father P. J. M. Chaumonot, of the Society of Jesus, Missionary in New France. Written by himself by order of his Superior.]
No. 11 of Shea's *Jesuit Relations.*

Father Chaumonot, born at Chatillon in 1611, was a missionary in Canada from the 1st of August, 1639, until his death, which happened in Quebec, February 21, 1693. During this long period he was a missionary either to the Hurons or the Iroquois. He wrote a Dictionary of the radical words of the Huron language, with a grammar and catechism in the same tongue. These three works remain in MSS. A translation of the Grammar was printed in the second volume of the Quebec Historical Society.

CHAUMONOT (J. M.).

Suite de La Vie du R. P. Pierre Joseph Marie Chaumonot, De la Compagnie de Jesus, Par un Pere de la meme Compagnie avec la manierre d'Oraison du venerable Pere ecrite par lui-meme. 4° *pp.* 66. *Nouvelle York, Isle de Manate A la Presse Cramoisy de Jean-Marie Shea,* 1858. 289

No. 12 of Shea's *Jesuit Relations.*

[Continuation of the Life of the Rev. Father P. J. M. Chaumonot of the Company of Jesus, by a Father of the same Society, with the method of Prayer of the venerable Father written by himself.]

Mr. Shea says: "If we may be permitted a conjecture regarding the author, we should say that this supplement was from the hand of Father Sebastian Rasle, put to death some years later at Norridgewock; but whom we find at Quebec on his return from his mission in the country of the Illinois, and ready to enter upon the field, which he enriched with his labors and his blood."

CHEROKEE TESTAMENT.

[*Title in Cherokee Character.*] *Cherokee* 12° *pp.* 408. *New York, American Bible Society,* 1860. 290

CHEROKEE MEMORIAL.

Memorial of a Delegation from the Cherokee Indians, presented to Congress January 18, 1831. 8° *pp.* 8. *n. d.* 291

CHEROKEE CONSTITUTION.

Constitution of the Cherokee Nation, made and established at a General Convention of Delegates duly authorized for that purpose at New Echota July 27, 1827. 12° *pp.* 16. *Printed for the Cherokee Nation, Georgia, n. d.* 292

CHEROKEE LAWS.
The Constitution and Laws of the Cherokee Nation, passed at Tah-le-quah Cherokee Nation, 1839. 12° *pp.* 36. *Washington*, 1840. 293

CHEROKEE ALMANAC, 1858.
[*Two lines in Cherokee Character*] 1858. Cherokee Almanac, 1858. [*Three lines Cherokee.*] Calculated by Benjamin Greenleaf, author, etc., for the Latitude and Longitude of Tahlequah Cherokee Nation. 12° *pp.* 36. *Park Hill, Mission Press, Edwin Archer, printer.* [*One line Cherokee*]. 294

Alternate Cherokee Character and English.

CHEROKEE AFFAIRS.
Report from the Secretary of War in compliance with a Resolution of the Senate of the 18th of October, 1837, in relation to the Cherokee Treaty of 1835. 8° *pp.* 1090. (*Washington*, 1838.) 295

CHENEY (T. Apoleon).
Illustrations of the Ancient Monuments in Western New York. T. Apoleon Cheney, Del., 1859. 296

Pages 37 to 52 of Thirteenth Annual Report of Regents of University of State of New York, on the State Cabinet of Natural History and the Historical and Antiquarian Collection, with twenty-four plates and folding map.

CHILD (L. M.).
The First Settlers of New England or Conquest of the Pequods, Narragansets, and Pokanokets, as related by a Mother to her Children. By a Lady of Massachusetts. 12° *pp.* 282. *Boston, printed for the author*, 1829. 297

CHILD (L. Maria).
An appeal for the Indians. **By L. Maria Child. 12° *pp.* 24.** *New York*, 1868. **298**

CHIMALPOPOCA (F.).
Silibario de Idioma Mexicano, dispuesto por el Lic Faustino Chimalpopoca Galicia Catedratico propietario del mismo idioma en la Nacional y Pontificia Universidad de esta Capital. 12° *pp.* 32. *Tipografia de Manuel Castro. Mexico*, 1859. 299

CHIQUITOS.
Erbauliche und angenehme Geschichten derer Chiquitos und andberer von denen Patribus der Gesellschafft Jesu in Paraguaria neu bekehrten Volcker famt einem ausfuhrlichen Bericht von dem Amazonem Strom wie auch einigen Nachrichten von der Landschaft Guiana in der neuen Welt. Alles aus dem Spanisch und Franzosischen in das Deutsche ubersettet von einem aus ertwebnter Gesellschafft. 16° *Frontispiece, title, and prel. leaves* 7 + *pp.* 744 + (xiv.). *Wienn*, 1729. 300

[Edifying and amusing Histories of the Chiquitos and other peoples of their Country, newly converted by the Society of Jesus, together with a large account of the River of the Amazones, also a Relation of the Country of Guiana in the New World. All translated from the Spanish and French into German by one of the said Society.]

CHOCTAW TESTAMENT.
The New Testament of Our Lord and Saviour Jesus Christ, translated into the Choctaw Language. — Pin Chitokapa pi okchalinchi Chisus Klaist in Testament Himona Chata anumpa atoshoba hoke. 12° *pp.* 818. *New York, Bible Society*, 1854. 301

CHOCTAW.
The books of Joshua, Judges, and Ruth translated into the Choctaw language. Choshua nan apesa Uhlema holisso micha luth holisso aiena kut toshovot. Chata anumpa toba hoke. 12° *pp.* 151. *New York, American Bible Society*, 1852. 302

CHOCTAW.
The first and second Books of Samuel and the First Book of Kings translated into The Choctaw Language. Samuel I. Holisso Unomona, Atukla Itatuklo micha Miko Chleha, Isht anumpa Ummona aiena kut toshwoet. Chata anumpa toba hoke. 12° *pp.* 236. *New York, American Bible Society*, 1852. 303

CHOCTAW GIRL (The).
Written for the American Sunday School Union, and Revised by the Committee of Publication. 18° *pp.* 16. *Philadelphia, n. d.* 304

CHOULES (Rev. John O.).
The Origin and History of Missions; A Record of the Voyages, Travels, Labors, and Successes of the various missionaries who have been sent forth by Protestant societies and churches to evangelize the heathen; compiled from authentic documents; forming a Complete Missionary Repository illustrated by numerous engravings from original drawings made expressly for this work by the Rev. John O. Choules, A. M. of New York and the Rev. Thomas Smith late minister of Trinity Chapel London. Ninth edition. In Two Volumes. 4° Vol. I. *pp.* 622 + 23 *plates*. Vol. II. *pp.* 610 + 3 *plates*. *New York, Robert Carter and Brothers*, 1851. 305

The authors of these volumes, who give minute details of Protestant missions among the Indians, most strangely fail to more than incidentally notice the labors of John Eliot and Experience Mayhew. They wholly ignore the existence of the first Protestant Missionary Society in England, "The Society for the Propagation of the Gospel among the Indians of North America," and of course utterly fail to mention the heroic labors of the Jesuit Missionaries in Christianizing the Indians of Canada and New York near a quarter of a century before the Puritans landed in New England.

CHRISTIAN INDIAN (The).
Or Times of the First Settlers. (The first of a Series of American Tales). 8° *pp.* 231. *New York, published by Collins & Hannay — J. & J. Harpers, printers*, 1825. 306

CHRISTIAN (James).
In the Supreme Court of the State of Kansas, January term 1870, ss. Albert Wiley, plaintiff vs. Keokuk Chief of the Sac

and Fox Indians, defendant on petition in error. Argument and brief for the defendant, by James Christian. 8° *pp.* 41. n. p. (1870.) 307

CHRONICLES

Of the North American Savages. 1835. 8° *pp.* 80. 5 Nos.: May 1835 to Sep. 1835. n. p. 308

A periodical of sixteen pages devoted to the history, traditions, language, etc. of the Indians.

CHURCH (Thomas).

The History of Philip's War, commonly called The Great Indian War, of 1675 and 1676. Also, of the French and Indian Wars at the Eastward in 1689, 1690, 1692, 1696, and 1704. By Thomas Church, Esq. With Numerous Notes to explain the situation of the places of Battles, the particular geography of the ravaged country, and the lives of the principal persons engaged in those wars. Also an Appendix containing an account of the treatment of the natives by the early voyagers, the settlement of N. England by the fore-fathers, the Pequot War, narratives of persons carried captive, anecdotes of the Indians, and the most important late Indian Wars to the time of the Creek War. By Samuel G. Drake. Second edition with plates. 12° *pp.* 360 + 2 *plates. Boston, printed by J. H. A. Frost,* 1827. 309

CHURCH (Thomas).

The History of Philip's War, commonly called the Great Indian War of 1675 and 1676. Also of the French and Indian Wars at the Eastward in 1689, etc. With Notes by Samuel G. Drake. Second edition. 12° *Boston*, 1827. 310

CHURCH (Thomas).

The History of Philip's War, commonly called the Great Indian War of 1675 and 1676. Notes and Appendix by Drake. 12° *Exeter*, 1829. 311

CHURCH (Thomas).

The History of the Great Indian War of 1675 and 1676 commonly called Philip's War, also The Old French and Indian Wars from 1689 to 1704. By Thomas Church, Esq. With numerous Notes and an Appendix by Samuel G. Drake. 12° *Hartford*, 1852. 312

CHURCH (Benj.).

The History of King Philip's War, by Benjamin Church, With an Introduction and Notes by Henry Martyn Dexter. 2 vols. 4° *pp.* 234, 261. *Boston, J. K. Wiggin*, MDCCCLXV. 313

CIEZA (Pietro).

* La Prima Parte dell' historie del Peru dove si tratta l'ordine delle Provincie delle citta nuoue in quel Paese edificate, i riti, & costumi d gli Indiani, con molte cose notabili, et degne et consideratione. Composta da Pietro Cieza di Leone Cittadi no di Siuiglia. Con la tavola delle cose piu notabili. Con Privi-

leglo per Anno xx. 12° *pp.* (xvi.) + 215 *numbered leaves* + 1 *leaf Registro. In Venitia Appresso Giordano Ziletti, al segno della Stella*, MDLX. 314

[The first part of the History of Peru. Which treats of its division into provinces, and their description. The foundation of its new cities, the religious rites, and the customs of the Indians. And many other strange things worthy of being known, composed by Pedro Cieza, of Leone.]

The first edition of this much esteemed work was printed in Spanish at Sevilla in 1553, or seven years prior to this the first Italian imprint. Two other editions are noted as printed in Venice during the same year. Only the first of this work, to the everlasting regret of scholars, has ever been printed. The second and third parts were known to exist in Madrid before Mr. Rich's period; of which the abiding-place to-day of only one has been discovered. It rests in the collection of Mr. Lenox. The second and third parts of this edition were written by Gomara.

CIEZA (Pietro).

La Seconda Parte Delle Historie dell India. Con tutte le cose notabili accadute in esse dal principio sin' a questo giorno, & nuovamente tradotte di Spagnuolo in Italiano. Nellequali oltre all'imprese del Colombo & di Magalanes si tratta particolarmente della presa del Re Atahallippa, delle perle, dell'oro, delle spetierrie ritrovate alle Malucche & delle guerre civili tra gli Spagnuoli con privilegio. 12° *pp.* (xxxii.) + 324 *numbered leaves. In Venetia Appresso Giordan Ziletti, al segno della Stella*, MDLXV. 315

The second and third parts of this edition, commonly attributed to Cieza, were written by Gomara, whose work was first printed at Medina in 1553. Having fallen under the ban in Spain, and strictly prohibited from circulation, it found a place of refuge in Venice, from whence five editions were issued in a period of seven years. The uniform testimony of scholars has placed the work of Cieza in the same rank with that of Beumal. Both are remarkable for affording us the most authentic views of the primitive condition of the Indians before tyranny had crushed, or civilization had corrupted them. Both are the narrations of those who saw with intelligent eyes the memorable things they described.

CIEZA (Peter de).

The Seventeen Years Travels of Peter de Cieza Through the Mighty Kingdom of Peru and The large Provinces of Cartagena and Popayan in South America: From the City of Panama, on the Isthmus, to the Frontiers of Chile. Now first Translated from the Spanish, and Illustrated with a Map and Several Cuts. 4° *pp.* (viii.) + 244 + (xii.) + *folding map and folding plan of Cusco, and four engravings in the text. London, printed in the year* 1709. 316

This is the first English edition of Peter de Cieza's work. It was published in Stevens' Collection of Voyages and Travels, in which also Lawson's *Carolina* first appeared. Both of these works were also issued separate from the collection, with the addition of distinct titles. The work purports to be a translation of the First Part of Pedro di Cieza's *History of Peru*, and in the main is a fair rendering of the original, except that it is somewhat abridged, as instead of one hundred and nineteen chapters it has but ninety-four. It is a curious and very interesting history, particularly of the secret mysteries of the worship of the Incas, and the peculiarities of each tribe of Indians inhabiting Peru.

Cist (Charles).

The Cincinnati Miscellany, or Antiquities of the West, and Pioneer History and general and local statistics, compiled from the Western General Advertiser from October 1st, 1844 to April 1st, 1845, Vol. I., and to April 1st, 1846, Vol. II. (Complete in two volumes). By Charles Cist. 8° *pp.* 272 *and* 364, *with pp.* lv. *of index of both volumes. Cincinnati,* 1845 & 46. 317

This collection is largely composed of original narrations of scenes of border life, personal experiences in Indian warfare, or reminiscences of Indian fighters and warriors. It is a very valuable repertory of that mass of historic material that is so fleeting and evanescent, that only a serial journal can seize and perpetuate it.

Cist (Charles).

Cincinnati in 1841: Its Early Annals and Future Prospects. By Charles Cist. *pp.* 300. *Cincinnati, printed and published for the Author,* 1841. 318

Pages 17 to 23 and 155 to 232 are occupied with Historical Sketches, Early Annals and Pioneer Sketches. Among the latter is included the Journal of John Cleves Symmes, here first printed from the original MS. In this Judge Symmes narrates many incidents of Indian warfare, particularly the death of John Filson, the author of *The Discovery of Kentucky.*

Claesse (Lawrence).

Morning and Evening Prayer. See Mohawk. 319

Claiborne (Nathaniel Herbert).

Notes on the War in the South, with Biographical Sketches of the lives of Montgomery, Jackson, Sevier, The late Governor Clairborne and others. By Nathaniel Herbert Claiborne, of Franklin County, Va., A Member of the Executive of Virginia during the late War. 12° *Richmond,* 1819. 320

Claiborne (J. F. H.).

Life and Times of Gen. Sam Dale, the Mississippi Partisan. Illustrated by John McLenan. 12° *pp.* 233. *New York,* 1860. 321

General Dale was an Indian fighter of great renown on the Southern frontier, and in the Creek and Seminole wars accomplished some feats of personal prowess, in conflicts with the warriors of those nations, which would appear the inventions of romance, were they not so well fortified by contemporaneous testimony.

Clarke (William).

Observations on the late and present Conduct of the French, With Regard to their Encroachments upon the British Colonies in North America, together With Remarks on the Importance of these Colonies to Great Britain. By William Clarke M. D. of Boston in New England. [3 *lines.*] 8° *pp.* 54. *Boston, printed* (1755). *London, reprinted,* 1755. 322

The Boston edition does not announce the author on the title-page.

Clark (J. V. H.).

Onondaga: or, Reminiscences of Earlier and Later Times. Being a series of Sketches relative to Onondaga, with Notes on the Several Towns in the County and Oswego, by Joshua V. H.

Clark. In Two Volumes. 8° Vol. I. *Map and 4 plates* + *pp.* 402. Vol. II. 8 *plates and pp.* 393. *Syracuse, Stoddard and Babcock*, 1849. 323

The Onondagas were the central tribe of the Six Nations, the guardians of the great council fire, and the custodians of the important records of the Confederacy. From their chiefs was selected the highest officer, styled by Europeans the King. Residing near them, as the author did for many years, familiar with their observances, and often present at the great councils of the Confederacy, when numerous representatives of the tribes assembled from their colonies around the upper lakes, he could not but be imbued with the desire to make his history of the county, a record of the great tribes which once inhabited it. Mr. Clark has evidently examined almost every source of information regarding the Six Nations, we possess in the English, French, and Spanish languages, and accordingly the first seventy-eight pages are occupied with a *resumé* of what he thus gleaned. But it is in chapter v. pp. 79 to 125, that he adds entirely new material to their history in his "Biographical Sketches of Distinguished Chiefs of the Onondaga Tribe." This valuable work was principally derived from chiefs or planters then living. Chapter vi. pp. 126 to 209, is devoted to an account of the French Jesuit and Recollect Missions among the Onondagas, and chapter vii. pp. 210 to 245, to a history of the English, German, and American Missions in the tribe; the last chapter being entirely new material in their history. Chapters viii. and ix. pp. 246 to 321, is occupied with the early history of the Onondagas, being a collection of much original matter, combined with gleanings from documentary and printed accounts. Chapter x. pp. 322 to 363, entitled "Reminiscences," is filled with a list of aboriginal names and their signification, expeditions against the tribe, treaties, and sketches of Indian traders resident in it. It will thus be seen that the first volume of this work is in fact a history of the Onondaga tribe of the Six Nations, and holds the highest rank among treatises on Aboriginal affairs for original and valuable information.

CLARK (J. V. H.).

Lights and Lines of Indian Character and Scenes of Pioneer Life. 12° *pp.* 375. *Syracuse*, 1854. 324

In this work the author produces those lighter results of his research into Indian history, which the dignity of his greater work did not permit to be introduced. The traditions, legends, and the romantic shades of the character and life of the aborigines here find a place.

CLARK (Col. George Rogers).

Col. George Rogers Clarke's Sketch of his Campaign in the Illinois, in 1778–9, with an Introduction by Hon. Henry Pirtle, of Louisville, and an Appendix containing the Public and Private Instructions to Col. Clark, and Major Bowman's Journal of the taking of Post St. Vincents. 8° *pp.* 8 + 119. *Cincinnati, Robert Clarke.* 1869. 325

CLAVIGERO (D. Francisco).

The History of Mexico, collected from Spanish and Mexican Historians, from MSS. and Ancient Paintings of the Indians. Illustrated by Charts and other Copper Plates. To which are added Critical dissertations on the Land, the Animals and Inhabitants of Mexico. By Abbe D. Francesco Saverio Clavigero. Translated from the original Italian, by Charles Cullen, Esq. *In two volumes.* Vol. I. *pp.* xxvi. + 476 + *map*,

and 24 plates. Vol. II. *pp.* (11) + 436 + *map and* 1 *plate.* 4°
London, 1787. 326

The Abbe Clavigero resided for forty years in the provinces of New Spain, and expended a vast deal of labor in becoming familiar with the languages and dialects of the Aborigines of those countries; in examining their pictographic MSS., their monuments, and their traditions. His "Account of the Authors who have written upon Mexican History," pages 13 to 28, is exceedingly important and interesting. He names thirty-nine, Indian and Spanish authors, with critical notices of their works, besides noting that his attention had been given to numerous other writers in various languages. On pages 28 to 31, Clavigero describes the Mexican historic paintings he has examined. His work is esteemed the most valuable and complete of all works on the Toltec and Aztec races, as he collected all their authentic material from works already published, and added thereto the valuable results of his own examinations.

CLAY (Hon. Henry).
Speech of the Hon. Henry Clay, in the House of Representatives of U. S. on the Seminole War. 12° *pp.* 30. [*Washington*, 1819.] 327

CLEMENS (Orion).
City of Keokuk, in 1856. A View of the City, embracing its Commerce and Manufactures, and containing the Inaugural Address of Mayor Curtis, and Statistical Local Information: also a Sketch of the Black Hawk War, and History of the Half Breed Tract. Historical and Statistical Matter written by Orion Clemens. 8° *pp.* 44. *Keokuk*, 1856. 328

CLINTON (De Witt).
Discourse delivered before the New York Historical Society, at their anniversary meeting, 6th December, 1811. By the Honorable De Witt Clinton, one of the Vice Presidents of the Society. 8° *pp.* 82. *New York, published by James Eastburn*, 1812. 329

One of the best geographical, political and historical, views of the Red Men, who inhabited the State of New York, ever written.

CLINTON (De Witt).
A Memoir on the Antiquities of the Western Parts of the State of New York, read before the Literary and Philosophical Society of New York. By De Witt Clinton, President of the said Society. 8° *pp.* 16. *Albany, printed by E. & E. Hosford*, 1820. 330

The origin, history, and ethnological traits of the Indians of America, seem to have occupied much of the attention of this statesman and philosopher. In the first edition of this pamphlet, dated 1818, of which but one copy (now in the State Library of New York) seems to have survived to our day, Governor Clinton stated, with some degree of positiveness, that there were evidences of a Spanish colony having existed in the Onondaga Valley among the Six Nations. Nothing of this appears in the second edition, and probably the rarity of the first is occasioned by its destruction at the hands of the author.

COATES (B. H.).
Annual Discourse delivered before the Historical Society of Pennsylvania on the 28th day of April, 1834. On the Origin

of the Indian Population of America. By B. H. Coates, M. D. 8° *pp.* 64. *Philadelphia*, 1834. 331

Coats (Captain W.).

The Geography of Hudson's Bay; being the remarks of Captain W. Coats, in many Voyages to that locality between the years 1727 and 1751. With an Appendix, containing extracts from the log of Captain Middleton on his Voyage for the discovery of the North-West Passage in H. M. S. Furnace in 1741–82. Edited by John Barrow, Esq. 8° *pp.* x. + 147. *London, printed for the Hakluyt Society*, 1852. 332

Captain Coats' narrative of his voyages and travels along the shores of Hudson's Bay, and the rivers emptying therein, occupies pp. 1 to 92 of this volume, and is largely composed of curious details of the numerous tribes of Indians that occupied the country a century and a half ago. Some of the customs he mentions, have been the subject of no little controversy, in proof and rebuttal of their actual existence. Of cannibalism especially, Captain Coats narrates with corroboratory details more than one instance. Not the least in interest to us, is his enumeration of tribes of savages, so long extinct their very names had been forgotten but for his narrative.

Coates (D.) Beecham and Ellis.

Christianity the Means of Civilization: Shown in the Evidence given before a Committee of the House of Commons, On Aborigines. By D. Coates Esq., Rev. John Beecham and Rev. William Ellis. To which is added selections from the evidence of other witnesses bearing on the same subject. 12° *pp.* 360. *London*, 1837. 333

There is but little in this volume regarding the American Aborigines, and that is of little value, being derived from the estimates of persons who had no opportunity of verifying them, from observation or facts otherwise obtained.

Cockburn (John).

The Unfortunate Englishman; or a *faithful narrative* of the Distresses and Adventures of John Cockburn and Five other Mariners, viz., Thomas Bounce, John Holland, Richard Banister, John Balmain, and Thomas Robinson, Who were taken by a Spanish Guarda Costa in the John and Ann Captain Burt, And set on shore, naked and wounded at Porto Cavallo: containing A Journey over Land from the Gulph of Honduras to the Great South Sea; Wherein are many new and useful Discoveries of the Interior of those unknown Regions of America. Also An Account of the Manners, Customs, and Behaviour, of the several Indian Nations, Inhabiting an Extent of Country upwards of 2500 Miles; Particularly of their Disposition to the Spaniards and English. A new edition carefully corrected. 12° *Plate, title, reverse blank, preface* 4 *pp.* + *pp.* 1 *to* 126. *London*, 1794. 334

Cockburn (John).

The Unfortunate Englishman or a Faithful Narrative of the Distresses and Adventures of John Cockburn and Five other English mariners who were taken by a Spanish Guarda-Costa and set on shore at Porto-Cavallo naked and wounded, containing a journey over land from the Gulf of Honduras to the Great South Sea, As also An Account of the Manners and Customs of the Tribes of Indians Inhabiting a Tract of Territory 2000 miles in extent. A new edition. 16° *pp.* 197. *Plate. Edinburgh, printed for Waugh & Innes,* 1831. 335

COCKBURN (John).

A Journey over Land from the Gulf of Honduras to the Great South Sea. Performed by John Cockburn and Five other Englishmen, viz., Thomas Rounce, Richard Banister, John Holland, Thomas Robinson, and John Ballman, Who were taken by a Spanish Guarda-Costa in the John and Jane, Edward Burt Master, and set on Shoar at a Place called Porto-Cavallo naked and wounded as mentioned in Several News-Papers of October, 1731. Containing Variety of extraordinary Distresses and Adventures; [*etc.*, 2 *lines.*] As also An exact Account of the Manners, Customs, and Behaviour of the several Indians Inhabiting a Tract of Land of 2400 Miles; particularly of their Dispositions towards the Spaniards and English [*etc.*, 5 *lines*]. *pp.* viii. + 350. *London, printed for C. Rivington,* 1735. 336

The first edition of Cockburn's very curious account, at first believed to be fictitious; but in later years received as authentic. "A Brief Discovery of the East Indies by Nicholas Withington" is added, which gave rise to the attributing of Cockburn's account to the same author. His relations of incidents of travel among the Indians of Central America, and his descriptions of the peculiarities of their character and customs, are valuable on account of its filling a period in the history of their characteristics not elsewhere to be found. The work has been many times reprinted, with but slight variations in the title, except in prefixing the phrase, The Unfortunate Englishman.

CODMAN (John).

The Importance of Spiritual Knowledge, A Sermon delivered before the Society for Propagating the Gospel among the Indians and others in North America, in the First Church Boston, November 3, 1825. By John Codman. With the Report of the Select Committee. 8° *pp.* 44. *Cambridge, from the University Press, Hillyard and Metcalf,* 1825. 337

COFFIN (William F.).

1812 The War, and its Moral, A Canadian Chronicle by William F. Coffin, Esquire. 338

This work, by a personal observer of the events he narrates, contains much new matter relating to the conduct of the Indians, and charges the Americans with cruelties only equaled by the aborigines.

COHEN (M. M.).

Notices of Florida and the Campaigns, by M. M. Cohen, an officer of the left wing. 12° *pp.* 240 + *map. Charleston, S. C. Burgess and Honour; and New York, B. B. Hussey.* 1836. 339

This work is a personal narrative and journal, of incidents occurring in the war with the Seminole Indians.

COKE (Hon. Henry J.).

A Ride over the Rocky Mountains, to Oregon and California; with a Glance at some of the Tropical Islands, including the West Indies and the Sandwich Islands, by the Hon. Henry J. Coke. 8° *Portrait, and pp.* x. + 388 + (2). *London,* 1852. 340

Chapter iii. p. 81, contains the description of the author's commencement of his tour on the prairies, the narrative of which is continued through chapters iii. to ix. pp. 81 to 310. In the course of his foolhardy travels, he meets with the usual adventures with the Indians, from whose toils he, with the fortune of hair-brained scamps, constantly escapes. Coke's narrative of such incidents of Indian life and adventure which he saw and experienced, are interesting and well told.

COLDEN (Cadwallader).

The History of the Five Indian Nations Depending on the Province of New York. Reprinted exactly from Bradford's New York Edition (1727). With an Introduction and Notes by John Gilmary Shea. *Imp.* 8° *Portrait, and pp.* 199. *New York, T. H. Morrel,* 1866. 341

Large paper; only thirty copies printed.

Historical Introduction, pp. xl. "The History of the Five Indian Nations," Title and Pref. pp. xviii. + 141.

This fourth edition of Colden's work is a reprint of the first, printed by Bradford in 1727. The two subsequent ones have additions, interpolations to, and variations from, Colden's work, by English editors, who tagged their own valueless observations, and absurd changes upon his work, without marking them so as to be distinguishable. Dr. Shea gives in his Introduction, a valuable bibliographical notice of the editions, with collations of their contents, and an analysis of them, noting the changes made by the English editors or publishers. His notes, occupying pp. 121 to 141, are characterized by the fullness, research, and exactness, with which the writer always invests any subject he illustrates.

COLDEN (Cadwallader).

The History of the FIVE Indian NATIONS of CANADA, which are the Barrier between the English and French, in that part of the World, with Particular Accounts of their Religion, Manners, Customs, Laws, and Government; their Several Battles and Treaties with the European Nations; their Wars with the other Indians; And A true Account of the present State of our Trade with them. In which are shewn The great Advantage of their Trade and Alliance to the British Nation; and the Intrigues and Attempts of the French to engage them from us; nearly concerning all our American Plantations and highly meriting the Consideration of the British Nation. a Subject [*etc.,* 2 *lines.*] By the Honorable Cadwallader Colden, Esq. One of his Majesty's Counsel, and Surveyor-General of New York. To which are added: Accounts of the several other Nations of Indians in North America, their Numbers, Strength &c., and the Treaties which have been lately made with them. The Second Edition. 8° Part I. *pp.* xx + 1 *to* 90. Part II. *Pref. pp.* 2 + 91 *to* 204. *Papers relating to an Act for the Encouraging of the Indian Trade, pp.* 1 to 283. *Printed for John Whiston, London,* 1750. 842

COLESON (Miss Ann).

Miss Coleson's Narrative of her Captivity Among the Sioux Indians. An Interesting account of the terrible Sufferings and providential escape of Miss Ann Coleson, A victim of the late Indian outrages in Minnesota. 8° *pp.* 70. *Philadelphia,* 1864. 843

COLLINS.

Historical Sketches of Kentucky, Embracing the History, Antiquities, and Natural Curiosities, Geographical, with Anecdotes of Pioneer Life. And more than one hundred biographical sketches of distinguished Pioneers, Soldiers, Statesmen, Jurists, Lawyers, Divines, etc. Illustrated by forty engravings by Louis Collins. 8° *Map,* 16 *plates* + *pp.* 560. *Cincinnati,* 1850. 844

COLTON (C.).

Tour of the American Lakes, and among the Indians of the North-West Territory in 1830: Disclosing the Character and Prospects of the Indian Race. In two volumes. Vol. I. *pp.* xxxii. + 316. Vol. II. *pp.* vii. + 387. *Frederick Westley and A. H. Davis. London,* 1833. 845

Mr. Colton seems to have been imbued with the laudable design of affording such information regarding the Indians he visited, as would not only excite the interest of his readers in his narration of incident, but would arouse the sympathy of the humane to their wretched condition. Almost the entire work is devoted to the relation of Indian affairs. More than half of the first volume is occupied with personal observations of Aboriginal life, and statements made to him regarding it. The second volume is entirely filled with a collection of facts relating to their origin, wars, treaties, treatment by the governments of Great Britain and the United States, and the result of missions among them.

COLTON (Walter).

Three Years in California. By Rev. Walter Colton, U. S. N., Late Alcalde of Monterey. With Illustrations. 12° *pp.* 456. *New York, published by S. A. Rollo & Co.,* 1859. 846

Numerous incidents of Indian life, occur in the Journal of Chaplain Colton.

COLUMBUS (Christopher).

Personal Narrative of the First Voyage of Columbus to America, from a Manuscript recently Discovered in Spain. Translated from the Spanish. 8° *pp.* 303. *Boston,* 1827. 847

The personal narrative of the great discoverer affords as many views of the savages as they appeared to one of the fairest, most unprejudiced minds that ever existed, and before their manners or habits of thought were colored by the influences of civilization.

COMBS (Captain Leslie).

Col. Wm. Dudley's Defeat opposite Fort Meigs, May 5th, 1813. Official Report from Captain Leslie Combs to General Green Clay. Printed for William Dodge. 8° *pp.* 13. *Cincinnati, Spiller & Gates, printers,* 1869. 848

COMBS (Gen. Leslie).
Narrative of the Life of Gen. Leslie Combs; embracing Incidents in the History of the War of 1812. 8° *pp.* 20. *American Whig Review Office*, 120 *Nassau Street*, 1852. 349

The narrative, embracing incidents in the early history of the Northwestern Territory, was published in the *Whig Review*, and the columns re-paged and circulated in this form.

COMMUNICATION
From the Governor (of N. Y.) transmitting certain proceedings of the Seneca Nation of Indians. 8° *pp.* 80. *Albany*, 1849. 350

COMSTOCK (Joseph).
The Tongue of Time and Star of the States. A System of human nature with the phenomena of the heavens and earth, American Antiquities, Remains of Giants, etc. By Joseph Comstock, M. D. 8° *New York*, 1838. 351

CONDAMINE (M. De La).
Relation Abrege d'un Voyage fait dans L'Interieure De L'Amerique Meridionale Depuis la Cote de la Mer du Sud, Jusqu' aux Cotes du Bresil & de la Guyane, en descendant La Riviere des Amazones. Avec une Carte du Maragnon ou de la Riviere des Amazones levee par le meme. Nouvelle Edition. Augmentie de la Relation de l'Emeute populaire de Cuença au Perou. 8° *pp.* 379 + *map and plate.* *A Maastricht*, 1778. 352

CONDAMINE (Mons. de La).
A Succinct abridgment of a Voyage Made within the inland parts of South-America; from the Coasts of the South-Sea to the Coasts of Brazil and Guiana, down the River of Amazons: As it was read in the Public Assembly of the Academy of Sciences at Paris, April 28, 1745. By Mons. De La Condamine, of that Academy. To which is annexed A Map of the Maranon, or River of Amazons, drawn by the Same. 8° *Map, and pp.* xii. + 108. *London, printed for E. Withers*, 1747. 353

The author, having been fortunate enough to escape assassination in a popular *émeute*, excited against the French Academicians, in Cuenca, during which one of them fell a victim to the fury of the mob, returned to France with the results of his scientific expedition. This work purports to be an abridgment of his Relation, but it is a complete translation of the one published in France. The author abridged his MSS., and published the narrative portion, omitting the statistical and scientific parts. He examined with care the condition of the Indians, and has some novel and interesting particulars of their languages. He noted particularly that some tribes could enumerate no more than three in their own tongue, and that their articulation of words was performed wholly by inspiration, being utterly incapable of imitation by the vocal organs of other nations. Many other interesting particulars of the savages of Central South America are given by this savant.

"The observations of La Condamine on the Aborigines of the countries he visited, are very judicious." — *Leclerc Catalogue.*

CONDITION OF THE INDIAN TRIBES.

Report of the Joint Special Committee appointed under Joint Resolution of March 3d, 1865, with an Appendix. 8° *pp.* 532. *Washington, Government Printing Office,* 1867. 354

This volume contains the evidence of the horrible massacre of unoffending Indians at Sand Creek. Nothing in Las Casas' relations of Spanish atrocities surpasses it.

Eight hundred miners, gamblers, and adventurers of the border, were enlisted under Colonel Chivington, a preacher of the Methodist Church, to punish some thefts of horses and murders committed by Indians, who would not remain to be caught. A peaceable tribe of Cheyennes and Shoshones, with whom Major Wynkoop, United States agent, had made a treaty a few days before, lay in the route, and hailed the approach of the army with the highest demonstrations of friendship. On these wretched Indians, who absurdly trusted in the promises and good faith of their white brethren, with whom they had always remained at peace, the Christian whites determined to revenge all the outrages perpetrated by others. Having lulled all suspicion, by artfully pacific overtures for several days, Colonel Chivington's army silently surrounded the Indian camp, and a scene of most horrible massacre commenced. The chiefs ran forward with white flags, repeating in English, *We are friends; we are friends!* but the appeal was made in vain. No resistance was made, and one hundred and seventy men, women, and children were slain.

Colonel Chivington, good, pious clergyman, when appealed to, replied, "*Damn any man who sympathizes with Indians;*" and added, "*I want no prisoners.*" One Lieutenant Richmond distinguished himself so much that his name deserves to be damned to perpetual infamy. Observing that three squaws and five children had been taken prisoners, he killed and scalped the whole of them, while they were screaming for mercy.

The atrocities that were perpetrated upon the bodies of the slain would tax the cleverest ingenuity of devils to invent its parallel. Every one of the dead was scalped, but in this the Christian whites only equaled the savages. The genitals of both sexes were cut off. The skins of the males were dried for tobacco-pouches, and those of the genitals of the women were worn as hat-bands, and in one instance as a pair of mustachios. Colonel Chivington saw, without remonstrance, these horrible deeds performed around him. To the truth of these statements we so unwillingly believe, nearly one hundred witnesses testified before a committee of Congress, and their examinations are recorded in this volume.

CONDUCT OF THE PAXTON-MEN,

Impartially represented; The Distresses of the Frontiers, and the Complaints and Sufferings of the People fully stated [*etc.*, 2 *lines*]. With some Remarks upon the Narrative of the Indian-Massacre, lately published. Interspersed with several interesting Anecdotes, relating to the Military Genius and Warlike Principles of the People called Quakers [*etc.*, 1 *line*]. In a letter from a Gentleman in one of the Back Counties, to a Friend in Philadelphia [*etc.*, 17 *lines*]. 12° *Two titles. pp.* 34. *Philadelphia, printed by A. Steuart,* 1764. 355

This is an attempt to justify one of the foulest, most cruel, and cowardly massacres of an unoffending people that was ever committed. The Paxton-men were a mob of poltroons, who preferred to murder unarmed men and boys to risking their worthless carcasses on the frontier, fighting the savages who ravaged their homesteads almost unresisted.

CONSIDERATIONS ON THE INDIAN TRADE.

Originally published in the Detroit Gazette. *pp.* 15. *Detroit, printed by Sheldon & Reed,* 1821.

Indian Trade. From the Detroit Gazette, 22d December, 1820. Concluded. 8° *pp.* 1 *to* 10. 356

CONSTITUTION

Of the Seneca Nation of Indians. 12° *pp.* 14. *Baltimore, printed by William Wooddy & Son,* 1848; *and* Letter from William Medill to Senecas, 8 *pp.; and* To the Seneca Nation of Indians, 8 *pp.; — in total* 30 *pp.* 357

CONVERSATIONS

On the Mackinaw and Green Bay Indian Missions. In two parts. By the author of Conversations on the Sandwich Island Missions, &c. Revised by the Publishing Committee. 24° *pp.* 128. *Boston, printed by T. R. Martin for the Massachusetts Sunday School Union,* 1831. 358

COOKE (P. St. G.).

Scenes and Adventures in the Army; or Romance of Military Life, by P. St. G. Cooke, Lieutenant Colonel Second Dragoons, U. S. A. 12° *pp.* 432. *Philadelphia, Lindsay & Blakiston,* 1857. 359

The author was personally engaged in several battles with the Camanches and the Sacs and Foxes, and nearly half his volume is composed of narrations of events connected with Indian warfare.

COOPER (Thomas).

Strictures addressed to James Madison on the Celebrated Report of Wm. H. Crawford recommending the intermarriage of Americans with the Indian Tribes. Ascribed to Judge Cooper, and originally published by John Binns in the Democratic Press. 8° *pp.* 22. *Philadelphia,* 1824. 360

The humane but unpopular project of the excellent Secretary of the Treasury, was the occasion of such virulent abuse, as we find it difficult to comprehend at this day. He hoped to preserve the Indian race from utter destruction by infusing it with the blood of more civilized but not less barbarous nations.

COOPER (Rev. Mr.).

The History of North America containing A Review of the Customs and Manners of the Original Inhabitants; The first Settlement of the British Colonies, Their Rise and Progress, from The earliest Period to the Time of their becoming United free and Independent States. By the Rev. Mr. Cooper, Embellished with Copper-Plate Cuts. 24° *pp.* 184 *and* 5 *plates. London, printed for E. Newberry, the Corner of St. Paul's Church-yard,* 1789. 361

COPPIER (Guillaume).

Histoire et Voyage des Indes Occidentales, Et de plusiers Regions maritimes & esloignees. Diuise en Deux Liures. Par

Guillaume Coppier Lyonnois. *A Lyon Pour Iean Huguetan, rue Merciere, au plat d'Estain* 1645. *Avec Approbation & Privilige du Roy. Engraved Title Page [with 5 lines at the bottom.* Histoire et Voyage | Des Indies | Occidentales | A Lyon |] 1 *leaf. Title* 1 *leaf.* + *Epistre signed by Coppier,* 9 *pp.* + *Au Lecteur, etc.* 7 *pp.* + *Preface* 26 + *table* 4 *pp.; total prelim. pp.* 50 + 182 + (xviii.). 362

[History and Travels of the West Indies, and of many other Maritime Regions. Divided into two Books, by William Coppier of Lyons.]
Chapter viii. is entitled "Of the Savages of the West Indies." Chapter ix. "Of their Method of Navigation and Warfare;" and Chapters x. to xiv. contain descriptions of their ceremonies, dwellings, weapons, food, wine, and hunting. The work affords some particulars of interest concerning the now extinct Carib, recorded at an early day in the history of the country. It contains also some relations of Canada.

COPWAY (G.).
The Ogibway Conquest, A Tale of the Northwest by Kah-ge-gagah-bow, or G. Copway, Chief of the Ojibway Nation. 12° *pp.* 91. *New York,* 1850. 363

COPWAY (George).
The Traditional History and Characteristic Sketches of the Ojibway Nation. By G. Copway, Chief. 8° *pp.* 266. *London,* 1850. 364

COPWAY (George).
Same, by G. Copway or Kah-ge-ga-gah-bouh, Chief of the Ojibway Nation, illustrated by Darley. 12° *pp.* 266, 2 *plates. Boston, Benjamin J. Mussey,* 1851. 365

COPWAY (George).
The Life, History, and Travels of Kah-ge-ga-gah-Bouh (George Copway), a young Indian Chief of the Ojibwa Nation, A Convert to the Christian Faith, and a Missionary to his people for twelve years, with a sketch of the present state of the Ojibwa Nation [*etc.,* 6 *lines*], written by himself. 8° *pp.* 224. *Albany,* 1847. 366

COPWAY (George).
Organization of A New Indian Territory east of the Missouri River. Arguments and Reasons submitted to the Honorable the Members of the Senate and House of Representatives of the 31st Congress of the United States. By the Indian Chief Kah-ge-gah-bouh, or George Copway. 8° *pp.* 32. *New York,* 1850. 367

CORNELIUS (Elias).
The Little Osage Captive, an Authentic Narrative: to which are added some interesting Letters written by Indians. 18° *Plate, and pp.* 182. *York, printed and published by W. Alexander & Son, Castlegate.* 1821. 368

CORRESPONDENCE

On the Subject of the Emigration of Indians between The 30th November, 1831, and 27th December, 1833, with Abstracts of Expenditures by disbursing Agents in the removal and Subsistence of Indians, etc., etc. (Vol. IV.) 8° *pp.* 771. *Washington, printed by Duff Green*, 1835. 369

Document 512. The volume is No. 4 of Documents, but the subject of the Indian emigration is complete in this.

CORRESPONDENCE

On the Subject of the Removal of Indians, between the 30th November, 1831, and 27th December, 1833, with Abstracts of Expenditures by disbursing Agents, in the Removal and Subsisting of Indians, etc. etc., furnished in answer to a Resolution of the Senate of 27th December, 1833, by the Commissary General of Subsistence. 2 *volumes.* Vol. I. *pp.* 1179. Vol. II. *pp.* 972. *Washington, printed by Duff Green*, 1834. 370

CORRESPONDENCE

Between Gen. Andrew Jackson and John C. Calhoun, President and Vice President of the United States, on the Subject of the course of the latter in the deliberations of the Cabinet of Mr. Monroe on the occurrences in the Seminole War. 8° *pp.* 52. *Washington*, 1831. 371

CORTES (Hernando). See Folsom.

The Despatches of Hernando Cortes, the Conqueror of Mexico, Addressed to the Emperor, Charles V., written during the Conquest, and containing a narrative of its events. Now first translated into English from the original Spanish, with an Introduction and notes by George Folsom. 8° *pp.* xli. + 431. *New York and London*, 1843. 372

COSTA (B. F. De).

The Pre-Columbian Discovery of America by the Northmen. Illustrated by Translations from the Icelandic Sagas; edited with Notes and a general Introduction, by B. F. De Costa. 8° *pp.* 118. *Albany, Joel Munsel*, 1868. 373

COTTON (Josiah).

Vocabulary of the Massachusetts or Natick Indian Language. By Josiah Cotton. 8° *pp.* 112. *Cambridge, printed by E. W. Metcalf and Company*, 1829. 374

The author, born at Plymouth in 1679, received the impetus which impelled him to the construction of this work, from his father, John Cotton, who aided Eliot in the translation of the Bible into the same language. The Indian apostle acknowledged his obligation to the elder Cotton's knowledge of the Natick language. Beside the advantages of his father's instruction, the author's frequent intercourse with the Indians as a civil officer, a neighbor, and an occasional missionary among them, afforded him ample opportunities of becoming familiar with the intricacies of their speech.

The MS. of the work, written in 1708, had remained unedited until the year 1829.

The Vocabulary is very full, but is only a collection of arbitrary phrase translations, in which all the moods, tenses, and other conditions which govern the languages of civilized races, are forced upon a tongue which possessed few correlative parts.

Cowley (Charles).

Memories of the Indians and Pioneers of the Region of Lowell. By Charles Cowley. 8° *pp.* 24. *Lowell, Stone and House, book printers,* 21 *Central Street,* 1862. 875

Cox (Ross).

Adventures on the Columbia River; including the Narrative of a Residence of Six Years on the Western Side of the Rocky Mountains, among Various Tribes of Indians hitherto unknown; together with a Journey across the American Continent. By Ross Cox. In two volumes. 8° *pp.* 368 *and* 400. *London, Henry Colburn and Richard Bentley, New Burlington Street,* 1831. 876

Cox (Ross).

The Same. One volume. *New York,* 1832. 877

The narrative of the personal experience of a fur-trader, among the Indians of the Rocky Mountains and the Pacific Slope; full of adventure, history, and character. The narrations of Cox, as well as those of Alexander Ross and of Franchere, cover the same period, and afford us other views of the same events as are related by Washington Irving in his "Astoria."

Coxe (Daniel).

A Description of the English Province of Carolana. By the Spaniards call'd Florida, and by the French La Louisiane. Viz: [*Table of contents, double columns,* 36 *lines*], with a large and curious Preface demonstrating the Right of the English to that Country [*etc.,* 6 *lines*]. To which is added A large and accurate Map of Carolana and of the River Meschacebee. By Daniel Coxe, Esq. 8° *Title* 1 *leaf, preface* 25 *leaves, contents* 1 *leaf, folding map, and pp.* 1 *to* 122. [*London*], 1741. 878

Coyer (Abbe).

A Letter to Doctor Maty, Secretary of the Royal Society; containing An Abstract of the relations of travellers of different nations, concerning the Patagonians; with a more particular account of the several discoveries of the latest French and English navigators, relative to this gigantic race of men; including a full reply to the objections made to their existence. By Abbe Coyer. 24° *pp.* 137. *London, printed for T. Becket and P. A. De Hondt, in the Strand,* 1767. 879

The few evidences of the great stature of the Patagonians, which are cited by the witty Abbe, are used only as a cover for him to cast his shafts of satire at the English laws, customs, and government. After sufficiently proving the existence of gigantic Patagonians, he proceeds to describe a fancied code of domestic, social, and political laws, by the exercise of which this stature was reached and preserved. The whole imaginative scheme affords him a medium for exhibiting the deficiencies and absurdities of the practices of the subjects of his satire.

Coyner (David H.).

The Lost Trappers. A Collection of Interesting Scenes and

Events in the Rocky Mountains, together with a Short Description of California. Also some Account of the Fur Trade, etc. By David H. Coyner. 12° *pp.* 255. *Cincinnati*, 1859. 380

These Lost Trappers were a portion of Lewis and Clark's party.

Craig (Neville B.).

The Olden Time, A Monthly Publication devoted to the preservation of Documents and other Authentic information in relation to the early explorations and the Settlement and Improvement of the country, around the head of the Ohio. Edited by Neville B. Craig, Esq. *Large* 8° Vol. I. *pp.* viii. + 1 *to* 576 + 1 *plate.* Vol. II. *pp.* iv. + 1 *to* 572 + *map of Braddock's Route. Pittsburgh, printed by Dumas & Co., Chronicle Buildings,* 1846. 381

This excellent work is often incomplete in the second volume, of which the last signature is frequently wanting, few copies of that sheet having left the press when it was attached by the sheriff for debts due by its editor or printer. It is filled with materials for Indian history gathered from original sources. The book, in consequence both of its intrinsic value and the perversity of its fortune while the last sheet was printing, has become exceedingly difficult to procure.

Volume I. contains among other articles upon Aboriginal history, "Notices of the Settlement," which includes Washington's "Journal of his first Campaign in 1754," "Stobo's Letters," Colonel Armstrong's "Taking of Kittanning," Christian Posts, "Two Journals of Mission to Shawnees," "Colonel Boquet's Expedition," "Journal of George Croghan," Washington's "Journal of a Tour to the Ohio in 1770."

Volume II. contains Ormsby's "Narrative of Campaigns of Colonels Forbes and Boquet," "History of Lord Dunmore's War," "History of Logan's Speech," Lynn's "Narrative of Captivity," "Colonel Connolly's Plot." Translation of the celebrated and rare work upon Washington's Campaign against the French Indians of the Ohio, printed by the French Government, entitled *Memoire Precis des Faits*, covering pp. 140 to 237; "Colonel Brodhead's Expedition," Arthur Lee's "Journal of a Mission to the N. W. Indians," Journal of General Butler for the same purpose, and Letters upon the Iroquois, occupying more than 100 pages.

Craig (N. B.).

Memoirs of Major Robert Stobo of the Virginia Regiment. 16° *Map and pp.* 92. *Pittsburgh*, 1854. 382

Crantz (David).

The History of Greenland, containing a Description of the Country and its inhabitants, and particularly a Relation of the Mission carried on for above these Thirty Years by the Unitas Fratrum, at New Herrnhuth and Lichtenfels, in that Country. By David Crantz. Translated from the High-Dutch, and illustrated with Maps and other Copper-plates. In two volumes. Vol. I. *pp.* lix. + *pp.* 1 *to* 405 + 2 *folding maps and* 5 *folding plates.* Vol. II. *Title* 1 *leaf and pp.* 1 *to* 498 + 2 *folding plates; all illustrative of the life, habits, utensils, and habitations of the native Esquimaux. London, printed for the Brethren's Society for the Furtherance of the Gospel among the Heathen,* 1767. 383

This first English edition is a literal translation of the German, and vastly superior to that of 1820, which is not only an abridged, but an interpolated edition. The minute Journal of the noble Moravian Brethren, gives us in their own language the phases of Aboriginal life and peculiarities which daily presented themselves. No tribe of American savages has been more closely or intelligently studied. Specimens of their language are given at pp. 350 to 358, and 447 to 451. Another edition, edited by La Trobe, was printed in 1780.

CRANTZ (David).

The History of Greenland: Including An Account of the Mission carried on by the United Brethren in that country. From the German of David Crantz. With a Continuation to the present time; illustrative notes, and an Appendix, containing a Sketch of the Mission of the Brethren in Labrador. In two volumes. 8° Vol. I. *pp.* xl. + 359 (*2 maps, 6 plates*). Vol. II. *pp.* vi. + 323, 1 *plate. London, printed for Longman, Hurst, Rees, Orme, and Brown, Paternoster Row*, 1820. 384

The narration of the services of the Moravian missionaries, in the conversion and civilization of the Aborigines of Greenland, is not excelled in heroism and self-devotion by any beings whose actions history records, except the Evangelists of the Society of Jesus. The rigors of an Arctic winter, where the temperature falls to 80° below zero, the horrors of a residence amid the unrevealable filth of an Esquimaux hut, the constant dangers of starvation, shipwreck, and disease, did not deter them from suffering the experience which enabled them to record this interesting narrative of the native habits of the savages, as well as the steps by which so many of them approached civilization and Christianity.

CRAWFORD (Charles).

An Essay on the Propagation of the Gospel, in which there are numerous facts and arguments Adduced to prove that many of the Indians in America are descended from the Ten Tribes. By Charles Crawford, Esq. 12° *pp.* 154. *Philadelphia*, 1801. 385

CREEK INDIANS.

Emigrating Indians. Letter from the Secretary of War transmitting information of the inadequacy of the fund for defraying the expenses attending the emigration of the Creek Indians. January 7, 1828. *Washington*, 1828. 386

This volume contains six other important documents, illustrating the history of the treatment of the Indians by the government.

CREMONY (John C.).

Life among the Apaches, by John C. Cremony, Interpreter to the U. S. Boundary Commission, under the Hon. John R. Bartlett in 1849, '50, and '51, and late Major of California Volunteer Cavalry, operating in Arizona, New Mexico, Texas, and Western Arkansas. 12° *pp.* 322. *San Francisco, A. Roman & Co. publishers. New York*, 1868. 387

The life of an officer during one of the ordinary paroxysms of Indian war is not generally fertile in incidents, but what with skirmishes with the warlike Camanches, and hunts for the assassin Apaches, the service of Major Cremony was tolerably adventurous. The Apache, the Thug of American Aborigines, was more closely approached and studied by him during his twenty years of border life, than by any other writer.

[Crevecœur (Hector St. John de).]

Voyage dans la Haute Pensylvanie et dans l'Etat de New York. Par un Membre adoptif de la Nation Oneida. Traduit et publie par l'auteur des Lettres d'un Cultivateur Americain. De l'imprimerie de Crapelet. *A Paris. Chez Maradan Libraire rue Paree St. Andre-des-Arcs.* No. 16. *An* ix. 1801. 3 *vols.,* *Pp.* 459, 421, 448. 10 *plates and maps numbered.* 388

[Tour through Upper Pennsylvania and in the State of New York, by an adopted Member of the Oneida Tribe. Translated and published by the author of Letters of an American Cultivator.]

Many of the plates are portraits of Indian chiefs and plans of ancient fortifications. Much of the work is devoted to aboriginal affairs.

The author was a gentleman of Normandy who passed twenty-four years of his life in North America. He is styled in several works one of the first victims of the war of Independence, but this suffering must be understood as affecting his property rather than his person. His work contains some curious details on the state of the aborigines, before the arrival of Europeans in that part of North America which he visited. It is announced on the title-page as a simple translation, but it is well known to be the work originally of John Crevecœur, and is to be regarded probably as a continuation of his Letters of an American farmer (*Letters d'un Cultivateur Americain*).

[Cuoq (Rev. Mr.).]

Ainmie Tipadjimo8in, Masinaigan ka Ojitogobanen Kalat ka Nitna8ial Mekate8okonaie8igobanen kanactageng, 8ak8i enasindibanen. O ki Mag8abikickoton John Lovell, Moniag ate Mekate8ikonaie8ikamikong, Kanactageng. 1859. 12° *pp.* 339. 389

Stories of Bible History, translated into the language of the Algonquin Indians, by the Sulpitian Missionary, Mr. Cuoq.

[Cuoq (Rev. Mr.).]

Ka Titc Tebeniminang Jesus ondaje aking–Oom masinagan ki ojitogoban ka ojitogabanen. Aianrie tipadjimo8in masinaigan 8ak81 enа8indibanen Monniang [Montreal]. Ate Mekate8ikonaie8ikomikong kanactageng. 12° *pp.* 396. 1861. 390

The *Life* of Jesus in the Algonquin language, translated by the Rev. Mr. Cuoq. A singular self-abnegation characterises the works written by members of the Order of Sulpitians. Although adopting the rules and service of the order, without vows or obligations of any sort, they are more strict in secreting their authorship, than the most severe in self-denial of other orders; accordingly their works are almost without exception published anonymously.

[Cuoq (Rev. Mr.).]

Etudes Philologiques Sur quelques Langues Sauvages de L'Amerique. Par N. O. Ancien Missionnaire. 8° *pp.* 160. *Montreal, Dawson Brothers,* 1866. 391

[Philological Studies of some languages of the savages of America, by N. O. (formerly) missionary.]

The author has given unimpeachable evidence in his work, of that familiarity with his subject, which must precede ability to write a valuable treatise upon it. He has in its pages analyzed the Iroquois and Algonquin languages, compared, and treated them grammatically so as to afford a very clear and extensive comprehension of their structure to the student. He is equally severe upon Mr. Schoolcraft and Mr. Renan and curiously enough, in punishment of the same crime in each — audacious ignorance. The erudite and ingenious Renan, and the industrious but illiterate Schoolcraft, both suffer impalement, the one for constructing a hypothesis upon the structure of the Aboriginal tongues, and the other for scheming a similar edifice upon that of the Greek — while neither author knew a word of the languages on which he built his fabric. Mr. Schoolcraft determines to find a modern origin for the Iroquois word Haw-en-ni-io, "True God" and therefore says it is composed of Niio, corrupted from the French Dieu, and the Greek Deo, and the native prefix Hawen. Mr. Renan is equally unhappy in finding a good basis for some of his realistic dogmas in the assumed want of systematic structure of the American Aboriginal languages. Mr. Cuoq exhibits a regularity in grammatical arrangement that rivals the Latin, in the system and extent of the Iroquois and Algonquin, in which qualities indeed they are only excelled in his opinion by the monarch of languages.

The excellent author, who modestly conceals himself under the enigmatical letters N. O., is known to be the Rev. Father Cuoq, who for twenty years was in charge of the mission at the Lake of Two Mountains, an Indian village in Canada. Here for many years have resided a portion of two tribes representing the Iroquois and Algonquin races; the latter a branch of the great Chippewa nation called the Sauteaux. Here for nearly a century have the children of these two aboriginal races been in contact without blending, or even associating with that degree of familiarity which each exhibits for the more distant white race.

Half a century ago McLean found them the same. The Catholic church and seminary divide the village into nearly two equal parts, and the natives of each nation seldom pass their respective limits into the territory of the other. With few exceptions they cannot converse together, as the languages are so radically different as to be mutually perfectly unintelligible. Even within the sacred walls of the church of their common religion they do not meet; as Father Cuoq conducts the services of the Catholic faith alternately, morning and evening in their respective languages. Situated in these most fortuitous circumstances for obtaining a perfect comprehension of the radical differences of their formation, there has probably never existed any person better fitted to write the treatise he has presented us. The structure of these two representative tongues is complete, each in its own form, and yet nowhere touching, nowhere in common, either in enunciation, grammatical basis, radicals or derivatives. Were the natives of one nation emigrants from China, and the other from Wales, there would be equal points of similarity.

Cushing (Mr.).

Speech of Mr. Cushing, of Massachusetts, on the bill making appropriations for the current expenses of the Indian Department, delivered in the House of Representatives February 1st, 1837. 8° *pp.* 14. *Washington*, 1837. 392

Cusick (D.).

Sketches of Ancient History of the Six Nations. 8° *pp.* 35 + 5 *plates and printed covers. Lockport, N. Y.*, 1848. 393

Cusick (D.).

The same. *Tuscarora Village*, 1825. 394

Cutler (Lieut. J.).

Topographical Description of the State of Ohio, Indiana Territory, and Louisiana, comprehending the Ohio and Mississippi Rivers and their principal Tributary Streams, and a concise Account of the Indian Tribes west of the Mississippi. To which is added an Interesting Journal of Mr. Charles Le Raye, while a captive of the Sioux Nation, on the waters of the Missouri river. By a late Officer in the United States Army. 12° *pp.* 219. *Plates. Boston*, 1812. 395

Almost the whole value which attaches to this scarce book, is comprised in the narrative of the captivity of Le Raye. His Journal of personal experience among the fierce Sioux has much more than the usual modicum of real merit, to which such relations are entitled, as it is the result of the observations, regarding the habits of this nomad nation, of a man of some intelligence. Le Raye's Journal was never published in any other form than the present edition.

DABLON (Claude R. P.).

Relation de ce qui s'est passe de plus remarquable aux missions des peres de la Compagnie de Jesus en la Nouvelle France les annees 1673 a 1679. Par le R. P. Claude Dablon Recteur du College de Quebec & Superieur des Missions de la Compagnie de Jesus en la Nouvelle France. 8° *pp.* 290. *A la Nouvelle York, De la Presse Cramoisy de Jean-marie Shea*, 1860. 396

[Relation of the most remarkable events which took place in the Missions of the Fathers of the Society of Jesus in New France in the years 1673 to 1679, by the Rev. Claude Dablon.]

No. 16 of Shea's *Relations of the Missions of the Jesuits among the Indians of Canada.*

The first four chapters, pp. 1 to 134, are occupied with The Relation of the Mission of the Outaouacs; and chapter five, pp. 135 to 204, Relation of the Missions to the Iroquois. Part II., pp. 205 to 227, is entitled, "Of the Missions to the Montaignons and Algonquins at Tadousac;" and Part III., pp. 229 to 290, "Relation of the Missions to the Huron Colony near Quebec, and of the Iroquois Mission near Montreal." The most minute details of the character, conduct, and habits of life of the Christianized as well as Pagan Indians, are to be found recorded in these Reports of the Jesuit missionaries to their superior. They were not intended for the public, and yet there was nothing to conceal: they were not designed as a proclamation of their success, and therefore we may regard them as veracious.

DABLON (Claude R. P.).

Relation de ce qui s'est passe de plus remarquable aux Missions des Peres de la Compagnie de Jesus en la Nouvelle France les annees 1672 et 1673. Par le R. P. Claude Dablon Recteur du College de Quebec & Superieur des Missions de la Compagnie de Jesus en la Nouvelle France. 8° *pp.* 219. *A la Nouvelle York, De la Presse Cramoisy de Jean-marie Shea*, 1861. 397

[Relation of the most remarkable events in the Missions of the Fathers of the Company of Jesus in New France during the years 1672 and 1673, by the Rev. Claude Dablon.]

No. 15 of Shea's *Relations of the Jesuit Missions among the Indians of Canada.*

The first thirty-two pages are devoted to "Relation of the Mission among the Hurons," and pp. 33 to 144 are entitled, "Relation of the Missions among the Iroquois." "The Missions to the Algonquin People called Outaouacs," is the subject of pp. 115 to 219. The Relations are very minute, as they only cover the period of two years, and extend to 219 pages.

Father Dablon was a French Missionary, of the Order of the Jesuits, who travelled more than thirty years in the service of the Cross. He was rector of the College of Quebec and Father Superior of the Mission of Canada.

The two volumes are printed from manuscripts preserved at Quebec and Montreal in the Jesuit colleges, and form the last documents which exist of the Relations of the Missions of that order in that country.

DARNELL (Elias).

A | Journal | containing an accurate & interesting ac | count of the hardships, Sufferings, bat | tles, Defeat & Captivity of those he- | roic Kentucky Volunteers & Reg | ulars, commanded by General- | Winchester, in the year | 1812–1813. | Also | Two Narratives, | by men, that were wounded in the battles | on the river Raisin, and taken captive | by the Indians. | By Elias Darnell. | Printed for the Author. | *Paris, Kentucky:* | *Printed by Joel R. Lyle.* | 1812. | 8° *Title* 1 *leaf* + *Preface and Journal pp.* 1 *to* 37 + *Narrative of Mallary pp.* 1 *to* 7 + *The Battle of Raisin* (1) *p. Total pp.* 67. 398

The original edition of Darnell's Journal. So rare that Mr. Sabin announced at the sale of this copy that it was the first which he had ever seen or heard of.

DARNELL (Elias).

A Journal, containing an Accurate and Interesting Account of the Hardships, Sufferings, Battles, Defeat and Captivity of those heroic Kentucky Volunteers and Regulars, commanded by General Winchester, in the years 1812, 1813. Also, Two Narratives, &c., by men that were wounded in the battles on the River Raisin and taken captive by the Indians. By Elias Darnell. 24° *pp.* 100. *Philadelphia*, 1854. 399

DAVIES (John).

The History of the Caribby-Islands, viz., Barbadoes. St. Christophers, St. Vincents, Martinico, Dominico, Barbouthos, Montserrat, Mevis, Antego, &c. in all xxviii. In Two Books. The First containing the Natural; The Second the Moral History of those Islands. Illustrated with Several Pieces of Sculpture representing the most considerable Rarities therein Described. With a Caribbian Vocabulary. Rendered into English, by John Davies. *Folio.* 4 *plates. pp.* 366. *London*, 1666. 400

This book is an example of the most unblushing effrontery. The pseudo author assumes the credit of the performance with but the faintest allusion to its previous existence. It is a nearly faithful translation of Rochefort's *Histoire des Antilles.* There is, however, a gratifying retribution in Davies' treatment of Rochefort, for the work of the latter was fictitious in every part which was not purloined from authors whose knowledge furnished him with all in his treatise which was true.

DAVIS (A.).

Antiquities of America. The first Inhabitants of Central America and the Discovery of New-England by the Northmen, Five hundred years before Columbus, with important additions. A Lecture [3 *lines*], by A. Davis, fourteenth edition from the twelfth Boston edition. 8° *pp.* 30. *Troy, N. Y.*, 1846. 401

DAVIS (A.).

Ruins of Central America and Discovery of New-England by the Northmen. (Tenth edition.) 8° *pp.* 24. *Buffalo*, 1842. 402

DAVIS (George F.).

The St. Regis Bell. 8° (*n. d. or p.*) 403

Pages 311 to 321 of Massachusetts Historical Society's Proceedings for 1870. A few copies of Mr. Davis' article were printed separately. In it he attempts to disprove the romantic story of the bell taken by the Indians at Deerfield, and carried to St. Regis.

DAVIS (Solomon).

A Prayer Book in the Language of the Six Nations of Indians, containing the Morning and Evening Service, the Litany, Catechism, some of the Collects, and the Prayers and Thanksgivings upon several Occasions, in the Book of Common Prayer of the Protestant Episcopal Church: together with forms of family and private devotion. Compiled from various Translations and prepared for publication by request of the Domestic Committee of the Board of Missions of the Protestant Episcopal Church in the United States of America. By the Rev. Solomon Davis, Missionary to the Oneidas at Duck Creek, territory of Wisconsin. 12° *pp.* 168. *New York, Swords, Stanford, & Co. D. Fanshaw, printer*, 1837. 404

DAVIS (Rev. Sheldon).

Shekomoko; or the Moravians in Dutchess County. By Rev. Sheldon Davis, A. M. 8° *pp.* 29. *Poughkeepsie*, 1858. 405

DAVIS (W. W. H.).

The Spanish Conquest of New Mexico. By W. W. H. Davis. 8° *pp.* 438, *map and portrait. Doylestown. Pa.*, 1869. 406

Beside the narrations of Cabeça de Vaca, Niza, and other printed accounts of Spanish explorations, the author has availed himself of the MSS. which his official position, soon after the conquest of the country by the United States, placed in his custody. His narrative of the prolonged hostilities between the Spaniards and the Indians, the religious rites, method of warfare, and peculiar ceremonies of the latter, is fresh, vigorous, and highly interesting.

DAWSON (Moses).

A Historical Narrative of the Civil and Military Services of Major General Harrison, and a Vindication of his Character and Conduct as a Statesman, a Citizen, and a Soldier. With a Detail of his Negotiations and Wars with the Indians, until the final overthrow of the Celebrated Chief, Tecumseh, and his Brother the Prophet. The whole written and compiled from original and authentic Documents, furnished by many of the most respectable Characters in the United States. By Moses Dawson, Editor of the Cincinnati Advertiser. 8° *Title and prel. pp.* viii. + *pp.* 464 + *Appendix* 4 *leaves* + *Errata half page. Cincinnati, printed by M. Dawson, at the Advertiser Office*, 1824. 407

This is certainly one of the most thorough, complete, and authentic treatises, relating to the Border Wars of the West, ever printed. The fine portraiture of aboriginal character, the narration of the minutest incidents of camp, treaty, and war, and the style of simple candor adopted by a scholarly mind, all commend the narrative to our judgment, and attract our interest in its progress.

[DAY-BREAKING | (The) |

If not | The Sun-Rising | of the | Gospel | With the | Indians in New England. | Zach. 4, 10 | [*motto 5 lines*]. 4° *Title, reverse 'To the Reader' signed Nathan. Warde* + *A True Relation, pp.* 1 *to* 25. *London*, | *Printed by Rich. Cotes, for Fulk Clifton*, *and are to be | sold at his shop under Saint Margaret's Church on | New-fish-Street Hill*, 1647. | 408

No. 3 of the *Eliot Tracts*, reprinted under the following title.

DAY-BREAKING (The)
If not The Sun-Rising of the Gospel With the Indians in New England. 4° *pp.* 34. *New York, reprinted for Joseph Sabin*, 1865. 409

DEARBORN (Henry A. S.).
A Sketch of the Life of the Apostle Elliot, prefatory to a Subscription for erecting a Monument to his Memory. By Henry A. S. Dearborn. 8° *pp.* 32. *Roxbury*, 1850. 410

DEBATE
In the House of Representatives of the United States on the Seminole War, in January and February, 1819. 12° *pp.* 591. *Washington, printed at the Office of the National Intelligencer*, 1819. 411

DE COSTA (B. F.).
The Pre-Columbian Discovery of America by The Northmen. Illustrated from the Icelandic Sagas. Edited with notes, and a general introduction, by B. F. De Costa. 8° *pp.* 118. *Albany, Joel Munsel*, 1868. 412

D'ERES (Charles Denis Rusoe).
Memoirs of Charles Denis Rusoe D'Eres, A Native of Canada, Who was with the Scanyawtauragahrooote Indians eleven years, with a particular account of his Sufferings, &c. during his tarry with them, and his safe return to his Family Connections in Canada; To which is added An Appendix containing A brief account of their Persons, Dress, Manners, Reckoning Time, Mode of Government, &c. Feasts, Dances, Hunting, Weapons of War, &c. Making Peace, Diversions, Courtship, Marriage, Religious Tenets, Mode of Worship, Diseases, Method of Cure, Burying their Dead, Character of the Scanyawtauragahrooote Indians, Particular Description of the Quadrupeds, Birds, Fishes, Reptiles and Insects, which are to be met with on and in the vicinity of Scanyawtauragahrooote Island. Copy Right Secured. *Small* 12° *pp.* 176. *Printed for, and sold by Henry Ranlet, Exeter*, 1800. 413

If there ever existed a tribe of savages who were recognized by such a title, it was sufficient warrant for their extermination; and judged by this rule the author himself had but little advantage. He terminates his narrative by marriage with a maiden of Spencer in New Hampshire, where he fixed his habitation in 1794. Whether the author was ever a captive to any savage tribe is somewhat uncertain; his narrative is at all events little better than a fiction. It is one of the rarest of books relating to the aborigines.

DE FOREST (J. W.).
History of the Indians of Connecticut from the earliest known period to 1850. Published with the Sanction of the Connecticut Historical Society. 8° *pp.* 509. *Hartford*, 1852. 414

De Hass (Wills).

History of the Early Settlement and Indian Wars of Western Virginia; embracing an Account of the various expeditions in the West, previous to 1795, etc. Illustrated by numerous engravings. Also Biographical Sketches of Col. Ebenezer Zane, Major Samuel M'Colloch, Lewis Wetzel, Gen'l Andrew Lewis, Gen'l Daniel Brodhead, Capt. Samuel Brady, Col. Wm. Crawford; and other distinguished actors in our border wars. 8° *pp.* 416. *Wheeling,* 1851. 415

Delafield (John).

An Inquiry into the origin of the Antiquities of America by John Delafield Jr. with An Appendix containing Notes and a View of the Causes of the Superiority of the Men of the Northern over those of the Southern Hemisphere, by James Lakey, M. D. 4° *Folding engraving of Mexican Paintings.* 10 *plates, pp.* 142. *New York, published for subscribers by Colt, Burgess, & Co. London, Longman, etc. Paris, Galignani,* 1839. 416

Delano (A.).

Life on the Plains and among the Diggings; being scenes and adventures of an overland journey to California with particular incidents of the routes, mistakes, and sufferings of the emigrants, the Indian tribes, &c. 12° *pp.* 384. *Auburn,* 1854. 417

Denis & Famin.

Bresil par M. Ferdinand Denis. Colombie et Guyanes par M. C. Famin. 8° *pp.* 384 + *map and* 90 *plates on separate leaves. Total* 584 *pp. Paris,* 1837. 418

A large portion of the volume is devoted to the description of the history, ceremonies, character, and condition of the aboriginal tribes of Brasil, of which traits twenty-five of the plates are illustrative.

Denton (Daniel).

A Brief Description of New York formerly called New Netherlands with the places thereunto adjoining Likewise a brief Relation of the Customs of the Indians there by Daniel Denton. A new edition with an introduction and copious historical notes by Gabriel Farman. 8° *pp.* 17 + (4) + 57. *New York, William Gowans,* 1845. 419

De Pauw (M.).

Recherches Philosophiques sur les Americaines ou Memoires Interessants pour Servir a l' Histoire de l' espece Humaine Par M de P——. *Three vols.* 12° Vol. I. *pp.* xxx. + 326 + xxiv. Vol. II. *pp.* 366 + xxx. + 133. Vol. III. *pp.* 246. *Berlin,* 1770. 420

[Philosophical Researches on the Americans, or Interesting Memoirs to serve in the History of the Human Race; by M. de P(auw).]

Vol. III. has in addition to the above title, "Nouvelle edition augmentee d' une Dissertation Critique par Dom Pernetty; & de la Defense de l'Auteur des Recherches contre cette Dissertation."

["New edition augmented by the critical Dissertation of M. Dom Pernetty, and by the Defense of the Author of the Researches against that Dissertation."]

Vol. I. and pp. 366 of Vol. II. are occupied with the Philosophical Researches of M. De Pauw. Dom Pernetty wrote an able controversial reply, which is printed at the end of the Researches in Vol. II. with the title "Dissertation sur l' Amerique et les Americains, contre les Recherches Philosophiques de M. De P—, par Dom Pernetty." [Dissertation on America and the Americans, against the Philosophical Researches of Mr. De Pauw.] pp. 1 to 136. Vol. III. is entirely devoted to the rejoinder of M. De Pauw. A fourth volume of this controversy, written by Dom Pernetty, was subsequently printed (1771), entitled, "Examen des Recherches Philosophiques sur l'Amerique et les Americains et de la defense de cet ouvrage, par Dom Pernetty." [Examination of the Researches Philosophic on America and the Americans, and of the Defense of that work, by Dom Pernetty.] "This rejoinder," says Mr. Rich, "of Dom Pernetty, in which he exposes the blunders and unfair conduct of De Pauw, is much more ably written than his first work." A fifth work upon the same subject appeared in 1771, of which Mr. Rich has this note :—

"A lively and humorous defense of the American Indians, attributed by Monsel to M. Poivre; but Barbier says that it is either M. Bonneville or Dom Pernetty. Now Poivre was never in America, and Bonneville was only eleven years of age at this time. As it is not probable that Dom Pernetty wrote two works on the same subject in the same year, all these conjectures as to the authorship are probably erroneous." Mr. Sabin attributes it to Bonneville.

In volumes one and two De Pauw labors to prove the inferior scale upon which nature has organized men, animals, and vegetation in America. The character of the American Aborigines receives the principal force of his attack. Dom Pernetty, with forcible arguments, defended them in his "Dissertation." To this De Pauw rejoined in his "Defense," which was again answered by Dom Pernetty in his "Examen."

Depons (F.).

Travels in South America, during the years 1801, 1802, 1803, and 1804; containing a description of the Captain-Generalship of Caraccas, and an account of the discovery, conquest, topography, legislature, commerce, finance, and natural productions of the country; With a View of the Manners and Customs of the Spaniards and Native Indians, by F. Depons. In two volumes. Translated from the French. 8° Vol. I. *pp.* iii. + 503 *and map.* Vol. II. *pp.* (xii.) + 384. *London*, 1807. 421

Beside his account of the slaughter, and destruction, by various modes, of the Indians during the conquest of their nations, the author gives, in chapter iv. pp. 183 to 248, a "Portrait of the Indians before the arrival of the Europeans, — means employed to civilize them." This relation is drawn from documents, narrations of persons with whom he conversed, and from personal observation. On pp. 342 to 368 is a description of the locality and effect of the missions among the natives, and pp. 369 to 384 are devoted to expulsion of the Caribs, and expeditions in search of El Dorado.

Dewees (W. B.).

Letters from an Early Settler of Texas. By W. B. Dewees. Compiled by Cara Cardelle. 12° *pp.* 312 *and map.* *Louisville, Hull & Brother, printers,* 1854. 422

The adventures of a ranger in the border wars of Texas, against the Comanches and other tribes of the plains, are here narrated with spirit and apparent truthfulness.

DEXTER (H. M.).
The History of King Philip's War. By Benjamin Church. With an Introduction and Notes by Henry Martyn Dexter. 4° *pp. L + 3 prel. leaves + 54 leaves + 14 pp. Total pp. numbered on bottom margin* 205. *Boston, John Kimball Wiggin*, 1865. 423

DEXTER (H. M.).
The History of the Eastern Expeditions of 1689–1690–1692–1696–1704, Against the Indians and French, by Benjamin Church, With an Introduction and Notes By Henry Martyn Dexter. 4° *pp.* 203. *Boston, J. K. Wiggin and Wm. Parsons Lunt*, 1867. 424

DIAZ DEL CASTILLO.
The True History of the Conquest of Mexico. By Captain Bernal Diaz del Castillo, One of the Conquerors. Written in the year 1568. Translated from the Original Spanish by Maurice Keatinge. 4° *Plan, pp.* viii. *and* 514. *London*, 1800. 425

DICKENSON (Jonathan).
Gods Protecting Providence, Man's Surest Help and Defence in Times of Greatest Difficulty, and most Eminent Danger: evidenced In the Remarkable Deliverance of Robert Barrow, with divers other Persons, from the Devouring Waves of the Sea; amongst which they Suffered Shipwreck: And also From the cruel Devouring Jaws of the Inhuman Cannibals of Florida. Faithfully Related by one of the Persons concerned therein. Jonathan Dickenson. [Psalm xcii. 4 *lines.*] The Third Edition. 16° *Title and* 4 *prel. leaves + pp.* 94. *Printed in Philadelphia. Reprinted in London, and Sold by the Asigns of F. Sowle, at the Bible in George Yard, Lombard Street*, 1720. 426

DICKENSON (Jonathan).
God's Protecting Providence, Man's surest Help and Defence In times of Greatest Difficulty and Most Imminent Danger, Evinced In the Remarkable Deliverance of Robert Barrow, with divers other persons, from the devouring Waves of the Sea, amongst which they suffered Shipwreck; and also from the cruel devouring Jaws of the Inhuman Cannibals of Florida. Faithfully related by one of the persons concerned therein, Jonathan Dickenson. Sixth Edition. *London, printed and sold by James Phillips*, 1787. 427

The first edition of Dickenson's "Narrative of Captivity among the Indians of Florida" was printed in Philadelphia 1699, by Reinier Jansen, and is erroneously accredited with being the first book printed in that city. It is, consequently, one of the most costly, as it is certainly one of the rarest gems of the book collector. A perfect copy would be eagerly seized by half a score of this class at any price, less than one hundred and fifty dollars. An imperfect copy brought eighty-five dollars at Fisher's sale. The second edition is almost equally rare, at least I have never seen, or indeed known of a copy. Copies of the third edition, although not by any means so rare as the others, are far from common.

DIÈREVILLE.

Relation du voyage du Port Royal de L'Acadie, ou de la Nouvelle France, dans laquelle on voit un détail des divers mouvemens de la Mer; la Description du Pais, les Occupations des François qui y sont établies, les manieres des différentes Nations Sauvages, leurs, Superstitions et leurs chasses, avec une dissertation exacte sur le Castor. 12° *Plate.* 16 *pp.* + 236 + 7. *Amsterdam*, 1710. 428

[Relation of the Voyage from Port Royal to Acadia or New France. In which may be seen a detail of the various movements, &c. The Description of the Country, the Occupations of the French who are there established; the manners of the different Nations of Savages; their Superstitions and their hunting, with an exact dissertation on the Beaver.]

At page 236, commences a Relation of a combat between the French and the Acadians, against the English.

DILLON (John B.).

History of Indiana from its earliest exploration by Europeans to the close of the territorial government in 1816, with an Introduction containing Historical Notes of the discovery and settlement of the territory of the United States northwest of the river Ohio. By John B. Dillon. Vol. I. [*Only one volume published.*] *pp.* 456. *Indianapolis, Ia.*, 1843. 429

Indian missions, wars, and treaties form a large part of the volume. Historical notes of the French occupation of the territory, the visits of the Jesuits to the various tribes of Indians and of the nations of savages inhabiting it, occupy the first three chapters, pp. 1 to 78. Chapter iv., pp. 79 to 96, is devoted to the account of Pontiac's War. Chapter v., pp. 97 to 115, is filled with the narrative of Lord Dunmore's expedition, and the battle of Point Pleasant. Chapters vi., vii., viii., and ix., pp. 116 to 184, are devoted to Colonel Rogers Clark's journal of his famous expeditions. St. Clair's expedition, Indian wars and treaties, occupy with their details the rest of the volume.

DILLON (John B.).

A History of Indiana, from its Earliest Exploration by Europeans to the close of territorial government in 1816; Comprehending a history of the Discovery, Settlement, and Civil and Military Affairs of the Territory of the U. S. northwest of the River Ohio, and a general view of the progress of public affairs in Indiana from 1816 to 1856. By John B. Dillon. *Large* 8° *pp.* 637 + 2 *maps and* 4 *plates. Indianapolis*, 1859. 430

A new edition of the above work, continued to a later period.

DOBRIZHOFFER (Martino).

Historia de Abiponibus equestri bellicosaque Paraquariae Natione Locupletata. Copiosis Barbararum Gentium, Urbium, Fluminum, Terarum, Amphibiorum, Insectorum, Serpentium Praecipuorum, Piscium, Avium, Arborum, Plantarum, Aliarumque eiusdem Provinciae Proprietatum Observationibus. Authore Martino Dobrizhoffer Presbytero et per annos duo de Viginti paraquariae Missionario. *Viennae Typis Josephi Nob. De Kurzbek caes. Reg. Aul. Tipog. et Bibliop. Anno* 1784. Three vols. 8° Vol. I. *pp.* (x.) + 1 *to* 476 + (4) + *pl. and map.* Vol. II. *pp.* (iii.) + 3 *to* 499 + (2) + 1 *plate and* 1 *map.* Vol. III. *pp.* (vi.) + 3 *to* 424 + (2) + 2 *plates.* 431

DOBRIZHOEFFER (Martin).

An Account of The Abipones, an Equestrian People of Paraguay. From the Latin of Martin Dobrizhoeffer, eighteen years a Missionary in that Country. In three volumes. Vol. I. *pp.* xli. + 435. Vol. II. *pp.* v. + 446. Vol. III. *pp.* vi. + 419. *London, John Murray,* 1822. 432

This work is a translation of the preceding, made by the daughter of Robert Southey, the poet.

Martin Dobrizhoeffer, born in 1717, was one of those extraordinary men, who organized in Paraguay a government that has not ceased to excite the wonder and perplex the reason of all who tried to comprehend its strange anomalies. For a century and a half it existed as a pure hierarchy, insulated and intact; more mysterious than the fabled Amazonian Republic, or the equally mythical El Dorado. For a half century succeeding it has remained the only example of a people, professing to be free, existing under a tyranny supported solely by themselves.

Not the least of the wonders of that land of mysteries is it, to see occasionally emerge from its obscurity a mind of extraordinary ability in government, power of reasoning, or breadth of scholarship. The author of these volumes was a man of learning, who in 1736 entered the order of Jesuits, and in 1749, in obedience to the commands of his general, commenced the appalling labor of attempting the civilization and christianizing of one of the fiercest and most superstitious, of all the savage tribes of American Indians. His mission among them lasted through eighteen years of living martyrdom; which he survived to write and publish this work in the Latin tongue. It is the most complete, faithful, and interesting detail of the life, habits, and character of a savage tribe which was ever written. Southey, when praising the work, only speaks the language of every scholar or writer who has perused it. In chapters xvi. and xvii. of Vol. II., pp. 159 to 206, he treats of the language of the Abipones, with a grammatical analysis of the language, and in chaper xviii. is found a translation of the Symbol of the Cross into five Indian dialects.

DOBBS (Arthur).

An Account of the Countries adjoining to Hudson's Bay in the North West Part of America [*etc.*, 8 *lines*]. With an Abstract of Captain Middleton's Journal [2 *lines*]. [*Paragraphs i. to v. of Contents*] V. Vocabularies of the Languages of several Indian Nations adjoining to Hudson's Bay [3 *lines*]. 4° *Map and pp.* 211. *London,* 1744. 433

DOCUMENTS

And Proceedings relating to the Formation and Progress of a Board in the City of New York for the Emigration, Preservation, and Improvement of the Aborigines of America July 22d, 1829. 8° *pp.* 48. *New York,* 1829. 434

DOCUMENTS

And Official Reports, illustrating the causes which led to the Revolution in the Government of the Seneca Indians in the Year 1848, and to the recognition of their representative republican Constitution, by the authorities of the United States and of the State of New York. 8° *pp.* 92. *Baltimore, printed by Wm. Wooddy & Son,* 1857. 435

DOCUMENTS

In relation to the claim of the executor of John J. Bulow, Jr. to be Indemnified for the loss of property destroyed by the hostile Seminole Indians, Dec. 21, 1837. 8° *pp.* 12. *Washington,* 1837. 436

DODDRIDGE (Dr. Jos.).

Notes on the Settlement and Indian Wars of the Western parts of Virginia and Pennsylvania, from the year 1763 until the year 1783, inclusive. Together with a view of the State of Society and Manners of the First Settlers of the Western Country. By the late Rev. Dr. Joseph Doddridge. 12° *pp.* 316. *Printed at the Office of the Gazette for the Author, Wellsburgh, Va.,* 1824. 437

Doddridge's work was drawn from original sources, mostly of personal observation, or from the actors in the Border Wars he depicts. No one except Withers has approached him in fidelity or exactness, and both have the best attestation to the value of their works, in the frequent reproduction of them in Collections and Narratives of Border Warfare without acknowledgment of the sources from which all that is valuable has been taken. Some of these pirated reprints are as scarce as the originals, of which retributive rarity Kercheval's *Valley of Virginia,* and Bickley's *History of Indian Wars of Tazewell County, Virginia,* are instances. Perfect copies of all these works are rare.

DODDRIDGE (Dr. Joseph).

Logan, The last of the race of the Skillellimus, Chief of the Cayuga Nation, A Dramatic piece to which is added The Dialogue of the Backwoodsman and the Dandy, First Recited at the Buffaloe Seminary July the 1st, 1821. By Dr. Joseph Doddridge. 4° *pp.* 76. *Reprinted from the Virginia Edition of 1823, with an Appendix relating to the Murder of Logan's Family, for William Dodge, by Robert Clarke & Co., Cincinnati,* 1868. 438

DODGE (J. R.).

Red Men of the Ohio Valley, an Aboriginal History of the period commencing A. D. 1650 and ending at the treaty of Greenville A. D. 1795, embracing notable facts and thrilling incidents in the settlement by the Whites of the States of Kentucky, Ohio, Indiana, and Illinois. By J. R. Dodge. 12° *pp.* 435. *Springfield, O.,* 1860. 439

DOM PERNETTY.

Dissertation sur l'Amerique et les Americains contre les recherches philosophiques de M. de P(auw). 12° *pp.* iv. + 239. *Berlin, Samuel Pitra* (1770). 440

In this dissertation the author controverts the sentiment of Mr. de Pauw, that America occupies an inferior position in the scale of Nature, to other parts of the world; and that the degradation of the American Indians, as well as the inferior size, ferocity, and utility of its animals, proves it. Monsieur de

Pauw replied in his work, entitled *Defense de l' Auteur des Recherches.* Dom Pernetty rejoined in his second work, entitled *Examen des Recherches Philosophiques.*

Another attack on De Pauw's assumptions, entitled *Examen des Recherches*, a defense of the American Indians, was printed in 1771, which closed a controversy on the part of these writers that had been much more ably conducted, more than a century previous, by Grotius, Hornius, and De Laet.

DOM PERNETTY.

Examen des Recherches Philosophiques Sur l'Amerique et les Americaines, et de la defense de cet ovrage. 12° *Two vols.* Vol. I. *pp.* xx. + 319. Vol. II. *pp.* xx. + 604. *A Berlin*, 1771. 441

This rejoinder of Dom Pernetty to the Defense of M. de Pauw of his *Recherches Philosophiques*, exposing the blunders and assumptions of the latter, is said by Mr. Rich to be much more ably written than his former work, *Dissertation sur les Recherches de M. de Pauw.*

DOMENECH (Abbe Em.).

Manuscript Pictographique Americain precede d' une Notice sur l' Ideographie des Peaux-Rouges par Em. Domenech, Missionaire Apostolique, &c. Ouvrage publie sous les Auspices de M. le Ministre d'Etat et de la Maison de l' Empereur. 8° *pp.* viii. + 119 + 228 *plates.* *Paris, Gide Libraire-editeur*, 1860. 442

The First Section is entitled "Notice of the Ancient American Manuscripts, and of The Book of the Savages." This unhappy work afforded a sensation to the literary world of Europe, not less unusual than universal. From every study, library, and bookseller's rooms arose a shout of laughter, that the soul of Rabelais might have envied. No Frenchman, since that ribald wit left the earth, has excited such a chorus of unextinguishable cachinnation. Unfortunately for the Abbe Domenech the parallel between himself and Rabelais soon ceases, the world laughs not with him but at him. He has been the victim of an imposture so rank, that we should wonder not less than we admire his self delusion, if he had not dragged so many considerable people into the same net.

His MS. work received the sanction of the Emperor himself, so far as to direct the Minister of State to furnish the means of its publication. In his Dedication to M. Lacroix, he says: "You will recall among the men of all nations who thronged your drawing-rooms, a pale and young man recently returned from the solitudes of the New World. Poor child, among your exotics;" etc., etc. This poor child was informed by M. Lacroix that his destiny was literary eminence, and advised to set out on the road at once. Looking about for some subject to employ the talent so recently discovered, his ill fortune led him to the Arsenal Library purchased from the Marquis de Paulmy, where he encountered a MS. of 114 leaves, entitled *Livre des Sauvages.* It would seem impossible, on the merest glance at the sprawling pictures, that any person in this matter-of-fact world could have arrived at any other conclusion regarding the MS. than that it was a child's drawing-book. But the eyes of a pale enthusiast looking for his destiny, can see the history of a thousand years in the track of an ink-bedraggled fly. There is a persistence in self-delusion that carries the dupe on to his destruction. Besides, a French savant is ready to believe in anything except his God. Accordingly the Abbe Domenech wrote a treatise on the MS., which he declared to be the work of some Indian chief of Canada. He said that Boturini, Torquemada, Tschudi, and Kingsborough had done much to illustrate Aztec and Inca MSS., but hitherto nothing had been found to enlighten the darkness of the story of the Northern Indians. It was reserved for his fortune to draw aside the veil. Indeed, he was obliged to hasten, as he learned to his dismay that a copy had been made by an American savant, with the view to its publication by the United States Government. The glory of France, he declared to the Emperor's confidant, was involved in this attempt to snatch from her the fame of bringing to light so precious a document illustrative of her former renown in New France. Sufficient however is it for our mirth that the work was published only to discover that the MS. was either the work of some mischief-loving inventor, or of a sick child whiling away the hours of illness. Since then the Emperor, the Emperor's household, and Abbe Domenech have been industriously employed in destroying all the copies they can procure, consequently they are exceedingly rare.

DOMENECH (Abbe).

Missionary Adventures in Texas and Mexico. A personal narrative of six years sojourn in those regions. By the Abbe Domenech. Translated from the French under the author's superintendence. 8° *Map and pp.* xv. + 366. *London*, 1858 443

Little is to be said regarding this narrative, except that it is written by the author of *Livre des Sauvages.* But a very small portion of it relates to the Aborigines.

DOMENECH (Abbe Em.).

Seven Years Residence in the great Deserts of North America, by the Abbe Em. Domenech, Apostolical Missionary. [*etc.*, 2 *lines.*] Illustrated with fifty-eight wood-cuts by A. Joliet, three plates of Indian music, and a Map showing the actual situation of the Indian Tribes and the Country described by the Author. In two volumes. 8° Vol. I. *pp.* xxiv. + 1 *to* 445, *and* 34 *plates.* Vol. II. *pp.* xii. *and* 1 *to* 465 *and* 25 *plates. London.* 1860. 444

Whatever the length of time actually spent in the region which he professes to have traversed, the Abbe Domenech's heavy volumes contain but little more than a resumé of the Pacific Railroad Reports, with a reproduction of many of the plates published in them. He has also industriously gleaned from every source he found available, and compiled a mass of material not without value and merit. Beside the pictures of scenery obtained from various sources, the Abbe gives many representatives of Indian antiquities, utensils, and weapons. A category of the Indian Tribes of North America, and some short vocabularies of some of their languages, form perhaps the most valuable portion of these volumes. The entire absence of narrative of personal observations, effectually belies the suggestions of the title of a residence of seven years in the countries he depicts.

DOMENECH (L'Abbe Em.).

La Vèrità sur le Livre des Sauvages par L'Abbe Em. Domenech, Missionaire Apostolique, [*etc.*] 8° *Printed cover and pp.* 54 + 10 *full paged plates. Paris,* 1861. 445

The shout of laughter with which Europe resounded, at the expense of the Emperor Napoleon and his protege, the Abbe Domenech, on the appearance of his book *Le Livre des Sauvages*, had scarcely subsided when the Abbe issued this pamphlet as a defense of his unfortunate book. He founds his claim for its authenticity upon the resemblance between the schoolboy's drawings which had deluded him, and some inscriptions found on the rocks in New Mexico and Sonora, both of which he illustrates in the plates at the end of the work.

DOMINGUEZ (F.).

Catecismo de la Doctrina Cristiana puesto en el Idioma Totonaco de la Cierra Baja de Naolingo distinto del de la Cierra alta de Papantla por El Lic D Francisco Dominguez Cura itinerino de Xalpan. Reimpresso en Puebla en la imprenta del Hospital de San Pedro, 1837. 12° *pp.* 38 + 1. 446

D'ORBIGNY.

Voyage Pittoresque dans les Deux Ameriques resume general de tous les Voyages De Colomb, Las Casas, Oviedo, Gomara, Garcilaso de la Vega, Acosta, Dutertre, Labat, Stedman, La Condamine, Ulloa, Humboldt, [*and* 28 *others*, 4 *lines*] par les Redacteurs du Voyage Pittoresque autour du Monde. Publie sous la direction de M. Alcide D Orbigny Accompagne de Cartes et de Nombreusse Gravures, en taille-douce sur acier, d'apres les dessins de MM. de Sainson. *Folio.* *pp.* 568 + 268 *plates, of* 2 *on a page.* *A Paris.* 1836. 447

[A Pictorial Narrative of Voyages in the two Americas. A general resumé of all the voyages of Columbus, Las Casas, Oviedo, Gomara, Garcilaso de la Vega, Acosta, Dutertre, Labat, Stedman, La Condamine, Ulloa, Humboldt, etc., by the Editors of the Voyage Pittoresque autour du Monde. Published under the direction of M. Alcide D'Orbigny. Accompanied by Maps and numerous Engravings both Copperplate and Steel.]

This volume, comprising a resumé of the principal facts gleaned from the relations of the authors enumerated on the title-page, has little other value than is derived from the one hundred and thirty-four folio pages of steel and copper-plate engravings, of which there are two on each page. More than one half of these are illustrative of some phase in the life, customs, and history of the numerous tribes of the Indians of South America and Mexico. Brief descriptions of these facts are found in the text.

D'ORBIGNY (Alcide).

L'Homme Americain (de L'Amerique Meridionale) considéré sous ses Rapports physiologiques et Moraux; par Alcide D'Orbigny. Three vols. 2 *vols.* 8° 1 *vol. large* 4° Vol. I. *prel. pp.* 28 + 423, *two folding tables and* 1 *map.* Vol. II. *pp.* 372 + 2 *folding tables.* Vol. III. *Atlas, half title, title* + 15 *plates of crania aboriginal, Indian pottery, and monumental antiquities.* *Paris*, 1839. 448

[The American *Native* of South America, considered under his physiological and moral affinities. By Alcide D'Orbigny.]

Monsieur D'Orbigny brought to the task of examining and classifying the Aborigines of South America, a zeal, intelligence, and learning which fitted him admirably for the important labor he assumed. The peculiarities of the various races of South America had been noted with more or less discrimination by many writers, but their ethnological distinctions, the territorial boundaries of the great nations, the classification of their languages, and the grouping of the almost innumerable tribes into their parent nations, had never been treated by a man of science. The author examined personally both the natives and their locale, and accomplished as much as one man can do of the labor which will require the toil and thought of many to perfect.

DRAKE (Benj.).

The Life and Adventures of Black Hawk. with Sketches of Keokuk, the Sac and Fox Indians, and the late Black Hawk

War. Seventh edition. Improved. 18° *pp.* 288. *Cincinnati*, 1844. 449

Drake (Benjamin).
The Life and Adventures of Black Hawk, with Sketches of Keokuk, the Sac and Fox Indians, and the late Black Hawk War. By Benj. Drake. 12° *pp.* 288 + 8 *plates*. *Cincinnati*, 1838. 450

This edition differs from the subsequent ones only in some of the plates.

Drake (Benj.).
Life of Tecumseh, and of his Brother the Prophet; with a Historical Sketch of the Shawanoe Indians. By Benjamin Drake. 12° *pp.* 235. *Cincinnati, E. Morgan & Co.*, 1841. 451

Drake (S. G.).
Biography and History of the Indians of North America, from its first Discovery. By Samuel G. Drake. Eleventh edition. 8° *pp.* 720 + 8 *plates*. *Boston, Sanborn, Carter, & Bazin*, 1857. 452

The last and most complete edition of this very excellent and carefully compiled collection of the materials of Indian history. It is the result of a lifetime of labor, by one who spared no pains to be at the same time faithful to the completeness and truthfulness of history.

Drake (S. G.).
Catalogue of a Private Library principally on the antiquities, history, and biography of America, and especially of the Indians. 8° *pp.* 80. *Boston*, 1845. 453

Drake (S. G.).
The History of the Great Indian War, of 1675 and 1676, commonly called Philips War. Also the old French and Indian Wars from 1689 to 1704. By Thomas Church, Esq. With numerous Notes, and an Appendix by Samuel G. Drake. Revised edition. 12° *pp.* 360. *Hartford, Silas Andrews*, 1852. 454

Drake (S. G.).
Indian Biography. Containing the Lives of more than Two Hundred Indian Chiefs; also, such others of that Race as have rendered their names conspicuous in the History of North America, from its first being known to Europeans, to the Present Period. Giving at large their most celebrated Speeches, Memorable Sayings, Numerous Anecdotes and a History of their Wars, much of which is taken from Manuscripts never before published. 12° *pp.* 350. *Boston*, 1832. 455

The first edition of the work entitled, *Book of the Indians*, which has reached its eleventh edition.

Drake (Samuel G.).
Indian Captivities, or Life in the Wigwam, being True Narratives of Captives who have been carried away by the Indians, from the Frontier Settlements of the United States, from the earliest period to the present time. By Samuel G. Drake. 8° *pp.* 372 + 8 *plates*. *New York and Auburn, Miller, Orton, and Mulligan*, 1856. 456

Drake (Samuel G.).

A Particular History of the Five Years French and Indian War in New England and Parts Adjacent, from its declaration by the King of France, March 15, 1744, to the treaty with the Eastern Indians, Oct. 16, 1749. Sometimes called Governor Shirley's War, with a memoir of Major-General Shirley, accompanied by his portrait and other engravings. By Samuel G. Drake. 4° *pp.* 312, *and portrait. Boston, Samuel G. Drake,* 1870. 457

This very excellent and judicious collection of the principal incidents of the five years of French and Indian war, contains, beside the annals of that period, some personal narratives of much interest. In the Appendix is a reprint of a very scarce journal of captivity among the Indians, entitled "The Redeemed Captive," by the Rev. John Norton.

Drake (S. G.).

The History of King Philip's War. By the Rev. Increase Mather, D. D. Also a History of the Same War, by the Rev. Cotton Mather, D. D., to which are added, An Introduction and Notes, By Samuel G. Drake, Late President of the New England Historic-Genealogical Society. 4° *pp.* 281. *Albany, printed for the editor by J. Munsell,* 1862. 458

Editors' Preface, Explanation, and Introduction form pages xxxii. Pages 33 to 295 are occupied with a reprint of the rare work by Mather, *Brief History of the War with the Indians of New England from June 24, 1675, to August 12, 1676.* But the editor has very greatly marred the completeness of his edition by reproducing the abridged text of Cotton Mather's *The Troubles (etc.) had with the Indian Salvages,* from the Seventh Book of his *Magnalia* on the same pages, and blended with the material of the other work. The *Arma Virosq* and the *Decennium Luctuosum* would have formed a very desirable work if produced entire. The Appendix pp. 227 to 264, is composed of valuable additions to the history of the war with the Indians in the shape of narratives and letters printed from the original manuscripts. Of this work and the next following, the edition was limited to two hundred and fifty copies.

Drake (S. G.).

Early History of New England; being a Relation of Hostile Passages between the Indians and European Voyagers and First Settlers, and a full Narrative of Hostilities to the Close of the War with the Pequots in the year 1637; also a detailed account of the Origin of the War with King Philip. By Increase Mather. With an Introduction and Notes, by Samuel G. Drake. 4° *pp.* 309. *Albany, N. Y., J. Munsell,* 1861. 459

This book is a reprint of the very rare work of Increase Mather, entitled, *A Relation of the Troubles which have hap'ned in New England, By reason of the Indians there From the Year 1614 to the Year 1675. Boston John Foster* 1677. Mather's first work on the Indian Wars, was hurriedly brought forward to forestall the vastly superior one of his reverend brother, Wm. Hubbard. Nothing is more apparent than the jealousy of the eminent theologian, for as Mr. Drake observes, "When it is considered that the war was not ended until the autumn of 1676, the year in which it was printed, it must be apparent to every reader that the work was a hurried performance."

DREUILLETTES (Rev. P. Gabrielis).

Epistola Rev. P. Gabrielis Dreuillettes Societatis Jesu Presbyteri Ad Dominum Illustrissimum Dominum Joannem Wintrop Scutarium. 4° *pp.* 13. *New York*, 1864. 460

[Letter of Rev. Father Gabriel Dreuillettes, Presbyter of the Society of Jesus, to John Winthrop].

Another edition of a letter of Father Dreuillettes to John Winthrop which forms part of the *Recueil de Pieces sur la Negociation entre la Nouvelle France et Nouvelle Angleterre.* This edition is not recognized by Mr. Shea as a part of his Series of Relations.

See Historical Magazine.

No. 21 of Shea's *Jesuit Relations.*

DREUILLETTES (Pere Gabriel).

Recueil de Pièces sur la Negociation entre la Nouvelle France et la Nouvelle Angleterre, es annees 1648 et suivantes. 4° *pp.* 59. *Nouvelle York, De la Presse Cramoisy de Jean-Marie Shea*, 1866. 461

[Collection of Documents relating to the Negotiation between New France and New England in the year 1648, and subsequently].

This collection of documents consist of (1.) "The Narrative of the Voyage of Father Dreuillettes, made for the mission of the Abnaquis Indians, to induce the Magistrates of the Republique of New England to aid them against the Iroquois," pp. 5 to 24. (2.) "Reflections on the hope given the Abnaquis." (3.) "Letter of Father G. Dreuillettes to John Winthrop," in Latin. The same, translated into French. (4.) Extracts from the Journal of Father Lalemant, and the Letter written by the Council at Quebec to the New England authorities.

These documents narrate the story of that extraordinary negotiation between the authorities of Canada and the Christian Abnaquis, on the one part, and the colonies of Boston and Plymouth on the other. In September, 1651, Father Dreuillettes set out on his long and perilous mission through the wild forests intervening between Quebec and Boston, where he arrived on the eighth of September. The object of his mission was to induce the New England colonies to unite in a league with the Christian Abnaquis residing on the Kennebec against the terrible Iroquois. The minutes of this embassy were for a long period lost, which Father Charlevoix greatly lamented, and much desired to peruse. It was the good fortune of Mr. Shea to recover them, as it is ours that he possessed the generous enthusiasm of a historian in communicating them. They inform us that Father Dreuillettes was received with Christian kindness by the Puritans, and that Winthrop, Endicott, Winslow, and Bradford warmly approved his design. Four tribes of the New England Indians and a powerful Southern nation agreed to the Confederation, and Father Dreuillettes departed, with a firm conviction that his mission had succeeded. Had the Puritans carried out the terms of this treaty, it is more than probable, that New England would have escaped the bloody massacres inflicted upon her citizens during a century, by the Northern Indians.

DUDLEY (Rev. Thomas P.).

Western Reserve Historical Society, Cleveland, Ohio, August, 1870. Historical and Archaeological tracts, number one.

Battle and Massacre at Frenchtown, Michigan, January 1813. By Rev. Thomas P. Dudley, one of the Survivors. 4° *pp.* 4, *double columns. Cleveland*, 1870. 462

Four numbers have been issued, of which the last contains an account of the massacre of the Indians of Gnadenhutten, by John Heckewelder.

DUMONT (M.).

Memoires Historiques sur la Louisiane, Contenant ce qui y est arrivè de plus memorable depuis l'annee 1687, jusqu' a present; avec l'establissement de la Colonie Francoise dans cette Province de l'Amerique Septentrionale sous la direction de la Compagnie des Indes; le climat, la nature & les productions de ce pays; l'Origine & la Religion des Sauvages qui l'habiteut; leurs moeurs & leurs coutumes, &c. Composes sur les Memoires de M. Dumont, par M. L. L. M. Ouvrage enrichi de Cartes & de Figures. *A Paris, Chez ce J. B. Bauche, Libraire, Quai des Augustins, a l'image Ste Genevieve*, 1753. *Avec Approbation & Privilige du Roi. Two vols.* 24°. Vol. I. *Half title, title, 2 leaves + pp.* x. + 261 + *map and 2 plates.* Vol. II. *Half title, title 2 leaves + pp.* 338 + 4 *plans.* 463

[Historic Memoirs of Louisiana: Containing an account of that which passed the most memorable, from the year 1687 to the present; with the establishment of the French Colony in this Province of North America under the direction of the India Company; the climate, the nature, and the productions of the country; the Origin and the Religion of the Savages who inhabit it; their manners and their customs, etc. Composed from the Memoirs of M. Dumont by M. L. L. M.]

The author has in pp. 117 to 338, Vol. I., treated minutely the subject of the customs and ceremonies of the aborigines of the province, and almost the whole of Vol. II. is devoted to the history of the wars of the French with the various tribes which inhabited the vast territory then known as Louisiana. The editor of Dumont's Memoirs has told the story of the events of this border warfare in a style at once concise and interesting, but with few of the details and minute particulars which we so much desire at this period.

The work is embellished with maps and plates. It is found in some Catalogues under Butel-Dumont. Mr. French translated the Historical Narrative, and printed it in Volume V. of the *Louisiana Historical Collections.*

DUNCAN (William).

The Gospel in the Far West Metlahkatlah. Ten Years' Work among the Tsimsheean Indians. Third Edition. 12° *pp.* 130 + *map. Church Missionary House, Salisbury Square (London).* 1869. 464

The Tshimshean Indians occupy a district on the Pacific coast lying between Fraser and Simpson rivers, north of Queen Charlotte's Sound. They are divided into ten tribes, speaking the same dialect, each governed by three or four chiefs. The elevation of rank to which each is entitled is indicated by the height of a pole erected in front of his wigwam. So imperial is the dignity to which some eminent savages attain, that it can only be shown by a pole one hundred feet in height. Sanguinary fights are caused by the erection of too high a pole, and a beaten chief is literally obliged to eat his stick. Mr. Duncan spent ten years in his efforts to Christianize the members of this confederacy of savage tribes. The work is a relation of his labors and their results drawn up from his letters and reports, by some friend in England, principally in the language of their writer. In addition to the difficulties and dangers of a missionary's labors among a savage people, he had to contend with the most besotted stupidity, and mulish obstinacy and apathy, which ever characterized a race. One of the pleasing pastimes of the chiefs was to nourish a design, for three or four days, of killing some person, without any animosity against him or her except pure appetite for bloodshed, of which every Indian was aware except the doomed wretch himself.

DUNHAM (Captain John).
Journal of Voyages, containing an account of the authors being twice captured by the English and once by Gibbs the Pirate, his narrow escape when chased by an English War Schooner, as well as his being cast away and residing with Indians, to which is added * * *. With illustrations. 12° *New York*, 1831. 465

DUNN (John).
History of the Oregon Territory and British North-American Fur Trade; with An Account of the habits and customs of the principal native tribes on the northern continent. By John Dunn, late of the Hudson's Bay Company; eight years a resident in the country. 8° *pp.* viii. + 359 + *map.* *London, Edwards and Hughes*, 1844. 466

DUNN (John).
The Oregon Territory and the British North American Fur Trade. With an Account of the Habits and Customs of the principal Native Tribes of the Northern Continent. By John Dunn, late of the Hudson's Bay Company; eight years a resident in that country. 16° *pp.* viii. + 13–236. *Philadelphia, G. B. Zeiber & Co.*, 1845. 467

DUPAIX (Captain).
Antiquites Mexicaines. Relation Des Trois Expeditions du Capitaine Dupaix ordonnez en 1805, 1806 et 1807 pour la Recherche des Antiquites du Pays notamment celles de Milla et de Palenque; accompagnee des dessins de Castañeda et d'une carte du pays exploree [*for remainder of Title, see Lenoir, Warden*]; Farcy St. Priest. *Two vols. large folio.* Vol. I. *Texte pp.* 18 + 20 + 56 + 40 + 92 + 82 + 228, *total pp.* 537. Vol. II. *Plates*, 166. *A Paris, Imprimerie de Jules Didot l'Aine*, 1834 468

DU PONCEAU.
Memoire sur le Systeme Grammatical des Langues de Quelques Nations Indiennes de L'Amerique Du Nord; ouvrage qui a la Seance publique Annuelle de L'Institut Royal De France le 2 Mai 1835. A remporte le prix fondè par M. le Comte de Volney, Par M. P. et Du Ponceau, LL. D. 8° *pp.* 464. *Paris*, 1838. 469

[Memoir of a Grammatical System of the Languages of some Indian Nations of North America; a work which at a public session of the Royal Institute of France was reported for the prize founded by M. Count Volney. Written by Mr. P(ickering) and Du Ponceau.]

One of the first attempts subsequent to that of Mr. Gallatin to systematize the aboriginal languages; and determine the laws of their construction. The peculiarity of their formation, now styled the aggregative, as announced by that gentleman, excited great surprise among the savants of France.

DUPONCEAU & FISHER.
A Memoir on the History of the Celebrated Treaty made by

William Penn with the Indians, under the Elm Tree at Shackamoxon in the year 1682. By Peter S. Du Ponceau and T. Francis Fisher. 8° *pp.* 63. *Philadelphia*, 1836. 470

Report made to the Historical Society of Pennsylvania.

Du Pratz (Le Page). See Le Page Du Pratz. 471

Earle (John Milton).

Report to the Governor and Council concerning the Indians of the Commonwealth (Massachusetts), under the Act of April 6, 1859. By John Milton Earle, Commissioner. 8° *pp.* 147 + *pp.* lxxxiv. *Boston*, 1861. 472

Early History

Of Western Pennsylvania. And of the West and of Western Expeditions and Campaigns, from 1744 to 1833, by a Gentleman of the Bar. With an Appendix containing besides copious extracts from important Indian Treaties, Minutes of Conferences, Journals, etc. A topographical description of the Counties of Allegheny, Westmoreland, Washington, Somerset, Greene, Fayette, Beaver, Butler, Armstrong, etc. Illustrated by several drawings. 8° *pp.* 352 + *Appendix, pp.* 406 + *Index,* 10 *pp., total pp.* 768 + 2 *folding plans. Pittsburg, Pa., Daniel W. Kaufman; Harrisburg, Pa., William O. Hickox*, 1846. 473

The whole of the text of this volume is devoted to the history and incidents of expeditions against the Indians of Western Pennsylvania; the siege of frontier forts by the savages, and the massacres of white families along the border settlements. The Appendix, occupying more than half the work, is composed of long extracts from the journals of Conrad Weiser, George Croghan, General Washington, Christian Post, Alex. McKee, General St. Clair, the letters of General Braddock and General Harmar, and copies of the treaties made with the Indians. It is a good compilation of most of the material relating to Indian wars, already accessible in the original memoirs.

Eastburn (Robert).

A Faithful | Narrative, | of | The many Dangers and Sufferings, as well as | wonderful Deliverances of Robert East | burn during his Captivity among the | Indians: Together with some Remarks | upon the Country of Canada, and the | Religion and Policy of its Inhabitants; the | whole intermixed with devout Reflections. | By Robert Eastburn. | Published at the earnest Request of many | Friends for the benefit of the Author. | With a recommendatory Preface by the | Rev. Gilbert Tennent. | [*Psalm* cxxiv. 6 *and* 7, *six lines.*] *Title*, 1 *p.* "*Preface,*" *commencing on reverse,* 2 *pp.* "*Gilbert Tennent, Kind Readers,*" *middle of pp.* 3 *to* 4. "*A Faithful Narrative, &c.*" *pp.* 5 *to* 45, *reverse of p.* 45, *Advertisement. Philadelphia* | *printed by William Dunlap*, 1758. | 474

This is one of the rarest of Indian captivities, being exceeded in that quality only by Dickenson's *God's Protecting Providence*, and Gyles' *Odd Adventures and Captivity*. A second edition was printed in Boston the same year, and a third in Philadelphia, 1828, with a separate title, as a sequel to a memoir of the author.

Eastburn (Robert).
Same. Reprinted in Memoir of Joseph Eastburn. 12° *Philadelphia*, 1828. 475

Eastburn (James W.).
Yamoyden, a tale of the Wars of King Philip: In Six Cantos. By the late Rev. James Wallis Eastburn and his friend. 12° *pp.* xii. + 339. *Plate and vignette title. New York, published by James Eastburn*, 1820. 476

Two college youths (both authors being less than twenty years of age), having written a poem with Indian characters, proceeded to examine history a little for notes to illustrate it. They found, as the surviving editor frankly says, that history and their poem were quite divergent. They could not correct the poem without destroying its whole scheme, so they printed eight pages of historical notes at the end as a corrective.

Eastman (Mary H.).
Chicora and other regions of the Conquerors and the Conquered. By Mrs. Mary H. Eastman. *Small folio.* 126 *pp. and* 21 *fine steel engravings of scenes in Indian life and history. Philadelphia*, 1854. 477

A beautiful book upon aboriginal manners and history, written by a lady and illustrated by her husband, both of whom were well fitted for the task by long residence among the Indians. The book was reprinted under the title of *The American Annual.* The same work appeared also as the *Aboriginal Portfolio.*

Eastman (Mrs. Mary).
Dahcotah, or Life and Legends of the Sioux around Fort Snelling, by Mrs. Mary Eastman, with Preface by Mrs. C. M. Kirkland. Illustrated from drawings by Captain Eastman. 12° *pp.* xl. + 268. *New-York*, 1849. 478

Easton (John).
A | Narrative | Of the Causes which led to | Philip's Indian War, | of 1675 and 1676. | By John Easton, of Rhode Island, | With other Documents concerning this | Event in the office of the Secretary of | State of New York. | Prepared from the originals, with an | Introduction and Notes. | By Franklin B. Hough. | 4° *Map, title and pref. pp.* 1 *to* xxiii. + *pp.* 207. *Albany, N. Y.* | *J. Munsell*, 78 *State Street*, | 1858. | 479

Edition limited to one hundred copies.
The author of this Relation was a Quaker residing in Ipswich and Hampton, who was driven, by the intolerance of the Puritans, to Rhode Island in 1638. He suffered in person from the incursions of the Indians, who burned his house at Newport the next year. Easton is the only early writer upon the wars of the New Englanders with the Indians who ventures to doubt that the Almighty was on the side of the slaughtering Puritans; and Satan himself commanding the savages. He seems anxious to give an impartial and just relation of the war and its causes; but, like all the members of his sect, could not resist the sympathy which that sense of justice aroused. He shows clearly that the greed and cupidity of the stern Puritans, were as potent causes of an unnecessary and cruel war upon the wronged owners of the soil, as they are to-day in our age of Indian agents and speculators.

EATON (John Henry).

The Life of Andrew Jackson, Major General in the Service of the United States, comprising A History of the War in the South from the Commencement of the Creek Campaign, to the termination of Hostilities before New Orleans. By John Henry Eaton. *Large 8° Portrait, and pp.* 468. *Philadelphia, published by Samuel F. Blatchford,* 1824. 480

The history of the war with the Creek Indians is given with great minuteness in chapters ii., iii., iv., v., vi., pp. 28 to 217.

EATON (Cyrus).

Annals of the Town of Warren with the Early History of St. George's, Broad Bay and the Neighboring Settlements on the Waldo Patent. By Cyrus Eaton, A. M. 8° *pp.* 436. *Hallowell, Masters, Smith, and Co.,* 1851. 481

The narrative of the wars with the Eastern Indians, is illustrated with many new incidents and adventures derived from manuscript journals and from tradition.

ECKLEY (Joseph).

A Discourse before the Society for Propagating the Gospel among the Indians and others in North America, delivered November 7, 1805, by Joseph Eckley, D. D., minister of the old South Church in Boston. 8° *pp.* 36. *With an Appendix. Boston,* 1806. 482

EDWARDS (Frank S.).

A Campaign in New Mexico with Colonel Doniphan, by Frank S. Edwards, a Volunteer. With a map of the route, and a table of the distances traversed. 12° *pp.* 181. *Philadelphia,* 1847. 483

Some accounts of the Apaches and Mexican Indians are blended with the narrative.

EDEN (Richarde).

The Decades | of the newe Worlde or | west India, | Conteynyng the nauigations and conquestes | of the Spaniardes, with the particular de | scription of the most ryche and large landes | and Ilandes lately founde in the west Ocean | perteynyng to the inheritaunce of the Kinges | of Spayne. In the which the diligent reader | may not only consyder what commoditie may | hereby chaunce to the hole Christian world in | tyme to come, but also learne many secreates | touchynge the lande, the sea, and the Starres, | very necessarie to be knowne to al such as shal | attempte any nauigations, or otherwise | haue delite to beholde the strange | and woonderfull woorkes of | God and nature. | Wrytten in the Latine tounge by Peter | Martyr of Angleria, | and trans | lated into Englysshe by Richarde Eden. 4° 24 *leaves* + 361 *leaves folioed* + ' *Contentes and Faultes* ' | 13 *leaves* + *portrait. Londoni.* | *In aedibus Guilhelmi Powell* | *Anno* 1555. 484

The first English translation of a portion of Peter Martyr's work, containing the first three Decades. To Richarde Eden Mr. Rich devotes a page of eloquent praise, and quotes the glowing passage in his preface in which he recites the motive which prompted the work. These Decades, first printed in Latin in 1516, contain probably the first systematic and critical narration of the peculiarities of religion and customs of the American Indians. Both this and the subsequent edition of 1577 are considered among the rarities of bibliography. In catalogues of recent issue in England, the prices at which copies have been offered vary from £15 to £21. Although valued principally for that portion translated from Peter Martyr, the work is usually accredited to and catalogued under Eden, as he was the author, or at least the editor, of much the larger portion of it. Subsequent editions of the eight decades are noticed under the name of Peter Martyr.

EDEN (Richarde).

THE | History of Trauayle | In the | VVest and East Indies and other | countreys lying eyther way | towardes the fruitfull and ryche | Moluccaes. | As | Moscouia, Persia, Arabia, Syria, Ægypt, | Ethiopia, Guinea, China in Cathayo and | Giapan. VVith a discourse of | the Northwest pas | sage.

In the hands of our Lorde be all the corners of | the Earth Psal. 94 | Gathered in parte and done into Englyshe by *Richarde Eden.* Newly set in order, augmented and finished by Richarde VVilles | *Imprinted at London* | *by Richarde Iugge* 1577 *Cum Priuilegio.*

Small 4° *Title*, 1 *leaf. The Epistle*, 5 *leaves. To the Reader*, 3 *leaves. Certayne Preambles*, 1 *leaf, and* 1 *to* 466 *leaves, errata and table*, 6 *leaves.* 485

This second English translation of a part of Peter Martyr's (Anghiera) *Decades of the New World*, bears not the slightest recognition of its real author on the title-page. Willes added to this edition a translation of a part of the Fourth Decade of Peter Martyr's work, but without the division into books which Eden preserved. This additional portion is almost wholly descriptive of the peculiarities of the aborigines, and terminates with folio 178. A compilation from Oviedo and other writers occupies folios 183 to 236. The remainder of the work, like the edition of 1555, contains nothing relating to America.

EDWARDS (J.).

Some account of the Life of the Rev. David Brainard. Minister of the Gospel, Missionary to the Indians from the Honorable Society in Scotland. &c., who died at Northampton, in New England, October 9th, 1747, in the 30th year of his age; chiefly from his own Diary and other private writings. By Jonathan Edwards, A. M. To which are added Extracts from Mr. Brainard's Journal, comprising the most material things in that Publication. 8° *Worcester, Mass.,* 1793. 486

EDWARDS (Jonathan, D. D.).

Observations on the Language of the Muhhekanew Indians in which The extent of that Language in North America is shewn, its Genius is grammatically traced, some of its peculiarities and some Instances of Analogy between that and the Hebrew are Pointed out. Communicated to the Connecticut Society of Arts and Sciences, and published at the Request of the Society. By Jonathan Edwards, D. D. *New Haven, printed by Josiah Meiggs*, 1787. 8° *pp.* 15. *Reprinted London*, 1788. 487

The very able author of this treatise was not the first to analyze the Aboriginal language of New England, and reduce it to rules, yet his brief work is remarkable for suggesting the radical basis of the Muhhekaneew dialect, and exhibiting its structural difference from the Mohawk. He was however the first to show the affinity of all the Algonquin dialects, and trace the basal relationship of all the Eastern tongues with those of the Long Island, Delaware, Shawnese and Chippeway Indians. He was eminently fitted for this service to ethnology from his peculiar fortune in being associated with all these tribes. Commencing a familiar acquaintance with the Mohegans at Stockbridge, when only six years of age, and at a period when the town contained but twelve families of European lineage to one hundred and fifty of Indian birth, his youth was spent with the native boys for schoolmates and playfellows. Out of his father's house he seldom heard the enunciation of any language but that spoken by Indian tongues. To him, therefore, the Mohegan language became his vernacular. In his tenth year he was sent among the Six Nations to learn their language, and thus, although resident with them for less than a year, became fitted for his work of comparison of the two radically different tongues. The obvious difference between the guttural, harsh, and by civilized organs almost unpronounceable language of the Six Nations, and the liquid flowing tongue of the Mohegan and New England tribes, could not but elicit his attention and curiosity in after life to analyze the causes of this diversity. The following are the principal characteristics of these tongues he notices; No word of the Iroquois corresponds to any of the Algonquin. The Algonquin has no gender, no infinitive mood, or abstract verb. The action always is associated in expression with the noun, no relative pronouns, no abstract adjective, as quality is always expressed by varying the noun, a different noun being used to express differing qualities of the same thing. Thus, there are no abstract terms for things commonly expressed with relation to other nouns. The Iroquois dialects have few if any labials, the Algonquin abounds in them. It is impossible to express a simple action in either tongue as, *John strikes*. The action must always be connected with its nominative, and if transitive, in connection with both nominative and objective, and even then by the circumlocutory phrase "*John he strikes him Peter.*" All these curious philological traits are very clearly analyzed in this treatise.

EGEDE (Hans).

A Description of Greenland. By Hans Egede, who was a Missionary in that Country for Twenty-five Years. A New edition, with an Historical Introduction and a Life of the Author. Illustrated with a Map of Greenland, and numerous engravings on wood, &c. *Second edition.* 8° *pp.* cliii. *and* 225. *London*, 1818. 488

Chapters vii. to xx., pp. 100 to 225, are devoted to descriptions of the occupations, implements, habitations, persons, customs, habits, mourning, pastimes, etc., of the natives of Greenland.

In chapter xv. is given a specimen of one of their songs in the Esquimaux language with the parallel passages in English, occupying four pages. Chapter xvi. treats of the principles of that tongue with a vocabulary and grammatical analysis of twelve pages. Although the quaint relation of the Danish missionary Egede affords us little information regarding the natives of Greenland which has not often been printed, yet his narratives of incidents among them, and descriptions of their characteristics at that early day (1721), are valuable as historical records.

ELDRIDGE (Eleanor).

Memoirs of Eleanor Eldridge. 2 *vols.* *Square* 16° *pp.* 128 *and* 128. *Providence, B. T. Albro, printer*, 1841. 489

The subject of this narrative was the granddaughter of a Narragansett Indian squaw and an African chief, and is interesting ethnologically, as portraying the characteristics of two aboriginal races blended.

ELIOT (John).

The | Glorious Progress | of the | Gospel | amongst the | Indians in New England. | Manifested | By three Letters under the Hand of that fa | mous Instrument of the Lord, Mr. John Eliot, | And another from *Mr. Thomas Mayhew*, Jun: both Preachers of | the Word as well to the *English as Indians in New England* | WHEREIN | the riches of Gods Grace in the effectuall calling of | many of them is cleared up: As also a manifestation of the hungring | desires of many People in Sundry parts of that Country after the | more full Revelation of the Gospel of *Jesus Christ* to the | exceeding Consolation of every Christian Reader. | Together, | with an Appendix to the foregoing letters hol | ding forth Conjectures Observations, and Applications. | By I D Minister of the Gospell | Published by Edward Winslow | *Small* 4° *Title, reverse blank + Epistle Dedicatory* 3 *leaves* + 4 *leaves not paged* + 9 *to* 28. *London, printed for Hannah Allen in Pope's-head-Alley*, 1649. 490

Reprinted pp. 68 to 98 of Vol. IV., third series, Massachusetts Historical Society's Collection.

This is the fourth of that series of reports of the "Corporation for Propagating the Gospel among the Indians of New England," which began in 1643, and continued at irregular intervals to 1671. The complete series consists of eleven, and is probably, next to the Jesuit Relations, the most difficult to reassemble in good copies, of any works relating to American History. Some of these Protestant relations of missions among the Indians, bring almost fabulous prices. One hundred and seventy dollars has been paid for that of 1659 (No. 9), and one hundred dollars was paid both by Mr. Menzies and myself for that of 1671. They are doubtless all written by the hand, or from material furnished by the writings of John Eliot. No series of works relating to American history are more sought for; and the collector who possesses a large part of either the Catholic or Protestant Relations of Missions, while he has something to boast of, has still a long period of expectancy to keep alive his interest, before he will complete either one of them.

Under the title of "Eliot Tracts," — nowhere recognized, perhaps, except in the caste nomenclature of bibliophiles, — the reports of John Eliot, Whitfield, and others, to the "Corporation for the Propagation of the Gospel among the Indians," are collectively designated. They were issued under the following titles and order: —

No. 1. *New England's First Fruits in respect . . . . of the Indians.* 4° London, 1643.

2. *The Day-Breaking if not the Sun-Rising of the Gospel with the Indians in New-England.* 4° London, 1647.

3. *The Clear Sun-shine of the Gospel breaking forth upon the Indians of New-England.* By Thos. Shepard, London, 1648.

4. *The Glorious Progress of the Gospel amongst the Indians in New-England.* Published by Edward Winslow, London, 1649.

5. *The Light appearing . . . . or A farther Discovery of the present State of the Indians.* Published by Henry Whitfield, London, 1651.

6. *Strength out of Weakness Or a Glorious Manifestation Of the further Progress of the Gospel among the Indians in New England.* London, 1652.

7. *Tears of Repentance Or A further Narrative of the Progress of the Gospel*

Amongst the Indians in New England. Related by Mr. Eliot. 4° London, 1653.

8. *A late and further manifestation of the Gospel amongst the Indians in New England.* London, 1655.

9. *A Further Accompt of the Progresse of the Gospel amongst the Indians in New England.* London, 1659.

10. *A further Account of the progress of the Gospel Amongst the Indians in New-England.* London, 1660

11. *A Brief Narrative of the Progress of the Gospel amongst the Indians in New England.* Given in By the Reverend Mr. John Eliot, London, 1671.

Only two entire sets of these tracts, it is believed, exist in this country. Nos. 9 and 8 I have never been able to obtain. Their full titles will be found in this catalogue under the Alphabetic Classification, except No. 2 attributed to Shepherd; No. 5 to Whitfield.

Eliot (John).

A Brief | NARRATIVE | of the | Progress of the Gospel amongst | the Indians in New-England, in | the year 1670. | Given In | By the Reverend Mr. John Elliot, | Minister of the Gospel there. | In a Letter by him directed to | the Right Worshipfull the Com- | missioners under his Majesties | Great-Seal for Propagation of the | Gospel amongst the poor blind Na- | tives in these United Colonies. | *London, | printed for John Allen, formerly living in Little-Britain at | the Rising-Sun, and now in Wentworth Street, near Bell- | Lane,* 1671. *Title, reverse blank, To the Right Worshipfull, pp.* 3 *to* 11, *reverse of* 11 *blank.* 491

Eliot (John).

A Brief Narrative of the Progress of the Gospel among the Indians of New England. 1670. By Rev. John Eliot. With Introductory Notes by W. T. R. Marvin. *Half title, Title and Prefatory Note, 8 pp. "Bibliographic Note" (of the Works of John Eliot)* 9 *to* 16. *"A Brief Narrative," reprint of the edition of* 1671, *pp.* 17 *to* 36. *Boston, John K. Wiggin & Wm. Parsons Lunt,* 1868. 492

This is a reprint of one of the rarest of the series of reports of the progress of the Missions among the Indians of New England.

Eliot (John).

A Late and Further | Manifestation | of the | Progress of the Gospel | amongst the | Indians | in | Nevv England | . Declaring their constant Love and Zeal | to the Truth: With a readinesse to give | Accompt of their Faith and Hope as of | their desires in Church Commu- | nion to be Partakers of | the Ordinances of | Christ. | Being a Narrative of the Examinations of the Indians about their | Knowledge in Religion, by the Elders of the Churches. | Related by Mr. John Eliot. | Published by the Corporation, established by Act of Parliament, for Propagating the Gospel there. | Acts 13, 47. [2 *lines.*] *Title* 1 *p., reverse blank. Certificate* 1 *p., reverse blank. "To all that pray," etc.,* 3 *pp., reverse blank. "A Brief Narration," pp.* 1 *to* 10. *"The Examination of the Indians at Roxbury," pp.* 11 *to* 23. *Total pp.* 31. *London, printed by M. S.,* 1655. 493*

ELIOT (John) and Mayhew, Mr.

Tears of Repentance: | Or, A further | Narrative of the Progress of the *Gospel* | Amongst the | Indians | In | New-England: | Setting forth, not only their present state | and condition, but sundry confessions of sin | by diverse of the said *Indians*, wrought upon | by the saving Power of the Gospel; Together | with the manifestation of their Faith and Hope | in Jesus Christ, and the Work of Grace upon | their Hearts. | Related by Mr. Eliot and Mr. Mayhew, two Faithful Laborers | in that work of the Lord. | Published by the Corporation for propagating the Gospel there, for the | Satisfaction and comfort of such as wish well thereunto. [*Motto.*] *London: Printed by Peter Cole in Leaden-Hall, and are to be Sold at | his Shop, at the Sign of the Printing-Press in Cornhill | near the Royal Exchange.* 1653. | 4° 18 *prel. leaves, viz. Title* 1 *leaf;* "*To His Excellency*" 1 *leaf;* "*To the Corporation;*" "*Letters from Mayhew and Eliot;*" "*To the Reader;*" "*To the Christian Reader*" + *pp.* 47 *entitled* "*A Brief Relation.*" 494

ELIOT (John).

The | Holy Bible: | containing the | Old Testament | and the New. | Translated into the | Indian Language, | and | Ordered to be printed by the Commissioners of the Vnited Colonies | in New-England. | At the Charge, and with the Consent of the | Corporation in England | For the Propagation of the Gospel amongst the Indians | In New England. | Cambridge: | Printed by Samuel Green and Marmaduke Johnson. | MDCLXIII. 495

The collation of this memorable work of the Apostle Eliot is rendered much more difficult by the entire absence of pagination; and the variations made apparently by the translator himself. A few copies, said by Thomas to have been not more than twenty, were sent to England, with a dedication to King Charles of two leaves. Others have an English title, in place of the Indian, and a few have both. A perfect copy may be deemed to consist of the following named contents: Title 1 leaf + Contents 1 leaf + Text A to M.m.m.m.m. in fours, or 416 leaves for the Old Testament. *Title of New Testament*: Wusku | Wuttestamentum, | Nul-Lordumun | Jesus Christ | Nuppoquohwussuaeneumun. | Cambridge: Printed by Samuel Green and Marmaduke Johnson | MDCLXI. 1 leaf. Verso blank. Text: Matthew to the end of Luke, signatures A[4] to reverse of L[4]. John to Revelations, Aa to reverse of Xx[4] all in fours. *Psalms*: VVame-Ketoohomaeuketoo homaoe gush | David, signatures U to N, in fours. Noowomoo (Catechism) 1 leaf. Total leaves of New Testament, Psalms, and Catechism, 178, or 594 leaves for the complete work.

It will be seen that the New Testament was printed two years previous to the other portion of the Scriptures. Not the least of the many features of interest which concentrate in this volume, are the statements of undoubted authorities, that Eliot was engaged for ten years in its translation; that it was the first Bible printed in America; that a large portion of the composition in the printing of the second edition at least, was performed by Indian James; and that the work was three years in passing through the press. But it exists for us like some vast monolith erected by a race which has passed away. Every individual who could speak, or understand the divine words uttered in that tongue, perished a century ago. It remained for a scholar of our generation, Mr. J. Hammond Trumbull, to revive this extinct language, and he has found in its study something more than the mere gratification of literary curiosity. The edition of fifteen hundred copies recommended to be printed by the Corporation, was exhausted in twenty years. Even the "two hundred copies of the New Testament, strongly bound in leather for the immediate use of the Indians," were probably worn out. Accordingly in 1680 another edition of two thousand of the New Testament was printed; and in 1685, the same number of the Old Testament. The second edition is complete with 607 leaves, the Old Testament containing 425; the New Testament 131; Psalms and Catechism 51 leaves. Eliot did not receive from the Pilgrim fathers that aid in his great work which he had a right to demand. The funds raised in England for Christianizing the Indians were diverted from that purpose, by the Puritan authorities; and it was not until peremptory orders from the Corporation compelled them to restore them that he found them available for his designs.

Although this work was considered so exceedingly rare a few years since, that it was asserted that but three copies were known to exist, the zeal of American bibliophilists has brought to light in this country no less than 23 copies of the first edition. They are distributed in the libraries of the following named gentlemen: Hon. Henry C. Murphy, Brooklyn, L. I., 2; Mr. T. W. Field, Brooklyn, L. I., 1; Mr. John H. King (deceased), Jamaica, L. I., 1; Mr. John G. Gardiner, Gardeners, L. I., 1; Long Island Historical Society (very imperfect), L. I., 1; Mr. James Lenox, New York, 2; Mr. William Menzies, New York, 1; Mr. Edward Everett (deceased), Boston, 1; Mr. George Brinley, Hartford, 1; Mr. J. Hammond Trumbull, Hartford, 1; Mr. John Carter Brown, Providence, 1; Mr. George Livermore (deceased), Cambridge, 1; Harvard University, 1; American Antiquarian Society, 1; New York Historical Society, 1; Boston Athenæum, 1; Massachusetts Historical Society, 1; Brown University, 1; Congregational Church, Newport, 1; Loganian Library, Philadelphia, 1; American Phil. Society, Philadelphia, 1.

Notwithstanding this considerable number of known copies in this country, in addition to at least nine in Europe, the price of each successive copy offered for sale has been greatly augmented above the last. The copy belonging to Mr. John A. Rice had been bought for £100 in 1863, but was sold in 1869 for $1,050. Twenty years since Mr. Murphy bought one of his copies in London for twenty shillings, and in 1870 Mr. Quarritch sold another for £250, or nearly two thousand dollars of the United States currency of that date.

ELIOT (John).

See Mather, Life of Eliot; Moore, Life of Eliot; Francis, Life of Eliot; Vol. V. Sparks' Biographies. 496

ELLIS (Edward S.).

The Life of Tecumseh the Shawnee Chief, including Biographical Notices of Black Hoof, Cornplanter, Little Turtle, Tarhe (the Crane), Captain Logan, Keokuk, and other distinguished Shawnee Chiefs. By Edward S. Ellis. 12° *pp.* 98. *New York, Beadle and Company, publishers.* 497

A cheap publication of a cheap collection of the principal incidents in the life of the Shawnee chief, easily available in half a score of publications.

ELLIS (M.).

New Britain. A Narrative of a Journey, by Mr. Ellis, to a country so called by its inhabitants, discovered in the vast plains of the Missouri in North America, and inhabited by a people of British Origin. [*etc.*, 9 *lines.*] 8° *pp.* 336. *London*, 1820. 498

There is not the slightest attempt made in this work to conceal its fictitious character, except on the title-page. It is a romance of the allegorical class, written to illustrate some notions of government which infested the author's brain.

ELIZA.

The Chippeway Indian. 8° *pp.* 8. *American Tract Society, (New York.)* 499

EMORY (W. H.).

Notes of a Military Reconnoissance from Fort Leavenworth in Missouri to San Diego in California including parts of the Arkansas, Del Norte, and Gila Rivers. By W. H. Emory. 8° *Plates and maps. Washington*, 1848. 500

This work contains some interesting particulars concerning the Pimo, Apache, Navajo, and Maricopa Indians, with several engravings of Indian antiquities, portraits of women and chiefs of these tribes, and of scenes in the country inhabited by them. One of these plates represents the Aztec temple of Pecos, where the sacred fire of Montezuma was kept burning by the zeal of his worshippers until 1841.

E[NGEL] (E. B. d').

Essai Sur Cette question. Quand et Comment L'Amerique A-T-Elle ete peuplée, d'hommes et d'animaux par E. B. d' E[ngel]. 2 vols. 12° Vol. I. *pp.* xxii. + (vi.) + 454. Vol. II. *pp.* (ii.) + 384. *Amsterdam*, 1767. 501

E[NGEL] (E. B. d').

Essai Sur Cette question: Quand et Comment L'America A'telle ete peuplee d'hommes et d'animaux? Par E. B. d'E[ngel]. 4° *pp.* xiv. + 610. *A Amsterdam, Chez Marc Michel Rey*, 1767. 502

[Essay on this question: When and how has America been peopled with men and animals? by E. B. d'Engel.]

D'Engel, with great sounding of trumpets, that he is about to propound a theory of the population of America both novel and impregnable, asserts that it was antediluvian in its origin. He berates Grotius, DeLaet, and Hornius in detail, but he groups Acosta, Lescarbot, Brerewood, and Mornay with "plusiers ecrivains," and dismisses them altogether with contempt. He argues at great length to reconcile his theory with the sacred writings, and to account for the but partial submersion of the surface of the globe.

ESQUEMELING (John).

Bucaniers | of | America: | Or, a true | Account | of the | Most remarkable Assaults | Committed of late years upon the Coasts of | The West-Indies, | By the Bucaniers of Jamaica and Tortuga, | Both English and French. | Wherein are contained more especially, | The unparallel'd Exploits of Sir Henry Morgan, our En | glish Jamaican Hero, who Sack'd Puerto Velo, burnt Panama &c. | Written originally in Dutch, by John Esquemeling, one of the | Bucaniers, who was present at those Tragedies; and thence | translated into Spanish by Alonso de Bonne-Maison, Doctor of | Physick and Practitioner at Amsterdam. | Now faithfully rendered into English. | 4° *Pref. pp.* (xli.) *Text in Three Parts.* Part I. *pp.* 115. Part II. *pp.* 152. Part III. *pp.* 124. *The Table (of the 3 books) pp.* xl. + *nine plates, three of which are double. London, Printed for William Crooke, at the Green Dragon with | out Temple Bar*, 1684. | 503

This is the first English edition complete in three parts, the text of which is a beautiful specimen of the quaint clear typography of the day, being greatly superior to the following.

ESQUEMELING (John).

Bucaniers of America, &c. [*Same title*]. Second Edition, Corrected and Inlarged, with two Additional Relations, viz., the one of Captain Cook, and the other of Captain Sharp. Now faithfully rendered into English. Part I. *pp.* 53. Part II. *pp.* 80. Part III. *pp.* 84 + *table* (xii.). Second volume, Part IV. *pp.* 8 + 212 + *table* 17 + *four portraits and six plates. London,* 1684. 504

This, although with the same date, is really a different, somewhat later, and generally inferior edition to the first. The only point of superiority consists in the addition of the fourth part. The type from which it was printed, was much smaller, of a meaner style and worn, the paper of a poorer quality, and the general appearance greatly inferior.

The first three books of the second edition are not unfrequently found unaccompanied by the fourth, and the imperfect work is believed to be complete on account of the finis and the table.

The relations of the Buccaneers are full of particulars of the Indians who two centuries since inhabited the islands and the main of the Caribbean Sea. A description of the customs of the natives of Yucatan may be found in Part II. pp. 43 to 47 of the first edition, and of the encounters of the Buccaneers with them on pp. 51 to 57 and pp. 36 to 43 of Part III. Chapters vii. and viii., pp. 77 to 105 of the same part, are almost wholly occupied with a description of the habits, religion, and mode of warfare of the Indians of Costa Rica, with cuts of their weapons. The fierce French and English marauders, who so constantly overcame the Spaniards, were as constantly checked or defeated whenever they assailed the Indians of the Isthmus or the adjacent countries. But the most noteworthy historical fact elucidated by this volume, is the proof of the retributive fruit of vengeance forever produced from the vile seeds of cruelty. The Spaniard, who for a century and a half had devastated the countries of the Indians, with cruelties born of hell, was now to become the prey of fiends as ferocious and vindictive but more powerful than himself. There were burnings at the stake, there were venerable men flayed alive, beautiful women forced to submit to the lust of the most loathsome of the human race, children impaled on bayonets, and men hung by their privates; but the victims were no longer miserable Indians. Alas, they were not even the perpetrators of the cruelties suffered by the natives. The sins of the fathers shall be visited upon the children.

ESQUIMAUX.

Testamentetak tamedsa nalegapta pluti-Jiptа Jesusib Kristusib Apostelingitalo, pinniarningit okausingillo. Printed for The British and Foreign Bible Society, For the use of the Christian Esquimaux in the Mission-Settlements of the United Brethren on the Coast of Labrador. 12° *pp.* 637. *London, W. McDowell, printer,* 1840. 505

The New Testament of our Lord Jesus Christ translated into the Esquimaux language.

ESQUIMAUX VOCABULARY.

See Washington, Capt. John. 506

ESQUIMAUX (Gospel of St. John).

Tamedsa Johannesib aglangit, okautsinik tussarnertunik Jesuse Kristusemik Gudim erngninganik. Printed for The British and Foreign Bible Society For the Use of the Christian Esquimaux

In the Mission-Settlements of the United Brethren at Nain, Okkak, and Hopedale on the Coast of Labrador. 12° *Title and pp.* 124. *Londonnnne*, 1810. 507

EVANS (Governor).

(Massacre of the Cheyenne Indians.)

Reply of Governor Evans of the Territory of Colorado. To that part referring to him of the Report of the Conduct of the War, headed Massacre of the Cheyenne Indians. Statement of Mrs. Ewbank's Captivity. 8° *pp.* 21. *Denver, Colorado Territory*, 1865. 508

Mr. Evans was the Governor of Colorado Territory at the time of the horrible Sand Creek Massacre of friendly Indians. Although not in the immediate command of the murdering horde under Colonel Chivington, who perpetrated the frightful atrocities narrated under the title of "Condition of the Indian Tribes," yet he organized the force, and is charged with having given the instruction to Colonel Chivington, which has made his name infamous. Governor Evans' popularity was so much augmented with the cruel borderers and bloodthirsty adventurers of the territory, that he was elected to the United States Senate, where he met a civilized community, who were horrified at the crimes he had authorised, and was compelled to print this lame exculpation of them.

EVANS (Estwick).

A Pedestrian Tour of four thousand miles through the Western States and Territories, during the winter and spring of 1818, interspersed with brief reflections upon a great variety of topics, religious, moral, political, sentimental, &c. By Estwick Evans. 12° *pp.* 256. *Printed by Joseph C. Spear. Concord, N. H.*, 1819. 509

The slight value which attaches to this book is entirely in the few pages in which the author describes his visits to some western tribes of Indians.

EVANS (Jonathan).

A Journal of the Life, Travels, and religious Labours of William Savery, late of Philadelphia, a minister of the gospel of Christ, in the Society of Friends, compiled from his original memoranda. By Jonathan Evans. 12° *pp.* vii. + 316. *London*, 1844. 510

William Savery in 1793, was in conjunction with John Heckewelder and the agents of the government, and by the desire of General Washington, sent on a mission to the Indians of Ohio, on the occasion of the meeting of a grand council at Sandusky. He kept a daily journal of his tour and of the incidents of his intercourse with the Indians, which occupies pp. 13 to 103 of this volume. It is a narrative of more than ordinary interest and value, as it adds the observations of an intelligent and scrupulous journalist, to our store of historical material of that early period.

EVENTS IN INDIAN HISTORY.

Beginning with an Account of the Origin of the American Indians and Early Settlements in North America, and embracing Concise Biographies of the principal Chiefs and head Sachems of the different Indian Tribes, with Narratives and Captivities. Including [*etc.*, 9 *lines*], illustrated with eight fine engravings. 8° *pp.* 633. *Lancaster*, 1841. 511

EVERETT (Edward).

An Address delivered at Bloody Brook in South Deerfield, September 30th, 1835, in Commemoration of the fall of the "Flower of Essex," at that Spot, in King Philips War, September 18 (O. S.) 1675. By Edward Everett, published by request. 8° pp. 44. *Boston, Russel, Shattuck, and Williams*, 1835. 512

EVERETT (Mr.).

Speech of Mr. Everett of Massachusetts on the Bill for Removing the Indians from the East to the West Side of the Mississippi, delivered in the House of Representatives, on the 19th of May, 1830. 8° *pp.* 28. *Washington, printed by Gales and Seaton*, 1830. 513

EVERETT (Mr.).

Speech of Mr. Everett of Massachusetts in the House of Representatives, on the 14th and 21st of February 1831. On the execution of the laws and treaties in favor of the Indian Tribes. 8° *pp.* 23. (*Washington*, 1831.) 514

[EVARTS (Jeremiah).]

Essays on the Present Crisis in the Condition of the American Indians; first published in the National Intelligencer. under the Signature of William Penn. 8° *pp.* 116. *Philadelphia*, 1830. 515

EXPLICACION

Clara y Sucinta de los principales misterios DE Nuestra Santa Fe. Oracion Dominical. Mandamientos y Sacramentos en el Idoma Mexicana. A beneficio de los Indios y en el Castellano para los que Aspiran al Ministeriod Estos. Compuesta por un Cura del Obispado de la Puebla, puesta al honor, y amparo de la Majestad de Ntro. Sr. Jesucristo y de la Madre Ima De la Luz. Con la licencia necesaria. 24° *pp.* 267. *Puebla, Imprenta del hospital de S. Pedro*, 1835. 516

[Clear and Succinct Explanation of the principal mysteries of Our Holy Faith. Dominical Discourse. Ordinances and Sacraments in the Mexican tongue, for the benefit of the Indians and in Spanish for those who aim at ministering to them. Composed by a Curate of the Bishopric of La Puebla, prepared for the honor and Increase of the Majesty of Our Lord Jesus Christ and of the Holy Mother (of light, or De la Luz), with the necessary License. Puebla, Printing-office of the Hospital of San Pedro.]

FACTS

Relative to the Canadian Indians, published by direction of The Aborigines Committee, of the Meeting for Sufferings. 8° *pp.* 24. *London, Harvey & Darton, Grace Church Street*, 1839. 517

Tracts Relative to the Aborigines, No. 4. See Friends.

FAILLON (P. de St Sulpice).

Histoire de la Colonie Francaise en Canada. *Three vols. royal* 8° Vol. I. *pp.* (xvi.) + xxiii. + 551. Vol. II. *pp.* (4) + xxiii. + 548. Vol. III. *pp.* (ii.) + xxiv. + 568 + *Portrait of Cartier. Villemarie Bibliotheque Paroissiale*, 1865. 518

[History of the French Colony in Canada.]

This remarkable work is designed to fill the hiatus in Canadian colonial history over which the works of Sagard, du Creux, and Charlevoix have only thrown a narrow causeway. A continuous narrative of the motive for the establishment of the French Colony in Canada, its progress and the numerous obstacles it overcame, has never before been written with such attention at once to detail and completeness.

The romantic story of French domination over some of the Indian tribes, the fierce wars with the Iroquois, which more than once nearly exterminated their civilized foes, and the establishment of the Catholic faith among the savages of the Algonquin race, is here told with spirit and elegance.

FALCONER (Captain Richard).

The Voyages, Dangerous Adventures And imminent Escapes of Captain Richard Falconer Containing The Laws, Customs, and Manners, of the Indians in America, his Shipwrecks; his Marrying an Indian Wife, his narrow Escape from the Island of Dominico &c. Intermixed with the Voyages and Adventures of Thomas Randal of Cork Pilot; with his Shipwreck in the Baltick, being the only Man that escap'd: His being taken by the Indians of Virginia &c. Written by Himself, now alive. 12° *Title and Preface* viii. *Book I. pp.* 1 *to* 72. *Book II. pp.* 1 *to* 186. *Part III. pp.* 1 *to* 179 — *verso last numbered page Advertisement. London,* 1720. 519

The subject of the North American Indians must have early been one of great interest to the English mind, for a large number of the works of fiction, of which copies cannot be readily obtained, have the locality in America and involve a captivity among the savages. They are generally written, like the adventures of Falconer, with such a profound gravity, and freedom from dramatic colloquialisms, that they leave the reader vexed with a doubt if they are wholly fictitious, or not as generally truthful as the boasted veritable narratives.

FALCONER (Capt. Rich.).

The Voyages, Dangerous Adventures. And Imminent Escapes of Capt. Rich. Falconer. Containing The Laws, Customs, and Manners of the Indians of America, his Shipwrecks; his Marrying an Indian Wife; his narrow Escape from the Island of Dominico, &c. Intermixed with The Voyages and Adventures of Thomas Randal of Cork Pilot; with his Shipwreck in the Baltick; being the only Man that escap'd: His being taken by the Indians of Virginia &c. And an Account of his Death. The Fourth Edition Corrected. To which is added, a Great Deliverance at Sea, by William Johnson, D. D. Chaplain to his Majesty. 18° *pp.* viii. + 216 + vi. *London, printed for J. Marshall at the Bible, Grace-Church-Street,* 1734. 520

FALKNER (Thomas).

A Description of Patagonia, and the Adjoining Parts of South America: containing an Account of the Soil, Produce, Animals, Vales, Mountains, Rivers, Lakes, &c. of those Countries; the Religion, Government, Policy, Customs, Dress, Arms, and Language of the Indian Inhabitants; and some Particulars relating to Falkland Islands. By Thomas Falkner, Who resided near Forty Years in those Parts. Illustrated with A New Map of the Southern Parts of America. Engraved by Mr. Kitchen. Hydrographer to His Majesty. 4° *Pref. leaves* (4) + *pp.* 144. *Hereford*, 1774. 521

The relation of Father Falkner, a Jesuit missionary in Patagonia, is said to have been privately printed in English. Chapters iv. and v., pp. 96 to 131, are occupied with "An Account of the Indian Tribes inhabiting the Southern part of America," and of "The Religion, Government, and Customs of the Moluches and Puelches." Chapter vi., pp. 132 to 144, is entitled "An Account of the Language of the Inhabitants of those Countries." It includes a short grammatical analysis, translations of the Creed and Lord's Prayer, and a vocabulary of the language of the Moluches.

FANCOURT (C. St John).

The History of Yucatan from its discovery to the close of the Seventeenth Century. By Charles St. John Fancourt recently H. M. Superintendent of the British Settlements in the Bay of Honduras. With a Map. 8° *pp.* xvi. + 340, *and map.* *London, John Murray*, 1854. 522

This volume is devoted almost entirely to the aboriginal history of the peninsula of Yucatan; the wars, treaties, and association of the Spaniards, and the missions established by them. The author's long residence in the country should, however, have afforded him more material for a general view of the peculiarities, language, and condition of its aboriginal inhabitants.

FARMER.

Collections, Topographical, Historical, and Biographical, relating principally to New Hampshire. Edited by J. Farmer and J. B. Moore. 3 *vols.* 8° Vol. I. *pp.* 296 + (7) *pp. of Contents.* Vol. II. *pp.* 388 + *Appendix, pp.* 103 + *Index*, (6) *pp.* Vol. III. *pp.* iv. + 388 + *Appendix, pp.* 88 + *Index*, 9 *pp.* *Concord, published by Hill & Moore*, 1822; *Reprinted by H. E. & J. W. Moore*, 1831. 523

The first subject announced as the purpose of these volumes in the Preface, is certainly well sustained by their contents, "Historical Sketches of Indian Wars, battles, and Exploits; of the adventures and sufferings of the Captives." The work is in fact a copious cyclopædia of Indian history; narratives of captivities in their original style without abridgment; descriptions of Indian antiquities, with memoirs and anecdotes of Indian chiefs, and border fighters of the whites.

It may be considered the model of a historical magazine, or of a collection of material relating to the early history of any locality.

FARNHAM (Thomas J.).

Travels in the Great Western Prairies, the Anahuac and Rocky Mountains, and in the Oregon Territory, by Thomas J. Farnham. In two volumes. 8° Vol. I. *pp.* xxiii. + 297. Vol. II. *pp.* viii. + 315. *London*, 1843. 524

This is by far the best edition of Farnham's *Travels*, which work is an entirely distinct one from his *Life in California*. Much the greater portion of the work is devoted to the narration of his observations of Indian life and character, with incidents of adventure, or association, with almost every tribe of the Great Plains and the Rocky Mountains. His work is full of interest, and as it is evidently written with fidelity to actual observation, it possesses not a little value, in contributing to the historic materials of the once formidable border of the American Desert.

FARNHAM (Thomas J.).
Travels in the Great Western Prairies, and in the Oregon Territory. 8° *New York*, 1843. 525

FARNHAM (THOMAS J.).
The Same. 12° *pp.* 197. *Poughkeepsie*, 1841. 526

FARNHAM (Thomas J.).
Life and Adventures in California and Scenes in the Pacific Ocean, by Thomas J. Farnham. 8° *pp.* 416. *New York, published by Wm. H. Graham*, 1847. 527

A large part of this work is devoted to a narrative of the Jesuit mission among the Indians of California, and of personal adventures among them.

FARNHAM (J. T.).
Pictorial Edition. Life, Adventures, and Travels in California. By J. T. Farnham, to which are added, Conquest of California and Travels in Oregon. 8° *pp.* 468. *New York, Sheldon, Lamport, & Blakeman*, 115 *Nassau Street*, 1855. 528

Pages 117 to 298, are occupied with a history of the Jesuit Missions among the Indians, and pp. 364 to 378 with a description of the Indian tribes of California.

FAR WEST (The).
The Far West or a Tour beyond the Mountains embracing outlines of Western Life and Scenery. Sketches of the Prairies, Rivers, Ancient Mounds, Early Settlements of the French, etc. etc. In two volumes. 12° *pp.* 263 *and* 241. *New York, published by Harper & Brothers*, 1838. 529

Much of the text and most of the notes of these volumes convey interesting information, of personal examination of ancient fortifications, and other aboriginal monuments in the Western States.

FEATHERSTONHAUGH (G. W.).
A Canoe Voyage up The Minnay-Sotor with an Account of the Lead and Copper deposits in Wisconsin; of the gold region in the Cherokee Country; and Sketches of popular Manners; &c. &c. &c. By G. W. Featherstonhaugh. In two volumes. 8° Vol. I. *pp.* xiv. + 416. Vol. II. *pp.* vii. + 351. *London, Richard Bentley, New Burlington Street*, 1847. 530

The author narrates many particulars of Indian life and manners, obtained by the aid of traditional and documentary evidence, as well as from personal observation.

FEDERMANN LE JEUNE (Nicolas).
Belle et agreable Narration du premier Voyage de Nicolas Federman le Jeune, d'Ulm, aux Indes de la mer Oceane, et de tout ce qui lui est arrive dans ce pays jusqu a son retour en Espagne, ecrit brievement, et divertissante a lire. Haguenau, 1557. 8° *pp.* 227. *Paris, Arthus Bertrand, Libraire-editeur*, 1837. 531

[Excellent and agreeable Narrative of the first voyage of Nicolas Federman

pher Wilkinson at the Black-Boy against St. Dunstan's Church in Fleetstreet, 1688. 592

The author of the three works on the Conquest of the Aboriginal Nations in Peru and Florida, was the son of one of the conquerors of Peru, Garcilasso de la Vega, by the daughter of the Inca Huallpa Tupac, and sister of Huayna Capac Inca, the last native monarch of Peru. He was so proud of both paternal and maternal origin, that while he assumed the Spanish name of the first, he was careful to assert his Incarial descent. He was evidently a gentleman of refinement, and possessed of much more learning than was usually acquired by the conquistadors themselves. That one of Indian blood, and a descendant of the proud race of the Incas, should have been the most industrious and careful historian of the evil fortunes of his race, and the chronicler of the victories of their conquerors, may well excite our surprise. He was not, however, alone in this scholarly and mournful labor, for Clavigero cites the names of fifteen other noble and royal Indians who wrote histories of the events which either preceded or followed the conquest of their heroic race. The high state of civilization, reached by the Incas of Peru, can be no better evidenced, than by the fact that sixteen of that ill-fated nation, were so imbued with literary fervor as to chronicle the fortunes of their race.

Ferdinand Ixtlilxochitl, son of the last king of Acolhuacan, and Antonio Montezuma Ixtlilxochitl, a descendant of the royal house of Montezuma, wrote a genealogy of their houses, and some historical memoirs which were preserved in the Jesuits' College in Mexico.

The son of the first named Indian noble wrote Historical Memoirs of his ancestors' kingdom which greatly aided Torquemada in writing his *Monarchia Indiana.*

Niza, a noble Indian of Tlascala, wrote a *History of the Conquest by Cortez*, which was authenticated by the signatures of thirty Indian nobles of Tlascala.

Ayala, a noble of Tezcuco, wrote Historical Commentaries in the Mexican language of that kingdom, from the year 1243 to 1562.

Mendoza, a Tlascalan Indian noble, wrote in his native tongue, the chronicles of his country. Pedro Ponce, another Indian, wrote in the Spanish, *An Account of the Gods and the Rites of Mexican Paganism.*

The native chiefs of Colhuacan wrote the annals of that kingdom, or province of Mexico.

Camargo, a native noble of Tlascala, wrote a *History of the City and Republic of Tlascala*, of such merit that Torquemada made large use of his work in compiling his *Monarchia Indiana*, as he did of the Historical Memoirs of Cholula, written by the Indian Juan Poman.

Fernando Alba Ixtlilxochitl wrote four works of great erudition, which will be found noted under his name.

Domingo Chimalpain, a noble Indian of Mexico, wrote four works in the Mexican language, which were much esteemed by the learned. These were preserved in the library of the College of St. Peter and St. Paul in Mexico, and were copied by Boturini, who also procured copies of most of the other Indian works mentioned.

Fernando Tezozomoc, a Mexican Indian, wrote in Spanish, a Mexican Chronicle, which was also preserved in the same library.

Garcilaso de la Vega, the author of the works under consideration, is said by Irving to have conceived such an ardent desire to view the land of his father's nativity, that he abandoned the country of the Incas, and took up his residence at Cordova. His *Royal Commentaries of Peru* obtained for him the favor of the sovereigns of Leon and Castile, and the esteem of the learned throughout Spain. Barcia says, in his Preface to his edition of *La Florida del Inca*, that Garcilaso was during his lifetime eminent for his religion, nobility, virtue, modesty, and devotion to literature, and was always held in the highest estimation as a historian. The Friar Buenaventura de Salinas, in his *Memorial de la Historia del Nuevo Mundo*, says "the Inca Garcilaso, a Captain, native of the city of Cusco, was highly esteemed for his great talents and capacity." "His fame extended over all the world."

So great was the veneration in which his character was held, that he was buried in the great cathedral of Cordova, and the portion of the sacred edifice where his remains were deposited was denominated thereafter the Chapel of Garcilaso.

On each side of the chapel is a monument of black marble, on which is chiseled this inscription, "To the Inca Garcilaso de la Vega — a noble man, whose memory is worthy of preservation. Illustrious by birth; an accomplished writer, and valiant in arms. He was the Son of Garcilaso de la Vega, and of Elizabeth Palla, Sister of Huayna Capac, last Emperor of the Indies. Author of *Commentaries of Florida*, Translator of *Leon Hebreo*, and author of the *Royal Commentaries*. He lived at Cordova with great piety, and there died with exemplary resignation, 22d of April, 1616. Pray to God for his Soul."

It has been so much the fashion, during the last century, for writers to treat lightly the merit and historical value of Garcilaso's works, that I have introduced these testimonies of his contemporaries and of later historians to his character. He had access to sources of information that no longer exist, such as the MS. documents and relations of the conquerors, and the quipu records of the Incas. His friends and relatives of his native race were at that period still learned in the Incarial history. This gave him access to, and enabled him to decipher them. He had, beside, the most intimate personal relations with some of the great conquerors and commanders, and probably drew confirmation of his researches from their own lips. He obtained a great portion of the material for his history of De Soto's expedition from an old friend who accompanied him on that fatal invasion. Garcilaso had determined to preserve the details, thus narrated to him, from oblivion, but his service to the king separated him from his friend for more than twenty years. At last freed from his duty in the field, he established himself in the village where his friend resided, and with the zeal of a missionary, recorded the narrations of his brother soldier. For the character of this hidalgo, he vouches in the most solemn manner, averring that he was incapable of uttering an untruth. While engaged in thus perpetuating the facts, which he had long grieved to think must die with his friend, he received most fortunately two manuscripts of soldiers engaged in that famous expedition. One was written by Alonso de Carmona, and was entitled *Wanderings in Peru and Florida*. The other, a somewhat meagre diary of the events of the invasion, was the work of a soldier named Juan Coles. Fortified by these documents, Garcilaso incorporated their principal details, or used them to corroborate those obtained from his noble friend. Not the least valuable testimony to the veracity and worth of his histories, is the fact that the celebrated Herrera, who is regarded as "The Prince of Spanish Historians," incorporated the whole of *La Florida del Inca* into his *Decadas de las Indias*. This acute and learned writer, living so near the period in which Garcilaso wrote, could not have been deceived regarding the value of Garcilaso's works, and by adopting, certified their truthfulness to us.

The opinions of the learned have differed much regarding the historical value of his works. Charlevoix, who has not a ready stock of praise for his brother historians, says that "this work is well written, but the author has evidently exaggerated the riches and power of the Floridians."

Charlevoix declares, however, that it is to be received as authentic regarding the expeditions of De Soto and Louis de Moroso. For many years the dicta of Mr. Robertson, denying the authenticity of Garcilaso's writings, was received without question, but that historian's own credit has so waned, as to affect but few opinions at this day.

GARDINER (Capt. A. F.).
A Visit to the Indians on the Frontiers of Chili. 8° *pp.* 195.
London, 1841. 598

GARRARD (Lewis H.).
Wah-to Yah, and the Taos Trail; or, Prairie Travel and Scalp Dances. With a look at Los Rancheros, from Mule back and the Rocky Mountain Camp Fire. 12° *pp.* 367. *New York and Cincinnati*, 1850. 594

GASS (Patrick).
Journal of the Voyages and Travels of a Corps of Discovery. Under the command of Captain Lewis and Captain Clarke of the army of the United States; From the mouth of the river Missouri through the Interior parts of North America to the Pacific Ocean; During the Years 1804, 1805, and 1806. Containing An Authentic Relation of the most interesting Transactions during the Expedition; A Description of the Country; And an Account of its Inhabitants, Soil, Climate, Curiosities, and Vegetable and Animal Productions. By Patrick Gass, One of the Persons employed in the Expedition. 8° *pp.* 381. *Pittsburgh, printed for David McKeehan; London, reprinted for J. Budd*, 1808. 595

GASS (Patrick).
Same. Fourth Edition, with Six Engravings. 12° *Philadelphia*, 1812. 596

GASS (Patrick).
A Journal of the Voyages and Travels of a Corps of Discovery under the command of Captain Lewis and Captain Clarke of the army of the United States, from the mouth of the river Missouri through the interior parts of North America to the Pacific Ocean. During the years 1804, 1805, and 1806. Containing An authentic relation of the most interesting transactions during the expedition, a description of the country, and an account of its inhabitants, soil, climate, curiosities, and vegetable and animal productions. By Patrick Gass, one of the persons employed in the expedition, with geographical and explanatory notes. Fourth Edition. With Six Engravings. 12° *Philadelphia*, 1812. 597

GENDRON (Le Sieur).
Quelques Particvlaritez dv pays Des Hvrons en la Novelle France. Remarquees par le Sieur Gendron Docteur en Medicine qui a demeuré dans ce Pays-la fort long-temps. Redigées par Iean Baptiste de Rocoles, Conseiller & Aumonier du Roy, & Historiographe de Sa Majestie. A Troyis & A Paris, 1660. 4° *pp.* 26. *New York*, 1868. 598

[Some Particulars of the Country of the Hurons in New France. Remarked by the Sieur Gendron, Doctor of Medicine, who resided in that Country for a long period. Collected by Jean Baptiste de Rocoles.]

These particulars, taken from the letters of Dr. Gendron, who claimed to have remained among the Hurons for a long time, are very curious as affording us information of that nation at the early period of his visit, in 1644 and 1645.

GENESIS, EXODUS, LEVITICUS, NUMBERS, AND DEUTERONOMY
(The Books of) translated into the Choctaw Language. Chene-

sis, Ekssutu, Lefitekra, Nambaa, Micha Tutelonomi Holbaa. Aieua Kut Toshowit. Chata anumpa toba hoke. 12° pp. 564. *New York Bible Society*, 1867. 599

GIBBONS (Charles).
An Address delivered before the Northern Lyceum of the City and County of Philadelphia, At their Anniversary Meeting, November 1839. By Charles Gibbons, Esq. (On the Native Character of the Aborigines of America). 8° pp. 27. *Philadelphia*, (1839). 600

GIBBS (George).
Alphabetical Vocabularies of the Clallam and Lummi, by George Gibbs. *Large* 8° *pp.* 40. *New York, Cramoisy Press*, 1863. 601

No. 11, Shea's *American Linguistics.*

The tribe of Clallams, so called by the inhabitants of Washington Territory where these Indians reside, on the southern shore of the Straits of Fuca, are a branch of the Nootka family; their language is similar to that of the Songles and Sokes of Vancouver's Island. The Lummi tribe live on a river emptying into the Gulf of Georgia, to which they are emigrants from a group of islands in the Strait, separating Vancouver's Island from the Continent. Both vocabularies were collected by Mr. Gibbs, during a residence of a few months at Port Townshend and its adjacent territory. A historical preface occupies pp. v. to viii. Vocabulary of the Clallams, pp. 9 to 20. Vocabulary of the Lummi, pp. 21 to 40.

GIBBS (George).
A Dictionary of the Chinook Jargon, or trade language of Oregon, by George Gibbs. *Large* 8° *pp.* 44. *New York, Cramoisy Press*, 1863. 602

No. 12, Shea's *American Linguistics.*

GIBBS (George).
The Same. Smithsonian Institute, Miscellaneous Collections. 8° *pp.* 44. *Washington*, 1863. 603

And also in a pamphlet, with the same title, date and place. *pp.* 44.

The fur-traders of the eighteenth century, and the early part of the present, in coasting along the shores of Vancouver's and Nootka Sounds, carried with them some of the words of each of the tribes whom they visited; until at the mouth of the Columbia they found a quick-witted people who adopted the mongrel jargon they heard from the lips of the strangers, and blended the fragments of twelve native tongues, with some English and French terms, into a sort of language possessing nearly five hundred words. Mr. Gibbs, with the zeal of a philological apostle, undertook to resolve this wretched jargon into its original elements, and this is the result of his labors. This curious history of the degradation of a language is doubly interesting, as the declension has taken place in our own day. It affords a valuable key to the methods by which languages have been revolutionized and corrupted. On pp. 13 and 14 is a bibliography of the Chinook Jargon, containing the titles of fifteen works which contain vocabularies of that mongrel dialect. The Chinook-English Dictionary occupies pp. 15 to 29, and the English-Chinook embraces the remainder of the work.

GIBBS (George).

Alphabetical Vocabulary of the Chinook Language, by George Gibbs. *Large* 8° *pp.* 23. *New York, Cramoisy Press*, 1863. 604

No. 13, Shea's *American Linguistics.*

GIBBS (George).

Instructions for research relative to the Ethnology and Philology of America. Smithsonian Miscellaneous Collections. 8° *pp.* 33. *Washington*, 1863. 605

GIDDINGS (Joshua R.).

The Exiles of Florida; or, the Crimes Committed by our Government against the Maroons who fled from South Carolina, and other Slave States seeking protection under Spanish laws. By Joshua R. Giddings. 12° *pp.* 338. *Columbus, O.*, 1858. 606

This treatise, written by the celebrated advocate of the abolition of slavery, is a glowing arraignment of the government of the United States for its complicity in the outrages perpetrated upon the Seminoles, in the interests of the slaveholders of Florida. The heroic Indians of the hammocks defied for a quarter of a century the armies of the United States, and to the shame of that government, it only succeeded in conquering them by the foulest treachery, and the most shameless violation of their plighted word by generals of the United States army. The long and bloody war, in which every captured and slain Indian cost the lives of more than fifty white soldiers, and an expenditure of one hundred and forty thousand dollars, originated in the seizure of the handsome wife of the Chief Osceola, and her sale into slavery. The war thus begun in treachery was only ended by it. General Jessup having pledged his word of honor to Osceola, foully violated it, and threw him into prison where he died.

GILBERT (Benjamin).

A Narrative of the Captivity and Sufferings of Benjamin Gilbert and his Family, who were surprised by the Indians, and taken from their Farms on the Frontiers of Pennsylvania, in the Spring 1780. 12° *pp.* 123. *Philadelphia printed; London, reprinted and sold by James Phillips*, 1785. 607

This work was written by William Walton, to whom it was verbally narrated by Mr. Gilbert and his family after their return, and published by Jos. Cruikshank, Philadelphia, 1784.

Account of Benjamin Gilbert. p. 278. Vol. 3. Hazard, Register of Pennsylvania.

Narrative reprinted with some additional particulars, pp. 314.

GILBERT (Benjamin).

A Narrative of the Captivity and Sufferings of Benjamin Gilbert and his Family. Who were surprised by the Indians, and taken from their farms on the frontiers of Pennsylvania. In the Spring 1780. *pp.* 124. *Philadelphia printed; London, reprinted and sold by James Phillips, George Yard, Lombard Street*, 1790. 608

GILES (John).

Memoirs of Odd Adventures, Strange Deliverances, etc. In the Captivity of John Giles Esq., Commander of the garrison on Saint George river, in the district of Maine. Written by himself. Originally Published at Boston, 1736. 8° *pp.* 64. *Printed for William Dodge, Cincinnati*, 1869. 609

Copies of the original edition of this captivity are very rarely found. Only one has ever been offered for sale to my knowledge, and that was contained in the Collection of *Mr.* S. G. Drake.

Godard-Lange.

La Congregation ou une Mission Chez les Iroquois; poeme Asceti-epique en 9 chants, avec des notes critiques, historiques, anecdotiques et edifiantes, tirees pour la plupart, des ouvrages des Benoits Peres Jesuits, et orne d'une Jolie vignette de frontispiece par Ignace Gr; gravee sur bois par Brevirre. Par Godard-Lange. 8° *Frontispiece* + *pp.* xiv. + 397. *Paris*, 1846. 610

[La Congregation or a Mission to the home of the Iroquois. A Satiric-epic poem in 9 cantos, with critical and historical notes, both anecdotal and edifying, taken for the most part from the writings of the Benoit Jesuit Fathers, and ornamented with a handsome vignette and frontispiece, par Ignace Gr.; engraved on wood by Brevirre. Par Godard-Lange.]

A satire, without a word either in the poem or the notes regarding the Iroquois or any other savages, except those of Paris.

Gomara (Lopez de).

The Pleasant Historie of the Conquest of the West India, now called new Spaine. Atchieued by the most woorthie Prince Hernando Cortes, Marques of the Valley of Huaxacac, most delectable to reade. Translated out of the Spanish tongue by T. N. Anno. 1578. *Small* 4° *Title, reverse blank. Epistle and other prel. matters* (x.) *pp.* + 1 *to* 405 + *Table, pp.* (vi.). *London, printed by Thomas Creede*, 1596. 611

This is the second English Edition of Gomara's *Cronica de Nueva Espana.* The first edition of the translation was printed in 1578, by Henry Bynneman. The dedication is signed by Thomas Nicholas, who is therefore supposed to be the translator. The conquest of the Aztecs, their peculiarities of religion, warfare, and government, are portrayed here by one of the earliest, as he was one of the most able of the Spanish historians. The *Cronica* of Gomara was first printed in 1554 as the second part of his General History.

Good Indian Missionary (The).

Written for the American Sunday-School Union and revised by the Committee of publication. 18° *pp.* 86. *Philadelphia, n. d.* 612

Goodrich (S. G.).

History of the Indians of North and South America. By the author of Peter Parley's Tales. 16° *pp.* 320. *Boston*, 1855. 613

Goodwin (Isaac).

An Oration delivered at Lancaster, February 21, 1826. In Commemoration of the One Hundred and Fiftieth Anniversary of the Destruction of that town by the Indians. By Isaac Goodwin. 8° *pp.* 15. *Worcester, Rogers & Griffin, printers*, 1826. 614

GOODWIN (H. C.).

Pioneer History of Cortland County and the Border Wars of New York from the earliest Period to the Present Time. By H. C. Goodwin. 12° *pp.* 456 *and* 3 *plates.* *New York, A. B. Burdick, publisher, No.* 8 *Spruce Street,* 1859. 615

The author has gathered in the first six chapters of his book, the well-known incidents of the border wars of New York, which had been many times printed before.

They are entitled "Aboriginal French and English History," "Cherry Valley," "Border Wars, Battle of Oriskany and Siege of Fort Schuyler," "Flight of St. Leger, Brant gathering his Forces, and the Massacre," "Sullivan's Campaign, Pioneer movements, Indian reflections, Revenge and Destruction of Mohawk Valley." In chapter xi., entitled "Legend of Tioughnioga Valley," he adds something more or less authentic to our aboriginal literature.

GUMILLA (Joseph).

Historia Natural, civil y geograpica de las Naciones situadas en las Riveras Del Rio Orinoco. Su autor el Padre Joseph Gumilla, Missionero que fuè de las Missiones del Orinoco Meta y Casanare. Neuva Impression; Mucho mas correcta que las anteriores, y adornada con oche laminas finas, que manifestan las costumbres y ritos de aquellos Americanos. Corregido por el P. Ignacio Obregon de los Clerigos Menores. *Two volumes.* 4° Vol. I. *pp.* xvi. + 360 + 1 *map and* 5 *plates.* Vol. II. *prel. leaves* 2 + *pp.* 352 + 2 *plates.* *Barcelona, Ano* 1791. 616

[Natural, civil, and geographical History of the (Indian) Nations situated on the River Orinoco by Father Joseph Gumilla Superior of the Missions of Orinoco, Meta, and Casanare. New Edition, with many corrections of the first, adorned with eight copperplate engravings illustrative of the customs and religious ceremonies of these Indians.]

This is the third Spanish edition of this work first printed in 1741, and reprinted in 1745. Subjected to sharp criticisms for a long time, for its supposed want of veracity, further explorations only confirmed the author's statements. The French edition published in 1758, in three volumes, was much abridged, and with a title invented by the unscrupulous translator. The object of the work is indeed but poorly expressed in the author's own title, as more than three fourths of it is devoted to a minute description of the government, peculiar customs, religious rites, domestic habits, and ceremonies of the Indians inhabiting the shores of the Orinoco and its tributaries. The plates are copied from drawings intended to illustrate some of the peculiarities of their life and habits.

GUMILLA (P. Joseph).

Histoire Naturelle, Civile et Geographique de L'Orenoque, et des princepales Rivieres qui s'y Jetent Dans laquelle on traite du Govvernment, des Usages, & des Coutumes des Indiens qui l' habitent, etc.; Par le P. Joseph Gumilla. Superieur des Missions d l'Orenoque, traduite de l'Espagnol. Avignon et Marseille 1758. *Three vols.* 18° Vol. I. *pp.* xxv., *map, plate,* + 392. Vol. II. *pp.* 338 *and plate.* Vol. III. *pp.* 336. 617

[Natural, Civil, and Geographical History of the Orinoco, and of the principal rivers which empty into it. In which is treated, the Government, the Habits, and Customs, of the Indians which inhabit the Country. By Father Joseph Gumilla, Superior of the Missions of Orinoco, translated from the Spanish second edition.]

All of Vol. I. after p. 94, the whole of Vol. II. and Vol. III. from p. 146 to the end, are occupied solely with minute and faithful descriptions of the Indians. Every peculiarity affecting their customs, mode of life, wars, religion, and government, is treated by this intelligent observer.

In the Leclerc Catalogue, is affixed this note: "The work of Father Gumilla is one of the most curious and interesting hitherto published upon the country of the Orinoco. Although the reverend Father passed many years of his life in America, his work is derived principally from the historic MSS. of the Fathers Mercado and Ribera." Father Gumilla was born in 1690, and appointed Superior of the Missions of Orinoco, and more than once travelled along the shores of almost the entire course of this great river. As late as 1743 he returned from Spain to America, but the period and place of his death is unknown.

GUINNARD (A.).

Three years' Slavery among the Patagonians: an Account of his Captivity, By A. Guinnard, member of the Geographical Society of France. From the third French edition. By Charles S. Cheltnam. *Post 8° Map. pp.* x. + 375. *London, Richard Bentley and Son,* 1871. 618

The English translator speaks with some confidence of the authenticity and truthfulness of M. Guinnard's narration of the incidents of his captivity, and I am inclined to believe them veritable, but it lacks so notably that Anglo-Saxon simplicity, which marks and distinguishes unalloyed historical relations, that we may subject it to an unjust suspicion. With true French exaltation of style, he so begilds his narrative, as to give his true story the color of fiction. It is, however, a very valuable collection of material relative to the habits, religion, and mode of life of the but little known race of savages inhabiting the vast Pampas between Buenos Ayres, Chili, and Northern Patagonia.

GRAAH (Capt. W. A.).

Narrative of an Expedition to the East Coast of Greenland, sent by order of the King of Denmark, in search of The Lost Colonies, under the Command of Capt. W. A. Graah of the Danish Royal Navy, Knight of Dannebrog, &c. Translated from the Danish by the late G. Gordon Macdougall for the Royal Geographical Society of London, with the original Danish Chart completed by the Expedition. 8° *pp.* xxi. + 199 + *map. London, John W. Parker, West Strand,* 1837. 619

This expedition traversed the inhospitable regions of Greenland for nearly three years, and during that time found ample opportunity of becoming acquainted with those traits of character, which mark its aboriginal inhabitants. The narrative will not disappoint the reader greatly, in its details of the dreary life of these residents of a land of perpetual winter, if he but considers that it is the product of an antiquarian, as well as a scientific expedition.

GRANADOS Y GALVEZ,

Joseph Joaquin. Tardes Americanas: Gobierno Gentil y Catolico breve y particular noticia de toda la historia Indiana: Sucesos, casos notables y cosas ignoradas, desde la entrada de la Gran Nacion Tulteca a esta tierra de Anahuac, hasta los presentes tiempos. Trabajados por un Indio, y un Espagnol. Sacalas a luz El M. R. P. Fr. Joseph Joaquin Granados y Galvez, Predicador General de Jure ex-Definidor de la Provincia de

Michoacan, y Guardian que Sue de los Conventos de Xiquilpan, Valladolid, Rio Verde, y Custodio de todas sus Misiones. [*Dedication, 6 lines.*] *Mexico: En la nueva Imprenta Matritense de D. Felipe de Zuniga y Ontiveros, Calle de la Palma, ano de* 1778. 4° 36 *prel. leaves* + *pp.* 1 *to* 540 + 3 *plates.* 620

No. 1 of *Tulteras and Chicimeras.*

[American Evenings: Government, Pagan and Catholic, with concise and particular notices of all the events of Indian History: followed by a narration of the remarkable and unknown incidents which transpired from the invasion of the Grand Nation of the Toltecs into the land of Anahuac, up to the present time. A work obtained from the conversation of an Indian and a Spaniard. By Father Joseph Joaquin Granados y Galvez.]

This interesting history of ancient Mexico, written in the form of a dialogue between an Indian and a Spaniard, and divided into seventeen "Nights," is very little known in Europe, and is very rare in Mexico. The author held several important offices in the latter country, among which was the superintendence of the Missions among the Mexican Indians, which even a century before his time had become very important civil as well as religious institutions. On pp. 90 to 94, will be found a fragment of Aztec poetry, written by a poet of the euphonious name of Notzahualcoyotl, and translated into Spanish by the author. One of the most curious subjects treated in this work, is that of the Mexican Calendar with the names of the days in Mexican and in Spanish. On pp. 141 to 150 are given the Mexican names of the kings of the empire of Tezcuco.

Grantland (Mr.).

Speech of Mr. Grantland of Georgia while in Committee of the whole on Mr. Adams' motion to strike out the appropriation for carrying into effect the Cherokee Treaty delivered in the house of Representatives, June 29, 1836. 8° *pp.* 7. *Washington,* 1836. 621

Gravier Jacques (R. Pere).

Relation De Ce Qvi S'est passe dans la' Mission de l' Immaculate Conception au Pays des Ilinois depuis le Mois de Mars, 1693, jusqu' en Fevrier 1694. Par le R. Pere Jacques Gravier de la Compagnie de Jesus. *A Manate De la Presse Cramoisy de Jean-Marie Shea.* 4° *pp.* 65. 1857. 622

No. 2, Shea's *Jesuit Relations.*

[Relation of that which occured at the Mission of the Immaculate Conception in the Country of the Illinois (Indians), from the month of March 1693, to February 1694, by the Rev. Father Jacques Gravier of the Society of Jesus.]

Gravier Jacques (R. P.).

Relation ou Journal du Voyage du R. P. Jacques Gravier, *de la Compagnie de Jesus* en 1700 depuis le pays des Illinois jusqu' à l'embouchure du Mississipi. *Nouvelle York Isle de Manate de la Presse Cramoisy de Jean-Marie Shea. Small* 4° *pp.* 68. 1859. 623

No. 10, Shea's *Jesuit Relations.*

[Relation or Journal of the Voyage of the Rev. Father Jacques Gravier, of the Society of Jesus from the Country of the Illinois (Indians), to the mouth of the Mississippi.]

GRAVIER, PERE JACQUES.
Lettre Du Pere Jacques Gravier de la Compagnie de Jesus, Le 23 Fevrier 1708. Sur les Affaires de la Louisiane. 8° *pp.* 18. *Nouvelle York, De la Presse Cramoisy de Jean-Marie Shea*, 1865. 624

No. 24, Shea's *Jesuit Relations*.
[Letter from Father Jacques Gravier of the Society of Jesus, written the twenty-third of February 1708, on the affairs of Louisiana.]

GREGG (Josiah).
Commerce of the Prairies or the Journal of a Sante Fe Trader during eight expeditions across the Great Western Prairies and a residence of nearly nine years in Northern Mexico. Illustrated with Maps and Engravings. By Josiah Gregg. In two volumes. 12° *pp.* 320 *and* 318. *New York, Henry G. Langley*, 1844. 625

GREGG (Josiah).
Scenes and Incidents in the Western Prairies during eight expeditions and including a residence of nearly nine years in Northern Mexico. Illustrated with Maps and Engravings by Josiah Gregg. Two volumes in one. *pp.* 320 *and* 318 + *plate*. *Philadelphia*, 1857. 626

The same work published seven years previously under the title of *Commerce of the Prairies*.

Gregg (Alexander).
History of The Old Cheraws Containing An Account of the Aborigines of the Pedee, The first White Settlements, their subsequent progress, civil changes, the Struggle of the Revolution, and growth of the Country afterward; extending from about A. D. 1730 to 1810, with notices of families and sketches of individuals. By the Right Rev. Alexander Gregg. 8° *pp.* vii. + 543 + *maps*. *New York, Richardson and Company*, 14 *Bond Street*, 1867. 627

GREENE (Max.).
The Kansas Region — Forest, Prairie, Desert, Mountain, Vale, and River, descriptions of Scenery, Climate, Wild productions, Capabilities of Soil and commercial resources interspersed with Incidents of Travel and anecdotes illustrative of the character of the Traders and Red Men, to which are added [*etc.*, 3 *lines*]. 12° *pp.* 192. *New York*, 1856. 628

GREENLAND ESQUIMAUX.
A Greenland Family or the power of the Gospel, A Narrative of facts. 24° 54 *pp.* *Dublin*, 1830. 629

GROTIUS (Hugo).
Hugonis Grotii de Origine Gentium Americanarum Dissertatio. *Small* 4° *pp.* 15. (*Paris*), 1642. 630

[Hugo Grotius on the Origin of the American people.]
This is the first treatise of that long series which provoked such animosity, between the learned scholars Grotius, Laet, Hornius, and others. Grotius maintains, that as the Isthmus of Darien had been deemed impassable by the

natives of the two continents of America, they must therefore have had a different origin. North America, excepting Yucatan, was peopled by the Norwegians, and other northern nations of Europe. The ancestors of the Peruvians, he asserts, migrated from China, and the Moluccas furnished the original settlers of the more southern territory.

HAKLUYT (Richard).

The Principal Navigations, Voiages, and Discoveries of the English Nation, made by Sea or ouer Land, to the most remote and farthest distant Quarters of the earth at any time within the compasse of these 1500 yeares. Deuided into three seuerall parts, according to the positions of the Regions whereunto they were directed. The first containing the personall trauels of the English vnto [*Asia and Africa, 5 lines*]. The second comprehending the worthy discoueries of the English towards the North [*of Europe, 4 lines*]. The Third and last including the English valiant attempts in Searching almost all the corners of the vaste and new world of America from 73 degrees of Northerly latitude Southward to Meta Incognita, Newfoundland, the Maine of Virginia, the point of Florida, the Baie of Mexico, all the Inland of Noua Hispania, the coast of Terrafirma, Brasill, the riuer of Plate, to the Streight of Magellan: and through it, and from it to the South Sea to Chili, Peru, Xalisco, the Gulfe of California, Noua Albion vpon the backside of Canada, further than euer any Christian hitherto hath pierced. Whereunto is added the last most renowned English Nauigation round about the whole Globe of the Earth. By Richard Hakluyt Master of Artes, and Student sometime of Christ Church in Oxford. *Folio. 8 prel. leaves + pp. 1 to 825 + (x.). Imprinted at London by George Bishop and Ralph Newberie, Deputies to Christopher Barker printer to the Queens most excellent Maiestie*, 1589. 631

HALE (Salma).

Annals of the Town of Keene, from its first Settlement in 1734, to the year 1790; with corrections, additions, and a Continuation from 1790 to 1815. By Salma Hale. 8° *pp.* 120, *map. Keene, printed by J. W. Prentiss and Company*, 1851. 632

The first thirty-four pages are almost exclusively occupied with a narration of the Indian hostilities, from which the town suffered for nearly thirty years.

HALKETT (John).

Historical Notes respecting the Indians of North America with remarks on the attempts made to convert and civilize them. By John Halket, Esq. 8° *pp.* vii. + 408, *London, printed for Archibald Constable & Co., Edinburgh*, 1825. 633

Mr. Halkett was the son-in-law of Lord Selkirk, the founder of the Red River Settlement, and nephew of the unfortunate and gallant Sir Peter Halket killed in the Braddock campaign against Fort DuQuesne. He wrote the defense of Lord Selkirk's claim, entitled *Statement respecting the Earl of Selkirk's Settlement of Kildonan upon the Red River in North America,—Its Destruction and the Massacre of Governor Semple and his Party.* London, 1817. He was also the author of *A Letter to the Earl of Liverpool* upon the same subject. The tragedy of the Red River Settlement, the wars of the Fur-traders and Indians, having thus attracted his attention and aroused his interest in the Aborigines, he visited Canada in 1822, and traveled so far as the scene of the murder of Governor Semple. He must therefore have written his notes immediately after his return. His work is a concise narration of the attempts to civilize and convert the Indians made by both Catholic and Protestant.

See *Historical Magazine*, Vol. III. p. 60.

With the intensest Scotch prejudice against everything French, he speaks in severe terms of the French policy towards the Indians. Something of his animus may be gleaned from the subject-title of Chapter iv.: "Treacherous conduct of the French government with regard to the Indian Nations." — "Absurd accounts of the Jesuit Missionaries relative to their Success in Converting the Indians." At the same time he calls the murderous forays of the New Englanders upon unoffending, and even friendly Indians, in retaliation for outrages perpetrated by others, "Imprudent conduct of the Puritans."

HALL (Henry).

The History of Auburn; by Henry Hall. Auburn, N. Y. 12° *pp.* 579. *Auburn, published by Dennis Bros. & Co.,* 1869. 634

Chapter first, entitled "The Cayugas," pp. 1 to 31, is occupied with notes and observations upon the history of that branch of the Six Nations.

HALL (Frances and Almira).

Narrative of the Capture and Providential Escape of Misses Francis and Almira Hall, two respectable Young Women (Sisters), of the ages of 16 and 18, who were taken Prisoners by the Savages at a Frontier Settlement, near Indian Creek, in May last, when 15 of the Inhabitants fell Victims to the Bloody Tomahawk. Likewise is added the Narrative of the Captivity and Sufferings of Phillip Brigdon, a Kentuckian. 8° *Plate, pp.* 24, *printed covers. St. Louis,* 1832. 635

HALL (James).

Sketches of History, Life and Manners in The West. By James Hall. In two volumes. 12° *pp.* 282 *and* 276 + *plan of the fort at Boonesboro. Philadelphia, Harrison Hall,* 1833. 636

Narratives of frontier warfare with the Indians, and incidents of Indian life, fill almost all the pages of these interesting volumes.

HALL (Sherman) and George Copway.

Odizhijigeuiniua igiu Gaanoninjig Anishinabe enuet Anikunotabiung, au Sherman Hall gaie au George Copway. Acts of the Apostles in the Ojibwa Language. 12° *pp.* 108. *Boston,* 1838. 637

HALL (S.) and G. Copway.

Minuajimouin Gaiuajoinot au St. Luke Anishnabe enuet Giishkanikunotabiung au S. Hall Mekvdenikonaie. Gaie au George Copway. Anishinabe Gugikueuiniui. 12° *pp.* 112. *Boston,* 1837. 638

Ojibway Translation of St. Luke.

HALL (C. F.).

Arctic Researches and Life among the Esquimaux, being the

Narrative of an Expedition in Search of Sir John Franklin, in the years 1860, 1861, and 1862, by Charles Francis Hall. With Maps and One Hundred Illustrations. *Large* 8° *pp.* 595 *and map. New York, Harper & Brothers, publishers*, 1866. 639

HALL (C. Francis).

Life with the Esquimaux: The Narrative of Captain Charles Francis Hall, of the Whaling bark "George Henry" from the 29th May 1860, to the 13th September 1862. With the results of a long intercourse with the Innuits, and full description of their Mode of Life, the discovery of Actual relics of the Expedition of Martin Frobisher of three centuries ago, and deductions in favor of yet discovering some of the survivors of Sir John Franklin's Expedition. With Maps and One Hundred Illustrations. In two volumes. Vol. I. *pp.* xvi. + 324 *and map.* Vol. II. *pp.* xii. + *map and pp.* 352. *London, Sampson Low & Co.*, 1864. 640

Thirty-five of the engravings illustrate some phase in Esquimau life, of which the work also is mainly descriptive.

HALLETT (Benjamin F.).

Rights of the Marshpee Indians | Argument of Benjamin F. Hallett, Counsel for the memorialists of the Marshpee Tribe, before a Joint Committee of the Legislature of Massachusetts; Messrs. Barton and Strong of the Senate, and Dwight of Stockbridge, Fuller of Springfield and Lewis of Pepperell, of the House; to whom the complaints of the Indians for a change of Government and redress of grievances were referred. Published at the request of Isaac Coombs, Daniel Amos, and William Apes, The Marshpee Delegation, March 1834. 8° *pp.* 36. *Boston, J. Howe, printer* (1834). 641

HAMOR (Raphe).

A True Discourse of the present Estate of Virginia, and the Successe of the affairs there till the 18 of Iune, 1614. Together With a Relation of the Severall English Townes and fortes, the assured hopes of that Countrie and the peace Concluded with the Indians. The Christening of Powhatan's daughter and her marriage with an English-man. Written by Raphe Hamor the yonger late Secretarie in that Colony. Alget qui non ardet [*coat of arms.*] *Folio. Prel. pp.* (viii.) + 70. *Printed at London by John Beale &c.*, 1615. 642*

HAMOR (Raphe).

Same. *Reprinted Richmond*, 1860. 643

Copies of the original edition of Hamor's *Virginia* are of exceedingly rare appearance for sale. Only two have been offered in this country. That in the sale of the collection of C. O. Barney brought $150, the other, from the Brace library, sold for $170. Mr. Neil's Monogram on Pocahontas would hardly have been printed had he given credit to the letters written by Sir Thomas Dale and Alex. Whittaker, announcing the marriage of Pocahontas to John Rolfe, and the long one by the latter gentleman himself, minutely relating his alternate qualms of conscience, and paroxysms of love, the latter finally victoriously compelling him to lead the Indian princess to the altar. Hamor visited the *Court of Powhatan*, and his minute relations of the characteristics of the Indians of Virginia are full of interest, as being among the earliest accounts of them printed.

HANNA (John Smith).
A History of the life and services of Captain Samuel Dewees, A native of Pennsylvania, and Soldier of the Revolutionary and Late Wars. Also Reminiscences of the Revolutionary Struggle (Indian War, Western Expedition, Liberty Insurrection in Northampton County Pa.) and Late War with Great Britain. In all of which he was patriotically engaged. The whole written (in part from manuscript in the handwriting of Captain Dewees) and compiled By John Smith Hanna. Embellished with a lithographic likeness of Captain Dewees, and with eight wood-cut engravings, illustrative of portions of the work. 12° *pp.* 360. *Baltimore, printed by Robert Neilson*, 1844. 644

HANSER (Elizabeth).
God's Mercy surmounting Man's Cruelty, exemplified in the Captivity and Redemption of Elizabeth Hanser, Wife of John Hanser of Knoxmarsh at Keacheachy in Dover Township, who was taken captive with her children and maid servants by the Indians in New England in 1724, etc. To be sold by Samuel Keimer in Philadelphia and by Hewston Goldsmith in N. Y. 1724, Dec. 24. 645*

HANSON (Elizabeth) or Bownas (Samuel).
An Account of the Captivity of Elizabeth Hanson Late of Kakecky in New England who with Four of her children, and Servant-Maid was taken Captive by the Indians and carried into Canada. Setting forth The various remarkable occurrences, sore Trials and wonderful Deliverances which befel them after their Departure to the Time of their Redemption. Taken in Substance from her own Mouth by Samuel Bownas. *New Edition.* 12° *pp.* 28. *London*, 1787. 646

Mr. Rich must have taken this title orally from some cockney, as he speaks of the captive as Elizabeth *Anson*. "The captivity took place in 1725, and a relation of it made in 1741 to Samuel Hopwood, about which time it was probably first printed." The third edition was printed at Danvers in 1780, it is therefore to be supposed that this is the fourth.

HANSON (J. W.).
History of the Old Towns Norridgewock and Canaan, comprising Norridgewock, Canaan, Starks, Skowhegan, and Bloomfield, from their early Settlement to the year 1849; including a Sketch of the Abnakis Indians, By J. W. Hanson, Author of the History of Danvers. 12° *pp.* 372 + 4 *plates*. *Boston, published by the Author*, 1849. 647

HANSON (J. W.).
History of Gardiner, Pittston, and West Gardiner, with a Sketch of the Kenebec Indians, New Plymouth Purchase, com-

prising Historical Matter from 1602 to 1852; with Genealogical Sketches of many Families. Engravings. 12° *pp.* 343. *Gardiner*, 1852. 648

HANSON (John H.).

The Lost Prince, or the Identity of Louis XVIII. and the Rev. Eleazer Williams, missionary among the Indians of North America. 12° *pp.* 479 + *three portraits. New York*, 1854. 649

Part II. of this work, entitled "The Wigwam, the Camp, and the Church;" commences with a narrative of the capture of the reputed ancestress of Eleazer Williams by the Indians at Deerfield, her marriage to an Indian, and the fortunes of her descendants, until the subject of this memoir appears in the family.

The circumstances attending his first appearance and the incidents of his youth, were related to the author by Skenondoah, an Oneida chief, who was himself a half-breed, his father being an Irishman named O'Neal. The life of the missionary among his reputed aboriginal kindred is minutely related, taken in great part from his own diary. A great mass of evidence, more traditional than circumstantial, and more circumstantial than positive, is adduced to prove Eleazer Williams to be the son of Louis XVI. Mr. Hanson's theory of the causes which prevented his recognition are summed up in the statement that Williams was a Protestant; and the Catholics who only were in the secret, caused his rejection.

HARBISON (Massy).

Narrative of the Sufferings of Massy Harbison from Indian Barbarity giving an account of her captivity, the murder of her two children, her escape with an infant at her breast, Together with some account of the cruelties of the Indians on the Allegheny River &c. during the years 1790, '91, '92, '93, '94. Communicated by Herself. 16° *pp.* 66. *Pittsburgh, printed by S. Engles*, 1825. 650

HARDY (Lieut Campbell).

Sporting Adventures in The New World, or Days and Nights of Moose-Hunting in The pine forests, of Acadia. By Lieut. Campbell Hardy, royall artillery. In two volumes. 12° *pp.* xii. + 304 *and* viii. + 299. *London, Hurst & Blackett, publishers*, 1855. 651

The author's intimate associates in his sporting adventures, the Micmac Indians, occupy the largest share of his very interesting narrative. Some particulars regarding the numbers and characteristics of the aborigines of the provinces that have not been printed elsewhere, may be found in his volumes.

HARDY (Captain Campbell).

Forest Life in Acadia. Sketches of Sport and Natural History in the Lower Provinces of the Canadian Dominion. By Captain Campbell Hardy, Royal Artillery. 8° *pp.* 371 *and* 12 *plates. London, Chapman & Hall*, 1869. 652

Incidents of personal association with individuals of the Micmac and Milicete tribes of Indians, fill the volume.

HARIOT (Thomas).

Admiranda Narratio fida tamen de Commodis et Incolarum ritibus Virginiae, nuper admodum ab Anglis qui a Dn. Richardo Greinvile Equestris ordinis viro eo in Coloniam anno MDLXXXV deducii sunt inventae sumtis faciente viro fodinaru stanni praefecto ex auctoritate serenissime reginae Angliae. Anglico Scripta Sermone. A Thoma Hariot, eiusdem Walteri Domestico in eam Coloniam misso ut regionis situm diligenter observaret nunc autem primum Latio donata a C. C. A. Cum gratia et privilegio caes. Ma^tis Spec^ll ad quadriennium. *Francoforti ad moenum. Typis Ioannis Wecheli Sumtibus vero Theodori de Bry anno* CIϽ IϽXC (1590.) *Venales reperiuntur in officina Sigismundi Feirabendii. Folio.* 653

Collation, sixty-four leaves, namely, plate of Adam and Eve, reverse blank + 34 numbered pp. including engraved title + 4 unnumbered pp. + folding map of Virginia and 22 plates of Virginia Indians numbered in Roman letters from ii. to xxiii. The xiii., xvii., xix., xx., and xxii. are full-page or folding plates with the description on the reverse of five separate leaves. The xvii. is a folding plate counted as two leaves + 1 p. text, reverse blank + 5 full-page plates of Picts and 5 leaves of description of the same; recto of all but the first, blank + 2 pp. text + 3 pp. Index.

The illustrations, from plates engraved by Theodore de Bry, are of extraordinary beauty. They are all representations of savage life, principally of the Indians of Virginia, and although more or less imaginative, have been reproduced in a score of works, from Montanus to Lafitau, and of all sizes from folio to duodecimo. The English edition printed in the same year is extremely rare, having brought one thousand dollars in the Stevens' sale at Boston in 1870. It has been reproduced in fac-simile by the photo-lithographic process by Mr. Sabin, with the following title:—

HARIOT (Thomas).

A Briefe and True Report of the New Found Land of Virginia, of the Commodities and of the nature and manners of the Natural Inhabitants. Discouered by the English Colony there seated by Sir Richard Greinvile Knight In the Yeere 1585. Which remained Vnder the gouernment of twelve monethes, At the speciall charge and direction of the Honourable Sir Walter Raleigh Knight lord Warden of the Stanneries, who therein hath beene fauored and authorised by her Majestie and her letters patents: This fore booke Is made in English by Thomas Hariot [*etc.*, 11 *lines*]. *Folio. Franckfort*, 1590. *Reprinted by J. Sabin. Folio. New York*, 1871. 654

HARLOW (Lawrence).

The Conversion of an Indian in a letter to a friend by Lawrence Harlow. *London*, 1774. 655*

HARMON (Daniel Williams).

(A) Journal of Voyages and Travels in the Interior of North America between the 47th and 58th degrees of North Latitude, extending from Montreal nearly to the Pacific Ocean, a distance of about 5,000 miles, Including an account of the principal occurrences, during a residence of nineteen years, in different parts of the country. To which are added, a concise description of the face of the country, its Inhabitants, their Manners, Customs, Laws, Religions, *etc.* and considerable specimens of the two Languages most extensively spoken; together with an account of the principal animals, to be found in the forests and prairies of this extensive Region. Illustrated by a map of the Country. By Daniel Williams Harmon, a partner in the North West Company. *Portrait of Author, and pp.* 432. *Andover,* 1820. 656

This Journal purports to have been only revised and published by Mr. Daniel Haskell, but he is said to have introduced religious reflections not made by the author. Harmon's narration of events among and peculiarities of the Indian tribes is believed by those familiar with him, and the regions he visited, to be correct; but the life of a fur-trader, dispensing fire-water to the Indians, while daily witnessing the murders it produced, was not favorable to religious emotions. Mr. Haskell makes the writer reject the proffer of an Indian concubine by her father, with very proper pious emotions; but Mr. Schoolcraft intimates that the latter were not more consonant with his character than the story of his continence. A copious vocabulary of the Cree or Knistenaw language is given on pp. 385 to 412. The journal of events in his life as an Indian trader, terminates at page 373, and two subdivisions entitled "Account of the Indians living East of the Rocky Mountains," and "Account of the Indians living West of the Rocky Mountains," are evidently written by another hand, perhaps from Harmon's dictation.

HARRIS (Thaddeus Mason).

The Journal of a Tour into the Territory Northwest of the Alleghany Mountains; Made in the Spring of the year 1803. With a geographical and historical account of the State of Ohio. Illustrated with Original Maps and Views. By Thaddeus Mason Harris. 8° *pp.* 271 *and* 4 *maps. Boston,* 1805. 657

A portion of the book is devoted to a "Sketch of the Wars and Treaties with the Indians."

HARRISON (W. H.).

The Life of William Henry Harrison comprising a brief account of his important civil and military services and an accurate description of the Council at Vincennes with Tecumseh, as well as the Victories of Tippecanoe, Fort Meigs, and the Thames. 8° *pp.* 96 + 4 *plates. Philadelphia, published by Grigg & Elliot,* 1840. 658

This panegyric upon the candidate for the Presidency, possesses little merit except in its quotations from McAfee.

HARRISON (Wm. H.).

The Life of Major-General William Henry Harrison, comprising a brief account of his Important Civil and Military Services, and an accurate description of the *Council at Vincennes with Tecumseh,* as well as the victories of Tippecanoe, Fort Meigs, and the Thames. *pp.* 96, *and* 8 *wood-cuts. Philadelphia, Grigg & Elliot,* 9 *North Fourth Street,* 1840. 659

HARRISON (William Henry).

A Discourse on the Aborigines of the valley of the Ohio. In which the opinions of the conquest of that valley by the Iroquois or six Nations, in the Seventeenth Century supported by

Cadwallader Colden of New York, Governor Pownall of Massachusetts, Dr. Franklin, the Hon. De. Witt Clinton, of New York, and Judge Haywood of Tennessee, are examined and contested. [*etc., 5 lines.*] 8° *pp.* 47. *Boston*, 1840. 660

HARTLEY (Cecil B.).

Life and Adventures of Lewis Wetzel, The Virginia Ranger, to which are added Biographical Sketches of General Simon Kenton, General Benjamin Logan, Captain Samuel Brady, Governor Isaac Shelby and other heroes of the West. Illustrated with engravings from original designs by G. G. White. 12° *pp.* 320. *Philadelphia*, 1860. 661

HARTLEY (Cecil B.).

Life and Times of Colonel Daniel Boone, comprising History of the Early Settlement of Kentucky. By Cecil B. Hartley. To which is added Colonel Boone's Autobiography complete, as dictated to John Filson, and published in 1784. Illustrated with Engravings from original drawings by G. G. White, and other eminent artists. 12° *pp.* 351. *Philadelphia*, 1860. 662

HARVEY (Henry).

History of the Shawnee Indians, from the year 1681 to 1854 inclusive. by Henry Harvey, a member of the Society of Friends. 12° *Portrait, and pp.* 316. *Cincinnati, Ephraim Morgan and Sons*, 1855. 663

The author says of himself, "Having for a number of years been engaged in endeavors to ameliorate the condition of the Shawnee Tribe of Indians, I have become very much attached to them, on account of a near intimacy with them, which enabled me to become acquainted with the character of this noted and very interesting people. I was connected with them, too, at a time when one of those severe trials overtook them, of which the Indians so much complain, more bitterly by far than they do of the most desolating wars, by which they have ever been visited,— which was the procuring (*the wresting from them*) their reservations of land at Wa-paugh-koo-netta, in the State of Ohio, containing near one hundred thousand acres. I have been an eye-witness to most I have related in regard to this people, and in all my intercourse have ever found them a noble, generous hearted, honest and ever confiding people, of strong minds, powerful intellect, warmly attached to their friends, ever true to their word in matters of self interest, when treated fairly, and patient under suffering." If the story of the wrongs of the Shawnees, whose high character is attested in such eloquent language, does not stir the indignation of the reader, it can only be because his heart is dead, or his brain torpid. It tempts one to doubt the justice of God. The work is one of the most simple and veritable narrations of facts relating to the Indians ever printed. The author gives us in the first 138 pages, a history of the tribe to the year 1812, at which period the Society of Friends undertook their amelioration. From this period the narrative is almost entirely from the personal observation of the writer, and is the most sadly interesting that can be conceived.

HATFIELD AND DEERFIELD.

Papers concerning the Attack on Hatfield and Deerfield, by a Party of Indians from Canada September 19, 1677. *Imp.* 8° *Map, and pp.* 82. *Bradford Club, New York*, 1859. 664

HAVEN (Samuel F.).

Archaeology of the United States, or Sketches, historical, and bibliographical of the progress of information and opinion respecting vestiges of Antiquity in the United States. By Samuel F. Haven, Washington City. Published by the Smithsonian Institution, July 1856. 4° *pp.* 168. *New York, G. P. Putnam & Co.* 665

HAWES (Barbara).

Tales of the American Indians and Adventures of the Early Settlers in America. By Barbara Hawes. 12° *pp.* 862. *London, printed for Longman & Co.*, 1844. 666

A collection of anecdotes and narratives of Indian life and warfare, some of which are from sources not now easily accessible.

HAWKINS (Sir Richard).

The Observations of Sir Richard Hawkins K^nt^ in his voyage into The South Sea in the year 1593, reprinted from the edition of 1622, edited by C. R. Drinkwater, Captain R. N. 8° *pp.* xvi. + 246. *London, printed for the Hakluyt Society*, 1847. 667

Some particulars relating to the Indians of Florida, the Caribbean Islands, and parts of South America, are given by the worthy and credulous knight, which interest us, as data of their history and mode of life two and a half centuries ago.

HAWKINS (Col. Benj.).

Sketch of the Creek Country with a Description of the Tribes, Government, and Customs of the Creek Indians by Col. Benj. Hawkins, for Twenty Years Resident Agent of that Nation. Preceded by a Memoir of the Author and a history of the Creek Confederacy. Published by the Georgia Historical Society. 8° *pp.* 88. *Savannah*, 1848. 668

The author of this treatise was for more than thirty years employed by the Government of the United States in its intercourse with the Indians. He was styled by the Creeks, Choctaws, Chickasaws, and Cherokees, the Beloved Man of the Four Nations. He wrote eight volumes of material relating to the history of the various Indian tribes with whom he treated. These volumes of MSS. are filled with details of treaties, his correspondence on the behalf of the tribes with the general and state governments, vocabularies of Indian languages, and records of the manners and customs, religious rites and civil polity of these wonderful aboriginal nations. This treatise is filled with sketches of all these particulars as existing in the Creek nation.

HAYNE (Mr.).

Speech of Mr. Hayne of Georgia delivered in the House of Representatives January 21, 1831, in reply to Mr. Everett of Massachusetts on the Indian Question. 8° *pp.* 13. *Washington*, 1831. 669

HAYWOOD (John).

The | Natural and Aboriginal | History | of | Tennessee, | up to the | First Settlements therein | by the | White People | in the | year 1768. | By John Haywood | of the County of Davidson, in the State of Tennessee. | 8° *Half title*, 1 *leaf. Title* 1 *leaf. Contents and Preface pp.* v. *to* viii. *Natural and Aboriginal His-*

tory of Tennessee, pp. 1 *to* 390. *Commentaries, pp.* I. *to* II. *Errata, two pp. Nashville,* | *printed by George Wilson,* | 1823. | 670

In this book, now exceedingly rare and highly prized, the author has brought together a very large number of curious facts, relating to the origin and character of the natives of his State, prior to the settlement by the whites. He does not favor the hypothesis of great antiquity in the Indian nations of America, and believes in their common origin with the Caucasian race. He describes with great minuteness and care the relics of the race which once inhabited the territory, its utensils, skeletons, crania, and fortifications, most of which he appears to have personally inspected.

HAYWOOD (J.).
The | Civil and Political | History | of the | State of Tennessee | from its | Earliest Settlement | up to | the year 1796 | Including the | Boundaries of the State | By John Haywood | . 8° *Title, reverse blank, slip of copyright. Preface,* 1 *p. reverse blank* + *pp.* 1 *to* 504. *Printed for the author* | *by Heiskel and Brown* | *Knoxville Tenn.* | 1823. | 671

This work, only less rare than the Aboriginal History of Tennessee by the same author, contains a large portion of the material relating to the border warfare with the Indians, narrated in the last mentioned work. The speculative and antiquarian portions and descriptions of mounds are omitted in this volume, but the story of Indian conflicts and massacres is narrated with greater detail and minuteness, filling much the larger portion of the work. The story of the formation of the State of Franklin, and the civil war which ensued, is a chapter of American history but little known, and scarcely exceeded in interest by any other.

HAZART (P. C.).
Kerckelycke Historie vande ghehele Wereldt etc. Inde welcke verhaelt worden de gheleghentheden der landen, manieren, ceremonien, ende Inwoorders maer naemelijck de Verbreydinghe des H. Gheloofs Martelaren, ende andere Cloecke Roomsche Catholijcke daeden, Inde vier ghewesten des wereldts, met over de 40 Copere platen verciert. Beschriven Door den Eerw P. Cornelius Hazart Priester der Societeyt Jesu. Het eerste deel. Vervatteude de Rijcken ende landen van Japonien China Mogor Bisnagar, Peru, Mexico, Brasilien, Florida, Canada, Paraguarien, Maragnan. T'Antwerpien. *Folio. By Michael Cnobbaert,* 1682. 672

HAZART (P. C.).
The Same in German. Two Volumes. *Folio. Same plates half page size. printed in* 1634. 673

[Church History of the whole world principally of the foregoing and present century: In which is narrated the situation of the Countries, the Manners, Ceremonies, and Religion of the Inhabitants but more especially of the Propagation of the Holy Gospel, of the Martyrs, and other acts of the Roman Catholics.]

This is the title of the fourth volume of Hazart's Church History in Dutch, published in four volumes, folio, of which only this contains anything relating to America. Pages 311 to 457 are occupied with the history of the Jesuit Missions among the Indians of Peru, Brazil, Mexico, Florida, Canada, Paraguay, and Maragnan. This portion of the work is illustrated with eighteen full-page copper-plate engravings, of which seven are portraits of

Indians of each of the countries named, and eleven represent the martyrdom of the missionaries by the natives. Most of these plates are beautifully drawn and engraved, and exhibit the various forms of torture and massacre by which the missionaries and their converts were put to death, with the most vivid and painful fidelity. The account of missions in Florida and Canada, fills thirty-four pages. One of the plates in this part of the work represents the martyrdom of Father Jogues and two French associates by the Mohawks; another exhibits the tortures by which Fathers Brebeuf and Lallemant were killed in Canada; and a third the murder of Fathers Daniel and Garnier by the Indians of the same country.

HEAD (Captain B. F.).

Rough Notes taken during Some Rapid Journeys across The Pampas and among the Andes. By Captain B. F. Head. 12° *pp.* 204. *Boston*, 1827. 674

Besides his descriptions of the rude life of the savage Guachos, and the fearful atrocities of the Saltendores, both of the Creole or Mestiso race, the author gives on pp. 61 to 114 an account of "The Indians of the Pampas."

HEARD (Isaac V. D.).

History of the Sioux War and Massacres of 1862 and 1863. By Isaac V. D. Heard. With Portraits and illustrations. 12° *pp.* 354 *with* 33 *plates. New York, Harper & Brothers*, 1865. 675

The gloomy details of this dreadful massacre, lead us to inquire the cause of such an apparently unexplainable frenzy for slaughter. Although the author affords us little light upon this part of the sad history, yet from other sources we discover that it was but a repetition of the old story, of the red man made desperate by a sense of unbearable wrongs, avenging them upon the innocent. Pushed back from their fertile and game-thronged hunting-grounds, to sterile lands unfrequented by the animals upon which they subsist, deluded by promises of annuities which fail to come, while their wives and children perish by famine or cold, the unreasoning savages, made furious by their sufferings, overwhelmed the innocent German settlers, in their undistinguishing thirst for blood.

HEARNE (Samuel).

A Journey from Prince of Wale's Fort in Hudson's Bay, to The Northern Ocean. Undertaken by order of the Hudson's Bay Company, for the Discovery of Copper-Mines, A North West Passage &c., In the Years 1769, 1770, 1771, & 1772. By Samuel Hearne. *Large* 4° *pp.* xliv. + 500 + 9 *folding maps and plans. London, printed for A. Strahan and T. Cadell: and sold by T. Cadell, Jun. and W. Daviess (successors to Mr. Cadell), in the Strand*, 1795. 676

HEARNE (Samuel).

A Journey from Prince of Wale's Fort in Hudson's Bay to the Northern Ocean undertaken by order of the Hudson's Bay Company, for the Discovery of Copper Mines, a Northwest Passage, &c. In the Years 1769, 1770, 1771, & 1772. By Samuel Hearne. 8° *pp.* l + 460 + 9 *folding maps and plates of northern Indians, etc. Dublin, printed for P. Byrne*, 1796. 677

The most satisfactory narration of the life and peculiarities of the northern Indians is by honest old Hearne. Nothing can be more vivid than his descriptions of their savage customs, their brutal indifference to their own as well as others' sufferings, and their horrible massacres of rival tribes. It is to a most singular fortune of war, that we owe the publication of this interesting journal. When the fort on Hudson's Bay was surrendered by the unfortunate and heroic La Perouse, he recommended that the British authorities should cause Hearne's MS. Journal which he found at the fort, to be printed. He declared that it possessed so much interest that he had read it with the greatest pleasure, and it is believed that a copy he had made accompanied him in his last voyage. Narrated by Albert Gallatin, and confirmed, as Mr. Stevens says, in the prologomena of the French edition of Hearne. Paris, 1799, 2 vols. 8°.

HECKEWELDER (John).

A Narrative of the Mission of the United Brethren among the Delaware and Mohegan Indians, from its commencement, in the year 1740, to the close of the year 1808. Comprising all the Remarkable Incidents which took place at their Missionary Stations during that Period. Interspersed with Anecdotes, Historical Facts, Speeches of Indians, and other interesting matter. By John Heckewelder, who was many years in the service of that Mission. 8° *Portrait and pp.* 429. *Philadelphia, published by McCarty & Davis.* 1820. 678

The narrative of this mission is a history of the noblest labors of the human race, for the civilization of a savage people, and at the same time the record of the most horrible crime perpetrated by a civilized people turned savages. It is the account of a large number of the aborigines, collected into a community; governed by all the refinements of a gentle and admirable humanity, sacrificed to the brutal and cowardly vengeance of a murderous mob. Ninety Christian men and women with their children were slaughtered and scalped without attempting resistance, to revenge the outrages of Pagan Indians whom the civilized wretches dared not attack. The massacre was terribly avenged by their Pagan kindred. The frontier was desolated for ten years, and the Colonel Crawford who was present, was afterwards burnt at the stake in avowed retaliation for this very deed of blood. Heckewelder's narrative is a full and undoubtedly faithful record of all the details of the Mission, its wonderful success and its appalling destruction. He was able to give a thousand particulars from personal experience, and it is at once an interesting story abounding in veritable incidents, and a valuable history, fortified by impregnable facts.

There could be no better guarantee of the value of a treatise on the American Indians, than the names of Rev. John Heckewelder and Peter S. Duponceau. Forty years of missionary life among the Delaware and Shawnese tribes, had amply fitted the author of the history to record the facts which fell under his own knowledge. Although his want of familiarity in ethnological and philological science, have caused his deductions and hypotheses to be somewhat derided, yet it must be conceded that his statements regarding the history of the aboriginal tribes with which he was personally familiar, are those of a conscientious and faithful, if not an accurate observer.

It is unfortunate for us, as for the author, that his history was written at a late period of his life; and that when it was suggested to him, he was not prepared with notes and journals written during his long period of service as a missionary. The first six chapters, pp. 29-83, are occupied with the history of the Indian Nations as derived from tradition, and an account of the various tribes which inhabited Pennsylvania. Chapters vi. to vii., pp. 83 to 103, are devoted to "General Character, Government, and Education of the Indians." Chapters ix. to xiii. treat of "Languages of the Tribes, Signs and Hieroglyphics, Oratory, Metaphorical Expressions, and Indian Names." Chapters xiv. to xviii. are entitled "Intercourse with each other, Political Manœuvres, Marriage, Respect for the Aged, and Pride and Greatness of Mind." Chapters xix. to xxii. are filled with a "Relation of their manner of making War, Peace, and Treaties." The remainder of the work is occupied with a relation of their domestic and public life.

HECKEWELDER (John).

An Account of the History, Manners, and Customs of the Indian Nations, who once inhabited Pennsylvania and the neighboring States. By the Rev. John Heckewelder, of Bethlehem. Pp. iv. + 347, of Transactions of the Historical and Literary Committee of the American Philosophical Society, Held at Philadelphia for promoting useful knowledge. 8° *Portrait and pp.* l. + iv. + 465. *Philadelphia*, 1819. 679

Contents: Report on the general character and forms of the languages of the American Indians, by Peter S. Duponceau, pp. xvii. to l. Catalogue of manuscript works, on the Indians and their languages, presented to the American Philosophical Society, or deposited in their library, pp. xlvii. to l. No. I. An Account of the History, etc. of Indian Nations, by Heckewelder, pp. iv. + 1 to 348. No. II. A Correspondence between the Rev. John Heckewelder of Bethlehem, and Peter S. Duponceau respecting the Languages of the American Indians, pp. 351 to 448. Containing vocabularies and grammatical analyses of the Delaware and Shawnese tongues. No. III. Words, Phrases, and Short Dialogues, in the Language of the Lenni Lenape, or Delaware Indians. By John Heckewelder, pp. 451 to 464. A vocabulary prepared by Heckewelder, very full, and undoubtedly very accurate.

HECKEWELDER (Jean).

Histoire Moeurs et Coutumes des Nations Indiennes qui habitaient autrefois la Pennsylvanie et les etats voisins, par le Reverend Jean Heckewelder Missionnaire Morave Traduit de l'Anglais Par le Chevalier Du Ponceau. 8° *Half title, title + pp.* 522. *A Paris*, 1822. 680

With the exception of the Preface by the translator, this work is a French translation of Heckewelder's "History of the Manners and Customs of the Indian Nations, etc." by the learned Du Ponceau, whose interest in the aboriginal history of America has never been exceeded by any scholar of Anglo-Saxon origin.

HELPS (Arthur).

The Life of Las Casas "The Apostle of the Indies." By Arthur Helps. 12° *Map and pp.* xix. + 292. *Philadelphia, J. B. Lippincott*, 1868. 681

The execution of this work could hardly have fallen into more worthy or competent hands. Prepared by his investigations for several years into the documents that would illustrate his Spanish conquest of America, Mr. Helps' work was half accomplished when designed. The apostle of the Indians deserves the grandest monument which human genius has yet conceived for the heroes of humanity. He was not satisfied, like many of his priestly order, with the salvation of the souls of his savage flock; he constituted himself by gigantic efforts the saviour of their bodies. In accomplishing this he has been for three centuries subjected to the taunt of being the first suggestor of African slavery. Mr. Helps most irresistibly refutes that slander; and adds a statement which will account for the malignity of the aspersion; "Las Casas had, it may be fearlessly asserted, a greater number of bitter enemies than any man who ever lived."

HELPS (Arthur).

The Spanish Conquest in America, and its relation to the History of Slavery and to the Government of the Colonies. By Arthur Helps. *Four vols.* 8° *London: Parker, Son, and Bourn,* 1861. 682

The whole of this noble work is devoted to a history of the relations of the Indians of America to its Spanish invaders; and the effect of their occupation, and conquest upon the population, religion, and manners of the aborigines. The various narratives and histories, which describe the awful destruction of many Indian nations by the Spaniards, are criticised with true philosophical acumen, and the veracity and capability of their authors fairly examined. It treats the whole story of the Indians and their conquerors, during the sixty years which immediately succeeded the discovery, in that continuous narrative style, by which our curiosity is aroused, and our interest perpetuated, without losing the dignity of veracious history. The mind of the learned author was evidently inspired by that divine spirit that is born only of the wedlock of humanity and scholarship. Every page affords evidence of historical lore, and almost every sentence glows with the warmth of his philanthropy.

Henderson (James).

A History of Brazil comprising its geography, commerce, colonization, Aboriginal Inhabitants, &c., &c., &c. By James Henderson, recently from South America, illustrated with twenty-eight plates and two maps. 4° *pp.* 522. *London, printed for the author, and published by Longman, Hurst, Rees, Orme, and Brown, Paternoster Row,* 1821. 683

Henderson (George).

Account of the British Settlement of Honduras, being a view of its commercial and agricultural resources, Soil, climate, Natural history, &c. To which are added Sketches of the Manners and Customs of the Mosquito Indians and Journal of a Voyage to the Mosquito Shore. Illustrated with a Map. Second edition enlarged, by Capt. Henderson 44th Regt. 8° *Map, and pp.* xi. + 237. *London,* 1811. 684

A division of the work commencing on p. 211 is entitled "Sketches of the Manners and Customs of the Mosquito Indians," which terminates at page 229; the last three pages being occupied with a vocabulary of their language. With this brief fulfillment of the promise on the title-page, the purchaser must content himself, if he procured the work for a relation of the Mosquito Indians.

Hennepin (L.).

A New Discovery of a Vast Country in America Extending above Four Thousand Miles between New France and New Mexico With a Description of the Great Lakes, Cataracts, Rivers, Plants, and Animals. Also the Manners, Customs and Languages of the several Native Indians and the Advantage of Commerce with those different Nations. With a Continuation, Giving an Account of the Attempts of the Sieur De la Salle upon the Mines of St. Barbe &c. The Taking of Quebec by the English. With the Advantages of a Shorter Cut to China and Japan. Both Parts Illustrated with Maps, and Figures, and Dedicated to his Majesty K. William. By L. Hennepin now Resident in Holland. To which are added, Several New

Discoveries in North America not publish'd in the French Edition. 12° *London*, 1698. 685

Frontispiece, Title 1 leaf, Dedication 4 leaves, Preface 8 leaves, Contents 4 leaves, Map and pp. 1 to 243, Plates at pp. 24, 60, 80, and 98. Continuation Title 1 leaf, Dedication 4 leaves, Preface 12 pp., Contents 7 pp., Map and pp. 1 to 228, Plates at pp. 9 and 33.

The work was translated and printed in London, 1698, as above described. But there is an English edition purporting to be of the same year, with an entirely different collation. The printing of this edition is inferior, the type of the second part being so much smaller that instead of 228 pages, it has but 178. At the end of this part is an additional relation commencing with page 301, and ending at page 355. Dr. O'Callaghan enumerates twenty-three editions in his bibliography of Hennepin's works in the *Historical Magazine*, Vol. II. p. 24.

It has been the fashion until late in this age, to deride the work of Father Hennepin, as smacking of the marvelous. Indeed, some of our savants have endeavored to prove that the very excellent Father Recollect never saw any of the wonders he narrates. This severe criticism proceeds from sources which entitle him to the benefit at least of a doubt of its impartiality. First. Father Charlevoix, who cast the first cloud of suspicion, was a missionary priest of the Jesuits, who were at one time under the ban in New France through the influence of the Recollects, to which order Father Hennepin belonged. Second. The author lost the support of his own brethren of the order of Recollects by neglecting or refusing to return to his duties in America as a missionary. He accordingly retired to Utrecht in Holland, where in 1697 he reprinted his book published at Paris in 1683 (some copies have the date of 1684). In the course of the next year it was reissued as printed at Amsterdam 1698. Mr. Rich places the date of 1698 also on an edition printed at Utrecht. The first book of Father Hennepin is entitled, *Description de la Louisiane.* 12° Paris, 1683. The same, 1688. Reprinted with additional matter as *Nouvelle Decouverte d'un tres Grand Pays situé dans Am. Utrecht.* 12° 1697. The same title, Amsterdam, 1698. Then in the same year, in the form which the reverend father calls his third volume, *Nouveau Voyage d'un Pais plus grand que l'Europe.* This however is not the same work as the two former. *See Addenda.*

HENRY (Alexander).

Travels and Adventures in Canada and the Indian Territories between the years 1760 and 1776. In Two Parts. By Alexander Henry Esq. 8° *Portrait and pp.* viii. + 330. *New York, printed and published by I. Riley*, 1809. 686

In PART I. the author relates the incidents of his life as a fur-trader among the Indians on the shores of the upper great lakes; of the surprise and massacre of the garrison of Fort Michillimackinac, of his own narrow escape from the slaughter, and his capture. His narrative of the details of his long captivity is very interesting, and has been deemed the most authentic we have, relating to the domestic habits of the northern Indians. PART II. is a narrative journal of travels through the Indian countries, and supplies much additional information regarding the natives.

HERIOT (George).

Travels through the Canadas, containing a description of the picturesque scenery of some of the rivers and lakes with an account of the productions, commerce and inhabitants of those provinces, to which is subjoined a Comparative View of the Manners and Customs of the Indian Nations of North and

South America by George Heriot. Illustrated with a map and numerous engravings from drawings made at the several places by the author. 4° *24 colored plates, pp. 602. London*, 1807. 687

Part Second is entitled, "Manners and Customs of the American Indians," and occupies Chapters xii. to xx., pp. 271 to 602, which are entirely devoted to a minute description of the peculiarities of various nations of American aborigines, principally derived from other printed works. The last thirty-one pages are filled with Father Rasle's vocabulary of the Algonquin language.

HERNDON (Lewis) and LARDNER GIBBON.

Exploration of the Valley of the Amazon made under the direction of the Navy Department, by Wm. Lewis Herndon and Lardner Gibbon. Four vols. 8° *Two vols. text with many plates, and two vols. map. Washington*, 1854. 688

These volumes contain minute, accurate, and very interesting accounts of the aborigines of the Andes, and the Amazon and its tributaries.

HERRERA (Antonio de).

Historia General de los Hech^s de los Castellanos en las Islas i Terra Firme del Mar Oceanos escrita por Antonio de Herrera Coronista Mayor de Sum^d de las Indias y sv Coronista de Castilla. En quatro Decadas desde el Ano de 1492, hasta el de (1)531. *En Madrid en la Imprenta Real de Nicolas Rodriguez franco, Año de* 1720. *Folio* 689

[General History of the Proceedings of the Castilians in the Isles and Mainland of the Ocean Sea, written by Antonio de Herrera, First Chronicler of His Majesty for the Indies and his Chronicler for Castille. In Four Decades, from the year 1492 to that of 1531. In Madrid in the Royal Printing-office of Nicolas Rodriguez Franco. In the year 1720.]

Four volumes, containing Eight Decades. Each decade has an engraved title and separate pagination. Vol. I. Title and pp. (xlvi.) + Engraved Title of Decade 1 dated 1730 + 78 pp. + 292 + (iv.). Decade 2. Title dated 1726, and pp. 268 + eleven maps. Decade 3. Title dated 1726, and (ii.) prel. pp. + 296. Decade 4. Title dated 1730, and (iv.) prel. pp. + 232. Decade 5. Title dated 1728 and (vi.) prel. pp. + 252. Decade 6. Title dated 1730, and (iv.) prel. pp. + 236. Decade 7. Title dated 1730 and (iv.) prel. pp. + 245. Decade 8. Title dated 1730 + (iv.) prel. pp. + 251 + (452). Each engraved title is divided into from ten to fourteen compartments, in which is represented some scene of the conquest of the Indians by the invading Spaniards, or a portrait of some eminent Conquistador; seventy-two battle-scenes, views of human sacrifices, or Indian life, and thirty-nine portraits are thus exhibited. This is the edition edited and published by the celebrated Barcia, the original of which was printed in 1601 and 1615.

HERRERA (Antoine de).

Histoire Generale des Voyages et Conquestes des Castillans dans les Isles & Terre-Firme des Indes Occidentales Traduite de l'Espagnol d'Antoine D'Herrera, Historiographe de la Majeste Catholique, tant des Indes, que des Royaumes de Castille. Par N de la Coste. Ou l'on voit la prise de la grande ville de Mexique, & autres Provinces par Fernand Cortes; Sa Fon-

dation, Les rois qui la gouvernerent; La Commencement & fin de cet Empire; Leurs Coutumes & Ceremonies; Les grandes revoltes qui y sont arrivez; Les Contestations qui eurent les Castillians & les Portugais sur l affiette de la ligne de partage de leurs conquestes; La decouverte des Isles Philippines par Hernando de Magellan; Sa mort, & autres choses remarquables. Dedidie a Monseigneur le premier President. 4° *pred. pp.* xviii. + 790 + (xii). *A Paris,* 1671. *Three vols.* 690

[General History of the Voyages and Conquests of the Spaniards in the Islands and Continent of the West Indies. Translated from the Spanish of Antonio Herrera by N. de la Coste. In which history will be found, The Conquest of the great city of Mexico and other Provinces by Hernando Cortes, with its Foundation; The Native Kings who governed it; The Commencement and end of that Empire; The Customs & Ceremonies of the Natives; The great insurrections which occurred. The Contests between the Spaniards and Portuguese regarding the boundaries of their respective Conquests, etc.]

HERRERA (Antonio de).

The General History of the vast Continent and Islands of America, Commonly call'd the West-Indies from The First Discovery thereof: With the best Accounts the People could give of their Antiquities. Collected from the Original Relations sent to the Kings of Spain. By Antonio de Herrera, Historiographer to his Catholic Majesty. Translated into English by Capt. John Stevens. Illustrated with Cuts and Maps. The Second Edition. *Six vols.* 8° *with* 15 *plates and three maps. London, printed for Wood & Woodward in Paternoster-Row,* 1740. 691

No one has ever disputed the fidelity of old Herrera, styled the Prince of Historians, to the sources of information then accessible, and no one has ever exceeded him in careful research, and interesting narration of aboriginal history. He sought and obtained many of the original documents, which the industry and spirit of the old missionaries and explorers made so numerous and voluminous. He copied, almost bodily, the MS. History of the Indies by Las Casas. Mr. Squire notices that he has transferred almost the entire MS. Relacion of Palacio, to chapters 8, 9, and 10 of the Eighth Book of his Fourth Decade. His work is a perfect treasure-house of the most valuable details, regarding the original state of the religion and manners of the Indians. Of Herrera, Ternaux says, "Among the historians of America this author holds the first rank." He was born in [illegible], and was for some time secretary of the Viceroy of Naples, being afterwards appointed Historiographer of the Indies. His work is the most complete of all those which we possess upon that subject of the epoch it embraces. Herrera incorporated into his work, almost the whole of Garcillaso de la Vega's work, *La Florida del Inca.* It is unfortunate for the student of history, that the translation is performed with the same unscrupulous license which most English editors of works on American history assumed a century ago. Captain John Stevens has left in his translation a monument of his own impertinent vanity, in the liberties he has taken with this noble history. He has transposed, abridged, and interpolated, and thus greatly impaired the value of his work, and yet it is the best translation we have of the whole of Herrera. Mr. Henry C. Murphy considers the French translation, which extends only to the first three decades, to be much the best, as it is so exact as to reproduce the original,—book for book, chapter for chapter, and almost phrase for phrase."

[HILDRETH (James).]
Dragoon Campaigns to the Rocky Mountains, being a History of the Enlistment, Organization and first Campaigns of the regiment of United States Dragoons, together with incidents in a Soldier's life and Sketches of Scenery and Indian Character by a dragoon. 8° *pp.* 250, *with Appendix* 250 *to* 288. *New York*, 1836. 692

HILDRETH (Samuel P.).
Contributions to the Early History of the North-West, including the Moravian Missions in Ohio, by Samuel P. Hildreth. 18° *pp.* 240. *Cincinnati, published by Poe & Hitchcock*, 1864. 693

The incidents of border warfare and Indian life narrated in this book, seem to have been gathered from the personal experience of the author, during fifty years' residence among the actors whose deeds are narrated.

HILDRETH (S. P.).
Biographical and Historical Memoirs of the early Pioneer Settlers of Ohio with Narratives of Incidents and Occurrences in 1775, by S. P. Hildreth. To which is annexed A Journal of Occurrences which happened, in the circles of the Author's personal observation in the detachment commanded by Col. Benedict Arnold, consisting of two Battalions from the United States Army at Cambridge, Mass., in A. D. 1775, by Colonel R. J. Meigs. 8° *pp.* 539. *Cincinnati*, 1852. 694

I have never seen a copy of this book with Meigs' Journal, announced in the title as "annexed."

HILDRETH (S. P.).
Pioneer History: being an Account of the first Examinations of the Ohio Valley, and the Early Settlement of The Northwest Territory. Chiefly from Original Manuscripts; Containing the Papers of Col. George Morgan; those of Judge Barker; The Diaries of Joseph Buell and John Mathews; The Records of the Ohio Company, &c., &c., &c., by S. P. Hildreth. 8° *pp.* xiii. + 1 *to* 525 + 8 *Pl. & Map. Cincinnati and New York, H. W. Derby & Co., Publishers*, 1848. 695

The journals and narratives of Indian scouts and rangers, of Indian agents for forming treaties with the tribes of the West, and of captives among them, are transcribed in this volume in the exact language of the authors. These are all interwoven in the history, with a multitude of incidents of Indian warfare, and the wild fortunes of the borderers who survived the conflicts.

HILL (A.).
The Gospel of our Lord and Saviour Jesus Christ, according to St. Matthew. Translated into the Mohawk Language by A. Hill, and Corrected by J. A. Wilkes, Jr. 12° *pp.* 197. *New York*, 1836. 696

HILL (H. A.).
The Acts of the Apostles in the Mohawk Language. Translated by H. A. Hill, with Corrections by William Hess and John A. Wilkes, Jr. 12° *pp.* 121. *New York*, 1835. 697

HILL (H. A.).

The Epistle of Paul the Apostle to the Romans, in the Mohawk Language, translated by H. A. Hill, with corrections by William Hess and John A. Wilkes, Jr. 12° *pp.* 56. *Published by the Young Men's Bible Society, New York*, 1835. 698

HIND (Henry Youle).

Narrative of the Canadian Red River Exploring Expedition of 1857, and of the Assinniboine and Saskatchewan Exploring Expedition of 1858, by Henry Youle Hind. In charge of the Assinniboine and Saskatchewan Expedition. In Two Volumes. *Thick* 8°. Vol. I. *pp.* xx. + 494. Vol. II. *pp.* xvi. + 472. *London*, 1860. 699

Each volume has a half title. The work contains twenty colored plates of scenery and portraits of the aborigines, and seventy-six wood-cuts of the same in the text, and eleven colored maps and plans. During this exploration, Mr. Hind lived almost constantly among the Crees and Chippeways, whose habits and peculiarities he was most eager to study, and prompt to record. Everything in their life had not only the charm of novelty, to him, but as a man of science, he was anxious to observe all the facts which may prove stepping-stones in tracing their origin and their history. Besides the incidents of Aboriginal life, which crowd almost every page, the author has devoted Chapters xxviii. to xxxii., pp. 103 to 205, Vol. II., to the subjects entitled, Indian Wealth, Indian Customs and Superstitions, Indian Population, Indian Title, and Missionary Labors among Indians.

HIND (Henry Youle).

Explorations in the Interior of The Labrador Peninsula, the Country of the Montagnais and Nasquapee Indians, by Henry Youle Hind. In Two Volumes. 8° Vol. I. *pp.* xv. + 351. Vol. II. *pp.* xiii. + 304 + 14 *plates, numerous wood-cuts in text. London*, 1863. 700

All that Mr. Hind undertakes, is done so thoroughly that little more could be indicated, to complete the exhaustion of his subject. All the peculiarities of the aboriginal races of Labrador, which a stranger would be permitted to observe, he noted. We are enabled to see how the territory, swept of its animal tenants to furnish the white man with skins and furs, has become no longer capable of furnishing its savage inhabitants with food; how the unhappy Indian has been pushed towards the frigid zone until he has reached a point beyond which human constitutions are unfitted for enduring its rigors, and how thus, from want of the wild food his wild habits and tastes demand, the aborigines have dwindled to a handful.

Mr. Hind's volumes are almost entirely occupied with incidents of Indian life and character, particularly of the Montagnais, Abenakis, and Esquimaux Indians. The engravings are illustrative of scenes in aboriginal life, or of their customs, features, and other peculiarities.

Chapter xxvii., pp. 96 to 111, of Vol. II., is entitled, "The Nasquapees, or the people standing upright." Chapter xxviii., pp. 112 to 124, has the heading, "The present Condition of the Montagnais Indians." "The Labradorians," is the subject of Chapter xxx., pp. 150 to 166, in which the habits and character of the Esquimaux are illustrated. "The Roman Catholic Missions of the Labrador Peninsula," is the title of Chapter xxxi., pp. 167 to 180. In the Appendix No. I., the Indians of the Youcon are the subject of a report by the Rev. W. W. Kirby. "The Esquimaux of Anderson's River," is the subject of Appendix No. IV. "Census of the Indian Tribes" of No. V. "Indian Races north of the Cree hunting-grounds," of No. VI. And "Moravian Missions among the Esquimaux," of No. VII., all of which occupy pp. 254 to 266. Although these particular sections of the work upon aboriginal affairs are cited, yet it must be said that the whole work is a great repository of facts relating to them.

HINES (Rev. Gustavus).
(Life on the Plains of the Pacific.) Oregon, its History, Condition, and Prospects. Containing a description of the Geography, Climate, and Productions, with Personal Adventures among the Indians during a residence of the Author on the Plains bordering the Pacific while connected with The Oregon Mission, embracing extended notes of a voyage around the world. 12° pp. 437. *Buffalo*, 1851. 701

HINMAN (S. D.).
Journal of the Rev. S. D. Hinman, Missionary to the Santee Sioux Indians, and Taopi, by Bishop Whipple. 12° pp. 87. *Philadelphia, McCalla & Stavely*, 1869. 702

HISTORY
Of the Deleware and Iriquois Indians, Formerly inhabiting the Middle States. With Various Anecdotes Illustrating their Manners and Customs. Embellished with a variety of original Cuts. 16° pp. 158. *Philadelphia*, n. d. (1832). 703

HODGSON (Adam).
Remarks during a Journey through North-America in the Years 1819, 1820, and 1821, in a series of letters with An Appendix Containing An account of several of the Indian Tribes, and the principal Missionary Stations &c., [4 *lines*]. By Adam Hodgson, Esq. of Liverpool Eng. Collected, arranged, and published by Samuel Whiting. 8° pp. 335. *New York*, 1823. 704

The author gives on pp. 260 to 290 an account of his "Journey among the Creeks, Choctaws, Chickasaws, and Cherokees."

HODGSON (Adam).
Letters from North America written During a Tour in the United States and Canada. By Adam Hodgson. Two Volumes. 8° pp. 405 *and* 459. *Two plans of ancient aboriginal fortifications. London*, 1824. 705

Mr. Hodgson's account of his visit to the Creek and Choctaw Indians, and the Appendix, contain interesting particulars relating to the aborigines and their antiquities.

[HOFFMAN (Charles Fenno)].
A Winter in the (Far) West. By a New Yorker. In Two Volumes. 12° Vol. I. pp. xii. + 282. Vol. II. pp. viii. + 286. *New York, published by Harper & Brothers*, 1835. 706

The numerous incidents of personal intercourse with Indians of various western tribes, the interesting details which the author's ardent curiosity regarding them drew from persons familiar with their life and habits, and the voluminous notes appended to these volumes, extracted from works not easily accessible, entitle them to a high rank in aboriginal literature.

HOFFMAN (C. F.).

Wild Scenes in the Forest and Prairie. By C. F. Hoffman, Esq. Author of "A Winter in the Far West." In Two Volumes. Vol. I. *pp.* vi. + 292. Vol. II. *pp.* 284. *London, Richard Bentley, New Burlington Street*, 1839. 707

The Indian legends and stories narrated in these volumes, though tinged with the graceful romance, in which the imagination of the author's genius clothed his writings, are still truthful to the phases of aboriginal life which the author had witnessed.

HOLLISTER (G. H.).

Mount Hope; or Philip, King of the Wampanoags, an historical romance, by G. H. Hollister. 12° *pp.* 280. *New York, Harper & Brothers*, 1851. 708

Fiction, tinged with a little fact.

HOLMES (Abiel).

The History of Cambridge. By Abiel Holmes, A. M. 8° *pp.* 1 *to* 67. *Printed by Samuel Hall in Cornhill, Boston*, 1801. 709

HOLMES (Abiel).

A Memoir of the Mohegan Indians, written in the year 1804. s. d., s. l. *Half title.* 8° *pp.* 1 *to* 27. (*Boston*, 1804.) 710

Printed in a collection of the works of Mr. Holmes.

HOLMES (Abiel).

A Discourse delivered before the Society for Propagating the Gospel among the Indians in North America, at their Anniversary Meeting in Boston, November 3, 1808. By Abiel Holmes. 8° *pp.* 68. *Boston*, 1808. 711

Including thirty pages of Appendix, and historical notes of aboriginal affairs.

HOLMES (John).

Historical Sketches of Missions of the United Brethren, for Propagating the Gospel among the Heathen, from their commencement to the year 1817. By the Rev. John Holmes, Author of History of the Protestant Church of the United Brethren. Second improved edition. 8° *pp.* viii. + 472. *London*, 1827. 712

HOOPER (W. H.).

Ten Months among the tents of the Tuski, with incidents of an Arctic boat Expedition in Search of Sir John Franklin, as far as the Mackenzie River and Cape Bathurst. By Lieut. W. H. Hooper, with a Map and Illustrations. 8° *pp.* xvi. + 417 + *map* + 6 *full page plates. London, John Murray*, 1853. 713

That portion of the narrative of the Expedition in Arctic America, is entitled, Part II. Boat Expedition, and commences with Chapter xiv., pp. 212 to 417. It is filled with relations of encounters with the Esquimaux, and particulars of their mode of life, personal appearance and character, more particularly valuable and interesting, as the observations of one, who had so recently and intimately examined those of their congenors on the opposite shore of Behring's Straits. His long journey up Mackenzie's River on his return, furnishes us with many particulars of the Red-Indians of the Coppermine and other tribes, their wars with the Esquimaux, and the horrible massacres of these unwarlike people.

HOSMER (H. L.).
Early History of the Maumee Valley. By H. L. Hosmer. 8° *pp.* 70. *Toledo, published by Hosmer & Harris*, 1858. 714

This little volume is one of that limited number which disappoints us with its brevity. The very interesting incidents of border warfare at the River Raisin, Fort Meigs, and other terrible tragedies of the West, are apparently derived from original and authentic sources.

HORN (MRS.).
A Narrative of the Captivity of Mrs. Horn, and her two Children, with Mrs. Harris, by the Camanche Indians, after they had Murdered their Husbands and travelling Companions; with a brief account of the Manner and Customs of that Nation of Savages, of whom so little is Generally known. 12° *pp.* 60. *St. Louis*, 1839. 715

HORN (MRS.).
An Authentic and Thrilling Narrative of the Captivity of Mrs. Horn and her two children with Mrs. Harris, by the Camanche Indians and the murder of their husbands and travelling companions. 8° (n. d.) *Portrait and plate, and pp.* 32. *Cincinnati, published by the author.* 716

HORNII (Georgi).
De Originibus Americanis. Libri quatuor. Societas Illaeus. *Hagæ Comitis, Sumptibus Adriani Vlacq*, clc Ic cIII. [1652.] 16° *pp.* 20, *unnumbered* + 1 *to* 282. 717

This is the celebrated treatise, *Origin of the Americans*, published in answer to Grotius' *De Origine Gentium Americanorum*. It provoked an angry rejoinder from the latter, which was answered by a counter-treatise from De Laet. All of these essays display a degree of learning and refinement, which we shall look for in vain, to find bestowed on this vexed question in later days.

HOPKINS (Gerard T.).
A Mission to the Indians, from the Indian Committee of Baltimore yearly meeting, to Fort Wayne in 1804. Written at the time, by Gerard T. Hopkins, with an Appendix. Compiled in 1862, by Martha E. Tyson. 18° *pp.* 198. *Philadelphia: T. Ellwood Zell*, 1862. 718

Pages 1 to 120 are occupied with a Journal of a Mission, as it was termed, among the Indians of Ohio. It is in fact a narrative of the incidents of a visit of a committee of the Society of Friends, to the Miamis and Pottawatomies. It is filled with interesting details of these tribes, with some historical particulars relating to the defeat of St. Clair, not elsewhere printed. The Appendix, occupying the last seventy-eight pages, is a collection of additional incidents of the same tour, from the manuscripts of George Ellicott, who accompanied friend Hopkins, not less valuable as historical material, than the Journal.

The work was first printed in the *Friend's Intelligencer*, at the request of Mathew Tyson, in order to recall the somewhat dormant interest of the Society of Friends to the state of the Indians. Martha E. Tyson, his daughter, added the Appendix; and prepared the whole for printing in its present shape, at the expense of her father and brother. It was never offered for sale, but all the copies were presented to Friends and others interested in Indian affairs.

HOUGH (F. B.).

Diary of the Siege of Detroit in the War with Pontiac. Also a Narrative of the Principal Events of the Siege by Major Rogers; A Plan for Conducting Indian Affairs, by Colonel Bradstreet, and other Authentic Documents, never before printed. Edited with Notes, by Franklin B. Hough. 4° *Half title, pp.* i. *to* xxiii. + *Second half title, pp.* 301. *Albany, N. Y., J. Munsell,* 1860. 719

The Diary of the Siege of Detroit by Pontiac, and the confederated Indian tribes, occupies pp. 1 to 119, and Major Robert Rogers' journal of the Siege of Detroit, fills pp. 121 to 135. Colonel Bradstreet's plan for conducting Indian affairs is on pp. 137 to 157. "Papers relating to the Indian wars of 1763 and 1764, and the Conspiracy of Pontiac," occupy the remainder of the volume. In the frenzied era of book collecting, culminating in 1868, this book brought fifty and even sixty dollars. With other objects of fashion of that period, it has fallen in price to less than half the lower sum.

HOUGH (F. B.).

Notices of Peter Penet and of His Operations among the Oneida Indians, including a plan prepared by him for the government of that Tribe, read before the Albany Institute, January 23d, 1866. By Franklin B. Hough. 8° *Map and pages* 36. *Lowville, N. Y.,* 1866. 720

Edition limited to fifty copies. Peter Penet was a French adventurer, sometime employed as an agent by the Continental Congress, but absconded from Paris without accomplishing anything, except to bring undeserved annoyance and vexation upon Franklin, from the creditors Penet swindled. He fixed himself sometime after among the Oneidas, where he proved an equal torment to the excellent missionary Kirkland, got large grant lands from the credulous Indians, and again absconded.

HOUGH (F. B.).

Papers concerning the attack upon Hatfield and Deerfield by a party of Indians from Canada September 19, 1677. With an Introduction by F. B. Hough. Bradford club publication. 8° *pp.* 82. *New York,* 1859. 721

HOUGH (Franklin B.).

Proceedings of the Commissioners of Indian Affairs appointed by law for the extinguishment of Indian Titles in the State of New York. Published from the original manuscript in the library of the Albany Institute. With an Introduction and Notes by Franklin B. Hough (with maps). *Large* 4° *pp.* 498. *Albany,* 1861. 722

The same work, as the following in two volumes.

HOUGH (F. B.).

Proceedings of the Commissioners, Appointed by Law for the Extinguishment of Indian Titles in the State of New York. Published from the Original Manuscript in the Library of the Albany Institute. With an Introduction and Notes by Franklin B. Hough. Two vols. 4° Vol. I. *pp.* 255 + 8 *folding maps.* Vol. II. *Title and pp.* 256 *to* 501. *Albany, Joel Munsell,* MDCCCLXI. 723

The two volumes form ix. and x. of *Munsell's Historical Series*, and contain most of the documents, which record the extinguishment of the title of the Six Nations to a great portion of the State of New York in 1784. All of these tribes except the Oneidas, were to be punished for having taken part with the British against the colonists, and immediately on the ratification of peace, the Legislature appointed commissioners to treat with, or in other words, obtain from the Indians great tracts of fertile lands. The maps exhibit the divisions of lands claimed by the several tribes, and the boundaries of those obtained by the commissioners.

HOUSTON (Sam).

Nebraska bill. Indian Tribes. Speech of Hon. Sam Houston of Texas delivered in the Senate of the United States Feb. 14 and 15, 1854, in favor of maintaining the public faith with the Indian Tribes. 8° *pp.* 15. *Washington*, 1854. 724

HOW (Nehemiah).

A Narrative of Nehemiah How, who was taken by the Indians at the Great Meadow Fort above Fort Dummer, Where he was an inhabitant, October 11th 1745. Giving an account of what he met with in his travelling to Canada, and while he was in prision there. Together with an account of Mr. How's death at Canada [*Motto*]. *Boston N. E., printed and sold opposite to the Prision in Queen Street*, 1748. 725*

HOWE (Mrs. Jemimah).

An Account of the Captivity of Mrs. Jemimah Howe Taken by the Indians at Hinsdale N. H. July 27, 1755. 12° *pp.* 12 *to* 23. n. l., 1824. 726

In *Two Orations*, *by John Hancock and Joseph Warren.*

HOWSE (Joseph).

A Grammar of the Cree Language; with which is combined an analysis of the Chippeway Dialect. By Joseph Howse, Esq. F. R. G. S. and Resident twenty years in Prince Ruperts Land in the Service of the Hon. Hudson's Bay Company. 8° *pp.* 324. *London*, 1844. 727

HOYT (E.).

Antiquarian Researches, comprising a History of the Indian Wars in the Country bordering Connecticut River, and Parts Adjacent, and other interesting events, from the Landing of the Pilgrims to the Conquest of Canada by the English in 1760: With Notices of Indian Depredations in the Neighboring Country, &c. 8° *pp.* xii. + xii. + 312. *Greenfield, Mass.*, 1824. 728

HUBBARD (John N.).

Sketches of Border Adventures in the Life and Times of Major Moses Van Campen A Surviving Soldier of the Revolution. By his grandson John N. Hubbard, A. B. 8° *pp.* 310. *Bath, N. Y.*, 1841. 729

HUBBARD (W.).

The | Present State | of | New England | being a | Narrative

| of the Troubles with the | Indians | in | New England from the first planting | thereof in the year 1607 to this present year 1677 : | But chiefly of the late Troubles in the two last | years 1675 an 1676 | To which is added a Discourse about the War | with the Pequods in the year 1637. | By W. Hubbard Minister of Ipswich. [*Motto 6 lines.*] 4° *London: | printed for Tho Parkhurst at the Bible and Three Crowns in Cheapside, | near Mercers Chappel, and at the Bible on London Bridg*, 1677. 730

Order for Printing and Licence, verso of leaf 1 + title, 1 leaf + Epistle Dedicatory, two leaves + Advertisement to the Reader, 1 leaf + Poem to Hubbard, 1 leaf + Poem by Hubbard, 1 leaf + map + Narrative, pp. 1 to 131 + Table, 132 to 138 + Postscript, 139 to 144 + A Narrative, etc., pp. 1 to 88; total leaves, 123.

HUBBARD (W.).

A | Narrative | of the Troubles with the | Indians | in New-England from the first planting thereof in the | year 1607 to this present year 1677. But chiefly of the late | Troubles in the two last years 1675 and 1676. | To which is added a Discourse about the Warre with the | Pequods | In the year 1637. | By W. Hubbard Minister of Ipswich. | Published by Authority. 4° *Boston, printed by John Foster in the year* 1677. 731

Certificate signed Simon Bradstreet, Daniel Denison, Joseph Dudley, Boston, March 29, 1677 1 page, recto blank + title 1 p. reverse blank + "The Epistle Dedicatory," signed William Hubbard, 4 pp. + "An Advertisement to the Reader," 2 pp. + verses "To the Reverend Mr. William Hubbard," signed J. S., 1 p. + "Upon The elaborate Survey of New England's Passions," signed B. T., 2 pp. + "The printer to the Reader," 1 pp. + A Map of New-England Being the first that ever was here cut. [Total unnumbered preliminary leaves, seven.] "A Narrative of the Troubles," etc., pp. 1 to 132. + "A Table," etc., 7 unnumbered pp. "A Postscript" commencing on the eighth unnumbered page, covers seven pp. of which the last six are numbered 7 to 12 (but should be 9 to 14). A narrative, etc., pp. 1 to 88. On the eighty-eighth page twelve lines of errata in some copies, and in others only ten. Total number of leaves, 124.

This is the original of Hubbard's *Present State of New England, being a Narrative, &c.*, in every respect except the wording of the title, the table of errata, and the errors in the text. It has remained a matter of some doubt whether the London edition is not complete without the map, as the one in the few copies possessing it, has been found so often to correspond perfectly with the one in the American edition announced as "the first ever printed in this country;" and may have been inserted from the other edition.

I have seen two copies of the map varying so much, as to prove almost beyond doubt, that there were two editions of it, as well as of the text. To establish this, so far as to defy skepticism, I caused a photolithographic copy of one to be made, to place beside the other. The third line of the title in one edition ends with the word "done;" in the other that line terminates with the word "by." In one the fourth line ends with "being," in the other with "in;" fifth line, "less," fifth line of the other with "exact." Of the six remaining lines only two end similarly. In the centre of the right hand side of the map, the "Wine Hills" of one copy are the "White Hills" of the other. There are several other slight discrepancies, particularly in the number of place lines which form the shading.

It is evident, therefore, that one of these editions of the map was executed for the London edition of the text. We have only internal evidence to direct us in determining this fact, and no bibliographer would hesitate to declare that the one executed in the best manner is the one engraved in London. It is evident, on the slightest inspection, that this is the one having "Wine Hills" engraved below the title in place of "White Hills" as in the other more rudely executed one. In the first, the letters are more perfectly formed, the shading is finer, and the lines representing the ocean sharper, clearer, and more than twice the number of the other.

A still more curious discrepancy exists between copies of the text of the Boston edition. There is evidence in the table of errata on the last page, that there were two issues, if not two Boston editions, bearing date 1677. I have two copies of that date, precisely similar in every respect, except that the errata in one occupies ten lines, and in the other twelve. It is probable that after some copies had been disseminated, other errors were discovered, and two lines of corrections added. Another peculiarity of the Boston edition, of less consequence, is the error in pagination from pages 84 to 92. Pages 84, 86, 88, and 90, are not numbered at all, while pp. 85, 87, 89, 91, and 92, are numbered 84, 85, 86, 87, and 88, respectively.

The London edition has no errata, which is so remarkable a feature in that printed in Boston. Mr. Hubbard printed in the Boston edition an apology, commencing "The Printer to the Reader. By reason of the Author's long absence from the Press, many faults have escaped in the printing, etc." This is omitted in the London edition, which is comparatively free from the errors indicated, is printed on better paper, and the typography greatly superior. In both editions the title-page is preceded by a recommendation of the work signed by Simon Bradstreet, Daniel Denison, and Joseph Dudley, and dated March 29, 1677; immediately following this on the same page in the London edition, is the license signed Roger L'Estrange, June 27, 1677. Thus it will be seen that the longest period which could have elapsed between the printing of the two editions, was three months; a period entirely too short for the work to be printed in Boston, sent across the ocean, and printed in London, when we consider the great length of the voyages at that day. It is probable that the first part of the work was printed nearly simultaneously, and from manuscript, in both places. The first poem, addressed to the Rev. William Hubbard, is signed J. S., which is conjectured to mean the Rev. Jeremiah Shepherd of Lynn. The second poem, signed B. T., is supposed to have been written by Benjamin Trumbull.

In both editions "A Narrative of the Troubles" begins with page 1 and ends with page 115, but in the London edition "A Supplement Concerning the War with the Pequods" commences on p. 116, while in that printed in Boston, that page is blank, and the "Supplement" begins on page 117. "A Table shewing the Towns," etc., begins in the London edition on the 132d, in the other on the 133d page. The Table and Postscript in the London, occupy 13 unnumbered pp., which in the Boston edition occupy 14 pp., the first eight unnumbered, and the last six erroneously numbered 7 to 12, while they should be 9 to 14.

But it is in the last division of the book that the coincidence is so striking, that the hypothesis of both editions having been printed entirely from manuscript, seems almost untenable. Both have the same title occupying the upper half of page one. "Narrative of the Troubles with the Indians of New England, From Pascataqua to Pemmaquid." Both commence in the middle of page 1, and end at the seventeenth line of the 88th page. They have the same number of lines on the page, and have the same catch words on every page except the first, and even the words printed in Italics in one, are exactly repeated in the same letter in the other. The title of this section is printed in the London with large type, while the same division heading, is in small and mean letters in the Boston edition. The lower half of page 88, in this last edition, is occupied with errata, which in the other is entirely wanting.

The remarkable coincidences of typographical execution in the last 88 pages, and the almost simultaneous printing in the distant capitals of old and New

England, will always continue as now, sources of surprise and conjecture. The work is exceedingly rare, complete with the map, and in good condition; and preference is given to the one printed in Boston. The latest sold in this country was purchased at the sale of Mr. John Rice's library, for one hundred and eighty dollars. The Rev. William Hubbard was the minister of Ipswich, Mass., where he died September 14th, 1704, aged eighty-three. He was remarkable in an age and country of bigots, for his liberality, moderation, and piety. His narrative has been regarded for two hundred years by historians as a standard of authority. It is sometimes accompanied by a tract bound in the same volume, entitled *The Happiness of a People in the Wisdome of their Rulers*, etc., a sermon preached in Boston. Printed by John Foster, 1676, a year previous to the publication of the Narrative. It was reissued with the Narrative, although an entirely separate publication. The second edition of the Narrative was printed in Boston, 1775, in 24°, much altered and abbreviated. The third at Worcester, 1801, in 24°. Three editions in 1802 and 1803, at three different localities. In 1834 in 4°. The best reprint is that of Mr. S. G. Drake, in two octavo volumes, with numerous notes.

The Rev. William Hubbard was born in England in 1621, and emigrated at the age of fourteen to New England. He wrote a *History of New England*, which remained in manuscript for nearly a century and a half, or until 1815, when it was printed by the Massachusetts Historical Society. In 1848 the *History* was reprinted in the Historical Collections of that Society, forming Vols. V. and VI. of the second series. His narrative seems to have excited the envy of the Rev. Increase Mather, who wrote and published two books on the same subject.

HUBBARD (W.).

The Happiness of a People In the Wisdome of their Rulers Directing, And in the Obedience of their Brethren. Attending Unto what Israel ought to do: recommended in a Sermon Before the Honorable Governour and Council and the Respected Deputies of the Massachusets Colony in New-England. Preached at Boston, May 3d, 1676, being the day of Election there. By William Hubbard, Minister of Ipswich. 4° *Prel. pp.* (viii.) + 61. *Boston, printed by John Foster*, 1676. 732

This tract is frequently bound in with Hubbard's *History of Indian Wars*, of which it is believed never to have formed a part, having been printed a year previously. As it is however so often found appended to the Narrative, collectors have not felt that work to be complete, unless associated with the sermon.

HUBBARD (William).

The History of the Indian Wars in New England, from the First Settlement to the Termination of the War with King Philip in 1677. From the Original Work by Rev. Wm. Hubbard, Carefully revised, and accompanied with an Historical Preface, Life, and Pedigree of the Author, and Extensive Notes. By Samuel G. Drake. Two vols. *Large* 8° Vol. I. *pp.* xxxii. + 292. Vol. II. *pp.* 303. *Roxbury, Mass., printed for W. Elliot Woodward*, 1865. 733

Three hundred and fifty copies were printed of this beautiful edition of Hubbard's Narrative. Prefixed to this is a Bibliographical Preface by the very capable editor, Mr. Samuel G. Drake, occupying pp. v. to xviii. in which all the editions of Hubbard's work are described. The life of the author fills pp. xix. to xxxii. It is a splendid specimen of typography, on thick paper, uniform with Fouchet's Memoirs.

HUBBARD (Rev. William).
A General History of New England from the Discovery to MDCLXXX. By the Rev. William Hubbard, Minister of Ipswich Mass. Published by the Massachusetts Historical Society. 8° *pp.* 676. *Cambridge*, 1815. 734

HUBBARD (Rev. Wm.).
A Narrative of the Indian Wars in New England, from the first Planting thereof in the Year 1607 to the Year 1677; containing a Relation of the Occasion, Rise and Progress of the War with the Indians, &c. 12° *Danbury*, 1803. 735

HUGHES (John T.).
Doniphan's Expedition. Containing an Account of the Conquest of New Mexico; Gen. Kearney's Overland Expedition to California; Doniphan's Campaign against the Navajos; His unparalleled march upon Chihuahua, &c. Illustrated with Plans and a Map. 12° *pp.* 407. *Cincinnati*, 1850. 736

HUGHES (John T.).
Doniphan's Expedition, with an account of the Conquest of New Mexico. Col. Kearney's overland expedition to California. Doniphan's march against the Navajos, his unparalleled march upon Chihuahua and Durango. 12° *Cincinnati*, 1848. 737

HULL (William)
Memoirs of the Campaign of the North Western Army of the United States A. D. 1812, in a Series of letters addressed to the Citizens of the United States. With an Appendix Containing a brief Sketch of the Revolutionary Services of the Author. By William Hull, late Governour of the Territory of Michigan, and Brigadier General in the Service of the United States. 8° *pp.* 229, *and* x. *Boston*, 1824. 738

HUMBOLDT (Baron Von).
Vues des Cordilleras et Monumens des Peuples Indigines de l'Amerique. *Large folio pp.* 16 + 830 *and* 69 *plates* (*many beautifully colored*). *Paris*, 1810. 739

Every class of Mexican or Aztec, and Peruvian Antiquities, receives in this work the clearest philosophical analysis.

HUMBOLDT (Alexander de).
Researches Concerning the Institutions & Monuments of the Ancient Inhabitants of America with Descriptions & Views of some of the most Striking Scenes in the Cordilleras written in French by Alexander de Humboldt & Translated into English by Helen Maria Williams. Two vols. *pp.* 411 *and* 324 + 19 *plates*. *Published by Longman and Co.* *London*, 1814. 740

This translation of the text of Humboldt's celebrated *Vues de Cordilleras'* is a valuable adjunct to the great folio of plates, for all students not familiar with the language of the original.

HUMPHREY (H.).
Indian Rights and our Duties. An Address delivered at Am-

herst, Hartford, etc., December 1829, by Heman Humphrey. Stereotyped for the Association for diffusing information on the Subject of Indian Rights. 12° *New York*, 1831. 741

This little pamphlet was the effort of an earnest and learned man, to arouse the people of the United States, to the wrongs perpetrated on the Indians. How many such men shall rise and fall, before these wrongs shall be redressed!

HUMPHREYS (Col. David).

An Essay on the Life of the Hon. Major-General Israel Putnam, Addressed to the State Society of the Cincinnati, in Connecticut, and first Published by their Order. By Col. David Humphreys, with notes and additions. With an Appendix containing an Historical and Topographical Sketch of Bunker Hill Battle. By S. Sweet. 12° *Boston*, 1818. 742

HUNTER (John D.).

Manners and Customs of the Several Indian Tribes located West of the Mississippi. Including some accounts of the Soil, Climate, &c. To which is prefixed the History of the Author's Life during a residence of several years among them. 8° *pp.* 468. *London*, 1824. 743

HUTCHINS (Thomas).

A Topographical Description of Virginia, Pennsylvania, Maryland, and North-Carolina, Comprehending the Rivers Ohio, Kenhawa, Sioto, Cherokee, Wabash, Illinois, Mississippi, &c.; the climate, soil, and produce, whether Animal, Vegetable, or Mineral, The Mountains, Creeks, Roads, Distances, Latitudes, &c., and of every Part, laid down in the annexed Map. Published by Thomas Hutchins, Captain in the 60th Regiment of Foot; with a Plan of the Rapids of the Ohio, a Plan of the Several Villages in the Illinois Country, a Table of the Distances between Fort Pitt and the Mouth of the Ohio, all Engraved upon Copper. And An Appendix containing Mr. Patrick Kennedy's Journal up the Illinois River and a correct List of the different Nations and Tribes of Indians, with the Number of Fighting Men, &c. 12° *Title and Preface pp.* 4 + 67 *and three folding plans. London, printed for the author, and sold by J. Almon*, 1778. 744

HUTCHINSON (C. C.).

A Colony for an Indian Reserve in Kansas. Climate, Soil, Products, Timber, Water, Kind of Settlers Wanted, &c. Persons desiring copies of this pamplett can address C. C. Henderson, Indian Agent, Ottawa Creek, Kansas. 8° *pp.* 15. (*Lawrence*, 1863.) 745

This pamphlet narrates the steps by which the Ottawa Indians became citizens, acquired the fee of part of their lands, and endeavored to induce the settlement of the remaining portion by industrious whites, from whom they could learn the art of agriculture.

HUTCHINSON (Abijah).

A Memoir of Abijah Hutchinson a Soldier of the Revolution by his grandson R. M. Hutchinson. 8° *pp.* 22. *Rochester, William Alling, printer,* 1843. 746

The narrative of Hutchinson's captivity among the Indians of Canada forms the principal subject of the memoir.

IMLAY (Gilbert).

A Topographical Description of the Western Territory of North America; containing A succinct Account of its Soil, Climate, Natural History, Population, Agriculture, Manners, and Customs, with an ample Description of the Several Divisions into which that Country is partitioned. To which are added I. The Discovery, Settlement, and present State of Kentucky; with an Essay towards the Topography and Natural History of that important Country by J. Filson. Also the Minutes of the Piankashaw Council 1784. II. An Account of the Indian Nations inhabiting within the Limits of the XIII. States; their Manners and Customs, and Reflections on their Origin. III. The culture of Indian Corn [*etc.*, 8 *lines*]. IV. Observations on the ancient Works, the native Inhabitants of the Western Country, &c., by Major Jonathan Heart. V. Historical Narrative of Louisiana and West Florida by Thomas Hutchins. [VI. *and* VII. 8 *lines.*] VIII. Topographical Description of Va. [*etc.*, 4 *lines*], by Thos. Hutchins. IX. Mr. Patrick Kennedy's Journal up the Illinois River. [*Sections* X. + XI. + XII. + XIII. *eleven lines*]. By Gilbert Imlay. A Captain in the American Army during the War, and Commissioner for laying out Lands in the Back Settlements [4 *lines*]. The Third Edition, with great additions. 8° *pp.* xii. + 598 + *Index pp.* (28) *Advertisement,* (2) + 4 *maps. London,* 1797. 747

The work consists for the greatest part of reprints of works relating to the Kentucky country, now become quite rare. Filson's "Discovery and Settlement of Kentucky, with the Adventures of Col. Dan' Boone, and The Piankashaw Council," occupy pp. 306 to 376. Hutchins' "Two Historical Narratives" fill pp. 387 to 456, and 485 to 506. Patrick Kennedy's "Journal," pp. 506 to 511. "An Account of the Savages inhabiting the Western Territory, with an enumeration of their tribes and numbers" occupies pp. 283 to 296, and Heart's "Observations on the ancient Mounds, Inhabitants, &c.," 297 to 305.

INCIDENTS

And Sketches connected with the Early History of and Settlement of the West. With numerous Illustrations. 8° *pp.* 72 *and frontispiece. Cincinnati, n. d.* 748

This book is a collection from newspapers, and other equally authentic sources, of fragments of narratives of border life and Indian warfare. It is only to be noted for its worthlessness for historical purposes.

INDIAN ATROCITIES.

Affecting and Thrilling Anecdotes respecting the hardships and sufferings of the brave and venerable forefathers in their bloody and heart-rending skirmishes and Contests with the ferocious Savages, containing numerous engravings illustrating the most general traits of Indian Character their customs and deeds of cruelty, with interesting accounts of the Captivity, Sufferings and heroic Conduct of many who have fallen into their hands. 8° *pp.* 32. *Boston.* 749

INDIANS (The).

A Tragedy performed at the Theatre Royal, Richmond. 12° *Prel. pp.* (viii.) + 58. *Dublin,* 1791. 750

In this most heroic aboriginal tragedy, written by one whose sole knowledge of Indian character was obtained from the midnight brawls of the ruffian Mohocks of London, Onoutlio-Neidan and Maraino speak after the fashion of Brutus and Coriolanus.

INDIANS (The). |

Or | Narratives | of | Massacres and Depredations on the frontiers | in Wawasink and its Vicinity | during | The American Revolution | By a descendant of the Huguenots. | 8° *pp.* 79. *Rondout, N. Y., For sale at the printing office of Bradbury & Wells | and at the office of the Christian Intelligencer | No.* 103 *Fulton Street, New York,* 1846. 751

INDIAN (The).

Fairy Book. From the original legends, with illustrations by McLenan engraved by Anthony. 12° *pp.* 338. *New York,* 1856. 752

An edition of 1869, has the name of Cornelius Mathews, as author on the title-page.

INDIAN LAWS.

Laws of the Colonial and State Governments, relating to Indians and Indian Affairs from 1633 to 1831 inclusive; with an Appendix Containing the Proceedings of the Congress of the Confederation; and the Laws of Congress from 1800 to 1830 on the Same Subject. 8° *pp.* 250 *and Appendix pp.* 72. *Washington,* 1832. 753

INDIAN TREATIES

And Laws and Regulations relating to Indian Affairs, to which is added, An Appendix Containing the proceedings of the Old Congress, and other important State papers in relation to Indian Affairs. 8° *pp.* 661. *Washington City,* 1826. 754

This volume contains an abstract of almost all the treaty stipulations of the government with the Indians. Besides the more legal statement of the obligations, by which the savage tribes and the United States authorities mutually bound themselves, there is a vast mass of historical data, the names and numbers of the tribes, the names of the chiefs, and their significations, and on page 485 is George Guess (Sequoyah's) alphabet of syllables of the Cherokee language.

INDIAN HISTORY.

The History, Manners, and Customs of the North American Indians. 24° *pp.* 245. *Philadelphia, n. d.* 755

INDIAN MISSIONS.

The American Board and the American Missionary Association. 8° *pp.* 16. *n. d., n. p.* 756

This tract contains a curious narration of the adoption of the slave code by the Cherokee Indians, themselves fugitives from the acquisitiveness of the slave owners of Georgia.

INDIAN NARRATIVES:

Containing A Correct and Interesting History of The Indian Wars, from The Landing of our Pilgrim Fathers, 1620, to Gen. Wayne's Victory, 1794. To which is added A correct Account of the Capture and Sufferings of Mrs. Johnson, Zadoc Steele and others; and also a thrilling Account of the burning of Royalton. 12° *pp.* 276. *Claremont, N. H.*, 1854. 757

INFORMATION

Respecting the Aborigines, in the British Colonies. Circulated by Direction of the Meeting for Sufferings. Being principally extracts from the Report presented to the House of Commons, by the Select Committee appointed on that Subject. 8° *pp.* xii. + 60. *London, Darton and Harvey*, 1838. 758

See Friends.

INSTRUCTIONS

For treating with the Eastern Indians given to the Commissioners appointed for that Service. By the Hon. Spencer Phipps . . . in the year 1752. Now first printed from the Original Manuscript. 4° *pp.* 8. *Boston, printed for S. G. Drake*, 1865. 759

IRVING (Washington).

Astoria; or, Anecdotes of an Enterprise beyond the Rocky Mountains. By Washington Irving. Two vols. 8° Vol. I. *pp.* 285; Vol. II. *pp.* 279 *and map. Philadelphia*, 1836. 760

IRVING (Washington).

Astoria; or, enterprise beyond the Rocky Mountains, by Washington Irving. In three volumes. 12° Vol. I. *pp.* xvi. + 317. Vol. II. *pp.* ix. + 320; Vol. III. *pp.* vii. + 294. *London, Richard Bentley*, 1836. 761

This book is the narration of one of those attempts to found a viceroyalty, in a distant and unexplored territory, which smacks of the romance and chivalric enterprise of the old Spanish adventurers. In 1810, two expeditions, having the common object of establishing a settlement on the Pacific, left New York. The one by sea, sailed on board the ill-fated *Tonquin*, which with its master and crew fell into the vengeful hands of the savages on the northwest coast. The other passed over the same route which Sagard and Hennepin traversed — the Ottawa River, and along the string of small lakes to Mackinaw, and then onward to St. Louis. From thence the expedition entered upon the realms of savage life, and for a year fought or negotiated its way, through nation after nation, and tribe after tribe, of crafty and hostile Indians. The details of its progress, pictured with the warm coloring of Washington Irving's pen, rivals the stately march of De Soto, or the equally adventurous, and more prolific exploration of La Salle. The narrative is crowded with incidents of Indian subtlety or ferocity, as well as with descriptions of the manners and peculiarities of the fierce lords of the great plains, and the vaster mountains, before civilization had enervated or corrupted them. This is much the best edition of the work.

It is fortunate for the memory of the great millionaire Astor, that his attempt to establish the first American settlement on the Pacific coast, found such a historian. Irving has done much more to perpetuate the fame of his friend than any act of his own life, or even the reputation of possessing the greatest wealth acquired in a single lifetime could afford.

IRVING (Washington).

The Adventures of Captain Bonneville in the Rocky Mountains and the Far West. Digested from the Journal of Captain B. L. E. Bonneville of the army of the United States and illustrated from various other Sources, by Washington Irving. 12° Two vols. *pp.* 248 *and* 248. *New York*, 1847. 762

Captain Bonneville was an officer of the United States army who had served for several years on the frontier, where the service required constant association with the Indians, either in making peace or war. Instead of becoming satiated with the incidents of a frontier life, Bonneville's imagination was so fired with the relations of trappers and fur-traders, of the wonders of the Plains and Rocky Mountains, that he obtained the permission of the authorities to undertake their exploration. His journal of the incidents and adventures of his wonderful journey, is not less interesting as a narrative than valuable as a history. The perils his party survived, perils from the elements, from starvation, and hostile tribes of Indians, would seem the offspring of an ingenious imagination, were they not authenticated by the word of honor of a gentleman, who satisfied the fastidious judgment of Washington Irving, with the veracity of his statements. The book is crowded with descriptions of the savage tribes of the unexplored regions bordering the Rocky Mountains, with sketches of their warriors and chiefs, with accounts of skirmishes with their war parties, and the marvelous adventures of fur-trappers among the Indians, whom their own atrocities had made their enemies.

IRVING (Washington).

A Tour on the Prairies. By the author of the Sketch Book. 12° *Philadelphia*, 1835.

Serial Title Crayon Miscellany. By the author of the Sketch Book. No. 1. A Tour on the Prairies. *pp.* 274. 763

Everything relating to aboriginal life or manners, had an attraction for Washington Irving which he could not resist. The hardy fur-trapper, with his trusty rifle, and his dusky bride, scorning with the fierce pride of independence the sweets of civilization; the wild warrior of the plains, in his swift foray on the herds of the civilized intruders on his domains, or in bloody invasion of a neighboring tribe, all had for the author a warm coloring which he loved to paint. It is of such scenes, blended with the softer traditions of Indian lore, and dreams of the better land, this book is composed. Irving eagerly seized the opportunity offered by a government mission to the Pawnees, of observing for himself the peculiarities of a savage race; and of what he saw he has made the most charming picture ever painted of its life.

IRVING (John T.).

Indian Sketches taken during an Expedition to the Pawnee Tribes. In Two Volumes. 12° Vol. I. *pp.* 272; Vol. II. *pp.* 296. *Philadelphia, Carey, Lea, & Blanchard*, 1835. 764

In all the copies of this work I have seen, there appears to have been an omission of four pages immediately succeeding page 4, Vol. I. The dedication ends with page 4, and the introduction begins with page 9.

The object of this expedition was of a higher humanitarian order, than those which the government has usually organized for Indians affairs. Under its direction there had been settled on lands claimed by the fierce tribes of the Plains, those unfortunate victims of civilization, the remnants of the Delawares and other eastern nations. The wild savages of the great prairies resented this forced intrusion, in their simple distrust not reckoning that their red brethren were exiles, driven from their homes by a power which would soon press them from their own hunting grounds. Between the exiles and the natives arose a fierce warfare, and over the debatable ground was fought many a bloody battle. It would have been in conformity with the greedy policy of the white man, to permit the unsophisticated savages to mutually exterminate each other, and thus leave the land free for the speculator. It was, however, to induce peaceable relations between these warring tribes, that the government sent out Mr. Elsworth as its commissioner. Mr. Irving accompanied the expedition, and his work affords us many interesting incidents of savage life. The work abounds in such fragments of the traditions, history, and peculiarities of the Indian tribes of the Plains as the opportunity offered the author. The method of dealing with a savage nation to induce it to forego its savage instincts (ending as usual in a surrender of its land), is fully detailed in the work.

IRVING (Theodore).

The Conquest of Florida, by Theodore Irving. Complete in one volume. 12° *pp.* 457. *New York, G. P. Putnam & Co.* 1857. 765

This very interesting narrative of the celebrated expedition of Ferdinando de Soto, is a compilation from *La Florida del Inca* of Garcilaso de la Vega, and the English translation of the Portuguese work by a gentleman of Elvas, entitled *A Relation of the Invasion and Conquest of Florida by the Spaniards Under the Command of Ferdinando de Soto.* Aided by Mr. Fairbanks of St. Augustine, by Buckingham Smith, and by Alfred Pickett, author of the *History of Alabama*, Mr. Irving gives in the Appendix a sketch of the route, and places occupied by the expedition. The descriptions of the various tribes of Indians, the bloody battles between them and the Spaniards, and the obstinate resistance of the populous and thriving nations of savages, through which De Soto and his devoted band passed, are not more historically valuable; but the narrative is more popularly interesting, than in the grave and quaint language of the original authors.

IXTLILXOCHITL (Don Fernando D'Alva).

Histoire des Chichimiques ou des Anciens Rois de Tezcuco, par Don Fernando D'Alva Ixtlilxochitl, traduite sur le Manuscrit Espagnol inedite. Two vols. 8° Vol. I. *pp.* 16 + 340; Vol. II. *pp.* 356. *Paris, Arthus Bertrand, Libraire-editeur libraire de la Société de geographié de Paris Rue Hautefeuille No.* 23, 1840. 766

[History of the Chichemecas or ancient Kings of Tezcuco, by Don Fernando d'Alva Ixtlilxochitl; translated from the unedited Spanish Manuscript.]

In the full title the subject title is preceded by the serial one thus: *Voyages, Relations, et Memoires originaux pour servir a l'histoire de la decouverte de l'Amerique, publies pour la premiere fois en Francais, par H. Ternaux Compans.* "Original Voyages, Relations, and Memoirs, to aid in the history of the discovery of America, published for the first time in French by Ternaux Compans." Clavigero, himself an authority of the highest rank, speaks of the author as extremely conversant with the antiquities of his nation, and as having written the very learned and valuable works which bear his name, at the request of the viceroy of Mexico.

Don Fernando d' Alva Ixtlilxochitl, who was a lineal descendant of the kings of Tezcuco, in Mexico, wrote many very learned works of great estimation, upon the antiquities of his nation, in which he was profoundly versed. Among these were *The History of New Spain; The History of the Chicmecas; An Historical Compendium of the kingdom of Tezcuco;* and *Some Historical Memoirs of the Toltecas and other Nations.* Dr. Cabrera says that Ixtlilxochitl was so cautious in what he wrote, that in order to remove all suspicion of invention or fiction, he caused a document to be executed in legal form, authenticating his narrative, as perfectly corresponding to the relations in the historical paintings which he inherited from his ancestors.

The second work is the only one of the series which has been printed entire. The MSS. of all the works named, are said to be preserved in the Jesuits College of St. Peter and St. Paul in the city of Mexico. *The History of the Chicmecas* was first printed in the ninth of Kingsborough's great volumes, in the Spanish language. Ternaux Compans translated the work into the French, and produced it as two of the twenty volumes of his series of Voyages and Travels.

IXTLILXOCHITL (F. d'Alva).

Cruates Horribles des Conquerants du Mexique et des Indiens qui les aiderent a Soumettre cet empire a la Couronne d'Espagne, Memoire de don Fernando D'Alva Ixtlilxochitl; Supplement a l histoire du Pere Sahagun, public et dedie au gouvernement Supreme de la Confederation Mexicaine par Charles-Marie de Bustamente. Mexico, 1829. 8° *Half title, title, and pp.* xlvii. + 312. *Paris, Arthus Bertrand Editeur,* 1838. 767

[Horrible Cruelties of the Conquerors of Mexico, and of the Indians who aided them in the subjecting that empire to the crown of Spain. A Memoir by F. de A. Ixtlilxochitl. Supplement to the history of Father Sahagun and published by C. M. Bustamente in Mexico, 1829.]

Bustamente, the Mexican editor, gives an account of thirteen noble Indians, who wrote memoirs and histories of their country, in both Aztec and Spanish. Ixtlilxochitl's entire work, which remained in MS. until brought to light by Bustamente, comprehended three relations, and commenced at the most ancient period of the history of his race. Bustamente and Ternaux published only the third, which narrated the conquest of Mexico.

All his works were preserved in MS. in the library of the Jesuits' College in Mexico, and guarded by the Spaniards with great jealousy until that power lost its hold on the country. The authenticity of the history is certified on page 356 of the fourth volume of the manuscript, in the Mexican archives before the notary Ortiz, in 1608, by eleven principal officers who attest that it conforms with the Aztec records, painted by the native historians with which it had been compared. The only questionable statement evolved in its perusal, is that this royal Tezcucan historian makes his countrymen so often heroic, and deserve victory if they did not achieve it.

JACKSON (Isaac R.).

The life of William Henry Harrison of Ohio. The people's candidate for the presidency. With a history of the Wars with The British and Indians on our North-Western frontier. Fifth edition. 24° *pp.* 222. *Philadelphia, Marshall, Williams, & Butler,* 1840. 768

JACOB (John J.).

A Biographical Sketch of the Life of the late Capt. Michael Cresap. 12° *Cumberland, Md., printed for the author, by J. M. Buchanan,* 1826. 769

Title 1 leaf, reverse blank. Advertisement 1 leaf, reverse blank. To the Hon.

John E. Howard, 2 pp. Preface, 3 pp. Signed by John J. Jacob. Introduction, 3 pp. and pp. 15 to 120; reverse of last page, errata.

The strange fate which led this border warrior from the silent forests, prowled only by angry savages or by the scarcely less savage frontiersmen, to die in the crowded city, and lie within a few feet of the ceaseless sounding of the million feet which tread Broadway, is not less remarkable than the fortune which befell his memory when dead. Made the object of the hatred and detestation of the civilized world, by Jefferson's publication of Logan's speech, he has not lacked for three quarters of a century the warmest and most active defenders of his memory, from the charge which has made him infamous. Captain Cresap, worn down with anxiety and ill health, did not hesitate to collect a company of his formidable riflemen, and marched to aid his countrymen at the siege of Boston. He however was only able to reach New York, where he died in October, 1775, and was buried in Trinity church-yard.

JACOB (John J.).

A Biographical Sketch of the Life of the late Captain Michael Cresap [*motto*]. By John J. Jacob. 4° *pp.* 158. *Cincinnati, Ohio. Reprinted from the Cumberland edition of* 1826, *with notes and Appendix for William Dodge, by Jno. F. Uhlhorn,* 1866. 770

JACOBS (Rev. Peter).

Journal of the Reverend Peter Jacobs, Indian Wesleyan Missionary from Rice Lake to the Hudsons Bay Territory and returning, commencing May 1852 with A Brief Account of his Life, and a Short History of the Wesleyan Mission in that Country. 12° *Portrait and pp.* 96. *New York,* 1857. 771

JAMES (Edwin).

Narrative of the Captivity and Adventures of John Tanner (U. S. Interpreter at the Saut de Saint Marie), during Thirty Years residence among the Indians, in the interior of North America. Prepared for the Press by Edwin James, M. D. Editor of an Account of Major Longs Expedition from Pittsburgh to the Rocky Mountains. 8° *pp.* 426, *and portrait. New York, G. & C. & H. Carvill,* 1830. 772

The editor of this work obtained the material for its construction from the lips of John Tanner, a captive white who had resided among the Indians for thirty years. Mr. James was a man of much information upon Indian affairs, and must have been able to discriminate between the probable and the uncertain portions of Tanner's narrative. The renegade himself (for he had during his long sojourn among the Indians become even more savage than they) was a person of retentive memory and fair intelligence. His relation of his life among the Northern Indians, is probably the most minute if not authentic detail of their habits, modes of living, and social customs, ever printed. The perils and privations in which they constantly exist, the tribal distinctions, and family associations and quarrels, the hunter's painful struggles to overmatch the cunning and instinct of the animals upon which he must feed or starve, and the labor of the squaws, alternated with days and weeks of gnawing famine, awaiting his return, are all minutely and vividly related. The details of Tanner's captivity, given in his own language as it fell from his lips, are related by him in the first person, pages 23 to 281. Part II, pp. 282 to 293, is entitled "Indian Feasts." On pages 294 to 312, is given a "Catalogue of Plants and Animals Found in the Country of the Ojibbeways," with their Indian names. Whenever the English name could be ascertained, it is also given. Next follows a catalogue, also in Chippeway, of the Totems among the Ottawas and Ojibbeways, with their description in English, occupying pp. 314 to 315. "Knowledge of Astronomy," is the title of a division of the work, extending over pp. 316 to 323. A comparison of Chippeway numerals with nearly fifty other American dialects, occupies pp. 324 to 333. On pp. 341 to 381, are given a large collection of songs in the Indian language, with their English translation in parallel lines, and the hieroglyphic signs, or rather pictographs of these chants. Chapter ix, occupying pp. 383 to 426, is entitled "Languages of the American Indians," of which by far the largest portion is filled with a copious vocabulary of words and phrases in the Ottawa and Chippeway languages. Dr. James is said by Schoolcraft to have been imposed upon by Tanner, whom Mr. Schoolcraft declared to be "more suspicious, revengeful, and bad tempered than any Indian he ever knew." After the publication of Tanner's narrative, the people of St. Mary's were accustomed to call him the Old Liar. This so enraged him against Dr. James, that he made efforts to kill him, for printing what those acquainted with him called lies. Schoolcraft was, however, strongly prejudiced against Tanner, who had assaulted himself, and who in 1846, actually murdered James Schoolcraft, his brother, by shooting him from behind a cedar thicket. The renegade then fled back to the hills of the upper lakes. During his residence in a civilized community he had married a white girl, who, unable to endure his brutality longer than a year, fled from him and was divorced. Mr. James was also the editor of *Long's Expedition to the Source of the Mississippi.*

JARVIS (Samuel Farmar).

A Discourse on the Religion of the Indian Tribes of North America, delivered before The New York Historical Society, December 20, 1819. By Samuel Farmar Jarvis. 8° pp. 1 to 111. *New York*, 1820. 773

Also printed in Volume III. of the New York Historical Society's Collections.

JEFFERSON (Tho's).

Notes on the State of Virginia. With an Appendix relative to the Murder of Logan's Family. By Thomas Jefferson. 12° pp. 363. *Trenton, printed by Wilson & Blackwell, July* 12, 1803. 774

This is the first edition in which the Appendix relating to the murder of Logan's family by Captain Cresap, was announced on the title-page, having been first printed in 1800, as an answer to the charge that Jefferson had invented the narrative in the Notes to cover the alleged literary imposture of Logan's speech. The number of books and pamphlets to which this charge against Captain Cresap gave birth, is already scarcely computable. Of this Appendix some copies were printed separately, under the title of *An Appendix to the Notes on Virginia relative to the Murder of Logan's Family. By Thomas Jefferson*, pp. 1 to 51. 8° Philadelphia, 1800. This has become quite rare.

JEFFERYS (T.).

The Natural and Civil History of the French Dominions in North and South America. Giving a particular Account of the Climate, Soil, Minerals, Animals, Vegetables, Manufactures, Trade, Commerce, and Languages together with The Religion, Government, Genius, Character, Manners and Customs of the Indians and other Inhabitants. Illustrated by Maps and Plans of the principal Places, Collected from the best Authorities and engraved by T. Jefferys Geographer to his Royal Highness the

Prince of Wales. Part I. Containing A Description of Canada and Louisiana. *Folio. Prel. pp.* (viii.) + 163. Part II. *Title and pp.* 246. *with* 18 *large folding maps. London, printed for Thomas Jeffreys at Charing-Cross*, 1760. 775

The third section of Part I. is entitled, "Of the Origin, Languages, Religion, Government, Genius, Character, Manners and Customs, of the different Indian Nations inhabiting Canada," and occupies pp. 42 to 97. Almost all the remaining portion of Part I. is devoted to a relation of the wars and treaties of the French with the Indians, more particularly pp. 161 to 168, which are entirely to the peculiarities which distinguish the Indians of Louisiana. Similar divisions of Part II. are occupied with descriptions of the Indians of Hispaniola and Cayenne.

JEMISON (Mary).

See Seaver. 776

JEWETT (John R.).

A Narrative of the Adventures and Sufferings of John R. Jewett only survivor of the crew of the Ship Boston during a captivity of nearly three years among the Savages of Nootka Sound with an account of the Manners, Mode of living and Religious opinions of the natives. Illustrated with a plate representing the ship in possession of the Savages. 12° *pp.* 203 + 2 *plates. Middletown, printed by Loomis & Richards*, 1815. 777

The narrative of Jewett's captivity, was written by Richard Alsop, of Middletown, Connecticut, author of several books of poems, and translator of Molina's *History of Chili.* The details of the adventures of Jewett were drawn from him by the indefatigable queries of Alsop, who after some years declared that he feared he had done Jewett but little good, in furnishing him with a vagabond mode of earning a livelihood, by hawking his book from a wheelbarrow through the country.

The narrative of Jewett affords us many new and interesting particulars of the life and habits of the most savage of American aborigines. It is probably as faithful a portrayal of them as could be made by an unlettered man, after the lapse of several years. A vocabulary of the Nootka language, containing nearly one hundred words, occupies page 4.

JEWITT (John R.).

Narrative of the Adventures and Sufferings of John R. Jewitt, only survivor of the crew of the ship Boston, during a captivity of nearly 3 years among the Savages of Nootka Sound: with an account of the Manners, Mode of living, and Religious Opinions of the Natives. 12° *pp.* 166. *Ithaca, N. York*, 1851. 778

JOSSELYN (John).

New-England's | Rarities | Discovered: | In | Birds, Beasts, Fishes, Serpents, | and Plants of that Country. | Together with | The Physical and Chirugical Remedies | wherewith the Natives constantly use to | Cure their Distempers, Wounds, | and Sores. | Also | A perfect Description of an Indian SQUA. | in all her Bravery; with a Poem not | Improperly conferred upon her. | Lastly | A Chronological Table | of the most remarkable Passages in that | Country amongst the English. | Illustrated with Cuts. | By John Josselyn, Gent. | 24° *Frontispiece, a dragon. Title and dedication, each* 1 *leaf. Text pp.* 1

to 114. *Advertisement*, 1 *leaf. London, printed for G. Widdowes at the* | *Green Dragon in St Paul's Church Yard*, 1672. | 779

The description of the Indian Squaw and her bravery, together with the poem not improperly conferred upon her, occupy pp. 99 to 102. The description of Indian medicaments, and the use made of various herbs by the natives, occupies much of the remainder of Josselyn's work.

JOSSELYN (John).

An | Account | of two | Voyages to | New-England. | Wherein you have the Setting out of a Ship | with the charges; | The prices of all necessaries for | furnishing a Planter and his Family at his first Com- | ing; A Description of the Countrey, Natives and | Creatures, with their Merchantel and Physical use. The Government of the Country as it is now pos | sessed by the English &c. A Large Chronological Ta- | ble of the most remarkable passages, from the first dis- | covering of the Continent of America, to the year | 1673. By John Josselyn, Gent. | *Small* 18° *4 prel. leaves* + *pp.* 279. *Books &c. pp.* 8. *London, printed for Giles Widdows at the Green Dragon, in St. Paul's Church Yard*, 1674. 780

JOGUES (Father Isaac).

Narrative of a Captivity among the Mohawk Indians and a Description of New Netherland in 1642–3 by Father Isaac Jogues of the Society of Jesus. With a Memoir of the Holy Missionary. By John Gilmary Shea of the New York Historical Society. 8° *pp.* 69. *New York* (*Press of the Historical Society*), 1856. 781

This work is the first publication, of the manuscripts in the handwriting of the martyr Father Jogues himself, preserved in the Hotel Dieu at Quebec, and of the letters of Governor Kieft, announcing his death. They consist, I. Narrative of Captivity among the Mohawks. II. Account of his Escape. III. Description of New Netherlands. IV. Father Jogues' last Letters. V. Captivity and Death of Rene Goupil. VI. Letters of Governor Kieft. They are the most astonishing relation of sufferings in the holy cause of religion, and of the persistent cruelties of a savage race, ever written. They afford us the most intimate, as they do the most authentic account of the character of the Mohawks, that we are now cognizant of. But our gratification in perusing these valuable relics of a race now extinct, is almost overpowered by the wonder blended with horror, which we feel at the gigantic fortitude, and the awful sufferings of this unconquerable hero missionary. From the period of his captivity, to his escape through the humanity of the good Dutch pastor Megapolensis, and his reception by Queen Anne of France, who kissed with reverence his mutilated hands, to his return to the Mohawk lands, and final martyrdom by that tribe, we read with bated breath and unabated interest.

JOGUES (Isaac).

Novum Belgium, Description de Nieuw Netherland et Notice Sur Rene Goupil Par le R. P. Isaac Jogues de la Compagnie de Jesus. 8° *pp.* 44 *and map. A New York dans l' Ancient Nieuw Netherland Presse Cramoisy de J. M. Shea*, 1862. 782

[New Belgium, a Description of New Netherlands, and Notice of Rene Goupil, by the Rev. Father Isaac Jogues of the Society of Jesus. New York in the former New Netherlands.]

No. 17 Shea's *Jesuit Relations.*

JOHNS (Kensley).

Speech of Kensley Johns Jr. of Delaware on the Indian Bill in the House of Representatives May 1830. 8° *pp.* 19. *Washington*, 1830. 783

JOHNSON (Charles).

A Narrative of the Incidents attending the Capture, Detention and Ransom, of Charles Johnson, of Botetourt County, Virginia; who was made Prisoner by the Indians on the River Ohio, 1790. Together with an Interesting Account of the Fate of his Companions, five in number, one of whom suffered at the Stake. 8° *pp.* 264. *New York*, 1827. 784

JOHNSON (Mrs.).

A Narrative of the Captivity of Mrs. Johnson Containing An Account of her Sufferings during Four Years with the Indians and French. Published according to Act of Congress. 18° *pp.* 144. *Printed at Walpole, Newhampshire, by David Carlisle, Jun.*, 1796. 785

JOHNSON (Mrs.).

The Captive American, or a Narrative of the Sufferings of Mrs. Johnson during Four Years Captivity with the Indians and French. Written by herself. [*motto 6 lines*] 18° *pp.* 72. *Newcastle, printed and sold by M. Angus*, 1797. 786

JOHNSON (Mrs.).

Narrative of the Captivity of Mrs. Johnson, containing an account of her Sufferings, during Four Years with the Indians and French. Together with an Appendix containing the Sermon Preached at her Funeral, &c. Third edition. Corrected and Considerably Enlarged. 12° *pp.* 178. *Windsor, Vt.*, 1813. 787

JOHNSTON (Dr. James).

A History of the haunted Caverns of Magdelama, An Indian Queen of South America, with her likeness, Written by Dr. James Johnston. During a Captivity of three years, being taken up as a Spy by the above queen, and near the expiration of his time, tried by their laws for attempting his escape, found guilty, and sentenced to death in their barbarous way, to be stuck full of light wood splinters, set on fire, and kept dying for several days. With the author's trial, and last speech to the Indian Kings and Chiefs, together with his oration on the Stage, at the Kings request, in order to teach them the better to govern their Country, and numerous Subjects. With the rise and progress of the Indian Tribes, and that of the white inhabitants of South America. Published for the relief of the Author who lost his all by that tremendous fire at Savannah as before stated in the public papers. 12° *Plate and pp.* 206. *Price* 87½ *cents. Philadelphia, printed for James Sharon*, 1821. 788

If after having been stuck full of light wood splinters, set on fire and dying for several days, and then being burnt out in the tremendous fire at Savannah, the author does not win the sympathy of his reader, I cannot conceive what amount of dying will do it.

JOHNSON (Col. Richard M.).

Authentic Biography of Col. Richard M. Johnson, of Kentucky. 12° *pp.* 94. *Boston*, 1834. 789

The oft told story of the battle of Tippecanoe, and Col. Johnson's share in it, and whether he killed Tecumseh, and other particulars relating to his participation in Indian wars, are narrated in this thin volume, without adding much to the common stock of information on those subjects.

JOHNSON (Theodore T.).

California and Oregon, or Sights in the Gold Region and Scenes by the way. By Theodore T. Johnson with a map and illustrations fourth edition. With an Appendix containing [5 *lines*] also particulars of the march of the regiment of U. S. riflemen in 1849, together with the Oregon land bill. 12° *pp.* 348. *Philadelphia, J. B. Lippincott*, 1865. 790

There would be no reason for classing this work among those treating upon the aborigines, had not the author incidentally noticed, the perpetration of one of those indiscriminate slaughters of the Indians of California, which have disgraced the name of humanity. He relates in Chapters xix., xxi., and xxii. the massacre of an Oregon party of white men by Indians, and the horrible revenge taken by the miners upon a tribe, entirely innocent.

JOHNSON (Anna C.).

The Iroquois, or The Bright Side of Indian Character. by Minnie Myrtle. 12° *pp.* 317 + 8 *plates. D. Appleton and Company, New York*, 1855. 791

A compilation of material relating to the Six Nations, legendary, historical, and biographical, written under the pseudonym of Minnie Myrtle, by Miss Anna C. Johnson. The lady took more pains to make herself familiar with the subject upon which she had determined to write a book, than her sex has been usually accredited with doing, for such a purpose. She lived among the Senecas for several months, in the society of educated Indians, and was adopted into the tribe under the name of Gui-ee-wa-zay, "The narrator of new things." The name could not, however, have been conferred on account of the material of her book. Among the things not new, are the illustrations, which were copied from Morgan's *League of the Iroquois*, and not improved in the transfer.

JOHONNOT (Jackson).

The Remarkable Adventures of Jackson Johonnot of Massachusetts, who served as a Soldier in the Western army, in the Expedition under Gen. Harmar and Gen. St. Clair. Containing an Account of his Captivity, Sufferings and Escape from the Kickapo Indians. Written by himself, and published at the earnest request and importunity of his friends for the benefit of American Youth. 12° *pp.* 24. *Greenfield, Mass. Printed by Ansel Phelps*, 1816. 792

JONES (Charles C.).

Indian Remains in Southern Georgia. Address delivered before the Georgia Historical-Society on its twentieth Anniversary. February 12th, 1859, by Charles C. Jones, Jr. 8° *pp.* 25. *Savannah*, 1859. 793

JONES (Charles C.).
Ancient Tumuli on the Savannah river, by Charles C. Jones, Jr. *Map and* 14 *pp.* (*no p. or d.*) 794

JONES (Charles C.).
Monumental Remains of Georgia, by Charles C. Jones, Jr. Part First. 8° *pp.* 117. *Savannah, John M. Cooper and Company*, 1861. 795

This work is the result of a personal examination of the aboriginal monuments of Georgia, aided by such fortuitous circumstances as seldom fall to the lot of the explorer. These were, the existence of great numbers of unexplored mounds near his residence, the possession of sufficient means to provide the manual labor for their exploration, and a large provision of the taste and zeal for archæological discoveries, which only can give the requisite endurance of the tedious and often fruitless labor. Whatever Colonel Jones commences to investigate, he is satisfied with nothing less than completeness, of which quality of mind, his works are sufficient evidence.

JONES (C. C.).
Historical Sketch of Tomo-Chi-Chi, Mico of the Yamacraws, by C. C. Jones, Jr. 8° *pp.* 133. *Albany, N. Y., Joel Munsel*, 1868. 796

The large-minded and heroic Indian chief, who welcomed Oglethorpe to the lands of his nation, and fed and protected the infant colony during those early years, when disease and the Spaniards threatened its existence, well deserved a biography. No hero of the colonies of North America, even the loud boasting Captain John Smith, the zealous yet humane Roger Williams, or the noble Oglethorpe himself, better deserved an enduring monument than Tomo-Chi-Chi. The qualities of mind which he possessed, would have added honor to many of the great names, recorded in the annals of the early settlements of our country. Mr. Jones has done full justice to his subject, by fortifying the facts of his biography with undoubted authorities. Some particulars of the life of this chief, with his portrait, may be found in the Urlsperger tracts.

JONES (Peter).
History of the Ojibway Indians; with especial reference to their Conversion to Christianity. By Rev. Peter Jones (Kah, ke-wa-quon-a-by) Indian Missionary. With a brief Memoir of the writer; and introductory notice by the Rev. G. Osborn D. D. Secretary of the Wesleyan Missionary Society. 12° *pp.* viii. 278 + 16 *plates*. *London, A. W. Bennet*, 1861. 797

JONES (John).
The Gospel according to St. John. Translated into the Chippeway tongue by John Jones, and revised and corrected by Peter Jones, Indian teachers. 12° 280 *unnumbered pp.* *London*, 1831. 798

Alternate English and Chippeway, with the verses in each language opposite. English and Indian titles, each one leaf.

JONES (James Athearn).
Traditions of the North American Indians; being a second and revised edition of "Tales of an Indian Camp," by James Athearn Jones. In Three Volumes. 8° Vol. I. *pp.* xxxiii. + xxviii. + 312 *and plate*. Vol. II. *pp.* iv. + 336 *and plate*. Vol. III. *pp.*

iv. + 341 *and plate. London, Henry Colburn and Richard Bentley*, 1830. 799

The first Introduction was an author's puerile whim. Having once conceived this precious piece of absurdity, his parental affection for it would not permit him to throw it entirely aside, and accordingly while he prints it in the initial pages of his book, on pp. i. to xxxiii., he adds another Introduction, also numbered pp. i. to xxviii., in which he soberly informs us that this time he is telling the truth. In the second Introduction (the first being taken to be pure fiction), he informs us that he spent his boyhood among the Gayhead Indians of Martha's Vineyard Island, and heard their stories of Indian ghosts and witches. In after-life he strolled among the Cherokees, Creeks, Chickasaws, Shawnees, and Chippeways, of whom he set all the idle brains to work inventing tales for his note-book. He asserts a firm belief in them for himself, and solemnly asserts that the many weird and dreary hobgoblin stories he narrates, are the veritable emanations of aboriginal annalists. In the last thirteen pages of his second introduction, Mr. Jones gives the sources of a large number of his traditions, and of these it may be said that the origin was from such respectable authorities, that they may be taken as representative of the characteristics of the Indian intellect and emotions. The copious and numerous notes scattered through the volumes upon Indian history and customs, have also an authenticity, which entitles them to respect.

JONES (Miss Electa F.).

Stockbridge, Past and Present, or Records of An Old Mission Station, by Miss Electa F. Jones. 12° pp. 273. *Springfield, Samuel Bowles & Company*, 1854. 800

Stockbridge, in Massachusetts, was the residence of the Stockbridge Housatonic Muh-he-ka-ne-ok (Mohegan) Indians. They were called by the English, 'River Indians,' a fair translation of their name, which signified "The people of the ever flowing waters."

In Section II. entitled "Indian History," the authoress reproduces a fragment of a work said to be written by the Indian "Captain Hendrick Aupaumut." It consists of ten closely printed pages, of very valuable information regarding the habits and mode of life of the Stockbridge Indians. Section III. is entitled "Further particulars relating to Manners, Customs, Religion, etc.," and Section IV., "Language of the Muh-he-ka-ne-ok." Sections V. to XIX. are entirely occupied with a history of the Missions among the tribe until 1785, when it removed to Madison County in New York, upon a tract of land donated to them by the Oneidas, as a mark of gratitude for their aid in the Revolutionary War, during which the latter were threatened with destruction by the Senecas. Chapters xx. and xxi. narrate their removal to New Stockbridge, and Chapters xxiii. and xxiv. their emigration again to Lake Winnebago. Their fourth removal in 1848 to Minnesota, to which they were driven by the greed of speculators, aided by an unscrupulous and faithless government, is narrated in Chapter xxv. Sections XXVI. and XXVII. are entitled "Biographical Notices of Indians, and of Individuals engaged in the Stockbridge Missions."

JONES (George).

An original history of Ancient America, Founded upon the Ruins of Antiquity, the Identity of the Aborigines with the People of Tyrus and Israel, and the Introduction of Christianity by The Apostle St. Thomas, by George Jones. 8° pp. 479. *London, New York, Berlin, and Paris*, 1843. 801

The author of this work was afterwards known as the Count Johannes, a title said to have been conferred by one of the threescore German princes. It is entirely speculative in its character, and might rank well with the seven hundred treatises on the origin of the American Indians, said to have been offered for consideration to a French Society, on the first meeting after the announcement of the subject. The *learned* Count traces the Tyrian exiles directly to the shores of America, with almost as much definiteness, as he would had he accompanied them. It only needs an Appendix, tracing the ancestry of the American aborigines through the Tyrians, from the planet Herschel, to complete his scheme.

JONES (Elizabeth).

Memoir of Elizabeth Jones a little Indian girl, who lived at the River-Credit Mission, Upper Canada. 18° *pp.* 36 + *plate.* *New York, published by Carlton & Porter, n. d.* 802

JONES (N. W.).

Indian Bulletin for 1867, containing a brief Account of the North American Indians and the Interpretation of many Indian Names. By N. W. Jones. 8° *pp.* 16. *New York,* 1867. 803

A poor piece of charlatanism.

JONES (Rev. David).

A Journal of two Visits made to some Nations of Indians on the West Side of the River Ohio, in the years 1772 and 1773. By the Rev. David Jones, minister of the Gospel at Freehold, in New Jersey. With a Biographical Notice of the author, by Horatio Gates Jones, A. M., Corresponding Secretary Historical Society of Pennsylvania. *Large* 8° *pp.* xi. + 127. *New York, reprinted for Joseph Sabin,* 1865. 804

The original edition of this journal, printed in Burlington in 1774, is very rare. Of this size only fifty copies were printed.

JONES (Hugh).

The Present State of Virginia. Giving A particular and Short Account of the Indian, English, and Negroe Inhabitants of that Colony. Shewing their Religion, Manners, Government, Trade, Way of Living, &c., with a Description of that Country. From whence is inferred a Short View of Maryland and North Carolina. To which are added Schemes [*etc., 7 lines*] [*motto 3 lines*]. By Hugh Jones, A. M., Chaplain to the Honorable Assembly, and lately Minister of James-Town, &c., in Virginia. *London,* 1724. *Reprinted for Joseph Sabin, New York,* 1865. 805

Title of reprint 1 leaf, title of original 1 leaf, contents 1 leaf, and pref. pp. viii. + pp. 152. Part I. occupies the first twenty pages, and is divided into two chapters entitled, "Of the Original of the Indians, Europeans and Negroes," but is entirely devoted to a disquisition upon the natives. Chapter ii. has the heading, "Of the Government, Religion, Habit, Wars, Lives, Customs, &c., of the Indians of North America."

JOURNAL OF A TOUR IN THE INDIAN TERRITORY.

Performed by order of the Domestic Committee of the Board of Missions of the Protestant Episcopal Church, in the Spring of 1844, by their Secretary and General Agent. 8° *pp.* 74. *New York,* 1844. 806

JOURNAL DE LA GUERRE

Du Micissippi Contre les Chicachas, en 1739 et finie en 1740 le

1er d'Avril. Par un Officer de l'Armee de M. de Nouaille. 4°. *Nouvelle York, Isle de Manate de la Cramoisy de Jean-Marie Shea,* 1859. 807

No. 9 of Shea's *Jesuit Relations.*

[Journal of the War of the Micissippi against the Chi-ca-chas (the Chicasaws), in 1739 and ending April 1st, 1740. By an Officer of the Army of M. de Nouaille.]

This expedition against the Chicasaw Indians, embarked from New Orleans about the first of August, 1739, with one hundred and forty men, having lost by the terrible fever, fifty-eight of its number, besides leaving seventy in the hospital. They proceeded in eight bateaux up the Mississippi. On the 11th of October, reinforced by one hundred and ninety French, from Canada, and three hundred Indians, principally Iroquois, the expedition departed from Fort Assumption near Memphis. From that time the commander, Mr. Bienville, was embarrassed with the number of the savages, who offered to accompany him. Thus the poor Indians were induced, by the gratification of their mutual hatred, to destroy each other. In 1736, the Chicasaws had defeated the French, with a loss of one hundred and twenty men, in an attack upon their fort, and the French had induced the Choctaws, then so powerful as to be able to raise four thousand warriors, to make war upon the Chicasaws, but they had also been driven back. Mr. Bienville was fortunate enough on this occasion, through the intrepidity of Lieut. St. Laurent (who went alone to the Chickasaw fort), to make a lasting peace with this warlike nation.

JOUTEL.

A Journal of the Last Voyage performed by De la Salle to the Gulph of Mexico, to find out the Mouth of the Mississippi River. Containing an Account of the Settlements he endeavoured to make on the Coast of the Aforesaid Bay, his Unfortunate Death, and the Travels of his Companions for the Space of Eight Hundred Leagues, across that Inland Country of America, now call'd Louisiana (and given by the King of France to M. Crozat) till they came into Canada. Written in French, by Mons. Joutel, a Commander in that Expedition, and Illustrated from the Edition just Published in Paris. With an exact Map of that vast Country, and a Copy of the Letters Patents granted by the K. of France to M. Crozat. 8° *Title,* 1 *leaf; to the Reader,* xxi. *pages; Preface* 6 *pages, not numbered; Advertisement,* 1 *page; maps, and pp.* 1 *to* 205; *Index* 5 *pp. London,* MDCCXIV. 808

JOUTEL. (Mr.)

Mr. Joutel's | Journal | of his | Voyage | to | Mexico | His Travels Eight hundred | Leagues through Forty Nations | of Indians in Louisiana | to Canada. | His Account of the great | River Missasipi | to which is Added | A Map of that Country; | with a De | scription of the great Water Falls in the | River Missouris. | Translated from the French published at Paris. | 8° *Title,* 1 *leaf; to the Reader,* 2 *pp.; Letter to Author,* ii. *to* xxi. | *Pref.* 6 *pp., not numbered; Advertisement* 1 *p., and* 205 *pp.; Index,* 5 *pp. not numbered. London,* | *Printed for Bernard Lintot* | 1719. | 809

The same as the edition of 1714, with a new title.

In accordance with the somewhat questionable honesty of the English publishers of the period, this book was produced as a new work in 1719, although it differs from that of 1714, in nothing except the title. The edition of 1719 is believed to have been published without the map. I have seen two copies at least without evidences of their having ever possessed it. The curious relation of Joutel, was the last which the public received of the unfortunate expedition, in which La Salle perished. It was written by one of the companions of that celebrated traveller, who seems to have been the only one on whom La Salle could rely. Joutel was fortunate enough to render him some important services. The original edition of this work, was printed at Paris in 1713, one year prior to the first English publication.

KALADLIT.

Assilialiait. Gronlandske traesuit [*Woodcut*] Kriken, Seminariet og Inspekteurbolingen red kolonien. Godthaab. 4° 27 *leaves. Godthaab, trykt i inspektoratets, bogtrykkeri, af L: Møller og R Bethelsen,* 1860. 810

An Esquimau of Greenland, with his pencil, has in this work attempted to give representations of the traditions, manners, weapons, and habits of life of his own race. It consists of a title, two pages of text, thirty-nine numbered engravings, and a folding colored plate. As the work of one of the aborigines it is not without interest.

KANE (Paul).

Wanderings of an Artist among the Indians of North America, from Canada to Vancouver's Island and Oregon through the Hudson's Bay Company's Territory, and back again. 8° *pp.* 455. 8 *colored lithographs,* 16 *woodcuts, map, and Appendix.* "*Indian Census of Indian Tribes,*" 4 *leaves. London,* 1859. 811

The author, after four years study of art in Europe, returned to Canada filled with the determination to fulfill an early formed design of executing a series of drawings, of scenes in Indian life. To accomplish this, he traversed, almost alone, the territories of the Red River Settlement; the valley of the Saskatchewan; across the Rocky Mountains, down the Columbia River; the shores of Puget Sound, and Vancouver's Island. The book is a transcript of his daily journal, thrown into the narrative form; and the beautiful engravings are copies of the labors of his pencil. It is an interesting collection of the incidents of life and travel, among the Indian tribes inhabiting the regions over which he passed.

KANE (Elisha Kent).

Arctic Explorations: The Second Grinnell Expedition in search of Sir John Franklin, 1853, '54, '55. By Elisha Kent Kane. Illustrated by upwards of three hundred Engravings, From Sketches by the Author. The Steel Plates executed under the superintendence of J. M. Butler, the wood engravings by Van Ingen and Snyder, Philadelphia. *Two vols., pp.* 464 *and* 467, *and Life in one vol. In all three vols. London, Truebner & Co.,* 1856. 812

Although the explorations to the Arctic Regions have all had for their object the discovery of an open channel between the two great oceans, or the relief of the survivors of Sir John Franklin's expedition, yet the aboriginal tribes which inhabit those gloomy regions have always attracted a large share of the attention of the explorers. A great part of these volumes of Dr. Kane, is occupied with descriptions of the Esquimaux, portraits of their women and principal men, and illustrations of scenes in their life.

KEIM (De B. Randolph).

Sheridan's Troopers on the Borders: A winter campaign on the

Plains, by De B. Randolph Keim. With Numerous Engravings. 8° *pp.* 308, *with frontispiece and 6 plates. Philadelphia, Claxton, Remsen, & Haffelfinger,* 1870. 813

The author narrates in this work, the incidents of a campaign against the Indians of the Plains, in which the usual military rule of fighting the Indians when they were best prepared, was not adhered to. General Sheridan assailed them in the depth of winter, when the resources which make them so difficult to find or overtake were unavailable. A winter's campaign upon the ocean wastes of the prairies, skirmishes with the savage enemy, and at last a great battle with the despairing tribes, cooped up in a frozen plain, with details of some bloody massacres, afford a sufficient scope for the writer, who seems to have given us a faithful and accurate narrative of them.

KEITH (Capt. Thomas).

Struggles of Capt. Thomas Keith in America, including the Manner in which he, his wife and child, were Decoyed by the Indians; their temporary Captivity, and happy deliverance; Interspersed with occasional descriptions of the United States, Soil, Productions, &c. 12° *pp.* 28 *and folding plate of "Capt. Keith and family betrayed and made prisoners by the American Indians." London, printed for Thomas Tegg,* 111 *Cheapside (n. d.) price only Sixpence.* 814

KEITH's Captivity.

The thrilling and romantic story of Sarah Smith and the Hessian, an original tale of the American Revolution, to which is added Female heroism exemplified. An interesting story founded on fact. Together with Mr. Keith's Captivity among the American Indians. 8° *pp.* 24. *Philadelphia,* 1844. 815

KELLEY (A.).

The Mental Novelist and amusing companion, a collection of histories, essays, & Novels; containing Historical Description of the Indians in North America [*etc.*, 10 *lines.*] Unheard of Sufferings of David Menzies amongst the Cherokees and his Surprising Deliverance [*etc.*, 8 *lines*]. With many other Literary Productions of Alexander Kelley, Esq. 12° *pp.* 283. *London,* 1783. 816

This curious medley contains, besides the "Letter concerning the Indians," occupying the first thirty-two pages, the most surprising narrative of captivity, and sufferings among them ever printed. It is entitled, — Paper IV., "A true Relation of the unheard of Sufferings of David Menzies, Surgeon, among the Cherokees, and of his Surprising Deliverance." It is the personal narration of the captive himself, and bears the marks of veritability, from accurate local references.

KENDALL (James).

A Sermon delivered before the Society for Propagating the Gospel among the Indians and others in North America. At their Anniversary, November 7, 1811. By James Kendall. 8° *pp* 44. *Boston,* 1812. 817

The last ten pages are in the Appendix, and consist of historical notes on the Indian missions.

KENDALL (Geo. Wilkins).

Narrative of the Texan Sante Fé Expedition comprising a description of a Tour through Texas and across the great Southwestern prairies, the Camanche and Caygüa Hunting-Grounds, with an account of the Sufferings from want of food, losses from hostile Indians, and final capture of the Texans and their march as prisoners to the city of Mexico, with Illustrations and a map. Two vols. 8° *pp.* 405 *and* 406. *New York,* 1844. 818

KENDALL (Edward Augustus).

Travels through the Northern Parts of the United States in the years 1807 and 1808. Three vols. 8° *New York,* 1809. 819

The personal visits of the author to various tribes of Indians, and the oral information obtained by him from others, afford us much interesting matter concerning them.

KENNEDY (James).

Probable Origin of the American Indians with particular reference to that of the Caribs. A Paper read before the Ethnological Society The 15th March 1854. And printed at their special request. By James Kennedy, Esq. LL. D. [*etc.*] 8° *pp.* 42. *London, E. Lumley,* 126 *High Holborn,* 1854. 820

KER (Henry).

Travels through the Western Interior of the United States, from the year 1808, up to the year 1816, with a particular description of a great part of Mexico, or New-Spain. Containing A particular account of thirteen different tribes of Indians through which the author passed; describing their Manners, Customs, &c., with some account of a tribe whose customs are similar to those of the ancient Welch. Interspersed with valuable historical information, drawn from the latest authorities. By Henry Ker. 8° *pp.* 372. *Elizabethtown, N. J., printed for the author,* 1816. 821

An absurd preface which assures us of the veritability of the author's narration, and at the same time begs us to excuse what shall be proved false; a puerile account of his childhood in the first chapter, and an occasional attempt to throw a sentimental and melodramatic glow over his narrative, do not establish a perfect confidence in its historic truthfulness. In the seventh chapter he commences an account of his adventures among the Indians west of the Mississippi, which he continues through the twelve succeeding ones, or from pp. 90 to 192. If it is history, it is intolerably like fiction; and if it is a romance, it has too much resemblance to history to be amusing.

KERCHEVAL (Samuel).

A History of the Valley of Virginia. By Samuel Kercheval. 12° *pp.* 486. *Samuel H. Davis, Winchester,* 1833. 822

Although the author announces in his second edition, that it is extended as well as revised, yet on comparison it will be found that the revision consisted, in excluding from it the narrative of Manheim's and others' captivity which was printed in the first edition, as well as the chapter on slavery, a subject which in the interval of seventeen years, could not be safely treated in the manner of the author, for which he substituted a chapter on the Revolution in the second. Mr. Brantz Mayer says, "Some liberties have been taken with Mr. Doddridge's 'Notes on the Indian Wars, and Settlement of the Western Parts, of Pennsylvania, and Virginia,' *in this reprint of it by way of transposition.*"' The Appendix to the second volume, however, does contain some additional and interesting matter relating to conflicts with the Indians, which was collected by Kercheval. Copies of either editions have become scarce, the first being much the most difficult to procure.

KERCHEVAL (Samuel).

A History of the Valley of Virginia. By Samuel Kercheval. Second Edition: revised and extended by the author. 8° *pp.* 347. *Woodstock, Va., John Gatewood, printer,* 1850. 823

KETCHUM (William).

An Authentic and Comprehensive History of Buffalo, with some account of its early inhabitants both Savage and Civilized, comprising historic notices of the Six Nations or Iroquois Indians, including a sketch of the life of Sir William Johnson, and of other prominent white men, long resident among the Senecas. Arranged in chronological order. In Two Volumes. By William Ketchum. 8° Vol. I. *pp.* xvi. + 432. Vol. II. *pp.* vii. + 443. *Buffalo, N. Y., Rockwell, Baker, & Hill, printers,* 1864 *and* 1865. 824

The Indian traditions regarding the Eries and their destruction, the narratives of the early explorers, Champlain, Le Moine, and Hennepin, an account of the expeditions of La Barre, De Nonville, and Frontenac against the Six Nations, and an abridgment of the Journal of La Salle's Exploration, form the subjects of the first seven chapters, to page 108. The wars of the Senecas with the French during the first half of the eighteenth century; "The Senecas in Rebellion," and the history of the war of the Six Nations against the Colonies during the Revolution, fill the remainder of the volume. The narrative of Col. Thomas Proctor, a daily journal of the incidents of a Mission of a Commissioner of the Government to the Six Nations in 1791, forms the Appendix to Vol. I. pp. 413 to 436, and pp. 305 to 318 of Appendix to Vol. II. An account of Sullivan's Expedition against the Senecas, with a description of the obsequies of Lieut. Boyd and his men, slaughtered during the passage of that army, is given in pp. 319 to 344 of the Appendix to Vol. II. Nearly half of the second volume is also devoted to the history of Indian affairs, as connected with that of Buffalo.

KE-WA-ZE-ZHIG.

An Address delivered in Alston Hall, Boston, February 26, 1861, before a Convention met to devise ways and means to elevate and improve the condition of the Indians in the United States. By Ke-wa-ze-zhig, A son of the Chief of the Chippeways. With a report of the Proceedings of the Convention, and a poem by a friend. 12° *pp.* 27. *Boston, published by the author,* 1861. 825

KIDDER (Frederic) and UNDERWOOD (A. B.).

Report on the Sudbury Fight April 1676, (Read at the October meeting of the Society 1866, and reprinted from the N. E. Historical and Genealogical Register) n. d. a. l. 8° *pp.* 1 *to* 12. (*Boston*, 1866.) 826

KIDDER (Frederic).

The Expeditions of Capt. John Lovewell, and his Encounters with the Indians; Including an Account of the Pequaket

Battle, with a History of that Tribe; and a Reprint of Rev. Thomas Symmes' Sermon. *Map.* 4° *Boston*, 1865. 827

Large paper; only twenty-five printed. See Symmes (T.).

KIDDER. The same. *Small* 4°. *Boston*, 1865. 828

Edition two hundred copies in this size.

KIDDER (F.).

The Abnaki Indians; Their Treaties of 1713 and 1717, and a Vocabulary: with a Historical Introduction. By Frederic Kidder of Boston. 8° *pp.* 25. *Portland, printed by Brown Thurston*, 1859. 829

KIDDER (Frederick).

Military Operations in Eastern Maine and Nova Scotia, during the Revolution, chiefly compiled from the Journals and Letters of Colonel John Allan, with Notes and a Memoir of Col. John Allan, by Frederick Kidder. 8° *pp.* x. + 336, *and map. Albany, Joel Munsel*, 1867. 829

This narrative of the sufferings and devotion of a Revolutionary hero, hitherto but little known to the people whose cause he espoused, is entirely devoted to the minutiæ of seven years' residence among the Micmacs, Marachects, Passamaquody, and Penobscot Indians, during which he acted as their chief or superintendent, and influenced their neutrality during the conflict. The eastern settlements of New England, in consequence, entirely escaped the massacre and conflagration which desolated the Mohawk and Wyoming valleys. His Journals kept with great minuteness, and the letters and documents sent to the Indians, with those dictated and signed by them, form the great bulk of the volume. They are most interesting memoirs of the life and character of those tribes, which are the last remnants of the powerful nations which once controlled the territory of New England.

KING (Col. J. Anthony).

Twenty-four years in The Argentine Republic, embracing its civil and military history and an account of its political condition, before and during the Administration of Governor Rosas [*etc.*, 5 *lines*]. By Col. J. Anthony King, An officer in the army of the Republic and twenty-four years a resident of the Country. 12° *pp.* 324. *New York and Philadelphia, D. Appleton & Co.*, 1846. 830

Chapter vii. contains a curious account of the Chirriowe tribe of Indians, and the escape of Colonel King and his party from them.

KING (Richard).

Narrative of a Journey to the Shores of Arctic Ocean in 1833, 1834, and 1835, under the Command of Capt. Back, R. N. By Richard King, Surgeon and naturalist to the Expedition. In Two Volumes. Vol. I. *pp.* xviii. + 312 + 1 *plate*; Vol. II. *pp.* viii. + 321 + 3 *plates*. *London, Richard Bentley*, 1836. 831

Dr. King's narrative is full of the details of Indian life, as it was presented to the members of Captain Back's expedition. He looked at the same transactions with the natives, and the same phases of their character which Captain Back portrays, from a different point, and their coloring to his eye bears another tinge. His journal, filled with descriptions of interviews with the Chippewyans, Crees, Dog-Ribs, and Esquimaux, is therefore exceedingly interesting even after the perusal of Captain Back's narrative. Although every chapter is largely devoted to incidents associated with the natives, and anecdotes illustrative of their character, Dr. King yields the whole of Chapter xii. to an examination and relation of the present condition of the tribes inhabiting the Hudson's Bay territories.

The Doctor does not attempt to conceal the chagrin he felt, at the cool absorption of his own careful researches in the narrative of Captain Back. In the splendid work of that really eminent explorer, there appears a little, and but a little of that want of generosity which the relation of Dr. King insinuates. Both give the most minute narrations of the peculiar traits of the Northern Indians, their destructive wars, their wasting from disease, and famine, and debauchery, all of which are directly traceable to their communication with the whites. Dr. King, however, finds in them traces of some of the nobler, as well as the more tender emotions, the possession of which Captain Back somewhat superciliously derides. Dr. King very justly reminds him that the gallant Captain owed his life, and that of his entire party, to the devotion and self-denial, through two long starving winters, of the Chippewyan chief Akaitcho. This remarkable Indian deserves an honorable fame. While his tribe in common with himself were starving, he shared with Captain Franklin in his two expeditions, and with Captain Back in a third, the scanty food, which his superior hunter-craft enabled him to obtain, when the duller white reason failed. Captain Franklin would never have sailed upon his fateful voyage, but for the humanity of Akaitcho, as he would have perished of starvation on his first exploration.

[Kinzie (Mrs. J. H.).]

Narrative of the Massacre at Chicago August 15th, 1812, and of some preceding events. 8° *pp.* 1 *to* 34. *Chicago*, 1844. 832

Kinzie (John H., Mrs.).

Waubun, The Early Day of the North-West. By Mrs. John H. Kinzie of Chicago. With Illustrations. 8° *pp.* 498 + 6 *plates. New York, published by Derby & Jackson; and Cincinnati, H. W. Derby*, 1856. 833

This picture of the early days of the Northwest, drawn from the lips of an aged pioneer, is replete with authentic details of aboriginal manners, and the association of the frontiersmen with them in peace or war.

Kip (William Ingraham).

The Early Jesuit Missions in North-America. Compiled and translated from the letters of the French Jesuits, with notes by the Right Rev. William Ingraham Kip, Bishop of California, &c. 12° *pp.* 325. *Albany, N. Y., Pease & Prentice*, 82 *State Street*, 1866. 834

This edition, having an index, is superior to the others in that respect; a work of this size upon the Jesuit missions in America, could scarcely be more than a collection of annals of the Society of Jesus, or much more than a chronological statement of their establishment and efforts. The gigantic operations of this society, reaching from the great lakes of Canada through almost every tribe of savages to Patagonia; their wonderful success in Christianizing whole nations, in forming missionary establishments which became hierarchies, in combining these until they became kingdoms with priests for monarchs, could only be told in many volumes of folios. The story of the martyrdoms of Jesuit missionaries among the Indians, would alone fill a book much greater than this. Father Kip's work is composed of the journals and letters of missionaries, among which is the very interesting and important account of the massacre at Fort George, by Father Roubaud.

KIP (Rev. William Ingraham).
The Early Jesuit Missions in North America; Compiled and Translated from the Letters of the French Jesuits, with Notes. By the Rev. William Ingraham Kip, M. A. 12° *pp.* 321. *New York*, 1846. 835

KIP (Lawrence).
The Indian Council in the Valley of the Walla-Walla 1855 [*printed not published*]. 8° *pp.* 32. *San Francisco*, 1855. 836

"These pages are the expansion of a journal, kept while with the escort from the fourth infantry at the Indian council." — *Preface.*

KIP (Lawrence).
Army Life on the Pacific. A Journal of the Expedition against the Northern Indians, the tribes of the Coeur D'Alenes Spokans, and Pelouzes in the Summer of 1858, by Lawrence Kip, Second Lieut. 12° *pp.* 144. *New York, Redfield*, 1859. 837

KNAPP (H. S.).
A History of the Pioneer and Modern Times of Ashland County (Ohio), from the earliest to the present date, by H. S. Knapp. 8° *pp.* 550. *Philadelphia*, 1863. 838

There is scarcely a page in this voluminous work, to justify the expectation which the word Pioneer on the title may arouse, that the book will contain any information regarding the Indians, or their enemies the borderers.

KNIGHT (Dr.).
Narrative of a late Expedition against the Indians with an Account of the Barbarous Execution of Col. Crawford and the wonderful escape of Dr. Knight and John Slover from Captivity in 1782. To which is added A Narrative of the Captivity & Escape of Mrs. Frances Scott, An Inhabitant of Washington County Virginia. 24° *pp.* 46. *Andover, n. d.* ( ). 839

KNIGHT and CRAWFORD.
A | Remarkable | Narrative | of an | Expedition | against the | Indians | with an account of the | Barbarous Execution | of | Col. Crawford, | and | Dr. Knight's | Escape from | Captivity. | 12° *pp.* 24. *Printed for Chapman Whitcomb*, | (*n. p., n. d.*). 840

KOCH (Albert).
Description of the Missourium Theristo caulodon (Koch) or Missouri Leviathan, Leviathan Missouriensis, together with its supposed habits and Indian Traditions, [4 *lines*,] by Albert Koch. Fifth edition enlarged. 8° *pp.* 28. *Dublin*, 1843. 841

KOHL (J. G.).
Kitchi Gami. Wanderings around Lake Superior. By J. G. Kohl, author of travels in Russia, &c. *London, Chapman & Hall*, 1860. 842

Under this repellant name, suggestive of sensational or fictitious writing, the eminent German traveller Mr. Kohl, has given one of the most exhaustive and valuable treatises on Indian life ever written. It is wholly the result of personal experience, and one which only the most fervent scientific zeal and earnest self-abnegation, as well as a very high order of intelligence, could produce. He surrendered all the repugnances to filth, barbarism, and exposure with which civilization and self-indulgence invest us, to live intimately and confidentially with the Indian tribes around Lake Superior. He endeavored to penetrate the thick veil of distrust, ignorance, and superstition which conceal the mind of the Indian, and learn the innate traverses of thought which give motive to his soul. How well he succeeded, every one will know who commences to read his book, for its interest will compel him to finish it.

LABAT.

Nouveau Voyage aux Isles de l'Amerique contenant L'Histoire Naturel de ces pays, l'Origine, les Moeurs, la Religion & le Gouvernement des Habitans anciens & moderns. Les Guerres & les Evenemens singuliers qui y sont arrivez pendant le long sejour que le Auteur y a fait. Le Commerce & les Manufactures qui y font etablies & les Moyens de les augmenter. Avec une Description exacte & curieuse de toutes ces Isles. Ouvrage enrichi de plus de cent Cartes Plans & Figures en Tailles-donces. *Six vols.* 12° *A Paris, Rue S. Jacques*, 1722. 843

[A New Voyage to the American Islands, containing the Natural History of those Countries. The Origin, the Manners, the Religion, and the Government of the Inhabitants ancient and modern. The Wars and most remarkable Events which occurred during the long residence of the author there. The Commerce and Manufactures which have been established, and the means of increasing them. The work illustrated with more than one hundred copperplate engravings and maps.]

The principal interest of these volumes is found in Chapters II. and III. of Vol. II., pp. 6 to 96, in which the author gives an account of the prominent characteristics of the Caribs, the last surviving remnant of whom on the island of Martinique he visited in 1694. The destruction of the race had proceeded so far at that time that he found only forty-seven persons alive. Since then the last of the tribe has disappeared.

Most of these plates are from drawings of plants, animals, or manufacturing establishments.

LA BORDE (Sieur de la).

Relation de l'Origine, Moeurs, Coustumes, Religion, Guerres, et Voyages des Caraibes, Sauvages des Isles Antilles de l'Amerique. Faite par le Sieur de la Borde Employe a la Conversion des Caraibes, estant avec le R. P. Simon Jesuite; Et tiree du Cabinet de Monsieur Blondel. 4° *pp.* 1 *to* 40 + 3 *plates, divided into* 12 *compartments, exhibiting the utensils, dwellings, and manufactures of the Caribs.* (*Paris*, 1674). 844

[Relation of the Origin, Manners, Customs, Religion, Wars, and Voyages of the Caribs; Savages of the Antilles Islands, in America. Made by Sieur de la Borde, formerly engaged in the Conversion of the Caribs with the Jesuit Father Simon.]

See Recueil de Divers Voyages.

LACOCK (Mr.).

Seminole War. Mr. Lacock's Report upon the Execution of Arbuthnot and Ambrister, with the evidence before the Committee, on the Conduct of the Seminole War. 8° *pp.* 40. (*Washington*, 1818). 845

No title printed.

Laet (Ioannis de, Antwerpiani).

Notae ad Dissertationem Hvgonis Grotii De Origine Gentium Americanarum: et Observationes Aliquot ad meliorem indaginem difficillimae illius Quaestionis Parisiis Apud Viduam Gvilielmi Pelé Via Iacobaea Sub Signo Crucis aurea M.DC.XLIII. *Square* 16° *pp.* 223. 846

[Notes on the Dissertation of Hugo Grotius on the Origin of the American Indians and other Observations to facilitate the Understanding of some difficult Questions upon them. Paris, Widow G. Pele, Jacob Street under the Sign of the Golden Cross, 1643.]

Laet (Ioannis de, Antwerpiani).

Notae ad Dissertationem Hugonis Grotii De Origine Gentium Americanarum: et Observationes aliquot ad meliorem indaginem difficillimae illius Quaestionis. *Amstelodami Apud Ludovicum Elzevirium* clↄ.Iↄc.xliii. 16° *pp.* 223. 847

This learned essay upon the origin of the American Indians, was written to refute the arguments of Hugo Grotius, who controverted the theory of their Scythian descent. In 1642, Grotius maintained that the Indians of America north of Yucatan derived their origin from the Norwegians, who emigrated by way of Iceland, Greenland, and Labrador. That Yucatan was peopled from Ethiopia, he established from some rumor which had reached him of their practice of circumcision. That Peru was populated by the Chinese, he finds proof from their worship of the sun, their architecture, and their laws, which he confirms by repeating some tradition, which he fathers upon Herrera, of the wrecks of Chinese vessels found on the coast of Patagonia. Lastly, he asserts the origin of the inhabitants of the southerly portions of South America, in the natives of New Guinea, and the Moluccas. Laet controverted these theories in the treatise first printed in 1643, and effectually demolishes most of the arguments of Grotius, by proving the statements on which they were founded to be fallacious. On the ruins of his antagonist's theoretic structures, Laet erected a hypothetical edifice quite as frail. The Canaries afforded a convenient half-way station, and having read in Pliny that the remains of ancient buildings had been seen on some islands on the coast of Africa, he thinks the Spaniards, troubled by the Carthaginians, modeled some vessels after those of their enemies, sailed to the Canaries and subsequently drifted to Brazil, which they peopled. Laet inclines also to credit the story of Prince Madoc's Welsh immigration, and argues favorably to its adoption. He however gives the greatest credence, to the hypothesis of the Scythian population of North America, and labors hard to establish it. He also thinks it probable, that the Pacific Islands contributed to populate the western coasts of South America. Grotius, in a treatise printed in 1643, replied with much more hauteur than logic; and with scarcely any addition of argument. To this Laet responded with his second treatise entitled, *Responsio ad dissertationem secundam, Hugonis Grotii de Originibus gentium Americanarum, Amsterdam*, 1644.

Laet (Joan de).

Responsio ad dissertationem secundam Hvgonis Grotii, de Origine Gentium Americanarum. *Amstelrodami, Lud. Elzevirium*, 1644. 8° *Map.* 848

["Response to the second dissertation of Hugo Grotius on the Origin of the American Races."]

Not fully satisfied with his success, Laet induced the learned George Horn to enter the lists against Grotius, and he accordingly produced his *De Originibus Americanis*," in 1652.

LAET (Jean de).

L'Histoire | dv | Noveau Monde | ou | description | des Indes | Occidentales, | Contenant dix' huict Liures, | Par le Sieur Iean de Laet, d Anuers; | Enrichi de nouuelles Tables Geographiques & Figures des | Animaux, Plantes & Fruicts | *A Leyde,* | *Chez Bonauenture & Abraham Elseviers Imprimeurs ordinaires de l Universite* | 1640. *Folio* (28) *prel. pp.* + 632 + (xii.) + 14 *folding maps.* 849

[The History of the New World or description of the West Indies. Contained in eighteen books.]

Book II. is occupied with a description of Canada, of which division of the work Chapters ii., xii., xiii., xvi., and xix., are descriptive of the different tribes of savages inhabiting New France. Chapters xi., xvi., and xviii., of Book III. are devoted to the narration of the manners and customs of the Indians of Virginia; and in Chapters xiv., and xvi., of Book IV. will be found descriptions of the peculiarities of Florida. Six chapters of Book V. on Mexico, nine of Book XI. on Peru, five of Book XV. on Brazil, and four of Book XVII. on Guiana, are entirely occupied with dissertations on the language and origin, with descriptions of the appearance and manners of the aborigines of the respective countries. Vocabularies and grammatical analyses of the languages of the various nations of savages who inhabited the countries described, will be found on pages 52, 57, 80, 81, 153, 156, 406, 536, 537, 589, 583. Charlevoix says: "This work is full of the most excellent and curious details of the natural history, and the character, manners, and customs of the American aborigines, derived from the reports of the European mission establishments in America. It contains many documents upon American philology, taken for the most part from the collection of Ramusio, upon the languages of the natives of Canada, and the relation of Lery of those of Brazil."

LAFITAU (Joseph Francois).

Moeurs des Sauvages Ameriquains comparees aux Moeurs des Premiers Temps. Par le P. Lafitau de la Compagnie de Jesus. Ourage enrichi de Figures en taille-douce. *Two vols.* 4° Tome I.: 19 *plates, frontispiece, title, and* 10 *prel. leaves, pp.* 610. Tome II.: *Title,* 5 *prel. leaves,* 22 *plates, pp.* 490, *and* 21 *leaves Index. A Paris,* 1724. 850

[Manners of the Savages of America compared with those of Ancient Times. By Father Lafitau of the Order of Jesuits. The work enriched with many engravings on copperplate.]

Lafitau gives very extended and very exact details of the customs, manners, and religion of the savages of America, though principally of the Indians of Canada. He knew well the subject of which he treated, as his acquaintance with Indian customs was acquired by having lived a long time among the Iroquois. Charlevoix says: "We have nothing so exact upon the subject of which he treats. His parallel of ancient nations with the American Indians is very ingenious, and exhibits as great familiarity with the nations of antiquity in the Old World, as with the aborigines of the new."

The author undertook in his lengthy treatise upon the American Indians, to prove, from the similarity of their customs with those of the ancient nations inhabiting northern and central Asia, that they must be the descendants of emigrants from Tartary. He is confident that although it may be proved in time that the two continents do not quite connect their lands, yet that the arm of the sea separating them will prove so narrow, that it could have offered but little obstacle to the crossing of the Tartar horde, which peopled America. Aside from all the designs of proving the probability of this hypothesis, the work is a grand cyclopædia of Indian history, and customs at that date. The numerous engravings, although most of them remind us of De Bry, are finely executed illustrations of aboriginal life and peculiarities.

LA FITEAU.

De Zeden der Wilden Van Amerika Zynde Een nieuwe uitvoerige en zeer kurieuse Beschryving van derzelver Oorsprong Godsdienst, manier van Oorlogen, Huwelyken, Opvoeding, Oeffeningen Feesten Danzeryen, Begravenissen en andere zeldzame gewoonten; Tegen De Zeden der oudste Volkeren Vergeleken, en met getuigenissen uit de oudste, Grieksche enandere Schryveren getoetsst en bevestigt. Door den zeer geleerden J. F. La Fiteau, Jesuit en Zendeling in Amerika In't Fransch beschreven. Eerste Deel. In's Gravenhage. By Gerard Vander Poel Boekverkoper. 1781. *Folio. Two vols.* 41 *plates.* 851

This is a Dutch translation of Lafitau's Manners of the American savages. The fine copperplate engravings are from the same plates as in the original, and somewhat better impressions.

LA HONTAN (Baron).

New Voyages to North America. Containing an Account of the several Nations of that vast Continent; their Customs, Commerce, and Way of Navigation upon the Lakes and Rivers; the several attempts of the *English* and *French* to dispossess one another; with the reasons of the Miscarriage of the former; and the various adventures between the *French*, and the *Iroquese* Confederates of *England*, from 1683 to 1694. * * * Also a Dialogue between the Author and a General of the Savages, giving a full View of the Religion and strange Opinions of these People: with an account of the Author's Retreat to *Portugal* & *Denmark*, and his Remarks on those Courts. To which is added, a Dictionary of the *Algonkine* Language, which is generally spoke in *North-America*. Illustrated with twenty-three maps & cutts. Written in *French*, by the Baron La Hontan, Lord Lieutenant of the *French* Colony at *Placentia* in *Newfoundland*, now in *England*. Done into *English*, in Two vols, a great part of which never Printed in the Original. 8° *London*, 1703. 852

Vol. I., Title, 1 leaf, Dedication, 1 leaf, Preface, 4 leaves, Table of Contents, (all.) pp. and pp. 1 to 280 + 12 maps and plates. Vol. II., Title, 1 leaf + pp. 302 + Books lately printed, 1 leaf + Index (all.) + 11 plates.

The work of La Hontan has not received the amount of credit to which it is really entitled, although written by a man of more than ordinary learning and intelligence. Had he written no other work than the *New Voyages*, it is probable that it would have experienced no lack of esteem, but his Relations even when scrupulously exact, have felt the malign influence of the skepticism and infidelity which he infused into his subsequent work, *Dialogues between the Author and a Sauvage*. The present work is a translation of his Voyage originally published in French in two volumes, 1703, and of his *Dialogue* in the same language in one volume, 1704.

The first work, *New Voyages to N. A.*, occupies the whole of Vol. I. of the translation, and pp. 1 to 89 of Vol. II. "A Conference or Dialogue between the Author and Adario," occupies pp. 90 to 183. "Voyages to Portugal and Denmark," pp. 185 to 286. And on pp. 287 to 303, is "A Short Dictionary of the most Universal Language of the Savages," being a vocabulary of the Algonquin tongue.

The Voyages are almost wholly devoted to a description of the manners, customs, domestic habits, and method of warfare of the Indians of Canada. All of the nineteen plates are illustrative of the same characteristics of the savages.

The Baron La Hontan went to Canada in 1683, when only sixteen years old, and remained in that country nearly twenty years. He was required by his patron to write to him a detailed statement of the affairs of the colony in his letters, as a recognition of the yearly assistance he received from him. In this correspondence he did not flatter the priests, and imputed the evils which the colony suffered from the war with the Iroquois to their counsels. Becoming aware that steps were being taken by the Governor of Newfoundland to send him a prisoner to France, he fled to Portugal and thence to England. He says in his Preface, that had the King of France restored him to his offices, he would have given his book to the flames. But the rich and powerful ministers Pontchartrain were inexorable, and in consequence the book was printed. He asserts that the Dialogue which has generally been viewed as a fiction, is a true and faithful relation of conversations held with a Huron Indian named The Rat. La Hontan showed his MS. notes of the various reflections and sentiments of the Huron to Count Frontenac, who was much pleased with them, and aided him in stripping them of their metaphorical dress. This unfortunate meddling with the savage phraseology has also stripped the Dialogue of all its authenticity and value. La Hontan was in England while these volumes were printing, and in consequence of his supervision they are more correct than the French edition.

LAHONTAN (Baron).

Dialogue de Monsieur de Baron de Lahontan et d'un Sauvage Dans l'Amerique. Contenant une description exact des Moeurs & des Coutumes de ces Peuples Sauvages. Avec les Voyages du meme en Portugal [*etc.*, 4 *lines.*] Le tout enrichi de Cartes & les Figures. 18° *pp.* (16) + 103 + 1 *plate*. *A Amsterdam, Chez la Veuve de Boeteman et se vend A Londres, chez David Mortier, Libraire dans le Strand a l'Enseigne d'Erasme*, 1704. 853

[Dialogue between the Baron La Hontan, and an American Indian. Containing an exact description of the Manners and Customs of the Savage Natives; with the Voyages of the same in Portugal. The whole embellished with Maps and Figures.]

The dramatical part of the work is probably imaginary. The traits of the savages are doubtless fairly illustrated in its course, but it was used as a medium by the author to proclaim his deistical theories, and is of as much historical consequence as Rogers' *Ponteach*, or Count Johannes' *Tecumseh*, a *Drama*.

LANCASTER MASSACRE.

Serious Address, To such of the Inhabitants of Pennsylvania, As have connived at, or do approve of, the late Massacre of the Indians at Lancaster, or the Design of killing those who are now in the Barracks at Philadelphia. Re-printed from the First Edition (printed by Mr. Armbrister) and diligently compared and revised with the same. [*Price, two old Pennies.*] 12° *pp.*

8. *Philadelphia, printed by Andrew Stewart, at the Bible-in-Heart in Second-Street*, 1764. 854

A not inconsiderable number of pamphlets, were printed soon after the period of these Massacres, to exculpate the murderers, or to incriminate them. Some of these bloody men, afterwards aided in the destruction of Salem, and Gnadenhutten, when nearly one hundred Christian men, women, and children were inhumanly slaughtered.

The work is little more than a sermon, interspersed with historical sketches of the events which led to, and attended the dreadful massacre of the Christian Indians, by the dastardly wretches called Paxton Boys, whose cowardice had made them ferocious

Lang (John D.) and Taylor (Samuel, Jun.).

Report of a Visit to some of the Tribes of Indians, located West of the Mississippi River, by John D. Lang and Samuel Taylor, Jun. 8° *pp.* 34. *New York*, 1843. 855

Lanman (James H.).

History of Michigan, civil and topographical, in a compendious form, with a view of the surrounding lakes, by James H. Lanman, with a map. 8° *pp.* 398. *New-York, E. French*, 146 *Nassau Street*, 1839. 856

A minute narration of the early dealings of the whites with the aborigines of the territory, the Jesuit missions, and border wars, is given in the first ten chapters of the work.

[La Peyrere Is de]

Relation | dv | Groenland | [*Cut of Palm-tree with the motto Curvata Resurgo*] A Paris, | Chez Augustin Courbe, dans la | petite Salle du Palais, a la Palme. | M DCXL VII | Avec Priuilege du Roy. | 24°. 857

Prel. pp. (16)+278+(4)+a folding map of Greenland and one folding plate. The last is a sheet divided into five compartments, exhibiting cuts of the native Esquimaux, their fishing, weapons, etc.

This is the original edition of La Peyrere's curious Relation of Greenland, and is considered among the bibliographical rarities. It was afterwards printed in *Recueil de Voyages du Nord*, and a German edition was issued in 1674. The work contains some relations of the Esquimau savages of Greenland, which are of value, as being observations made upon them at that early day.

Lapham (I. A.).

The Antiquities of Wisconsin as surveyed and described by I. A. Lapham, civil engineer. On behalf of the American Antiquarian Society, Washington City. Published by the Smithsonian Institution, April, 1855. 4° *pp.* 95 + 55 *full-paged plates. New York, G. P. Putnam & Co.* 858

Larimer (Sarah L.).

The Capture and Escape. Or Life among the Sioux, by Mrs. Sarah L. Larimer. 12° *pp.* 252 + 5 *plates. Philadelphia; Claxton, Remsen, & Haffelfinger*, 1870. 859

The writer gives a vivid, and apparently candid narrative, of the terrible experience of a delicate woman, the survivor of the massacre of a train of emigrants to Idaho, in her captivity among the savages. She combines with her own, the narrations of several captives who escaped or were ransomed.

LAS CASAS (Bartholomew de las).

Breuissima re la | cion de la destruycion de las In | dias: colegida por el Obispo dō | fray Bartolome de las Casas | o | Casaus de la orden de Sācto Do | mingo. | Ano 1552. | [*Colophon on the 50th leaf:*] Fue impressa la presente O" | bra en la muy noble y muy leal ciudad de Seuilla | en casa de Sebastian Trugillo impressor de libros. A nuestra senora de Gracia. | Ano de M. D. L ij. | 4° 50 *leaves* + 4, *entitled,* "Lo que se sigue es un pedaco de una Carta," etc. 860

[A very brief narrative of the destruction of the Indies collected by the Bishop Don Bartholomew de Las Casas, or Casaus, Friar of the Order of Saint Dominick. In the year 1552. *Colophon:* Printed in the very noble and loyal city of Seville.]

LAS CASAS.

Lo quese sigue un peda | ço de una carta y relacion que escriuio cierto hombre: . . . | [*No title, place, or date.*] 4° 4 *leaves.* 861

[That which follows is a portion of a letter or narrative, written by a man who traversed these countries and records what his captain did or permitted to be done in the country through which he travelled.]

LAS CASAS.

Entre los re- | medios q̄ dō fray Bartolome de las Casas: | obispo d la ciudad real de Chiapa: refirio | por mandado del Emperador rey nro se- | ñor: en los ayuntamiētos q mādo hazer su | magestad de perlados y letrados y perso | nas grādes en Valladolid el año de mill & | quiniētos y quarēta y dos: para reforma- | ciō de las Indias. El octauo en ordō es el | siguiēte. Dōde se asignā veynte razones: | por las qles prueua no deuerse dar los in- | dios á los Españoles en encomiēda: ni en | fendo: ni en vassallaje: ni d' otra manera al | gūa. Si su majestad como dessea quiere li | brarlos de la tyrania y perdicio q̄ padecē | como de la boca delos dragones: y q̄ total- | mēte no los cōsumā y matē y q̄de vazio to- | do aq̄l orbe d' sus ta infinitos naturales ha | bitadores como estaua y lo vimos poblado | [*Colophon:*] Fue impressa . . . Seuilla, en las casas de Jacome Crōberger. Año de . . . mill & quinientos & cinquenta & dos años . . . 4° 53 *unnumbered leaves.* 862

[Among the remedies which Friar Don Bartholomew de Las Casas, Bishop of the royal city of Chiapa, has presented by order of our Lord, the Emperor King, at the councils of prelates, learned and great men ordered to be held in Valladolid in the year one thousand five hundred and forty-two for the reformation of the Indies. The following is the eighth in order, in which are given twenty reasons, which prove that the Indians ought not to be given to the Spaniards in commanderies, in feudal bondage, or in vassalage, or in any other manner; if his majesty should desire to free them from the tyranny and perdition which they are suffering: as from the jaws of dragons; and that they may not wholly consume and destroy them, and depopulate that world, which was as we saw filled with an infinite number of native inhabitants. *Colophon:* Printed in Sevilla, 1552.]

LAS CASAS.

Aqui se cōtienē vnos | auisos y reglas para los confessores q | oyeren confessiones delos Españo | les que son, o han sido en cargo a | los Indios delas Indias del | mar Oceano: colegidas por | el obispo de Chiapa don | fray Bartholome d | las | casas o casaus dela | orden de Sancto | Domingo. | [*Colophon:*] . . . Fue impressa . . . en . . . Seuilla, en casa de Sebastian Trugillo. Año de mil & quinientos & cin | cuenta y dos. 4° 16 *unnumbered leaves.* 863

[Here are contained some advices and rules for the confessors who receive the confessions of the Spaniards who possess, or have possessed commanderies of the Indians of the West Indies; composed by the Bishop of Chiapa, Don Bartholomew de Las Casas, or Casaus, brother of the Order of Saint Dominick. *Colophon:* Printed at Sevilla, 1552.]

Las Casas.

Aqui se contiene | vna disputa, o controuersia: entre el | Obispo don fray Bartholome de las | Casas, o Casaus, Obispo que fue de la | Ciudad Real de Chiapa que es en- | las Indias, parte de la nueua Espa- | ña, y el doctor Gines de Sepulueda | Coronista del Emperador nuestro Se | ñor, sobre q̃ el doctor cõtendia, que las | conquistas de las Indias contra los | Indios eran licitas, y el Obispo por | el contrario defendio y affirmo auer si | do y ser impossible no serlo: tyranicas | injustas & iniquas. La qual question | se ventilo & disputo en presẽcia de mu | chos letrados theologos & juristas, | en vna congregacion que mãdo suma | gestad juntar el año de mil yquiniẽtos y cincueta en la villa de Vallad. Año. | 1552 | [*Colophon:*] Aloor gloria de nuestro | señor Jesu Christo y de la sacratissima virgen sancta | Maria su madre. Fue impressa la presẽte obra | en lay muy noble & muy leal ciudad de Se- | uilla, en casa de Sebastiã Trugillo im | pressor de libros frõtero de nue | stra señora de gracia. Acabo | sse a. x. dias del mes de Se | trembro Año de mil & | quiniẽtos & cincuẽta | y dos Anos. | 864

Two editions of this tract were issued bearing the same date. From evidence offered in another place, I conclude this to have been printed first. The title is taken from the copy in my possession, the one below from that in the library of Mr. Brevoort.

Las Casas.

Aqui se contiene | vna disputa, o controuersia: entre el | Obispo dõ fray Bartholome de las | Casas, o Casaus, obispo q fue dela | ciudad Real de Chiapa, que es en- | las Indias, parte dela nueua Espa- | ña: y el doctor Gines de Sepulueda | Coronista del Emperador nuestro se- | ñor: sobre q el doctor contendia: q las | conquistas delas Indias contra los | Indios eran licitas: y el obispo por | el cõtrario d' fendio y affirmo auer si | do y ser ĩpossible no serlo: tiranicas, | injustas & iniquas. La qual questio | se vatilo & disputo en presencia d' mu | chos letrados theologos & juristas | en vna cõgregacion q mando su ma- | gestad juntar el año de mil & quiẽtos | y cincuẽta en la villa d Valladolid. | Año. 1552. | [*Colophon:*] Seuilla: | en casa de Sebastian Trugillo impressor de | libros. Frntero de nuestra señora de Gra | cia. Acabosse a. x. dias lel mes de Se- | tiembre. Año de mil & quinien | tos & cincuenta y dos. | 865

[Here is contained a dispute or controversy between the bishop Friar Bartholomew de Las Casas and Dr. Gines de Sepulveda, historiographer to our Lord the Emperor, wherein the Doctor contends that the conquests of the Indies from the Indians were lawful; and the bishop on the contrary, contended and affirmed that they were tyrannies, unjust and iniquitous, and that it was impossible they should be otherwise. The which question was examined and defended in the presence of many learned theologians and jurists in a council ordered by his Majesty to be held in the year one thousand five hundred and fifty, at Valladolid. *Colophon:* Printed at Sevilla, 1552.] 4°. Sixty-one unnumbered leaves in each edition.

Las Casas.

Este es vn tratado q̃ | el obispo dela ciudad Real de Chiapa dō | fray Bartholome de las Casas, o Casaus | compuso, por comision del Consejo Real | delas Indias: sobre la materia de los yn- | dios que se han hecho en ellas esclauos. El | qual contiene muchas razones y aucto- | ridades juridicas: que pueden apro | uechar a los lectores para deter- | minar muchas y diuersas | questiones dudosas | en materia de re- | stitucion: y de | otras que al | p̃sente los | hōbres | el tiēpo de agora tratan. | Año 1552. | [*Colophon:*] Fue impressa . . . en . . Seuilla, en casa de Sebastian Trugillo . . . Año de mill y quinientos cincuēta y dos. 4° 86 *unnumbered leaves, the last page blank.* 866

[This is a treatise which the Bishop of the Royal City of Chiapa, Don Friar Bartholomew de las Casas, composed by commission of the Royal Council of the Indies, upon the matters of the Indians who have been made slaves there. In which are contained many reasons, and judicial authorities, which will be profitable to the readers, in determining many different and doubtful questions in relation to restitution, and of others which men are discussing at the present day. *Colophon:* Printed at Sevilla, 1552.]

Las Casas.

Aqui se cōtienē tre | ynta proposiciones muy juridicas: en | las quales sumaria y succintamente se | toca muchas cosas perteneciētes al de | recho q̃ la yglesia y los principes chri- | stianos tienen, o puedē tener sobre los | infieles de qual quier especie que sean. | Mayormente se assigna el verdadero | y fortissimo fundamento en que se asie | nta y estriba: el titulo y señorio supre- | mo y . . . vniuersales señores y | Emperadores enellas sobre muchos re- | yes. Apuntā se tambien otras cosas co | cernientes al hecho acaecido en aql or | be notabilissimas: y dignas d' seruistas | y sabidas. Collijo las dichas treynta p | posiciones El obispo dō Fray Bartho- | lome de las Casas o Casaus: Obispo | q̃ fue d'la ciudad Real de Chiapa: cier | to Reyno de los dela nueua España. | Año 1552. | [*Colophon:*] Impresso en seuilla en casa de sebastiā trugillo. 4° 10 *leaves.* 867

[Here are contained thirty propositions most rightful, in which are treated and examined, in a summary and succinct manner, many things pertaining to the rights which the church, and Christian princes hold or can hold over the infidels of whatever kind they may be. More particularly, the true and strongest foundation is assigned, on which is based the title and supreme and universal dominion, by which the kings of Castile and Leon hold the world called the West Indies. By which they are constituted universal lords and Emperors over many kings. With other very remarkable things pointed ent, concerning transactions there, which are important to be seen and known. Anno 1552. *Colophon:* Printed in Sevilla at the house of Sebastian Trugillo.]

LAS CASAS.

Principia quedā ex quibus | procedendum est in disputatione ad manifestan | dam et defendendam Iusticiam Yndorum: | Per Episcopū. F. Bartholomeu a Ca- | saus ordinis predicatoru, collecta. | [*Colophon:*] Impressum Hispali in ineb Sebastiani Trugillo. 4° 10 *leaves.* (n. d.). 868*

[Principles upon which to proceed in discussions for sustaining and defending the rights of the Indians. *Colophon:* Printed in Spain by Sebastian Trugillo, [1552.]]

LAS CASAS.

Tratado cōpro | batorio del Imperio soberano y | principado vniuersal que los Re | yes de Castilla y Leon tienen so- | bre las indias: compusto por el | Obispo don fray Bartholome d | las Casas, o Casaus de la orden d | Sancto Domingo, Año 1552. | [*Colophon:*] ... Fue impressa ... en Seuilla | en casa d' Sebastiā Trugillo .... Año 1553. 4° 80 *unnumbered leaves.* 869

[A Treatise which proves the sovereign empire and universal dominion by which the kings of Castile and Leon hold the West Indies. *Colophon:* Printed by Sebastian Trugillo, 1553.]

LAS CASAS (D. Bartholomæi de).

D. Bartholo | maei de Las Casas, | Episcopi Chiapensis, Viri | in Omni doctrinarum genere | exercitatissimi, erudita & elegans explicatio Quaestionis | Vtrum Reges vel Principes iure aliquo vel titulo, & Salua con | scientia Cives ac Subditos a Regia Corona alienare, & alterius | Domini particularis ditioni Subijcere possint? Antehac | nunquam ab vllo Doctorum ita lucu | -lenter tractata. | Edita cura & studio Vuolffgangi Griesstetteri. | Cum gratia & priuilegio Caesareae Maiestatis. | 4° 4 *prel. leaves* + *pp.* 1 *to* 67. *Francoforti, ad Mœnum,* | 1571. 870

[D. Bartholomew de Las Casas Bishop of Chiapas, a man learned in every class of science; his wise Examination of the Question whether kings and princes have the right to dispose of their Subjects to other powers. Never before treated at such length, by any learned men. Published by Wolfgang Griesstetter. Frankfort, 1571.]

This piece of Las Casas' was not included in his Spanish works, first issued in 1552-53, and has never been printed in Spain (*Stevens*). It is even more rare than the other pieces of Las Casas which are so seldom reunited.

The Works of Las Casas — the first Catholic priest ordained in America, the first advocate of the abolition of American Slavery, the Apostle to the Indians — deserve from their intrinsic excellence as well as the excessive rarity of the original editions, an extended bibliographical notice.

For more than three hundred years, there has been known to exist in one or more libraries of Europe, a series of treatises, written by one of the companions of Columbus, who survived his friend the discoverer, more than sixty years. Of all the names, associated with the discovery and conquest of America, that of the author, Don Bartholomew de Las Casas, is second in eminence only to that of Columbus. The treatises consist of nine, or by some notations (when the *Carta* is separated from the *Brevissima Relacion*), of ten small quarto volumes, whose rarity has caused more than one of their number to be unknown to the collectors and editors of his works. Three nearly complete series of the original editions of Las Casas's treatises, are gathered in as many private libraries of Brooklyn; and two in those of New York.

It is probable that so great a number do not exist in any country in Europe. No public library in America claims to possess the whole series. Even as early as 1646, within one hundred years after the date of their first publication, an edition entitled *Las Obras de B. de Las Casas*, contained only six of the ten treatises; and when in 1822, Llorente printed his audacious paraphrase of them, under the title of *Coleccion de las Obras del Venerable Obispo de las Casas*, with a French edition entitled *Oeuvres de Las Casas* (each published in two volumes, 8° Paris, 1822), he only used the same number as the basis of his work.

In fact, it is altogether probable, that Llorente never saw the originals, and knew of Las Casas' works only by the edition of 1646. In America, six private libraries possess the original edition of Las Casas' treatises nearly or quite complete. These are, the collections of the Hon. Henry C. Murphy, J. Carson Brevoort, T. W. Field, of Brooklyn. James Lenox, S. M. L. Barlow, of New York, and John Carter Brown, of Providence.

Mr. Brevoort's copy was obtained at the sale of the Emperor Maximilian's library in Leipsic, 1869. A curious incident, illustrative of some of the peculiarities of book collecting, occurred in connection with the sale of this copy. Order had been transmitted by this gentleman, and the writer, to different agents for its purchase. So that at the distance of four thousand miles, we were made to compete for its possession, until it reached five hundred francs.

The career of the author of these distinguished treatises, was not less eminent than varied. Born in Seville in 1474, Las Casas, at the age of twenty-four, accompanied Columbus in his third voyage to America, in 1498, and was the first priest ordained on the soil of the New World. This event took place in San Domingo in 1510, where he sang the first *new mass*, ever celebrated, on a Continent now containing 80,000,000 Catholics. Every career, which ambition could incite to attain, or self interest prompt him to seek, was open and possible to him; yet he chose the humble self abnegation of a priest. The scenes of bloodshed which he narrates in his works, have thrilled the world with horror for more than three centuries.

Judging from circumstances attending their composition, internal evidences, and the dates of their titles, we may approximately fix their respective order of issue from the press. Thus, the *Brevissima*, having been written twelve years prior to its publication, would naturally take the first rank. The *Tratado Comprobatorio*, dated in the colophon 1553, and being a summary of all, except the *Explicatio Regia* printed in 1571, was doubtless, the latest printed with that exception. The *Thirty Propositions*, written in defense of the Twelve Rules of the Confessional, must of course have been printed subsequently to them, and therefore the *Avisos Reglas y Confesionario* takes the third place in order of publication. Examined by similar analysis, the bibliographical history of his treatises should, it appears to me, have the following chronological sequence:—

I. The first work of Las Casas was written in 1540, and submitted to the Emperor and Council in MS. It is, in substance, the same as the one afterwards known under the title of *Brevissima Relacion de la Destruccion de las Indias*. Although we now wonder at the boldness of this wonderful treatise, and esteem the courage of Las Casas as little less than superhuman, it is probable that it once contained much more to surprise us with its temerity. The allusions to persons who perpetrated the dreadful acts of cruelty he related, were doubtless well understood; but Mr. Helps's assumption that the memoir when first presented contained their names, is not warranted by the assertions of Las Casas himself. In his *Prologo* to the *Replicas* in the *Disputa* the Bishop says "I have before been permitted to present to you, some works to prove the injustice of the wars upon the Indians, ... and without going beyond the circle of generalities, I have rigorously imposed a law upon myself, never to name any one of my adversaries."—(*Disputa con Sepulveda*, verso of folio 29, edition Sevilla, 1552.) Wherever he found it necessary to refer to any one of the perpetrators of the cruelties he describes, he generally terms him, "this tyrant" or "that oppressor."

The *Brevissima Relacion* remains to-day almost unparalleled in the vigor of its composition and the nobility of its design. Yet this noblest work of philanthropy was, by a strange perversity of fortune, dedicated to Prince Philip, fated to become one of the most inhuman monsters who ever filled a throne. The work is divided into nineteen Articles, each portraying in detail the condition of the Indians, in one of the provinces of Spanish America, and is concluded by a Summary, and Addition for the year 1546.

II. The date of the tract which I place as the second work of Las Casas, is very uncertain, as it has neither title-page or colophon. It commences *Lo que Se sigue es un pedazo de una Carta*, and is usually found appended to the *Brevissima Relacion*. It consists of four leaves, and contains the fragment of a letter, written by a Spaniard, who witnessed some of the dreadful scenes of slaughter of the Indians which he narrates.

III. His third work was probably written soon after the *Brevissima Relacion*, and followed in the same order of publication. It is entitled, *Entre los Remedios para reformacion de las Indias*. (Among the Remedies for the reformation of the Indies.) The treatise is divided into twenty sections, entitled *Razones*, or "Reasons why the Indians should not be disposed of in Repartimientos."

IV. The fourth printed work of the venerable prelate, was probably the one entitled *Aqui se cotiene unos avisos y reglas para los Confessores*, or the twelve rules to govern the confessors, appointed by him to act in his diocese of Chiapa, while he was attending the council in the City of Mexico, 1547. It is not impossible that these rules were first printed in that city, as a press had been established there seven years previously. By these rules, the offices of the church were prohibited to all persons who held repartimientos, or who did not restore the avails of unrequited labor, by the Indians.

V. But it was in his fifth work that the fervent energy, the massive intellect, and great learning of the good bishop was exhibited most illustriously. His renowned controversy with the eminent scholar and casuist Sepulveda, was the origin of this treatise, entitled, *Aqui se contiene una disputa del Dr. Gines Sepulveda.* This remarkable man, whose learning and elegance of style obtained for him the title of "The Livy of Spain," had written a work entitled, *Democrates Secundus*, in which he maintained, with wonderful power of reasoning, the right of the Catholic monarch to dispose at pleasure of the lives and property of the Indians. Mr. Harrisse, in his *Bibliotheca Vetustissima*, says that after diligent search, he could not ascertain that the *Democrates Alter* had ever been published; and with good reason, for its printing was absolutely prohibited by Charles V., although Sepulveda was on terms of great intimacy with that monarch. The conscience of the emperor, now satiated with conquest, was alarmed by the awful narratives of Las Casas; and Sepulveda's work slept in MS., from which it has never awakened. The author, however, partially evaded the royal mandate, and printed three years after at Rome, some of its principal arguments in a work called *Apologia pro Libro de Justis Belli Causis.*

Of this fifth printed work, more than one edition bearing the date of 1552, was published. The copy in my possession has thirty-three variations in the title and colophon from the one in the library of Mr. Brevoort. The work is divided into three sections, of which the first is a summary of the motives which have given rise to the contradictory opinions of Las Casas and Sepulveda; prepared by the learned monk Domingo de Soto. Article II. contains the objections of Dr. Sepulveda to the reasons of Las Casas, both as stated by De Soto and as drawn from Las Casas' memoir. Article III. is composed of the answers of Las Casas, to the responses of Dr. Sepulveda, arranged in twelve sections entitled *Replicas*.

VI. The sixth publication of Las Casas is entitled, *Este es un Tratado q el Obispo de Las Casas . . . sobre la materia de los Indios*, or "A Treatise upon the Indians who have been made slaves in the Indies; containing some reasons for settling the doubtful questions of restitution to them."

VII. The seventh in the probable order of publication, is that entitled, *Aqui se contienen Treynta proposiciones* or "Thirty propositions regarding the work called Confesionario." The Bishop, during his absence in Mexico attending a council, had, as already noted, written twelve rules to the confessors whom he had appointed in his diocese to govern them in giving absolution. The rites of the Church were by a bull of Pope Paul III. refused to all who held Indians in slavery, and restitution of goods obtained by violence from them, was required by the rules of the Bishop founded upon this great authority. Complaint having been made to the Council of the Indies, of the rigor of these rules, the thirty propositions were written to sustain them.

VIII. The eighth work of the Bishop of Chiapas was written and printed in Latin, under the title *Principia quedam ex quibus procedendum*, etc. "Certain principles to be established in disputations regarding the government of the Indians." It was evidently an attempt to familiarise the minds of the clergy with the principles upon which he based his whole theory of the right of the Indians to person and property.

IX. The ninth printed work of Las Casas is the *Tratado Comprobatorio*, dated in the title 1552, but in the colophon 1553. It is the largest of the series, containing eighty-four leaves in one edition, and only eighty in the other. The fact that two editions were printed with the same date, seems hitherto unsuspected. From comparison of several copies of this work, it seems clear to me that it cannot be questioned. The Gothic characters, the size of the page, and even the number of lines in each page, are preserved in all the copies of either treatise I have seen except the ninth. It is, therefore, still uncertain whether more than one edition of the others was printed with the date of 1552.

Which of the two editions of that treatise is the first, it is probably now impossible to determine. So much at least may be conjectured, that both were printed in the lifetime of Las Casas, as there are orthographical changes, which would be more readily suggested to the fastidious sensitiveness of an author. These emendations being found in the copies containing eighty-four leaves, indicate that the edition complete in eighty leaves was the first printed.

X. The tenth and last of the series was not printed until 1571, five years after his death. It is entitled, *D. Bartholomaeo de Las Casas, . . . Quaestionis utrum Reges vel Principes jure aliquo vel titulo, etc.* "Examination of the Question whether kings and princes have the right to dispose of their subjects to other princes."

It is a wonderful enunciation of the inalienable right to person and property, which found its practical exemplification in America more than two centuries afterwards. Its doctrines had met a sympathetic and hearty response from the Emperor Charles the Fifth, and the hearts of the Catholic clergy. Long before, many devout and holy men had stimulated his zeal, and warmed his conscience while pondering over those mighty propositions. They afford us ground for astonishment and admiration. First, that those despotic and ambitious princes, Charles V. and Philip II., should have listened and assented to them. Second, that the first Catholic priest ordained in the New World should have been the first great casuist, to announce the principles upon which all its governments should one day be established. They attracted the attention of princes, prelates, and philosophers in every country of Europe.

XI. But the mind of this wonderful man, who seemed destined never to feel the infirmities of age, was not in repose even when approaching his ninetieth year. In 1555 he had written his eleventh work, in the form of a letter of great length, characterized by all his wonderful reasoning, addressed to the Archbishop of Toledo, then acting as adviser and confessor of Philip II. in England, in which he urges with all the fervent vehemence of his nature, and the massive reason and learning of his mind, the injustice of the contemplated sale of the Encomiendas in perpetuity, or in other words the fastening of unending slavery on the wretched Indians of America. This latter was printed for the first time by Llorente in his edition of the works of Las Casas (Paris, 1822), and occupies sixty pages of the second volume. His appeal was communicated to the king, and even that stern monarch was convinced. The sale of perpetual "Repartimientos" was prohibited, by an edict from the very monster whose cruelties depopulated Holland.

XII. In the seclusion and repose of his convent, Las Casas was still engaged upon a work which he had commenced as early as 1522, on his first entering the Dominican order, and which in 1566 he left uncompleted. This was his greatest work, the "History of the Indies;" which to the regret of all the lovers of historic truth has never been printed. The Manuscript has more than once been faithfully copied, and one of these transcripts rests in the library of Mr. James Lenox of New York. Two other copies are said to exist in the United States. The MS. copy made for Mr. Rich is comprised in four folio volumes covering 3,847 pages. The work is characterized by all the vigor of expression, elevation of style, and minuteness of statement, which give such decided personality to his other writings. It has proved a mine of almost exhaustless riches to other writers. The prince of historians, Antonio Herrera, filled his decades with its wealth, and later writers, Robinson, Prescott, and Helps, have enriched their pages from its stores.

XIII. His last work was written in 1564, when he was in his ninetieth year; and when repose had been earned by almost a century of labor. But it would seem as if he was constantly impelled by the awful enunciation of Pedro de Cordova, "I charge you as you would escape the pains of hell,"—and once more he armed himself for battle, to rescue his beloved Indians from oppression. This treatise remained in manuscript for two hundred and fifty-eight years, when it was printed by Llorente in 1822, under the title, *Réponse aux questions qui lui ont été proposées, sur les affaires du Pérou en* 1564. It occupies 156 pages of the second volume of the French edition. The editor fixes the date of the Response in 1504, several years before the discovery of Peru. It is probable, however, that the error is only typographical.

Llorente has done but scanty justice to the works of Las Casas. He wholly omits the *Principia Quædam*, and the *Reglas para los Confessores*, and seems to have been unaware of their existence. He printed what he styled a translation of the treatise entitled, *Quæstio de imperatoria vel regia potestate*, printed at Frankfort in 1571. ("Essay upon the question whether kings have the right to dispose of their subjects, their cities, and their government.") Llorente says in his Notes, "This extremely curious work was not published by the author with his other treatises in 1552. I have not attempted to translate each word and phrase of my author . . . . Unhappily this celebrated man paid tribute to a bad scholastic taste . . . . in quoting authors who convince nobody to-day." ("Enfin je publie une traduction libre de Las Casas avec l' intention de rendre la lecture de cet auteur plus supportable pour notre temps.")—*Llorente*, Vol. II. p. 117.

In the note to the writings of Las Casas the theory that Las Casas had printed other works is founded upon his enunciation to the council in his dispute with Sepulveda: "Esta materia emos largamente explicado en muchos nuestros tractados que en latin y romance auemos escritos." ("These matters I have more particularly explained in many other treatises, which may be found both in Latin and in Spanish in my writings.") It will be seen that Las Casas says "writings," and several of his works it is said, still remain only "writings," having never been printed. Several of his treatises also were written some years before the Dispute; and circulated very extensively among the learned in manuscript, for several years before they were printed. Such was indeed at that period the usual form of publication.

Thirteen other treatises are noticed in Mr. Sabin's Dictionary as having been written by Las Casas, which remain in manuscript, or are lost. But a careful examination of the catalogue of their titles, I think would reduce their number to five. Numbers 6 and 13 are without doubt identical, as are also probably 5-8, and 14. Of No. 4, entitled "Discussion of the Bishop of Chiapa with the Bishop of Darien in 1517," it needs only to be said that there was no Bishop of Chiapas until twenty-six years after that date, and the discussion with the warlike Bishop of Darien, the friend and patron of Balboa, did not take place until 1520. The belief in the existence of treatises 5, 6, and 7, of this list, is founded only upon the relation of Llorente, whose knowledge of Las Casas' works was imperfect, and his statements inexact. Nos. 8 and 12, also, as stated in the list, are believed to be identical. No. 9 is identical with the work noticed in my catalogue as *Explicatio Quæstionis Utrum Reges*, etc., printed at Frankfort, 1571. Nos. 10 and 11 were printed by Llorente in his collection, so that there remain unpublished, in all probability, only five of the works of Las Casas. Of these it is certain that the *History of the Indies* is an original work, but all the others have yet to be identified, as Las Casas himself produced his works in various forms more or less identical. His writings have been copied with interpolations, abridgments, and paraphrases not only, but two or more of them have been occasionally fused into one. They have been translated into many languages with the greatest license, and for various political designs. In Holland, where the works of Las Casas appeared as *Narratio Regionum Spiegels and Warrachtigers*, without number, the genius of De Bry was called into requisition to illustrate them with scenes of frightful atrocity, in order to fire the hearts of the Netherlanders with hatred of the Spaniard. In France every war with Spain produced an edition of *Mirroir des Cruautés par Las Casas*. The Spanish Armada, and the Falkland Islands' dispute produced popular editions of *Tears of the Indians*, *Accounts of Spanish Cruelties*, and *Old England Forever*, in endless number, and hopeless confusion of the works of the good Bishop. His ten printed works have appeared with more than eighty distinct titles, and we have yet to learn whether all that is attributed to him by some titles is authentic. A noble work by Mr. Arthur Helps, *The Spanish Conquest of America*, of which his *Life of Las Casas* is an offshoot, does such justice to the labors of the apostle, as learning, genius, and love of goodness may do, in its best.

The Spaniards have not been unaffected by the terrible denunciations of Las Casas, and more than one treatise has been written for the purpose of softening their severity. One that has fallen under my notice does not by weight of argument, or veracity of testimony, much affect the massive structure of his arraignment. It is printed in Italian and Spanish, the title of which, translated into English, is —

"Impartial reflections upon the Humanity of the Spaniards in the Indies, in answer to the pretended philosophers and politicians. To explain the Histories of Messrs. Raynal and Robertson. Written in Italian by the Abbé Don Juan Nuix, and translated with some Notes, by D. Pedro Varela y Ulloa. Small 4° Madrid, 1782."

More than one writer has attempted to cast a shade on the humanitarian character of Las Casas, by attributing to him the recommendation of the introduction of negro slaves into America. The facts regarding this charge are very far from complex, being wonderfully clear and conclusive in his exculpation. Negro slaves had been introduced into Hispaniola some years, when Las Casas, looking about for some means of ameliorating the horrible sufferings of the Indians in the mines, where they were perishing by thousands, suggested that possibly the labor of the hardier negroes might be found available. It was not until he had exhausted every expedient for putting an end to the forced labor of the aborigines, that his despair drove him to this unfortunate conception.

LAS CASAS.

Narratio | regionum | Indicarum per | Hispanos quosdam | devastatarum verissima: prius quidem | per Episcopum Bartholomæum Casaum, | natione Hispanum Hispanice Conscripta, | & Anno 1551. Hispali, Hi | spanice, Anno vero hoc | 1598. Latine ex | cusa, | *Francofurti*, | *Sumptibus Theodori de Bri, & Io | annis Saurii typis.* | *Anno* MDXCVIII. | 871

Small 4° Title in the centre of an engraving + 3 prel. leaves + pp. 141.

Seventeen engravings are printed in the text. This is the first edition of Las Casas' works with the plates engraved by De Bry.

LAS CASAS (B.).

Narratio | Regionum | Indicarum per | Hispanos qvondam | devastatarum verrissima: per Episco | pum Bartholomaeum Casaum, natione Hi | spanum Hispanice Conscripta, & | Hispali Hispanice, postalibi | Latine excusa: | Jam verò denuò Iconibus illustrata edita est. | *Oppenheimii,* | *Sumtibus Johan-Theod de Bry.* | *Typis Hieronymi Galleri* | MDCXIV. | 872

[Relation of the Countries in the (West) Indies devastated by the Spaniards; written in Spanish by the Bishop Bartholomew de Las Casas, a Native of Spain, and translated into Latin by a citizen of Hispalis in Spain. Now first published and illustrated with plates. Oppenheim, for J. T. de Bry. Printed by Hieronimus Gallerius.]

Title engraved, reverse blank. Pref. pp. 3 to 36. "Indicarum Devastatarum," pp. 37 to 138; with 17 copperplate engravings in the text.

The impressions of the plates in this edition are scarcely inferior to those of the first, so highly esteemed for their beauty of execution. From this period, however, they exhibited strong proofs of the wear and dimming of use and age. The text, it will be seen, covers twenty-four pages more than in the subsequent edition of 1664, in which the sixteen pages of preliminary matter of those of 1598 and 1614 are omitted.

LAS CASAS.

Tyrannies et Cruautez des Espagnols perpetrees es Indes Occidentales, quon dit le Nouveau Monde; traduictes par Jaques de Miggrode Anvers 1579. *Small* 8°. 873*

This is a translation of the first, second, and sixth of Las Casas' Tracts, in which the horrible cruelties recorded by the Bishop, are softened so as not too greatly to offend the ears of the Spaniards.

LAS CASAS.

The Same. *Reprinted at Rouen,* 1630. 874*

LAS CASAS.

Regionem Indicarum per Hispanos olim devastatarum accuratissima descriptio, insertis Figuris aeneis ad vivum fabrefactis. Authore, Bartholomaeo de las Casas. Episcopo Hispano. Editio nova, Priori longe correctior. 4° *Heidelbergae, Typis Guillelmi VValteri Acad. Typogr. A. S.,* 1664. 875

Engraved title, 1 leaf; second title, 1 leaf; "Bibliopola Lectori Felicitatem," 1 leaf + pp. 1 to 112, with seventeen copperplate engravings in the text.

[Accurate Description of the Indian Countries formerly desolated by the Spaniards. With Wood-cuts taken from life. Author, B. de las Casas. New Edition, corrected and enlarged. Heidelberg, printed by G. Walter, printer of the Academy.]

The plates are illustrative of the horrible cruelties perpetrated by the Spaniards upon the Indians, natives of the countries they conquered; which Las Casas' Relations narrate. The frightful tortures to which they subjected the wretched Indians, the awful slaughters of whole tribes, the burnings, the mutilations, the heaped-up masses of disjointed and half-roasted human forms; the wanton, frantic, and incredible pleasure these monsters seemed to feel in this work of devils, would almost compel the belief that hell had indeed broken its gates, and poured the torments of the damned upon the earth. The contemplation of these hideous acts of cruelty leaves some sense of gratification in the consideration of a punishment greater than death.

LAS CASAS (Bartholome).

Le Miroir | De la | Tyrannie Espagnole | Perpetree aux Indes | Occidentales. | On verra icy la Cruaute plus | que inhumaine, commise par les | Espagnols, aussi la description de | ces terres, peuples, et leur nature. | Mise en lumiere par un | Evesque Bartholome de las Casas, | de l'Ordre de S. Dominic. | Nouvellement refaicte, avec les | Figures en cuyvre. | tot | Amsterdam. | Ghedrucht by Jan Evertsz | Cloppenburg op't Water | tegen over de Koor Beurs | in Verguldén Bijbel, | 1620. | 4° *Engraved title and 68 folios.* 876

[The Mirror of Spanish Tyranny perpetrated in the West Indies. We see in it a Cruelty more than inhuman committed by the Spaniards, also a description of the countries, natives, and their nature. Illustrated by the Bishop Bartholomew de las Casas, of the Order of Saint Dominick. Newly re-collected, with copperplate Figures.]

Seventeen copperplate engravings from De Bry are printed in the text. This work is not the same as the *Tyrannies et Cruautez des Espagnols*, printed at Anvers, 1579, at Paris, 1582, and at Rouen, 1630. It differs materially also from that afterwards reprinted at Lyons, 1642, under the title of *Histoire des Indes Occidentales*, and at Paris in 1697 and 1701, as *La Decouverte des Indes Occidentales*, and *Relation des Voyages*, Amsterdam, 1698. Neither of these editions of the French translation were published with plates. This book is a translation of one of the Spiegels, with the plates engraved by the De Brys for the edition of 1598, *Narratio regionum Indicarum*, and is the only French edition possessing them. It has been considered as the sequel of a work illustrated by the same engravers, entitled, *Tyrannie Espagnole perpetree au Pays Bas*, although it is entirely independent in subject and pagination. The Hollanders took every pains to render the cruelty of the Spaniards immortally infamous, and the genius of De Bry was exhausted in illustrating their hellish ingenuity of torture. It contains only a portion of the *Brevissima Relacion* and *Carta*, rearranged and distorted, with a small fragment of the *Controversia*.

LAS CASAS.

The Tears of the Indians: | Being | An Historical and true Account | Of the Cruel | Massacres and Slaughters | of above Twenty Millions | of innocent People; | Committed by the Spaniards | In the Islands of | Hispaniola, Cuba, Jamaica, &c. | As also, in the Continent of | Mexico, Peru, & other Places of the | West-Indies, | To the total destruction of those Countries. | Written in Spanish by Casaus, | an Eye-witness of those things; | And made English by J. P. | *London,* | *printed by F. C. for Nath. Brook, at the Angel* | *in Cornhil,* 1656. | *Small* 8° 15 *leaves* + *pp.* 134 + *folding plate in four compartments.* 877

LAS CASAS.

La Decouverte | des | Indies Occidentales, | par | les Espagnols. | Ecrite par Dom Balthazar de Las- | Casas, Eveque de Chiapa. | Dedie a Monseigneur le Comte | de Toulouse. | A Paris, | Chez Andre Pralard, rue Saint | Jacques, à l' Occasion. | M D C XCVII. | Avec Privilige du Roi. | 12° *Engraved title* + *full title* + 4 *prel. leaves* + *pp.* 382 + (2). 878

This translation of four of Las Casas' treatises, was reproduced the following year in Amsterdam, with the title as in No. 879. The Holland publisher added the Relation of Montauban.

LAS CASAS.

Relation | des | Voyages | et des | de'couvertes | Que les Espagnols ont fait dans les | Indes Occidentales; | Ecrite par Dom B. de Las Casas Eve- | que de Chiapa. | Avec la Relation curieuse des Voyages du | Sieur de Montauban, Capitaine des | Filibustiers, en Guinèe l'an 1695. | *A Amsterdam,* | *Chez J. Louis de Lorme Libraire sur le* | *Rockin, a l' enseigne de la Liberte'.* | MDCXCVIII. | 12° *Frontispiece* + 5 *leaves* + *pp.* 402 + il. 879

[Relation of the Voyages and Discoveries made by the Spaniards in the West Indies, written by Don B. de Las Casas Bishop of Chiapas. With the Relation of the Sieur Montauban, Captain of Buccaneers in Guinea, 1695.]

This is a translation of five of Las Casas' treatises, entirely different from that of Miggrode, under the title of *Tyrannies et Cruautez.* "The Brevisima Relacion" occupies pp. 1 to 147. "Lo que se Sigue es un pedazo," pp. 147 to 161. "Entre los Remedios," pp. 161 to 196. "Treynta Proposiciones," 196 to 210. "Disputa con Sepulveda," pp. 211 to 354. The treatises are all much abbreviated, having been printed, as avowed in the Preface, to arouse the Hollanders against the Spaniards. The Relation of Montauban with a separate title occupies pp. 359 to 402. The work seems to be identical with the two French editions entitled *Histoire des Indies Occidentales*, 1642, and *La Decouverte des Indes Occidentales*, 1697.

Mr. Rich says the translation was made by the Abbe de Bellegarde, whose politeness (*or perhaps fear of the Spanish influence at the French court*), induced him to soften some of *the cruel parts*, lest they should give pain to delicate persons.

LAS CASAS (B.).

A | Relation | Of the First | Voyages and Discoveries | Made by the Spaniards in America, | With | An Account of their unparallel'd Cruelties | on the Indians, in the destruction of a | bove Forty Millions of People. | Together with the Propositions offer'd to the | King of Spain, to prevent the further Ruin | of the West-Indies. | By Don Bartholomew de las Casas, Bishop of Chiapa; | who was an Eye-witness of their Cruelties. | Illustrated with Cuts. | To which is added, | The Art of Travelling, shewing how a Man may | dispose his Travels to the best advantage. | 8° *London,* | *printed for Daniel Brown at the Black-Swan and Bible* | *without Temple-Bar, and Andrew Bell at the Cross* | *Keys and Bible in Cornhill, near Stocks-market,* 1699. | 880

Title, 1 leaf + Preface, 2 leaves, Contents, 1 leaf + pp. 248. "Art of Travelling," 40 pp. + 4 and two folding plates, one in sixteen and the other in six compartments, representing the most horrible torments, butcheries, and massacres perpetrated upon the Indians, which the genius of devils could invent or the pencil of the most imaginative artist could portray. This edition is not noticed in Mr. Sabin's Dictionary, or in his Monograph of Las Casas' works.

This work professes to be a translation of the French book entitled *Tyrannies et Cruautez des Espagnols.* The Relations of Las Casas proved a most formidable weapon for any nation on ill terms with the Spaniards. Ten editions at least of Spiegel's, with prints portraying the horrible cruelties perpetrated by the Spanish upon the Indians, were printed in Holland, while struggling with the murderous bandits of Philip II. Three were printed in

France, during the prevalence of hostilities with Spain, and four in England under similar animus.

The first of the English translations of Las Casas' Relations was printed in Cromwell's Protectorate, 1656, under the title of *Tears of the Indians*. The present Relation contains a translation of the "Brevissima Relacion," pp. 1 to 99, the "Treynta Proposiciones," "Disputa con Sepulveda," and "Tratado de los Remedios," or of such portion of them as the French translator saw fit to print. The latter is said to have politely softened some of the worst features of Las Casas' charges of cruelty. It is worthy of note, however, that while the English editor of *Tears of the Indians* places their slaughter at twenty millions, the editor of this Relation doubles the number and calls it forty millions. It is to be hoped that the real number inhumanly tortured and slain has been fictitiously doubled many times, otherwise we should be compelled to believe that the torments of purgatory were too moderate for the Spaniards.

LAS CASAS.

An | Account | Of the First | Voyages and Discoveries | Made by the Spaniards in America. | Containing | The most Exact Relation hitherto pub | lish'd, of their unparall'd Cruelties | on the Indians, in the destruction of a | bove Forty Millions of People. | With the Propositions offer'd to the King of Spain, | to prevent the further Ruin of the West Indies. | By Don Bartholomew de las Casas, Bishop of Chiapa, | who was an Eye- | witness of their Cruelties. | Illustrated with Cuts. | To which is added, | The Art of Travelling, Shewing how a Man may | dispose his Travels to the best advantage. | 8° *London,* | *printed by F. Darby for D. Brown at the Black Swan* | *and Bible without Temple-Bar, F. Harris at the* | *Harrow in Little Britain, and Andr. Bell at the* | *Cross Keys, and Bible in Cornhill,* M.D.C.XC.IX. | 881

Four prel. leaves + pp. 248 + 40 + 2 folding plates, one of which is in sixteen, and the other in six compartments. With the exception of the title, this work seems to be identical with the one entitled, *A Relation of the First Voyages*, etc.

LAS CASAS (B.).

Umbstandige warhafftige | Beschreibung | Der | Indianischen — Landern | so vor diesem von den Spa- | niern eingenommen und | verwust worden | Durchgehends mit schonen | kupfferstucken und lebhafften | Figuren auszgezieret | erst in Lateinischer Sprach auszgeben | durch Bartholomoeum de las Casas. | Bischoffen in Hispanien | Jetzt aber in das Teutsche übersetzt und au vielen Orten verbessert. indieser neu | und letztern Edition | Anno MDCLXV. 4° *Engraved title and prel. pp.* (iv.) + 119. 882

This is a German reprint of the French *Tyrannies and Cruautez Espagnols*, or the *Narratio regionum Indicarum*, of 1598. It has the same engraving surrounding the text of the title, and the seventeen plates two thirds the size of the page printed with the text. They, however, are much less clear than in the other editions. Mr. Sabin says that a copy exists in Mr. J. C. Brown's library with six preliminary leaves but with only a printed title. It will be seen that this possesses the engraved title with but two preliminary leaves, and the catch-words do not indicate any leaves wanting.

Las Casas.

Den Vermeerderden Spiegel Spaenssche tierannije geschiet in Westindien waerin te sien is de onmenschelijcke wreede feijten der Spanjarden met samen de beschrivinge der selver laut en Volcken aert en nature allen Vaderlant lievende en vrome voersta ders ten exempel voorgestelt. In Spans beschreven door den E bischop don fray bartholme de las Casas van S dominicu soorden. 4° *Gedruckt tot Amsterdam by Cornelis Lode Wijcke, vander Plasse inde Italiaensche Bijbel Anno* 1621. 883

[The Augmented Looking Glass of the Spanish Oppression happened in the West-Indies, wherein is to be seen the inhuman cruel acts of the Spaniards together with a Description of the Country and the manners and customs of the People. At the Service of and as an Example for all good and patriotic Men Described in Spanish by the Bishop B. de las Casas from the Order of St. Dominicus. Printed at Amsterdam by C. L. Wijcke at the Italian Bible. 1621.]

One hundred and four unnumbered pages, namely, engraved title, reverse blank, Christopher Columbus reverse plate, and sixteen engravings in the text, of scenes of Spanish cruelty towards the Indians. These are reproductions of De Bry's plates as first issued in the Latin edition of 1598, except that the one on pp. 10 of the Latin edition is omitted in the Dutch translation of 1621. Most of the plates in this last edition are reversed.

Las Casas.

Conqvista | dell' Indie | Occidentali | de Monsignor | Fra Bartolmeo dalle Case, | o Casaus, Siuigliano, Vescouo di Chiapa. | Tradotta in Italiano per opera di Marco Ginammi. | All' Illmo & Ecc^mo Sig^r Sig^r & mio Padron Col^mo | Il Sig^r Pietro Sagredo | Procvratore di S. Marco. | *In Venetia*, M DC XXXXV. *Presso Marco Ginammi.* | Con Licenza de' Superiori, & Priuilego. | 4° *pp.* 8 + 2 *leaves* + *pp.* xvii. + 30–184. 884

This is the only Italian edition of the *Disputa*, and the *Principia Quidam*, numbers eight and nine of Las Casas' tracts.

Las Casas.

Istoria, | ò Breuissima Relatione | della Distrvttione | dell' Indie Occidentali | di Monsig. reverendiss. | Don Bartolomeo dalle Case, o Casaus, Siuigliano dell' Ordine | de Predicatori; & Vescouo di Chiapa. | Conforme al suo vero Originale Spagnuolo gia stampato in Siuiglia. | Tradotta in Italiano dall' Excell. Sig Giacomo Castellani, | gia sotto nome di Francesco Bersabita. | Al Molt' Ill^re & Ecc^mo Sig^r Sig^r mio Col^mo Il Sig. | Nicolo' Perulco. | *In Venetia Presso Marco Ginammi*, M. DC. XLIII. | Con Licenza de' Superiori, & Priuilegio. | 4° 4 *leaves* + *pp.* 150 + 1 *leaf.* 885

This Italian translation of the *Breuissima Relation* was made by Castellani: is printed in double columns, (?) Italian and Spanish. It is the third edition, printed at Venice.

Las Casas.

Il svpplice | schiavo Indiano | di Monsig. Reverendiss. | D. Bartolomeo | Dalle Case, ò Casaus, Siniglíano, dell Ordine | de' Predicatori, & Vescouo di Chiapa, | Città Regale dell' Indie. | Conforme al suo vero Orignale Spagnuolo già stampato in

Siuglia. | Tradotto in Italiano per opera di Marco Ginammi. | Al Molto Illustre Sig. Sig. Osseruandiss. Il Sig. | Berando Moro. | *In Venetia, Per li Ginammi*, 1657. | Con licenza de' Superiori, & Priuilegio. | 4° *pp.* 96. 886

This is the third Italian edition (with the Spanish version in parallel columns) of Las Casas' tract, *Matters relating to the Indians who have been held as slaves*, numbered six in our arrangement.

Las Casas.

La Liberta | Pretesa | Dal supplice Schiano Indiano | di Monsignor Reverendiss | D Bartolomeo dalle Case | ò Casaus Siuigliano dell' Ordine de Predicatori, & Vescouo | di Chiapa, Citta Regale dell Indie. | Conforme al suo vero Originale Spagnuolo gia Stampato in Siuiglia. | Tradotto in Italiano per Opera di Marco Ginammi. | All' Altezza etc. 4° *pp.* 155 (3). *In Venetia, Presso Marco Ginammi*, M DC XXXX. | 887

Las Casas.

Old England for Ever, or, Spanish Cruelty display'd; wherein The Spaniards right to America is impartially Examined and found Defective; their Pretensions founded in Blood, Supported by Cruelty, and continued by Oppression. [*etc.*, 6 *paragraphs, the* V*th* *declaring*] Spanish Tyranny, exemplify'd in the intolerable Oppression and barbarous Treatment of the poor Indians, which is so severe and inhuman, that they would gladly become subject to the British Crown. 12° *Folding plate* + *pp.* 320. *London*, 1740. 888

There is no more foundation for attributing this work to Las Casas (as the Catalogues not unfrequently do), than that he is quoted as an authority in common with other writers. Not the slightest original information regarding the Indians is afforded us; what we find in it is commonplace, and of no consequence.

Las Casas.

Oeuvres de don Barthelemi de Las Casas, Eveque de Chiapa, Defenseur de la liberte des naturels de l'Amerique; precedees de sa vie, et accompagnees de notes historiques additions, developments, etc., etc., avec portrait, par J. A. Llorente dedices A. M. C. Comte de Las Casas. 8° Vol. I. *Half title, title, portrait, dedication, and table each* 1 *leaf*, cx. *prel. pp.* + 409 + 2. Vol. II. (iv.) *prel. pp.* + 503. *Paris*, 1822. 889

[Works of Don Bartholomew de Las Casas, Bishop of Chiapas, Defender of the liberty of the Natives of America, preceded by his biography, and accompanied by historical notes, additions, developments, etc., with portrait.]

This is the only collection of the works of the Apostle of the Indians, which was ever printed in a foreign language. It was published by order of the king, at a period when the long absence of employment, and consequent starvation, had driven the printers of Paris to the verge of revolution. It is not a faithful translation of those wonderful treatises of the extraordinary man, whose humanity has made his name immortal.

Las Casas,

Life of. *pp.* 367 *to* 432 *of New York Quarterly*, Oct. 1853. 890

A very excellent history of the life and services of the Apostle of the Indians

LAS CASAS.

A List of the printed editions of the works of Fray Bartholomé de las Casas, Bishop of Chiapa. Extracted from a Dictionary of Books relating to America. By Joseph Sabin. 8° *pp.* 27, *printed covers. New York, J. Sabin & Sons*, 84 *Nassau Street*, 1870. 691

LAS CASAS (Bartholomew).

Personal Narrative of the First Voyage of Columbus to America. From a manuscript recently discovered in Spain. Translated from the Spanish. 8° *pp.* 303. *Boston: Published by Thomas B. Wait & Son*, 1827. 692

This work, already noticed at number 347, where it was attributed to Columbus, has also some claims to attention here, as it owes its existence to Las Casas.

The original manuscript, in the well-known handwriting of the venerable Bishop, was discovered by Navarrete, near the close of the last century; but on account of the disturbed condition of Spanish affairs, did not make its appearance in print, until 1825. The title of the two volumes which it filled, was, *Coleccion de los Viages, y Descubrimientos que hicieron por mar los Españoles desde fines del Siglo XV.*, etc. The narrative is an English translation of only a small portion of the Spanish work. The Manuscript of Las Casas, from which these volumes were printed, is evidently itself an abridgment of the original journal of Columbus, made by the Bishop to aid him in writing his *History of the Indies.* The portions of the work written by Las Casas, are distinguished by speaking of Columbus as the Admiral, while the journal of the latter is in the first person.

LATHROP (John).

A Discourse before the Society for Propagating the Gospel among the Indians and others in North-America delivered On the 19th of January, 1804. By John Lathrop. 8° *pp.* 44. *Boston*, (1804). 693

This is the first anniversary discourse delivered before the Society formed in 1787. Seventeen years previously, the Appendix of twelve pages contains a historical sketch of the Society and its missions among the Indians.

LATROBE (Charles Joseph).

The Rambler in North America 1832, 1833, by Charles Joseph Latrobe. Two vols. 8° *pp.* 321 *and* 335. *London*, 1835. 694

The author accompanied Washington Irving in his tour on the prairies, and a large part of each volume is occupied with personal observations of Indian life.

LAWRENCE (A. B.).

Texas in 1840, or the Emigrant's Guide to the New Republic; being the result of observation, enquiry and travel in that beautiful country. By an Emigrant late of the United States. With an introduction by the Rev. A. B. Lawrence of New Orleans. 12° *pp.* 275. *New York*, 1840. 695

A journal of travels across the Plains, fills the first six chapters, pp. 23 to 80, with numerous incidents of adventures with the Indians. Chapter xix., pp. 245 to 256, treats of the Indian tribes of the State.

LAWSON (John).

A New | VOYAGE | to | CAROLINA ; | Containing the | Exact Description and Natural History | of that | COUNTRY: | Together with the *Present State* thereof | and | A Journal | Of a Thousand Miles Travel'd thro' several | Nations of INDIANS. | Giving a particular Account of their Customs, | Manners &c. | By John Lawson, Gent, Surveyor | -General of North-Carolina. | 4° *London,* | *printed in the Year* 1709. | (*no publisher*). 896

Map; Title, reverse blank; Dedication, 1 leaf; Preface, 1 leaf; Introduction, pp. 1 to 5; Journal, pp. 6 to 60; Description N. C., pp. 61 to 168; Account of Indians of N. C., pp. 169 to 235; Charters of N. C., 236 to 258; Advertisement, 1 p.; Plate of Animals, at p. 115.

LAWSON (John).

The | History | of | Carolina ; | containing the | Exact Description and Natural History | of that | Country. | Together with the Present State thereof. | And | A Journal | Of a Thousand Miles, Travel'd thro' Several | Nations of Indians. | Giving a particular Account of their Customs, | Manners &c. | By John Lawson, Gent. Surveyor-General | of North-Carolina. | *London: Printed for W. Taylor at the Ship, and T. Baker at the Black* | -*Boy, in Pater-Noster-Row,* 1714. | 897

Collation the same as above.

LAWSON (John).

The | History | of | Carolina ; | containing the | Exact Description and Natural History | of that | Country ; | Together with the Present State thereof. | And | A Journal | Of a Thousand Miles, Travel'd thro' several | Nations of Indians. | Giving a particular Account of their Customs, | Manners, &c. | By John Lawson, Gent. Surveyor-General | of North-Carolina. | *London,* | *printed for T. Warner, at the Black-Boy in Pater-Noster* | *Row,* 1718. *Price Bound Five Shillings.* | 898

Collation the same as above.

LAWSON (John).

The History of Carolina, containing the Exact Description and Natural History of that Country, together with the Present State thereof and a Journal of a Thousand Miles Traveled through Several Nations of Indians, Giving a particular Account of their Customs, Manners, &c. By John Lawson, Gent. Surveyor-General of North Carolina. *pp.* 390. *London,* 1714. *Reprinted.* 12° *Raleigh,* 1660. 899

This work, first published in 1709, was issued as a part of Stevens' Collection of Voyages in 1711. In 1714 it appeared again with a new title commencing *The History of North Carolina,* etc., but in all other respects perfectly identical. Another edition was issued in 1718, precisely similar to the last. The fourth edition was printed in Dublin, 1737, on the title-page of which it is attributed to John Brickel. The fifth and last was printed in Raleigh in 12°, 1660.

It is the relation of a man of acute habits of observation, some intelligence, and doubtless entire veracity regarding the Indians of North Carolina, at a very interesting period of their existence. Lawson was a land surveyor in the employment of the government, and was the unhappy cause of the exile of the Tuscarora tribe to New York, and its consequent incorporation into the Iroquois Confederacy, by which its name was changed to the Six Nations. As the surveyor was the precursor of the settler, who seized upon and occupied the lands of the savages, he was always the especial object of their detestation. A great conspiracy, it is asserted by Dr. Hawks, had been previously organized, but whether true or false, Lawson was the first victim of the Indian vengeance. Accompanied by Baron Graffenried in September, 1811, the surveyor-general was ascending the Neuse River in a boat, when he was seized by the Indians a few miles above Newbern. After some hours of captivity, the Indian council determined to put him to the cruel death of burning at the stake. All the appalling tortures, which savage ingenuity could invent, were exhausted on this unfortunate man, and the author of the first history of the Carolinas, perished at the hands of the savages, whose humanity he had in its pages so highly commended. The massacre at Bath, in which one hundred and thirty poor Huguenots perished under the hands of 1200 Tuscaroras, followed in a few days. The war which succeeded proved so disastrous to them that the Tuscaroras abandoned their native soil, and fled to New York. Neither of the first three editions of Lawson's work is often found complete with the map, and animal plate.

LANSON (Henry).

The Life and Adventures of Henry Lanson the only Son of a Wealthy Planter in the West Indies who when on his Voyage to England was put on Shore on an uninhabited Island where on his perambulation up the country he discovers the Ruins of an Ancient Temple; and near it the Oracle of the Sun, a large rude carved Idol made of pure brilliant gold of a wonderful construction, which contained an Immense and inestimable Collection of precious Indian Curiosities. The manner of his Converting the Natives of a neighboring Island, etc. 12° *Frontispiece* + *pp.* 42. *London*, (n. d.). 900

A wretched fiction.

LE BEAU (Sr C.).

Avantures du S^r. C. Le Beau, avocat en parlement, ou Voyage Curieux et nouveau, Parmi les Sauvages de l'Amerique Septentrionale. Dans le quel On trouvera une Description du *Canada*, avec une Relation tres particuliere des anciennes Coutumes, Moeurs, & Façons de Vivre des Barbares qui l'habitent & de la maniere dont ils se comportent aujourd' hui. Ouvrage enrichi d' une Carte & des figures necessaires. *Two vols.* 24° Vol. I. (14) *prelim. pp.* + 370 + (6) + *map and 3 plates.* Vol. II. *Title* + *pp.* 430 + (6) + *three plates.* *A Amsterdam, Chez Herman Uytwerf*, 1738. 901

[Adventures of the Count Le Beau, advocate in Parliament; Or New and Curious Travels among the Savages of North America. In which will be found a Description of Canada, a very particular Relation of the ancient Customs, Manners, and Habits of Life, of the Barbarians who inhabit that country, and of the manner in which they practice the same at this day. The work embellished with a map, and the necessary illustrations.]

How much of truth, and how much of fiction, are blended in the narratives of the class to which this of Sieur Le Beau belongs, is not often easy to decide.

It has the air of veracity with that want of authenticity which attaches to fiction. The writer had some acquaintance certainly with the peculiar habits of American savages, but whether the result of personal experience, or derived from others, and where the boundary line is to be drawn between the incidents of intercourse with them, and the offspring of his imagination, we are left without any guide to determine.

His narrative has, it *is* fair to say, been deemed by good scholars a veracious history, and this is not improbable, for in the eccentric whims of the writers of veritable statements, there have not been wanting some who have attempted to make their true history look like fiction.

Le Clercq (Pere Chrestien).

Nouvelle | Relation | de la | Gaspesie, | qui contient | les Moeurs & la Religion, des Sau | vages Gaspesiens Porte-Croix, | adorateurs du Soleil, & d'autres | Peuples de l'Amerique Septen | trionale, dite le Canada. | Dedie'e a Madame la | Princesse d'Epinoy, | Par le Pere Chrestien Le Clercq, | Missionaire Recollet de la Province de | Saint Antoine de Pade en Artois, & | Gardien du Convent de Lens. | *A Paris,* | *Chez Amable Auroy, rue Saint* | *Jacques, a l'Image St. Jerome, attenant* | *la Fontaine S. Severin,* | 1691. | Avec Privilege du Roy. | 24° *Title and prel. pp.* 8 + (32) + *pp.* 1 *to* 572. 902

[New Relation of Gaspe, containing the Manners, and Religion of the Savage Gaspesiens Cross-Bearers, Adorers of the Sun; and of other Natives of that part of North-America called Canada. By Father Chrestien Le Clercq, Missionary Recollect, etc.]

Le Clercq (Chrestien).

Premier etablissement de la foy dans la Nouvelle France, contenant la publication de l'evangile, l'histoire des Colonies francoises, et les fameuses decouvertes depuis le fleuve St. Laurent, La Louisiane et le fleuve Colbert jusqu au golphe Mexique, achevees sous la conduite de feu M. de la Salle par ordre du Roy. Avec les Victoires remportees en Canada par les armes de Sa Majeste sur les Iroquois en 1690. *Two volumes. Small* 8° Vol. I. *Prelim. pp.* 18 + 559. Vol. II. *pp.* 454, *numbered* 458 + 4 *leaves* + *Catalogue* 10 *leaves. Paris, Amable Auroy,* 1691. 903*

[First establishment of the faith in New France, containing the announcement of the Gospel, the history of the French Colonies, and the famous discoveries from the river St. Lawrence, Louisiana, and the river Mississippi to the Gulf of Mexico, achieved under the direction of the late M. de la Salle by order of the King. With the victories gained in Canada by the forces of his Majesty over the English and the Iroquois in 1690.]

Father Le Clercq has left a remarkable record of the labors of his brethren the Recollects, in converting the Pagan tribe of Gaspesien Indians. He not only recorded the results of his own missionary life among the savages inhabiting the shores of the St. Lawrence, but he has left us what has always been considered, an authentic account of their peculiar traits of character, religious rites, and mode of life, before these had been modified by contact with civilization. Two subjects, or rather the manner in which they were treated, have notwithstanding the general respect for his ability, and truthfulness, caused some hesitation in scholars to fully trust his judgment. Having found among some of their nation, the cross worn on their garments, and occasionally carried in their hands, he somewhat credulously adopted their traditions, that its worship was of very ancient origin with them. Father Le Clercq himself was half inclined to believe, that the worship of the sacred emblem came to them through the preaching of St. Thomas. This simplicity of the excellent missionary, ought by no means to weigh against his fidelity as a historian. The second ground of criticism is of a different character, somewhat more important, but does not affect the Relation of the Gaspesiens.

Le Clercq was a most zealous Recollect missionary, who having spent five years in the dreary country of the Gaspesiens, both of his Relations would have merited the highest credit, if the last of them, entitled *Etablissement de la Foy*, did not contain so many satirical reflections upon the labors of his brethren of the Jesuit order, who were equally zealous in the labor of Christianizing the savages. It is impossible to account for the misrepresentations found in his work by attributing them to jealousy, as he lived in the most cordial and friendly relations with them, especially with Father Bigot. The most plausible solution of the enigma must be sought for in the political relations of the two orders to the viceroyal government. The Bishop Laval, observing the terrible destruction and suffering caused by the sale of ardent spirits to the Indians, denounced the traffic, with the ecclesiastical penalties of the Church attaching to the offense. The Jesuit missionaries, who saw their flocks wasting under the ravages of the infernal beverage, strongly supported him. The community of fur-traders which almost wholly composed the colonies of New France, became desperate with rage, and as the missionaries and priests of the order of Recollects were not so rigid in their spiritual demands, the war assumed presently a sectarian coloring. Frontenac, the Governor, had also a cause of pique against the order, as the Jesuit missionaries had strongly opposed his favorite project of domiciliating the Indians in the white settlements, and entirely breaking up their tribal and village organizations. The Recollects, on the contrary, found favor with the Governor by espousing his impracticable theory. Sometime before this period, the missionaries of this order had been recalled to France, and the Jesuits placed in charge of all the mission establishments. Under the influence of Frontenac, the Recollects were now restored to favor, and the Jesuits placed under the ban. The Recollect missionaries are by no means to be charged with complicity, in bringing the controversy to this climax, but they were involved in it by a difference of opinion with their brethren of the other order. Father Le Clercq, and Father Charlevoix, as the representatives of the two orders, felt and expressed the bias of their respective interests in their histories of New France and their Missions. Made antagonistic by the relations of their societies to the government, they each belittle the labors and the discoveries of the society to which the other belonged. Charlevoix makes light of Father Sagard's Huron Dictionary, and doubts the authenticity of Hennepin's discoveries, because they were of the order of Recollects, and Le Clercq, in his *Etablissement de la Foi*, derides the claim of the Jesuits to extensive reclamation of savage tribes, or important discoveries. From what we know of the character of Father Le Clercq, we must conclude that the satirical portion of his work was by another hand. Mr. Shea, from whose work most of this detail of the "wars of the orders" is taken, says that Le Clercq's *Relation of the Gaspesie* is a description of his own field and his own labors; and the *Etablissement de la Foi*, is a well written history of the Recollect missions and La Salle's voyages. In an historical point of view, its fidelity to the documents upon which it professes to be founded, has never been questioned. It is then only when the writers on the history of New France speak of the work of other orders that we must read with caution.

According to Charlevoix, the *Etablissement de la Foy* was partly the work of Count Frontenac, then Governor of Canada. The great work of that historian has caused this important one to be forgotten. There is a curious bibliographical fact in the history of this work, which was brought to notice by Mr. Lenox in the *Historical Magazine* of January, 1858. The work issued under this title in 1691, was, he says, strictly suppressed. In the following year it appeared without the author's name, under the title of *Histoire des Colonies Françoises et les fameuses decouvertes, &c. . . . de la Louisiane, Sous la conduite du feu M. de la Salle. Paris et Lyon, Chez Thomas Amaulry,* 1692. Two vols. 12° Vol. I. pp. 559. Vol. II. pp. 458. It will be seen that the volumes of each edition agree in the numbered pages, and that in the second the name of the author is suppressed. The first edition was dedicated to Count Frontenac, and this may have had something of an influence in its suppression. The conflict of authorities upon the early history of the French Colonies, has been so puzzling, that historians and scholars have summarily rid themselves of trouble hitherto, by adopting one narrator and rejecting all whom he decides. It seems to me that this is not logically tenable ground. When Jontel contradicts Le Clercq's *Etablissement*, and Hennepin asserts that it was really written by Father Valentine le Roux; when Le Clercq doubts the authenticity of the Relation of Lalemant; and when Charlevoix says the Count Frontenac was the real author of a portion of Le Clercq's *Etablissement de la Foy*, we must conclude these charges, and counter-charges, as attributable to the weaknesses of human jealousy, belittling the strength of these good men, but not invalidating the truth of their positive statements.

Lee (D.) and Frost (J. H.).

Ten Years in Oregon. By D. Lee and J. H. Frost, late of the Oregon Mission of the Methodist Episcopal Church. 8° pp. 344. *New York*, 1844. 904

A minute and doubtless veracious journal of incidents of an arduous mission among the Northwestern Indians, with vocabularies of their dialects.

Lee (Nelson).

Three Years among the Camanches, the Narrative of Nelson Lee, The Texan Ranger. Containing a detailed Account of his Captivity among the Indians, his singular escape Through the Instrumentality of his Watch, and fully illustrating Indian Life as it is on the War Path and in the Camp. Portrait. 12° pp. 224. *Albany*, 1859. 905

This narrative of a captivity of three years among the Camanches, is accredited by the testimony of well known citizens of Albany, and other places in New York. They vouch for the veracity of the author, and accord to his statements their own credence. The appalling and monstrous cruelties of this untamable nation of nomads, reconciles us somewhat to their rapid extinction. Unlike the savages of the Algonquin and Iroquois races, who invariably respected the chastity of their female prisoners, the savages of the southern plains ravish and torture them, with the combined fury of lust and bloodthirst.

Le Moine (J. M.).

La Memoire de Montcalm Vengée ou Le Massacre au Fort George. Documents Historiques recueillis par J. M. Le Moine, Ecr. 12° pp. 91. *Quebec, J. N. Duquet & Cie. Editeurs*, 1864. 906

The details of this frightful massacre by the Indians under Montcalm, are given by an eye-witness, and go far to prove him innocent of conniving at it. The principal portion of this defense is a journal of the events of the siege, surrender, and massacre, written by a French missionary. It may be found in the *Lettres Edifiantes*, Vol. VI. A translation of this journal was made by Father Kip, and printed in Part II. of his *Early Jesuit Missions in America*, where it is attributed to Father Roubaud, Abnaquis missionary. It is an almost perfect exculpation of Montcalm, from the charge of horrible cruelty, of which he had been found guilty by historians, without trial or examination of the evidence. The slaughter is amply proven, by the evidence adduced in this little volume, to have been the result of one of those sudden and overwhelming phrensies for blood, to which the savages of all nations are predisposed in battle.

LENOIR (Alexandre).

Parallele (Suivie d'un) Parallele de ces Monuments avec ceux de L'Egypt, de L Indostan et du reste de l'ancien Monde. *A part of "Antiquites Mexicana." Folio, Paris,* 1834. 907

See Dupaix.

LEON Y GAMA.

Descripcion Historica y Cronologica de las dos Piedras que con ocasion del nuevo empedrado que se esta formando en la plaza principal de Mexico, se hallaron en ella el ano de 1790. Explicase el sistema de los Canlendarios * * * *. de los Indios. * * * a que se anaden otras curiosas e instructivas sobre la Mitologia de los Mexicanos, sobre su Astronomia, y sobre los ritos y ceremonias que acostumbraban en tiempo de su Gentilidad. Por Don Antonio de Leon y Gama. 4° *pp.* (vi.) + 116 + (ii.) + *three folding plates. Mexico, en la imprenta de don Felipe de Zuniga y Ontiveros, Ano de* M.DCC.XCII. 908

LEON Y GAMA (Antonio de).

Descripcion Historica y Cronologica de las Dos Piedras que con ocasion del Nuevo Emperado que se esta formando en la Plaza principal de Mexico, se hallaron en ella el ano de 1790. Explicase el sistema de los Calendarios de los Indios, el metodo que tenian de dividir el tiempo, y la correccion que hacian de el para igualar el ano civil, de que usaban, con el ano solar tropico. Noticia muy necesarie para la perfecta inteligencia de la segunda piedra: a que se anaden otras curiosas e instructivas sobre la mitologia de los Mexicanos, sobre su astronomia y sobre los ritos y ceremonias, que acostumbraban en tiempo de su gentilidad. Por Don Antonio de Leon y Gama. Dala a luz. Con notas, biografia de su autor y augmentada con la segunda parte que estaba inedita, y bajo la proteccion del Gobernio general de la Union: Carlos Maria de Bustamente. Segunda edicion. *Small* 4° *Title,* 1 *leaf* + *pp.* viii. + 114. *Segunda Parte, pp.* 1 *to* 148 + 5 *folding plans. Mexico,* 1832. 909

[Historical and Chronological description of the two stones which at the time of the new pavement being laid in the principal Plaza of Mexico, were found in it in the year 1790. The calendar system of the Indians is explained, the method which they had for dividing time, and the correction which they made to adjust the civil year, which they made use of, with the solar tropical year. A notice very necessary for the perfect understanding of the second stone; to which are added others curious and instructive on the Mythology of the Mexicans, on their Astronomy, and on the rites and ceremonies they usually practiced at the period of their heathenism. By Don Antonio de Leon y Gama. Published, with notes, and a biography of its author, and augmented with the second part which was unpublished, and under the protection of the general government of the Union, by Carlos Maria de Bustamente. Second edition. Mexico, 1832.]

LE PAGE DU PRATZ.

Histoire de la Louisiane, Contenant la Decouverte de ce Vaste Pays, sa Description geographique, un Voyage dans les Terres; l'Histoire Naturelle; les Moeurs, Coutumes & Religion des Naturels avec leurs Origines; deux Voyages dans le Nord du Nouveau Mexique, dont un Jusqu a la Mer de Sud; ornee de deux Cartes & de 40 Planches en Taille-douce. Par Mr. Le Page du Pratz. *Three vols.* 12° Vol. I. *Half title, title, pp.* xvi. + 359. Vol. II. *Half title, title + pp.* 441. Vol. III. *Half title, title, and pp.* 454. *A Paris*, 1758. 910

[History of Louisiana; Containing the Discovery of that vast Country; A geographical Description of it, and a Tour through its Territories; Its Natural History, and the Manners, Customs and Religion of the Natives, with their Origin. Also two Voyages through the Northern part of New Mexico to the South Sea. Ornamented with two Maps and 40 Copperplate engravings.]

This is Le Page du Pratz's work as it issued from the hands of the author. The English translator, with an assurance which is perfectly satire proof, not only abridges the work, but reconstructs and distorts it, and then calls upon us to admire his dexterity in subverting the labor and plan of the author. The work teems with facts and particulars relating to the Natchez and other tribes of Louisiana.

Le Page du Pratz resided in Louisiana fifteen years, and it is from his relation that most of the details of the life of the Natchez and other Mississippi tribes have been derived. Later historians have largely availed themselves of his materials. It is difficult to procure his work complete in all the plates and maps, which should number forty-two.

LE PAGE DU PRATZ.

The History of Louisiana, or of The Western Parts of Virginia and Carolina: containing A Description of the Countries that lye on both Sides of the River Missippi: with An Account of the Settlements, Inhabitants, Soil, Climate, and Products. Translated from the French, (lately published), by M. Le Page Du Pratz; with Some Notes and Observations relating to our Colonies. In Two Volumes. 12° Vol. I. 2 *maps and pp.* l. + vii. + 368. Vol. II. *prel. pp.* (vi.) + 272. *London, Printed for T. Becket (&c.)*, 1763. 911

The long preface is the work of the English editor, who informs us that because the author descends to trifles, he "has left out many things that appeared to be trifling, and abridged some parts of it." It will also be perceived, on comparison of the titles, that he has even constructed one for the work to suit himself. All of Book I., Chapter v., p. 21, to Chapter xlv. p. 117, is devoted to "The author's residence among the Natchez Indians;" Their wars with the French and Spaniards; "The Massacre of the French by that nation, and its extirpation;" "The War with the Chitimachas," and "The War with the Chicasaws." The English editor has combined in Books II. and III., with the journal of the author's tour through the northern parts of Louisiana, his own worthless lucubrations, and scraps from Charlevoix and Dumont. Book IV., pp. 291 to 387, is divided into chapters with the following headings: "Origin of the Americans (Indians);" "An Account of the Several Nations (of Indians) East of the Miss.;" "An Account of those West of the Miss.;" "A Description of the Natives of La., their Manners, etc.—those of the Natchez;" "Of their Language, government, religion, ceremonies, etc.;" "Of their Marriages, Nobility, etc.;" "Of the Indian Art of War," all of which may, or may not be Du Pratz's work.

LE PAGE DU PRATZ.

The History of Louisiana, or of the Western parts of Virginia and Carolina: Containing a Description of the Countries that lie on both Sides of the River Mississippi: With an Account of the Settlements, Inhabitants, Soil, Climate, and Products. Translated from the French of M. Le Page Du Pratz; with Some Notes and Observations relating to our Colonies. A new edition. 8° 2 *Maps, title* 1 *leaf Contents* (vi.) *pp.* + *Preface, pp.* xxxvi. + 1 *to* 387. *London, printed for T. Becket,* 1774. 912

LE RAYE (Charles).

[An Interesting Journal of Mr. Charles Le Raye, while a captive with the Sioux nation, on the Waters of the Missouri river.] *Pages* 156 *to* 219, *of* "*Topographical Description of Ohio.*" 12° *pp.* 1 *to* 219. *Boston,* 1812. 913

See Cutler.

LERY (Jean de).

Histoire d'un Voyage faict en la Terre du Bresil, autrement dite Amerique. Contenant la Navigation & Choses remarquables, veues sur mer par auteur. Le Comportement de Villegagnon en ce pays la. Les moeurs & facons de Viure estranges des Sauvages Brasilliens; aec un colloque de leur langage. Ensemble la description de plusieurs Animaux Herbes & autres choses singulieures & du tout incannues pardeca: dont on verra les sommaires chapitres au commencement du liure. Avec les figures reveve, corregee & bien augmentee de discours notables, en ceste troiseme Edition. Le tout recueilli sur les lieux par Jean de Lery, natif de la Margelle terre de Sainct Sene au Duchè de Bourgonne.— Pour Antoine Chuppin [*Paris*] 1585. 8° *Title and pref. pp.* (lxvii.) + 427 + *Index* (xiv.) + *Errata* 1 *p.* + 8 *plates in the text, and map.* 914

[History of a Voyage made to the Land of Brazil, otherwise called America. Containing the Voyage and the noticeable events which occurred to the author on the Sea. The Conduct of Villegagnon in the Country. The Manners and habits of life most singular of the Brazilian Savages. With a dialogue in the language of the Indians. Together with a description of many Animals, Trees, Plants and other remarkable things, entirely unknown before. And of all of which a true summary of the chapters will be found at the commencement of the book. With figures. Third Edition. The whole collected from the works of Jean de Lery].

The author sailed for Brazil in 1563, and after a residence of nearly eighteen years returned to France, and from his journals and writings composed this book. It has a high value as a historical work, being the results of a long experience among the savages of South America. In a bibliographical view it is also not without merit, as it is uncommon, and brings a not inconsiderable price when offered for sale. The greater portion of the work is composed of observations upon the peculiarities of the Indians.

Chapter vii. is entitled, "On the Nature, Power, Stature and Nudity of the Indians." Chap. viii., Of the roots and grain which the Indians eat in lieu of bread." Chap. xiv., "Of the Wars, battles, hardihood, and armes of the Savages." Chap. xv., "How the Indians treat their prisoners, their Cruelties and Cannibalism." Chap. xvi., "Of their Religion, or what they term Religion." Chap. xvii., "Of their Marriages and Polygamy and degree of Consanguinity." Chap. xviii., "Of what the Savages term their laws and police." Chap. xix., "How the Indians treat their diseases." Chap. xx., "Dialogue in French and the Indian language Toupinonkin." These subjects occupy all the space from pages 100 to 140, and from 207 to 379. The colloquy in the Indian and French language, and the accompanying Vocabulary, fill pages 347 to 379. The plates are all illustrative of savage life and manners. The folding plate represents the combat of the Tou-ou-pin-am-boult savages with the Margais Indians, which in most copies is lost. The work was translated into Latin and printed in the following year, and this translation was used by De Bry as a portion of Part III. of his Grand Voyages, illustrated by eleven plates.

LESCARBOT (Marc).

Histoire | de la Nouvelle- | France, | Contenant les navigations, decouvertes, & ha- | bitations faites par les Francoises Indies Occi- | dentales & Nouvelle-France, par Commission | de nos Roys Trez-Chretiens, & les diverses | fortunes d'iceux en l'execution de ces choses, | depuis cent ans jusques a hui. | En quoy est comprise l'histoire Morale, Naturale, & | Geographique des provinces cy decrites; avec | les Tables & Figures necessaires. | Par Marc Lescarbot Advocat en Parlement | Temoin oculaire d' vne partie des choses ici recitees. | Troisiesme Edition enriche de plusieurs choses singulieres, | outre la suite d l'Histoire. | [*Printer's Emblem.*] 12° *A Paris,* | *Chez Adrian Perier, rue saint* | *Iacques, au Compas d'or.* | M.D.C. XVIII. | 915

Collation: Title and other preliminary leaves together, 28, numbered only on the recto of each, as 55 pp. + pp. 1 to 970 + "Fautes" 1 p. + Les Muses | de la Nouvelle | France. | A Monseigneur le Chancellier. | [Motto two lines and Printer's emblem]. Paris, | Chez Adrian Perier, rue saint | Iaques, au Compas d'or. | M.D.C.XVIII. pp. 1 to 76. Map 1 of Florida "de la Main de M. Lescarbot." Map 2. Figure du Porte Ganabara au Bresil. Map 3. Figure de la Terre Nevve. Map 4. Figure du Port Royal.

[History of New France, containing the voyages, discoveries and settlements, made by the French in the West Indies, and in New France, by Commission of our very Christian Kings; and the various fortunes of those engaged in them, during one hundred years to the present time. In which is comprised, the Moral, Natural and Geographic History of the said Provinces, with the necessary Tables and Plates.]

This edition, as well as those of 1609 and 1611, is usually accompanied by another work, entitled *Les Muses de la Nouvelle France*, which is nothing more than a collection of poems by the same author separately paged.

This edition of Lescarbot's rare work on the History of New France, differs greatly from both the former. It has 139 pages more than that of 1609, with a very large addition of matter, and the arrangement much altered. The edition of 1611 has four less preliminary pages, and 94 pages less of text, than that of 1618; while *Les Muses* occupy the same number in each. The form and size of all the French editions is the same, 12° or small 8°. That of 1609 is thought to be complete with only two maps; those of 1611 and 1618 are only complete when containing four. The last received the final touches of Lescarbot's hand, and may therefore be well considered the most desirable of all. One copy at least has been announced with the date of 1617 on the title, but it is declared to be identical with this, which the publisher asserts to be the third edition. All of the French editions, as well as the translation of a part of that of 1609 into English by Erondelle, are very rare. A copy of the French of 1609, from the library of Bolton Corney, sold in 1871 for £27, and in the same collection a copy of Erondelle's translation sold for £37. A copy of the edition of 1618, without the maps, from Leclercq's collection, in 1817 sold for 251 francs; equal to $100 of the currency of the day.

Lescarbot's history is highly esteemed not only for its great veracity, but as the work of a candid and intelligent writer, and the first history of the French settlements in Canada. Charlevoix's praise of him is flavored with a little of his characteristic acidity. "Marc Lescarbot, advocate in the Parliament of Paris, was a man of sense and learning, but a little addicted to the marvelous." The good father, however, subsequently neutralizes the sharpness of his criticism by saying, "Lescarbot has collected with much care all that had been written before him, relating to the discoveries of the French in America, all that passed in French Florida, etc. — He was sincere, well educated, and impartial." His descriptions of Indian Life and peculiarities are very interesting, on account both of their fidelity, and from being among the first authentic relations, we have of them after Cartier. Lescarbot wrote two other works relating to Canada; copies of which are still rarer than either edition of his *Histoire de la Nouvelle France*. The first is entitled, *La conversion des Sauvages qui ont été baptisés dans la Nouvelle France cette année* 1610, *avec a brief recit du Sieur Poutrincourt*. The other appeared under the title *Relation derniere de ce qui s'est passe au voyage du Sieur de Poutrincourt en la Nouvelle France depuis vingt mois en ça.*" Paris, 1612, 8°.

LESCARBOT (Marc).

Nova Francia: | Or the | Description | of that part of | New France, | which is one continent with | Virginia. | Described in the three late Voyages and Plantation made by | *Monsieur de Monts, Monsieur du Pont—Graué*, and | *Monsieur de Poutrincourt*, into the countries | called by the Frenchmen *La Cadie*, | lying to the Southwest of | Cape Breton. | Together with an excellent seuerall Treatie of all the commodities | of the said countries, and maners of the naturall | inhabitants of the same. | Translated out of French into English by | P. E. | *Londini*, | *Impensis Georgii Bishop.* | 1609. | 4° *prel. pp.* 18 + 1 *to* 307. 916

Of the preliminary pages the "Title" forms 1; reverse blank. "To the bright Starre of the North," signed P. Erondelle, 3 pages. "To the Reader," 2 pages. "The Table of the Contents," 12 pages, all unnumbered. The text is divided into Two Booke's of xviii. and xxvi. chapters respectively. In the Table of Contents the First Booke is entitled, "Wherein are described the three late Voiages, Nauigations and Plantation of New France, etc; pages 1 to 136. "The Second Booke, Containing the Customes and maners of life of the West Indians of New France, etc.," Preface, pages 133 and 136; text 139 to 307. From the correspondence of the letters P E on the title with the initials of the name signed to the dedication, this translation of a portion of Lescarbot's work has been generally attributed to P Erondelle. He expressly avows in his Preface that: "The whole volume of the navigations of the French nation into the West Indies (comprised in three bookes) was brought to mee, to be translated by M. Richard Hakluyt, * * and by him this part was selected from the whole work, to the end, that comparing the goodnesse of the lands with that of Virginia, etc." "Which translation is but a part of a greater volume." It thus appears that the *Histoire de la Nouvelle France* was ignominiously devoted to an advertising scheme, for selling the lands in Virginia, distant more than seven hundred miles. Nor was it sufficient to rob Lescarbot of hard-earned fame, by utterly ignoring his authorship of the work, but it was greatly abridged; not however past recognition, for the preservation by the translator, of the divisions of the original, is almost exact.

Erondelle's book is a very faithful translation of the Fourth and Sixth Books of Lescarbot's History, with the same number of chapters in the first, and twenty-six instead of twenty-five chapters in the second, the third chapter of the original being divided into chapters iii. and iiii. It contains therefore a trifle less than half of the matter of the work, and it is but justice to add, much the best portion. So exact is Erondelle's reproduction of the original in English, that he has retained almost every word of the elaborate chapter headings. It is to be regretted that the honesty he evinced in translation, did not survive that labor long enough to place the author's name on the title-page.

Lescarbot (Marc).

Histoire de la Nouvelle France par Marc Lescarbot, suivee des Muses de la Nouvelle France. Nouvelle Edition publiee par Edwin Tross avec quatre cartes geographique. 3 *vols. Small* 8°. *Paris, Librairie Tross*, 1866. 917

This edition purports to be a reproduction of the second, which was printed in 1611, and which indeed he announces as the second in his biographical sketch of Lescarbot. Notwithstanding this, his reproduction of the title-page gives the date of 1612 (Chez Jean Milot, M.DC.XII.). Each volume contains one half and three full titles. The pagination of the text of the "Histoire" is continuous through the three volumes = pp. 851. Bars in the text indicate the termination of the pages of the original, and figures in the margin their corresponding number. Vol. I. has (viii.) + xx. preliminary pages. In Vol. III. the "Sommaire des Chapitres" occupies pp. xxviii.; "Les Muses de la Nouvelle France," pp. 84.

Mr. Tross gives us but a meagre sketch of the life of Lescarbot, in which he guesses at the period of his birth and death. The bibliographical account of his works is quite as carelessly drawn, for he omits in his list of editions and works, that of *Erondelle*, London, 1609, *Le Conversion des Sauvages*, of Paris, 1610, and the *Relation du Voyage du Sieur de Poutrincourt*, Paris, 1612. The publisher has reproduced, with very creditable exactness, the four maps, as belonging to the edition of 1611.

The works of Lescarbot are more numerous than seems to have been suspected by bibliographers.

Those which appear with his name, and their various editions, rank as follows: —

1. *Discours sur les reunion des Eglises d' Alexandrie et de Russie, a la Sainte Eglise Catholique par Marc Lescarbot.* 8° Paris, Morel, 1599. Library of J. Carson Brevoort.
2. *Histoire de la Nouvelle France.* Paris, Chez Jean Milot. 8° pp. 888 + 2 maps, 1609 Library of Hon. H. C. Murphy.
3. *Histoire de la Nouvelle France.* Second edition. Paris, Jean Milot. 8° (24) preliminary leaves not numbered + text, pp. 1 to 897 + 4 maps + "Muses," pp. 76, numbered erroneously 66. 1611. Library of Hon. H. C. Murphy.
4. *Histoire de la Nouvelle France.* Second edition, Paris, Jean Milot. Astor Library: —
5. *Histoire de la Nouvelle France*, Troiseme Edition. Paris, Adrian Perier. Collation as in edition of 1613. 8° 1617. Leclercq Catalogue.
6. *Histoire de la Nouvelle France*, Troiseme Edition. Paris, 1618, as in No. 915. All of these editions are accompanied by *Les Muses*, separately paged.
7. *Nova Francia.* English translation of *Erondelle.* Small 4° London, 1609, as in No. 916.
8. *Nova Francia.* Translation in German. Small 4° Augsburg, 1613.
9. *Les Muses de la Nouvelle France.* Paris, Jean Milot, 1609. As copies of

this date have been found annexed to the history, it is believed a separate edition was issued.

10. *Le Tableau de la Suisse, auquel sont decrites les singularitez des Alpes.* 4° Paris, pp. 79, 1613.

11. *La Conversion des Sauvages qui ont este baptizes en la Nouvelle France cette Anne* 1610, *avec un recit du Voyage du Sieur de Poutrincourt.* Paris, Jean Milot. 8° (n. d.). This work is rarer even than either of the others.

12. *Relation derniere de ce qui s'est passe au voyage du Sieur de Poutrincourt, en la Nouvelle-France depuis 20 mois en ça. Par M. Lescarbot. Advocat en Parlement.* 8° Paris, 1612. This work was reprinted in the *Archives Curieuses de l' Histoire France,* Vol. XV., 1st Series.

LESTRANGE (HAMON).

Americans No Iewes or Improbabilities that the Americans are of that race. [*Motto, 7 lines.*] 4° *Title,* 1 *leaf* + *To the Reader,* 1 *leaf* + *Americans no Jews,* 80 *pp. London, printed by W. W., for Henry Seile, over against St. Dunstans church, in Fleet Street,* 1652. 918*

This is a rejoinder to the work of Thomas Thorowgood, printed two years before entitled, *Jews in America,* London, 1650. The work of Lestrange was followed by Thorowgood's replication, entitled, *Jews in America, or Probabilities that those Indians are Judaical,* London, 1660.

LETTRES EDIFIANTES

Et Curieuses, ecrites des Missions Etrangeres. Nouvelle edition. (Memoires d'Amerique, Vols. VI. to IX.). *A Toulouse, Chez Noel-Etienne Sens &c.,* 1810. 26 *volumes* 12° 919

Vols. V. to VIII. are filled with Relations, Narratives and Letters from Jesuit Missionaries, written subsequently to the celebrated and rare Relations of the Jesuit Missionaries of Canada to their superiors. They are undoubtedly among the most authentic sources of information, regarding some of the most obscure and mysterious of aboriginal customs, languages, and religions. Vol. V. is principally occupied with the Relations of the Missionaries among the Indians of Paraguay and Brazil. Vol. VI. contains the Relations of the Indian Missions in Canada, and among the Abenakis. The letters regarding the latter are written by the celebrated Father Rasles, who fell a martyr to his zeal for his flock at Norridgewock. The most important historic portion of this volume, perhaps of the whole collection, is the Journal of an Abenakis missionary who was present at the massacre, by the Indians, of the English garrison of Fort George, after it had surrendered. In this series the name of the Father who wrote it is not given, but Father Kip, in his book *Early Jesuit Missions in America,* says the author was Father Rouband. The facts, as narrated by this very credible witness, certainly exculpate the heroic Montcalm from the taint of cruelty. Vol. VII. is composed of Letters and Relations of the missionaries among the Natches, the Illinois, the Indians of Saint Domingo, and of Guiana. A curious identification of the name of the city of Chicago, is found in the letter of Father Petit, pp. 1 to 60, which gives minute details of the visit of the Illinois chief Chicagou to the mission. This chief had visited Paris, and become somewhat noted, and doubtless it was from him that the name of that once opulent city is derived. Vol. VIII. contains the Relations of the missionaries among the Indians of Guiana, Peru, California, and Chili, in which the characteristics of the Moxes, Chiquitos, Pulchas, and Payas Indians, are given with great minuteness and fidelity. Every one of these volumes is crowded with interesting details for the history of the aborigines of the countries in which these wonderful men held their missions.

LETTER

From the Commissioner for Indian Affairs to Colonel Benton. 8° *pp.* 15. *Washington,* 1855. 920

LETTERS

From Buenos Ayres and Chili, with an Original History of the latter Country. Illustrated with Engravings, by the author of Letters from Paraguay. 8° *pp.* xl. *and* 323. *London, printed for R. Ackermann,* 101 *Strand,* 1819. 921

The author gives an interesting account of the Jesuit missions among the Indians, and the peculiar customs of some tribes hitherto unnoticed, derived from personal observation or inquiry, among those whose intimate relations with the savages entitled their information to credence.

LETTER

To a Member of Congress in relation to Indian Civilization. By the domestic Secretary of the united foreign missionary Society. 8° *pp.* 16. *New York,* 1822. 922

LETTERS

On the Chickasaw and Osage Missions. By the author of Conversations on the Sandwich Island Missions, &c., revised by the publication committee. 24° *pp.* 161. *Boston, printed by T. R. Marvin, for the Massachusetts Sabbath School Union,* 1831. 923

LEWIS (Hannah).

Narrative of the Captivity and Sufferings of Mrs. Hannah Lewis and her three children, who were taken Prisoners by the Indians, near St. Louis on the 25th May, 1815, & among whom they experienced all the cruel treatment which savage brutality could inflict. Mrs. Lewis & her eldest son fortunately made their escape on the 3d of April last, leaving her two youngest children in the hands of the cruel barbarians. Second edition. 12° *pp.* 24. *Boston, printed by H. Trumbull,* 1817. 924

LEWIS AND CLARKE.

Message from the President of the United States, communicating Discoveries made in exploring the Missouri, Red River and Washita, by Captains Lewis and Clarke, Dr. Sibley and Mr. Dunbar; with a Statistical Account of the Countries adjacent. Read in Congress February 19, 1806. 8° *pp.* 176. *New York,* 1806. 925

LEWIS AND CLARK.

Travels in the Interior Parts of America; communicating Discoveries made in exploring The Missouri, Red River and Washita, by Captains Lewis & Clark, Doctor Sibley and Mr. Dunbar; With A Statistical Account of the Countries adjacent. As laid before the Senate, by the President of the United States. In February, 1806, and never before published in Great Britain. 8° *pp.* 116 + *folding table. London: printed for Richard Phillips,* 1807. 926

This work is nearly an exact copy of the original government publication, of Lewis and Clarke's report of their expedition, without addition or interpolation. It is one of a series of travels published by Sir Richard Phillips, bookseller and baronet, who is the only example I recollect of that combination of trade and title.

Lewis (Meriwether).

The Travels of Cap^ns Lewis and Clarke, from St. Louis, by way of the Missouri and Columbia rivers, to the Pacific Ocean; performed in the years 1804, 1805, and 1806, by order of the government of the United States, containing delineations of the manners, customs, religion, &c. Of the Indians, compiled from Various Authentic Sources, and Original Documents, and a Summary of the Statistical View of the Indian Nations, from the official communication of Meriwether Lewis. Illustrated with a Map of the Country, inhabited by the Western Tribes of Indians. 8° *pp.* ix. and 309. *London*, 1809. 927

"As far as relates to Lewis and Clarke's travels, this work is not what it pretends to be, for it contains no further account of them than was given in the official communication of Meriwether Lewis, with the addition of some private letters from Captain Clarke." In other respects it possesses much interest, as it contains some documents not published in any other edition. Among them are a description of the manners and customs of the Missouri Indians; a statistical view of the Northwestern tribes; historical sketches of the several Indian tribes of Louisiana; observations on the voyage of William Dunbar and Dr. Hunter extracted from their journals, and a vocabulary of the languages of some of the tribes of Indians.

Lewis and Clarke.

History of the Expedition under the Command of Captains Lewis and Clark, to the Sources of the Missouri, thence across the Rocky Mountains and down the River Columbia to the Pacific Ocean. Performed during the years 1804–5–6. By order of the Government of the United States. Prepared for the Press by Paul Allen, Esquire. *Two vols.* 8° Vol. I. *pp.* xxviii. + 470, *large folding map and two plans.* Vol. II. *pp.* ix. + 498 + 3 *plans and table of names, localities, and numbers of Indian tribes. Philadelphia*, 1814. 928

This work was commenced by Captain Lewis himself, who was on his route to Philadelphia to engage in its completion, when the derangement seized him, under the influence of which he committed suicide at St. Louis. It was then undertaken by Mr. Nicolas Biddle, who in conjunction with Captain Clarke, arranged the numerous notes, and copious diaries and journals, kept by each of the principal explorers, and enlarged the skeleton of many incidents from the recollections of the survivor. To this mass of authentic material was added such additional particulars as were noted in the journals of Gass and another sergeant, — that of the last still unpublished, and said to be the most minute and valuable. Another intelligent member of the expedition, Mr. George Shannon, also contributed some material to confirm or correct the details already acquired. At this stage of the growth of the "History" of the expedition, Mr. Biddle from caprice, or business abstraction, abandoned its direction, when his literary structure was nearly or quite complete. It was thus left to the editor, (whom popular esteem has credited with the labor of forming the work,) only to obtain a sketch of the life of Captain Lewis from President Jefferson, and to place his name on the title-page. All of this he states in the Preface, but neglects to name the industrious and judicious editor who wrought his work ready to his hand; yet emblazons his own name in the place of honor on the title.

Mr. Samuel G. Drake says that he was informed by Mr. Nicholas Biddle that he was himself the editor who is referred to in the preface, as having nearly completed the work for the press. This is by far the most complete edition of this interesting work, whose value to the historian, the student, or the reader for amusement, has in no degree been superseded by the numerous relations of expeditions which have succeeded it. The explorers even anticipated our interest in the remains of aboriginal fortifications, by half a century; and constructed accurate plans of such as they discovered, even then disappearing, and scarcely traceable. This edition contains the Appendix of sixty-four pages, omitted in the English edition of three volumes.

Lewis and Clarke.

Travels to the Source of the Missouri River and across the American Continent to the Pacific Ocean. Performed by order of the Government of the United States, in the years 1804, 1805, and 1806. By Captains Lewis and Clarke. Published from the Official Report, and illustrated by a map of the route and other maps. 4° *pp.* xxiv. + 663 + *folding map and two full page maps. London: printed for Longman* (*&* Co.), 1814. 929

This is the most beautiful in typography and mechanical execution of all the editions of Lewis and Clarke's work. Its large margin, clear impression, and noble appearance, are worthy of this model of works of travel and exploration. The edition in three octavo volumes printed in the succeeding year by the same house, is an exact reprint of this. How large a portion of the work is devoted to Indian affairs may be ascertained by the headings of chapters: ii. "Some Account of the Pawnee Indians;" iii. "Superstition of the Sioux, and Council with the Sioux Indians;" iv. "Council with the Tetons, Their Manners, &c.;" v. "Council with the Mandans;" vi. "The Party increase in favor with the Mandans — Description of their Ceremonies;" vii. "Indian mode of attacking the Buffalo on the ice;" xiv. "Interview with the Shoshonies;" xv. "Council with that Nation." Nineteen of the remaining twenty-one chapters are devoted to the narration of the peculiarities of the savage nations which were encountered.

Lewis and Clarke.

Travels to the source of the Missouri River and across the American Continent to the Pacific Ocean. Performed by order of the government of the United States, in the years 1804, 1805, and 1806. By Captains Lewis and Clarke. Published from the official report, and illustrated by a map of the route, and other maps. A new edition in three volumes. 8° Vol. I. *pp.* 26 + 411. Vol. II. *pp.* 12 + 434. Vol. III. *pp.* 12 + 394. *London,* 1815. 930

This edition, announced as prepared for the press by Thomas Rees, is an exact reproduction of that really edited by Mr. Biddle, but formally claimed by Paul Allen, and published at Philadelphia in two volumes. Thus one literary brother robs another. The London edition, however, lacks the Appendix of "Observations on the Government of the Indians," by Captain Lewis, which with meteorological tables occupies sixty-four pages.

Another edition of Biddle's history of Lewis and Clarke's expedition was printed in Dublin, under the same title as the London edition of three volumes, from which it was copied with the addition on the title-page of, —

"With the Life of Captain Lewis, by T. Jefferson, President of the United States of America." In Two Volumes. Dublin, J. Christie. 1817. 8° Vol. I. prel. pp. xxxix. + 385. Vol. II. prel. pp. xiv. + 843 + 7 plates and map.

Lewis and Clarke.

History of the Expedition under the Command of Captains Lewis and Clarke, to the Sources of the Missouri, thence across the Rocky Mountains, and down the River Columbia to the

Pacific Ocean, performed during the years 1804, 1805, 1806, by order of the Government of the United States. Prepared for the press by Paul Allen Esq. revised, and abridged by the omission of unimportant details, with an introduction and notes, by Archibald M'Vicar. In Two Volumes. Vol. I. *Map and pp.* 371. Vol. II. *pp.* 395. *New York, Harper & Brothers, Publishers,* 1868. 931

Nicholas Biddle is once more ignored in this reproduction of his work, and the name of the modest Paul Allen emblazoned on the title-page to company with the Rev. Dr. M'Vicar.

LEWIS AND CLARK.

The journal of Lewis and Clark to the mouth of the Columbia river beyond the Rocky Mts. in the years 1804, 5 & 6. Giving a faithful description of the river Missouri and its source — of the various tribes of Indians through which they passed — manners & customs — soil — climate — commerce — gold and silver mines — animal and vegetable productions, &c. New Edition, with notes, revised, corrected and illustrated with numerous woodcuts. To which is added a complete dictionary of the Indian Tongue. 16° *pp.* 240 + 15 *plates. Dayton, O.,* 1840. 932

This is an almost exact reproduction of the octavo London edition of 1809. The variations are merely verbal, and the substitutions of synonymical terms appear dictated by mere whim and caprice.

LEWIS & CLARKE.

Journal of Voyages & Travels. *Philadelphia.* 12° 1812. 933

See Gass, Patrick.

LEWIS & CLARKE.

Journal of Voyages & Travels. *London.* 8° 1808. 934

LEWIS & CLARKE.

Journal of Lewis & Clarke. *Pittsburgh.* 12° 1807. 935

LEWIS, J. O.

Aboriginal Portfolio. 936

Two large folios containing each thirty-six lithographed Indian portraits. Each number is prefaced with a page commencing "Advertisement to The First — (and Second) — number of the Aboriginal Portfolio." No other text accompanies the prints, and nothing bearing the remotest relation to a title. No. 1 is dated "*Phil. July* 20th, 1835." No. 2, "*Phil. June*, 1836."

The portraits are each entitled with the name and rank of the Indian personage represented. They have the appearance of being authentic, although no voucher, or explanation of the circumstances under which they were executed, accompanies the plates.

LEWIS (Alonzo).

The History of Lynn including Nahant, by Alonzo Lewis, the Lynn Bard. Second Edition. 8° *pp.* 278 + *two plates of Indians. Boston,* 1844. 937

The work contains many particulars of Indian history.

LEWIS (Jane).

Narrative of the Captivity and Providential Escape of Mrs. Jane Lewis, Wife of James Lewis, Who, with a son and daughter, (the former in his 16th, and the latter in the 10th year of her age) and an infant babe were made prisoners, within a few miles of Indian Creek, by a party of Indians of the tribes of Sacs and Foxes, commanded by Black Hawk. [*etc.*, 7 *lines.*] 8° *Plate and* 24 *pp.* n. l. (*N. Y.*) 1833. 938

LIANCOURT (La Rochefoucault).

Travels through the United States of North America, the Country of the Iroquois, and Upper Canada, in the Years 1795, 1796, and 1797, by the Duke de la Rochefoucault Liancourt. With an authentic account of Lower Canada. Three Maps, severall Tables, &c. Second edition. 4 Vols. 8° Vol. I. *pp.* xxiii. + 607. Vol. II. *pp.* xviii. + 523. Vol. III. *pp.* 739. Vol. IV. *pp.* 618. *London:* 1800. 939

The usual addenda to this title in the Catalogues is, "The author exhibits pictures of Indian manners, which, though mournful, and disgusting to taste, are yet interesting to philosophy, in conjunction with his accounts of the settlers before whom the Indian tribes are gradually vanishing from the earth. The striking contrasts of savage life to the hackneyed phases of the society of Europe, forcibly impressed the mind and attracted the curiosity of this exiled Frenchman." With this comment it would be supposed, that the work is largely composed of his observations of the peculiarities of the Indian tribes he visited, as well as narratives of adventures among them, copied from printed works. But the whole of his so-much vaunted relations of aboriginal life in America, are found in Vol. I., pages 312 to 332, where the author describes the condition of the Senecas and other Indians in the vicinity of Buffalo, and on pages 339 to 379, where he gives the narrative of the captivity of Mr. Johnson by the Shawnese in 1794, as dictated to the Duke by the captive himself, with a few occasional observations on other tribes.

LINCOLN (Luther B.).

Address delivered at South Deerfield August 31, 1838, at the Completion of the Bloody Brook Monument, erected in memory of Capt. Lothrop and his associates, who fell at that spot, September 18 (O. S.) 1675. By Luther B. Lincoln. Published by request. 8° *pp.* 16, *with printed covers. Greenfield, Kneeland and Eastman,* 1838. 940

LINSCHOTEN (Jean Hugues).

Histoire de la Navigation De Iean HVGVES de Linschot Hollandais Aux Indes Orientales. Contenant diverses Descriptions des lieux iusques a present descouverts par les portugais: Observations des Coustoumes & singularitez de dela, & autres declarations. Avec annotations de B. Paludanus sur la matiere des Plantes & Espiceries: Item quelques Cartes Geographiques & autres Figures. Deuxiesme edition augmentee. *A Amsterdam, Chez Iean Evertz Cloppenburch, Marchand libraire, demeurant sur le Water a la Bible Doree. Avec Privilige pour* 12 *Ans.* 1619. 941

Folio. Engraved Title, Preface, Index and Portrait of Linschoten + pp. xiii. + 205 + 37 large folding maps and plates.

LINSCHOTEN (Jean Hugues).

Le Grand Routier de Mer de Jean Hughes de Linschot [*etc.* 14 *lines.*] *A Amsterdam,* 1619. 942

Engraved title, 1 leaf; preface, 1 leaf + pp. 1 to 181.

LINSCHOTEN (Jean Hugues).
Description de L'Amerique & des parties d' icelle, comme de la Nouvelle France, Floride, des Antilles Iucaya, Cuba, Jamaica &c. Item de l'estendue & distance des lieux, de la fertilite & abondance du pays, religion & coustumes des habitans, & autres particularitez. Avec une Carte Geographique de l'Amerique Australe, qui doit estre enfree en la page suivante. *Engraved title* + *pp.* 86. *A Amsterdam* 1619. 943

[LIVINGSTON (Wm.).]
A Review of the Military operations in North America, from The Commencement of the French Hostilities on the Frontiers of Virginia in 1753, to the Surrender of Oswego, on the 14th of August 1756. Interspersed With various Observations, Characters, and Anecdotes; necessary to give Light into the Conduct of American Transactions in general; and more especially into the political Management of Affairs in New York. In a Letter to a Nobleman. To which are added Colonel Washington's Journal of his Expedition to the Ohio in 1754, and Several Letters and other Papers of Consequence, found in the Cabinet of Major General Braddock, after his Defeat near Fort Du-Quesne; and since published by the French Court. None of these Papers are contained in the English Edition. 24° *pp.* 275. *Dublin, printed for P. Wilson and J. Exshaw*, 1757. 944

Washington's Journal commences at page 191, and with Braddock's Papers occupies the remainder of the volume. This portion of the work is a translation of the *Memoire contenant le Precis des Faits*, printed by the French Court, charging Washington with the assassination of Jumonville, and reprinted by Hugh Gaines in 1757, under the title of *Memorial containing a Summary View of Facts, etc.*

LIVINGSTON (John H.).
A Sermon delivered before the New York Missionary Society at their annual meeting, April 3, 1804. To which are added an Appendix and other papers relating to American Missions. 8° *Worcester*, 1807. 945

LONG (J.).
Voyages and Travels of an Indian Interpreter and Trader, Describing the Manners and Customs of the North American Indians; with an Account of the Posts situated on the river St. Laurence, Lake Ontario, &c. To which is added, A Vocabulary of the Chippeway Language. Names of Furs and Skins, in English and French. A List of Words in the Iroquois, Mohegan, Shawanee, and Esquimeaux Tongues, and a table, showing The Analogy between the Algonquin and Chippeway Languages. By J. Long. 4° *pp.* xl. *and* 295. *London:* 1791. 946

The author engaged in the service of the Hudson's Bay Company in 1768, and journeyed as a fur trader among the Indians of Canada for nineteen years. His knowledge of the character, customs, and domestic life of the Indians was therefore the most thorough and intimate. His relations are characterized by candor and intelligence, tinged a little with the disappointments, which most of the servants of the Company who have written accounts of their experiences, seem to have suffered.

The titles of his chapters will best indicate the range of the subjects treated in his work: "A Description of the Village and Inhabitants of Cahnuaga, a branch of the Mohawks." "Of the Indians of the Six Nations." "Indian Scouts and Manner of Scalping." "Account of the Connecedagas and Iroquois." "Indian Dances." "Ceremony of Indian Adoption." "Indian Manner of going to War." Such, with a narrative of the author's own personal adventures, is the character of the *Travels* and *Voyages* for 181 pages. The Vocabularies of the languages noted in the title occupy 112 pages, the entire remainder of the volume.

LONG (J.).

Voyages chez differentes nations Sauvages de l'Amerique Septentrionale; Renferment des détails curieux sur les moeurs, usages, cérémonies religieuses, le systême militaire, &c., des Cahnuagas, des Indiens des cinq & six Nations, Mohawks, Connecedagas, Iroquois, &c., des Indiens Chippeways, & autre sauvages de divers tribus; sur leurs langues, les pays qu'ils habitent, ainsi que sur le commerce de pelleteries & fourrure qui se fait chez ces peuples: Avec un état exact des postes situes sur le Fleuve S. Laurent, le Lac Ontario, &c., &c. Par J. Long, traiquant, & interpréte des langues Indiennes. Traduits de l'Anglois, avec des notes & additions interessantes, par J. B. L. J. Billecocq, citoyen Francais. *A Paris. Chez Prault l'aîné, Imprimeur, quai des Augustins, à l'Immortalité, No. 41. Fuchs, libraire, même quai, au coin de la rue Gît-le-Coeur, No. 28. II. Année de l'ère Républicaine.* 947

A French translation of Long's *Travels of an Indian Trader*, in which is omitted the most valuable portion of the original work, — the vocabularies, a fact which has been not a little regretted by French philologists.

LONG (Major S. H.).

Account of an Expedition from Pittsburgh to the Rocky Mountains, performed in the Years 1819, 1820. By order of the Hon. J. C. Calhoun, Secretary of War, under the command of Maj. S. H. Long, of the U. S. Top. Engineers. Compiled from the Notes of Major Long, Mr. T. Say, and other gentlemen of the party By Edwin James, botanist and geologist to the Expedition. In Three Volumes. 8° Vol. I. *pp.* vii. + 344 + *large map and 3 plates.* Vol. II. *pp.* vii. + 356 + 8 *plates.* Vol. III. *pp.* vii. + 347 + 2 *plates and folding map. London:* 1823. 948

In all of Major Long's explorations, the natives of the territories through which he passed received the largest share of his attention. This will be evident from an examination of the table of contents of each volume. Chapters vi. to xii. of Vol. I. are entitled: "Account of the Konza nation — Councils with the Otois, Missouries, Ioways, Pawnees," &c. — Sioux & Omahaw Indians. Account of the Omahaws, Manners, Customs & Religious Rites. History of Blackbird their principal chief. Of their Marriage, Infancy & Old Age, Diseases, Medical Knowledge, Vices, Ideas of God, Superstition and expiatory Tortures. Vol. II.: The subject of Mourning for the deceased. War, Legend, and Language is pursued in chapters i. to iv. Chapter xii.

An account of the Kaskaskias. A great part of Volume III. is devoted to observations upon the Shienne, Arapaho, Pawnee, and other tribes of the Plains. Of the eight plates seven are illustrative of Indian life and manners.

LONG (Stephen H.).

Narrative of an Expedition to the Source of St. Peter's River, Lake Winnepeg, Lake of the Woods, &c., &c., performed in the year 1823, by order of the Hon. J. C. Calhoun, Secretary of War, under the Command of Stephen H. Long, Major U. S. T. E. Compiled from the notes of Major Long, Messrs. Say, Keating and Calhoun, by William H. Keating. In Two Volumes. 8° Vol. I. 5 *plates and map* + *pp.* 439, *and page of Indian Music.* Vol. II. *pp.* 459 + 10 *plates.* 8° *Philadelphia, H. C. Carey,* 1824. 949

The work is almost a cyclopædia of material, relating to the Indians of the explored territory. Nothing escaped the attention, or record of the gentlemen who accompanied the expedition; and their statement regarding the customs, character, and numbers of the Sioux and Chippeway tribes, are among the most valuable we have of those people. Much the largest portion of the volumes is devoted to recording their observations upon these Indians. Six of the plates are representations of their practices, habitations, or features. Pages 449 to 459 of Volume II. are occupied with a comparative vocabulary of the Sawk, Sioux, Chippeway, and Cree languages.

LONG (Major Stephen H.).

Voyage in a Six-oared Skiff to the Falls of Saint Anthony in 1817, by Major Stephen H. Long. topographical engineer U. S. Army. With introductory notes by Edward D. Neill (Collec. Minnesota His. Soc). 8° *pp.* 88. *Philadelphia,* 1860. 950

This voyage of the veteran explorer, Major Long, was made while he was Superintendent of Indian affairs for the Northwest Territories, and in pursuance of the duties of his office, to visit the Indian tribes of his superintendency. It has never been published in any other form.

LONG (R. Cary).

The Ancient Architecture of America, Its Historical Value and parallelism of development with the Architecture of the old world. A Discourse delivered before the N. Y. Hist. Soc. at its meeting April 3d, 1849. By R. Cary Long, A. M. Architect. 8° *pp.* 87, *and nine plates, the 9th numbered xi. New York,* 1849. 951

LOSKIEL (George Henry).

History of the Mission of the United Brethren among the Indians in North America. In three parts. By George Henry Loskiel. Translated from the German by Christian Ignatius La Trobe. *pp.* xiii. Part I. *pp.* 1 *to* 159. Part II. *pp.* 1 *to* 234. Part III. *pp.* 1 *to* 233 + *Index, eleven leaves not paged; total pp.* 656. 8° *London,* 1794. *Printed for the Brethren's Society for the furtherance of the Gospel.* 952

Part I. is divided into eleven chapters, whose subject titles indicate a much wider range for the work, than the mere report of missions among the Indians. Among them are, "Hints concerning the Origin of the Indian Nations."—"Of the Language, Arts, and Sciences, known among the Indians." "Of their Religious Ceremonies and Superstition." "Of their Dress, Dwellings, and Housekeeping." "Marriages and Education of Children." "Agriculture and Breeding of Cattle." "Of their Manner of Hunting and Fishing." "Diseases and Method of Cure, Funerals and Mourning." "Political Constitution of the Delawares and Iroquois." "Indian Manner of making War and Peace." Parts II. and III. are devoted to the history of the Indians under the charge of the Moravian Mission. Among the subjects, is the narrative of that saddest of stories, the massacre of Gnadenhutten and Salem, — saddest, most atrocious, most damnable record of human infamy and bloody shame.

A remarkable omission occurs in La Trobe's translation. A copy of the first edition had been presented to Zeisberger, who expressed the greatest regrets that the names of Eliot McKee, and other former enemies of the mission had been recorded, as they had since repented. At his request the names of many who had brought terrible misfortunes upon the missionaries and their converts, were omitted in this translation.

LOSSING (Benson J.).

The Marriage of Pocahontas. **By Benson J. Lossing.** *s. l. s. d.* 8° *Engraving and 8 pp.* **953**

LOUDON (Archibald).

A | Selection, | of Some | of the most interesting | NARRATIVES, | of | Outrages, Committed | by the | INDIANS, | in | Their Wars, | with the White People. | Also, | An Account of their Manners, Customs, Traditions, | Religious Sentiments, Mode of Warfare, Military | Tactics, Discipline and Encampments, Treatment | of Prisoners, &c. which are better Explained, and | more Minutely Related, than has been heretofore | done, by any other Author on that subject. Many | of the Articles have never before appeared in print. | The whole Compiled from the best Authorities, | By Archibald Loudon. | Vol. I. | *Small* 12° *Prel. pp.* 12 + 5 *to* 355. *Carlisle: | from the Press of A. Loudon,* | (*Whitehall*), 1808. 954

Collation of Vol. I.: Title, reverse copyright; "Preface," pp. 5; "Mr. Archibald Loudon," etc., pp. 3; "Contents," pp. 2 (total prelim. pp. xii.); "The Narrative of Dr. Knight," etc., pp. 5 to 355. Page 355 terminates with "End of First volume," and on reverse "Advertisement." There are no pp. 1 to 4.

Collation of Vol. II.: Title, reverse copyright; "Contents," pp. 2; "A Selection, etc.," pp. 13 to 369. There are no pp. 1 to 12. The title of the second volume terminates "| By Archibald Loudon. | Vol. II. | Carlisle, | From the Press of Archibald Loudon, | 1811."

This rarest of books on American history has some bibliographical peculiarities, which that very rarity has hitherto prevented the recognition of. A large correspondence with book collectors, and not a little familiarity with the best of public and private libraries, have brought to my notice but three perfect copies of this work. The popularity of its subject, which caused its constant perusal at country firesides, combined with the fragility of the soft cotton paper upon which it is printed, insured its rapid destruction.

It will be observed that in Vol. I. there is an apparent omission of four pages in those numbered in Arabic figures, as the preliminary pages end with twelve and the narrative begins with five. The second volume has also some peculiarities not a little perplexing to the collator. It is dated three years later than the first volume, and the word "Whitehall" is omitted in the title.

From the Roman numbered page iv. to the Arabic numbered page 13, of

Volume II., there is an apparent hiatus of eight pages, and all the copies of both volumes would appear to be imperfect. This omission of eight numbers is doubtless to be accounted for as follows: The narrative portion of Volume I. was as usual printed before the Title, Preface, and Table of Contents. The printer provided for only a form of four pages to contain them, and therefore commenced the narrative with page 5. On making up the volume, London found a necessity for more room, and let the preliminary matter run on to page xii. When, however, the second volume was printed, the compositor flattered himself that he was too adroit to be caught in a similar blunder, and accordingly commenced the narrative with page 13, without reflecting that the second volume would require neither Preface or Introduction. On making up the form, containing the Title and Table of Contents, it was found that only four pages could be used, and in consequence there is a hiatus of eight pages (*in numbers only*). Other irregularities of less importance occur in this volume. Signature E ends with page 72. Signature G commences with page 85. The intervening twelve pages are therefore also signed E. This has led to the omission of this signature in some copies, by the carelessness of the folder, and for this reason, perhaps, few were ever perfect. The reverse of page 161, is numbered erroneously 134, in place of 162. The next page is numbered 164 erroneously instead of 163, and the error is continued to page 169, which is followed by another 169, thus restoring the correct enumeration, so that the true account of the number of pages is at last represented by the figures. At page 216 the mischievous demon which presides over types, again destroyed the consecutiveness of the numbers, by printing the succeeding page 215. The next page is also numbered 216, thus presenting us with two pages 216, and two pages 215. The omission which this originated, of dropping two pages in the notation, is perpetuated through the whole volume, so that there would really be two more pages than are indicated by the numbers, were it not for the first error of numbering, in putting 13 at the top of the page immediately following page iv. Allowing for this, there are therefore six pages less in Vol. II. than the notation represents. . . .'

But there are other complications attending the work, which will embarrass the bibliographer. Indeed, it would seem as if the spirit of mischance had rioted in schemes of perplexity, to confound everything associated with it. Where is Carlisle and Whitehall? And who was Archibald London? Whitehall in New York at the foot of Lake Champlain has its Carlisle in a secluded hamlet a few miles distant; and Carlisle in Pennsylvania has its Whitehall, not much more populous or distant. This question happily can be disposed of very readily, as Archibald London printed a book of poems unknown to fame, "By Isabella Oliver of Cumberland Co. Pennsylvania, Carlisle, From the Press of A. London, Whitehall, 1805." So Archibald London, printer, publisher, and author, resided at Whitehall in Pennsylvania, and printed his book at Carlisle in the same State. The author-printer also published a volume of miscellanies, an octavo serial. He is believed to have been a descendant of the Samuel London, whose printing-office was sacked, and his type thrown into the East River, by the Revolutionary mob under Chris. Duyhinck in 1775.

LOUISIANA.

The Present State of the Country and Inhabitants, Europeans and Indians, of Louisiana [*etc.*, 2 *lines*] containing The Garrisons, Forts and Forces, ... also an Account of their drunken, lewd Lives, which led them to Excesses of Debauchery and Villainy. To which are added, Letters . . . . on the Trade of the French and English with the Natives . . . . Annual Presents to the Savages. [*etc.*, 6 *lines.*] 8° *pp.* 55. *London*, 1744. 955

LOUISIANA.

Historical Collections of Louisiana, embracing many rare and valuable documents relating to the Natural, civil and political History of that State. compiled with Historical and biographical notes, and an Introduction, by B. F. French, 8° *Six vols. pp.* 300 *to* 360 *each. New York:* 1846 *to* 1869. 956

This collection is remarkable for the immense amount of material relating to the aborigines of America, being almost wholly composed of memoirs and narratives, in the language of the original explorers.

Vol. I. contains, with other historical material, La Salle's memoir of discovery of Mississippi, Joutel's journal of Mississippi, and Hennepin's account of Mississippi.

Vol. II. Marquette and Joliet's voyage to discover the Mississippi, narrative of De Soto's expedition, and Coxe's "Carolana."

Vol. III. La Harpe's journal of establishment of the French in Louisiana, Charlevoix's journal — with biography of; Account of the Southern tribes of Indians; Account of the antiquity of the Natchez Indians; Account of the massacre of the French by the Natchez.

Vol. IV. contains the narratives of the voyages, missions, and travels among the Indians, of Marquette, Joliett, Dablon, Allouez, Le Clercq, La Salle, Hennepin, Membre, and Douay, with biographical and bibliographical notices of these missionaries and their works. By J. G. Shea.

Vol. V. is occupied from pp. 1 to 126 with a translation of Dumont's memoir of transactions with the Indians of Louisiana, from 1712 to 1740.

Vol. VI. contains Penicaut's Annals of Louisiana, and account of the manners, customs, and religion of the Indian tribes. pp. 19 to 175, Laudonniere's History of Jean Ribault's three voyages to Florida (with account of its native inhabitants), pp. 177 to 362.

LOUGHRIDGE (R. M.).

Narcokv Esyvhiketv. Muskogee hymns, collected and revised by Rev. R. M. Loughridge of the Presbyterian Mission and Rev. David Winslett, Intrepreter. Fourth edition, revised and enlarged. By Rev. W. S. Robertson. 24° *pp.* 221. *New York, Mission House* 23 *Centre Street,* 1868. 957

LOWRIE (John C.).

A Manual of the Foreign Missions of the Presbyterian Church in the United States of America. By John C. Lowrie. 8° *pp.* 859. *New York, William Rankin, Jr.,* 23 *Centre Street,* 1868. 958

Chapter II., entitled "Missions among the Indian Tribes," occupies pp. 34 to 55, and is accompanied by a valuable colored map of the localities in the United States, which are occupied by Indian tribes.

LUDEWIG (Herman E.)

The Literature of American Aboriginal Languages. By Herman E. Ludewig. With additions and corrections By Professor Wm. W. Turner. Edited by Nicolas Trübner. 8° *Half title,* 1 *leaf and pp.* xxiv. + 258. *London,* 1858. "*Trübner's Bibliotheca Glottica.*" 959

The learned author of this treatise on the languages of the American Indians, did not live to see his work issue from the press. His memory has been preserved, not only by his refined taste and scholarship exhibited in his works, but the remembrance of his warm and generous nature, and tireless zeal in literature and science. He died in December 1856, when only 156 pages of this volume had been printed. It was completed under the supervision of Dr. Nicholas Trübner of London, and Professor Turner of Washington. It contains notices of treatises on the languages and dialects spoken by 1,030 tribes, or by aboriginal peoples, known under as many names; and as a monument of industry is scarcely excelled.

LUMPKIN (Mr.).

Speech of Mr. Lumpkin of Georgia, on the Indian Territory Bill. Delivered in the Senate of the United States April 30, 1838. 8° *pp.* 7. *Washington*, 1838. 960

LYON (Captain G. F.).

The Private Journal of Captain G. F. Lyon, of H. M. S. Hecla, during the recent Voyage of Discovery under Captain Parry. With a Map and Plates. A New Edition. 8° *pp.* xii. + 468 + *map and 7 plates. London: John Murray*, 1825. 961

Almost the entire volume is devoted to the narration of the peculiarities of the Aborigines of the Arctic regions. Captain Lyon's curiosity led him to observe with great attention, the habits of life, and traits of character of the different tribes of Esquimaux, which his humanity, and good management attracted to his winter quarters. They built their villages near his ships, and permitted a closer familiarity, than any other of the Arctic voyagers was able to attain. His narrative, therefore, abounds with incidents of their intercourse, and curious anecdotes of Esquimaux life.

LYON (Captain G. F.).

A Brief Narrative of an unsuccessful attempt to reach Repulse Bay, through Sir Thomas Rowe's Welcome, in his Majesty's Ship Griper, in the year 1824 by Captain G. F. Lyon, R. N. with a chart and engravings. 8° *pp.* xvi. + 199 + *map and* 6 *plates and diagram. London: John Murray, Albemarle street.* 1825. 962

This is an entirely distinct work from the private journal of Captain Lyon, being in fact his official report. The work contains some material regarding his intercourse with the Esquimaux, not repeated in the Journal; and of the plates, three are illustrative of their sea-craft, burials, and comparative physiognomy,— also used only in this narrative.

LYON (L.).

The Military Journals of two Private Soldiers, 1758–1775, with numerous illustrative notes, to which is added a supplement containing official papers on the skirmishes at Lexington and Concord. 8° *Plate and pp.* 128. *Poughkeepsie*, 1855. 963

The journal of Lemuel Lyon, containing some incidents of the fatal expedition during the French and Indian war of 1758, against Fort Ticonderoga, occupies pages 11 to 45 of this volume. There is but little detail in the meagre diary, but the notes by Mr. Lossing add to it material value.

M'AFEE.

History of the Late War in the Western Country, comprising a full account of all the Transactions in that quarter, from the commencement of hostilities at Tippecanoe, to the termination of the contest at New Orleans on the return of peace. 8° *pp.* viii. + 534 + (ii.). *Lexington, K. published by Worsley & Smith*, 1816. 964

The author of this now scarce work, sought and obtained a large amount of information, regarding the Indian wars of the western frontier, from the actors engaged in them. His narrative, therefore, contains much material, which later histories either do not possess, or only copy from his pages.

MACFIE (Mathew).

Vancouver Island and British Columbia. Their History, Resources, and Prospects. By Mathew Macfie, five years resident in Victoria. 8° *pp.* 574 + 9 *maps and plates. London: Longman,* 1865. 965

"The Indians of Vancouver Island, and British Columbia," is the title and subject of Chapter xvi., pp. 423 to 492, in which many interesting details of the life and customs of the Northwestern Indian are given.

MACKENTOSH (John).

Receipts for the cure of most diseases incident to the Human Family. By the celebrated Indian Doctor, John Mackentosh, of the Cherokee Nation; none of which have ever been communicated to the world. 12° *pp.* 12. *New York,* 1827. 966

MACKENZIE (Alexander).

Voyages from Montreal, on the river St. Laurence, through the Continent of North America, to the Frozen and Pacific Oceans; In the years 1789 and 1793. With a preliminary Account of the Rise, Progress, and Present State of the Fur Trade of that Country. Illustrated with Maps. By Alexander Mackenzie, Esq. 4° *London, printed for T. Cadell,* 1801. 967

Half title, portrait, title, "Dedication," each one leaf; "Preface," pp. viii.; "General History of the Fur Trade," pp. i. to cxxxii.; "Journal of a Voyage," 1 to 412; "Errata," two pages + three large folding maps. Pages cxxix. to cxxxii. are occupied with a vocabulary of the Chepewyan Tongue, and pp. 257 and 258 with a short vocabulary of the Atnah dialect, and another of an unknown tribe, on page 376. Both parts of the work of this intrepid traveller, are filled with accounts of the tribes of Indians, who inhabited the regions traversed by him three quarters of a century ago. No writer upon the subject of Indian customs and peculiarities, has given us a more minute, careful and interesting relation of them, as indeed none were better fitted to do, by long experience among them as a fur trader. His investigations, although pursued at so early a period of Arctic exploration, were remarkable for their accuracy; Sir John Franklin more than once expressing his surprise at being able to corroborate their correctness in his own explorations.

MACKENZIE (Alexander).

Voyages from Montreal, on the River St. Laurence, through the Continent of North America, to the Frozen and Pacific Oceans; in the years 1789 and 1793. With a preliminary account of the Rise, Progress, and Present State of the Fur Trade of that Country. Illustrated with a general Map of the country and a portrait of the Author. By Sir Alexander Mackenzie. 8° *Philadelphia: published by John Morgan.* 1802. 968

Half title, portrait, title, and "Dedication," each one leaf; "Preface," pp. viii.; map, and pp. i. to cxxvi. + 1 to 392.

An American edition of Mackenzie's voyages and fur trade, of which it is a complete, unmutilated copy.

MACKINTOSH (J.).

The Discovery of America, by Christopher Columbus; and the

Origin of the North American Indians. By J. Mackintosh. 8° *pp.* 149. *Toronto*, 1836. 969

[Macomb (Gen.).]

Pontiac: or the Siege of Detroit. A Drama, in three Acts. 12° *pp.* 60. *Boston:* 1835. 970

McBride (James).

Pioneer Biography. Sketches of the Lives of some of the Early Settlers of Butler County, Ohio. By James McBride, of Hamilton. *Large* 8° Vol. I. *pp.* xlv. + 352 *and portrait. Cincinnati: Robert Clarke & Co.*, 1869. 971

The author of this volume adopted a plan for narrating his reminiscences, which has something more than novelty to commend it to our attention. He selected some prominent character among the pioneers, and while sketching a biographical portrait, fills all the spare canvass with those agreeable pictures of border life with which his subject was associated. His biographies are crowded with the most interesting incidents of Indian warfare, and other scenes in aboriginal life. Of the seven persons whose lives are commemorated in this volume, four were Indian fighters, the narration of whose exploits fill the first three hundred pages.

McCall.

The History of Georgia, containing Brief Sketches of the most Remarkable Events, up to the present day. By Capt Hugh McCall. In Two Volumes. Vol. I. *Pref. pp.* viii. + 376. Vol. II. *Pref. pp.* viii. + 424. *Savannah: printed and published by Seymour & Williams*, 1811. 972

Although the title indicates the intention to bring the history down to the date of publication, the narrative is suspended with the declaration of peace in 1783. Both volumes are largely devoted to the history of the border warfare with the Creeks and Cherokees. Numerous incidents relating to the savages of these nations, and their sanguinary attacks upon the frontiers, with sketches of their chiefs, and of the loyalist refugees who led them, are narrated. These were derived in many instances directly from the lips of some of the survivors of these bloody scenes, from manuscripts, or from printed documents, no longer accessible to the student of history.

McCall (General George A.).

Letters from the Frontiers written during a period of thirty years' Service in the army of the United States. By Major General George A. McCall, late commander of the Pennsylvania reserve corps. 12° *pp.* 539. *Philadelphia, J. B. Lippincott & Co.*, 1868. 973

These letters form an exceedingly interesting, and doubtless truthful narrative of the astonishing endurance of the United States troops, and the fortitude and courage of the Indians, during the Seminole war.

McLellan.

The Fall of the Indian, with other Poems. By Isaac McLellan, Jun. 8° *pp.* 99. *Boston*, 1830. 974

McClung (John A.).

Sketches of Western Adventure: containing an Account of the most interesting Incidents connected with the Settlement of the West, from 1755 to 1794: together with an Appendix. By John A. McClung. 12° *pp.* 360. *Philadelphia.* 1832. 975

McClung (John A.).
Sketches of Western Adventure, containing an account of the most Interesting Incidents connected with the Settlement of the West. 12° *pp.* 360. *Cincinnati*, 1851. 976

McClure (A. K.).
Three Thousand Miles through the Rocky Mountains, by A. K. McClure. 12° *pp.* 456 *and Portrait. Philadelphia, J. B. Lippincott & Co.*, 1869. 977

This book is a well written miscellany of personal adventures and incidents. A large portion of it is devoted to details of Indian warfare, which at the period of the author's tour, made every step across the plains and through the mountains, eminently hazardous.

McClure (David) and Parish (Elijah).
Memoirs of the Rev. Eleazer Wheelock, D. D. Founder and President of Dartmouth College and Moor's Charity School; with a Summary History of the College and School. To which are added, copious extracts from Dr. Wheelock's correspondence. Portrait. 8° *pp.* 336. *Newburyport*, 1811. 978

McConkey (Harriet E. Bishop).
Dakota War Whoop: or, Indian Massacres and War in Minnesota, of 1862-3. Revised Edition. 12° *pp.* 429. *St. Paul*, 1864. 979

McConnel (J. L.).
Western Characters, or Types of Border Life in the Western States, by J. L. McConnel, with illustrations by Darley. 12° *pp.* 378 + 6 *plates. Redfield, New York*, 1853. 980

A collection of didactic pieces, having little history of any kind, and none of the aborigines, blended with its great mass of fine writing. It is of course as worthless as a novel, or a poem, for any purpose in which facts are of the slightest consequence.

McCormick (R.).
Indians, Friendly and Unfriendly. Remarks of Hon. Richard C. McCormick of Arizona, delivered in the House of Representatives February 28, and March 2 and 3, 1870. 8° *pp.* 7, *double columns. Washington*, 1870. 981

Mr. McCormick's speech is a document of more interest and value than many more lengthy treatises.

It is the testimony of an intelligent gentleman, who had spent several years near the haunts of the Apaches, and knew personally of the matters of which he spoke. His relations of their atrocities, and the attempts to subdue them, confirm the prevalent belief, that they are the only untamable savages of the continent. The wild and fierce Camanches, as well as the degraded and cowardly Digger Indian tribes, have succumbed to the strong hand of civilized warfare, while the Apache alone defies it. Mr. McCormick enumerates one hundred and fifty-four citizens who had been massacred within four years, out of a population of little more than ten times that number, in Tucson alone.

McCoy (Isaac).
History of Baptist Indian Missions: embracing remarks on the former and present condition of the Aboriginal Tribes; their Settlement within the Indian Territory, and their future pros-

pecta. By Isaac McCoy. [*Motto 4 lines.*] 8° *pp.* (viii.) + 611. *Washington and New York*, 1840. 982

The author resided more than twenty years among the Ottawas, Pottawatamies, and Miamis as a missionary. During this period, he kept a journal of events and incidents of Indian life, which with his letters and reports, formed a great mass of material from which to form his history. It is largely composed of the records of personal experience; but is far from being a mere missionary report of religious progress. It is in fact the work of a highly intelligent man, who recorded with the judgment of a historian, while he labored with the zeal of an ecclesiastic; and the result of his early philosophical observations has been, to give us a very valuable record of the characteristic traits of the Indian tribes he lived among. The first forty pages are occupied with remarks on the origin of the Indian tribes. The awfully rapid destruction of the aboriginal race, by contact with the whites; the murders, the debauchery, and superstition of the Indians, as well as their nobler traits, receive a large share of the author's attention.

M'Coy (Isaac).

The Annual Register of Indian Affairs within the Indian (or Western) Territory. Published by Isaac M'Coy. Shawanoe Baptist Mission House, Indian Territory, May 1837. 8° *Nos.* 1 *to* 4, *each* 85 *to* 91 *pp.* *Shawanoe Baptist Mission*, 1835 *to* 1838. 983

McCoy (Isaac).

Periodical Account of Baptist Mission within the Indian Territory, for the year ending December 31, 1836. 8° *n. d. n. l.* *pp.* 52. 984

McCoy (Isaac).

Remarks on the practicability of Indian Reform embracing their Colonization, by Isaac McCoy. 8° *pp.* 47. *Boston, December*, 1827. 985

McCulloch (James H.).

Researches on America; being an attempt to settle some points relative to the Aborigines of America, &c., by James H. McCulloch. *pp.* 220. *Baltimore:* 1817. 986

McCulloch (J. H.).

Researches, Philosophical and Antiquarian, concerning the Aboriginal History of America. By J. H. McCulloch. 8° *Map, and pp.* 535. *Baltimore:* 1829. 987

The first edition of this work was published without the author's name. It however, as well as the second, was a mere sketch of the design and scope of his later work, which his labor and talent formed into the most complete and valuable essay upon the subject of which it treats. The character of the author's researches may be ascertained from the division titles of his work: Chap. I. "Complexion and physical appearance of the Aborigines." II. "Languages of the American Indians." III. "Social and moral institutions of the Barbarous American tribes." IV. "Of the Natches and other Indians of Florida." V. "Institutions of the Mexican Empire." VI. "Of the Nations inhabiting Guatemala." VIII. "Of the institutions of the Peruvians." X. "Of the Manner in which men and animals reached America." Appendix II. "Of the monuments, mounds, and fortifications of North America." Appendix III. "Of the invasion of Florida by De Soto," with an analysis of the statements concerning his route, and an attempt to trace it, and identify the localities mentioned by the narrators of the expedition, with a map of the route.

McDonald (A.).

A Narrative of some passages in the history of Eenoolooapik, a young Esquimaux, who was brought to Britain in 1839, in the ship Neptune of Aberdeen: an Account of the Discovery of Hogarths Sound: remarks on the Whale Fishery, and suggestions for its improvement, &c. By Alexander McDonald. *Portrait, map, folding letter.* 12° *pp.* iii. + 149. *Edinburgh*, 1841. 988

McDonald (J.).

Biographical Sketches of General Nathaniel Massie, General Duncan McArthur, Captain William Wells, and General Simon Kenton: who were early settlers in the western country. By John McDonald, of Poplar ridge, Ross County, Ohio. 8° *pp.* 267. 14 *plates. Dayton, O.* 1852. 989

This work was first printed at Dayton, Ohio, in 1838. The author had the advantage of personal communication with the families and neighbors of these Indian fighters, and thus secured many details of their exploits among the savages, which would otherwise have been lost. His own experience reaches back to the latter part of the last century.

McGaw (Rev. James F.).

Philip Seymour or Pioneer Life in Richland County, Ohio. Founded on facts. By Rev. James F. McGaw. 8° *pp.* 296. *Mansfield, published by R. Brinkerhoff*, 1858. 990

The author has filled out the skeleton of facts in his possession, from his own imagination, and has not thus improved their value.

McIntosh (John).

The Origin of the North American Indians; with a faithful description of their Manners and Customs, both civil and military; their religions, languages, dress, and ornaments: [*etc.*, 8 *lines*]. *Plates.* 8° *pp.* 345. *New York*, 1853. 991

M'Kenney and Hall.

History of the Indian tribes of North America, with Biographical Sketches and Anecdotes of the Principal Chiefs. Embellished with one hundred and twenty Portraits, from the Indian Gallery in the Department of War, at Washington. By Thomas L. M'Kenney, late of the Indian Department, Washington, and James Hall, Esq. of Cincinnati. *Philadelphia, published by Edward C. Biddle*, 1837. 992

Three volumes, elephant folio. Vol. I. pp. iv. + 206 + Table of Plates and forty-eight plates. Vol. II. pp. 237 + 48 plates. Vol. III. pp. 196 + 24 plates. The last two volumes have each a table of plates numbered with the text. At page 45 commences, "An Essay on the History of the North American Indians by James Hall," which occupies the remainder of the volume.

The work is one of the most costly and important ever published on the American Indians. The plates are accurate portraits of celebrated chiefs, or of characteristic individuals of the race; and are colored with care, to faithfully represent their features and costumes.

M'Kenney (Thomas L.).

Memoirs, Official and Personal; with Sketches of Travels among the Northern and Southern Indians; embracing a War Excursion, and descriptions of scenes along the Western borders. By Thomas L. M'Kenney, late chief of the Bureau of Indian Affairs, author of the History of the Indian Tribes of North America. etc., etc. Two volumes in one, second edition. 8° *pp.* 340 + 136, *and twelve plates. New York: Paine & Burgess,* 1846. 993

McKenney (Thomas L.).

Sketches of a Tour to the Lakes, of the Character and Customs of the Chippeway Indians. And of Incidents connected with the Treaty of Fond du Lac. By Thomas L. McKenney, of the Indian Department, and joint Commissioner with his Excellency Gov. Cass, in negotiating the Treaty. Also, a Vocabulary of the Algic, or Chippeway Language, formed in part, and as far as it goes, upon the basis of one furnished by the Hon. Albert Gallatin. Ornamented with twenty-nine Engravings, of Lake Superior, and other scenery, Indian likenesses, Costumes, &c. 8° 29 *plates, and pp.* 493. *Baltimore: published by Fielding Lucas, junr,* 1827. 994

The author was for many years superintendent of Indian affairs at Washington, and was brought in constant association with the principal men of the nations and tribes which sent representatives to the seat of government. In this tour he formed a more intimate association with the great mass of the Indian population, and was able to present much valuable information regarding it. The vocabulary occupies the last seven pages of the volume.

McKenney (Col. Tho's.).

Documents and Proceedings relating to the formation and progress of a Board in the city of New York for the emigration, preservation and improvement of the Aborigines of America. July 22d, 1829. 8° *pp.* 48. *New York,* 1829. 995

The half title announces the tract as *Proceedings of the Indian Board in the City of New York, with Colonel McKenney's Address.*

McLean (John).

Notes of a Twenty-five Years' service in the Hudsons Bay Territory. By John McLean. In Two Volumes. 12° Vol. I. *pp.* 308. Vol. II. *pp.* 328. *London: Richard Bentley,* 1842. 996

Much the largest portion of these volumes, is devoted to the narration of incidents of travel among the Indians of the territory; descriptions of the life, habits, and character of the different tribes inhabiting it, and the relations of the Hudson's Bay Company to them. All of the statements of the author confirm the most authentic accounts of others, and some of them have the novelty which the experience of a quarter of a century must afford to an author. The last volume terminates with a vocabulary of Indian dialects, occupying the last six pages. Besides the relation of personal adventures among the Indians, the author has narrated the circumstances connected with some of those appalling massacres, by which the employees of the Hudson's Bay Co., at several of their lone posts, have been swept off.

He believes in the American origin of syphilis, but without offering much argument that will convince others. One statement, for the truth of which he is sufficient authority, is very interesting to ethnologists, — that he could make himself sufficiently understood, for business purposes, to all the tribes from Labrador, to Columbia on the Pacific, by speaking the Abenaquis dialect.

McMasters (Guy H.).
History of the Settlement of Steuben County, N. Y. Including notices of the old Pioneer Settlers and their Adventures. By Guy H. McMasters. 12° *pp.* 302. *Bath:* 1853. 997

McVicar (Archibald).
See Lewis & Clarke. 2 vols. Harpers' Edition. 998

Magalhanes de Gondaro (Peru de).
Histoire de la Province de Sancta-Cruz que nous nommons ordinairement Le Bresil par Pero de Magalhanes de Gonduro. *Lisbonne, A. Gonsalvez,* 1576. 8° *pp.* 162. *Paris,* 1837. 999

[History of the Province of Santa Cruz, ordinarily called Brazil, by Pedro de Magalhanes de Gondaro].

The author of this history passed a number of years in Brazil, returned to his own country, established a school near Douro, and wrote this history, which was first published in 1572. These principal events in his life, established sufficiently his ability to perform well the task, the results of which he offers us. His work would, however, have received but little if any of our attention, if he was not the only narrator of the characteristics of the Indians of Brazil at the early day of his narrative. The Portuguese have always been cold to the influence of literature, and their explorers and warriors have accordingly left few records of their experience and adventures. Chapters x. to xiii., pp. 108 to 153, are devoted to descriptions of the manners, customs, wars, treatment of prisoners by the Indians, and accounts of the missions among them.

Maillard (Abbe).
Grammar of the Mikmaque Language of Nova Scotia, edited from the manuscripts of the Abbe Maillard, by the Rev. Joseph M. Bellenger. *Large* 8° *pp.* 101. *Cramoisy Press, New York,* 1864. 1000

Abbe Maillard's work forms No. 9 of Shea's *American Linguistics.* It should have two titles, one of which is in French. The tribe of Mikmaks occupied formerly all the peninsula of Nova Scotia and New Brunswick, and part of Maine. Scattered fragments of the tribe are still to be found in the great woods, or near the salmon rivers of the English colonies.

Ma-ka-tai-me-she-kia-kiak,
Or Black Hawk, and Scenes in the West, a national poem, in six cantos, embracing an account of the life and exploits of this celebrated chieftain, the Black Hawk War [*etc.,* 7 *lines*], by a Western tourist. 12° *New York,* 1848. 1001

Two hundred and ninety-nine pages of verse, without a single note of prose.

Manheim (Frederick).
Affecting History of the dreadful distresses of Frederick Manheim's family. To which are added, the Sufferings of John Corbly's family. An encounter between a White Man and two savages. Extraordinary bravery of a Woman. Adventures of Capt. Isaac Stewart. Deposition of Massey Herbeson. Adventures and Sufferings of Peter Wilkinson. Remarkable Adventures of Jackson Johonnot. Account of the destruction of the Settlement at Wyoming. 8° *pp.* 48 *and plate. Philadelphia, printed (for Mathew Carey) by D. Humphreys,* 1794. 1002

Mante (Thomas).

The History of the Late War in North America, and the islands of the West Indies, including the Campaigns of MDCCLXIII and MDCCLXIV, against His Majesty's Indian enemies. By Thomas Mante, Assistant Engineer during the Siege of the Havana, and Major of a brigade in the Campaign of 1764. 4° *pp.* 542, *and* (18) *maps and plans. London: printed for W. Strahan; and T. Cadell in the Strand.* 1772. 1003

Mante's association with the frontier war between the American colonists and the Canadian French and Indians, did not commence until 1764, the last year of hostilities with these allies. He seems, however, to have made good use of his opportunities to gain information. He describes with great detail the campaigns of Washington and Braddock, of Generals Abercrombie and Amherst, and of Colonels Bradstreet and Bouquet. The last chapter gives the principal incidents of Pontiac's war. The eighteen large folding maps and plans which should accompany the text, are often missing.

Marcoy (Paul).

Voyage a Travers L'Amerique du Sud de l'Ocean Pacifique a l'Ocean Atlantique par Paul Marcoy illustre de 626 Vues, Types et Paysages par E. Riou et accompagne de 20 Cartes gravees sur les dessins de l'-auteur Tome Premier Islay. Arequipa — Acopia — Cusco — Echara — Chulituqui — Tunkini — Sarayacu Tome Deuxieme Terra Blanca — Nauta — Taratinga. — Santa-Maria De Belem de Para. *Two Vols.* 4° Vol. I. *pp.* 701. Vol. II. *pp.* 509. *Paris Librairie de L. Hatchette et Cie*, 1869. 1004

It is difficult to speak of this splendid work in such terms as its excellence deserves, without seeming to be extravagant in laudation. The author has brought the art of photography to aid for the first time, in illustrating a work principally treating of the aborigines of America. Much more than half of the plates, so beautifully executed as we find them in these volumes, are illustrative of phases in the common life of the Indians of South America, of scenes in their warfare, or barbarous rites; or of physiognomical peculiarities of the different tribes; exhibited by portraits of representative individuals. Nothing effected by engraving has been published, since the days of the brothers De Bry, so elaborate, so rich, and so perfect in drawing, scenery, costume, and anatomical correctness. The greatest difference we perceive is in the marks of that advance of art, in more faithful portraying nature according to nature, instead of attempting it by blind adherence to the rules of art. The savages in these pictures are not endowed with the noble features of the Greek deities.

Marcy (William L.).

A Traditional Account of the Life of Tammany, an Indian Chief, famed for his friendship toward the Whites, and for his virtues as a man. By William L. Marcy. 8° *pp.* 20. *Providence, from the Phenix Press*, 1810. 1005

This is an essay written in such grave historic strain, as to be often taken for veritable biography. It is, however, nothing but pure fiction, and not even original at that. Mr. Marcy levied upon Dr. Samuel Mitchell for the material to construct his essay, and carried it away bodily. Dr. Mitchell wrote and printed an account of Tammany several years before. Mr. Marcy's oration and life of Tammany were first printed at Troy, N. Y.

MARCY (Randolph B.).

Exploration of the Red River of Louisiana, in the Year 1852, by Randolph B. Marcy, Captain fifth infantry, U. S. Army; assisted by George B. McClellan, Brevet Captain U. S. Engineers. With Reports on the natural history of the Country, and numerous illustrations. 8° *pp.* 286 + 66 *plates. Washington,* 1854. 1006

Captain Marcy's report affords the reader some authentic information regarding the peculiar customs of the Indians of the southern plains. Their mode of warfare, their invariable violation of the chastity of female prisoners, and the construction of their dwellings and villages, are more particularly described in Chapters viii. and x. The Appendix contains a comparative vocabulary of the Comanches and Wichitas, of five pages; and one of the plates is a view of a Wichita village.

MARCY (Colonel R. B.).

Thirty Years of Army Life on the Border. Comprising descriptions of the Indian Nomads of the Plains; explorations of new territory; a trip across the Rocky Mountains in the Winter; descriptions of the habits of different animals found in the West, and the methods of hunting them; with Incidents in the life of different frontier men, &c., &c., By Colonel R. B. Marcy. With Numerous Illustrations. 8° *pp.* 442 + 13 *plates. New York: Harper & Brothers, publishers,* 1866. 1007

Colonel Marcy's volume is the result of a lifetime of frontier experience, during which period almost everything which he describes has changed or passed away, except the natural features of the country. No writer has had more intimate communication with the warlike tribes of the plains, and his official relation gives authenticity to his statements. One of the most interesting portions of his work is the narration of the subjection of one of the fierce tribes of the Comanches, numbering more than eight thousand, and of the selection, after long explorations, of a beautiful valley, thirty miles long, by more than half that breadth, for their settlement. Here, expatriated from their native plains and imprisoned by high mountains, beyond which they could not stray without danger of being declared at war with the government, they were deported. Even here the cupidity of the whites could not give them peace. The Texan hordes of banditti coveted the fertile valley, and murdered or drove away its occupants.

MARKHAM (C. R.).

Cuzco: A Journey to the Ancient Capital of Peru; with an Account of the History, Language, Literature, and Antiquities of the Incas. And Lima: a visit to the capital and provinces of modern Peru; with a sketch of the viceregal government, history of the Republic, and a review of the literature and society of Peru. With Illustrations and a Map. By Clements R. Markham. 12° *pp.* iv. + 419 + 8 *plates and map. London: Chapman & Hall,* 1856. 1008

The first moiety of the title well expresses the scope of a greater part of the book. It is principally devoted to a study of the physical and mental works of the ancient rulers of Peru, the wonderful race of the Incas. Few persons have, in later years, been better fitted for this task than Mr. Markham. His familiarity with the Quichua language has been more lately exhibited, in the production of a treatise on that language. In the present work he gives translations of the poems and dramas, composed by the Indians, with a grammatical analysis and vocabulary of their language.

MARKHAM (Clements R.).

Contributions towards a Grammar and Dictionary of Quichua, The Language of the Yncas of Peru. Collected by Clements R. Markham. 8° *pp.* 223. *London*, 1864. 1009

Pages 1 to 61, are occupied with a Grammar, and pages 63 to 193, with a Dictionary of Quichua, Spanish, and English, while the remainder of the book is devoted to a Dictionary of Quichua and English alone. The learned author was secretary to the French Royal Society of Geography, and composed his work during a long residence in Peru.

MARKHAM (C. R.).

Travels in Peru and India, while superintending the collection of Chinchona plants and seeds in South America, and their introduction into India. By Clements R. Markham. With Maps and Illustrations. 8° *pp.* xviii. + 572 + 2 *maps* + 16 *plates*. *London*: 1862. 1010

Mr. Markham did not exhaust the subject of the Incas, in his first work, *Cusco & Lima.* In this he devotes Chapters vii. to x., pp. 108 to 180, to "The Aymara Indians, their antiquities, their condition, Narrative of the Insurrection of the last of the Incas in 1780." Chapters xii. to xiv., pp. 199 to 240, are filled with a "Description of The Province of Caravaya, its Aboriginal Inhabitants, their cultivation and use of the Coca," etc. The wonderful story of Tupac Amaru, the last of the Incas, his insurrection, defeat, and horrible execution, are nowhere related at length as in Mr. Markham's volume.

MARKHAM (C. R.).

Ollanta. An ancient Ynca drama. Translated from the original Quichua. By Clements R. Markham. 12° *Title* + *pp.* 128. *London: Trübner & Co.*, 1871. 1011

This remnant of the literature of the Incas, was preserved until about 1770, by the quipus, or knotted calendar; when Dr. Valdez, who had often witnessed the representation of the drama by Indian actors, before the ill-fated Inca, Tupac Amaru, reduced it to writing. From this copy, written by the Cura in pure Quichua, Mr. Markham has translated this English version. Its great antiquity is authenticated, not so much by the existence of several copies in MS. as by the conformity of wide-spread traditions, and the entire absence of every Spanish word. There is not the slightest trace of ideas, derived from civilization or Christianity. It has received the sanction of such scholars as Drs. Riviero, Tschudi, and Barranca, who were convinced that it was composed long before the Conquest of Peru by Pizarro.

MARMONTEL (M.).

Les Incas ou La Destruction De L'Empire du Perou, Par M. Marmontel, Historiographe de France, l'un des Quarante de l' Academie Francoise. 8° *Two vols. in one.* Vol. I. *pp.* xxviii. + 207. Vol. II. *pp.* 260. *Paris*, 1777. 1012

MARTYR PETER.

The | Historie Of | The West-*Indies*, | Containing the Actes and Aduentures | *of the Spaniards, which haue conquered* | and peopled those Countries, Inriched with var | ietie of pleasant relation of the Manners, | Ceremonies, Lawes, Gouernments, | and Warres of the | Indians. | Published in Latin by Mr. *Hakluyt*, | and translated into English by M. *Lok.* Gent. | In the hands of the Lord are all the corners of | the earth. Psal. 95.

| *Small* 4° *London,* | *printed for Andrew Hebb, and are to be sold at the signe* | *of the Bell in Pauls Church-yard.* [1597.] 1013

Collation: Title, 1 leaf, reverse blank + To the Reader, 2 leaves signed M. Lok + folios 318, numbered on the recto.

There is not a little discrepancy in the views of bibliographers, regarding the issue of this edition. White Kennett makes it the first of the complete English editions, placing it under the date of 1597. What authority he had for his conclusion, is not even guessed at by the authorities of the present day. Mr. Sabin simply quotes Mr. Rich's note, to the edition of 1612: "Some copies are without date." Ternaux and Stevens do not notice it. It would seem from this negative testimony, to have been even rarer than the editions of 1612 and 1628. The name of the author of this work, was Pietro Martir, of Anghiera, in Milan, a name which he latinized into Angleria. There is no more warrant for styling him Anglerius than Milanoise. He is recognized by all Spanish writers by his patronymic, anglicized to Peter Martyr.

He was an Italian scholar of a noble family of Milan, born 1455, and died at Granada in Spain, 1526. He possessed eminent ability and learning, and is believed to be the first writer who noticed in his works the discovery of America by his countryman Columbus; as he is the first who published a treatise descriptive of the peculiarities of the natives of the New World, the first decade having been printed in 1504, and the first three decades in 1516. It was not until 1530, that the complete work in eight decades was printed. Eden translated the first edition of three decades, and printed it with some matters copied from Oviedo and other authors, in 1555. Willes followed his example, and produced the three decades with part of the fourth, and some additional material drawn from several historians. The first complete English edition was printed in 1597.

Martyr accompanied the Count Tendilla to Spain, in 1487, and was ordained a priest two years after the discovery of America. He was in such high esteem, that he was appointed tutor to their children, by Ferdinand and Isabella. He was sent in 1501, on a diplomatic mission to Egypt, of which he gives a relation in one of his works, entitled *Delegatione Babylonica.* Pope Leo X. appointed him Prothonotaire Apostolique, and in 1505 he was made Dean of the Chapter of Granada Cathedral. In this city he died in 1525 or 1526. He was the contemporary and friend of the great navigators, discoverers and conquerors, — Columbus, Vasco de Gama, Cortes, Magellan, Cabot, and Vespucius. Beside the great advantage thus acquired, his official position as member of the council for the Indies, afforded him the inspection of documents of undoubted authenticity. His work therefore, composed from sources of such importance, and with such aids, has always been placed in the highest rank of authorities, on the history of the first association of the Indians with Europeans. Munoz qualifies these encomiums, and criticises severely Martyr's want of order, and neglect to consult original documents. Perfect copies of either of the English translations, as well as of the first edition in Latin, are rare. A copy of the edition of 1597 has been recently sold in New York for seventy-five dollars.

MARTYR PETER.

De Nouo Orbe, | or | the Historie of | the West Indies, Contayning the actes | and aduentures of the Spanyardes which haue | conquered and peopled those Countries | Inriched with varietie of pleasant re | lation of the Manners, Ceremonies, | Lawes, Gouernments, and | Warres of the Indians. | Comprised in eight Decades. | Written by Peter Martyr a Millanoise of Angleria, Cheife | Secretary to the Emperour Charles the fift, | and of his Priuie Councell. | Whereof three haue beene formerly translated in | to English, by R. Eden, Whereunto the other | fiue, are newly added by the Industrie, and | painefull Trauaile of M. Lok, Gent. | [*Motto 2 lines.*] *Small* 4° *London.* | *Printed for Thomas Adams.* | 1612. | 1014

Collation: Title, one leaf, reverse blank + "Epistola Dedicatoria" in Latin, two leaves. Signed Michael Lok, the first page indorsed as Signature A. 3 + To the Reader, two leaves indorsed as Signatures B and B 2. Total preliminary pp. 10.

It will be seen that this edition possesses double the preliminary pages of either the preceding or succeeding titles. This would give some color to the hypothesis, that the edition of 1612 was the first complete English one; as the omission of the "Epistola Dedicatoria" from them both would seem to have been an after-thought. Yet there is nothing less certain than a deduction drawn from common sense, in analyzing the motives of an English publisher, two centuries ago. The text of the three editions, and the address "To the Reader," are in every particular identical.

Martyr (Peter).

The | famous | Historie of | the Indies: | Declaring the aduentures of | the Spaniards, which haue conque | red these Countries, with varietie of Relations | of the Religions, Lawes, Gouernments, Manners | Ceremonies, Customes, Rites, Warres | and Funerals of the People. | Comprised into Sundry Decads. | Set forth first by M^r. Hakluyt, and now pub | lished by L. M. Gent. | The Second Edition. | *London: Printed for Michael Sparke dwelling at the Signe | of the blue Bible in Green Arbor.* 4° *3 preliminary leaves + text 318 folios*, 1628. |. 1015

Marrant (John).

An interesting Narrative, of the life of John Marrant, (A man of Color.) Containing an account of his birth, extraordinary conversion, and remarkable success among the Cherokee Indians, his arrival in England, and departure as a Missionary to America. Compiled originally By the Rev. J. Aldridge, Late Minister of Jewry-Street Meeting, London. A new edition — 12° pp. 27. *Printed cover and extra title. Brighton: published and sold by T. Sharp, (etc.)* 1813. 1016

An edition was printed in 1810 at Leeds, in octavo, with the title, *A Narrative of the Life of John Marrant, of New York in North America, giving an account of his conversion when only 14 years of age, and being at last taken by an Indian Hunter among the Cherokees, and condemned to die. With an account of his conversion of the king of the Cherokees, and his daughter, etc.*

This book is the relation of a religious enthusiast, or of an impostor, the two characters, unhappily for our trust in humanity, exhibiting sometimes remarkably similar traits. Although the pamphlet has little or no value, except what its rarity bestows, it has arrived at the distinction of being printed in two editions; but the bibliopole has learned little of books who has not discovered that this is no insignia of merit.

Marshall (Chief Justice).

Opinion of the Supreme Court of the United States, at January term, 1832, delivered by Mr. Chief Justice Marshall, together with the opinion of Mr. Justice McLean, in the Case of Samuel C. Worcester versus The State of Georgia. 8° *Washington*, 1832. 1017

In this case of the Cherokee Indians against Georgia, the whole history of Indian treaties with the United States is reviewed.

MARSHALL (H.).

The History of Kentucky. Exhibiting an account of the modern discovery; settlement; progressive improvement; civil and military transactions; and the present state of the country. In Two Volumes. By H. Marshall. 8° *Frankfort: Geo. S. Robinson, printer.* 1824. 1018

Vol. I.: Preface and Introduction, pp. viii. "Rafinesque Ancient Annals of Kentucky," 10 to 47. "The History of Kentucky," 1 to 465. Appendix, 6. Vol. II.: pp. v. + 1 to 524. Rafinesque's tract is an essay towards the aboriginal history of Kentucky, with an account of the antiquities and native tribes found in it. Marshall's history is very largely composed of minute relations of the border wars, and the massacres by the Indians.

MARSHALL (Orsamus H.).

The Niagara Frontier: embracing Sketches of its early history, and Indian, French and English Local Names. Read before the Buffalo Historical Club, Feb. 27, 1865, By Orsamus H. Marshall. Printed for private circulation. 8° *pp.* 46. (*Buffalo,* 1865.) 1019

MASSACHUSETTS.

Collections of the Massachusetts Historical Society. 1020

Four series of ten volumes each, and the fourth series of eight. Boston, 1792 to 1871. 8° Generally more than 300 pages. Almost every volume of the first three series is nearly filled with material illustrating the aboriginal history of the country. Not only were very rare works of that class reprinted, but original treatises and MSS. of the most valuable character were published, and very precious documents, like Gookins' *Historical Collections of the Indians of N. E.*, and Niles' *History of the Indian Wars of N. E.*, were for the first time made accessible to the public. It is to be regretted that the later volumes have assumed more the character of state documents. The first series of ten volumes contains fifty-two treatises on Indian history, languages, or origin; including Roger Williams' *Key into the Languages of N. E.*, 35 pages; Gookins, *His Collection of Indians*, 141 pages, etc. The second series has fifteen tracts on the same subjects, including Edwards' *Observations on the Mohegan Language, with Duponceau's Notes*, Winslow's *Account of the Religion, Manners, and Customs of the Indians of N. E.* But it is in the third series that these collections excel in the number and value of their essays and histories of the aborigines. Sixty-one tracts, illustrating almost every feature of their character and history, are either reproduced, or for the first time brought to light in these volumes. Seven of the eleven reports, to the "Corporation for the Propagation of the Gospel among the Indians," commonly known as the *Eliot Tracts*, are reprinted in this series. Captain John Underhill's *History of the Pequot War*; Vincent's *Relation of the Battell with the Pequods*; Waymouth's *Voyage to Va.* in 1605; Levett's *Voyage to N. E.* in 1623; Lion Gardiner's *Relation of the Pequod War*; Cotton's *Vocabulary of Indian Language*; *Account of Hugh Gibson's Captivity*; Niles' *History of the French and Indian Wars in New England*, of which the first part was printed in Vol. VI. of the third series, pp. 154 to 279, was completed in Vol. V. of the fourth series, pp. 309 to 589.

MASON (John).

A Brief History of the Pequot War, written by Major John Mason, A Principal Actor therein. With an Introduction, and Some Explanatory Notes, by the Reverend Mr. Thomas Prince. 8° *New York, Reprinted by J. Sabin & Sons*, 1869. 1021

Title, half title, and title of Edition of 1736, with a half title of do., each one page, and reverse blank; Introduction pp. 1 to vi. "Address" pp. 1 to ix. "Brief His." pp. 1 to 20.

The second title is a copy of the original edition: "A Brief History of the Pequot War: Especially of the memorable Taking of their Fort at Mistick, in Connecticut. Written by Major John Mason, A principal Actor therein, as their chief Captain, and Commander of Connecticut Forces. With an Introduction, &c., &c. Boston: Printed & sold by S. Kneeland and T. Green, in Queen-street, 1736." *Small 8°.*

MATHER (Increase).

A brief | History | of the | War | with the | Indians | in | New-England. | From June 24. 1675. (when the first Englishman was Murder | ed by the Indians) to August 12. 1676. when Philip, | alias Metacomet, the principal Author and | Beginner of the War, was slain. | Wherein the Grounds, Beginning, and Progress of the War, is summarily | expressed. Together with a serious Exhortation to the | Inhabitants of that Land. | By Increase Mather, Teacher of a Church of | Christ, in Boston in New-England. [*Mottoes 7 lines*]. *London, Printed for Richard Chiswell, at the Rose and Crown in St. Pauls | Church-yard, according to the Original Copy Printed in New-England.* 1676. 1029

Small 4° Half title, the "Wars of New England," reverse blank; full title, reverse "Licence," "To the Reader," 4 unnumbered pages; "A Brief History of the War with the Indians of New-England," pp. 1 to 51; reverse of last page blank; "Postscript," pp. 1 to 8.

This work, printed in London in 1676, as will be seen by the title, covers a period of but little more than a year. An edition was printed in Boston nearly simultaneously; but the reverend author, not entirely free from an author's vanity, in the next year hurried through the press another work, entitled, *A Relation of the Troubles which have hap'ned in New-England by reason of the Indians there. From the year* 1614 *to the year* 1675. He was stimulated to this literary labor by the knowledge that his reverend brother, Wm. Hubbard, was engaged upon the same work. Indeed, the two treatises were probably almost simultaneously passing through the press of John Foster. In his preface, Mather exhibits a little trace of acerbity, when he asserts, "This following relation was written neer upon a year ago; since which a reverend author hath emitted a narrative of the troubles which happened by the Indians: * * nevertheless * * most of the things here insisted on, are not so much as once taken notice of in that narrative." Both of Mather's histories of Indian wars, are exceedingly rare. They have been reprinted by Mr. Drake. The present one is included in his work entitled, *History of King Philip's War.* The second Mr. Drake reprinted with the title, *Early History of New England.*

MATHER (Cotton).

The | Life and Death | Of the Reverend | Mr. John Eliot, | Who was the | First Preacher | of the | Gospel | to the | Indians in America. | With an Account of the Wonderful Success | which the Gospel has had amongst the Heathen | in that Part of the World: And of the many | strange Customs of the Pagan Indians, | In New-England. | Written by Cotton Mather. | The Third Edition carefully Corrected. | 18° *pp.* viii. + 168 + *Advertisements* (iv.). *London: | Printed for John Dunton, at the Raven in | the Poultry.* MDCXCIV. 1023

MATHER (Cotton).

De | Successu Evangelii | Apud | Indios | Occidentales, | In

Nova-Anglia; | Epistola. | Ad Cl. Virum | D. Johannem Leusdenum | Linguae Sanctae in Ultrajectina Acade | mia Professorem, Scripta, | A Cresentio Mathero | Apud Bostonienses V. D. M. nec non Collegii | Harvardini quod est Cantabrigia Nov-An | glorum, Rectore. | Londini, Typis J. G. 1688 | Jam recusa & Successu Evangelii apud In | dos Orientales aucta. | 24° pp. 16. *Ultrajecti, | apud Wilhelmum Broedeleth.* | *Anno* 1699. 1024

[Of the Success of the Gospel among the American Indians, in New England.] This is the third edition, having been printed in London in 1688, and at the same place as this in 1697. Copies of either edition are not easy to procure, but that of 1696 is rarer than the others.

MATHER (Cotton).

Magnalia Christi Americana: | or, the | Ecclesiastical History | of | New-England, | from | Its First Planting in the Year 1620 unto the Year | of our Lord. 1698. | In Seven Books. | I. Antiquities: In Seven Chapters. With an Appendix. | [*Titles of Books II to VI. 15 lines.*] *VII. The Wars of the Lord.* Being an History of the Manifold Afflictions and | Disturbances of the Churches in *New England,* from their Various Adversa- | ries, and the Wonderful Methods and Mercies of God in their Deliverance: | In Six Chapters: To which is subjoined, An Appendix of Remarkable | Occurrences which *New England* had in the Wars with the *Indian* Salvages, | from the Year 1688, to the Year 1698. | By the Reverened and Learned Cotton Mather, M. A. | And Pastor of the North Church in *Boston, New-England. London: Printed for Thomas Parkhurst, at the Bible and Three Crowns in Cheapside.* MDCCII. 1025

Folio. Title 1 leaf (full page title to each book). 14 prel. leaves unnumbered. Book I. pp. 38. Book II. pp. 75. Book III. pp. 238. Book IV. pp. 124, 222 Book V. pp. 100. Book VI. pp. 88. Book VII. pp. 118. Advertisement 2 leaves. Map. Book VIII. pp. 60 to 95, are occupied with Mather's "Remarkables of a Long War with Indian Salvages," among which are narratives of massacres of whites by Indians, aided by the devil, and massacres of the Indians by the whites aided by the Lord.

Of captivities of whites among the Indians, and of their restoration to liberty; but no account of the release of the wretched Pequods and Wampanoags, sold into slavery in the West Indies. Even at this early day, the *dilettanti* notion of large paper editions, was in fashion. In the *Post Angel,* a periodical published in London in 1701, we find a notice of Mather's forthcoming history, in these words: "I had the Happiness to be acquainted with Mr. Mather, and have heard him preach many Excellent Sermons, in New England; being once in his Company, he shewed me his Library and I do think he has one of the best (for a Private Library) that I ever saw. . . To Encourage Subscribers to this Great and Useful Work, he that brings the first payment for Six Books, is promised a Seventh Gratis, in *Larger* or *Smaller Paper.*" The "Magnalia" was therefore printed in two sizes, of which the larger brings $100 to $150, being much the rarer form of a book by no means common in either.

MATHER (Cotton).

Duodecennium Luctuosum. | The History of a Long | WAR | with Indian Salvages, | And their Directors and Abettors; | From the Year 1702. To the Year, 1714. | Comprised in A | Short Essay, to declare the Voice of the | Glorious God, in the

Various Occurrences | of that War, which have been thought Mat | ters of more Special Observation. | A Recapitulation made in the Audience, | of his Excellency the Governour. | and the General Assembly of the | Massachusett Province; At Boston, | 30. d. vii. m. 1714. | [*Motto, 2 lines.*] 24° *Title,* 1 *leaf* + *pp.* 80. *Boston: Printed by B. Green, for Samuel Gerrish,* | *at his Shop on the North-side of the T. House.* 1714. 1026

MATHER (Rev. Cotton).

| India Christiana | A Discourse | Delivered unto the Commissioners | for the Propagation of the Gospel among | the American Indians | which is | Accompanied with Several Instru | ments relating to the Glorious | Design of Propagating our Holy | Religion, in the Eastern | as well as the Western Indies | An Entertainment which they that are | Waiting for the Kingdom of God | will receive as Good News | from a far Country. | By Cotton Mather D. D. | and F. R. S. | 12° *pp.* 2 + 11 + 94 + *Corrigenda,* 1 *leaf.* *Boston in New England* | *Printed by B. Green,* 1721. 1027

The other works of the Mathers relating to the Indians are: —

1. *Masukkenukeeg,* etc., being (Five Sermons of Increase Mather, translated into the Indian Language of Mass. by Samuel Danforth.) 16° Boston, 1698.
2. *Soldiers Counselled and Comforted. A Discourse by Increase Mather, unto Some part of the Forces, Engaged in the Just War of New England, against the Northern and Eastern Indians.* Sept. 1, 1689. 16° Boston, 1689. By the Massachusetts Historical Society Catalogue, this is attributed to Cotton Mather.
3. *A Letter about the Present State of Christianity, among the Christianized Indians of New England; written to Sir William Ashhurst, by Cotton Mather.* 16° pp. 15. Boston, 1705.
4. *Just Commemorations. The Death of Good Men considered; with a Brief Account of the Evangelical Work, among the Christianized Indians of N. E., by Cotton Mather.* 8° pp. 58. Boston, 1715.
5. *History of Remarkable Occurrences in the long War with the Indian Savages, by C. Mather.* 18° Boston, 1699.
6. *Wussukwhonk, en Christianeue, asuh peantam wae Indianog.* 8° Mushauwomuk, 1706, by C. Mather.
7. *To the Christian Indians. Giving them A short Account, of what the English Desire them to Know, and to Do, in order to their Happiness. Written by an English Minister,* (C. Mather,) *at the Desire of an English Magistrate, who sends unto them this Token of Love.* Boston, 1700. 16° pp. 28. Indian Title on reverse of first leaf.

MATHER (Cotton).

The Life of the Rev. John Eliot, the First Missionary to the Indians in North-America. By Cotton Mather, a new edition. 18° *pp.* 112. *London, printed and sold by D. Jacques, &c.,* 1820 1028

[MATHER (Samuel).]

An Attempt to Shew, That America must be Known to the Ancients; Made at the Request, and to gratify the Curiosity, of An Inquisitive Gentleman: to which is added An Appendix, Concerning the American Colonies, and some modern managements against them. By an American Englishman. Pastor of a Church in Boston, New England. [*Motto 8 lines*]. 8° *Half title, reverse "To the Gentleman," title, reverse blank and pp. 5 to 35. Boston New England: printed by J. Kneeland, in Milk Street, for T. Leverett and H. Knox in Cornhill.* 1773. 1029

MATHER.

The History of King Philip's War, by the Rev. Increase Mather; also a History of the same War, By the Rev. Cotton Mather. 1030

See Drake.

MATHEWS (Cornelius).

Behemoth, a Legend of the Mound Builders. By Cornelius Mathews, 12° *pp.* vi. + 192. *New York:* 1843. 1031

[MATHEWS (Cornelius).]

The Indian Fairy Book. From the original legends. With illustrations by John McLenan, engraved by V. S. Anthony. 12° *pp.* 338. *New York, published by Mason Brothers,* 1856. 1032

MAUN-GWU-DAUS.

An Account of the North American Indians, written for Maun-gwu-daus, A Chief of the Ojibway Indians, Who has been travelling in England, France, Belgium, Ireland, and Scotland. [*etc.*, 10 *lines*]. 8° *pp.* 24. *Leicester:* 1848. 1033

MAW (Henry Lister).

Journal of a passage from the Pacific to the Atlantic, crossing the Andes in the Northern Provinces of Peru, and descending the River Maranon, or Amazon. By Henry Lister Maw. 8° *Map and pp.* xv. + 485. *London: John Murray,* 1829. 1034

The author was very assiduous in collecting facts relating to the condition, history, and character of the Indians of Peru and Brazil, particularly of the unexplored districts, in the valley of the Maranon. He studied them with the zeal of a scholar, and the analysis of an ethnologist, and although his opportunities were comparatively narrow, and his tour very rapid, he gleaned with great industry. He copies, in pp. 463 to 563, from the *Mercurio Peruano*, the report of the re-establishment of the missions among the savage tribes of Manoa, where fifteen missionaries had been murdered a few years before. At pages 474 to 477, is given the official report of the discovery and exploration of a valley, hitherto unapproached by the whites, and in which resided a tribe of Indians, whose unappeasable hostility had heretofore utterly forbidden intercourse with them.

MAXIMILLIAN (Prince).

Travels in Brazil, in the years 1815, 1816, 1817. By Prince Maximillian, of Wied-Neuwied. Illustrated with Plates. 4° *pp.* x. + 335 + *portrait, map, and 6 plates. London: printed for Henry Colburn & Co.,* 1820. 1035

The work is largely devoted to Indian affairs. The royal author is the same who subsequently exhibited his zeal for explorations among the savage races of America, by publishing the princely volumes of *Travels in the Interior of N. A.* in 1832 and 1833. The attention of the author was, in both tours, drawn primarily to the aborigines, though not so distinctly, in his travels in Brazil, as subsequently in North America. The greater shyness of the wild natives of South America, the impenetrable forests through which they roam, and their indisposition to gather in large communities, offer almost insuperable obstacles to intimate association with them. The plates are principally illustrative of the habits and appearance of the Indian tribes he encountered.

MAXIMILLIAN (Prince).

Travels in the Interior of North America. By Maximillian prince of Weid. With numerous engravings on wood, and a large map. Translated from the German, by H. Evans Loyd. To accompany the original series of eighty-one elaborately colored plates, size, Imperial folio. 1 Vol. 4° 10 *prel. pp.* + 520, *and* 1 Vol. *folio, of plates. London, Ackerman & Co.*, 1843. Two volumes *of text in German.* 4° 1837. 1036

The quarto volume is the text of one of the most beautiful and costly of works, having the American Indians for their subject. The wiseacre who gave it an English dress, takes credit to himself in his preface, for omitting the very extensive vocabularies found in the German edition, occupying nearly one quarter of volume second, or pp. 455 to 560. The volume of plates contains eighty-one vignettes and full-page colored engravings of the most perfect drawing, and beautiful execution. Forty-nine of these are illustrative of some phase in Indian life and character. Two English editions of these plates have been issued, the last, so much inferior to the other as to be unworthy of comparison, was published by Mr. Bohn to meet a continued demand for the work. The first edition brings a large price, usually 100 to 125 dollars.

MAYER (Brantz).

Observations on Mexican History and Archaeology, with a special notice of Zapotec Remains, as delineated in Mr. J. G. Sawkins's drawings of Mitla, etc. By Brantz Mayer. 4° *pp.* 33 + 4 *full page plates. Washington City. Published by the Smithsonian Institution. December*, 1856. *New York, G. P. Putnam & Co.* 1037

MAYER (Brantz).

Mexico, Aztec, Spanish and Republican: A Historical, Geographical, Political, Statistical and Social account of that country from the period of the invasion by the Spaniards to the present time; With a view of the Ancient Aztec Empire and Civilization; A Historical Sketch of the late War: and notices of New Mexico and California. By Brantz Mayer, formerly secretary of legation to Mexico. In Two Volumes *pp.* 399 & 433. *Hartford:* 1853. 1038

Mr. Mayer's work is probably the most complete and exhaustive history of Mexico. The narration of the conquest of the Aztec race, with a view of its civilization, occupy the first 124 pages. The remainder of the work is largely devoted to the history, character, and condition of the native races. It is particularly valuable for its statistics obtained from governmental documents, regarding the number and tribes of Indians residing in each state. He enumerates 153 nations or tribes of aborigines, with a total population in 1842, of 4,354,000. Of the numerous illustrations, more than forty exhibit some phase in the life, habits, or antiquities of these native tribes.

MAYER (Brantz).

Tah-gah-Jute; or, Logan and Captain Michael Cresap. A discourse by Brantz Mayer, delivered in Baltimore, before the Maryland Historical Society. On its Sixth Anniversary, May 9, 1851. 8° *pp.* 86. *Baltimore*, 1851. 1039

MAYER (Brantz).

Tah-gah-jute; or, Logan and Cresap, an historical essay. By Brantz Mayer. *Large* 8° *pp.* x. + 204. *Albany: Joel Munsell*, 1867. 1044

The address delivered before the Maryland Society, is in this work, by notes, biographical sketches, and an appendix, increased to a volume. When Mr. Mayer commenced his defense of Colonel Cresap, he, in common with all who had given the subject any attention, believed that the letter of General Clarke, which fully vindicated the memory of Colonel Cresap from the charge of murdering Logan's family, had never reached President Jefferson, to whom it was addressed, as he never modified his aspersions. But later examinations of Mr. Jefferson's papers, have resulted in the discovery of an unhappy fact, for the candor of that statesman. He had received the vindication two years before he published his testimony in 1800, to the veritability of Logan's speech. The testimony regarding the celebrated speech of the Indian chief, does not, however, disprove its delivery by him, in all its essential elements of eloquence and pathos. In fact, to doubt its utterance by Logan, is to credit Colonel Gibson, a gentleman who never before or after wrote or spoke in other than the plainest terms, with the composition of the wonderful speech. Mr. Mayer narrates at length, the manner and period of the death of Logan, which were for a long time in doubt. The chief was assassinated by one of his own tribe, in revenge for chastising his wife, — a privilege which Indian sachems claimed over every member of their clan.

MAYHEW (Experience).

Indian Converts: or, some Account of the Lives and Dying Speeches of a considerable Number of the Christianized INDIANS of Martha's Vineyard, in New England. Viz. I. Of Godly Ministers. II. Of other Good Men. III. Of Religious Women. IV. Of Pious young Persons. By Experience Mayhew, M. A. Preacher of the Gospel to the Indians of that Island. To which is added, Some Account of those ENGLISH MINISTERS who have successively presided over the Indian work in that and the adjacent Islands. By Mr. Prince. [*Motto 7 lines.*] 8° *London, Printed for Samuel Gerrish, Bookseller in Boston in New England: and sold by F. Osborn and T. Longman in Paternoster Row*, 1727. 1045

Title, 1 leaf; Dedication, 3 leaves; Preface, ix. to xiii.; Attestation, xiv. to xix.; Introduction, xx. to xxiv., and pp. 1 to 310; Advertisement, 1 leaf, do. pp. 1 to 16.

In this extraordinary relation of the effects of the Gospel upon the aborigines, are narrated biographical sketches of one hundred and twenty-nine Indians, who gave unexceptional tokens of conversion by Christian lives. The humane labors of this noble missionary contrast so strikingly with the bloody massacre of the Cheyennes in 1863, by the forces under the Rev. Colonel Chivington at Sand Creek, that we cannot but wonder if their religion was the same. We are reminded, however, that Mr. Mayhew's own sect instigated wars between the tribes of New England, in order to weaken their forces, slaughtered the entire adult members of some tribes, and sold their children into slavery in the West Indies.

MAYHEW (Experience).

Narratives of the Lives of Pious Indian Children, who lived on

Martha's Vineyard, more than one hundred years since. By Experience Mayhew, A. M., preacher to the Indians of Martha's Vineyard at that time. Carefully revised from the London edition, originally printed for Samuel Gerrish, Bookseller in Boston, New England. 1727. 24° *pp.* 108. *Boston* (1829). 1046

This is a reprint of the fourth division of Mayhew's *Indian Converts*, or rather of extracts from it for the use of Sunday-schools.

MAYNE (R. C.).

Four Years in British Columbia and Vancouver Island. An account of their forests, rivers, coasts, gold fields, and resources for colonization. By Commander R. C. Mayne. With Map and Illustrations. 8° *pp.* 468. *London: John Murray, Albemarle Street.* 1862. 1047

Several engravings illustrative of aboriginal life, and two chapters devoted to that subject, form a sufficient claim of this volume to a place in a collection of works relating to Indian history. The portion of the book exclusively devoted to aboriginal affairs, occupies pp. 242 to 352. The facts narrated are largely derived from Mr. Duncan's letters, which also formed the source of the work entitled *Metlahkatlah.*

MEEK (A. B.).

Romantic Passages in Southwestern History, including Orations, Sketches, and Essays. By A. B. Meek, author of The Red Eagle, etc. 12° *pp.* 330. *New York and Mobile,* 1857. 1048

Pages 210 to 330 are occupied with a biography of Weatherford, the Creek chief, massacre of Fort Mimms, and other sketches of Indian history, bearing marks of personal research, as they convey information that is novel and evidently authentic.

MEEK (A. B.).

The Red Eagle, a poem of the South. By A. B. Meek. 12° *pp.* 108. *New York, D. Appleton and Company,* 1855. 1049

The poem is accompanied with the usual stereotyped notes on Indian life.

MEGINNESS (J. F.).

Otzinachson; or, a History of the West-Branch Valley of the Susquehanna: embracing a full Account of its Settlement — trials and privations endured by the first Pioneers — full accounts of the Indian Wars, predatory Incursions, Abductions, Massacres, etc., together with an Account of the fair play System; and the trying Scenes of the Big Runaway; interspersed with Biographical Sketches of some of the leading settlers, families, etc., together with pertinent anecdotes, statistics, and much valuable matter entirely new. By J. F. Meginness. 8° *pp.* 518 + 14 *plates.* *Philadelphia: published by Henry B. Ashmead,* 1857. 1050

The author, a land surveyor, was by his occupation, brought in contact with the last of the race of pioneers, or perhaps their immediate descendants. He brought to his work the genuine zeal of an antiquary, and was peculiarly fortunate in obtaining a rich store of incidents and narratives, which had not been stated with repetition. His large volume is, therefore, one mass of new material in the history of border warfare, Indian massacres, biographical sketches of Indian fighters, and Indian warriors.

MEMOIRE,

Contenant le Precis des Faits, avec leurs Pieces Justicatives, pour servir de Reponse, aux Observations envoyees par les Ministres d'Angleterre, dans les cours de l'Europe. 24° *A Paris, de l'Imprimerie Royale*, 1756. 1051*

["Memorial containing a statement of facts responsive to the observations sent by the Ministers of England to the Courts of Europe."]

The very curious history of this memoir deserves attention from all students of American history. At the surrender of Fort Necessity by Washington, his Journal of the Expedition, together with the letters of Braddock to the British Ministry, and his instructions to Washington, were seized by the French victors. They were immediately transmitted to France, and by order of the French king, printed and sent to every court of Europe, as indicating the aggressive character of the British. From evidence drawn from these documents, they charge Washington with the murder of Jumonville. This was the second publication of any of Washington's writings, and the first notice the public had of his Journal. It was translated and printed in New York, in 1757, under the title of *A Memorial, etc.*, and the same year in Dublin under the title of *Review of Military Operations in N. A., and Journal of Major Washington*. It is very clear from the French relation that Jumonville was approaching Washington on an embassy of peace, but that Washington, unwilling to trust him, had ordered his advance to be fired upon.

MEMORIAL (A).

Containing a summary view of facts with their authorities, in answer to the observations, sent by the English Ministry to the Courts of Europe. Translated from the French. *New York, printed and sold by H. Gaine, at the printing office, at the Bible and Crown, in Hanover-Square*, 1757. 1052*

This is a translation of the preceding work. It contains Washington's Journal of mission to the Indians of Western Pennsylvania, with a narration of his interviews and negotiations with Half-King, and other Indian chiefs. This Journal, as well as the whole of the Memorial, is reprinted in the second volume of *Olden Time*.

MEMORIAL

and Remonstrance of the Committees appointed by the yearly meetings of Friends, of Genesee, New York, Philadelphia, and Baltimore, to the President of the United States, in relation to the Indians of the State of New York. 8° *pp.* 19. *New York, Mercein & Posts' press*, 1840. 1053

MEMORIAL AND PROTEST

Of the Cherokee Nation. 1054

See John Ross.

MENGARINI (Rev. Gregory).

A Selish or Flat-Head Grammar. By the Rev. Gregory Mengarini, of the Society of Jesus. *Large* 8° *New York, Cramoisy Press*, 1861. 1055

Number two of Shea's *Library of American Linguistics*. English and Latin titles each 1 leaf + pp. viii. + 122.

The work is printed as in the original, in Latin. The grammatical analysis of the language occupies pages 1 to 116. The Appendix, pp. 117 and 118, is devoted to the relation of terms expressive of consanguinity, of matrimonial and other affinities.

MESSAGE
From the President of the United States, transmitting an extract from the Occurrences at Fort Jackson, in August, 1814, during the negotiation of A Treaty with the Indians, and recommending the ratification of certain donations of land, made By the said Indians, to Gen. Jackson, Col. B. Hawkins, and others therein named. 8° *pp.* 11. *Washington, printed by William A. Davis,* 1816. 1056

MESSAGE
From the President of the United States, transmitting information, in relation to the War with the Seminoles, and the measures which have been adopted by the government, in consequence thereof. 8° *pp.* 29. *Washington,* 1818. 1057

MESSAGE
From the President of the United States, transmitting sundry documents, in relation to the Various Tribes of Indians within the United States, and recommending a plan for their Future Location, and Government. 8° *pp.* 21 + 3 *charts. Washington,* 1825. 1058

MESSAGE
From the President of the United States, transmitting sundry documents, in relation to the Various Tribes of Indians, within the United States, and recommending a plan for their future Location, and Government. January 27, 1825. 8° *Washington,* 1825. 1059

This document consists of thirteen pages of text, and four tabular sheets of names of tribes, and the estimated numbers of Indians composing each of them.

METLAH KATLAH.
See Duncan William. 1060

METCALF (Samuel L.).
A | Collection | of some of the most interesting | Narratives | of Indian Warfare in the West, | containing an account of the adventures of | Colonel Daniel Boone, | one of the first settlers of Kentucky, | Comprehending the most important occurrences relative to its early | history — Also, an account of the Manners, and Customs of the Indi | ans, their Traditions and Religious Sentiments, their Police or Civ | il Government, their Discipline and method of War: | to which is added, | an account of the expeditions of | Genl's. Harmer, Scott, Wilkinson, St. Clair, & Wayne: | The whole compiled from the best authorities, | By Samuel L. Metcalf. | 8° *pp.* 270. *Lexington, Ky.* | *Printed by William G. Hunt,* | 1821. | 1061

This very rare work has comparatively little of intrinsic value perhaps to merit the avidity with which it is sought. It is a compilation, principally from available sources, of the narratives which in their original form had, even at the date of its publication, become scarce or difficult to procure. These have since been so often reprinted, that they would seem to have superseded the necessity which called for the publication of this volume.

But every succeeding year brings with it an augmentation of the price at which it is sold. It has in turn become as rare as the works it sought to preserve from oblivion. Colonel Boone's *Narrative*, first printed in Filson's *Kentucky*, at Wilmington, 1784; Dr. Knight's and Slover's *Narrative of Captivity*, originally published (s. l. s. d.); Colonel James Smith's *Narrative of Captivity*, printed in 1799; are all here reproduced, in whole or in part. As one of the earliest imprints of the West, and as a specimen of really excellent typography, as well as a contribution to the literature illustrative of aboriginal and frontier life, it will probably always preserve its rank among rare and costly books.

MICKMAKIS AND MARICHEETS.

An | Account | of the | Customs and Manners | of the | Mickmakis and Maricheets | Savage Nations, | Now Dependent on the | Government of Cape-Breton, | from | An Original French Manuscript-Letter, | Never Published, | Written by a French Abbot, | Who resided many Years, in quality of Missionary, amongst them. | To which are annexed, | Several Pieces, relative to the Savages, to Nova | -Scotia, and to North-America in general. | 8° *Half title, and title, each* 1 *leaf* + *pp.* viii. + 138. *London*: | MDCCLVIII. | 1062

MILET (R. P. Pierre).

Relation de sa Captivité parmi les Onneiouts en 1690–1. Par le R. P. Pierre Milet de la Compagnie de Jesus. 4° *pp.* 56. *Nouvelle York: Presse Cramoisy de Jean-Marie Shea.* 1864. 1063

[Narrative of his Captivity among the Oneidas, by the Rev. Father Pierre Milet, of the Society of Jesus.]

The Manuscript of this narrative of Father Milet's captivity among the Oneidas, written by himself, was found by the Hon. H. C. Murphy in Holland; and we owe this fine historic relic of the early history of the Colony of New York, in addition to many others of importance, to the research and good fortune of that gentleman. Father Milet, during his captivity of nearly two years, acquired such an intimate knowledge of the peculiar characteristics of the Onondagas and Oneidas, among whom he was a prisoner, that we can now only regret that he did not leave us a more full and complete narrative than his brief account affords. Such as it is however, it gives us, in connection with Father Jogues' narrative, nearly all we know from personal observation, of the Five Nations at this period.

MILITARY HISTORY (The)

of Great Britain, for 1756, 1757. Containing A Letter from an English Officer at Canada, Taken Prisoner at Oswego. Exhibiting The Cruelty and Infidelity of the French, and their Savage Indians, in Times of Peace, and War. [*etc.*, 6 *lines*]. Also, A Journal of the Siege of Oswego, the Articles of Capitulation. [*etc.*, 9 *lines*]. 8° *pp.* 125. *London*: 1757. 1064

"The Narrative of the English Officer's Captivity," occupies pp. 5 to 25; "The Journal of the Siege of Oswego," evidently from the same hand, pp. 26 to 60; "A letter, giving a Narrative of the Captivity among the Indians, of Peter Lewney," occupies pp. 66 to 88. These narratives and journals are all very interesting and doubtless authentic. They have been printed in no other form.

MILFORT (General).

Memoire ou Coup-d'Œil rapide Sur mes differens voyages et

mon sejour dans la nation Creck. Par le G^d Milfort, Tastenegy ou grand Chef de guerre de la nation Creck, et General de brigade au service de la Republique Francaise. 8° *Half title and title 2 leaves + pp. 1 to 332. A Paris, de l'imprimerie de Giguet et Michaud An* XI. (1802). 1065

[Memoir, or rapid view of my different voyages, and of my residence in the Creek Nation. By General Milfort, Tastenegy, or Great War Chief of the Creek Nation, and Brigadier-General of the French Republic, Paris, 1802.]

The narrative of this extraordinary man's career among the Creek Indians, has so much of the romantic in the design of the author, that the reader is at first predisposed to think lightly of its veracity. There are, however, corroborative circumstances which confirm his statements, and induce us to give a fair degree of credence to his narrative.

At the time of his arrival among the Creeks, a half breed named McGillivray, had obtained so great an influence over them by his talent for organization, that he had actually acquired the rank of head chief. Milfort was received by McGillivray with great cordiality; married his Indian sister, and in a short time was made the commander of the warriors of the nation. He led them against both the Spaniards and the Americans, and by his aid the Indians defeated the forces of each in several skirmishes. Milfort remained with the Creeks, until the breaking out of the revolution in his own country. His Memoir affords us some general information of the tribes he visited, but not of such value as we might have anticipated from his opportunities.

Miller (Samuel).

A Sermon delivered before the New-York Missionary Society, at their annual meeting April 6th, 1802. To which are added, the annual report of the directors, and other papers relating to American Missions. 8° *pp.* 81. *New York*, 1802. 1066

Pages 63 to 81, are occupied with reports of Indian councils.

Milton (Viscount) and Cheadle (W. B.).

The North-West Passage by Land. Being the narrative of an expedition from the Atlantic to the Pacific, undertaken with the view of exploring a route across the Continent to British Columbia through British Territory, by one of the northern passes in the Rocky Mountains. By Viscount Milton, and W. B. Cheadle. Fifth Edition. 8° *pp.* 24 + 400 + *map and* 23 *plates. London: Cassell, Petter, and Galpin, Ludgate Hill*, (1865). 1067

This narrative of a frightful journey, across the continent through British America, is crowded with details of aboriginal life as seen by the author, who gained an additional claim to his title of nobility, by the fortitude with which he endured the privations and extremities which befell his party. From the imminent dangers of drowning, assassination, and starvation, the authors were rescued by the adroitness, daring, and fidelity of an Assiniboine Indian, and his squaw. Several of the plates are illustrative of these scenes of peril, and of his rescuers.

Miner (Charles).

History of Wyoming, in a series of letters, from Charles Miner, to his Son William Penn Miner. [*Motto two lines*]. 8° 2 *maps*, 2 *plates, and pp.* 488 + *Explanation of Maps*, 2 *pp.* + *Appendix, pp.* 1 *to* 104. *Philadelphia: published by J. Crissy*, 1845. 1068

This is the most nearly complete of all the histories of the valley, which has been the scene of such tragic events, as have elicited the interest of some in every civilized land. The work is much the largest of these narratives, and is more documentary in its character. It contains an Appendix of 104 pages, in which the author gives forty-five biographical sketches of the pioneers of the valley, and incidents of their participation in its warfare with the Indians. Pages 62 to 104, are occupied with "Copy of Lt. Col. Adam Hubley's Journal on the Western Expedition, against the Indians under the Command of Major General Sullivan, 1779. By Simon Stevens, Lancaster, Pa. Aug. 9, 1845."

MISSIONS IN NEW YORK.

Missions in Western New York, and Church History of the Diocese of Buffalo, by the Bishop of Buffalo. 12° *pp.* 258. *Buffalo:* 1862. 1069

This work, written by the venerable Bishop, is a narration of some of the principal incidents in the lives and sufferings of the Jesuit and Franciscan missionaries among the Indians of New York. Obtaining his materials from the documents and relations of the missions, his history could not but be authentic. Chapters iv. and v., pp. 39 to 60, are occupied with descriptions of the Indians, and vi., vii., and viii., with "The Host of Martyrs," "Chaumonot compiling his grammar on the frozen earth," "Brebeuf with his collar-bone broken, crawling on the frozen ground, and sleeping in the snow," and finally, with "Father Lallemant, burnt at the stake, under incredible tortures." The work also narrates how Fathers Viele, Garnier, Jogues, and Goupil followed them, through the same road, to heaven; how others, beaten, robbed, and tortured, dragged their worn and wounded bodies from village to village, to baptize a dying child, or bestow the last offices of their religion on a captive, perishing at the stake.

MISSION DU CANADA.

Relations Inedites de la Nouvelle-France (1672-1679) pour faire suite aux anciennes relations 1615-1672 Avec deux Cartes Geographiques. Two vols. 12° Vol. I. *pp.* xxviii. + 356. Vol. II. *pp.* 384 + 2 *maps.* *Paris Charles Douniol, Editeur Rue de Tournon,* 29. 1861. 1070

[Missions in Canada. Unedited Relations of New France (1672 to 1679) in continuation of the Early Relations of 1615 to 1672, with two Maps.]

These very interesting volumes narrate the wonderful story of nearly nine years of Jesuit missions among the Iroquois, Huron, Ottawa, Montagnais, and Abenaquis Indians, during which the immortal heroism of these Christian soldiers carried civilization into central and western New York, a century and a half before the English settlement of that frontier.

MITCHEL (Joseph).

The Missionary Pioneer, or a brief memoir of the life, labours, and death of John Stewart, (man of colour,) founder, under God of the mission among the Wyandotts at Upper Sandusky, Ohio. Published by Joseph Mitchell. 24° *pp.* 96. *New York, printed by J. C. Totten, No.* 9 *Bowery.* 1827. 1071

This extraordinary man, whose labors are rivaled only by those of the early Jesuit missionaries, was a negro born in Virginia, about 1790, who, in 1816, conceived that he was directed by divine authority to preach the Gospel to the northwest Pagan Indians. He arrived among the Wyandots, then located in the vicinity of the present site of Sandusky, during the performance of one of their wild, heathenish festivals. Fierce as they were, the melody of one of his religious hymns, sung in the rich, expressive voice, for which he was remarkable, struck the savage fancy and gave him at once a powerful hold upon their interest. For five years this unlettered African not only retained the power he had acquired, but step by step increased his influence, until a great portion of the tribe was redeemed from drunkenness and paganism. The fiercest vindictiveness of the revengeful Pagans, melted before the mild zeal and pure life of the fervent missionary. It was not until 1820, that the attention of the Methodist Church authorities was attracted to the wonderful labors of this black apostle, and they then determined to assume jurisdiction over the Christian Church, organized by the descendant of African savages, among American aborigines. There are few in any generation of men, who may not envy the labors of this negro missionary and his reward. Some details of his labors will be found in Finley's autobiography.

MOHAWK.

The | Morning and Evening Prayer, | The Litany, | Church Catechism, | Family Prayers, | and Several Chapters of the Old and New-Testament, | Translated into the Mahaque Indian Language, | By Lawrence Claesse, Interpreter to William | Andrews, Missionary to the Indians, from the | Honourable and Reverend the Society for the Propagation | of the Gospel in Foreign Parts. | Ask of me, and I will give thee the Heathen for thine Inheritance, | and the Utmost Parts of the Earth for thy Possession, Psalm | 2. 8. *Printed by William Bradford in* *Small* 4° *New York*, 1715. | 1072

Ne | Orhoengene neoni Yogaraskhagh | Yondereanayendaghkwa, |
Eno Niyoh Raodeweyena, |
Ne | Onoghsadogeaghtige Yondadderighwanoa | doentha, |
Siragonoogheode, Enyondereanayendagh | kwagge, |

Yotkade Kapitelhogough ne Karighwadaghkwe | agh Agayea neoni Ase Testament, neoni Niyadegari | wagge, ne Kanninggahaga Siniye wenoteagh. | Tehoweyhadenyough *Lawrence Claesse*, Rowenagaradatsk | *William Andrews*, Ronwanhaugh *Oeguehorneraghne*. | Rodirigh hoeni Raddiya danorongh neoni Ahoenwadi | gonnyostbagge Thoderighwawaakhogh ne Wahooni | Agarigh howanha Niyoh Raodeweyena Niyadadegoh | wisenjage. | Eghtseraggwas Eghtjeragh ne ong-wehoonwe, neoni ne | aiyodgowhanjooktanaighoegh ethoahadyran dough. |

Collation: English title, 1 leaf, printed on reverse, recto blank + Indian title, 1 leaf, printed on recto, reverse blank + The Order for Morning and Evening prayer, pp. 1 to 40, The Church catechism and prayers, pp. 1 to 21, reverse blank. Psalms, selections from Scriptures, Bible history and songs, pp. 41 to 115. Total No. of pp., 141.

MOHAWK.

The Book of | Common Prayer, | and Administration of the | Sacraments, | and other | Rites and Ceremonies | of the | Church, | according to the use of the | Church of England: | together with | A Collection of Occasional Prayers, and | divers Sentences of | Holy Scripture, | Necessary for Knowledge and Practice. | Formerly collected, and translated into the Mohawk Language | under the direction of the Missionaries of the Society for the | Propagation of the Gospel in Foreign Parts to the Mohawk | Indians. | A New Edition: | to which is added | The Gospel according to St. Mark, | Translated into the Mohawk Language, | By Capt[n] Joseph Brant, | An Indian of the Mohawk Nation. | 8° *London:* | *Printed by C. Buckton, Great Pulney Street,* | *Golden Square*, 1787. 1073

Collation: Preliminary pp. 11, viz., English title, 1 leaf, Indian title, 1 leaf, reverse of each blank, Preface 2 leaves, reverse of last blank, "The Contents," 1 page + text, pp. 3 to 505 + observations on Mohawk Language p. 1 + frontispiece and 18 other plates.

This is the fourth edition of the Book of Common Prayer, first translated into Mohawk by the missionary Freeman, and by Lawrence Claesse. The Society for the Propagation of the Gospel in Foreign Parts sent the first missionary to the Mohawks in 1702, but it was not until 1709, on the occasion of the visit of some of that nation to London, accompanied by Colonel Schuyler, that the Society was stirred to provide them with the offices of the church, printed in their own language. The Book of Common Prayer had been in part translated by Mr. Freeman, was enlarged by the interpreter, Lawrence Claesse, and printed by William Bradford, in New York, in 1715. It was in medium quarto, containing 141 pages. One or two copies of this very rare edition have been seen without date or imprint; three that I have examined have both. As copies of this edition had become scarce in 1762, Sir William Johnson caused another to be prepared which was printed in New York, in 1769. Very considerable additions were made to it, and as the quarto form had been found inconvenient, it was, by Sir William's direction, changed to small octavo, of 208 pages. In the terrible devastations which the Mohawk valley suffered during the War of the Revolution, together with the expatriation of the nation in 1777, most of the copies in their possession were lost. Governor Haldiman of Canada, moved by their petitions, caused an edition of one thousand copies to be printed in 1780, at Quebec. This was also in octavo and contained 213 pages. In a few years this edition had also become exhausted, and the Society, which seventy years before had caused the first translation to be printed, again directed the work of furnishing to the Indians a more enlarged and correct version. Colonel Daniel Claus, who had under the direction of Governor Haldiman supervised the printing of the Quebec edition, was engaged by the Society to revise the impression as it issued from the press. The edition of 1787 is declared in the Preface to be much more correct than any previous one, — a merit which it probably owes to the accurate knowledge of the Mohawk language, possessed by Colonel Claus. All the other editions were solely in the Indian tongue, but in this the English version on the verso of each leaf, is rendered as closely as possible into Mohawk on the recto of the next. The chronological history of the translation, may be summed up as follows: The Morning and Evening Prayers, the Gospel of St. Matthew and other portions of Scripture, were translated by the Rev. Mr. Freeman, a missionary among the Mohawks about 1706, but remained in MS. This translation was given to Mr. Andrews, and used as the basis of Lawrence Claesse's translation of the Catechism, the Litany, etc., printed in 1715. Colonel William Johnson employed William Weyman of New York, to print four hundred copies in 1763; but the death of Dr. Barclay, the Mohawk missionary who was to superintend it, caused a suspension of two years. His successor in the mission, the Rev. Mr. Ogilvie, then undertook the labor, but in 1768 the death of the printer, Mr. Weyman, again stopped its progress. Hugh Gaines, then having been induced to complete the printing, it was issued in 1769, having been six years in the press. The two succeeding editions followed as already described. See Humphrey's *History of the Society for Propagating the Gospel*, and Vol. I. *Historical Magazine.*

MOHAWK PRIMER.

A | Primer, | for the USE of the | Mohawk Children, | To acquire the Spelling and Reading of their | own, as well as to get acquainted with the | English, Tongue; which for that Purpose is put | on the opposite Page. | Wnerighwaghsawe | Iksaongoenwa | [*etc., 4 lines in Mohawk.*] *London,* | *printed by C. Buckton, Great Pulteney-Street.* | 1786. | 1074

Collation: Small quarto, pp. 96 + a frontispiece representing a School of

Indian Children, engraved by James Peachey. In Mr. Henry Stevens' catalogue of books sold by Puttick & Simpson, 1861, a copy of this rare little book is announced, as believed to be UNIQUE, price three guineas. A copy believed to be the same, was catalogued by Leclerc, to be sold in 1867, with the note, that an edition of the Primer was printed at Montreal, in 1781, in 12°. This copy brought about twenty-four dollars. I have seen two copies of the book, and become cognizant of the sale of another.

MOHAWK.

Book of Common Prayer. 1075

See Eleazer Williams; Solomon Davis.

MOHAWK BOOK OF ISAIAH.

Ne Kaghyadonghsera ne Roy ad adokenghdy, ne Isaiah. 24° *pp.* 243. *New York: printed for the American Bible Society. D. Fanshaw, Printer.* 1839. 1076

MOHAWK LANGUAGE.

Nene Karighwiyoston tsinihorighhoten ne Saint John. (The Gospel according to Saint John. 16° *pp.* 125 *and* 125, *alternate Mohawk and English. London: n. d.* 1077

MOLINA (J. Ignatius).

The Geographical, Natural and Civil History of Chili. By Abbe Don J. Ignatius Molina. Illustrated by a half-sheet map of the country. With Notes from the Spanish and French versions, and An Appendix containing copious extracts from the Araucana of Don Alonzo de Ercilla. Translated from the original Italian, by an American Gentleman. In Two Volumes. 8° Vol. I. *pp.* xii. + 271, *and map.* Vol. II. *pp.* viii. + 305 + 68. *Middletown, Conn., printed for I. Riley.* 1808. 1078

Vol. II. is entirely devoted to the history of the Araucanian Indians, their peculiar customs, and their wars with the Spaniards, with a grammar of the language, and a vocabulary. The wars of the Spaniards with the unconquered Araucanians, have afforded the most fertile material of all the chapters of South American history, for story and romance. Ercilla, the Spanish poet, whose epic has been compared to the Iliad and the Æneid, formed his *Araucana* on their story. The Abbe Molina has told in his volumes, in almost equally glowing prose, the narrative of the heroic struggle of these savages for freedom. He obtained from the Abbe Olivarez, MS. history written prior to 1665, and from the oral narration of actors in the wars, as well as from printed documents, the materials for his history. On pp. 285 to 304, Vol. II. he gives a grammatical essay, and vocabulary of the Araucanian language. The remainder of this volume is taken up with copious extracts from Ercilla's poem, as copiously annotated.

MOLINA (Luis de Neve de).

Grammatica della Lingua Otomi esposta in Italiano dal conte enea Silvio Vicenzo Piccolomini. Secondo la traccia del licenziato Luis de Nevę y Molina col vocabulario Spagnuolo-Otomi Spiegato in Italiano. 4° *pp.* 82. *Roma nella tipografia di propaganda fide* 1841. 1079

[Grammar of the Otomi Language, translated into Italian by Count Piccolomini, from the Spanish-Otomi of Molina.]

MOLLHAUSEN (Baldwin).

Diary of a Journey from the Mississippi to the Coasts of the

Pacific with a United States government expedition. By Baldwin Mollhausen, topographical draughtsman and naturalist to the expedition. With an Introduction by Alexander Von Humboldt and Illustrations in chromo-lithography. Translated by Mrs. Percy Sinnett. In Two Volumes. 8° *pp.* 352 + 7 *colored plates*, 397 + *five colored plates and eleven woodcuts. London, Longman & Co.*, 1858. 1080

The narration of the author's personal examination of Indian life, and aboriginal antiquities, occupy almost the whole of these volumes. The plates are principally illustrative of such phases of the one, and remains of the other, as seemed most noteworthy. Mollhausen's work received the approbation of Humboldt, who wrote the historical preface, pp. xi. to xxv.

MONETTE (John W.).

History of the Discovery and Settlement of the Valley of the Mississippi, by the three great European powers, Spain, France, and Great Britain, and the subsequent occupation, settlement, and extension of civil government by the United States, until the year 1846. By John W. Monette. In Two Volumes. Vol. I. *pp.* xxiii. and 567, *with* 2 *maps and* 1 *plate.* Vol. II. *pp.* xv. and 595, *with a map and* 5 *plates. Harper & Brothers, New York.* 1848. 1081

The first volume is principally occupied with a relation of the French and Spanish discovery of the territory, and the association of the colonial governments of these nations with the Indians, and their wars with the various tribes inhabiting it. Much the largest portion of Vol. II. is devoted to a narration of the Indian wars of the States bordering the Ohio. Chap. I. is entitled, "Manners and Customs of the Frontier Population." Chap. II. "Indian Warfare, and its effects upon the Frontier People." Chaps. III. and IV. "Indian hostilities upon the Ohio." Chap. IV. The same, and "Predatory Excursions into Kentucky and partisan Warfare." Chap. VIII. "Indian Relations with the U. S." Chaps. IX. and X. "Early Settlement and Indian hostilities from 1776 to 1796." Chap. XI. "Indian Wars, and Military Operations North of the Ohio River, 1787 to 1795." The work is probably the best of the numerous class of books on the subject of western history.

MONTANUS (Arnoldus).

De Nieuwe en Onbekende Weereld of Beschryving Van America en 't Zuid-Land Vervaetende d' Oorjprong der Americaenen en Zuid-Landers, geden kwaerdige togten derwaerds, gelegendheid Der vaste Kusten, Eilanden, Steden, Sterkten, Dorpen, Tempels Bergen, Fontemen, Stroomen, Huisen, de natuur van Beesten, Boomen Planten en Vreemde Gewasschen Gods-dienst en Zeden, Wonderlyke Voorvallen, Vereeuw de en Nieuwe Oorloogen: Verceot met Af-beeldfels na 't leven in America gemaekt en beschreeven door Arnoldus Montanus. t' Amsterdam. By Jacob Meurs. *Boek-verkooper*, 1671. 1082

[The New and Unknown World: or, Description of America by A. Montanus.]

Large folio. Engraved Title, Portrait, and (vi.) prel. pages + 585 + (xxvii.), and fifty-four plates and maps. Forty-one of the half-page plates printed in the text, are illustrative of the battles, festivals, religious rites, cannibalism, habitations, or customs of the aborigines of America. All of the finely executed engravings of this huge volume, were first used for Montanus' work, but were in the same year reproduced in Ogilby's *America*, and in 1673, in Dapper's German translation of Montanus. The impressions are far the most brilliant and clear, in this original Dutch edition. If the value of Montanus' relations of aboriginal life and customs, is to be estimated from his pictures of fabulous monsters, there is little to be learned from his tremendous tome.

MONTGOMERY (William).

The Extraordinary Adventures of William Montgomery in the unexplored regions of Amazonia; An account of his captivity among the Oromana Indians — a description of their manners, customs, and wars; — and the escape of the captive with the daughter of their chief. 16° pp. 30. *London: printed by W. Nicholson*, n. d. 1083

This narration begins with an air of veracity, like De Foe; it continues with a vein of rhapsody, like Richardson; and ends beautifully, like a fairy tale. Whether true or false is not of the least consequence, and yet it cost me a guinea.

MONTIGNY (M. de).

Relation de la Mission Du Missisipi du Seminaire de Quebec en 1700. Par M.M. de Montigny de St. Cosme et Thaumur de la Source. pp. 66. *Nouvelle York. A la Presse Cramoisy de Jean-Marie Shea*, 1861. 1084

No. 13 of Shea's *Series of Jesuit Relations*.
[Relation of the Mission of the Missisipi, of the Seminary of Quebec, in 1700, by Messieurs de Montigny, de St. Cosme, and by Thaumur de la Source.]
The principal portion of this relation is the narrative by Father de St. Cosme, of his travels and missions among the Indians, living on the rivers which empty into the Mississippi, from the northwestern territory of New France. Jean Francoise de St. Cosme, born in France, 1667, became a missionary in 1690, and was killed by the Chetimachas Indians in 1707.

MOORE (Francis).

A Voyage to Georgia, Begun in the Year 1735. Containing An Account of the Settling of the Town of Frederica, in the Southern Part of the Province; and a Description of the Soil, Air, Birds, Beasts, Trees, Rivers, Islands, &c. With the Rules and Orders made by the Honorable the Trustees for that Settlement; Including the Allowances of Provisions, Cloathing, and other Necessaries to the Families and Servants which went thither. Also A Description of the Town and County of Savannah in the Northern Part of the Province; the Manner of dividing and granting the Lands, and the Improvements there: With an Account of the Air, Soil, Rivers, and Islands in that Part. By Francis Moore, Author of Travels into the Inland Parts of Africa. 8° *Half title* + *pp.* 1 *to* 108 + (2). *London: printed for Jacob Robinson in Ludgate Street*, 1744. 1085

The numbers of the Indian tribes, the location of their territories, and the dealings of the wise and pacific Oglethorpe with them, form the subject of much of the volume. Many incidents in the life of the good chief Tomo-chi-chi, are given.

MOORE (Jacob B.).

Annals of the Town of Concord in the county of Merrimack, and state of New Hampshire, from its first settlement, in the year 1726, to the year 1823. With several biographical sketches. To which is added, A Memoir of the Penacook Indians. By Jacob B. Moore. [*Motto 5 lines.*] 8° *pp.* 112. *Concord: published by Jacob B. Moore.* 1824. 1086

MOORE (Martin).

Memoirs of the Life and Character of Rev. John Eliot, apostle of the N. A. Indians. By Martin Moore. 24° *pp.* 174. *Boston: published by T. Bedlington. Flagg & Gould, printers.* 1822. 1087

MOORE (William V.).

Indian Wars of the United States. From the Discovery to the Present Time. With accounts of the Origin, Manners, Superstitions, etc., of the Aborigines. From the best authorities. By William V. Moore. 8° *pp.* 328 + 100 *plates. Philadelphia;* 1858. 1088

This compilation of events in Indian history, although issued under the imputed authorship of Mr. Moore, is said to be really another guise for that Protean character, John Frost, LL.D. The clipped and mis-used narratives, and the mixture of harsh, dark, unsightly woodcuts, with tawdry colored lithographs, would induce the editor, we could readily believe, to hide his name under any convenient synonym.

MORALES (A. Bachiller y).

Antiquedades Americanas. Noticias que tuvieron los Europeos de la America antes del descubrimiento de Cristobal Colon, recogidas por A. Bachiller y Morales. 4° *pp.* 156 + *map. Habana. Oficina del Faro Industrial,* 1845. 1089

[American Antiquities. Evidences which the Europeans had of America before the discovery by Christopher Columbus, collected by A. Bachiller y Morales.]

MORAVIAN MISSIONS.

The History of the Moravian Missions among the Indians in North-America, from its commencement to the present time. With a preliminary account of the Indians. By a Member of the Brethren's Church. 16° *pp.* vi. + 318. *London: T. Allman,* 1838. 1090

MORGAN (Lewis H.).

League of the Ho-de-no-sau-nee or Iroquois. By Lewis H. Morgan. 8° *pp.* 477 + 23 *maps, plates, and plans. Rochester: Sage & Brother, publishers.* 1851. 1091

Beside the large map, there is a folding sheet of comparative vocabularies, a large folding plate, and twenty full-paged engravings. It is evident on examination, that this is the work of a writer more than ordinarily fitted for the task. It is indeed rare that taste and learning so well combine with the experience of a lifetime to favor the researches of a historian in examining the scanty records of the American Indians. In early youth Mr. Morgan was so familiarly associated with the Senecas, that he was adopted as a member of the tribe. Under such favorable circumstances, he was permitted to closely study their social organization, and the structure and principles of their ancient league. Year after year his materials grew, until his copious notes became volumes, and thus the production of the first systematic treatise, regarding the internal structure of Indian society and government was made easy of accomplishment. The laws of descent among the Iroquois, first claimed the author's attention, and his treatise fully exhibits that marvelous and sagacious legislative restriction, by which tribal and national rank was always derived from the mother. Not the least valuable feature of his work, crowded as it is with original investigations and logical deductions, is the map of the territory belonging to, or once occupied by the Six Nations, in which all the localities of their numerous villages are shown, with the aboriginal names of the streams, lakes, valleys, and other geographical features. The Appendix, pp. 465 to 477, is entitled "Schedule explanatory of the Indian Map." It is a table giving the English names of the localities, streams, etc., on the map, and opposite thereto the Indian name, while a third column exhibits its signification. Nearly four hundred geographical names are thus rendered and translated.

MORGAN (Lewis H.).

Laws of Descent of the Iroquois. By Lewis H. Morgan of Rochester. 8° *pp.* 16. *New York.* 1092

A sheet of eight closely printed pages, designed to be sent to persons having some knowledge of Indian history, and domestic or social customs, in order to elicit information regarding them. It contains an analysis of their tribal divisions, marital relations, and a series of questions regarding the same. 8° *pp.* 8. *Rochester, Monroe Co., New York, October* 1, 1859.

Everything which passes the hands of this indefatigable student of aboriginal history, bears the marks of so much thoughtful analysis, that even these fugitive leaves have a distinct and peculiar value. In most treatises upon the mysterious subject of the origin, progress, and other ethnological data of the Indians, hypothesis has run mad, and the wildest speculations have not been without their advocates. These, the grim silence of their history, forbids ever to be proven true or false. Mr. Morgan, however, deals only with facts, of which his residence among the Iroquois affords him an abundant store. He leaves his reader himself to deduce the almost inevitable conclusion, which his data suggest.

MORGAN (Lewis H.).

The American Beaver and his Works. By Lewis H. Morgan, Author of the League of the Iroquois. 8° *pp.* 330 + 23 *full page plates. Philadelphia: J. B. Lippincott & Co.*, 1868. 1094

This elegant treatise on the habits and life of the animal, which has been so greatly the innocent cause of the ruin of his fellow aborigines, by provoking the greed of the white, and the fatal thirst of the red man, incidentally treats of some of the phases of the life of the latter.

MORRIS (Capt. Thomas).

Miscellanies in Prose and Verse. By Captain Thomas Morris. 8° *pp.* 178. *London:* 1791. 1095

Under this unpromising title, the author has printed a journal of an expedition against Pontiac, in which he was made a captive by the Indians. On pp. 1 to 39, he gives his narrative of the incidents of his hazardous mission to Pontiac, a savage general, who in a six weeks' campaign, overthrew the British authority in all the territories of the northwest. Captain Morris accepted the service at the request of General Bradstreet, sensible that to place himself in the power of the vindictive Indian chief, was little short of a sentence to death. General Bradstreet, who had the ill luck to bear a reputation too great for his capacity, had the additional misfortune of seldom knowing what he really wanted. Captain Morris, by the combined force of good fortune, and good conduct, escaped the perils which inclosed his course and secured irresistibly to close behind him and forbid his return to life. With the fire kindled around the stake to which he was tied, he was more than once rescued at the last minute. The original MS. of his journal is preserved in the London Colonial Archives. Other particulars of his mission, captivity, and escape, can be found in Captain Morris' letter to Bradstreet, in the MSS. of Sir William Johnson, belonging to the New York State library, and in Parkman's *Conspiracy of Pontiac.*

MORRIS (I.).

A Narrative of the Dangers and Distresses: Which befel Isaac Morris, and Seven more of the Crew Belonging to The Wager Store-Ship, etc. An Account of their Adventures, etc., till they were Seized by a Party of Indians and carried above a Thousand Miles into the Inland Country, with whom they resided upwards of Sixteen Months [*etc., 5 lines*]. Interspersed with A Description of the Manners, and Customs of the Indians in that Part of the World, particularly their Manner of taking the Wild Horses in Hunting, as seen by the Author himself [*etc., 3 lines*]. By I. Morris late Midshipman of the Wager. 12° *London* (1749). 1096

MORSE (Jedidiah).

Annals of the American Revolution; or a Record of the Causes and Events which produced, and terminated in the establishment, and independence of the American Republic. [*etc., 4 lines*] a Summary Account of the first Settlement of the Country, and some of the principal Indian Wars, [*etc., 7 lines*] and Biography of the Principal Military Officers. [*etc., 3 lines*] Compiled by Jedediah Morse. 8° *pp.* 400 + 5 *plates* + *Appendix pp.* 50. *Hartford:* 1824. 1097

MORSE (Rev. Jedidiah).

A Report to the Secretary of War of the United States, on Indian Affairs, comprising a narrative of a tour performed in the summer of 1820, under a commission from the President of the United States, for the purpose of ascertaining, for the use of the government, the actual state of the Indian Tribes in our Country. Illustrated by a map of the United States; ornamented by a correct portrait of a Pawnee Indian. By the Rev. Jedidiah Morse, D. D. 8° *Portrait and map* + *report pp.* 96 + *Appendix pp.* 400. *New Haven:* 1822. 1098

This is certainly the most complete and exhaustive report of the condition, numbers, names, territory, and general affairs of the Indians, ever made. It affords us the details of almost every particular which we could desire, relating to the accessible tribes, in the territory of the United States, as they existed in the year 1820. They are the result of the indefatigable labors, of a humane and learned man, who personally visited, and investigated the affairs of many of the tribes enumerated. The most elaborate tables accompany the work, and afford a vast amount of statistical information regarding the Indians within the jurisdiction of the government.

On page 361 commences "A Statistical Table of all the Indian Tribes in the United States, with their names, number of souls in each tribe, residence, and references to the page and map." This and similar tables cover thirty-seven pages, and give the above designated information, regarding two hundred and fifty-nine tribes, numbering 471,148 individuals. On pages 359 and 360, is a translation of the Nineteenth Psalm, into the Mohegan language, with the English version in parallel columns.

MORSE (Jedidiah).

Signs of the Times: A Sermon preached before the Society for Propagating the Gospel among the Indians, and others in North-America, at their Anniversary. Nov. 1, 1810. By Jedidiah Morse. 8° *pp.* 72. (*Boston*), *printed* 1810. 1099

The Notes and Appendix occupy pp. 39 to 72.

MORTON (Dr. S. G.).

Crania Americana; or a comparative view of the Skulls of Various Aboriginal Nations of North and South America: To which is prefixed an essay on the varieties of the human species. Illustrated by Seventy-Eight Plates and a Colored Map. By Samuel George Morton, Philadelphia: *Folio. pp.* 296 + 78 *folio plates. London:* 1839. 1100

This treatise is highly esteemed by ethnologists, and is certainly the result of a vast amount of original research, by a learned and zealous investigator. The cranial forms of more than forty Indian nations once inhabiting the two Americas, from Canada to Brazil, are examined and compared. Both in this country and in Europe, wherever learning and science are reverenced, Mr. Morton's work has been recognised, as one of the best contributions to exact knowledge of the history of man, ever offered as the work of one individual, excepting always the works of Humboldt. The large plates at the end of the text are numbered 1 to 72; 11 A, B, C, and D, 17 A, and 18 A, each occupying a full folio page, reverse blank.

MORTON (S. G.).

An Inquiry into the Distinctive Characteristics of the Aboriginal Race of America. By Samuel George Morton. Second Edition. 8° *pp.* 44. *Philadelphia:* 1844. 1101

MORTON (S. G.).

Catalogue of Skulls of Man, and the Inferior Animals, in the Collection of Samuel G. Morton. Third Edition. *Philadelphia,* 1849. 1102*

MORTON (S. G.).

Some Observations on the Ethnography and Archaeology of the American Aborigines. From the American Journal of Science, Vol. II., Second Series. 8° *pp.* 19. *New Haven,* 1846. 1103*

MOULTON (Joseph W.) and YATES (J. V. N.).

History of the State of New-York, including its Aboriginal and Colonial Annals. By John V. N. Yates and Joseph W. Moulton. 8° Vol. I. Part I. *Title, sub-title 2 leaves, pp.* xi. + 325. *New York: published by A. T. Goodrich.* 1824. 1104

MOULTON (J. W.).

History of the State of New York. By Joseph W. Moulton. Part II. Novum Belgium. 8° *pp.* viii. + 333 *to* 428 + *folding plan. New York: published by E. Bliss & E. White,* 1826. 1105

Bound with these is a work also by Mr. Moulton, entitled *View and Description of New Orange, as it was in the year* 1673. New York, 1825; folding plan; pp. 40; and another entitled *New York 170 years ago*, New York, 1843. In Vol. I., Parts I. and II., the aboriginal history of New York is very ably treated, these divisions of the work being almost entirely devoted to an examination of the various questions, which have so vexed ethnologists regarding the "origin of the savages," the pre-Columbian history, and discovery of America, and a narrative of events connected with Indian history, to the year 1633.

MUNOZ (Juan Baptista).

The History of the New World, by Don Juan Baptista Munoz Translated from the Spanish, with notes by the translator, an engraved portrait of Columbus, and a map of Espanola. Vol. I. 8° *pp.* xv. + 552. *London: printed for G. G. and J. Robinson, Paternoster-Row*, 1797. 1106

After eighteen years of most laborious investigations, this excellent historian persuaded himself, that he was at length justified in printing his work. But exhausted with the intensity of his application, he had only vitality enough to aid in the issue of one volume, when his death forever interrupted the completion of his labors. The literary treasures of the Indies, which Spanish jealousy had hitherto secluded from all investigation, were by royal mandate placed at his disposal. Vast numbers of original MSS of the highest historical importance, were under his direction, copied and arranged for use. These authenticated much that was only conjectured, and disproved much that was thought to be known. A large portion of the volume we have, is devoted to narrations of the character of the Indians, and their treatment by Columbus, which Munoz declares to have been eminently humane, although he early countenanced, and even directed, their reduction to slavery. One incident he mentions, reveals the high elevation of religious sentiment, among the graver and more intelligent, of the once happy and innocent aborigines of San Domingo. An aged and venerable Indian, on witnessing one of the first acts of devotion by the Spaniards, expressed the highest gratification at their evident belief in a Supreme Being, declaring his pleasure with tears of joy, that these white strangers and his own naked countrymen, worshipped the same King of Heaven, who would, after this short life, reward the good of all tribes with happiness, and punish the wicked with misery. Of less importance, yet not without significance, is the statement on Oviedo's authority, that Europeans first imitated the natives in smoking tobacco, to alleviate the pangs of syphilis.

MURATORI (Mr.).

A Relation of the Missions of Paraguay. Wrote Originally in Italian, by Mr. Muratori, And now done into English from the French Translation. 12° *pp.* xvi. + 296. *London: printed for J. Marmaduke, in Long-Acre.* 1759. 1107

Muratori's relation of the Jesuit missions in Paraguay is very highly esteemed, having been composed in great part from documents written by various Jesuit missionaries and travellers, furnished to Muratori by Father Gaetan Cattanio, a missionary of the brotherhood of Jesus, in Paraguay. The latter was born in Modena, in 1696, and died in Paraguay, in 1733. His letters, published as an appendix to this work, are exceedingly interesting in affording descriptions of the Indians of Paraguay at this early day. The historian is said also to have derived no small portion of his work from the communications of Santo Bueno, Viceroy of Peru.

MURDER (The)

of the Christian Indians in North-America, in the year 1782. A Narrative of Facts. 12° *pp.* 16. *Dublin*, 1826. 1108

MURPHY (Timothy).

Life and adventures of Timothy Murphy the benefactor of Schoharie, including his History from the commencement of the revolution — His rencontres with the Indians — The siege of the three Forts, and the preservation by his unparalleled courage of all their inmates — his courtship and, marriage, and anecdotes of his adventures with the Indians &c. 8° *pp.* 32. *Printed by W. H. Gallup, Schoharie C. H., N. Y., January,* 1839. 1109

This very scarce pamphlet, narrates a few of the adventures and feats of the Indian fighter and scout, of the valley of the Mohawk. The authenticity of the stories narrated here and elsewhere, of his prowess, is better sustained, than most of those illustrating the heroism of border warriors.

MURPHY (Henry C.). 1110

See Vries.

MURRAY (Charles Augustus).

Travels in North America during the years 1834, 1835, & 1836. Including a summer residence with the Pawnee Tribe of Indians, in the remote prairies of the Missouri, and a visit to Cuba and the Azore Islands. By the Hon. Charles Augustus Murray. In Two Volumes. 8° Vol. I. *pp.* xvi. + 473 *and* 1 *plate.* Vol. II. *pp.* xi. + 372 *and* 1 *plate. London: Richard Bentley, New Burlington Street,* 1839. 1111

This is the first and best edition of a most interesting work, by an intelligent observer of the peculiarities of the Pawnees, before they had been modified by contact with the whites. His departure from St. Louis, and first encounter with the Pawnees, is narrated in Chap. xii. of Vol. I., and through the remainder of the volume, pp. 235 to 460, and pp. 1 to 96 of Vol. II., we follow him with unabated interest in his narration of his adventures during a three months' tour in the Indian territory. There is little of scientific value in his narrative, but it possesses a more than common charm in the vividness of his relation.

MURRAY (Hon. Charles A.).

Travels in North America; Including a summer residence with the Pawnee Tribe of Indians, in the remote prairies of the Missouri, and a visit to Cuba and the Azore Islands. Third edition. 2 *vols.* 12° Vol. I. *pp.* xl. *and* 343. Vol. II. *pp.* xi. *and* 336. *London:* 1854. 1112

MURRAY (Hugh).

Historical Account of Discoveries, and Travels in North America, including the United States, Canada, the Shores of the Polar Sea, and the Voyages in Search of a North West passage, with observations on emigration. Illustrated by a Map of North America. 8° 2 *vols., pp.* 530 *and* 556. *London,* 1829. 1113

This work contains a vast amount of information regarding the condition of the aborigines of America, before it was modified by association with Europeans, and a Bibliography of Voyages and Travels in America.

MURRAY (T. B.).

Kalle, the Esquimaux Christian. A Memoir. By the Rev. T B. Murray. 16° *pp.* 70. *New York, General Protestant Episcopal S. School Union and Church Book Society, n. d.* 1114

Murr (Christoph Gottlieb Von).

Reisen einger Missionarien der Gesellschaft Jesu in America. Aus ihren eigenen Aussaken herausgegeben Von Christoph Gottlieb Von Murr. Mit einer Landkarte und Kupfern. 8° *pp.* (viii.) + 615 + *map, and two folding plates. Nurnberg, bey Johann Eberhard Zeh,* 1785. 1115

[Voyages of some Missionaries of the Society of Jesus, in America. Published from their own declarations by C. G. von Murr. With Maps and Copperplates. Nurnberg, 1785. 8°]

A large portion of the work, pp. 325 to 450, is devoted to a grammatical analysis of the Indian languages of South America, accompanied by extensive vocabularies. The titles of a considerable number of works upon the Indians and their languages are given. The folding plates are designed to illustrate life and habits.

Narrative | (A) |

of the late | Massacres, | in | Lancaster County, | of a | Number of Indians, | Friends of this Province, | By Persons Unknown. | With some Observations on the same. | Printed in the Year MDCCLXIV. | 8° *pp.* 31. (*Philadelphia*). 1116

This is another story of the method in which the cowards of the frontiers revenged upon innocent and helpless old men, and young children, the outrages of Indian warriors whom they dared not meet. The pamphlet narrates the destruction of the feeble remnant of the Conestoga tribe, by those whose bodies must have been inhabited by fiends from hell, instead of human souls. The inhuman slaughter of Christian men and women with their babes, by the mob of Scotch and Irish frontier settlers, is the most horrible picture of human phrensy this continent ever saw. Among all the atrocities which have been attributed to the Spaniards, as having been perpetrated upon the Indians, no historian has ever charged them with the merciless slaughter of Christian and friendly tribes, to revenge the outrages of pagan and hostile savages. The pamphlet is said to have been written by Benjamin Franklin, and is among the rarest of works relating to the history of Pennsylvania.

Narrative (A)

of Occurrences in the Indian Countries of North America, since the connexion of the Right Hon. the Earl of Selkirk with the Hudson's Bay Company, and his attempt to establish a colony on the Red River; with a detailed account of his lordship's military expedition to, and subsequent proceedings at Fort William, in Upper Canada. 8° *pp.* 87. *London:* 1817. 1117

This narrative is the second of that long catalogue of statements, histories, and narratives to which the murder of Governor Semple by the half-breed Indians, in the service of the Northwest Fur Company, gave existence. The first publication was the "Sketch of the Fur Trade in North America," by the benevolent and enterprising Lord Selkirk. This narrative is the rejoinder of the Northwest Fur Company, covering pp. 1 to 152. The Appendix which follows, paged separately 1 to 87, is composed of affidavits of the traders, of Indian speeches, etc. The next work in order of this embroglio is entitled, "Statement respecting Lord Selkirk's Settlement, its Destruction, Massacre of Governor Semple, etc."

Narrative (A).

A Narrative of the early days and reminiscences of Oceola Nikkanochee, prince of Econchatti, a young Seminole Indian; son of Econchatti-Mico, king of the Red Hills, in Florida; with a brief history of his nation, and his renowned uncle, Oceola, and his parents; and amusing tales illustrative of Indian life in Florida. Written by his guardian. 8° *Prel. pp.* (viii.) + 328 *and 3 plates. London:* 1841. 1118

NARRATIVE

of A Voyage to the Spanish Main, in the Ship "Two Friends;" The occupation of Amelia Island by McGregor &c. Sketches of the Province of East Florida, and anecdotes illustrative of the habits and manners of the Seminole Indians: with an Appendix containing a detail of the Seminole War, and the execution of Arbuthnot and Ambrister. 8° *pp.* 14 *and* 1 *to* 328. *London: printed for John Miller,* 1819. 1119

The narrator gives in this work the results of his observations regarding the people and government of Florida, during the last days of its occupation by the Spaniards. Almost the whole of the volume subsequent to, and including Chapter x., pp. 147 to 328, is devoted to the Seminole Indians; the barbarous character of the war of the Americans with them; and anecdotes respecting the Seminoles. The Appendix is entitled "Seminole War: execution of Arbuthnot and Ambrister." The details of the seizure of these two Indian traders, on the soil of a friendly power, themselves citizens of another friendly government, engaged in a lawful commerce, their trial and execution by General Jackson, for selling arms to the Seminoles, whom they believed, and whom history records, to have been justly fighting against aggression, are all related at length, and principally by exact copies of historical documents.

NARRAGANSET CHIEF.

The Narraganset Chief; or the adventures of A Wanderer. Written by himself. 12° *pp.* 195. *New York: J. K. Porter, 144 Fulton Street,* 1832. 1120

This purports to be a veritable narration of incidents in the life of an Indian.

NARRATIVE

of recent proceedings of the committee, appointed by the yearly meeting of Friends of New York, in Relation to The Indians in that State. Published for the information of Friends. 8° *pp.* 23. *New York, Mercein & Post's Press,* 240 *Pearl Street,* 1839. 1121

NARRATIVE.

A very surprising Narrative of a Young Woman, discovered in a Rocky Cave, after having been taken by the Savage Indians of the Wilderness, In the year 1777. And seeing no human being for the space of nine years. In a letter from a gentleman to his friend. 16° *pp.* 12. *Brookfield, December* 1800. 1122

There is nothing in the composition of this pamphlet to forbid its being considered a puerile fiction. It is so poor indeed as to delude no one but a book collector.

NEILL (Rev. Edward D.).

Pocahontas and her Companions; a chapter from the history of the Virginia company of London. By Rev. Edward D. Neill. 4° *pp.* 32. *Albany,* 1869. 1123

In common with Beutre, a celebrated French wit, we may be compelled to ask every year of our iconoclasts what saints will be left canonized for us to worship. Mr. Charles Deane and Mr. Neill have attacked the authenticity of Captain John Smith's history, the chastity of Pocahontas, and the legitimacy of the Randolphs, in one breath. In this essay Mr. Neill quotes from the narrations of Smith, Strachey, Argall, Chamberlain, Hamor, Whitaker, Purchas, and others, to prove that Rolfe did not and could not marry Pocahontas, as he had brought a white wife from England. The evidence is at best only negative, plausible merely by omission, and very inconclusive.

NEW ENGLAND.

New | ENGLANDS | FIRST FRUITS; | in Respect, | First of the { Conversion of some / Conviction of divers / Preparation of sundry } of the *Indians.* | 2. Of the progress of *Learning*, in the *Colledge* at | Cambridge in *Massacusets* Bay. | With | Divers other speciall Matters concerning that *Countrey.* | Published by the instant request of sundry Friends who desire | to be satisfied in these points by many New England Men | who are here present, and were eye or eare- | witnesses of the same. | [*Motto 5 lines.*] *Small* 4° *Title, reverse blank* + *pp.* 1 *to* 26. *London,* | *Printed by R. O. and G. D. for Henry Overton, and are to be* | *sold at his Shop in Popes-head-Alley.* 1643. 1124

This is the first of the series of eleven tracts by John Eliot and others which were printed by the Corporation for the Propagation of the Gospel amongst the Indians in New England.

NEW ENGLAND'S FIRST FRUITS,

With Divers other Special Matters Concerning that Country. 4° *Two prel. leaves, and pp.* 47. *New York, reprinted for Joseph Sabin,* 1865. 1125

This reprint of the first of that series of reports to the Corporation for Propagating the Gospel among the Indians of New England, known as the Eliot *Tracts*, has the great defect of being published without note, comment, or biographical sketch. Indeed, the whole of Mr. Sabin's reprints are unedited, and thus an excellent opportunity, of adding to the common stock of knowledge regarding their bibliographical history as well as that of their author, editors, and the venerable society which printed them, was lost.

NEW HAMPSHIRE.

Collections of the New-Hampshire Historical Society for the year 1824 [*and other years*]. *Eight volumes.* 8° *pp.* 300 *to* 500. *Concord.* 1126

Vol. I. pp. 10 to 165, Penhallow's "Indian Wars," preceded by a Memoir of the author. Note on the Penacook Indians.

Vol. II. Captain Wheeler's "Narrative of Expedition against the Nipmucks." "Attack of the Indians on Walpole in 1755." "Annals of Keene." "Indian treaties."

Vol. III. Journal of John Pike.

Vol. IV. Abner Clough's "Journal of Expedition against Indians 1746."

Vol. V. Journal of Captain Stevens to redeem Indian Captives 1749. Journal of Captain Melvin.

Vol. VI. Journal of Daniel Livermore of the Western Expedition, 1779.

Vol. VIII. "Massacre at Dover by the Indians." "Character of the Penacooks." "Indian Names along the Merrimac."

NEWHOUSE (S.).

The Trappers Guide. A Manual of Instructions for Capturing all kinds of Fur-bearing Animals, and Curing their Skins; with Observations on the Fur trade; Hints on Life in the Woods, and Narratives of Trapping, and Hunting Excursions. By S. Newhouse, and other trappers and sportsmen. Second edition, with new narratives and illustrations. Edited by J. H. Noyes. 8° *pp.* 215. *Published by Oneida Community. Printed Wallingford, Ct.*, 1867. 1127

There is only the obvious reason for admitting this book into this Catalogue, that it is so fully illustrative of the habits of the animals, which form a great portion of the Indian's subsistence, and the subtle craft by which he is obliged to circumvent their sagacity and cunning instinct. It is the work, not of one man only, but of many acute and observing woodsmen, who have spent their lives watching the habits of the denizens of the forest, and in discovering the devices by which the sly, timid, and crafty beasts preserved their hunted lives. It is in fact a revelation of the secrets of all the wild animals which haunt the streams or woods, obtained from the reticent Indian and the garrulous fur-hunter.

NEW-JERSEY

Historical Society. Proceedings of the. *Ten volumes.* 8° *Newark*, 1847 *to* 1867. 1128

Vol. I. "Journal of Captain John Schuyler to Canada 1690."
Vol. II. "Journals of Lieutenant Barton, and Dr. Elmer during Sullivan's Expedition against the Seneca Indians," pp. 22 to 51. "Journal of Lieutenant Elmer of Expedition to Canada 1776," pp. 95 to 190.
Vol. III. "Journal of Lieutenant Elmer," continued pp. 21 to 90.
Vol. IV. "The Aborigines of New Jersey," by A. Gifford, pp. 159 to 200.

NEKAGH-YA-DOUGH-SE-RA.

Ne Royadadokenghdy, ne Isaiah. 16° *pp.* 248. *New York, printed for the American Bible Society*, 1839. 1129

The book of Isaiah, translated into the Mohawk dialect.

NEWMAN (John B.).

Origin of the Red Men. An authentic History of the peopling of America, by the Atlantians, and Tyrians. The origin of the Toltecs [*etc.*, 8 *lines*] illustrated with a portrait of Montezuma, the last of the Aztec Emperors. 12° *pp.* 48. *New York*, 1852. 1130

NEW SOCIETY (A).

for the Benefit of the Indians, organized at the City of Washington. February 1822. 8° *pp.* 15. 1131

NEWS FROM NEW ENGLAND,

Being A True and last Account of the present Bloody Wars carried on betwixt the Infidels, Natives, and the English Christians, and Converted Indians of New England, declaring the many Dreadful Battles, Fought betwixt them: As also the many Towns and Villages burnt by the merciless Heathens. And also the true Number of all the Christians slain since the beginning of that War, as it was sent over by a Factor of New-England to a

Merchant in London. 4° *pp.* 20. *London*, 1676. *Boston, N. E. Reprinted for Samuel G. Drake*, 1850. 1132

NEW YORK.

Collections of the New York Historical Society for the year 1809, Vol. I. 1814, Vol. II. 1814, Vol. III. 1826, Vol. IV. 1829, Vol. IV., reprint. 1830, Vol. V. Second series, Vol. I. 1841. Vol. II. 1847, and 1848. Vol. III. Part I. 1849. 8° *New York*, together eight volumes, besides reprint of Vol. IV. 1135

There are many papers of great merit in these volumes, relating to some characteristics of the aborigines. In Vol. II. will be found De Witt Clinton's "Discourse on the Geographical, Political, and Historical View of the Red Men of New York," pp. 37 to 116. La Salle's "Account of his last Expedition and Discoveries," pp. 317 to 368. Vol. III. Dr. Jarvis' "Discourse on the Religion of the Indian Tribes of N. A." Vol. I. second series, Verrazano's "Voyages," "Indian Tradition of first Settlement of New York," Lambrechtsens' "History of New Netherlands," Vander Donk's "Description of New Netherlands," "Extract from De Vries' Voyages," Juet's "Journal of Hudson's Voyages," "Dermer's letter, giving an Account of the Indians of N. E." Vol. II. of second series, Mr. H. C. Murphy's "Complete translation of De Vries' Voyages," pp. 9-137. "Narrative of Captivity, and Martyrdom of Father Jogues, by the Mohawks," pp. 161 to 236. "Short Sketch of the Mohawks," by J. Megapolensis, pp. 147 to 160. Vol. III. "Memoir on Dutch and Indian," by Beason, pp. 97 to 149. "Narrative of Marquis De Nonville's Expedition against the Senecas," pp. 149 to 193. -

NEW YORK HISTORICAL SOCIETY (Proceedings of the).

New York, Press of the Historical Society. 8° 7 *vols.* 1843 *to* 1849. 1136

Among the numerous papers read before the Society, and published in these volumes, will be found many of more than ordinary interest, upon the subjects connected with aboriginal history. In Vol. I. is printed, Mr. Bartlett's "Progress of Ethnology." Vol. II. Schoolcraft's "Aboriginal Names of New York." Vol. III. Thompson's "Indian Names of L. I." Schoolcraft's "Siege and Defence of Fort Stanwix." "Employment of the Indians by the English in the Revolutionary War." Vol. IV. 1846, Van Rensselaer's "Memoir on the French and Indian Expedition against N. Y. and the burning of Schenectady, 1689," pp. 101 to 123. Schoolcraft's "Notices of Tumuli in Florida, and burial places of Indian Tribes," pp. 124 to 136. Vol. V. Gilman's "Defeat of Gen. St. Clair," Morgan's "Territorial Limits of the Iroquois," Peter Wilson's "Address on the Iroquois," O'Callaghan's "Jesuit Relations, with a Bibliographical Sketch of each." Vol. VII. "Champlain in the Onondaga Valley." Long's "Ancient Architecture in America."

NOAH (M. M.).

Discourse on the evidences of the American Indians being the descendants of the Lost Tribes of Israel. By M. M. Noah. 8° *pp.* 40. *New York:* 1837. 1137

In this treatise, Mr. Noah, an eminent Jew, for many years the editor of the *Sunday Atlas*, by far the highest in literary rank of that class of journals, endeavors to establish the identity of the ten lost tribes of Israel, with the American Indians. It is by no means exhaustive, the editor having apparently consulted only the more easily accessible and not very erudite authorities.

NORMAN (B. M.).

Rambles in Yucatan, or, notes of travel through the peninsula, including a visit to the remarkable ruins of Chi-chen, Kabah,

Zayl, and Uxmal. With numerous illustrations. By B. M. Norman (third edition). 8° *pp.* 304. *New York: J. & H. G. Langley*, 1843. 1138

Vignette, title, and full title + 23 full-page lithographic plates of Maya and Aztec ruins, temples, pyramids, idols, and Indians. Chapter xiv., pp. 236 to 251, is occupied with a dissertation on the Maya Language. The Appendix contains "A Brief Maya Vocabulary," of nine pages in double columns, besides traditional and historical sketches. It is said that Mr. Norman was hurriedly sent to Yucatan, to anticipate the researches of Mr. Stevens, who expended so much time and labor in careful examinations of the vast works of the extinct races, who inhabited the peninsula of Yucatan.

NORTON (Rev. John).

Narrative of the Capture, and Burning of Fort Massachusetts by the French and Indians, in the time of the war of 1744-1749, and the captivity of all those stationed there, to the number of thirty persons. Written at the time by one of the captives, the Rev. Mr. John Norton, chaplain of the fort. Now first published with notes by Samuel G. Drake. 4° *pp.* 51. *Half title on cover. Albany: printed for S. G. Drake, of Boston, by Joel Munsell.* 1870. 1139

In this volume, Mr. Drake has not only reprinted the very rare narrative of the captivity of Mr. Norton, but he has added a biography, and many notes, explanatory of the very minute relations of the captive. The original narrative was printed in Boston, 1748, and in common with all the publications of its class and period, has become exceedingly rare.

NORTON (John N.).

Pioneer Missionaries, or the lives of Phelps and Nash. By John N. Norton. 16° *pp.* 193. *New York, General Protestant Episcopal S. School Union and Church Book Society, 762 Broadway,* 1850. 1140

In Chapters iv., v., vi., vii., the author gives many particulars of the early life of Brant, the Mohawk chief, who was a schoolmate of the missionary Phelps.

NOTE

Sur les Botecudos, accompagne d' un Vocabulaire de leur langue, et de quelqes remarques. 8° *pp.* 1 *to* 13. *Paris*, 1846. 1141

[Notes on the Botecudos, accompanied by a Vocabulary of their language, and some remarks.]

Preceding these thirteen pages is a leaf, on the reverse of which is printed, "Extrait du Bulletin de la Societe de Geographie Nov. et Dec. 1846." Two young Indians of the Botecudos, a savage tribe inhabiting the forests of Brazil, having arrived in Paris, drew forth all the interest of the savans exhibited in this brochure. The vocabulary was obtained by M. Pointe.

NOTICES

of Sullivan's Campaign, or the Revolutionary Warfare in Western New York: embodied in the addresses and documents connected with the Funeral Honors, rendered to those who fell with the gallant Boyd in the Gennesse Valley including remarks of Gov. Seward at Mount Hope. 18° *pp.* 192. *Plate. Rochester: published by William Alling*, 1842. 1142

This volume was edited by Henry S. O'Reilly. It is far from being exhaustive of Sullivan's celebrated campaign, of which abundant materials exist to form an interesting and valuable history. The massacre of Lieutenant Boyd and his party, has attracted the interest and sympathy of a vast number of readers, but there are few that have heard the story which makes his fate seem almost a just retribution. "When the company of which he was an officer, was forming for the march to the rendezvous, a young girl endeavored to draw him aside, to whose entreaties he offered only a contemptuous refusal. Rendered desperate by her wrongs, she declared that she was about to become a mother, through his promises of marriage, and then in the most solemn manner abjured him to fulfill them. As he turned a deaf ear to her entreaties, she terminated the scene, by beseeching his Maker to prevent his returning alive, if he abandoned her." Simms' *History of Schoharie County.*

NOTICES

of East Florida, with an account of the Seminole Nation of Indians. By a recent traveller in the province. 12° *pp.* 105. *Charleston: printed for the author*, 1822. 1143

The author kept a journal of his observations during his travels in the Seminole country, and on pp. 64 to 96, he gives "An Account of the Seminole Nation of Indians," drawn up from his notes. As the results of the personal intercourse of an intelligent observer of the character and peculiarities of that interesting people, it possesses more than common interest. "A vocabulary of the Seminole Language," occupies pp. 97 to 105, a portion of which is in MS. obtained (as a MS. note informs us), from the "unfortunate Arbuthnot, hanged as a British spy, by order of General Jackson."

NOVA-SCOTIA.

A Geographical History of Nova Scotia. Containing an Account of the Situation, Extent, and Limits thereof. [*etc.*, 12 *lines.*] Together with the Manners and Customs of the Indian Inhabitants. 8° *pp.* 110. *London:* 1749. 1144

NUTTALL (Thos.).

A Journal of Travels into the Arkansa Territory, during the year 1819. With occasional observations on the manners of the Aborigines. Illustrated by a map and other engravings. By Thomas Nuttall. 8° 5 *engravings and map* + *pp.* xii. + 9 *to* 296. *Philadelphia: printed and published by Thomas H. Palmer*, 1821. 1145

The naturalist records in almost every chapter some incidents of his personal intercourse with the Chickasaw, Cherokee, and Osage Indians, then inhabiting the territory he explored. It is in the Appendix, however, that he has grouped, more particularly, his observations regarding the Indians. Section I. pp. 247 to 267, is entitled, "An Account of the Ancient Aboriginal population of the banks of the Mississippi." Section II. is headed, "The History of the Natchez," and occupies pp. 268 to 282; and Section III. pp. 283 to 294, has the subject title, "Observations on the Chickasaws and Cherokees." The author was so capable, by his long scientific culture, of affording us the most valuable contributions to ethnology and philology, that it is much to be regretted that the manuscripts of which he speaks in the Preface have never been published. "Not wishing to enlarge the present publication, I reserve for a subsequent volume which will shortly be issued, 'A general View and Description of the Aboriginal Antiquities of the Western States,' and some '*Essays* on the Languages of the Western Indians.' The surveys and collections towards a history of the aboriginal antiquities, have remained unpublished in my possession for several years." Cannot some persevering and fortunate antiquarian unearth these treasures; the means of putting them before the world would not long be wanting.

O'CALLAGHAN (E. B.).

Jesuit Relations of Discoveries and other occurrences in Canada and the Northern and Western States of the Union. 1632–1672. By E. B. O'Callaghan, M. D. From the Proceedings of the New York Historical Society. 8° *pp.* 1 *to* 22. *New York, Press of the Historical Society*, 1847. 1146

In this biographical and bibliographical essay, Dr. O'Callaghan gives brief sketches of the writers of the relations or reports, to their superior, of the Jesuit missionaries among the Indians of New York and Canada. It also contains a synopsis of the contents of each Relation known to him, and on the last leaf, a Table showing the date and present owner of the copies, which he ascertained to be in existence. Dr. O'Callaghan enumerates only forty; of which Mr. J. C. Brown had thirty-six, Harvard College thirty-five, H. C. Murphy twenty-nine. Each of these libraries have increased their number, and of the forty-eight now known to exist, Mr. Murphy has secured all but three. Of all the objects of bibliographical acquisitions, there is none so difficult of completion as this. A perfect set of the Jesuit relations of the missions to Canada, is not known to exist, although it is believed one could be formed from the three collections named.

O'CALLAGHAN (E. B.).

A brief and true Narrative of the Hostile Conduct of the Barbarous Natives towards the Dutch Nation. Translated by E. B. O'Callaghan. 8° *pp.* 48. *Albany:* 1863. 1147

As late as 1655, the Indians of New York were revenging the murderous slaughter of four hundred of their countrymen at Pavonia, by that sanguinary coward, Governor Kieft. The petition shows that three hundred of the Dutch colony had been slain, and one hundred carried away captives. So audacious had the fierce Indians become, that several of the Dutch had been killed on the island of Manhattan; and on one occasion sixty four canoes loaded with the savages had landed on the shore of the North River, and before daylight, had filled the streets of New Amsterdam. The first objects upon which the eyes of the astonished Dutchmen rested in the morning, were the crowds of savages to whose forbearance alone they owed their lives. Only fifty copies of the work are said to have been printed.

OCCOM (Samson).

A Sermon, Preached at the Execution of Moses Paul, an Indian, Who was executed at New Haven, on the 2d of September, 1772, for the Murder of Mr. Moses Cook, Late of Waterbury, on the 7th of December, 1771. Preached at the Desire of the said Paul. By Samson Occom, Minister of the Gospel, and Missionary to the Indians. 12° *pp.* 32. *Boston: printed and sold by John Boyle, next door to the Three Doves in Marlborough-Street.* 1773. 1148

OCCOM (Samson).

A Sermon at the Execution of Moses Paul, an Indian; Who had been guilty of Murder. Preached at New Haven in America. By Samson Occom, A native Indian, and Missionary to the Indians, who was in England in 1766 and 1767, collecting for the Indian Charity Schools. To which is added a Short Account of the Late Spread of the Gospel among the Indians. Also Observations on the Language of the Muhhekaneew Indians;

communicated to the Connecticut Society of Arts and Sciences. By Jonathan Edwards, D. D. 8° pp. 24 + 16. *New Haven, Connecticut: Printed*, 1788. *London: Reprinted*, 1788. 1149

OCCOM (Sampson).

A Sermon preached at the Execution of Moses Paul, &c. By Samson Occom. 8° pp. 26. *Springfield, Henry Brewer, printer, n. d.* 1150

OCCOM (Samson).

A Sermon, preached at the Execution of Moses Paul, &c. By Samson Occom. 12° pp. 22. *Exeter: Printed for Josiah Richardson, the Lord's Messenger to the People*, 1819. 1151

Sampson Occom was a Mohegan Indian, born 1723. He was the first Indian pupil, of the celebrated Eleazar Wheelock, at his school in Lebanon, in 1748, where he remained four years, graduating at the age of twenty-three. He established a school among the Montauk Indians on Long Island, in 1755, which he continued for ten years. Being ordained as a clergyman of the Presbyterian church, he engaged as a missionary to the Oneida Indians for a year when he sailed for England, where he preached, in the course of a year and a half, nearly four hundred sermons. Wherever he spoke, the houses were thronged. The contributions for his schools reached five thousand dollars. On his return to America he again engaged as a missionary to the Indian tribes of Connecticut and New York, in which service he continued until his death in 1792. He was undoubtedly a zealous, pious minister, and his preaching is described by those whose judgment is conclusive, to have been more than ordinarily rational and eloquent. His sermon has been many times reprinted.

OGDEN (John C.).

Excursion to Bethlehem & Nazareth in Pennsylvania, in the Year 1799; with a succinct history of the Society of United Brethren, commonly called Moravians. By John C. Ogden. 16° pp. 167. *Philadelphia: printed by Charles Cist*, 1805. 1152

A short narration of the massacre of Christian Indians at Salem and Gnadenhutten, is all that entitles this book to a place in a collection of works on the aborigines.

OGLE COUNTY.

Sketches of the history of Ogle County, Ill., And the Early Settlement of the Northwest. Written for the Polo Advertiser. 8° pp. 88. *Polo, Illinois:* 1859. 1153

In this collection of memorabilia of a northwestern county, the association of its citizens both in peace and war, with the Indians, could not be omitted. Some particulars therefore of the neighboring tribes, in both relations, are to be found in its pages.

OJIBWAY LANGUAGE.

Ojibue Spelling Book. *Small* 4° pp. 96. *Boston*, 1846. 1154

OJIBWA NUGUMOSHANG.

Ojibwa Hymns. 16° pp. 95. *Published by the American Tract Society*, 150 *Nassau Street, New York.* 1155

OJIBWAY TESTAMENT.

Iu Otoshki-kikindiuin au Tebenim-nvng gale-bemajiinvng Jesus Christ Ima. Ojibue Inueuloing Gbzhitong. The New Testament of our Lord and Saviour Jesus Christ. Translated into the language of the Ojibwa Indians. 12° pp. 717. *New York. American Bible Society*. 1856. 1156

OLDEN TIME. See Craig (Neville B.). 1157.

ONTWA,

The Son of the Forest. A Poem (by an officer of the army at Detroit). 8° pp. 136. *New York*: 1822. With illustrative notes, from the MSS. of Lewis Cass, Governor of the Territory of Michigan. 1158

ON THE TEN TRIBES OF ISRAEL,

And the Aborigines of America, &c., &c. By a Bible Professor. This Publication is not made to gratify Man; but to aid the cause of God: therefore any one is at liberty to approve or disapprove the work, [*etc.*] Nett Sales of the Publication will be appropriated to the Canada Missions to the Indians. 8° pp. 32. *Providence, Indiana, May 2d* 1831. *New-Albany, Indiana*, 1831. *Printed by Collins and Green*. 1159

The real or fancied points of resemblance between the customs, language, and physical appearance of the American Indians and the Jews, has crazed the brains of thousands of theorists, and the author of this rhapsody adds one more to the category.

O'REILLY.

Greenland, the adjacent seas, and the North-West Passage to The Pacific Ocean, illustrated in a voyage to Davis's Strait during the summer of 1817. With charts and numerous plates, from drawings of the author taken on the spot. By Bernard O'Reilly, Esq. 4° pp. (viii.) + 293 + 2 *maps and* 17 *plates*. *London: printed for Baldwin, Cradock, and Joy*, 1818. 1160

The observations of the author on the natives of Greenland, are recorded on pp. 59 to 85, of which the last two are occupied with a vocabulary of their language. Five of the plates are illustrative of the features, or habits of life of the Esquimaux.

ORIGINE, ET PROGRESS

de la Mission du Kentucky, par un Temoin Oculaire. 8° pp. 32. *A Paris*, 1821. 1161

[Origin and Progress of the Missions in Kentucky, by an Eye-witness].

ORTON (J. R.).

Camp Fires of the Red Men, or A Hundred Years Ago. By J. R. Orton, New York. Illustrated by Wolcott. 12° pp. 401. *New York*, 1859. 1162

A novel in which the red men appear but seldom.

OVERTON (Judge).

Vindication of the Seminole War. 8° *Washington*, 1819. 1163

PAGAN (Count).

An | Historical & Geographical | Description | of the | Great Country & River | of the Amazones | in | America. | Drawn out of divers Authors, and reduced | into a better forme; with a Mapp of | the River, and of its Provinces being | that place which Sr Walter Rawleigh intended | to conquer and plant, when he made his Voy- | age to Guiana. | Written in French by the Count of Pagan, and | dedicated to Cardinall Mazarine, in order | to a Conquest by the Cardinals moti | on to be undertaken. | And now translated into English by William | Hamilton. and humbly offered to his Majesty, | as worthy his Consideration. | 12° *London, | printed for John Starkey at the Miter in Fleet | -Street near Temple-Barre*, 1661. 1164

Title, 1 leaf, Epistle and preliminary leaves, unnumbered 14 + map + pp. 1 to 153 + table (iii.). Several chapters of this curious work are devoted to descriptions of the aborigines of the valley of the Amazon; and those treating of the advantages of commerce with them, suggest an odd comparison with the works of our own day, written two centuries later, which do but little more than repeat the same statements.

It is compiled principally from that of Acuna. The map is almost without exception, missing from the copies offered for sale. It was first published in French, in Paris, 1655; another edition has the date of 1656. This is the first, and indeed only edition in English. The Count François de Pagan, engineer and astronomer, was born in 1604 near Avignon, and died in 1665. He distinguished himself in the wars of Italy and Flanders.

PALMER (Joel).

Journal of Travels over the Rocky Mountains, to the mouth of the Columbia River: made during the years 1845, and 1846: containing minute descriptions of the valleys of the Williamette, Umpqua, and Clamet; [*etc.*, 7 *lines*]. Also; a Letter from the Rev. H. H. Spalding, resident Missionary, for the last ten years, among the Nez Percé Tribe of Indians, on the Kooskooskee River; The organic laws of Oregon Territory; Tables of about 300 words of the Chinook Jargon, and about 200 words of the Nez Percé Language; a Description of Mount Hood; Incidents of Travel, &c., &c. By Joel Palmer. 8° *pp.* 189. *Cincinnati: J. A. & U. P. James*, 1847. 1165

This minute and carefully written journal affords us many new particulars of the life, manners, and customs of the savages of the Rocky Mountains, both in their wild and semi-civilized state. The description of the success of the mission of the unfortunate Dr. Widman, who with his family were soon afterwards massacred, is particularly interesting, as exhibiting the apparently irreclaimable ferocity of some savage tribes, even by the influences of Christianity.

PANDOSY (Rev. Mie Cles).

Grammar and Dictionary of the Yakama Language, by Rev. Mie Cles Pandosy oblate of Mary Immaculate. Translated by George Gibbs and J. G. Shea. *Large* 8° *New York, Cramoisy Press*, 1862. 1166

No. 6 of Shea's *Library of American Linguistics*.

The Yakamas were an Indian tribe inhabiting the banks of the Columbia and the Yakama rivers. The author of this grammar, Father Pandosy, resided for several years among them as a missionary, and thus became perfectly familiar with their language. The original manuscript, written in French, was lost in the conflagration, by which the mission establishment was destroyed. The descriptive preface occupies pp. vii. and viii. The Indian grammar, pp. 9 to 34, and the Dictionary, pp. 37 to 59.

PAPOONAHOAL.

An Account of a Visit lately made to the People called Quakers In Philadelphia, by Papoonahoal, An Indian Chief, And several other Indians, chiefly of the Minisink Tribe. With the Substance of their Conferences on that Occasion. 16° *pp.* 21. *London: Printed and Sold by S. Clark, in Bread-Street.* MDCCLXI. 1167

The extraordinary Indian chief whose visit is narrated in this account, deserved a memoir of greater extent, and a wider celebrity than has been conferred upon him. In his native forests, before communication from Christian advisers had reached him, he conceived the design of personal moral reform. To forward his purpose he visited the Quakers of Philadelphia, and as vouchers for his sincerity, he brought three white prisoners, and several stolen horses he had purchased from hostile tribes, after long journeys undertaken in search of them. His speeches to the Friends are models of good sense and religious conviction; but the most remarkable of all the numerous addresses by American Indians, was made by him to the Governor, who offered him a considerable, and to the chief very valuable amount of goods, as a present. The dignified and noble reply, in which he declined to receive them, on the ground that his visit was entirely for religious instruction, and therefore of too sacred a character to admit of the gross indulgence of personal desires, is worthy of a place on the same page with the most renowned sayings of the heroes of antiquity. The book is of considerable rarity.

PATTERSON (A. W.).

History of the Backwoods; or, the region of the Ohio: authentic, from the Earliest Accounts. Embracing many events, notices of prominent pioneers, sketches of early settlements, etc., etc., etc. Not heretofore published. By A. W. Patterson. 8° *pp.* 311 *and map.* *Pittsburgh:* 1843. 1168

Mr. Patterson's work is a very good compilation of the narratives, histories, and sketches of western adventure and frontier life, with a considerable proportion of that material described by the author as "Not heretofore published." He seems to have had access to documents containing some interesting details and to have availed himself of such information as could be derived from the actors in the scenes he describes, or their immediate descendants.

PARAVEY (Chev de)

Documens hieroglyphiques, emportes d' Assyrie, et conserves en Chine et en Amerique, sur le Deluge de Noe, les dix generations avant le deluge, l'existence d' un premier homme, et celle du peche original: Dogmes qui sont la base du Christianisme, mais qui sont nies en ce jour. Par le Chev de Paravey. *A Paris chez Treutel et Wurz et Masse Libraries,* 1838. 8° *pp.* 57 + 2 *plates & 1 folding chart.* 1169

[Hieroglyphic Documents brought from Persia, and preserved in China and in America, on the Deluge of Noah, the ten generations before the deluge, the existence of a first man, and that of original sin: Dogmas which are the base of Christianity, but which are denied in this day.]

This treatise attempts the authentication of the principal dogmas of the Jewish faith, as adopted by Christianity, from the sacred writings of the Chaldees, Chinese, and Aztecs. The portion devoted to the decipherment of such Mexican pictographs as the author believes aid in his hypotheses, occupy pp. 41 to 56. A large folding plate is entitled, "Copy of an ancient Mexican Picture, preserving the memory of the Deluge, and of some other biblical facts, and also indicating the route by the Aztecs in going to establish themselves in Mexico."

PARAVEY (M. de).

L'Amerique sous le nom de pays de Fou Sang, est-elle citee, des le 5ᵉ siecle de notre ere, dans les grandes annales de la Chine, et, deslors, les Sameneens, [*etc.*] . . . . discussion ou dissertation abregee, ou le' affirmative est prouvee, by M. de Paravey. *Paris*, 1844. 8° *pp.* 1 + 27. 1170

[America under the name of Fou Sang, as it is noticed in the fifth century of our era, in the great annals of China.]

PARAVEY (M. de).

Memoire sur l' origine Japonaise, Arabe et Basque de la civilisation des peuples du Plateau de Bogota, d' apres les travaux recens de MM. de Humboldt et Siebold. Par M. de Paravey. 8° *pp.* 33 + *plate*. *Paris, Dondey-Dupre libraire*, 1833. 1171

[Memoir on the Japanese, Arab, and Basque origin of the Natives of the Plains of Bogota from the recent travels of Messieurs Humboldt and Siebold.]

PARAVEY (M.).

Nouvelles Preuves que le pays du Fou-Sang mentionné dans les livres Chinois est l' Amerique. (*Paris*, 1847.) 8° *pp.* 12 & *plate*. 1172

[New Proofs that the Country of Fou-Sang, mentioned in the Chinese books, is America.]

The plate represents a man of the kingdom of Fou-Sang milking a *llama*, an animal only known in America; with a figure of Buddha, found at Uxmal, in Yucatan. M. Paravey, an eminent scholar of the Chinese and other Oriental languages, in these treatises brought the resources of his learning, to establish the theory of communication with America by the Chinese. He was successful at least, in adding another plausible hypothesis to the list of speculations, on a subject incapable of proof. Another pamphlet written by him is entitled *Dissertation sur les Amanmes, or the memory of them preserved in China.*

PARISH (Elijah).

A Sermon preached at Boston, November 3, 1814, before the Society for Propagating the Gospel among the Indians and others in North America. By Elijah Parish. 8° *pp.* 44. *Boston*, 1814. 1173

An Appendix of fifteen pages, is composed of historical notes of Indian missions.

PARKER (W. B.).

Notes taken during the expedition commanded by Capt. R. B. Marcy, U. S. A., through unexplored Texas. In the Summer and Fall of 1854. By W. B. Parker. Attached to the Expedition. 12° *pp.* 242. *Philadelphia, Hayes & Zell, No.* 193 *Market Street*, 1856. 1174

Under this unpretending title, the author has given us a volume crowded with the most interesting details of personal intercourse with the Indian tribes of the southern prairies, — the Bedouins of the American desert.

PARKER (Rev. Samuel).

Journal of an Exploring Tour beyond the Rocky Mountains, under the direction of the A. B. C. F. M. Containing a Description of the geography, geology, climate, productions of the country, and the Numbers, Manners, and Customs of the Natives, with a Map of the Oregon Territory. By Rev. Samuel Parker. 12° *Map + pp.* 416. *Fourth Edition. Ithaca, N. Y.*, 1844. 1175

First published at Albany, 1838, with the addition, after the sixth line of the title, of "Performed in the years 1835, 36, and 37." "A leading object of this Exploration," the author announces in his preface, "was to become acquainted with the situation of the remote Indian Tribes, and their disposition in regard to teachers of Christianity." This part of the duties was exceedingly well performed by an intelligent and discriminating man. The author's personal experience among the nomads of the plains, the root-diggers of the mountains, and the fish-eaters of the western slope, is given with sufficient detail to attract our interest, and with such evident adherence to fidelity of narration as to acquire our confidence and belief. In all the qualities which a historian would require, it has few equals. The author indeed anticipates the requirements of his day, and furnishes the philologist with a vocabulary of four Indian tongues, extending over sixteen pages (401 to 416).

PARKER (James W.).

NARRATIVE of the perilous adventures, miraculous escapes and sufferings of Rev. JAMES W. PARKER, during a frontier residence in Texas, of fifteen years; with an impartial geographical description of the climate, soil, timber, water, &c., &c., &c., of TEXAS; written by himself. To which is appended a NARRATIVE of the capture, and subsequent sufferings, of Mrs. Rachel Plummer, (his daughter) during a captivity of twenty-one months among the Cumanche Indians; with a sketch of their manners, customs, laws, &c., with a short description of the country over which she travelled whilst with the Indians; written by herself. *Printed at the Morning Courier, 4th Street, Louisville, Ky.*, 1844. 12° *pp.* 1 *to* 95 + *Narrative of Mrs. Rachel Plummer, pp.* 1 *to* 36, *numbered* 35, *total* 136 *pp.* 1176

Second Title, on 97th page: —

Narrative of the Capture and subsequent Sufferings, of Mrs. Rachel Plummer, during a captivity of twenty-one months among the Cumanche Indians, with a sketch of their manners, customs, laws, &c., &c. With A short description of the Country over which she travelled whilst with the Indians. 1839.

PARKMAN (Francis).

Prairie and Rocky Mountain Life; or, the California and Oregon Trail. By Francis Parkman. *Third Edition.* 12° *pp.* 448. *Frontispiece and engraved Title. New York: George P. Putnam*, 1852. 1177

The accomplished author of *Conspiracy of Pontiac; Jesuits in America;* and *Pioneers of New France*, caught in the experiences recorded in this volume, the incentive which led his researches in the direction of aboriginal life. Mr. Parkman had all the genuine love of adventure of a frontiersman, the taste for the picturesque and romantic of an artist, and the skill in narration of an accomplished raconteur. It is not too high praise of his work to say, that his pictures of savage life are not excelled by the narratives which had their birth in the personal experience of Washington Irving, or the imagination of

Fenimore Cooper. He had the advantage of both these authors in one respect. While he brought all the zeal of an antiquary, and the refinements of education to his researches, he lived in the wigwams and tents of the savages, and endured all the hardships of a hunter's every-day struggle for existence. His book is crowded with descriptions of Indian life, of which we have heard but one fault expressed, — that they are narrated with a mocking tone that tantalizes the sober reader with the suspicion that the author is covertly laughing at him.

PARKMAN (Francis).

History of the Conspiracy of Pontiac, and the War of the North American Tribes against the English Colonies after the Conquest of Canada. By Francis Parkman, Jr. *Large* 8° *pp.* xxiv. + 632. *Boston: Little, Brown, & Co.*, 1866. 1178

The charm which Mr. Parkman's books assert on the attention of every reader, is not wholly derived from the delicious style of his writing. His perfect knowledge of Indian life and manners, acquired by personal experience, and his exhaustion of the literature of his subject, as it is found in printed works, unedited manuscripts, and authenticated tradition, give new interest to a subject so often illustrated as the life of the Ottawa chief. Subsequent researches, elicited doubtless by Mr. Parkman's work, have brought new material to light, but it adds little to the historical value of his history.

PARKMAN (Francis).

Pioneers of France in the New World. By Francis Parkman. *Large* 8° *pp.* xix. + 420. *Boston: Little, Brown, and Company*, 1866. 1179

Part I. of the series "France and England in North America."

PARKMAN (Francis).

The Jesuits in North America in the Seventeenth Century. By Francis Parkman. *Royal* 8° *pp.* lxxxix. *and* 1 *to* 463. *Boston, Little, Brown, and Company*, 1867. 1180

PARKMAN (Francis).

The Discovery of the Great West. By Francis Parkman. *Large* 8° *pp.* xxi. + 425 + *map. Boston: Little, Brown, and Company*, 1869. 1181

The last three works have each the serial title of *France and England in North America. A series of historical narratives*, Parts I. to III. They are beautifully printed, the edition of this size being limited to one hundred copies.

PARKMAN (Francis).

Historical Account of Bouquet's Expedition. Against the Ohio Indians, in 1764. With Preface, by Francis Parkman, and a Translation of Dumas' Biographical Sketch of General Bouquet. *Large* 8° *pp.* xxiii. + 162 + *map and* 4 *plates and plans. Cincinnati, O., Robert Clarke & Co.*, 1868. 1182

PARSONS (Usher).

Indian Names of Places in Rhode Island. Collected by Usher Parsons, M. D. for the R. I. Historical Society. 8° *pp.* 32. *Providence*, 1861. 1183

PARRY (Captain W. E.).

Journal of a Second Voyage for the Discovery of a North-West passage from the Atlantic to the Pacific; performed in the years 1821–22–23 in his Majesty's Ships Fury and Hecla, under the orders of Captain William Edward Parry, R. N., F. R. S., and Commander of the Expedition. Illustrated with Numerous Plates. Published by authority of the Lords Commissioners of the Admiralty. 4° *London: John Murray*, 1824. 1184

Pages xxx. + 571 + 32 copperplate engravings, and 6 folding maps and plans drawn by Captain Lyon.

Throughout the whole of this splendid work, the characteristics of the Esquimaux, and incidents of intercourse with them, absorb the attention of the writer. The last seventy-nine pages are entirely devoted to the subject of the aborigines of the Arctic lands, under the sub-title of "Some Further Account of the Esquimaux of Melville Peninsula," fourteen of which are occupied with a vocabulary, in double columns. Of the thirty-two beautifully engraved copperplates, twenty-two are illustrative of the "Domestic Life of the Esquimaux," their fishing and walrus-hunting, their boats, summer tents, winter huts, villages, modes of travelling, building and hunting, interior of their dwellings, their villages, music, charts of the coast drawn by Esquimaux, implements of hunting, and portraits of characteristic individuals singly and in groups. The work is in truth a splendid treatise on aboriginal life, rather than a narrative of scientific discoveries.

PATON (Alexander).

Narrative of the loss of the schooner Clio, of Montrose, Captain George Reid; containing an account of the massacre of her crew by the Indians, on the north coast of Brazil, in October, 1835; with other interesting particulars, relative to the subsequent Adventures, and miraculous escape of the author from the hands of a savage people. By Alexander Paton, a native of Ferryden, the only Survivor. Second edition, enlarged and improved. 12° *pp.* 60. *Montrose: published by Smith & Co.*, 1838. 1185

Alexander Paton has the testimony of the minister of the kirk of his native village, in Scotland, to the veracity of his statements. At the period of his return from captivity, he was twenty years of age. The leading facts of the barbarous massacre of his captain and shipmates had reached his native land, some time before his escape. The narrative of his captivity, the murder of his comrades by the Indians, and of his escape, is told with the simple style of truth, and affords us a new view of the character of the natives of the coast of Brazil.

PATTIE (James O.).

The Personal Narrative of James O. Pattie, of Kentucky, during an expedition from St. Louis, through the vast regions between that place and the Pacific Ocean, and thence back through the city of Mexico to Vera Cruz, during journeyings of six years: in which he and his father, who accompanied him, suffered unheard of hardships and dangers, had various conflicts with the Indians, and were made captives, in which captivity his father died: Together with a description of the country, and the various nations through which they passed. Edited by Timothy Flint. 8° *pp.* 300. *Cincinnati: published by E. H. Flint.* 1833. 1186

The narrative of Pattie's expedition and captivity has more than the ordinary interest and value, which attaches to the stories of adventurers. He crossed the continent of America on a route which his party were the first to pursue. He encountered tribes of Indians who then saw a white man for the first time, and his narrative has the merit of being given in a candid, unexaggerated style, which impresses us with its veracity. The story of the perilous expedition, the frightful extremities to which his party were reduced, the fights with the savages, and his final capture, are all narrated with spirit and candor.

PAXTON MEN.

The Conduct of | The Paxton-Men, | Impartially represented; | The Distresses of the Frontiers, and the | Complaints and Sufferings of the People fully | stated; and the Methods recommended by the wisest | Nations, in such Cases, seriously consider'd. | With some | Remarks upon the Narrative, | Of the Indian-Massacre, lately published. | Interspers'd with several interesting Anecdotes, relating to the | Military Genius, and Warlike Principles of the | People called Quakers: Together with proper Reflec | tion and Advice upon the whole. | In a Letter from a Gentleman in one of the | Back-Counties, to a Friend in Philadelphia. | [*Motto* 17 *lines*]. 12° *Half title + full title + pp.* 3 *to* 34. *Philadelphia: Printed by A. Steuart, and Sold by John Creaig, Shop | keeper in Lancaster*, 1764. 1187

The sanguinary wretches of Pennsylvania, who have been pilloried before the world under the title of "Paxton-Men," thought it necessary to print their defense against the charges of monstrous cruelty and cowardice, made by Franklin in his *Massacre of Indians at Lancaster*. These fastidious murderers slaughtered a number of inoffensive Christian Indians, out of revenge for the outrages committed by their savage brethren, whom these cowardly frontiersmen feared to encounter. This tract is their attempted exculpation, but it has hitherto only monumented their own infamy.

PAXTON MEN.

See Conduct of Paxton Men; Serious Advice to inhabitants of Penn.; Narrative of Massacre of Indians; Brief State of Pennsylvania; Brief View of Conduct of Penn.; Brief and Impartial View of Penn. 1188

PECK (John M.).

Life of Daniel Boone the Pioneer of Kentucky. By John M. Peck. *Pages* 1 *to* 208 *of Vol. XIII. Sparks' "American Biography." Boston*, 1855. 1189

PECK (J. M.).

See Albach, Annals of the West. 1190

PECK (George).

Wyoming; its History, Stirring Incidents, and Romantic Adventures. By George Peck. With Illustrations. Third Edition. 12° *pp.* 432 + 12 *plates. New York: Harper and Brothers, publishers*, 1868. 1191

The author was familiar with the scenes, as well as many of the actors in the Wyoming tragedy, for a period of forty years commencing with 1820. He was thus enabled to glean many particulars regarding the Indians, the pioneers and their bloody skirmishes, which had escaped the eager inquiries of Chapman, Miner, and Stone. Beside the numerous anecdotes and incidents obtained from the lips of the survivors of the massacre, he had the good fortune to discover several manuscript narratives of captivities and expeditions, which had never been printed. These he reproduces in this work. Composed so largely of original material, the author has given even that portion which is merely compiled, an additional value.

PEQUOT (The)

of a Hundred Years. An Authentic Narrative. 8° *pp.* 4. (*American Tract Society*) (*New York*). 1192

PENNSYLVANIA.

Collections of the Historical Society of Pennsylvania. Vol. I. 8° *Philadelphia:* 1853. 1193

Only the first volume of this series in six numbers, was ever published. Conrad Weiser's "Narrative of a Journey to the Onondaga Indians, in 1737," and "Journal of Mission to the Indians of Ohio, in 1748," occupy pp. 1 to 34. "Account of March of Paxton Boys to Murder the Christian Indians in Philadelphia," pp. 73 to 78. Charles Thomson's "Essay on Indian Affairs, and Biography of the Writer," pp. 80 to 94. Buck's "Account of Indian Implements and Utensils," pp. 239 to 243.

PENNSYLVANIA.

Memoirs of the Historical Society of Pennsylvania. 8° *Eight volumes. Philadelphia:* 1826 *to* 1867. 1194

The first four volumes were published in eight parts. In Vol. II., pp. 61 to 131, will be found "A Narrative of an Embassy to the Western Indians from the original MS. of Hendrick Aupaumut," and "Minutes of a Conference with the Delaware and Susquehana Indians," pp. 206 to 213. Vol. III. Part I., pp. 1 to 166, is entirely occupied with a translation of Campanius' "Description of New Sweden," of which all subsequent to page 111 is devoted to the Indians of the Province, their history, manners, language, vocabularies, etc. Coates' address "On the Origin of the Indian population of America," occupies pp. 1 to 63 of Vol. III., Part II., and "Several papers relating to the Indians of Pennsylvania," pp. 129 to 213. Vol. IV. Part I., "Description of Engraving by the Aborigines of North America." Part II., "Incidents in the Early History of Crawford County," and "Notes respecting the Indians of Lancaster County," pp. 113 to 221. Vol. V. pp. 423, is entirely occupied with Sargent's "History of Braddock's Expedition against Fort Du Quesne." Vol. VII. contains Major Denny's "Journal of Campaign against the Ohio Indians, under General St. Clair," with a Vocabulary of Delaware and Shawanoe languages.

PENNSYLVANIA.

Bulletin of the Historical Society of Pennsylvania. Vol. I. 1845–1847. 8° *Philadelphia,* 1848. 1195

Only one volume was ever printed, and that was issued in thirteen parts, some of which are paged separately. No. 3, pp. 29 to 44, is occupied with "Remarks on the Traditions, &c. of the Indians of North America. By Rev. John Ettwein," with a Vocabulary of the Onondaga dialect. Nos. 8 and 9, pp. 121 to 181, are filled with Rev. John Heckwelder's "Memorandum of the Names and Signification of which the Delaware Indians gave to the Rivers, Streams, and Places in New Jersey, Pennsylvania, Maryland, and Virginia."

PEREYRE (Isaac).

Relation | dv | Groenland. | (*Cut of a Palm tree with the motto,* Curvata Resvrgo | .) 16° *Pref. pp.* (xvi.) + 1 *to* 278 + (iv.) + *map and plate. A Paris,* | *Chez Argvstin Covrbe, dans la* | *petite Salle du Palais, a la Palme.* | M. DC. XLVII. | Auec Priuilege du Roy. | 1196

The map and folding plate, representing the Esquimaux and their boats and utensils, are generally wanting. The work contains some of the earliest relations of the natives of Greenland, and their peculiarities.

PEREZ (Francisco).

Catecismo Otomi. Catecismo de la Doctrina Cristiana en Lengua Otomi, traducia literalmente al Castellano por El Presbytero D. Francisco Perez [*honorary titles 5 lines*]. 4° *pp.* 46. *Imprenta de la Testamentaria de Valdes, a cargo de Jose Maria Gallegos. Mexico*, 1834. 1197

[Catechism Otomi. Catechism of the Christian Doctrines in the Otomi Language, translated literally into the Spanish by the Rev. Dr. Francisco Perez.]

PERKINS (Samuel).

General Jackson's Conduct in the Seminole War, Delineated in a history of that period, affording conclusive reasons why he should not be the next President. By Samuel Perkins, Esq. 8° *pp.* 39. *Brooklyn, Con.* 1828. 1198

PERKINS (James H.).

Annals of the West. Embracing a concise account of the Principal Events which have occurred in the Western States and Territories, from the Discovery of the Mississippi Valley to the year 1850. By James H. Perkins. 8° *pp.* 808. *St. Louis*, 1850. 1199

A second edition was issued, revised, and enlarged, by J. M. Peck. A third edition is accredited to Albach, under which name it will be found.

PERNETTY (Dom).

Histoire d'un Voyage aux Isles Malouines, Fait en 1763 & 1764, avec des observations sur le Detroit de Magellan, et sur les Patagons. Par Dom Pernetty Abbe [*etc., 5 lines*]. Nouvelle Edition. Refandue & augmentee d'un Discours Preliminaire, de Remarquez sur l' Histoire Natural. *Paris*, 1770. 1200

Two vols. 8° pp. iv. + 385 + 11 folding maps and plates. Vol. II. pp. i + 334 + (ii.) + 8 folding maps and plates. Second edition of *Journal historique d'un Voyage*, printed 1769.

[History of a Voyage to the Malouines Islands, made in 1763 and 1764. With Observations on the Straits of Magellan, and on the Patagonians.]

At page 89, of Vol. II., the Abbe has made a division of his work, which he entitles "Observations on the Straits of Magellan, and on the Patagonians." This is the only part of the two volumes which entitles it to a place in our category of works on the aborigines, and is very meagre in its details. A large folding plate gives its testimony to the great stature of the gigantic inhabitants of Patagonia. It was translated into English, and printed in London 1771, under the title of "Bougainville's Voyage." 4°.

PEROUSE (J. F. de la).

A Voyage round the World, performed In the Years 1785, 1786, 1787, and 1788. By the Boussole, and Astrolabe; Under the Command of J. F. G. de la Perouse: published by order of the National Assembly under the Superintendence of L. A. Milet.—Mureau. In Two Volumes. Illustrated by a variety of charts, and plates in a separate folio volume. Translated from the French. *Large* 4° Vol. I. *pp.* lvi. + 539. Vol. II.

pp. viii. + 531 + (xiv.) *The folio volume of plates contains thirty folding maps and forty pages of plates. London,* 1799. 1201

The narrative of the enterprising but ill-fated Perouse, is full of interest in all portions, but his relations of the peculiarities he observed in the natives of the northwest coast of North America, are especially valuable in portraying their manners at that early day. He occupies chapters vii. to xi. pp. 354 to 470, almost entirely with descriptions of the appearance, disposition, and habits of the Indians of the coast tribes. On pp. 408 to 411, he gives a specimen of their music, a short vocabulary, and analysis of their language. Another brief vocabulary, and treatise on the language of the Indians of California, may be found on pp. 467 to 468. The folio of plates, Nos. 21–23 and 24, are illustrative of characteristics of the natives of Port St. Francais, on the northwest coast of America.

PENHALLOW (Samuel).

The | History | of the | Wars of *New-England,* | With the *Eastern* Indians. | or, A | Narrative | Of their continued Perfidy and Cruelty, | from the 10th of August, 1703. | To the Peace renewed 13th of July, 1713. | And from the 25th of July, 1722. | To their Submission 15th December, 1725. | Which was Ratified August 5th, 1726. | By Samuel Penhallow, Esqr. | [*Motto two lines.*] 12° *Boston; Printed by T. Fleet, for S. Gerrish at the lower* | *end of Cornhill, and D. Henchman over-against* | *the Brick Meeting-House in Cornhill,* 1726. | 1202

Title, reverse blank, the Preface, iv. pp., the Introduction (ii.), the History, pp. 1 to 134 + the Advertisement, 1 leaf, Total, pp. 144.

This work in any condition, ranks among the rarest of New England imprints, while a perfect copy with good margin, is very difficult to obtain. More than one collector would be glad to obtain it at even more than one hundred dollars. In this copy is a MS. note. "The Rev. N. M. wrote to his brother Rev. Increase Mather a letter received August 12, 1685. 'A good friend and near Relation of mine, one Mr. Rich' Lot, merch't in London, who married my sister Thompson, desires me to write in behalf of this gentleman ye bearer his kinsman, Mr. Penhallow of Falmouth in Cornwall, who designs to spend a year or two in New England, in your colledge, for ye p'fecting his learning.'" (from the original MSS. J. W. T.). The author was born in Cornwall, England, July, 1665, and arrived in Portsmouth, New Hampshire, July 1686. He held many important offices of public trust with great honor, being chief justice of the Province, at the period of his death, in December, 1726, at the age of sixty-one. His work on the Indian wars is esteemed as the highest authority on that subject. His design in emigrating was to serve the corporation for the propagation of the gospel among the Indians, as a missionary, after he had made himself acquainted with their language. Whether he ever really performed that service is uncertain. His MS. diary kept with great care, and covering a great portion of his life, was destroyed in the conflagration of Portsmouth, 1802.

PENHALLOW (S.).

The History of the Wars of New England, with the Eastern Indians. *Large* 4° *pp.* 129. *Cincinnati, reprinted from the Boston edition of* 1726, *with a Memoir and Notes, for W. Dodge,* 1859. 1203

Of this reprint the copies having a rubricated title are most esteemed, as they have an Appendix, not printed in those with only the black title, containing "Lovewell's Fight," "Gardener's Account of the Pequot Wars," and "The Gospel in New-England." The work was also printed in the first volume of the New Hampshire Historical Society's Collections.

PERRIN DU LAC.

Voyage dans les deux Louisianes, et Chez les Nations Sauvages du Missouri, par les Etat Unis, l'Ohio et les Provinces qui le bordent, en 1801, 1802, et 1803; avec un aperçu des moeurs, des usages, du caractere et des coutumes religieuses et civiles des Peuples de ces diverses contrees. Par Perrin du Lac. 8° *Half title, title, dedication,* 6 *pp.* + x. + 479 + 2 *maps. A Lyon, Chez Bruyset aîné et Buynand An* xiii. — 1805. 1204

[Travels in the two Louisianas, and to the homes of the Savage Nations of the Missouri, by way of the United States, the Ohio, and the Provinces which border it, in 1801, 1802, and 1803. With a relation of the Manners, the Habits, the Character, and the religious and civil Customs of the Natives of these different Countries.]

Chapters xxix. to xl., pp. 257 to 364, the author has entirely devoted to the narration of his observations on the Indians, then inhabiting the territory he visited. Chapter lii., pp. 456 to 472, is entitled, "Life of George Augustus Bowles, an Englishman, who abandoned civilization to become chief of the Creek Nation. The life of this worthy was printed in a small duodecimo volume, in England, whither he had gone to negotiate some treaty for his tribe.

The volume contains the narration of the personal experience of a traveller whose curiosity was not sated with what he saw, but who sought from books the particulars he did not himself observe, and thus fills out the form of which he himself observed but the mere outlines. Although there is little produced that is new, the author gives it to us in a pleasing and readable style, and thus, without adding much to our stock of information, makes that we already possessed more available.

PERRIN DU LAC.

Travels through the Louisianas, and among the Savage Nations of the Missouri; also, in the United States, along the Ohio, and the adjacent Provinces, in 1801, 1802, & 1803, with A Sketch of the Manners, Customs, character, and the civil and Religious Ceremonies of the people of those Countries. By M. Perrin Du Lac. Translated from the French. 8° *pp.* 106 + *Index* 2 *pp. London, printed for Richard Philips,* 1807. 1205

A translation of the preceding work, very much abridged.

PETERS (R.).

The case of the Cherokee Nation against the State of Georgia; argued and determined at the Supreme Court of the United States, January term 1831. With an Appendix, Containing the Opinion of Chancellor Kent on the Case; the Treaties between the United States and the Cherokee Indians, the Act of Congress of 1802, entitled "An Act to regulate intercourse with the Indian tribes, &c." And the Laws of Georgia relative to the country occupied by the Cherokee Indians, within the boundary of that State, by Richard Peters. 8° *Pml. leaves* (4) + 286. *Philadelphia,* 1831. 1206

PETERS (De Witt C.).

The Life and Adventures of Kit Carson, the Nestor of the Rocky Mountains; from facts narrated by himself. By De Witt C. Peters, M. D. With Original Illustrations drawn by Lumley. 8° *pp.* 534. *New York,* 1859. 1207

Pewani (A. M. D. G.).

Ipi Potewatemi Missinoikan, eyowat nemadjik, Catholiques Endjik. Baltimoiank: John Murphy, Okimissinakisan ote Missinoikan. 1846. 24° pp. 80. 1208

A primary book of religious instruction, in the Pottawatomie dialect, with plates; and translations of the Lord's Prayer, Apostles' Creed, and the Decalogue into that tongue.

Phelps (Noah A.).

A History of the Copper Mines, and Newgate Prison at Granby, Conn. Also of the Captivity of Daniel Hayes, Of Granby, by the Indians in 1707. 8° pp. 34. *Hartford*, 1845. 1209

Philo-Jackson.

The Presidential Election, written for the benefit of the people of the U. States, but particularly for those of the State of Kentucky; relating to the Seminole War, and the vindication of General Jackson. Third Series. By Philo-Jackson. 8° pp. 48. *Frankfort, printed for the author, May*, 1824. 1210

An attempt to vindicate General Jackson from the obloquy which followed his entrance upon the territory of a neutral power, seizing and hanging some of its subjects, without color of law. The halls of Congress resounded with the exclamations of horror, and indignant eloquence of such men as Clay, Lacock, and Mercer, at the atrocity of these murders.

Philoponus (Honorius).

Nova Typis | Transacta Na | vigatio. | Novi Orbis Indiae Occidentalis. | Admodum Re | verendissimorum PP. | ac FF. Reverendissimi ac Illustrissimi Domini, | Dn. Buelli Cataloni Abbatis montis | Serrati, & in universum Americani, sive Novum | Orbem Sacrae Sedis Apostolicae Romanae a Latere | Legati, Vicarii, ac Patriarchae: Sociorump, Mo | nach(or)um ex Ordine S. P. N. Benedicti ad supra | dicti Novi Mundi barbaras gentes Christi S. Evan | gelium praedicandi gratia delegatorum Sacerdo | tum. Dimissi per SDD. Papam Alexandrum | VI. Anno Christi. 1492. | Nunc Primum | Evariis Scriptoribus in unum colle | cta & figuris ornata. | Authore | venerando Fr Don Honorio Philopono | Ordinis S. Benedicti Monacho, 1621. | 1211

Folio, engraved title-page + (5) prel. leaves + pp. 1 to 101, and 18 folding plates.

The engraved title-page has portraits of St. Brandon, and Father Buell, on either side of the text. The latter personage accompanied Columbus in his second voyage. The title is sometimes an inch or two longer than the volume, and folded back, or torn away below the date, in which last condition, but little would appear to be missing. There is however in this portion an oval engraving of the two continents, on each side of which is a medallion cut. Most of the large folding-plates have numerous figures of the aborigines, exhibited in some stately pageant of homage to the discoverers and evangelists, or in a horrid festival of cannibalism, or in some appalling scene of massacre and torture perpetrated upon them. A curious bibliographical history attaches to this volume. The real name of the author was Caspar Plautus, who assumed the pseudonym of Philoponus, in order to admit of one of the most extraordinary devices of egotism, ever contrived.

He wrote a most fulsome piece of flattery, and in his character of Philoponus, dedicated it to himself, in his own proper cognomen. By this device, his work, everywhere it was read, advertised the merit and learning of Caspar Plautus, and the praise seemed vastly more important, as issuing from so learned a person as Philoponus. Mr. Henry Stevens first called the attention of English scholars to this curious chapter in the history of egotism. The work contains the relations of the first Catholic missionaries to the Indians of America, some of whom accompanied Columbus in his second voyage, and has the merit of affording as many incidents of their work among the savages of the first discovered islands. It is deformed, however, by nearly as many monkish tales of the miracles performed by them, on most whimsical occasions.

Father Boil, whose labors among the Indians the work principally commemorates, was a Benedictine monk of Montserrat, a man of learning and piety, chosen by their Catholic Majesties Ferdinand and Isabella to preach in the New World. Pope Alexander VI. decorated him with the pallium of Vicar-general in America, of which he is regarded as the first patriarch. Accompanied by two priests of his order, he embarked with Columbus in 1493. After his arrival in America, he formed one of the wretched cabal against the immortal Admiral, and went to Spain, in order to appear against him. He never returned to America. The author of this work on the discovery of the New World, and the first missions among its natives by the evangelists of the order of St. Benoit, was a monk in the convent of Seittenstent, in lower Austria.

Picard (Bernard).

Ceremonies et Coutumes religieuses des peuples Idolatres Representees par les Figures dessinees de la main de Bernard Picard: Avec une Explication Historique, & quelques Dissertations curieuses. Tome Premier, Premier partie, Qui Contient les Ceremonies Religieuses des Peuples des Indies Occidentales. *Folio pp.* 211 *and* 34 *plates. A Amsterdam, Chez J. F. Bernard,* 1723. 1212

[Religious Ceremonies, and Customs of Idolatrous Nations. Represented by Plates, designed by Bernard Picard. With an Historic Explanation, and some curious Dissertations. Vol. I. Part first. Which contains the religious ceremonies of the Natives of America.]

On the thirty-four folio pages of engravings, will be found seventy-five plates, illustrating the religious rites, amatory customs, funeral ceremonies, habitations, utensils, and weapons of various nations of American aborigines.

They are mostly copied from those in the celebrated series of De Bry, and are engraved with equal excellence of art. They are indeed so finely executed, both in the drawing and engraving, that there are few plates even at this day which excel them. Unfortunately the artist followed the fashion of his time, and represented the American savages with the Caucasian complexion and features. Pages 1 to 73 are occupied with a "Dissertation on the Natives of America." Pages 74 to 211 are devoted to a "Description of their Customs." Plates 1 to 15 are illustrative of the "Customs of the Indians of Florida, Virginia, and Canada."

Pickering (John).

An Essay on a Uniform Orthography for the Indian Languages of North America, as published in the Memoirs of the American Academy of Arts and Sciences. By John Pickering. 4° *pp.* 42. *Cambridge; Univ. Press Hilliard & Metcalf.* 1820. 1213

In every essay to reduce an American aboriginal language to writing, the difficulty of representing by alphabetic signs, vocal sounds produced by organs never used in civilized speech, has caused each writer to record his conception of them, in an arbitrary manner, which perhaps no other person would accurately comprehend. This has produced the greatest variety of orthographical forms, of the same Indian words. We are utterly unable at this day to recognise a single Indian nation, whose name is recorded by Cabeça de Vaca, in 1542. Mr. Pickering in his essay sought to remedy this defect by assuming certain diacritical signs, by the omission of C. J. Q. X. and by additional consonants, formed from combinations of our own. What hope, however, could be entertained of expressing by these means, the Maya and other Mexican languages, in the enunciation of which the lips, teeth, and tongue, have so little function, or in which the strong labial, dental, and even nasal sounds are so seldom used?

PIDGEON (William).

Traditions of De-coo-dah. And Antiquarian Researches: comprising Extensive Explorations, Surveys and Excavations of the wonderful and mysterious earthen remains of the Mound-Builders in America; The traditions of the last Prophet of the Elk Nation relative to their origin and use; and the evidences of an ancient population more numerous than the present Aborigines. By William Pidgeon. Embellished with Seventy Engravings descriptive of one hundred and twenty varying relative arrangements — forms of earthen effigies, antique sculpture, etc. 8° *pp.* 334 *and folding plate. New York:* 1858. 1214

This work is the record of personal examination of a great number of ancient mounds and fortifications, and of the traditions regarding them, obtained from an aged Sioux chief. The author was animated by an eager curiosity, which unhappily was directed by no familiarity with science, and accordingly what would otherwise have been really valuable results from his researches, are rendered almost useless by their blending with baseless hypotheses, and as unreliable traditions. If, however, read with care to discriminate between the fanciful and the real, the book will be found to add a large fund of information to our stock of knowledge of aboriginal antiquities. His development of Indian character is also not without interest, as it is the result of personal intercourse with many individuals of different tribes. The numerous plates afford very clear illustrations of many remains of Indian structures.

PIEDRAHITA (D. Lucas Fernandez).

Historia | general | de las conquistas | del nuevo | Reyno de Grenada. | A la S. C. R. M. | De D. Carlos Segvndo, | Rey de las Espanas, | y de las Indias. | Por el Doctor D. Lucas Fernandez | Piedrahita, Chantre de la Iglesia Metropolitana | de Santa Fè de Bogatà Calificador del Santo Oficio | por la Suprema y General Inquisicion, y Obispo | electo de Santa Marta. *s. d. n. p. Half title: Amberes. Por Juan Baptista Verdussen.* (1698?). 1215

Collation: Half title, 1 leaf + folding engraved title 1 leaf + 16 prel. pp. + 599 + Indice 6 + two engraved titles for Books I. and III. The principal title is surrounded by a border, containing the portraits of seven Indian kings of Bogota, and four plates of battles between the savages and the Spaniards.

[General History of the Conquest of New Grenada. By Doctor Lucas Fernandez Piedrahita.]

From the existence of engraved titles, before Books I. and III., it would seem that the twelve books had each been similarly ornamented, but it is believed that only the two noticed were ever engraved. Book I. is almost entirely devoted to a description of the peculiar rites and ceremonies of the Indians in New Granada. The remainder of the work is largely occupied with the narration of battles with the natives, their work in the mines, their revolts, subjugation, and their conversion. The work was composed during the residence of the author at Madrid, from the MSS. of Gonzales Ximenes de Quesada, the conqueror of the country, and the first European to penetrate its interior. This first volume is the only one ever printed, which is the more to be regretted, as it relates to a portion of America of which we possess the fewest documents. The work in any condition is very rare.

PIERCE (M. B.).

Address on the Present Condition and prospects of the Aboriginal Inhabitants of North America, with particular reference to the Seneca Nation. By M. B. Pierce, A Chief of the Seneca Nation, and a Member of Dartmouth College. 8° *pp.* 16. *Steele's Press*, 1838. 1216

PIKE (Z. M.).

An Account of Expeditions to the Sources of the Mississippi, and through the Western Part of Louisiana to the sources of the Arkansaw, Kans, La Platte, and Pierre Jaun rivers; performed by order of the Government of the United States during the years 1805–1806–1807. And a Tour through the Interior Parts of New Spain, when conducted through those Provinces, by order of the Captain General, in the year 1807. By Major Z. M. Pike. Illustrated with Maps and Charts. *Philadelphia:* 1810. 1217

8° Portrait, 5 maps, 2 folding tables, pp. 7 + 277, Meteorological table 2 pp. Appendix I., pp. 1 to 64 + 3 folding tables. Appendix II., pp. 1 to 53 + 2 tables, one folding. Appendix III., pp. 87 + 1 map. The American edition of Pike's exploratory travels, is the only complete one, containing as it does all the reports, appendices, maps, and tables, in most of which the larger and better printed English edition is lacking.

PIKE (Z. M.).

Exploratory Travels through the Western Territories of North America: comprising a Voyage from St. Louis, on the Mississippi to the source of that river, and a Journey through the Interior of Louisiana, and the North-Eastern Provinces of New Spain. Performed in the years 1805, 1806, 1807, by Order of the Government of the United States. By Zebulon Montgomery Pike; Major 6th Regt. United States Infantry. 4° 2 *maps, pp.* xx. + 436. *London: printed for Longman & (Co.)*, 1811. 1218

This accomplished officer was the first explorer under the government of the United States, of that vast portion of the republic now forming the States of Arkansas, Texas, and New Mexico. His accounts of the principal features of the country, and of the savage tribes which inhabited it, are accurate and interesting. Six years after completing this tour, he was killed at Little York, in Canada, by the explosion of a magazine in a fort, from which he had just before driven the garrison by assault.

Mr. Stevens notices that the French editor, Mr. Breton, detected innumerable errors in the French and Spanish names. "Meanwhile Humboldt in the *Moniteur*, complimenting the work highly as a whole, pointed out that his own map of New Mexico, a copy of which he had left with the Secretary of State at Washington, in 1804, had been appropriated with many erroneous additions." Captain Pike could be charged with no association in this misdemeanor, as the work was edited and published in his absence on duty.

PIKE (Albert).

Prose Sketches and Poems, Written in the Western Country, by Albert Pike. 12° *pp.* 200. *Boston, Light & Horton*, 1834. 1219

"A Narrative of a Journey in the Prairie," occupies the first eighty pages of the book. This tour, made in 1831, through the country of the Comanches, and other Indian tribes, gives some interesting particulars of their life and customs. The author, thirty years subsequently, organized and commanded a brigade of the half-civilized Indians, from the territory set apart for them, and fought at their head on several occasions in the civil war. Neither himself, or his brigade, acquired much reputation for military service.

PIMENTEL (D. F.).

Cuadro descriptivo y comparitivo de las Lenguas indigenas de Mexico por D. Francisco Pimentel Socio de numero de la Sociedad Mexicana de geografia y estadistica. *Two vols.* 8° Vol. I. *Prel. pp.* iii. + 539 + *Index* 1 *p.* Vol. II. *Prel. pp.* vi. + 427 + *Nota & Indice pp.* (ill.). *Mexico Imprenta de Andrade y Escalante* 1862. 1220

[Descriptive and Comparative View of the Indian Languages of Mexico.]

The first volume of this work is divided into twelve, and the second volume into twenty sections, each with a bastard title, and devoted to an analysis of one or more aboriginal languages, or dialects. Of these, forty-eight receive some attention, and most of them a critical examination. The peculiarities of each in grammatical construction, enunciation, and the varied particulars which distinguish them, are discussed with the skill of an intelligent philologist. No work on the Indian languages of America exhibits the tokens of more labor aided by learning than this, yet it is said by excellent authorities to be far from perfect.

PITCHLYNN (Peter P.).

Remonstrance, Appeal, and Solemn Protest, of the Choctaw Nation, addressed to the Congress of the United States. 8° *pp.* 21. (*Washington,* 1870.) 1221

PITOU (L. A.).

Voyage a Cayenne dans les deux Ameriques et chez les Anthropophages. Ouvrage orné de gravures, contenant le tableau [*etc.*] les moeurs des Sauvages, des noirs, des Creoles et des quakers. Par Louis-Ange Pitou. Deporte a Cayenne pendant trois ans. [*etc.*] 8° Vol. I. *pp.* 60 + 312 + *folding plate.* Vol. II. *Plate & title* + *pp.* 404. *A Paris.* An. xiii. 1805. 1222

[Voyage to Guiana, in the two Americas, to the home of the cannibals. The Work ornamented with engravings, and containing a view of the manners of the Savages, the blacks, the Creoles, and the Quakers.]

At page 191, Vol. II., the author commences a dissertation on "The Antiquity of the Discovery of America, drawn from its history, and the religion of the natives," which occupies eight pages. "Of the Indians of America," fills pp. 199 to 214. From this last page to p. 278, is occupied with a curious narrative entitled "Hyaona and Lisbe, or the Indians of the Torrid Zone," which in the table of contents is called "Tour to the Home of the Man-eaters, where the author narrowly escapes being devoured." All of which is intensely French and incredible.

PLUMMER (Clarissa).

Narrative of the captivity and extreme sufferings of Mrs. Clarissa Plummer, Wife of the late Mr. James Plummer, of Franklin County, State of New York; who, with Mrs. Caroline Harris, wife of the late Mr. Richard Harris, were, in the Spring of 1835, with their unfortunate families, surprised and taken prisoners by a party of the Camanche tribe of Indians, while emigrating from said Franklin County (N.-Y.) to Texas; and after having been nearly two years in captivity, and witnessed the deaths of their husbands, were redeemed from the hands of the savages by an American Fur Trader, a native of Georgia. (*Woodcut.*) Mrs. Plummer was made a prisoner and held in bondage at the same time with the unfortunate Mrs. Harris, with whose narrative the public have been recently presented. 8° *Frontispiece + pp.* 24. *New York:* 1838. 1223

PLAIN FACTS:

being An Examination into the Rights of the Indian Nations of America, to their respective Countries; and a vindication of the Grant, from The Six United Nations of Indians, to The Proprietors of Indiana, against the decision of the Legislature of Virginia; together with authentic documents, proving That the Territory, Westward of the Allegany Mountain never belonged to Virginia, &c. 8° *pp.* 165. *Philadelphia:* 1781. 1224

The author of this work is unknown. It has been attributed to Benjamin Franklin, and to Anthony Benezet. Its style is much more scholarly and judicial than that of either of these writers. It is declared by all to be the ablest treatise on the tenure of the Indian claim to the title of lands occupied by them, ever written.

POND (S. W.).

Wowapi Inonpa. Wowapi wakan etanhan taku wanjikji oyakapi kin he dee. Waumdiduta kaga. The second Dakota Reading Book. Consisting of Bible stories from the Old Testament. By Rev. S. W. Pond. 24° *pp.* 54. *Boston:* 1842. 1225

PONTIAC,

Or the Seige of Detroit. A drama, In three acts. 12° *pp.* 60. *Boston, Samuel Coleman,* 1835. 1226

A feeble, tawdry affair, without historical truth, poetic invention, or even a few scrappy notes to attach it to common sense.

POOR SARAH. (A pious Indian Woman.)

8° *pp.* 8. *New York: Published by the American Tract Society.* 1227

PORTER (Ebenezer).

Sermon (A) preached in Boston, November 1, 1827, before the Society for the Propagating the Gospel among the Indians, and others in North America. By Ebenezer Porter, D. D. Published by request of the Society. 8° *pp.* 42. *Andover,* 1827. 1228

The Appendix contains a statement of the condition of the Indian Missions.

PORTER (Ebenezer). The Same. 8° *pp.* 42. *Cambridge*, 1828. 1229

PORTER (Eliphalet).

A Discourse before the Society for Propagating the Gospel among the Indians and others in North America. Delivered Nov. 5th, 1807. 8° *Boston*, 1808. 1230

With an Appendix of historical notices of missions among the Indians.

PORTLOCK (Captain N.).

A Voyage round the World, but more particularly to the North West Coast of America: performed in 1785, 1786, 1787, and 1788, in the King George and Queen Charlotte, Captains Portlock & Dixon. Embellished with twenty copper-plates. Dedicated, by permission, to his Majesty. By Captain Nathaniel Portlock. 4° *pp.* xii. + 384 + xl. + 20 *maps and plans. London:* 1789. 1231

The accounts of Captain Portlock's traffic with the Indians of the north-west coast of America, and descriptions of their peculiarities, are narrated in Chapters x., xi., xii., and xiii., pp. 201 to 297. At page 293 is a short vocabulary of the language of one of the tribes.

POTTER (C. E.).

The History of Manchester, formerly Derryfield, in New Hampshire; including that of ancient Amoskeag, or the middle Merrimack Valley; together with the address, poem, and other proceedings, of the centennial celebration, of the Incorporation of Derryfield; at Manchester, October 22, 1851. By C. E. Potter. 8° *pp.* xiii. + 764 + 48 *plates. Manchester, C. E. Potter, publisher.* 1856. - 1232

Chapters iii., iv., v., ix., xii., xiv., and xv., are almost entirely devoted to the narration of the Indian wars; account of the different tribes inhabiting New England, biographies of their principal chiefs, with traditions and anecdotes of many of them, which are not familiar to many readers. There is much pains-taking and intelligence manifested in this local history, not common to its class.

POST (Christian Frederick).

The Second Journal of Christian Frederick Post, On a Message from the Governor of Pennsylvania to the Indians on the Ohio. 8° *pp.* 67. *London: Printed for J. Wilkie, at the Bible and Sun, in St. Paul's Church-yard.* 1759. 1233

This journal is the sequel to that printed by Charles Thompson, Secretary to the Continental Congress, in his *Enquiry into the Causes of the Alienation of the Delaware and Shawanese Tribe of Indians.* It exhibits in a still stronger light the intrepidity and self-devotion of this noble Quaker. Since the days of Regulus no more perilous mission has been undertaken by a single man. Braddock had been defeated, and eight hundred white soldiers slain. Forbes was preparing for his invasion of the Indian territory. Ruthless massacre reigned on both sides. Rewards that would have tempted all the fierce borderers a year before, were offered in vain, until Christian Post, rejecting all offers of compensation, and solely for peace and mercy's sake, set out upon his mission. Every step through the wilderness, the most appalling dangers thickened around him. A hundred times were savage arms raised to destroy him, and a hundred times by little less than miracles, the blows were averted.

It is impossible to exaggerate the importance of the work he accomplished. By his persuasions he detached the Ohio Indians from the French interest, and the empire of that nation in the west fell.

POSTON (Charles D.).

Speech of Hon. Charles D. Poston of Arizona, on Indian Affairs. Delivered in the House of Representatives, Thursday, March 2, 1865. 8° pp. 20. *New York*, 1865. 1234

The humane and sagacious policy indicated by this gentleman, for the conduct of Indian affairs, and especially as affecting the Apaches, contrasts strangely with the sanguinary and atrocious recommendations and practices, of most Western statesmen.

POWERS (Rev. Grant).

Historical sketches of the Discovery, Settlement, and Progress of events in the Coos Country and vicinity, principally included between the years 1754 and 1785. By Rev. Grant Powers. 12° pp. 240. *Haverhill, N. H., published by J. F. C. Hayes.* 1841. 1235

As this local history is almost wholly composed of personal narrations, and reminiscences of the pioneer settlers, it necessarily includes some information regarding the Indians of the locality, not otherwise recorded.

POUCHOT.

Memoir upon the Late War in North America, between the French and English, 1755–60; followed by Observations upon the Theatre of Actual War, and by New Details concerning the Manners and Customs of the Indians: with Topographical Maps. By M. —— Pouchot. Translated and edited by Franklin B. Hough, with additional Notes and Illustrations. Two vols. *Large* 8° Vol. I. *pp.* iv. + 268 + 8 *maps and plates.* Vol. II. *pp.* 283 + 12 *maps and plates.* *W. E. Woodward, Roxbury*: 1866. 1236

The publisher printed two sizes of this translation of Pouchot's memoir, fifty-seven of the edition of two hundred copies being in large quarto. The work is a faithful reproduction of the very minute journal of a French officer, engaged in the wars between the English Colonies and the French and Indians, from 1755 to 1761. The work is evidently written by a gentleman of education and intelligence, as an exculpation of himself, from some real or fancied charges, regarding the loss of Canada to the French monarchy. His work is full of the details of Indian warfare, the narratives of their skirmishes, and battles with the English, and of anecdotes and incidents of their association with the French. A division of the work commencing at page 180 of Vol. II. and ending at page 261, is entitled "On the Customs and Manners of the Indians of North America," in which the author more particularly relates the peculiarities of the natives of Canada.

[PREFONTAINE (M. de).]

Dictionnaire Galibi, presenté Sous deux formes; I° Commençant par le mot François; II° Par le mot Galibi. Precédé d'un essai de grammaire. Par M. D. L. S(auvage). 8° *pp.* xvi. + 128. *A Paris, Chez Bauche, Libraire, Quai des Augustins, a l'Image Sainte Genevieve & a Saint Jean dans le Desert,* M.D.CC.LXIII. 1237

[Dictionary of the Galibi language, presented under two forms. First, commencing with the French word. Second, commencing with the Galibi word, preceded by a grammatical essay.]

Mr. Ludwig informs us that the initials on the title-page are those of M. de la Sauvage, but leaves us in doubt whether he was the author of more than the grammar. The dictionary forms part of Prefontaine's *Maison Rustique*, and was compiled from the works of Boyer, Pelliprat, Biet, Barrere, Labat, and some manuscript relations.

PREFONTAINE (M. De).

Dictionaire Galibi. Dictionarium gallice, latine et gallibi. Digestum e libro: Dictionnaire Galibi, presente Sous deux formes, 1° commencant par le mot françois, 2° par le mot galibi, precede d'un essai de Grammaire, par M. D. L. S. a Paris 1763. 8° (Siute de la Maison rustique de Cayenne.) Autcum Sermone latino editit Car. Fr. Ph. de Martius. 8° *pp.* 48. (*n. d. n. l.*) 1238

PRESCOTT (W. H.).

History of the Conquest of Mexico, with a preliminary view of the ancient Mexican Civilization, and the life of the Conqueror. Hernando Cortez. By William H. Prescott, in Three Volumes. 8° *Philadelphia; J. B. Lippincott*, 1869. 1239

Book I., pp. 1 to 208, of Vol. III. is occupied with a "View of the Aztec Civilization," which comprises a summary of the history of that race of American aborigines, so far as the author's materials would furnish data, without venturing upon the gloomy territory of Indian mythology. Mr. Prescott made liberal use for this purpose of the MS. *Relaciones* of Fernando de Alva Ixtlilxochitl, the native Aztec historian, a sketch of whose life has been already given. The principal, and as Mr. Prescott asserts, the only complete work of Ixtlilxochitl, is the *Historia Chichemeca*, printed in Spanish by Lord Kingsborough, in his great collection; and by Ternaux in French, in his voyages and travels. The remainder of the volumes, is principally occupied with the narrative and incidents of the struggles of the warlike Aztecs, with the Spanish invaders. Here the author treads on safer ground, but his care in proving its firmness, step by step, has made us feel secure, even in his anti-Cortesian history.

There is but one point at which we hesitate to follow his leading. With the partiality of an author for his hero, he treats lightly the treachery of a Christian general, who broke his most solemn oaths with the indifference of a common swindler, who made the earth sodden with the blood of unresisting and almost impotent victims, and who exterminated a tribe, or a nation with equal indifference, to secure himself from the possible trouble of reconquering it. The English edition of Mr. Prescott's work is far superior to the late American, as indeed are the earlier ones published in this country.

PRESCOTT (W. H.).

History of the Conquest of Peru; with a preliminary view of the Civilization of the Incas. By William H. Prescott, in Two Volumes. 8° Vol. I. *pp.* xl. + 1 + 527. Vol. II. *pp.* xxviii. + 547, *map and two portraits. Philadelphia: J. B. Lippincott & Co.*, 1869. 1240

Book I., pp. 1 to 174 of Vol. I., is entitled, "View of the Civilization of the Incas." It is derived from sources which entitles it to a far greater credence for authenticity, than any other treatise on this subject, hitherto esteemed so mythical. Several contemporaneous authors who were familiar with the most cultivated and intelligent Incas, have left their records of what they learned from them. More than one of the Christianized Incarial race, has bequeathed his written history, and the correspondence of these independent accounts, may be derived ample fortification of their veracity. The Peruvian record of the knotted quipu, was decipherable only by one of those initiated from his youth in unraveling from them their mysterious narrative. Among those whose voluminous MSS. have enabled Mr. Prescott to present such a compact, lucid, and authentic account of the conquest of Peru by the Incas, and of their reign for two hundred years before they lost the empire, to the Spaniards, those of Sarmiento and Ondegardo excel in authenticity. The first compiled a history of the ancient Peruvians, derived from such materials as he obtained from the ancient Indian nobles and priests. Sarmiento's *History of the Government of the Incas*, covers four hundred folio pages of MS. The *Relaciones* of Ondegardo, occupying as much space as the last, have never been printed, and are derived from the most intimate and friendly relations, of a kind and prudent official, with the most learned of the Incas. We have therefore the strongest reasons for crediting the authenticity of Mr. Prescott's history.

PRIERES (L. J. C. & M. T.).

Cantiques et Catechisme en langue Montagnaise ou Chipeweyan [*characters 1 line. Motto in a Circle, with emblem*]. 24° *pp.* 180. *Montreal. Imprimerie de Louis Perrault, et Compagnie.* 1865. 1241

[Prayers, Sacred Songs, and Catechism in the Montagnaise or Chipewcyan language.]

The work is printed in characters invented to express phonetically the elementary sounds of the Chipewcyan language.

PRIERES (L. J. C. & M. T.).

Cantiques, Catechisme etc. en langue Crise. [*Indian characters one line, and Motto.*] 24° *pp.* 324. *Montreal: Imprimerie de Louis Perrault et Compagnie*, 1866. 1242

Prayers, Sacred Songs, Catechism, etc., in the Cree language. Printed in a species of phonetic characters.

PRIERES (L. J. C. & M. J.).

Cantiques et Catechisme, en Langue Montagnaise, ou Chipewyan. [*One line of Indian Characters, with Motto and Emblem in a Circle.*] 24° *pp.* 144. *Montreal, Imprimerie de Louis Perrault*, 1857. 1243

[Prayers, Sacred Songs, and Catechism, in the Montagnais, or Chipewyan language.]

PRIEST (Josiah).

Stories of Early Settlers in the Wilderness: Embracing the Life of Mrs. Priest, Late of Otsego County, N. Y., with various and interesting accounts of others: The first Raftsmen of the Susquehannah: A short account of Brant, the British Indian Chief: and of the Massacre of Wyoming. Embellished with a large and beautiful engraving. 8° *pp.* 40. *Albany*, 1837. 1244

Although Mr. Priest's works have not usually the stamp of veracity, yet most of them contain a large amount of historic material, obtained at some pains from sources more or less authentic. The present work is occupied principally with narrations of personal adventures on the frontiers, and among the Indians. The "large and beautiful engraving" is a coarse wood-cut of double-page size, exhibiting a fanciful scene of the massacre at Wyoming. Mr. Munsel's store of amusing anecdotes regarding this prolific, and it must be said, needy and unscrupulous author, would fill a volume of no mean dimensions.

PRIEST (Josiah).

American Antiquities, and discoveries in the West: being an exhibition of the evidence that an Ancient Population of partially civilized nations, differing entirely from those of the present Indians, peopled America, many centuries before its discovery by Columbus. And Inquiries into their Origin, with a copious description Of many of their stupendous Works, now in ruins. With Conjectures concerning what may have become of them. Compiled from travels, authentic sources, and the researches of Antiquarian Societies. By Joseph Priest. 8° *pp.* 400 + *plate and map. Albany*, 1838. 1245

Mr. Munsel, who printed this work, is accustomed to say with his quaint frankness, "Although 22,000 copies of this work were published in thirty months for subscribers, it is now scarce."

PRIEST (Josiah).

Stories of the Revolution. With an account of the Lost Child of the Delaware; Wheaton and the Panther, etc. Narrative of the Captivity of John and Robert Brice, by Tories and Indians. 8° *Plate and pp.* 32. *Albany:* 1838. 1246

PRIEST (Josiah).

The Fort Stannix Captive, or New England Volunteer, being the extraordinary life and adventures of Isaac Hubbell Among the Indians of Canada and the West, in the War of the Revolution, and the Story of his marriage with the Indian Princess; now first published, from the lips of the hero himself. By Josiah Priest. 8° *pp.* 63. *Albany*, 1841. 1247

PRITTS (J.).

Incidents of Border Life, illustrative of the times and condition of the first settlements in parts of the Middle and Western States, comprising Narratives of strange and thrilling adventure — Accounts of battles — Skirmishes and personal encounters with the Indians — Descriptions of their manners, customs, modes of warfare, treatment of prisoners, &c. &c., — Also, the history of several remarkable Captivities, and Escapes. To which are added brief historical sketches of the War in the North-West, embracing the expeditions under Gens. Harmar, St. Clair and Wayne. With an appendix and a review. Compiled from authentic sources. 8° *pp.* 507. *Chambersburg, Pa., printed and published by J. Pritts*, 1839. 1248

This is the first edition of Pritts' work, and contains a large amount of material, excluded from the one of two years later. The arrangement is also so widely different, as to render it an entirely distinct, and in some respects a more desirable work. In this edition, the actors are permitted to narrate their adventures in their own words, it being a reprint of the journals and narratives of the border warriors by themselves.

PRITTS (J.).

Mirror of Olden Time Border Life; embracing a History of the Discovery of America, [*etc.*, 4 *lines*] also, history of Virginia, [*two lines*] And a Narrative of the long continued and bloody struggle between the White Settlers and Indians in North-Western Virginia, Kentucky, &c. &c., [*etc.*, 12 *lines.*] Personal Narratives of Captivities and Escapes — of strange and thrilling Adventures — Personal Prowess &c. &c. Together with numerous Sketches of Frontier Men. [*etc.*, 3 *lines.*] Compiled from authentic sources, by J. Pritts, Chambersburg, Pa. 8°. *pp.* 700 + 13 *plates.* *Abingdon, Va.*, 1849. 1249

PROCEEDINGS

Of an Indian Council, held at the Buffalo Creek reservation, State of New York, Fourth month, 1842. 8° *pp.* 81. *Baltimore, printed by William Wooddy*, 1842. 1250

PROCEEDINGS

Of the Joint Committee appointed by the Society of Friends constituting the yearly meetings of Genessee, New York, Philadelphia, and Baltimore. For promoting the civilization, and improving the Condition of the Seneca Nation of Indians. 8° *pp.* 189. *Baltimore, William Wooddy, printer*, 1847. 1251

PUMPELLY (Raphael).

Across America and Asia, notes of a five years journey around the world and of residence in Arizona, Japan and China. By Raphael Pumpelly. Third edition, revised. 8° *pp.* xvi. + 454 + 25 *plates and* 4 *maps.* *New York, Leypoldt and Holt*, 1870. 1252

The first four chapters, pp. 1 to 64, are occupied with narrations of the dangers of frontier life, and the horrible massacres perpetrated by the Apache Indians.

RAE (John).

Narrative of an Expedition to the Shores of the Arctic Sea in 1846 and 1847. By John Rae, Hudsons Bay Service, and Commander of the Expedition. With maps. 8° *pp.* viii. *and* 1 *to* 248. *London, T. and W. Boone*, 1850. 1253

Like all other expeditions by land to the Arctic Ocean, the success of this was attributable largely to the aid derived from the Red Indians and the Esquimaux. In consequence, the volume is occupied to a great extent with a detail of incidents associated with Indian life and habits. The methods by which the hardy aborigines of the Arctic zone prolong their lives, which are one long struggle with starvation and famine, their craft and devices in hunting and fishing, and many other particulars of their condition, are interwoven with the journal.

RAFINESQUE (C. F.).

Ancient History; or, Annals of Kentucky, with a Survey of the Ancient Monuments of North America, And a Tabular View of the Principal Languages and Primitive Nations of the whole Earth. By C. F. Rafinesque. 8° *pp.* iv. + 39. *Frankfort, in Kentucky, printed for the Author*, 1824. 1254

Amidst much that borders on the whimsical, the author of this pamphlet has produced a vast collection of facts relating to the history, language, and antiquities of the Aborigines of America. He was a man of much learning.

insatiable zeal in pursuit of knowledge, and tireless industry, but he lived at a period when ethnology had not crystallized into a science, and his reports of his own investigations have the appearance of crudeness and hypothesis. To class him with the mere speculator upon science and history, would be an act of injustice, as he was undoubtedly an original investigator. This work first appeared as an introduction to Marshall's *History of Kentucky.* Rafinesque added a table, abridged from a survey of nearly 500 languages and dialects (principally found in Adelung), and printed a few copies in this form. This ethnological and philological table, compares four principal words of fourteen Indian languages with thirty-four primitive Asiatic and European dialects, and occupies two pages. Pages 1 to 26 are occupied with an examination of the period of the pre-Columbian history of the Aborigines, and down to 1510; and pp. 27 to 31, with the annals of Aboriginal history of Kentucky. The Appendix, pp. 33 to 37, is occupied with an "Enumeration of the Sites of Ancient Towns and Monuments of Kentucky," in which he describes 148 localities in that State alone, where he had found Aboriginal remains. He says, "The actual number of ancient seats of population, already ascertained by me in North America, is 541, while the ancient monuments found in these sites, amount already to 1830. I entertain no doubt that 1,000 sites and 4,000 monuments, exist still in the United States, exclusive of Mexico." Both Mr. Squier and Mr. Davis informed the writer, that they believed 10,000 mounds and fortifications existed in the Mississippi Valley alone unexplored.

RAFINESQUE (C. S.).

A Life of Travels and Researches in North America, and South Europe; or, outlines of the Life, Travels, and Researches of C. S. Rafinesque, A. M., [4 *lines of brag.*] Containing his travels in North America, &c., with sketches of his scientific and historical researches. 12°. *Philadelphia, printed for the Author. By F. Turner, No.* 367 *Market Street,* 1836. 1255

RAFINESQUE (C. S.).

The American Nations; or, outlines of their General History, ancient and modern: including the whole history of the earth and mankind in the Western Hemisphere; the philosophy of American history; the annals, traditions, civilization, languages, &c. of all the American Nations, Tribes, Empires, and States. By C. S. Rafinesque. *Two vols.* 12° *Philadelphia, C. S. Rafinesque,* 1836. 1256

Vol. I., both covers printed, and serial title 3 leaves + title 1 leaf + pp. 259. Vol. II., printed covers and serial title 3 leaves + pages.

This extraordinary mass of learning, hypothesis, and wretched meanings, is not without its large share of utility, if one had the patience to separate the veritable philological gold from the dross of conjecture. There seems to be in some minds every quality for obtaining vast stores of learning, patient investigation, rare scholarship, and admirable skill in research; but so little susceptible to the rigid control of logical selection, that their attainments and discoveries are almost useless. These volumes are largely made up of comparative vocabularies of Indian languages.

RAFINESQUE (C. S.).

The Ancient Monuments of North and South America. Second edition. Corrected, enlarged, and with some additions. By C. S. Rafinesque. 8° *pp.* 28. *Philadelphia, printed for the Author,* 1838. 1257

RAFN (Charles Christian).

Aperçu de l'Ancienne Geographie Des Regions Arctiques de l'Amerique selon les rapports contenus dans les Sagas du Nord. Par Charles Christian Rafn, extrait des Memoires de la Société Royale, des Antiquaires du Nord. 8° *pp.* 11 + *map and two fac-similes of ancient Sagas. Copenhague, Imprimerie de Berling,* 1847. 1258

[Sketch of the ancient geography of the Arctic regions of America, taken from the descriptions of them in the Northern Sagas. By Charles C. Rafn, extract from the Memoirs of the Royal Society of Northern Antiquaries.]

RAFN (Carl Christian).

Americas Arctiske Landes Gamle Geographie efter De Nordiske Old-Skrifter ved Carl Christian Rafn, Saerskilt aftryk af Gronslands. Historiske Mindesmaerker udgivne af det Kongelige Nordiske Oldskrift-Selskab. 8° *pp.* 48 + 3 *maps and* 8 *plates. Kjobenhavn,* 1845. 1259

RALEIGH (Sir W.).

The Discovery of the large, rich, and beautiful Empire of Guiana, with a relation of the great and golden city of Manoa, (which the Spaniards call El Dorado) etc. performed in the year 1595, by Sir W. Raleigh Kn't. Reprinted from the edition of 1596, with some unpublished documents relative to that country. Edited with copious explanatory notes and a biographical memoir. By Sir Robert H. Schomburgh. ***London*** *: printed for the Hakluyt Society.* 1848. 1260

8° Map + Introduction pp. lxxv. Title of original edition and pref. pp. xv. + 130 + Appendix, memoir of Sir Walter Raleigh, pp. 131 to 240.
This is a reprint of the edition of 1596, with copious notes by Schomburgh. The relation of his travels in Guiana, by Raleigh, is replete with curious information regarding the savage tribes which inhabited the great Delta of the Orinoco. It is made much more interesting, by the authentication of its details by Sir Robert Schomburgh, who two and a half centuries subsequently, spent eight years in travel among those Indians.

RAMSEY (J. G. M.).

The Annals of Tennessee to the end of the Eighteenth Century: comprising its settlement, as the Watauga Association, from 1769 to 1777: A part of North Carolina, from 1777 to 1784; The State of Franklin, from 1784 to 1788; A part of North Carolina, from 1788 to 1790; The Territory of the U. States, south of the Ohio, from 1790 to 1796; The State of Tennessee from 1796 to 1800. By J. G. M. Ramsey. 8° ***pp.*** 744. *Charleston : **John** Russel 256 King Street,* 1853. 1261

Almost the entire volume is filled with minute narratives of the Indian wars with the Colonists. The author, one of the first-born citizens of the *State* of Tennessee, found himself in 1820, by the death of his father, an early pioneer of the territory, in possession of a great mass of journals and papers relating to its early history. His zeal added to these, the documents of Governor Sevier and other public men. He sought out the old soldiers and frontiersmen, and obtained from them both written and oral narratives of border adventure. Most of these he reproduces in their original style and language. His history is therefore something more and better than the ordinary compilations, so styled. It is a mass of minute narrative material relating to the Indians, the border wars, and the principal pioneers, moulded into a consecutive and regular story. Although he has copied somewhat from the rare book of Haywood, his work is almost wholly original, and contains a vast amount of aboriginal history never before printed.

RANKING (John).

Historical Researches of the Conquest of Peru, Mexico, Bogota, Natches, and Talomeco. In the Thirteenth Century by The Mongols, accompanied with Elephants; and the local agreement of history, and tradition, with the remains of elephants, and mastodontes, found in the New World. Containing Invasion of Japan — A violent Storm — Mongols with Elephants, land in Peru; and in California — Very Numerous Identifications. — History of Peru and Mexico to the Conquest by Spain — Grandeur of the Incas, and of Montezuma. — On Quadrupeds supposed extinct — Wild Elephants in America — Tapirs in Asia — Description of Two living Unicorns in Africa. With two maps, and portraits of all the Incas and Montezuma. By John Ranking. 8° *Two maps, four plates, and pp.* vi. + 479. *London*, 1827. 1262

A very considerable amount of valuable historic material has been grouped in this volume, relative to Mexican antiquities, but as in every treatise written to maintain a fanciful hypothesis, its value is greatly deteriorated, from the bias given every fact, to maintain a theory incapable of either proof or denial.

RAU (Charles).

A deposit of Agricultural Flint Implements, found in Southern Illinois. By Charles Rau. From the Annual Report of the Smithsonian Institution, Washington, D. C. for the Year 1868. 8° *pp.* 9. *Washington, Smithsonian Institution, Nov.* 1869. 1263

This is a very interesting account of the discovery, characteristics, and uses of many singular Indian implements, found near the banks of the Mississippi.

RAU (Charles).

Drilling in Stone without the use of Metals. By Charles Rau. From the annual report of the Smithsonian Institution, Washington, D. C., for the Year 1868. 8° *pp.* 11. *Washington, Smithsonian Institution, Nov.* 1869. 1264

Professor Rau in this treatise most ingeniously proves and illustrates the method by which the aborigines of America and Europe produced some of their perforated stone tools and weapons.

RAU (Charles).

Indian Pottery. 8° *pp.* 9. *Washington*, 1866. 1265

An article by Professor Rau, printed in the Smithsonian Reports, of which a few copies were printed separately without repagination.

RAU (Charles).

An Account of the Aboriginal Inhabitants of the Californian Peninsula, as given by Jacob Baegert, a German Jesuit Missionary who lived there seventeen years during the second half of the last Century. Translated and arranged for the Smithsonian Institution, by Charles Rau, of New York City. 8° *pp.* 48. *Washington*, 1866. 1266

A small number of copies of *The Account* were printed separately, without repagination, from the Smithsonian Reports.

RECEUIL.

De divers Voyages Afrique et Amerique. 1267

See Billaine.

RED MEN.

The General Laws of the Improved order of the Red Men, to which are added the By Laws of Powhattan Tribe, of the City of Washington D. C. No. 1. Formed in the Grand Sun, 5605. 12° *pp.* 23. *Washington, D. C., printed by Wm. Q. Force*, 5606. 1268

RED BROTHERS (The).

Revised by the Committee of Publication, of the American Sunday-School Union. 18° *pp.* 23. *Philadelphia* (*n. d.*). 1269

REICHEL (William C.).

Memorials of the Moravian Church. Edited by William C. Reichel. Vol. I. Printed for the Association. Sold by John Penington & Son. 8° *pp.* 366. *Philadelphia, J. B. Lippincott & Co.*, 1870. 1270

The titles of the several papers forming this valuable collection, are sufficiently suggestive of the treatment, of the relations of the Moravians with the Indians. "Count Zinzendorf and the Indians 1742," "Christian Indians buried at Bethlehem, Pennsylvania," "Early Moravian Settlement in Georgia, and Pennsylvania," "Account of the Brethren with the Commissioners of Pennsylvania During the Indian War of 1755, 1756, and 1757," are some of the subjects treated in this volume.

REID (Samuel C.).

The scouting expeditions of McCulloch's Texas Rangers; or, The summer and fall campaigns of the army in Mexico, 1846; including Skirmishes with the Mexicans, and an accurate detail of the Storming of Monterey: also the daring scouts at Buena Vista; together with anecdotes, incidents, descriptions of country and sketches of the lives of the celebrated partizan chiefs, Hays, McCulloch and Walker. By Samuel C. Reid, Jr., late of Texas Rangers. 12° *pp.* 250 + 11 *plates.* *Philadelphia*, 1848. 1271

Although principally a journal of adventure in the Mexican war, some incidents of border warfare with the Comanches are given.

REIGN OF FELICITY (The).

Being a plan for civilizing the Indians of N. A., without infringing on their national, or individual independence, in a coffee house dialogue between a courtier, an esquire, a clergyman, and a farmer. 12° *pp.* 12. *London*, 1796. 1272

A political satire, in which the tenantry of England are alluded to as Indians, — a poor performance, of no interest at this period.

Registres

Des Baptesmes et Sepultures, qui se sont faits au Fort Du Quesne Pendant les annees 1753, 1754, 1755, & 1756. 4° *pp.* 51. *Nouvelle York, Isle de Manate De la Presse Cramoisy de Jean-Marie Shea*, 1859. 1273

[Register of Baptisms and Burials, which were made at Fort Du Quesne during the years 1753 to 1756.]

Relation (A).

of the Invasion and Conquest of Florida, by the Spaniards, Under the Command of Ferdinando de Soto. Written in Portuguese by a Gentleman of the Town of Elvas. Now Englished. To which is Subjoyned Two Journeys of the present Emperour of China into Tartary in the Years 1682, and 1683. With some Discoveries made by the Spaniards in the Island of California, in the year 1683. *London: Printed for John Lawrence, at the Angel in the Poultry over against the Compter*, 1686. 1274

16° License, 1 leaf + title, 1 leaf + Preface, pp. (vii.) + table of chapters, pp. (v.) + 1 to 272.

The original work printed in Portuguese, at Evora in 1557, of which this is a translation, may perhaps be considered as the rarest work relating to American history known to have been published. It was priced by Mr. Rich, forty years since, at thirty guineas. The present work is believed to have been translated from the edition in French, printed in Paris the year before. Mr. Rich says the translator seemed to be unaware that Hakluyt printed it in English, nearly eighty years previously, that is, in 1609. It is interesting as being the second printed account of Florida, the Commentaries of Cabeza de Vaca having been printed in 1555. The volume has an additional value in containing the first relation of the settlement of California printed in English, the new descent of the Spaniards on the Island of California having taken place in 1683. Both Relations are almost wholly occupied with the ceremonies, treaties, and battles with the Indians.

Relations

Between the Cherokees, and the Government of the United States. 8° *pp.* 15. *n. d. n. p.* 1275

Relation

Des Affaires du Canada En 1696. Avec des Lettres des Peres de la Compagnie de Jesus, depuis 1696, jusqu' en 1702. 8° *pp.* 73. *Nouvelle-York, De la Presse Cramoisy de Jean Marie Shea*, 1865. 1276

[Relation of the Affairs of Canada, in 1696. With the Letters of the Fathers of the Society of Jesus, from 1696 to 1702.]

These Relations were printed from copies, made by the Hon. H. C. Murphy, from the original MSS. in Paris. The first is entitled, "The War with the Iroquois." The second, "Mission of the Sault St. Xavier," among the Christian Iroquois. And the others are letters from missionaries in other tribes. There is another edition of a part of this collection, with the following title, *Relation des Affaires du Canada, En 1696, Et des Missions des Peres de la Compagnie de Jesus jusqu' en 1702. Nouvelle-York*, 1865. 4° pp. 42.

RELATIONS DES JESUITES.

Relationes des Jesuites contenant ce qui s'est passé de plus remarquble dans les Missions des Peres de la Compagnie de Jesus dans la Nouvelle France (ouvrage publie sous les auspices du Gouvernment Canadien). *Three thick vols. Royal 8°* *Quebec,* 1858. 1277

[Relations of the Jesuits, containing narrations of the most remarkable events which occurred in the Missions of the Fathers of the Society of Jesuits in New France. The work published under the auspices of the Canadian government.]

Vol. I. Contains Fourteen Relations, covering a period of twelve years, 1611 to 1636, and 1632 to 1641.

Vol. II. Contains Fourteen Relations, covering a period of fourteen years, from 1642 to 1655.

Vol. III. Contains Seventeen Relations, covering a period also of fourteen years, from 1656 to 1672.

The Relations of each year are paged separately, and form therefore forty-five distinct memoirs, which are required to make the work complete. A table of contents to each volume, divided into years and relations, facilitates the collation. At the end of the third volume will be found a general index to the whole work.

This is the most extraordinary and valuable collection of material, relating to the history and life of the Indians ever made. It is composed of the narratives of a class of men who, two centuries before what we boastingly term civilization, had prostrated the forests and exterminated their free occupants, —explored the vast territories covered by them, recorded the peculiarities of their natives, and in many instances bestowed the blessings of Christianity upon them. These relations, for many years looked upon through the haze of sectarian distrust, were lightly esteemed by the students of American history, but the more their character and statements were investigated, the more important and valuable they appeared. They have become the sources from which we must draw almost all the historic material of New York and Canada, during the first century and a half of their exploration by Europeans. From the manuscript relations sent to the head of the order, small editions were printed in 12° by the Cramoisy Press. Copies of these have become exceedingly rare. It is not known that a perfect series exists in any library, although several collectors have closely approached completeness. The library of the Canadian government at Quebec had nearly the number forming the series, when its collection was destroyed in the great conflagration of 1854. It was to perpetuate these monuments of the early history of Canada, that Parliament ordered their publication in this form.

REMOVAL OF THE INDIANS (The).

1. An article on the North American Review, on the removal of the Indians, for January, 1830. 2. The letters of William Penn, published in the National Intelligencer. 8° *pp.* 72. *n. d. n. p.* 1278

This pamphlet is an able review of the two treatises named. The first by Governor Cass, and the last by Wm. Evarts, with many quotations of facts from other authorities.

REMY (Jules).

A Journey to Great-Salt-Lake city, by Jules Remy, and Julius Brenchley. With a sketch of the History, Religion, and Customs of the Mormons, and an introduction on the religious movement in the United States. By Jules Remy. In two vols. *Large 8° pp.* cxxxi. + 508–605. *London:* 1861. 1279

Much of the space in these volumes is devoted to descriptions of the Shoshoni Indians, the author having travelled through their country, under circumstances which gave him, as he believed, some insight into their character.

RENVILLE (J.).

Extracts from Genesis and the Psalms, with the third Chapter of Proverbs, and the third Chapter of Daniel, in the Dacota Language. Translated from the French Bible, as published by the American Bible Society, by Joseph Renville Sr.; Compared with other Translations, and prepared for the Press by Thomas S. Williamson D. D. Missionary. 18° *pp.* 72. *Published by the American Board of Commissioners for Foreign Missions. Cincinnati, Kendall & Henry, printers,* 1839. 1280

Indian title on verso of English title.

RENVILLE (J.).

The Gospel according to Mark, and extracts from some other Books of The New Testament in the Language of the Dakotas. Translated from the French, by Joseph Renville Sr. Written and prepared for the Press by Thomas S. Williamson, M. D. Missionary. Published for the American Board of Commissioners for Foreign Missions. 18° *pp.* 96. *Cincinnati, Kendall & Henry, printers,* 1839. 1281

Indian title on recto of second leaf.

RENVILLE (J.).

Extracts from the Gospels of Mathew, Luke, & John, from the Acts of the Apostles, and from the First Epistle of John, in the Language of the Dacota, or Sioux Indians. Translated from the French, as published by the American Bible Society, by Joseph Renville Sr. Written and published by Thomas S. Williamson M. D. (Missionary). 18° *pp.* 48. *Cincinnati, Kendall & Henry, printers,* 1839. 1282

No Indian title.

REPORT

on the Sudbury Fight, April, 1676. Read at the October Meeting of the Society, 1866, and reprinted from the N. E. Historical and Genealogical Register. 8° *pp.* 12. *n. d.* 1283

REPORT

of the Commissioner of Indian Affairs. Thirty-six volumes. 8° *Washington,* 1835 *to* 1870. 1284

The reports of the Indian bureau, and of the commissioner for Indian affairs, form a body of material relating to the Indians, almost unrivaled for its minuteness in any department of history. The names, numbers, and condition of the Indian tribes, are given with all the attention to details and correctness, which a multitude of agents more or less efficient, and sometimes conscientious, could be induced by interest and discipline to collect. To no other source can we look for the progressive steps, by which the savage tribes retreated before the overwhelming charge of the army of civilization. The reports cover the whole history of the dealings of the government with its Indian wards. They have become exceedingly scarce, for no complete set is known to exist, even in the library of Congress or in the documents of the Indian Bureau.

REPORT

of the Memorials of the Seneca Indians and Others, accepted November 21, 1840, in the Council of Massachusetts. 8° *pp.* 28. *Boston, Dutton & Wentworth, State Printers,* 1840. 1285

This report exposes another of those schemes of villany which the agents of the government have been so fertile in producing. The details of carefully planned delusions, by which the Indians were cheated of their lands; of the connivance of the government; and of the bribed collusions of its commissioner with other plunderers; are so uniform and so constant wherever the Indian is concerned, as generally to lack the interest of novelty. In this case the story is more revolting than usual. The United States commissioner, Mr. Gillet (may his name be infamous), boldly announced himself on the side of the robbers. These *speculators* had procured the signatures of sixteen chiefs to their deed of cession, but when in the presence of the infamous Gillet, sixty-three others desired to execute a protest against being driven from their homes, he refused to permit them, and broke up the council. This pamphlet is the report of a committee of the Legislature of Massachusetts, which had a year previously, ratified the deed thus villianously procured. The committee report the facts with many civil regrets, that the State should have been deluded into aiding the robbery of the Indians, and recommend after the usual fashion of committees, that nothing be done. Thus the State of Massachusetts received money which was the proceeds of the robbery of two thousand Indians; of their forced exclusion from their homes, and declined to restore her share of the plunder.

REPORT

of the Committee for the gradual civilization of the Indian Natives; made to Yearly Meeting of the Religious Society of Friends, held in Philadelphia, in the fourth month 1838. 8° *pp.* 26. *Philadelphia,* 1838. 1286

REPORT (The)

of the Aborigines Committee of the Meeting for Sufferings, read at the yearly meeting 1840, with the address to Lord John Russel, on his becoming Secretary for the Colonies: That to Friends Settling in New Colonies; and some particulars calculated to give information, and promote interest respecting the Present state of Aboriginal Tribes. Published by Direction of the Meeting for Sufferings. 8° *pp.* 20. *London, Harvey & Darton,* 1840. 1287

(*Tracts Relative to the Aborigines,* No. 5.)
See Friends.

REPORT (The)

of the Meeting for Sufferings respecting the Aborigines, presented to the yearly meeting, 1841. Second Edition. 8° *pp.* 12. *London, Edward Marsh,* 1843. 1288

(*Tracts Relative to the Aborigines,* No. 7.)
See Friends.

REPORTS OF THE SECRETARY OF WAR.

With Reconnaissances of routes from San Antonio to El Paso, by Brevet Lt. Col. J. E. Johnson; Lieutenant W. F. Smith; Lieutenant E. I. Bryan; Lieutenant N. H. Micheler and Captain S. G. French of Q'rmasters Dep't. Also, The Report of Capt. R. B. Marcy's route from Fort Smith, to Sante Fee; and the report of Lieut. J. H. Simpson, of an Expedition into the Navajo Country; and the report of Lieutenant W. H. C. Whitings Reconnaissainces of the Western Frontier of Texas, July 24, 1850. 8° *pp.* 250 *and* 71 *plates.* *Washington*, 1850. 1289

All of the plates and most of the text of this volume, were reproduced under the title of *Simpson's Journal*. There is much interesting matter in the reports relating to Indian tribes, then first visited, and the plates are principally illustrative of Indian features, savage life, or aboriginal antiquities.

REPORTS
to the yearly Meeting of Friends held in Philadelphia, from its Committee for Promoting the Improvement, and gradual Civilization of the Indian Natives, in 1818 and 1819. 8° *pp.* 15. *London*, 1819. 1290

REPORT
of the Secretary of War, transmitting, in compliance with a resolution of the Senate, documents in relation to the difficulties which took place at the payment of the Sac & Fox annuities, last fall. 8° *pp.* 128. *Washington*, 1848. 1291

Senate Executive Document No. 70. 1848.

REPORT
on the Indians of Upper Canada, by a Sub-committee of the Aborigines Protection Society, 4 Blomfield Street. 8° *pp.* 52. *London, William Ball, Arnold, and Co.*, 1839. 1292

REPORT
of a Visit to Spotted Tail's Tribe of Brule-Sioux Indians, the Yankton and Santee Sioux, Ponkas, and the Chippewas of Minnesota. In September, 1870. 8° *pp.* 20 + *printed cover.* *Philadelphia, McCulla and Stavely*, 1870. 1293

REVERE (J. W.).
A tour of duty in California; including a description of the Gold Regions: and an account of the voyage around Cape Horn; with notices of Lower California, the Gulf and Pacific coasts, and the principal events attending the Conquest of the Californias. By Joseph Warren Revere, Lieut. U. S. Navy, edited by Joseph N. Balestierre, with a Map and Plates, from original designs. 12° *pp.* 305 + 6 *plates and map, New York*, 1849. 1294

Chapters XI. to XV., pp. 112 to 163, are devoted to a description of the Indians of California, their ceremonies, wars, and depredations.

REVIEW (A)
of the Military Operations in North America. 1295

See Livingston, Wm.

REVIEW
of an Article in the North American, for January, 1830, on the present relations of the Indians. *n. p. n. d.* 8° *pp.* 24. 1296

REYNOLDS (John).

The Pioneer History of Illinois, containing the Discovery, in 1670, and the history of the country to the year eighteen hundred and eighteen, when the state government was organized. By John Reynolds. 12° *pp.* 313. *Belleville, Ill. Published by N. A. Randall*, 1852. 1297

Reynolds' history is crowded with incidents of Indian life and border warfare, most of which are derived from the personal narrations of the actors or their families.

RHODES (John).

The | Surprising Adventures | and | Sufferings | of | John Rhodes, | A | Seaman of Workington. | Containing— | An account of his captivity and cruel treatment dur | ing eight years with the Indians, and five years in | different Prisons amongst the Spaniards in South- | America. | By a Gentleman perfectly acquainted with the unfortunate | sufferer. | 16° *pp.* 250. *New York: Printed for R. Cotton, by G. Forman, No.* 64 | *Water Street*, | 1798. 1298

RHODES (John).

The | Surprising Adventures | and | Sufferings | of | John Rhodes, | a | Seaman of Workington. | containing — | An Account of his Captivity and cruel Treatment dur- | ing eight Years with the Indians, and five Years in | different Prisons amongst the Spaniards in South- | America. | By a Gentleman perfectly acquainted with | the unfortunate Sufferer. | 16° *pp.* 268. NEWARK, *printed by Pennington and Dodge*, | *For R. Cotton, New-York*, | 1799. 1299

This is a reprint of the New York edition, in larger type, and extended to eighteen pages more than the first edition. An abridged and interpolated edition of the work, was printed in New York in 1818, entitled "*The Pow-wow, being an exact description of an Indian banquet, by John Rodes, thirteen years Captive, &c.*" It was a mean affair in every respect. There is nothing in this narrative to attest its truth, and the internal evidence is not sufficient to settle the question of its veracity. Without something more definite than we now possess regarding its authenticity, it must remain worthless for historical purposes. It contains some curious details of the customs of the Indians of Central America.

RICHARDSON (Sir John).

Arctic Searching Expedition: a journal of a boat-voyage through Rupert's Land and the Arctic Sea, in search of the discovery ships under command of Sir John Franklin. With an appendix in the physical geography of North America. By Sir John Richardson. In Two Volumes. Published by authority. *London: Longman, Brown, Green, and Longmans.* 8° 1851. 1300

Vol. I. pp. viii. + 431 + map and 9 colored plates, 6 wood-cuts inserted in the text. Vol. II. pp. vii. + 426 + 1 plate of Cree encampment.

This exceedingly interesting work of the eminent naturalist, is thronged with details of personal experiences of Indian life, besides which, chapters xi., xii., pp. 339 to 413, of Vol. I., and chapters xiii. and xiv., pp. 1 to 60, are entirely devoted to details of the customs and peculiarities of the five Indian tribes of Arctic America. The Eskimaux, — Kutchin, — Chippeway, — Cree, and Chipewyan. Appendix V., pp. 363 to 402, of Vol. II., is a treatise on the vocabularies of the languages of these tribes, obtained by the author's zeal and diligence.

RICHARDSON (Sir John).

The Polar Regions. By Sir John Richardson, LL. D. 8° *pp.* 400. *Edinburgh, Adam and Charles Black*, 1861. 1801

RIGGS (Rev. S. R.).

Grammar and Dictionary of the Dakota Language. Collected by the members of the Dakota Mission. Edited by Rev. S. R. Riggs, A. M., missionary of the Am. Board of Com. for foreign missions. Under the patronage of the Historical Society of Minnesota. 4° *Prel. pp.* xii. + 1 *to* 338. *Washington City: Published by the Smithsonian Institution. June*, 1852. 1802

The author of this Grammar and Dictionary was a resident missionary among the Dakota Indians for fifteen years. In its construction he was aided by the Messrs. Pond, who had resided with the same tribe for eighteen years. The grammar occupies pp. 1 to 64. The Dakota and English Dictionary comprises more than sixteen thousand Sioux words, and fills pp. 65 to 278, in double columns. The remainder of the work, pp. 279 to 338, is devoted to the English and Dakota Dictionary.

RIGGS (Stephen R.).

Tah-Koo Wah-Kan; or, the Gospel among the Dakotas. By Stephen R. Riggs, A. M., Missionary of the A. B. C. F. M., and author of the Dakota grammar and dictionary. With an Introduction by S. B. Treat. Written for the Congregational Sabbath School and Publishing Society and approved by the Committee of Publication. 12° *pp.* xxxvi. + 491 + 4 *plates. Boston: Cong. Sabbath-School and publishing Society, Depository* 13 *Cornhill* (1869). 1803

The wonderful self-devotion of the Jesuit missionaries among the Indians, during the sixteenth and seventeenth centuries, has of late years challenged the admiration and astonishment of historical students who have discovered the monuments of literary labor, raised by them in the translations of sacred books into dialects almost unpronounceable by European organs. Not less heroic and astonishing, are the devotion and labor of the modern avant-couriers of Christianity and civilization, who like the author, turn their backs on the soft enticements of the one, to diffuse the faith of the other among barbarous nations. Mr. Riggs, with the true spirit of an Apostle, not only gave his life to the dissemination of religious truths, but added to these exhausting duties, the task of constructing a monumental lexicon of the Dakota tongue.

RIGHTS OF THE INDIANS.

Meeting and Memorial of the Convention in Boston. 8° *pp.* 16. (*Boston*), *Jan.* 21, 1830. 1804

RIPALDI (P. Geronymo).

Catecismo Mexicano, | Que contiene toda la Doctrina Christiana con todas | sus Declaraciones: en que el Ministro de Almas ha | llara, lo que a estas debe ensenar: y estas hallaran lo | que, para salvarse, deben saber, creer, y observar. | Dispusolo primeramente en Castellano | El Padre Geronymo de Ripalda | de la Compania de Jesus. | Y despues para la comun utilidad de los Indios; y es | pecialmente para alguna ayuda de sus zelosos Minis | tros, clara, genuina, y literalmente lo traduxo del | Castellano, en el puro, y proprio Idioma Mexicano. | El Padre Ignacio de Paredes. | [*etc.* 14 *lines.*] 16° en | Mexico, en la Imprenta de la Bibliotheca. *Mexicana*, | *enfrente de San Augustin, Ano de* 1758. | 1305

Preliminary pages (xvii.), namely, Spanish title, one leaf, reverse Scripture extracts and morals, folding plate, one leaf, Mexican title, one leaf, reverse coat of arms + dedication, approbation, etc., fourteen leaves + pp. 1 to 170, Indice (ii.).

[Mexican Catechism, which contains the whole Christian Doctrine. By the Father G. de Ripaldi. Arranged for the common use of the Indians, and translated from the Spanish into the pure and proper Mexican Idiom. By the Father I. de Paredes.]

RIVIERO (Mariano Eduardo de).

Antiquedades Peruanas por Mariano Eduardo de Riviero, y Juan Diego de Tschudi. *Viena. Inprenta Imperial de la Corte y del Estado.* 1851. 1306

Two volumes. Text. 4° pp. xiv. + 328. Atlas of plates imperial oblong 4° lviii. pages of plates.

This work was the result of toilsome research, by two learned gentlemen, Dr. Tschudi, a German, long resident in Peru, and Dr. Riviero, a native of that country. Their contribution to ethnological and philological science, has been esteemed by the learned world among the most valuable, after that of Humboldt, of those relating to South America. The first volume containing the text is divided into ten chapters, each discussing some phase in the history, religion, civilization, arts, monuments, and language of the Incas. Chapter v., pp. 66 to 120, is entirely devoted to an examination of the principles and grammatical construction of the Quichua language; and on pp. 98 to 100 is a bibliography which gives the titles of sixteen printed works in that language.

The second volume is an oblong folio of fifty-eight pages, containing more than eighty plates, and representing more than twice that number of objects. The structures of the Incas, both as now existing and as restored to their original shape and dimensions, the mummied forms of the ancient inhabitants, their sacrificial and agricultural implements, are the subjects of these finely executed lithographic plates. These are all colored. Dr. Tschudi subsequently published a work which was translated into English, and printed in London and New York, under the title of *Travels in Peru*, in which slight evidences of jealousy of his associate appear.

RIVERO (Mariano Edward)

And John James Von Tschudi. Peruvian Antiquites, by Mariano Edward Rivero, and John James Von Tschudi. Translated into English, from the original Spanish, by Francis L. Hawks, D. D. LL. D. 8° *pp.* xxii. + 1 *to* 306, *plates. New York*, 1853. 1307

This is a translation of Riviero and Tschudi's great work, originally printed in Spanish at Vienna. It is, however, unaccompanied by any plates, unless exception be made in favor of twenty wood-cuts in the text and the frontispiece.

ROBERTSON (W. S.).

Come to Jesus. — Cesus a ob Vtes, Erkenvkv Hall Coyvte,

momen. W. S. Robertson, John Mekellop, Rev. David Winslett, Esyomat Mvskoke Enipunvkv Obtvlecicet os. 16° *pp.* 63. *s. d.* 1308

A religious tract in the Creek language.

ROBERTSON & WINSLETT.

Nukcokv es Keretv enhvtecesky Muskokee. Or Creek First Reader, by W. S. Robertson, A. M. and David Winslett. 12° *pp.* 48. *New York: Mission house,* 1856. 1309

A child's picture-book, with the names of the objects and animals in Muskogee, with their descriptions in the same language.

ROBINSON (Solon).

Me-won-i-toc. A Tale of Frontier Life and Indian Character: exhibiting Traditions, Superstitions, and Character of a race that is passing away. A Romance of the Frontier. By Solon Robinson. 8° *pp.* 133. *New York,* 1867. 1310

ROBINSON (Conway).

An Account of Discoveries in the West until 1519, and of the Voyages to and along the Atlantic Coast of North America, from 1520 to 1573. Prepared for the "Virginia Historical and Philosophical Society." By Conway Robinson. 8° *pp.* xv. + 491. *Richmond:* 1848. 1311

This is the second volume of the Virginia Historical Society's Collections, and contains a narration of the principal incidents of Cartier's voyages to Canada; De Soto's march through Florida, to the Mississippi; Laudonierre and Ribault's accounts of settlements in Florida; the massacre of the settlers and the revenge of the French under De Gourgues, with the description of the natives and their customs which are to be found therein.

ROBSON (Joseph).

An Account of six years residence in Hudson's Bay, From 1733 to 1736, and 1744 to 1747. By Joseph Robson, Late Surveyor and Supervisor of the Buildings to the Hudson's-Bay Company. Containing a Variety of Facts, Observations, and Discoveries, tending to shew, I. The Vast Importance of the Countries [*etc.,* 22 *lines*]. The whole Illustrated, By a Draught of Nelson and Haye's Rivers; a Draught of Churchill-River; and Plans of York-fort, and Prince of Wales Fort. 8° *pp.* vi. *and* 1 *to* 84 + 3 *folding maps and plans* + *Appendix pp.* 1 *to* 95. *London:* M.D.CC.LII. 1312

A residence of six years among the natives of the Hudson's Bay territories, could not but afford some original information regarding them. As the narrative portion is, however, confined to the first eighty-four pages, this addition to our stock of knowledge is far less than we had a right to expect.

ROCHEFORT (De).

Histoire Naturelle et Morale des Iles Antilles de l'Amerique. Enriche d'un grand nombre de belles Figures en taille douce, des Places & des Raretes les plus considerables, qui y sont decrites. Avec un Vocabulaire Caraibe. Seconde Edition. Reveue & augmentee de plusieurs Descriptions, & de quelques eclaircissemens, qu'on desiroit en la precedente. *A Rotterdam, Chez Arnout Leers*, MDCLXV. 1313

[The Natural and Moral History of the Antilles Islands, in America. Embellished with a great number of fine copperplate engravings of the most considerable Places and Rarities. With a vocabulary of the Carib language. Second edition. Revised and augmented with many Descriptions and some explanations which were wanting in the first.]

4° Engraved title and 17 prel. leaves + pp. 1 to 583 + (xliii.) + 3 folding plates and numerous copperplates in the text.

In this work, attributed to and claimed by De Rochefort, have been preserved very many curious and interesting particulars of the life, habits, and character of the Caribs, more especially of the Apalachites. The last eighteen chapters, pp. 344 to 583, are entirely devoted to the relation of these particulars, with a copious vocabulary of their language. But those relations which are true, are said to have been purloined from authors, whose personal experience relieved them from the necessity of furnishing details from their own imagination. Rochefort's Nemesis was John Davies of London, who in 1666 published a translation of the work, in which he utterly ignored the existence of the ci-devant French author.

It did not suffice, however, that Davies should rob Rochefort of his stolen laurels, but the partly fictitious, and partly abstracted materials of his work were successively plundered by Ogilby, Montanus, Dapper, Oldmixon, and a long heirship of literary thieves. There is something oddly fitting and harmonious as well as ludicrous, that each of these marauders believed that he was stealing the unadulterated gold of veracious history, from each of the mendacious robbers who preceded him.

It is now certain that Rochefort appropriated the labors of a savant named Du Tertre, whose name he utterly ignores. Davies levies upon Rochefort's supposed original material, and Ogilby, equally ignorant that the whole of the treasure had been purloined, absorbs it almost bodily into his great folio. The stolen wealth is constantly being unlawfully transferred from hand to hand. Mr. Rich relates the story of the original theft at length. Father Du Tertre, a missionary who had spent some years in the West Indies, wrote a history of the Antilles, the manuscript of which was borrowed from a friend with whom he had deposited it, by a general, for the inspection of another friend who was preparing a work on the same subject. This unknown author proved to be a Protestant clergyman of New Rochelle, named Rochefort, who had twice visited the islands.

On hearing of the unfaithful disposition of his labors, Father Du Tertre, fearing that his work would be anticipated by another, hurriedly brought it to press, in 1654, under the title of *Histoire Generale des Isles de S. Christophe, etc.*, which Mr. Rich says was in reality only a project of that work. The work of Rochefort was printed in 1658, and his second edition in 1665. Father Du Tertre published the first two volumes of his *Histoire Generale des Antilles*, in 1668, and the last two in 1671. In his preface to this work he narrates the story of the loan of his manuscript and its appropriation by Rochefort, affirming that it is so faithfully copied that even his errors have not escaped, but have, in common with his facts, been stolen by the latter. It was the fate of the second robber Davies to meet with retribution in a double shape. His work was published in the same year with the great conflagration which consumed one half of London, and in it disappeared nearly the whole edition of his history.

ROCKWELL (Rev. Charles).

The Catskill Mountains and the Region Around. Their Scenery, Legends, and History; with sketches in prose and verse by Cooper, Irving, Bryant, Cole, and others. By Rev. Charles Rockwell, revised edition. 16° *pp.* 351, *map and plates. New York: Tainter Brothers & Co.*, 1869. 1314

More than half of this modest little volume is devoted to new and interesting details of border warfare and Indian captivity.

ROGERS (Major Robert).

Journals of Major Robert Rogers: containing An Account of the several Excursions he made under the Generals who commanded upon the Continent of North America, during the late War. From which may by collected The most material Circumstances of every Campaign upon that Continent, from the Commencement to the Conclusion of the War. 8° *pp.* viii. + 347. *London: printed for the Author*, 1765. 1315

The Journal of this celebrated partisan chief affords as many interesting details of border warfare, in the French and Indian War, which ended seventeen years before the Revolution. It was while associated with Rogers that General Putnam is said to have experienced those wonderful adventures, with the relation of which our youthful nerves have so often thrilled. It is however remarkable, that Major Rogers does not even mention the name of Putnam. The last page (347), is unnumbered and entitled, "Advertisement." It announces a continuation, or second part of the Journal, which never appeared, as the subscriptions of a guinea a copy were probably not sufficiently numerous.

ROGERS (Robert).

A concise Account of North America: containing A Description of the several British Colonies, on that Continent, Including the Islands of Newfoundland, Cape Breton, [*etc.*, 8 *lines*]. To which is subjoined, An Account of the Several Nations and Tribes of Indians, residing in those Parts, as to their Customs, Manners, Government, Numbers, &c. Containing many Useful and Entertaining Facts, never before treated of. By Major Robert Rogers. 8° *pp.* vii. *and* 264, *map*. *London: printed for the Author*, MDCCLXV. 1316

This historical essay, by the famous partisan officer and Indian fighter, although by no means equal to his Journal in interest, is not without merit. In the "concise account" of the several colonies, he mingles many particulars of the Indian nations, but its especial interest is to be found in the section of his volume devoted to the "Customs, Manners, and Government of the Indians," pp. 205 to 264. These relations are the result of his own personal experience among the savages.

ROMANCE

Of Indian History; or thrilling Incidents in the Early History of America. 16° *pp.* 24. *New York, Kiggins & Kellogg, n. d.* 1317

This child's book contains the adventures of Kindago, a Mohawk chief, and his Christian wife, and of Adam Poe, with the Wyandot chief, Bigfoot.

RONDTHALER (Rev. Edward).

Life of John Heckewelder, by the Rev. Edward Rondthaler, of Nazareth, Pa. Edited by B. H. Coates, M. D. 12° *Philadelphia*, 1847. 1318

ROSNY (Leon de).

Archives Paleographiques de l'Orient, et de l'Amerique, publiee avec des notices historiques, et philologiques, par Leon de

Rosny, professeur etc. Recueil Trimestriel, destinee a publier la collection des alphabets de toutes les languages. Connues, des inscriptions, des medailles etc. Avec des fac-similes de manuscrits, orientaux. Imprimes en noir et en couleur. 8° *Paris, Maisonneuve*, 1870. 1319

[Paleographic Archives of America and the East, with historic and philologic notes, by Leon de Rosny. A quarterly publication, designed for the Collection of alphabets of all known languages, of inscriptions and medals, with fac-similes of oriental MSS. in black and colored. Each part is 8° pp. 80. Part II. contains, pp. 101 to 115, a bibliography of American works on paleography of no great value.]

Ross (John).

A Voyage of Discovery, made under the orders of the Admiralty, in his Majesty's ships Isabella and Alexander, for the purpose of exploring Baffin's Bay, and inquiring into the probability of a North-West passage. By John Ross K. S. Captain Royal Navy. 4° *Pref. pp.* xl. + 252 + cxliv. + *map*, 25 *plates and* 6 *charts. London: John Murray, Albemarle-Street.* 1819. 1320

This first volume of Sir John Ross's narratives of discovery, contains but little regarding the natives of the frigid zone. Chapters v. and vii. are occupied with an account of the discovery of an unknown tribe of Esquimaux, their customs, religion, and language. Several of the plates are illustrative of the same subjects.

Ross (Sir John).

Narrative of a Second Voyage in search of a North-West Passage, and of a residence in the Arctic Regions during the years 1829, 1830, 1831, 1832, 1833. By Sir John Ross, Captain in the Royal Navy. Including the reports of Commander, now Captain James Clark Ross, and the Discovery of the Northern Magnetic Pole. 4° *pp.* xxxiv. + 740 + 30 *plates and map. London: A. W. Webster*, 1835. 1321

Another of those wonderfully interesting narratives of human endurance, triumphing over the most awful peril and suffering. The sumptuous printing which makes every page a picture, has even its luxury enhanced by the splendid steel engravings and lithographs. The former are so excellent as to be worthy of preservation as gems of art. Although everywhere through the narrative is interwoven the records of aboriginal life as it appeared to the explorers, Chapters xvi., xvii., xviii., and xix. are especially devoted to a description of their peculiarities. Of the thirty plates seven are illustrative of some phase, in the lives of the natives of the Polar regions.

Ross (Sir John).

Appendix to the Narrative of a second voyage in Search of a North-West Passage; and of a residence in the Arctic Regions during the Years 1829, 1830, 1831, 1832, 1833. By Sir John Ross. Including the reports of commander, now Captain James Clark Ross, and The Discovery of the Northern Magnetic Pole. 4° *pp.* xii. + 120 + cxliv. + cii. + 18 *plates. London:* 1835. 1322

This appendix contains, besides the illustrations of Esquimaux life, forty-four pages of a vocabulary of the language of that people. The first twenty-four pages are descriptive of the general habits of life of the Esquimaux, and pp. 25 to 60 are occupied with biographical sketches of representative persons, of both sexes, of whom the plates are portraits.

Ross (John).

Letter in answer to inquiries from a Friend, regarding the Cherokee Affairs with the United States; with the Protest of the Cherokee Delegation. 8° *pp.* 31. (*Washington*, 1836.) 1323

Ross (John).

Letter from John Ross, the principal Chief of the Cherokee Nation to a Gentleman of Philadelphia. *s. l.* 8° *pp.* 40. (*Philadelphia*, 1837.) 1324

This letter of the Cherokee chief occupies twenty pages, and is an indignant remonstrance against the violent enforcement of one of those fraudulent treaties, by which the government of the United States have defrauded so many Indian tribes of their lands. It is accompanied by "Documents in Illustration of, or referred to in the foregoing Letter." The documents are such as would emanate from few councils of white men, engaged in the discussion of such wrongs. A number of outcast Indians of no influence in the nation, debauched with rum by designing whites, are by these swindlers dubbed chiefs, and made to sign a treaty of surrender of all the lands of the nation, in the presence of some of the United States authorities, parties to the robbery, and by virtue of a conveyance so forged, twenty thousand land proprietors are driven from their homes.

Ross (Alexander).

Adventures of the first settlers on the Oregon or Columbia River; being a Narrative of the expedition fitted out by J. J. Astor, to establish the "Pacific Fur Company." With an account of some Indian Tribes on the coast of the Pacific. By Alexander Ross, one of the adventurers. 12° *pp.* xvi. + 352 *and map. London: Smith Elder & Co.*, 1849. 1325

Although the narratives by Ross Cox and Washington Irving, of the adventures of the hardy traders, who first established a settlement at Astoria, seem to have left nothing to be said regarding it, yet the relation of the personal experiences of an intelligent and keen observer, such as the author was, is always welcome. Chapters vi. to xxi., pp. 87 to 341, are almost wholly devoted to descriptions of the peculiar habits and customs of the ten tribes inhabiting the western slope of the Rocky Mountains. The Appendix, pp. 342 to 350, is occupied with a vocabulary of the Chinooks.

Ross (Alexander).

The Fur Hunters of the Far West; a narrative of adventures in the Oregon and Rocky Mountains. By Alexander Ross. In Two Volumes. *Post* 8° Vol. I. *pp.* xv. + 333. Vol. II. *pp.* viii. + 262 + *portrait and map. London: Smith Elder & Co.*, 1855. 1326

The narrations of an intelligent observer of the peculiarities of savage life, always attract an amount of interest, which increases in proportion to the truthfulness of his coloring or shading. In all the qualities which should attract and hold our attention, it is rare to find the superior of Mr. Ross. For fifteen years he traversed the wastes of the Rocky Mountains, and thus became as familiar with every trait of Indian character and phase of savage life, as a white man may ever expect to be. As an Indian trader pushing his commerce among friendly but treacherous tribes, and even among hostile ones who are to be placated by resistless finery, or the equally omnipotent fire-water, he was often the first white man to burst upon their wild fastnesses. The Appendix, pp. 313 to 333, contains a vocabulary of the Nez Perces language.

Ross (Alexander).

The Red River Settlement: its rise, progress, and present state. With some account of the Native Races, and its general history, to the present day. By Alexander Ross, author of the Fur-Hunters of the far West. 12° *pp.* xvi. + 416, *frontispiece. London: Smith Elder & Co. 65 Cornhill,* 1856. 1327

After many years of toil and adventure among the fierce tribes of the northern plains of Oregon and Washington territory, the author sought repose among his associates in the Red River Colony. The successive disasters of massacre, famine, and inundation, drove him from this forlorn asylum, to writing books descriptive of the wild people and wild life he had seen. All of these works possess the unfailing interest, which attach to the details of an intelligent observer and a faithful narrator. His pictures are of savage life and manners, as seen by the adventurous voyagers and fur-traders of the Hudson's Bay Company.

Rouchefoucauld Liancourt.

(See Liancourt). 1328

Rowlandson (Mary).

A true | HISTORY | of the | Captivity & Restoration | of | Mrs. Mary Rowlandson, | A Minister's Wife in *New-England.* | Wherein is set forth, The Cruel and Inhumane | Usage she underwent amongst the Heathens, for | Eleven Weeks time: And her Deliverance from them. | *Written by her own Hand, for her Private Use: And now made* | *Publick at the earnest Desire of some Friends, for the Benefit* | *of the Afflicted.* | Whereunto is annexed, | A Sermon of the Possibility of God's Forsaking a Peo | ple that have been near and dear to him. | Preached by Mr. *Joseph Rowlandson,* Husband to the said Mrs. *Rowlandson:* | It being his Last Sermon. | *Small* 4° Printed First at *New England:* And Re-printed at London, and sold | by Joseph Poole, at the Blue Bowl in the Long Walk, by Christ's | Church Hospital, 1682. 1329

4° Title, 1 leaf, Pref., 2 leaves, Nar., pp. 1 to 36. A Sermon, pp. 37 to 46. This is the second edition of one of the earliest narratives of Indian captivities, and possibly one of the most authentic. The relation of the manners and peculiarities of the Indians of New England, in 1675, by one so observant and scrupulous in her statements, has more than ordinary interest and value. The original edition is very rarely found complete.

Rowlandson (Mary).

The Captivity and Deliverance of Mrs. Mary Rowlandson, of Lancaster, who was taken by the French and Indians. Written by herself. 18° *pp.* 80. *Brookfield, printed by Hori Brown, from the press of E. Merriam & Co. September,* 1811. 1330

Although printed with separate title and pagination, this edition actually forms a part of a work of the same date, entitled, *Captivity and Deliverance of Mr. John Williams and Mrs. Mary Rowlandson.* Williams' captivity occupies one hundred and sixteen pages.

Rupp (I. Daniel).

History of Lancaster County, to which is prefixed a brief sketch of the Early History of Pennsylvania. Compiled from authentic Sources. By I. Daniel Rupp. 8° *pp.* 528 + 5 *plates.* *Lancaster, Penn.: published by Gilbert Hills*, 1844. 1331

The history of the Moravians, their dealings with the Indians, the story of the massacre of Conestoga Indians, at Lancaster, by the Paxton Boys, and the particulars of the Border Wars of the county, are treated by the author with great minuteness.

Rupp (I. Daniel).

History of Northampton, Lehigh, Monroe, Carbon, and Schuylkill Counties: containing a brief history of the First Settlers. Topography of Townships, notices of leading events, incidents, and interesting facts in the early history of these counties: with an Appendix, containing matters of deep interest. Embellished by several engravings. Compiled from various authentic sources by I. Daniel Rupp. Published and sold by G. Hills, proprietor, Lancaster, Pa. 8° *pp.* xvi. + 568 + 4 *plates.* *Harrisburg: Hickok & Cantine, printers and binders*, 1845. 1332

Many incidents of Indian warfare, massacre, and captivity, with relations of treaties with the savages, and speeches of their chiefs, are given in the body of the work. The Appendix, from pp. 405 to 485, is entirely occupied with the journals of four persons, who were engaged in the campaigns against the Shawnese and Delawares from 1755 to 1758.

Rupp (J. Daniel).

History of the Counties of Berks and Lebanon. Containing a brief account of the Indians, and numerous murders by them; notices of the Swedish, Welsh, French, German, Irish, and English Settlers, giving the names of nearly 5000 of them, &c. Compiled by I. Daniel Rupp. 12° *Lancaster, Pa.*, 1844. 1333*

Ruttenber (E. M.).

History of the Indian Tribes of Hudson's River; their origin, manners and customs; tribal and sub-tribal organizations; wars, treaties, etc., etc. By E. M. Ruttenber. 8° *pp.* 415 + 5 *plates.* *Albany, N. Y.: J. Munsell*, 1872. 1334

The design, indicated in the title, is very well fulfilled in pp. 7 to 295; being a compilation of material, not readily accessible to all readers, in the original works. The Appendix is divided into three sections: Part I., pp. 300 to 331, entitled, "Biographical Sketches," rehearses in an agreeable manner, the familiar stories of the lives of prominent Indian chiefs. Part II., pp. 333 to 360, is devoted to language; and Part III., pp. 361 to 399, to geographical nomenclature and traditions.

Ruxton (George Frederick).

Life in the Far West. By George Frederick Ruxton, author of Adventures in Mexico and the Rocky Mountains. 12° *pp.* 285. *New York: Harper & Brothers*, 1859. 1335

We are assured by the author in his preface, that his work is a narration of veritable incidents of Indian and frontier life, with fictitious names to some of the characters, for prudential motives.

His relations of the awful ravages of the Apaches and Comanches in northern Mexico, are painfully vivid. He passes for weeks through ruined villages, whose inhabitants have perished in merciless slaughter, or have been carried into a captivity scarcely less horrible. Year by year the semi-civilization of the Mexican has been driven back, by the more vigorous savagery of the Indian, until a territory as large as France, once subjected to law, and thronged by active life, has been depopulated.' Melancholy as the story is, we read with perhaps not less regret, that the precious historical manuscripts of New Mexico, discovered by Mr. Ruxton, were irrecoverably lost by him in crossing the Arkansas.

RUXTON (George R.).

Adventures in Mexico and the Rocky Mountains. By George Ruxton, Esq. 12° pp. 312. *New York: Harper & Brothers.* 1860. 1336

RYCAUT (Paul).

The Royal Commentaries of Peru. 1337

See Garcilasso.

RYE (W. B.).

The discovery and conquest of Terra Florida, by Don Ferdinando de Soto, and six hundred Spaniards his followers. Written by a gentleman of Elvas, employed in all the action, and translated out of Portuguese, by Richard Hakluyt. Reprinted from the edition of 1611. Edited, With Notes and an Introduction, and a translation of a narrative of the expedition by Luis Hernandez de Biedma, factor to the same, by William B. Rye, of the British Museum. *London: printed for the Hakluyt Society,* MDCCCLI. 1338

The Introduction fills pp. lxvii. + "The Worthye and famous Historie," pp. 1 to 170 + Biedma's Relation, 173 to 200 + Index, v. + Map.

The relation of the gentleman of Elvas, first published in Portuguese at Evora, 1557, in small 8°, has a sufficient testimony of its great historical value, in the numerous editions through which it has passed. It first appeared in its English guise, as *Virginia Richly Valued*, translated by Richard Hakluyt, London, 1609. Small 4° The translator reissued it in 1611, as *The Worthye and famous historie of the travailes, Discovery and Conquest of Terra Florida.* An edition was printed at Paris, 1685, in 12° entitled, *Histoire de la Conqueste de la Floride*, which was translated into English, and the next year appeared in London in small 8° entitled, *Relation of the Invasion and Conquest of Florida by the Spaniards.*

It was reproduced in *Purchas Pilgrims*, in Peter Force's *Tracts*, in the Historical Collections of Louisiana, and has formed the basis of numerous works on the history of Florida. It ranks second only to the relation of Cabeça de Vaca, in the information it affords us, regarding the aborigines of the southern States, on their first introduction to Europeans.

SAABYE (Hans Egede).

Greenland: being extracts from a Journal kept in that country In the Years 1770 to 1778. By Hans Egede Saabye, Formerly ordained Minister in the Districts of Claushavn and Christianshaab, now Minister of Udbye, in the Bishopric of Fühnen; and grandson of the celebrated Hans Egede. (Now first published.) To which is prefixed an Introduction; containing some accounts of the manners of the Greenlanders, and of the Mission in Greenland; with various interesting information respecting the geography, &c. of that country; And Illustrated by a chart of Greenland, By G. Fries. Second edition. Translated from the German. 8° *Map and pp.* viii. + 298. *London:* 1818. 1339

This journal is a most complete relation of the character, peculiarities, and habits of life of the Greenlanders, both savage and Christian. The simple narrative of the every-day life of a missionary among the aborigines of the Arctic regions, is told by an intelligent, brave-hearted man, in that most pleasing of all styles, the natural, unaffected one, which carries conviction of its veritability.

SABBATH (A)

Among the Tuscarora Indians. A true Narrative. 24° pp. 69. *Glasgow*, 1821. 1340

SAGARD (Gabriel).

Le grand voyage | dv pays des Hvrons, | situé en l'Amerique vers la Mer | douce, es derniers confins | de la nouuelle France, | dite Canada. | Ou il est amplement traite de tout cequi est du pays, des | moeurs & du naturel des Sauvages, de leur gouvernment | & façons de faire, tant de dans leur pays, qu' allans en voya | ges: De leur foy & croyance; De leurs conseils & guerres, & | de quel genre de tourmens ils font mourir leurs prisonniers. | Comme ils se marient, & esleuent leurs enfans: De leurs Me | dicins, & des remedes dont ils usent a leurs maladies: De | leurs dances & chansons: De la chasse, de la pesche, & des | oyseaux & animaux terrestres & aquatiques qu' ils ont. Des | richesses du pays: Comme ils cultiuent les terres, & accom | modent leur Menestre. De leur deuil, pleurs & lamenta | tions, & comme ils enseuelissent & enterrent leurs morts. | Auec un Dictionaire de la langue Huronne, pour la commodi | te de ceux qui ont a voyager dans le pays, & n'ont | l'intelligence d' icelle langue. | Par F. Gabriel Sagard Theodat, Recollect de | S. Francois, de la Prouince de S. Denys en France. | *A Paris*, | *Chez Denys Moreau, rue S. Iacques, a* | *la Salamandre d'Argent*. | M.DC.XXXII. | Auec Priuilege du Roy. | 1341

[The Great Journey to the Country of the Hurons, Situated in America, upon the Fresh water Sea, at the farthest boundaries of New France, called Canada. In which everything relating to that country is copiously treated. Of the Manners of the Native Savages, of their government and habits of life as well in their country as in their travels. Of their faith and belief, of their counsels and wars, and of the torments they invent in killing their prisoners. Of the Manner of their marriages and rearing their children. Of their physicians and the remedies they use in diseases. Of their dances and songs: Of hunting and fishing, and of the birds and animals, both land and aquatic, which they have. Of the wealth of the country. How they cultivate the land, and conduct their household affairs. Of their mourning, tears, and lamentations, and how they shroud and bury their dead. With a Dictionary of the Huron language, for the convenience of those who travel in that country, and are not acquainted with the language.]

Collation: 16° Engraved title, 1 leaf + full title, 1 leaf, reverse of both blank. "Epistre Au Roy," 4 leaves + "Au Lecteur," 3 leaves + "Table des Chapitres and Priviliges," 3 leaves + "Voyage du Pays," etc., pp. 1 to 380 + "Table des Choses," 7 leaves + title to dictionary and pref. pp. 12 + 66 unnumbered leaves. Total, pp. 24 + 380 + 14 + 12 + 132 = 562.

SAGARD (Gabriel).

Dictionaire | de la langve | Hvronne, | Necessaire à ceux qui n'ont intelligence d'icelle. | & ont a traiter auec les Sauuages du pays. | Par Fr Gabriel Sagard, Recollect de | S. François, de la Prouince de S. Denys. | *A Paris,* | *Chez Denys Moreau, rue S. Jacques, a la* | *Salemandre d'Argent.* | M.DC.XXXII. | Auec Priuilege du Roy. | 1342

[Dictionary of the Huron Language, necessary to those who have no knowledge of it, and have to treat with the Savages of the country.]

This work is occasionally found separate from the *Grand Voyage*, and having a distinct title and pagination, has, by some, been considered a complete work, but its announcement on the title of the *Grand Voyage*, determines that question in the negative. It is said to have been the perusal of this Dictionary, that induced Lord Monboddo to undertake his work on the *Origin and Progress of Language*, but what book incited his theory, that mankind had progressed from the monkey, by asserting that a savage nation had been discovered with the rudiments of tails, is not stated.

Father Charlevoix speaks slightingly of Sagard's Dictionary, but his judgment upon the histories of New France is commonly sharp and censorious. Regarding Father Sagard, it is expressed in these words, "The author of this work spent some time among the Hurons, and relates naively all that he saw and heard on the spot, but he had not time to see things well enough, still less to verify all that was told him. The Huron vocabulary which he has left us, proves that neither he, nor any of those whom he consulted, was well versed in that language, which is a very difficult one. In other respects he seems a very judicious man. He gives us, on the whole, few interesting facts."

Few who read Father Sagard's *Grand Voyage and Histoire*, will coincide with Charlevoix in his severe judgment, regarding the interest of his history and narrative.

Father Sagard, a member of the Recollects in Paris, was directed by a congregation of his order to accompany Father Nicholas, in a mission to the savages of New France. He sailed from Dieppe in the latter part of March, 1624, and arrived at Quebec after a voyage of three months and six days, during which he endured such sufferings, that he says the whole of his life has not equaled in pain. He proceeded at once to the scene of his mission among the Hurons, one hundred and fifty leagues west of Quebec. Here he remained but a few months, when it was determined to send him to Quebec, for supplies. His fortitude was not equal to the emergency, and worn down with the privations and sufferings of a missionary's life, he allowed himself to be persuaded by his brethren that it was not his vocation. He accordingly returned to his convent in Paris, where he wrote the work we have considered, and four years subsequently, produced his *Histoire du Canada.* Both of these works were reprinted in Paris in 1864 and 1866. Copies of the original editions of both these works are excessively rare, the *Histoire du Canada* being much the most difficult to procure.

SAGARD (F. Gabriel).

Le grand voyage du pays des Hurons situe en l'Amerique vers la Mer douce es derniers confins de la Nouvelle France dite Canada avec un dictionaire de la langue Huronne par F. Gabriel Sagard Theodat, Recollect, &c. Two vols. 8° Vol. I. *pp.* xxvi. + 205. Vol. II. *pp.* 207 *to* 268, *Vocabulary* 12 + 148. *Paris,* 1865. 1343

SAGARD (F. Gabriel).

Histoire du Canada et Voyages que les Freres Mineurs Recollects y ont faicts pour la conuersion des infidelles. Diuisez en quatre liures. Où est amplement traicté des choses principales arriuées dans le pays, depuis l'an 1615 iusques à la prise qui en a esté faicte par les Anglois. Des biens & commoditez qu' ou en peut esperer. Des moeurs, ceremonies, creance, loix et coustumes merueilleuses de ses habitans. De la conuersion & baptesme de plusieurs, & des moyens necessaires pour les amener à la cognoissance de Dieu. L'entretien ordinaire de nos Mariniers, & autres particularitez, qui se remarquent en la suite de l'histoire. Fait & composé par le F. Gabriel Sagard Théodat, Mineur Recollect de la Prouince de Paris. A Paris, chez Claude Sonnius, rue S. Jacques à l'Efeu de Basle, & au Compas d'or, M.DC.XXXVI. Avec Privilege & Approbation. (Four vols. 12° *Paris, Libraire Tross*, 1864, 1865). 1344

[History of Canada, & Voyages that the Brothers Minors, Recollects, have made there for the conversion of Infidels, divided in four books. Where is fully treated some of the principal events which happened in the country since the year 1615 to the conquest by the English. The riches and commodities that they are able to hope from it. Of the manners, ceremonies, and remarkable customs of the inhabitants. Of the conversion and baptism of some of them, and of the means necessary to lead them to the knowledge of God. Made and Composed by the Brother Gabriel Sagard Théodat, Minor Recollect of the Province of Paris. Paris, Claude Sonnius, M.DC.XXXVI.]

This is the title of the original edition, which Mr. Tross has prefixed to the first volume of his issue, and to each of which he gives a separate title, although the pagination runs continuously through the whole four.

The second and fourth parts of the *Histoire du Canada*, are little more than extensions of the *Grand Voyage and Dictionary*. The travels and missionary labors of the Recollects among the Indians of Canada, for nine years before the arrival of Father Sagard, form the subject of Book I. The narrative of his *Grand Voyage to the Country of the Hurons*, which appeared three years before, is extended by additional particulars, from chapters xxii., in the edition of 1632, to xlvi. in Book II. of the *Histoire du Canada*. Book III. is a reproduction of Part II. of the *Grand Voyage*, with new matter increasing it from 85 to 135 pages. Book IV. contains the history of the Recollect missions to the end of 1629. The dictionary of the Huron language, which formed a part of Sagard's first work, is exactly reproduced in the *Histoire*, together with four pages of what he styles, an Indian hymn to the devil, with the musical notes of the drone or howl in which it was chanted. Mr. Tross has added to his edition, a brief sketch by M. Chevalier, of the Recollect missions, and a critique upon the works of Father Sagard, in which he arraigns Charlevoix with great severity, for his harsh judgment of them. M. Chevalier asserts with much reason, that Father Charlevoix, writing one hundred years after Sagard, could himself know little of the Huron language, as the people speaking it had in his time been long extinct as a nation, and the dialect of the few who remained much corrupted.

SAGE (Rufus B.).

Scenes in the Rocky Mountains, and in Oregon, California, New-Mexico, Texas, and the Grand Prairies; or notes by the way, during an excursion of three years, with a description of the countries passed through, including their geography, geology, resources, present condition, and the different nations inhabiting them. By a New Englander. 12° *pp.* 303. *Philadelphia:* 1846. 1345

SAGE (Rufus B.).

Rocky Mountain Life: or startling scenes and Perilous Adventures in the Far West, during an expedition of three years. By Rufus B. Sage. 12° *pp.* 363. *Boston: Wentworth & Co.,* 1857. 1346

This work is a second and enlarged edition of *Scenes in the Rocky Mountains.* The author says in his preface, that this work was written immediately after his return from the expedition, the events of which he narrates. He claims for it a veritability of which there is some internal evidence. It is much deformed by the spasmodic style he adopts, and the sentimental rhapsodies he indulges in, but it is crowded with incidents of Indian life, legends, and adventure.

SAGEAN (Mathieu).

Extrait de la Relation des Avantures et Voyage de Mathieu Sagean. 4° *pp.* 82. *Nouvelle York: A la Presse Cramoisy de J. M. Shea,* 1863. 1347

No. 16 of Shea's *Jesuit Relations.*

[Extract from the Relation of the Adventures and Travels of Mathew Sagean.]

Sagean was a Frenchman, possessed of considerable zeal and ambition, to rival La Salle, but so ignorant as to be unable to write, and scarcely to read his own language. He had doubtless visited some nations of Indians, living on the eastern tributaries of the Mississippi, but he was looked upon as an impostor, when he asserted that he had found a nation of cannibals on the Missouri, whose country abounded in gold mines. The late discoveries in Nevada and New Mexico, give a greater air of probability to his story. The manuscript of this hitherto unprinted narrative, was discovered at Paris, by Mr. Squier.

SAHAGUN (B. de).

Historia General de las Cosas de Nueva Espana, que en doce libros y dos volumenes escribio, el R. P. Fr. Bernardino de Sahagun, de la observancia de San Francisco, y uno de los primeros predicadores del Santo Evangelio en aquellos regiones. Dala a luz con notas y supplementos Carlos Maria de Bustamente, diputado por el estado de Oaxaca en el Congreso general de la federacion Mexicana; y la dedica a nuestro Santissimo Padre Pio VIII. Three Volumes 8° Vol. I. *pre. pp.* (6) + xx + 350 + (vii.) + *folding plan.* Vol. II. *pp.* (vi.) + 397 + xlvi. + (ix.). Vol. III. (iv.) + 339 + (iv.). *Mexico: Imprenta del Ciudadano Alejandro Valdes, Calle de Santo Domingo y esquina de Tacuba,* 1829. 1348

[General History of the affairs of New Spain, which was written in twelve books, and two volumes, by Father Bernardino de Sahagun, of the order of St. Francis, and one of the first preachers of the Gospel, in these countries. Edited with the addition of notes, and a supplement, by Carlos Maria de Bustamente, a deputy from the State of Oaxaca, to the General Congress of the Mexican Republic.]

This wonderful work, to which the entire life of Father Sahagun was devoted, is beyond question the most important, as it is the most authentic history of events, transpiring in the New World, before its discovery by Columbus. All that relates to the religion, customs, government, and wars of the Aztecs, was examined in a manner so critical, so patient and thorough that no history was ever conceived, or brought forth with more labor. Bernardino de Sahagun, born in a village of Spain, from which he derived his last name, became a Franciscan monk, and commenced his labors as a missionary to the Indians of Mexico, in 1529. Eminent for zeal, purity, and toil, even among the great number of pious and devoted men, who sought to redeem the New World from paganism, he resigned all the high functions his merit had procured him, after some years of service, in order to devote himself entirely to preaching, and to the examination of every Aztec pictograph and hieroglyph, which would illustrate the history of that race. To secure the greatest accuracy in his history, he lived for several years in an Indian village of Tescuco, where resided many of the learned natives, who had never been taught the Spanish tongue. Every day he examined some of them, regarding their antiquities, and their pictograph paintings. He arranged long series of questions regarding their ancient history, which they answered by writing their replies in their hieroglyphic style. To assure himself of the authenticity of his version of their answers, he submitted them to natives who had been educated at the College of Santa Cruz. These scholars wrote their translation of the hieroglyphic history, in the Mexican tongue, but with the use of Roman letters. These translations with the pictograph originals, were then subjected to revisal, by another body of learned Mexicans, educated in the Spanish language. After thirty years of almost incredible labor, he submitted his work to the brethren of his order, but the bigotry which had destroyed almost every vestige of Aztec literature, now opposed the terrible barrier of the churchman's disapprobation. The superior of his order seized his manuscripts, separated them, and sent the fragments to the several convents in Mexico. It was several years before Sahagun could procure an order for their restoration. His history, when he was eighty years of age, was still written only in the Mexican tongue, and he now commenced the labor of translation into Spanish. The manuscript in two great folios, with the two versions of Mexican and Spanish, in parallel columns, was sent to Madrid, where it slept unheard of for more than two hundred years. First brought to light by Munoz, who discovered it in a convent of Tolosa, in Navarre, it was first published in Mexico in these three volumes, by Bustamente, and the next year by Lord Kingsborough in his sixth volume. Some of the work, as it left the hands of Sahagun, has been lost, and among other parts which met this fate, are the hieroglyphic paintings which accompanied the text, and eighteen Aztec hymns. Sahagun died in Mexico in 1590, nearly ninety years of age. The second work of Sahagun was published for the first time in 1829, as a fourth volume of the *Historia General*. It was printed separately in Mexico, 1840. The MS. of a third work was found in Mexico, by Beltrami. It is entitled, *Evangeliarium, Epistolarium et Lectionarium Aztecum*. It is declared to be a translation of the Gospels and Epistles, into Nahuatl. It was edited by Biondelli who added a vocabulary in Latin and Nahuatl.

St. Clair (Maj. Gen.).

A Narrative of the manner in which the campaign against the Indians, in the year one thousand seven hundred and ninety one, was conducted, by Major General St. Clair, together with his observations on the statements of the Secretary of War and the Quarter Master General, relative thereto, and the reports of the committees appointed to inquire into the causes of the failure thereof: Taken from the files of the House of Representatives in Congress. 8° *Half title, title and Introduction, together pp.* xix. + 273 + (xx.). *Philadelphia*, 1812. 1849

General St. Clair's narrative, of the terrible defeat and slaughter, of eight hundred soldiers by the Ohio Indians, occupies pp. 1 to 58. The "Report of the Congressional Committee" of examination, pp. 59 to 82. St. Clair's observations on the report, pp. 83 to 134. — Supplementary Report and Letters, pp. 135 to 192. The Examination of Witnesses of the Battle, pp. 193 to 229. Appendix to 273 and subscribers' names, ten unnumbered leaves. All of St. Clair's voluminous defense is rendered nugatory and futile by the passionate ejaculations of Washington, when Major Denny called him from a dinner-party, to announce the defeat. Overcome with surprise and indignation, Washington cursed the beaten general with exceeding fervor, adding, "Did not my last words warn him against a surprise."

St. Priest (Bavaderre de).

(Et des) Notes explicatives, et autres documents. Part of Antiquites Mexicanes. See Dupaix. *Paris*, 1834. 1350

Sanders (Daniel C.).

A | History | of the | Indian Wars | with the | first settlers of the Uni | ted States, | particularly | in New England. | Written in Vermont. | (*motto 3 lines*) 24° *pp.* 319. *Montpelier, Vt.* | *Published by Wright & Sibley,* | 1812. | *Wright & Sibley, Printers,* 1812. 1351

The mystery which surrounded the authorship, history, and origin of this very rare volume, has been slowly dispelled by successive fragments of information. So few copies have survived the holocaust to which it was devoted, that its very existence was unknown to the most zealous collectors of Indian and Vermont history. Published anonymously, without preface, it was known to but few that the author was the Rev. Daniel Clark Sanders, President of the University of Vermont. Immediately after its appearance, some person, evidently a personal enemy of the author, published an acrimonious critique upon the book, in the *Liberal and Philosophical Repository*. The animus of the critic was evidenced, not only by the bitterness of his language, but by his ignorance of the subject of Indian wars, being more profound than that of the author of the book he scored. Such was the effect of the article upon either Mr. Sanders, or the publishers, that the work was suppressed. But very few copies could have escaped the hands that were now as zealous to destroy, as they had lately been to create. In fact, so nearly complete was the destruction of the book, that it was forgotten by those who professed to know most of its author, his biographers. Neither Thompson, Williams, or Hemmenway, who published memoirs of him, mention his authorship of the Indian wars.

Sanford (Ezekiel).

A history of the United States before the Revolution: with some account of The Aborigines. By Ezekiel Sanford. 8° *pp.* ccxii. + 341. *Philadelphia:* 1819. 1352

A very excellent *résumé* of what is known of the aborigines of America, occupies the first two hundred pages, divided into three sections, embracing the mythical, doubtful, and certain historical data recorded of them.

Sanford (Laura G.).

The History of Erie County, Pennsylvania. By Laura G. Sanford. 12° *pp.* 348, *map* + 9 *plates. Philadelphia: J. B. Lippincott & Co.,* 1862. 1353

The first seven chapters, pp. 1 to 93, are principally devoted to accounts of the Indian tribes, which once inhabited the county, explorations of the early discoverers, Indian wars, and biographical sketches of the pioneer settlers, without affording much information that was not already easily accessible.

Sargent (Winthrop).

The history of an expedition against Fort du Quesne, in 1755; under Major General Edward Braddock. Edited from the original manuscripts, by Winthrop Sargent. *Large* 8° *pp.* 423. *Eleven maps, plans, and plates. Philadelphia:* 1856. 1354

Mr. Sargent's *Introductory Memoir*, which gives a full, lucid, and continuous narrative of the ill-fated campaign, commanded by the debauchee, broken pimp, and brutal soldier, General Braddock, occupies pp. 13 to 280. The journals of participants in the expedition fill pp. 283 to 389. The appendix fills the remainder of the volume. The work was published as the fifth volume of the memoirs of the Pennsylvania Historical Society, and also as a distinct work by Lippincott.

SARYTSCHEW (Gawrila).

Account of a Voyage of Discovery to the North-East of Siberia, the frozen Ocean, and the North-East Sea. By Gawrila Sarytschew, Russian imperial major-general to the expedition. Two vols. Translated from the Russian, and embellished with engravings. 8° Vol. II. *pp.* 80 + *plate of Indians of Alaska. London: printed for Richard Philips*, 1807. 1355

Vol. II. of this narrative, gives us the first account of the Russian exploration of Alaska and the Aleutian Islands. It is very interesting, as affording us a view of the peculiarities of the savages of that portion of the United States at their first communication with the whites. It is very minute in its description of such of the ceremonies, manners, and life of the aborigines as fell under the observation of the author, a very frank and honest narrator.

SAVAGE (Timothy).

The Amazonian Republic, recently discovered in the Interior of Peru. By Ex-Midshipman Timothy Savage, B. C. *New York: Published by Samuel Colman* (*for the author*), 1842. 1356

An insignificant work of fiction.

SAVAGE (The).

The Savage, by Piomingo, a headman and warrior of the Muscogulgee nation. Philadelphia: printed for Thomas S. Manning; and sold by T. Cadell and W. Davies, Strand. 12° *pp.* 312. *London* (*no date*). 1357

A book of ethical essays, the author of which attempted a series of papers illustrative of American character after the manner of the celebrated British essayists. They have, of course, not the slightest relation to anything associated with the aborigines.

SCENES

In the Indian Country. 24° *pp.* 283. *Philadelphia: Presbyterian Board of Publication, No.* 821, *Chestnut Street* (1859). 1358

SCHERZER (Carl).

Sprachen der Indianer Central-Amerika's. Während seinen mehrjährigen reisen in der verschiedenen Staaten Mittel-Amerika's aufgezeichnet und zusammengestellt von Dr. Karl Scherzer. 8° *pp.* 11. (*Wien*), (1855). 1359

A comparative vocabulary of the languages of the Tlascan, Quiche, Pocomchi, Populaka tribes and the Indians of Costa Rica.

SCHWEINITZ (Edmund de).

The life and times of David Zeisberger, the Western Pioneer and Apostle of the Indians. By Edmund de Schweinitz. 8° *pp.* 747. *Philadelphia: J. B. Lippincott & Co.*, 1870. 1360

The wonderful man whose life is memorialized in this volume, though less celebrated than the Indian apostle, John Eliot, was not less saintly in his character, possessed equal accomplishments and learning, and performed far more labor as a missionary and a philologist For more than sixty years, commencing in 1744 and terminating in 1808, Zeisberger lived among the Delaware, Shawnese, and Iroquois Indians, or was associated with their interest. He resided for three years at Onondaga, the site of the council-fire of the Six Nations, nearly half a century before the arrival of the first white settlers. He was often employed on long and dangerous journeys, as an ambassador to distant tribes, and in every capacity in which a vigorous, intelligent, and humane man could be engaged, he exhausted his powers of endurance, to be useful. He was reverenced by the fiercest and most vindictive of the Pagan tribes, not only with the religious awe of an apostle, but almost with that due to a celestial being. He found savage nations at war with each other, and with the civilized hordes which were closing around them, and he soothed their angry warriors with the words of peace and divine love. He saw his converts living in Christian communities, slaughtered in a horrible massacre, which that of St. Bartholomew excelled only in its magnitude. He translated the sacred writings into the languages of the Indian tribes, among whom he labored, and painfully elaborated their harsh and difficult tongues into a grammatical system. Born in Moravia, 1721, he emigrated to America in 1739, and died at New Philadelphia in 1808. During the greater part of his sixty years of residence among the aborigines, Zeisberger and his fellow missionaries, wrote voluminous journals of the incidents of their every-day life, and complete reports of everything associated with the Indians which fell under their observation. These manuscripts amounting to many thousand pages, as the author assures us, are still preserved, and have formed the basis of his work. Zeisberger's printed works may be found under the following titles: —

1. *Essay of a Delaware Indian, and English Spelling Book*, pp. 113. Philadelphia, 1776.
2. The Same, reprinted. Philadelphia, 1806.
3. *A Collection of Hymns, for the use of the Christian Indians*, pp. 358. Philadelphia, 1803.
4. The Same, reprinted. Bethlehem, 1847.
5. *Sermons to Children*, translated into Delaware, pp. 90. Philadelphia, 1803.
6. *Something of Bodily Care for Children*, translated into Delaware, pp. 26. Philadelphia, 1803.
7. *The History of our Saviour Jesus Christ*, 12° pp. 222. New York.
8. *Verbal Bieguengen, or Delaware Conjugations*, Leipzig, 1821.

The Manuscript works of Zeisberger, are much more numerous than his printed books. Those deposited in the library of the American Philosophical Society in Philadelphia, are, — 1. *Deutsch und Onondaisches Worterbuch, or Dictionary of the German and Onondaga Languages*, in seven vols.

2. *Onondaga, and German Vocabulary.*
3. *Essay, toward an Onondaga Grammar.*
4. *Onondagaische Grammatica*, a complete grammar of the Onondaga language. This was translated into English by Peter S. Duponceau. This version also remains in manuscript in the same library. The library of Harvard College was presented with fourteen manuscript works of Zeisberger, on the Indian languages, by Edward Everett. These massive monuments of the labor and zeal of this eminent scholar and missionary, would form the worthy object of a Zeisberger Society to translate the German text into English, and print a series of volumes, as a testimony of the services of a great and good man.

SCHMIDEL (Ulrich).

Vera historia, | Admirandae cuius | dam navigationis, quam Hul | dericus Schmidel, Straubigensis, ab Anno 1534, | usque ad annum 1554, in Americam vel nouum | Mundum, iuxta Brasiliam & Rio della Plat a, confecit. Quid | per hosce annos 19. sustinuerit, quam varias & quam mirandas | regiones ac homines viderit. Ab ipso Schmidelio Germanice, | descripta: Nunc vero, emendatis & correctis Vrbium, Regio | num & Fluminum nominibus, Adiecta etiamtabula | Geographica, figuris & aliis notationi | bus quibusdam in hanc for | mam reducta. [*Plate of the Author mounted on a Llama, attended by two Indians.*] Noribergae, | Impensis Levini Hulsii, 1599. | 1361

Small 4° Title, 1 leaf, reverse blank + pp. 1 to 101, reverse blank. Map of Brazil, between pp. 94 and 95. Map of Patagonia and Straits of Magellan, at the end of the text; followed by sixteen plates in pairs, facing each other. Seven of the elaborate and very vivid representations are views of battles with the Indians, or assaults on their fortifications; five are representations of their dwellings, persons, or mode of life; one is a portrait of Schmidel, two are scenes of shipwreck and earthquake, and one a view of some bloody slaughter. This early relation of a traveller is very rare. It was translated by Ternaux and printed in his collection.

Schmidel (Ulrich).

Histoire veritable d'un Voyage Curieux fait par Ulrich Schmidel de Straubing, dans l'Amerique ou le Nouveau Monde, par le Bresil, et le Rio de la Plata, depuis l' annee 1534, jusq'en 1554. Ou l'on verra tout ce qu'il a souffert pendant ces dix-neuf ans, et la description des pays et des peuples extraordinaires qu'il a visites. Ouvrage ecrit par lui-meme, et publie de nouveau apres corrections des noms de villes, de pays et de rivieres, par Levinus Hulsius. 8° *pp.* 264. *Nuremberg*, 1599. *Paris, Arthus Bertrand-libraire-editeur*, 1837. 1362

[True History of a Curious Voyage made by Ulrich Schmidel of Straubing, in America or the New World, through Brasil and the Rio de la Plata, from the year 1534 to the year 1554. In which he relates all that he endured during these nineteen years, with a description of the country and the extraordinary people whom he visited. A work written by himself, and newly published, with corrections of the names of the cities, countries, and rivers, by Levinus Hulsius, Nuremberg, 1599.]

A French translation of Schmidel's narrative, printed by Ternaux-Compans, as number five of his collection of *Voyages, Relations, et Memoires.*

This first Latin edition, translated from the German of 1567, is much the most desirable, as it contains many corrections of errors, and is unabridged.

Ulrich Schmidel, the author of this narrative, was a common soldier who accompanied Mendoza and Cabeça de Vaca in their conquest of the countries south of Brazil. His history bears internal evidence of veracity, which is further attested by contemporaneous accounts. Its pages are one continuous record of massacre and enslavement of the Indians. Of the fifty-five chapters, eleven are descriptive of these battles or rather slaughters. Two we rejoice to read, because they narrate some considerable retributive killing of the Spaniards by the Indians. Thirteen chapters are filled with descriptions of the various tribes and nations he encountered. Ternaux published this work translated into French in his collection of voyages, with many corrections of names. Not the least of its interest to us is contained in his account of the character, adventures, and imprisonment of Cabeça de Vaca.

Schoolcraft (H. R.).

Narrative Journal of Travels from Detroit northwest through the Great Chain of American Lakes to the sources of the Mississippi River, in the year 1820. By Henry R. Schoolcraft. 8° *Map.* + *pp.* 424. *Albany, published by E. & E. Hosford,* 1821. 1363

The author has interwoven with his narrative a large number of incidents of Indian history, personal experience among the tribes he visited, and sketches of their principal characteristics, derived from persons living among them.

SCHOOLCRAFT (Henry R.).

Travels in the central portions of the Mississippi Valley: comprising observations on its mineral geography, internal resources, and aboriginal population. Performed under the Sanction of Government, in the Year 1821. By Henry R. Schoolcraft. 8° 5 *plates and maps, pp.* 459. *New York: Published by Collins & Hannay,* 1825. 1364

A large portion of this volume is devoted to descriptions of scenes in Indian history, occurring at localities visited by the author during his tour, as well as incidents, illustrative of the character of the aboriginal tribes which passed under his own observation. All of the last four chapters, pp. 337 to 459, are occupied with descriptions of ceremonies and incidents he witnessed, attending the treaty with the Ottawas, Pottawatomies, and Chippewas. Anecdotes and observations illustrative of Indian character, fill chapter xviii. Chapter xix. contains an analysis of the languages of the tribes present at the treaty, a vocabulary, and several songs, with their translations.

SCHOOLCRAFT (Henry R.).

Constitution of the Algic Society instituted March 28, 1832, for encouraging Missionary effort in evangelizing the North Western Tribes, and promoting education, agriculture, industry, peace, & temperance among them. To which is annexed an abstract of its proceedings together with an introductory address by Henry R. Schoolcraft, Esq. president of the Society. 8° *pp.* 23. *Detroit,* 1833. 1365

SCHOOLCRAFT AND ALLEN.

Expedition to Northwest Indians. Letter from The Secretary of War transmitting a Map and Report of Lieut. Allen and H. R. Schoolcraft's visit to the Northwest Indians in 1832. (Congressional Document.) 8° *pp.* 1 *to* 68. (*Washington,* 1834.) 1366

SCHOOLCRAFT (H. R.).

Narrative of an expedition through the Upper Mississippi to Itasca Lake, the actual source of this river; embracing an exploratory trip through the St. Croix and Burntwood (or Broule) Rivers: in 1832, under the direction of Henry R. Schoolcraft. 8° *pp.* 307, *two large folding maps. New York: Published by Harper & Brothers,* 1834. 1367

Most of this narrative is occupied with interesting incidents of Indian life and character, extracts from manuscript journals of the fur-traders, and traditions of the aborigines. Pages 169 to 310 of the Appendix, are devoted to an analysis and vocabulary of the Chippewa language. The remainder of the volume is filled with the official reports of the author, to the government, on the number, disposition, and characteristics of the Indian tribes he visited, and with biographical sketches of their principal chiefs.

SCHOOLCRAFT (Henry Rowe).

Algic Researches, comprising inquiries respecting the mental characteristics of the North American Indians. First Series. Indian Tales and Legends. In two volumes. By Henry Rowe Schoolcraft. 12° *pp.* 248 *and* 244. *New York: Harper & Brothers*, 1839. 1368

The term Algic was invented by Mr. Schoolcraft to indicate the Algonquin race. He composed it from the first and final syllables of Allegheny and Atlantic. He distinguishes the intruding tribes, into the vast territory covered by the nations of this race, as Otsic, which includes the Iroquois and Wyandots. He asserts the authenticity of these legends, by declaring that they were written down from the lips of the Indian raconteurs, during an intimate association with various tribes for seventeen years. There has not a little corroborative evidence in their favor, accumulated in the intervening forty years since their recording, by finding them rehearsed essentially identical, by other tribes to other recorders.

SCHOOLCRAFT (H. R.).

Cyclopedia Indianensis: Or a General Description of the Indian Tribes of North and South America. Comprising [*etc.*, 10 *lines.*] The whole alphabetically arranged. By Henry R. Schoolcraft. 8° *pp.* 16 + 4 *pp. printed covers. New York:* 1842. 1369

Issued as the prospectus of a contemplated work in two volumes, of seven hundred pages each, of which this sheet is the only portion which went beyond contemplation.

SCHOOLCRAFT (H. R.).

Notes on the Iroquois; or contributions to American History, Antiquities, and General Ethnology. By Henry R. Schoolcraft. 8° *pp.* xv. + 498 + *frontispiece and* 36 *wood-cuts in the text. Albany: Erastus H. Pease & Co.*, 1847. 1370

This is a much more pretentious but less valuable work than his official report on the same subject. It was intended to be a popular reproduction of the material embodied therein, but the substitution of a narrative history, based upon and composed of hypothesis, for substantial facts, even in the unattractive form of an official document, does not compensate for the lack of the solid structure of history.

SCHOOLCRAFT (H. R.).

Report Of Mr. Schoolcraft, to the Secretary of State, transmitting the census returns in relation to the Indians. Census of the Iroquois. *Tall* 8° *pp.* 285 + vii. (*Albany*), 1845. 1371

This is the most valuable of Mr. Schoolcraft's works, having been executed after personal examination in an official capacity of all the tribes inhabiting New York. There is an almost entire absence of the speculative and sentimental cogitations which so greatly marred his works. Section I. is entitled "Historical and Ethnological Minutes, made in taking the Census of the Iroquois 1845," commences at p. 25, and with Sections II. to X. embracing every item of the history, traditions, biography, antiquities, and statistics of the Iroquois, he was able to collect, occupy the volume to p. 190. The particulars of the census returns, fill pp. 191 to 202. An appendix extending to p. 285 is filled with letters from persons resident or familiar with the various Indian tribes, conveying minute and doubtless truthful information regarding them.

SCHOOLCRAFT (H. R.).

Report of the Aboriginal Names and Geographical Terminology

of the State of New York. Part I. — Valley of the Hudson. Made to the New York Historical Society, etc. By Henry R. Schoolcraft. Published from the Society's Proceedings for 1844. 8° *pp.* 43. *New York: printed for the author,* 1845. 1372

SCHOOLCRAFT (Henry R.).
Onéota, or characteristics of the Red Race of America. From original notes and manuscripts. By Henry R. Schoolcraft. 8° *New York & London:* 1845. 1373

This work was originally published in numbers, subsequently in the above form, and afterwards rearranged and printed under the title of *The Indian in his Wigwam.* In his personal narrative, the author has told us precisely what no one cares to know, and omitted all that would possess any interest,— incidents of his personal intercourse with the Indians.

SCHOOLCRAFT (Henry R.).
An Address delivered before the Was-ah Ho-de-no-son-ne or New Confederacy of the Iroquois, by Henry R. Schoolcraft a member, at its third Annual Council, August 14, 1846. Also Genundewah, a Poem by W. H. C. Hosmer, a member; pronounced on the same occasion; published by the Confederacy. 8° *pp.* 48. *Rochester,* 1846. 1374

SCHOOLCRAFT (H. R.).
The Indian in his Wigwam, or characteristics of the Red Race of America, from original notes and manuscripts. By Henry R. Schoolcraft. 8° *pp.* 416. *Buffalo:* 1848. 1375

SCHOOLCRAFT (H. R.).
A Bibliographical Catalogue of books, Translations of the Scriptures, and other publications in the Indian Tongues of the United States, with brief critical notices. 8° *pp.* 28. *Half title,* 1 *p. reverse prefatory remarks, Title, reverse synopsis. Washington: C. Alexander, printer,* 1849. 1376

SCHOOLCRAFT (Henry R.).
Personal Memoirs of a Residence of Thirty Years with the Indian Tribes, on the American Frontiers: with brief notices of passing events, facts, and opinions, A. D. 1812 to A. D. 1842. By Henry R. Schoolcraft. 8° *pp.* 703. *Philadelphia: Lippincott, Grambo, & Co.,* 1851. 1377

SCHOOLCRAFT (Henry R.).
The Myth of Hiawatha, and other oral legends, mythologic and allegoric, of the North American Indians. By Henry R. Schoolcraft. 12° *pp.* 343. *Philadelphia and London:* 1856. 1378

This volume is a reproduction of *Algic Researches,* printed in 1839, with some additions. Mr. Schoolcraft was not the only claimant for the honor of bringing to Mr. Longfellow's notice the Indian legends, from which the poet derived the foundation of his beautiful poem. Mr. Clark traces its origin to the Onondagas, the central tribe of the Iroquois. The legend by which the Indians accounted for the possession of that king of cereals, the Maize, was one of the most wide-spread and universal of all aboriginal myths. It would not be as difficult as many other propositions regarding the Indians, to trace it through almost every tribal organization in North America.

SCHOOLCRAFT (Henry R.).

Information respecting the History, Condition and Prospects of the Indian Tribes of the United States. Collected and prepared under the direction of the Bureau of Indian Affairs per act of Congress March 3d 1847. By Henry R. Schoolcraft LL.D. Illustrated by S. Eastman, Capt. U. S. Army. Published by authority of Congress. 6 vols. 4°. *Philadelphia: Lippincott, Grambo, & Co.,* 1853. 1379

Two editions of this work were published by the same house. One on thinner and somewhat smaller paper, of which, however, only five volumes were printed, and the edition is therefore incomplete. Schoolcraft's work was intended to be a great encyclopædia of information relating to the American Aborigines. With great earnestness, some fitness for research, and a good degree of experience of Indian life, Mr. Schoolcraft had but little learning and no scientific training. In consequence, his six volumes are little more than a magazine, of such matter relating to the Indians as fell to his hand, including a rehash of all which he had before written and printed in numerous other forms. Badly arranged, and selected as it is, the work contains a vast mass of really valuable material. It has indeed performed a very important service for Indian history, in collecting and preserving an immense amount of historic data. Vocabularies of Indian languages, grammatical analyses, legends of various tribes, biographies of chiefs and warriors, narratives of captivities, histories of Indian wars, emigrations, and theories of their origin, are all related and blended in an extraordinary and perplexing manner. A very large number of beautiful steel engravings, representative of some phase of Indian life and customs, are contained in the work, but the most valuable of its illustrations are the drawings of weapons, domestic utensils, instruments of gaming and amusement, sorcery and medicine, objects of worship, their sculptures, paintings, and fortifications, picto-graph writing, dwellings, and every form of antiquities, which have been discovered. The six volumes contain 336 full-page plates, representing thousands of the scenes and objects named.

SEAVER (James E.).

A Narrative of the life of Mrs. Mary Jemison, who was taken by the Indians, in the year 1755, When only about twelve years of age, and has continued to reside amongst them to the present time. Containing an account of the murder of her father and his family; her sufferings; her marriage to two Indians; her troubles with her children; Barbarities of the Indians in the French and Revolutionary Wars; the life of her last husband; And many Historical Facts never before published. Carefully taken from her own words, Nov. 29, 1823. To which is added An Appendix, Containing an Account of the Tragedy at the Devil's Hole, in 1763, and of Sullivan's Expedition; the Traditions, Manners, Customs, &c., of the Indians, as believed and practised at the present day, and since Mrs. Jemison's Captivity; together with some Anecdotes, and other entertaining Matter. By James E. Seaver. 24° *pp.* 160. *Howden: printed for R. Parkin: Sold by T. Tegg, 73, Cheapside, London:* 1826. 1380

SEAVER (James E.).

Life of Mary Jemison, Deh-he-wä-mis. By James E. Seaver. Fourth Edition, with geographical and explanatory notes. *New*

York and Auburn: Miller, Orton & Mulligan. Rochester: D. M. Dewey, 1856. 12° *pp.* 312 + 4 *plates*. 1381

This well written narrative, purporting to be only the biography of a captive among the Senecas, is really the best *resumé* we have of incidents in the history and common life of the Seneca Indians. Its truthfulness is vouched for by such veracious testimony as that of Eli Parker, an educated chief of that nation, though its authenticity can scarcely have greater corroboration than the fact that Mr. Seaver received almost the whole mass of incidents narrated in his book, directly from the lips of the aged captive herself. A portion of the book which future ethnologists will highly prize, is contained on pp. 300 to 312, where the Indian names of nearly 400 localities, in the State of New York, are given, with their English significations.

SELKIRK (Earl).

Statement respecting the Earl of Selkirk's Settlement upon the Red River, in North America; its destruction in 1815 and 1816 and the massacre of Governor Semple and his party, with observations upon a recent publication, Entitled "A Narrative of Occurrences in the Indian Countries," &c. 8° *pp.* viii. + 194. *Appendix pp. C. and folding map. London: John Murray*, 1817. 1382

For other works, relating to the murderous hostilities between the Indians, half-breeds, fur-traders, and desperadoes of the two great fur companies, see *Simpson's Trial of Bernhard; Report of Proceedings, etc.; Narration of Occurrences.*

SELKIRK (Earl).

Report of the proceedings connected with the disputes between the Earl of Selkirk and the North West Company, at the assizes, held at York, in Upper Canada, October, 1818. From minutes taken in court. 8° *pp.* xxv. + 1 *to* 225 *and* 1 *to* 203, *and Appendix* 1 *to* 48. *Montreal: printed. London: reprinted*, 1819. 1383

This is a report of the trial of certain members of the Northwest Fur Company, half-breed Indians, and others, for the murder of Governor Semple and several members of the Hudson's Bay Company.

SEMINOLE WAR.

Message from the President of the United States, transmitting, in pursuance of a resolution of the House of Representatives, such further information, in relation to our affairs with Spain, as, in his opinion, is not inconsistent with the public interest to divulge. December 28, 1818. 8° *pp.* 215. *Washington*: 1819. 1384

Under the forbidding title of a *President's Message*, is concealed an important mass of material, illustrating the origin of a war of the United States with a tribe of Indians, which lasted over a quarter of a century. The minutes of the trial of Arbuthnot and Ambrister are here furnished, and the feeble character of the evidence by which they were convicted and executed, only renders the horrible crime of murdering these men appear still more atrocious. Arbuthnot was a warm friend of the Seminoles, who as his intelligence discerned, were soon to be swept away by the encroachments and jealousy of the planters. He was guilty, at most, of endeavoring to save his Indian friends from extermination, and while in a foreign territory advising them what measures to pursue for their safety.

SEMINOLE WAR.

See Jackson's Correspondence. — Sprague History. — Clay's Speech. — Speeches on. — Notices of E. Florida. — War in Florida. — Cohen Notices. — Giddings Exiles. — Narrative of Voy — Sketch of. 1385

SENECA LANGUAGE

A Short Vocabulary of the language of the Seneca Indians, and in English. *Printed by W. & S. Graves, Cheapside, London:* 1818. 1386

SENECA INDIANS.

See
1. Constitution of.
2. Strong N. T. Appeal.
3. Memoirs & Remonstrance.
4. Report on Losses.
5. Report on Memorials.
6. Rep' of Com. on Civ.
7. Rep. on Ind' of Canada.
8. Pro' of Ind' Council.
9. Wa-o-wa-wa-na-onk.
10. Pro^{ss} of Joint Com.
11. Farther Proceedings.
12. Farther Illustration.
13. Pierce Address.
14. Case of Senecas.
15. Short Vocabulary. 1387

SENECA LANGUAGE

Dolohsawahgwah Gayádoshah. Gòwahas goyadoh, agaoyadih dowanandenyo. Neh Nadigehjih — shohoh dodiadoagoh; Wastok tadinageh. 12° *pp.* 42 (*Boston*), 1836. 1388

Elementary Reading Book in the Seneca language.

SERIOUS ADVICE

To Inhabitants of Penn. 1389

See Lancaster Massacre.

SEYMOUR (R. A.).

Pioneering in the Pampas, or the first four years of a settler's experience in the La Plata Camps. By Richard Arthur Seymour. With a Map. 8° *pp.* 180. *London: Longman & Co.,* 1869. 1390

This volume narrates the adventures of several English settlers on the Pampas, of the Argentine Republic, who suffered many hardships and losses, from the incursions of the equestrian savages of the plains. The narrative affords us many particulars of some of the least known tribes of South America, whose barbarities in their depredations are narrated in a manner so vivid and circumstantial, as to insure the interest of every reader.

SHEA (John G.).

Discovery and Exploration of the Mississippi Valley: with the original narratives of Marquette, Allouez, Membré, Hennepin, and Anastase Douay. By John Gilmary Shea, with a facsimile of the newly-discovered map of Marquette. 8° *Facsimile of letter of Allouez. Map and pp.* lxxx. + 268. *Redfield, New York.* 1853. 1391

Beside the valuable relations, which afford us the first accounts of the Indian tribes which inhabited the vast tract of territory, from the St. Lawrence to the Mississippi, Mr. Shea has added notes, biographical sketches, and bibliographical accounts of works upon aboriginal history, which are scarcely to be overestimated. The relations are preceded by a biography of Father Marquette, and a notice of the Sieur Joliet. The narratives of Fathers Membré, Douay, and Hennepin are also preceded by a bibliographical notice of Father Le Clercq's works, in pp. 78 to 82; and another similar account of Father Hennepin's works may be found on pp. 99 to 106. The last named author is treated by the editor with marked disesteem, but I believe his later convictions tend more favorably to the integrity of Hennepin, in what he actually wrote. Numerous editions of that author's works seem to have been printed without his connivance, and the unscrupulous publishers enlarged and abridged them at will. They made poor Hennepin the pack-horse to bear anything they wished to say, however foreign to his designs, and he is thus held responsible for much perhaps which he would have disclaimed.

All the relations, narratives, and notes in this volume are filled with the most interesting details of the Indians, at a period when many of them for the first time, beheld the white foreigners in the persons of the missionaries and explorers.

SHEA (John Gilmary).

History of the Catholic Missions among the Indian Tribes of the United States, 1529–1854. By John Gilmary Shea. 12° *pp.* 506 + 5 *portraits. New York:* 1855. 1392

A very large amount of information regarding the missions, and the Indians among whom they were established, is gathered in this volume. That it is undoubtedly authentic, will require no other voucher than the author's name.

SHEA (John Gilmary).

A French-Onondaga Dictionary, from a Manuscript of the Seventeenth Century. By John Gilmary Shea. *Large* 8° *pp.* viii. + 103. *New York: Cramoisy Press,* 1860. 1393

English and French title each 1 leaf, with historical preface.

No. 1, Shea's *American Linguistics.*

The Onondagas were the central tribe of the Six Nations, and in some respects the most important, as the records of the confederation were kept by them, and all its great assemblies were gathered around the council-fire, kept ever burning at Onondaga. They early attracted the attention of the Jesuit missionaries, and more than one of those who are known to have suffered martyrdom, doubtless perished in their beautiful valley. The original MS. of this work is still preserved in the Mazarin library at Paris, and is supposed to date from the close of the seventeenth century. It is undoubtedly the work of one of the Jesuit fathers, whose missions commenced at Onondaga in 1655, Fathers Le Moyne and Chaumonot having arrived there on the 5th of November.

SHEA (Jean Marie).

Relation Diverses sur La Bataille du Malangueulé. Gagné le 9 Juillet, 1755, par les François sous M. de Beaujeu, Commandant du Fort du Quesne sur les Anglois sous M. Braddock, Géneral en Chef des troupes Angloises. Recueillies par Jean Marie Shea. 8° *pp.* 51. *Nouvelle York, De La Presse Cramoisy,*, 1860. 1394

No. 14 of Shea's *Jesuit Relations.*

[Several Narratives of the Battle of Monongahela, gained the 9th of July, 1755, by the French under M. de Beaujeu, Commandant of the Fort Du Quesne, over the English under Mr. Braddock, General in chief of the English forces. Collected by Jean Marie Shea. (John Gilmary Shea).]

We owe to the zeal of the editor of this volume many valuable contributions to the history of America, but had he produced nothing more than the one whose title is given, he would be entitled to something more than ordinary gratitude. There is a chivalry not less noble than that exhibited in feats of arms, in rescuing from oblivion or unmerited reproach, the name of an unhonored hero. In these documents Mr. Shea produces the evidence, that M. Beaujeu was not a mere subordinate in the celebrated battle, which resulted in the defeat of General Braddock, and that he was actually commander-in-chief. Also, that instead of fortuitously blundering upon the plan of defense, Beaujeu had carefully considered it and skillfully adapted his means and forces to the exigencies of the contest, and with not more than five or six hundred Indians met the assault of 2,000 English soldiers. The documents are preceded by a biographical sketch of M. Beaujeu, which Mr. Shea terminates with an "Avant-Propos," that has this paragraph.

"Canada and France have forgotten Beaujeu. He has performed his duty as a soldier and a Christian, leaving to his country the care of his reputation. But another reaps the glory of the expedition in which he perished, and in the city of Pittsburgh, where repose his ashes, we seek in vain for a monument to his memory." The memoir is accompanied by a portrait of Beaujeu.

SHEA (John Gilmary).

Early Voyages up and down the Mississippi, by Cavelier, St. Cosme, Le Suer, Gravier, and Guignas. With an Introduction, Notes and an Index. By John Gilmary Shea. 4° *Albany: Joel Munsell.* 1861. 1395

Half title, title, and preface pp. viii. Contents 1 leaf, Introduction commencing at pp. vii. to xi. + second half title and pp. 15 to 191.

These relations of travels and voyages, are printed either from unedited MSS. or from such obscure sources, as to be accessible here for the first time. The journal of John Cavelier, La Salle's brother, and the letters of Montigni, were first printed from the manuscript by Mr. Shea. But the letter of La Salle was derived from a source which none would suspect of concealing a historic gem, — Tomasy's geology of Louisiana. These narratives of the first explorers of the valley of the Mississippi, are almost wholly composed of accounts of the Indian tribes they encountered. They are filled with the most interesting details of the peculiarities of these savages before civilization had corrupted, as it has since destroyed them. The edition was limited to one hundred copies.

SHEA (John G.).

Library of **American Linguistics. Thirteen volumes of Vocabularies,** Grammars, **and Dictionaries of Indian Languages.** 1396

For full titles, see No. 1, Onondaga and French Dictionary. No. 2, Mengarini, Selish Grammar. No. 3, Smith Grammar of the Ileve Language. No. 4, Arroyo, Grammar Mutsun Language. No. 5, Smith, Grammar of the Pima. No. 6, Pandosy, Grammar of the Yakama. No. 7, Sitjar, Vocabulary of the San Antonio Mission. No. 8, Arroyo, Vocabulary of the Mutsun. No. 9, Maillard, Grammar of the Mikmaque. No. 10, Bruyas, Radical Words of the Mohawk. No. 11 Gibbs' Vocabularies of the Clallam. No. 12, Gibbs' Dictionary of the Chinook. No. 13, Gibbs' Alphabet Vocabulary of Chinook.

SHEA (John G.).

Jesuit Relations. Twenty-four volumes. 4° *and* 8° **1397**

All of the series are printed upon a quarto page, although several numbers have a wide bottom margin, in order to permit them to be bound with the three volumes printed in Quebec, in 1858, of which they may be considered a continuation. For full titles, see No. 1, Milet, Captivity. No. 2, Gravier,

Relations Illinois Mission. No. 3, Cavalier, Relation. No. 4, Bigot, Relation, of Abnakis 1684. No. 5, Registre Baptismes Fort Du Quesne. No. 6, Bigot, Relations of Abnakis 1685. No. 7, Bigot, Relations Abnakis 1701. No. 8, Tranchepaine Voyage. No. 9, Nou' Jour' Chicachas. No. 10, Gravier, Journal of Voyages 1700. No. 11, Chaumonot, Vie. No. 12, Chaumonot, Suite de Vie. No. 13, Montigny, Relations du Mississippi. No. 14, Shea, Bataille du Mississippi. No. 15, Dablon, Relations of Missions 1672 to 1673. No. 16, Dablon, Relations of Missions 1673 to 1679. No. 17, Jogues, Novum Belgium. No. 18, Sagean Mathieu Avantures. No. 19, Relations des Affaire du Canada. No. 20, Recueil Nouvelle France. No. 21, Dreuillettes, Epistola. No. 22, Relation Affairs du Canada 1696 to 1702. No. 23, Bigot, Mission Abenaquis 1702. No. 24, Gravier, Lettre 1708.

SHELDON (E. M.).

The early history of Michigan, from the first settlement to 1815. By E. M. Sheldon. 8° *pp.* 409. *New York: A. S. Barnes & Company. Detroit: Kerr, Morley, & Co.*, 1856. 1398

The whole of this volume is devoted to details of the Jesuit missions among the Indians, and the association of the French with them, derived largely from unpublished manuscripts.

SHEPPARD (John H.).

A Memoir of Samuel G. Drake, A. M. author of the book of the Indians, History of Boston, etc., etc. By John H. Sheppard. 4° *pp.* 36. *Albany: printed for private distribution, by J. Munsell*, 1863. 1399

SHERRARD (Robert H.).

A Narrative of the Wonderful Escape and Dreadful Sufferings of Colonel James Paul, after the defeat of Colonel Crawford, when that unfortunate commander, and many of his men, were inhumanly burnt at the stake, and others were slaughtered by other modes of torture, known only to savages. By Robert H. Sherrard. 8° *pp.* 22. *Printed for J. Drake, Cincinnati: Spillis & Gates, printers*, 168 *Vine Street*, 1869. 1400

SHULTZ (T.).

The Acts of the Apostles, translated into The Arrawack Tongue. By the Rev. Theodore Shultz, in eighteen hundred and two. 16° *pp.* 119. *New York: published by the American Bible Society, instituted in the year* 1816: 1850. 1401

The Arrawak is a savage Indian tribe of Guiana, numbers of which were civilized, and brought within the influence of Christianity, by Berman, Brett, Schultz, and other heroic missionaries.

[SIGOURNEY (L. H.).]

Traits of the Aborigines of America. A Poem. 12° *pp.* 284. *Cambridge*, 1822. 1402

Pages 183 to 284, are occupied with historical notes, illustrative of the habits of the American Aborigines.

[SIMMS (William G.).]

Osceola; or Fact and Fiction; a tale of the Seminole War. By a Southerner. 12° *pp.* 50. *New York: printed by Harper & Brothers*, 1838. 1403

An amalgamation of history and romance, which like all hybrids, is a monstrosity less pleasing than the feeblest specimen of either pure race.

SIMMS (Jeptha R.).

History of Schoharie County, and Border Wars of New York; containing also a sketch of the causes which led to the American Revolution; and interesting memoranda of the Mohawk Valley; together with much other historical and miscellaneous matter, never before published. Illustrated with more than thirty engravings. By Jeptha R. Simms. 8° *pp.* 672 + *frontispiece. Albany: Munsell & Tanner, printers,* 1845. 1404

Mr. Simms' book is one of that limited class of historical works, for which the reader will feel from youth to age, that he owes a debt of gratitude to its garrulous and perhaps not over-scrupulous author. It is the very model of a local history. Crowded with details of the adventures of the early settlers of the Mohawk Valley, in their conflicts with their savage neighbors, we do not stop to question their authenticity. The midnight massacres, the long and weary captivities, the surprises of Indian camps, the bloody encounters between the scouts and their savage foes, are all narrated with a credulous faith, and an artless style that wins and preserves the reader's attention.

SIMMS (J. R.).

Trappers of New York, or a Biography of Nicholas Stoner & Nathaniel Foster; together with anecdotes of other celebrated hunters, and some account of Sir William Johnson, and his style of living. By Jeptha R. Simms. 12° *pp.* 287 + 4 *plates. Albany: T. Munsell,* 1860. 1405

The murderous hate between the scouts of the Revolution and their Indian foes, survived the war, and furnishes the principal incidents which fill this book. It narrates how the superior craft, and vengeful pursuit of the white hunters, thinned the woods of the Mohawk counties, of the remnants of the Indian tribes which once thronged them. Pages 208 to 232 are filled with the account of the murder of an Indian scout, by a hunter named Foster, and the minutes of his trial, for a crime of which all the evidence of angels and archangels would not have convicted him, with a jury of border settlers.

SIMMS (W. Gilmore).

The Life of Captain John Smith. The Founder of Virginia. By W. Gillmore Simms. 12° *pp.* 379. *New York:* (1846). 1406

SIMON (Fray Pedro).

The Expedition of Pedro de Ursua & Lope de Aguirre in search of El Dorado and Omagua in 1560–61. Translated from Fray Pedro Simon's "Sixth historical notice of the conquest of Tierra Firme." By William Bollaert. With an introduction by Clements R. Markham. 8° *pp.* liii. + 237 + *map. London: printed for the Hakluyt Society,* 1861. 1407

The history of this wonderful expedition affords us many relations of the character, condition, and customs of the Indians inhabiting the territories, drained by the northern tributaries of the Amazon, three centuries ago. The murderous wretch Aguirre, who by his sanguinary massacres became the leader of the force, was equally cruel in his thirst for the blood of the Indians and of his own countrymen. The progress of this bloody monster, through the lands of the fabled El Dorado, well illustrates the character of a thousand expeditions of the cruel Spaniard among the Aborigines, which have been unwritten because the victims were only Indians. The *Introduc-*

tion, occupying pp. liii., gives a general *resumé* of the expedition, and a sketch of the characters of the leaders; but Father Simon's narrative of the awful scenes of blood and massacre; through which it passed, cannot be excelled by any paraphrase or synopsis of its details. Mr. Markham's *Introduction* also contains a valuable examination of the authorities which corroborate the history of Father Simon. Only the first seven of Father Simon's historical notices were ever printed. Fourteen more exist in manuscript.

SIMON (B. A.).

The Hope of Israel; presumptive evidence that the Aborigines of the Western Hemisphere are descended from the ten missing Tribes of Israel. By Barbara Anne Simon. 8° *pp.* viii. + 328. *London:* 1829. 1408

SIMON (Mrs.).

The Ten Tribes of Israel historically identified with the aborigines of the Western Hemisphere. By Mrs. Simon. 8° *prel. pp.* xl. *folding plate* + *pp.* 370. *London:* 1836. 1409

In Mrs. Simon's first work, entitled *The Hope of Israel*, the authoress based her arguments almost wholly upon biblical and *presumptive* evidence. She brings evidence in this volume of extensive and scholarly research, to establish her hypothesis. Her semblances to Hebrew observances, are found almost entirely in the Aztec and Toltecan races, as portrayed in Lord Kingsbury's *Antiquities of Mexico*. She fortifies her position, from the histories and opinions of Las Casas, Botarini, Gomara, Garcilla, Sahagun, and Peter Martyr. It is a curious mass of learning, directed toward the demonstration of an unsolvable problem.

SIMPSON (William S.).

Report at large of the trial of Charles De Reinhard, for murder, (committed in the Indian Territories), at a court of Oyer and Terminer, held at Quebec, May, 1818. To which is annexed, a summary of Archibald M'Lellan's, indicted as an accessary. By William S. Simpson, Esquire. 8° *Half title and prel. pp.* xii. + 340. *Montreal: printed by James Lane, for the reporter.* 1819. 1410

This is a continuation of the trials of some Indian half-breeds, for the murder of Governor Semple, the first part of which will be found under Selkirk's *Proceedings*, etc.

SIMPSON (Thomas).

Narrative of the discoveries on the North Coast of America; effected by the officers of the Hudson's Bay Company, during the years 1836 to 1839. By Thomas Simpson. 8° *pp.* xix. + 419. *London:* 1843. 1411

In common with all the narratives of Arctic explorations, this work is largely composed of relations of the peculiarities of the Indian tribes inhabiting British America, and of incidents of personal intercourse with them.

SIMPSON (Alexander).

The Life and Travels of Thomas Simpson, the Arctic Discoverer. By his brother, Alexander Simpson. 8° *Portrait, pp.* viii., *map* + 424. *London:* 1845. 1412

Chapters vi. to viii., pp. 71 to 109, convey the explorer's views and experiences of the Indians and half-breeds of the Red River. A division of the work commences at pp. 403, entitled, "The Indians of North America: An Inquiry into their Character and Condition."

SIMPSON (James H.).

Journal of a Military Reconnaisance, from Santa Fé, New Mexico, to the Navajo Country, made with the troops under command of Brevet Lieut. Col. John M. Washington, chief of ninth military department, and governor of New Mexico, in 1849. By James H. Simpson. 8° *Philadelphia:* 1852. 1413

Seventy-four colored plates, representative of Indian life.

This is one of the most accurate and complete of all the narratives of exploration of the country of the Zuni and the Pueblos Indians. The examinations and journals were made by a most intelligent and scrupulous explorer, as is evidenced by the numerous carefully drawn pictures of the different phases of aboriginal life and history. Fifty-six of the engravings are portraits of representative Indians of the various tribes, scenes in their life and ceremonies, views of their pueblos or villages, their picture-writing, antiquities, ruins, and implements.

SITGREAVES (Captain L.).

Report of an expedition down the Zuni and Colorado Rivers, by Captain L. Sitgreaves. Accompanied by maps, sketches, views, and illustrations. 8° *pp.* 198 + 77 *plates. Washington:* 1854. 1414

Ten of the engravings represent the personal appearance, domestic habits, pueblos, and ceremonies of the Mojave, Zuni, and other Indian tribes of the Colorado plateau.

SITJAR (Father Bonaventure).

Vocabulary of the Language of San Antonio Mission, California. By Father Bonaventure Sitjar, of the Order of St. Francis. *Large* 8° *English and French title each* 1 *leaf, historical preface pp.* vii. *and* viii., *grammar pp.* ix. *to* xix., *diccionario* 9 *to* 53 + 1 *leaf advertisement. New York: Cramoisy Press,* 1861. 1415

No. 7, Shea's *Library of American Linguistics.*

This vocabulary, as well as No. 8, the Grammar of the Mutsun language, were the work of the missionaries. There is an apparent hiatus between the Roman and Arabic pagination, but in the notation the omitted pages were intended to be supplied by blank leaves. Fathers Sitjar and Pierras were the first to attempt the conversion of this tribe which occupied a mountainous range, twenty-five leagues southwest of Monterey, in California. Although it was once so numerous that more than twenty dialects were spoken by its branches, it was reduced to less than fifty individuals in 1860. The MSS. consist of four hundred and forty-two pages, and together with the Grammar, were obtained by Mr. A. S. Taylor, who deposited them in the Smithsonian Institute. Father Sitjar was born in Majorca, 1739, founded the mission of San Antonio in 1771, in which place he died in 1808. Father Pierras was also a native of Majorca, and died in 1795. The Grammar occupies pp. ix. to xix., the Interrogatories and Pater Noster the next two succeeding leaves, Dictionary, pp. 9 to 53.

SITTEN UND MEINUNGEN.

Der Wilden in America. Mit Kupfern. *Frankfurtham Mayn,* 1777. 1416

Four volumes. 16° pp. 503 + 12 plates; 476 + 12 plates; 461 + 12 plates; 460 + 8 plates; total plates in the 4 volumes, 44.

[Customs and Opinions of the Savages of America. With Plates.]

SIX NATIONS OF INDIANS.
Documents Relative to Indian Affairs. 8° *pp.* 28. (*New York*, 1794). 1417

Minutes of a Council of the Six Nations, and of a treaty with the commissioners of the United States.

SKETCH OF THE SEMINOLE WAR,
And sketches during a campaign. By a Lieutenant of the left wing. 12° *pp.* v.+311. *Charleston:* 1836. 1418

SKETCHES
of the West, or the Home of the Badgers: comprising an Early History of Wisconsin, with a series of familiar letters and remarks on Territorial Character and Characteristics, etc. 8° *pp.* 48 + *map and printed corr.* *Milwaukee:* 1847. 1419

SKETCHES
of Mission Life among the Indians of Oregon. 16° *pp.* 220 *and* 5 *plates.* *New York: published by Carlton & Porter*, 1854. 1420

SLIGHT (Benjamin).
Indian Researches; or, facts concerning the North American Indians; including notices of their present state of improvement, in their social, civil, and religious condition; with hints for their future advancement. By Benjamin Slight. 12° *pp.* 179. *Montreal: printed for the author, by J. E. L. Miller.* 1844. 1421

This unpretending little work is the expression of the personal experience of a candid and thoughtful man, on the structure of the Indian languages. He suggests, what has long been thought, the insuperable difficulty in the way of making our orthographic system, fairly interpret the involved and aggregated forms of the *sentence-words* of aboriginal tongues. The structure of every dialect of the Algonquin and Huron tongues, comprising every northern tribe, is monosyllabic, so that upon the radical syllable, the sentence is built up, by successive additions, of other syllables, until the idea is complete. These elemental syllables do not in most aboriginal dialects, exceed one hundred, and scarcely a single one of these can be perfectly represented by our system of orthographical analysis.

SMET (Father De).
The Indian Missions in the United States of America, under the care of the Missouri Province of the Society of Jesus. 12° *pp.* 34. *Philadelphia. King & Baird, printers*, 1841. 1422

SMET (P. J.).
Letters and Sketches with a narrative of a year's residence among the Indian Tribes of The Rocky Mountains. By P. J. De Smet, S. J. 12° *pp.* 252. *Philadelphia:* 1843. 1423

SMET (P. J.).
Oregon Missions and Travels over the Rocky Mountains, in 1845–46. By Father P. J. De Smet. Of the Society of Jesus. 12° *pp.* 412. *New York: published by Edwin Dunigan*, 1847. 1424

SMET (P. J.).
Missions de l' Oregon et voyages dans les Montagnes Rocheuses en 1845 et 1846, par le Pere P. J. De Smet, de la Societe de Jesus. Ouvrage traduit de l' Anglais, Par M. Bourlez. 12° *pp.* 408 + 12 *plates and engraved title.* *Paris*, 1848. 1425

[Missions of Oregon and Journeys in the Rocky Mountains in 1845 and 1846, by Father Paul de Smet of the Society of Jesuits. Translated from the English, by M. Bourlez.]

SMETT (P. J.).
Western Missions and Missionaries: A Series of letters, by Rev. P. J. De Smett, of the Society of Jesus, Author of Indian Sketches, Oregon Missions, etc. 12° *pp.* 532. *New York: James B. Kirker*, 1863. 1426

SMETT (P. J.).
New Indian Sketches. By Rev. P. J. De Smet, S. J. 12° *pp.* 175. *New York*, 1865. 1427

These volumes are the literary relaxation of one of those devoted missionaries to the Indians, of whom the Catholic Church has been so prolific. Although modestly concealing his own share in the divine labor of evangelizing the savage hordes beyond the Rocky Mountains, these books are monuments to his services, as well as of those he records performed by others. Father Smet is a modern example of those hero martyrs of the Jesuit order, who so nearly redeemed the savage tribes of America from Paraguay to Canada.

SMETHURST (Gamaliel).
A | Narrative | of an | Extraordinary Escape | out of the | Hands of the Indians, | in the | Gulph of St. Lawrence; | Interspersed | With a Description of the Coast, and Remarks on the Customs and Manners | of the Savages there: | Also, | A Providential Escape after a Shipwreck, in coming from | the Island St. John, in said Gulph; with an Account of the Fisheries | round that Island. | Likewise, | A Plan for reconciling the Differences between Great Britain and her | Colonies. | By Gamaliel Smethurst. *Large* 4° *pp.* 48. | *London:* | *Printed for the author;* | *And Sold by J. Bew*, MDCCLXXIV. 1428

SMITH (Buckingham).
See Cabeca de Vaca. 1429

SMITH (Buckingham).
Rudo Ensayo, tentativa de una Prevencional Descripcion Geographica de la Provincia de Sonora, sus terminos y confines; ó mejor, colleccion de materiales para hacerla quien lo supiere mejor. Compilada Asi de Noticias adquiridas por el Colector en sus Viages por casi toda ella, como Subministrados por los Padres Missioneros y Practicos de la Tierra. Dirigida al remedio de ella, por un Amigo del bien comun. 4° *pp.* x. + 208. *San Augustin de la Florida: Año de* 1863. 1430

[A Rough Essay, attempt at a Provisional Geographical Description of the Province of Sonora, its limits and boundaries: or rather, collection of materials to make it by any one knowing better. Compiled as well from notices acquired by the collector in his journeys through most all of it, as from statements by the Fathers Missionaries and domiciled in the land, for the purpose of its improvement, by a Friend of the Commonweal.]

As I reach this title in describing the works of this collection, the journals of the day announce that an unknown person was yesterday found in the streets of New York in an insensible condition; was taken by the police to a cell in the nearest station-house; was transferred to the hospital in a dying condition, and in a few hours, without a word or sign, the active, intelligent, and learned mind of the stranger, had ceased to animate his mortal part. The corpse was soon after death recognized as the editor of this work. The scholarly curiosity of this learned man, was absolutely insatiable; and his research stretched over an area of documentary evidence and historical data, which is scarcely less than appalling to contemplate. The vast storehouses of manuscripts by the early writers of the history of America, which Spain has so jealously guarded, were, page by page, assiduously examined by him, for new revelations regarding the country, whose half-told story constantly fired his brain with the desire to complete. This homage of an humble admirer of his patience, zeal, and learning, I could not resist the desire to leave on record here. Mr. Buckingham Smith was the translator and annotator of many works on American history. In 1851, Mr. Riggs printed at Washington his translation of the narrative of Cabeza de Vaca.

This relation of the missions, Indians, and Natural History of the Province of Sonora, was written by an unknown hand. The writer was a Jesuit Missionary, resident in that country eleven years, when by order or request of the authorities, the MS. was written in 1762. It is for the first time printed here, having been several times copied, and from one of the transcripts, made for the purpose of aiding Munoz in writing his history of the New World, this printed work is now produced. He resided at a place on the River Yaqui, where that stream flows through a cañon so deep, as to shut out three quarters of the heavens from sight. The first sixty-nine pages are occupied with a natural history of the country. At page 69 commences Chapter V., entitled, "Of The Nations which people this Province, in general; Their language, and of their disposition, genius and character. 2. Of the antiquity, idolatries, and conjurors of the Indians. 3. Of their absurd religious belief and superstitions. 4. Of their customs and ceremonies," etc., etc., to Section 6. Chapter VI., entitled "Of the Nations which inhabit this Province in particular," is divided into four sections, treating of the peculiarities of the Apaches, the Pimas, and the Papagos, tribes still inhabiting the provinces of Sonora, Arizona, and New Mexico. Chapter VII. is entitled, "The Missions of the Society of Jesus among the Indians of Sonora." Chapter VIII., "The Churches of the Missions." The subjects above noted relating to the Indians, occupy pp. 69 to 173. It is not without interest, that we read that the savages were spoken of at that day as the cruel Apaches.

SMITH (Buckingham).

Apalachian and Timuquean documents. Seven Sheets in the ancient languages of Florida, and in Spanish. *Folio.* 1860. 1431

Mr. Smith asserts that these documents are in the Apalachian tongue, as spoken and written by the Indians, and with the Timuquana marking. They denote an advancement made by the Timuquana Indians, under the Franciscan missionaries, in the seventeenth century in religion and civilization, superior, or at least equal to the farthest progress reached by the Aborigines anywhere in America. MS. letter of Mr. Buckingham Smith: "The documents are fac-similes of the handwriting of the Indians of Florida."

SMITH (Buckingham).

Grammar of the Pima or Névome, a language of Sonora, from

a manuscript of the XVIII. Century, edited by Buckingham Smith. *Large 8°* *Cramoisy Press, New York*, 1862. 1432

No. 5, Shea's *Library of American Linguistics*.

The author of this grammar, whose name is entirely unknown, was a Jesuit missionary among the Pimas, an Indian nation inhabiting New Mexico, and Sonora. The manuscript, discovered by Mr. Smith at Toledo in Spain, was probably carried thither in 1767, on the suppression of the order in Mexico. The work has three titles. In the French title, in addition to the description given in the English one, we find the words "With the Christian Doctrine and Confession" added. The Grammar occupies pp. 10 to 97. The third title in Spanish, *Christian Doctrine and Confession, in the language Nevome or Pima, of Sonora*, pages 1 to 32.

SMITH (Buckingham).

A Grammatical Sketch of the Heve Language, translated from an unpublished Spanish Manuscript, by Buckingham Smith. *Large 8°* *pp.* 26. *London*, 1862. 1433

No. 3, Shea's *Library American Linguistics*.

Pages 5 to 7, are occupied with "Notices of the Heve Nation." The grammar fills pages 9 to 24, and a vocabulary pages 25 and 26. The Heve tribe of Aborigines, more than a century ago, during the Spanish domination, occupied a portion of Sonora. The work is printed from an unpublished manuscript, obtained by the late Buckingham Smith. The unknown author entitled this fruit of his labors, *Arte y Vocabulario de la lingua Dohema Heve o Eudeva*."

SMITH (Buckingham).

Narratives of the career of Hernando de Soto in the conquest of Florida as told by a knight of Elvas and in a relation by Luys Hernandez de Biedma factor of the expedition. Translated by Buckingham Smith. 8° *New York*, 1866. 1434

No. 5 of the *Bradford Club Series*.

SMITH (John).

The | GENERALL HISTORIE | of | Virginia, New England, and the Summer | Isles: with the names of the Adventurers, | Planters, and Governours from their | first beginning An: | 1584, to this | present 1624. | With the Proceedings of those Severall Colonies | and the Accidents that befell them in all their | Journeys and Discoveries. | Also the Maps and Descriptions of all those | Countryes, their Commodities, people, | Government, Customes, and Religion | yet knowne. | Divided into sixe Bookes. | By Captaine John Smith sometymes Governour | In those Countryes & Admirall | of New-England. | *London*, | *printed by I. D. and* | *I. H. for Michael* | *Sparkes*, | 1624. | 1435

Folio, title in the centre of an engraved page, three portraits in medallions, on the upper border, the one at the right hand entitled Carolus Princeps, altered in subsequent editions, by placing a crown upon the head, with the word Princeps changed to Rex; reverse of title blank, engraving of the Duchesse of Richmond, and in some copies another plate entitled Matoarka Dedication to the Duchesse, (2) pp. — "Samuel Purchas of his friend Captain John Smith," eulogistic poems (4) pp. "The contents of the generall History," 4 pp. "A Preface" 1 p. "A Gentleman," &c., on reverse, 1 p. (total preliminary pp. 14) + "How Ancient Authors report the New World," pp. 1 to 248 + Map 1 of "*Ould Virginia*," surrounded by engravings in six compartments representing Smith's various adventures with the Indians + Map 2, of *Virginia*, 13 inches by 16, with a *Savage* depicted in the right upper corner, and *Powhatan Sitting in State* in the opposite corner + Map 3, Map of *The Summers Ils*, surrounded by engravings in eleven compartments + Map 4, *New England*, with portrait of Smith in left upper corner. Much the greater part of the value of copies of Smith's general history, consists in the perfection and identity of the maps. The first edition is the highest prized when it possesses the maps properly belonging to it. In the subsequent editions, the maps underwent such alterations as distinguish each of them from the others. It is so commonly the case, as almost to form the rule, that even the best copies of Smith's book have been made up by the substitution of later editions of some of the maps. This uncertainty extends even to the portraits. That of the Duchesse of Richmond, is generally supposed to have been reëngraved, and collectors have been somewhat puzzled to ascertain if their copies were originals. I have copies both of the original impression, and the so called replica, and am able to establish a criterion for testing the question. Only one plate of the portrait has been engraved, and that one is now in the possession of Mr. Dexter of New York. The distinction between the original impressions and the subsequent ones, consists in the cross hatchings which were made after the impressions were taken for Smith's history. In the first all the drapery is shaded by horizontal lines, the tapestry in the back ground alone being shaded by perpendicular lines, drawn at right angles to the others. In the second the cross hatching lines are diagonal to the others, producing a coarser and darker appearance. This is particularly observable in the cushion, above which the right hand rests.

SMITH (Captain John).

THE | TRUE TRAVELS, | ADVENTURES, | AND | OBSERVATIONS | of | Captaine John Smith, | In Europe, Asia, Affrica, and America, from Anno | Domini | 1593, to 1629. | His Accidents and Sea-fights in the Straights, his Service | [*etc.*, 3 *lines.*] | After how he was taken prisoner by the Turks, Sold for a Slave, sent into | Tartaria, [*etc.*, 4 *lines.*] | Together with a continuation of his general History of Virginia, | Summer-Isles, New England, and their proceedings since 1624. to this | present 1629, as also of the new Plantations of the great | River of the Amazons, the Isles of St. Christopher, Mevis, | and Barbados in the West Indies. | All written by actuall Authours, whose names | you shall finde along the History. *London.* | *Printed by F. H. for Thomas Slater, and are to bee* | *sold at the Blew Bible in Greene Arbour.* 1630. | 1436

Title 1 p., reverse plate of Smith's arms + dedication, 2 pp. + the contents of the several chapters, 2 pp. + Poems addressed to Captaine Smith, 6 pp. + "The True Travels," pp. 1 to 60 + folding plate in nine compartments, each representing a scene of Smith's adventures.

SMITH (Captain John).

The Trve Travels, Adventvres, and Observations of Captaine John Smith, in Europe, Asia, Africke, and America: beginning about the yeere 1593, and continued to this present 1629. 2 *vols.* 8° *From the London edition of* 1629, *Richmond*, 1819. 1437

The typographical and cartographical execution of these volumes is much more deserving of praise than their literary qualities. The maps are beautifully reproduced in fac-simile, and the text as admirably printed, but the various works of Captain John Smith, adventurer, poet, and historian, are blended in an exceedingly puzzling way, for ascertaining when the history of Virginia begins and the true travels end.

SMITH (Colonel James).

An Account | of the | Remarkable Occurrences | in the life and travels of | Col. James Smith (Now a Citizen of Bourbon County, Kentucky.) | during his captivity with the Indians, | in the years 1755, 56, 57, 58, & 59, | In which the Customs, Manners, Traditions, Theological Sen | timents, Mode of Warfare, Military Tactics, Discipline and | Encampments, Treatment of prisoners, &c., are better ex | plained, and more minutely narrated, than has been heretofore | done by any author on that subject. Together with a De | scription of the Soil, Timber and Waters, where he travel | led with the Indians, during his captivity. | To which is added, | A Brief Account of Some Very Uncommon Occurrences, which | transpired after his return from captivity; as well as of the | Different Campaigns carried on against the Indians to the | Westward of Fort Pitt, since the year 1755, to the present | date. Written by himself. | 8° pp. 88. *Lexington: | Printed by John Bradford, on Main Street*, | 1799. | 1438

This is the original edition of Colonel Smith's narrative, and one of the rarest works of western history. Indeed, in the quality of rarity, it is only exceeded by *Loudon's Narrative of Indian Wars*. Colonel Smith was himself the type of the chivalric, brave, and generous frontiersman, of which class Daniel Boone and Simon Kenton were famous examples. He possessed the advantage of an intellect, cultivated in the rude border schools, it is true, yet not ill cultivated in such places as heroes were not seldom bred.

SMITH (Colonel James).

A Treatise on the Mode and Manner of Indian War, their Tactics, Discipline and Encampment, the various Methods they Practise, in order to obtain the Advantage, by Ambush, Surprise, Surrounding &c. Ways and Means proposed to Prevent the Indians from obtaining the Advantage. A Chart, or Plan of Marching, and Encamping, laid down, whereby we may undoubtedly Surround them, if we have Men sufficient. Also — A Brief Account of Twenty-three Campaigns, carried on against the Indians with the Events since the year 1755; Gov. Harrison's included. By Col. James Smith. Likewise — Some Abstracts selected from his Journal, while in Captivity with the Indians, relative to the Wars: which was published many years ago, but few of them now to be found. 12° pp. 1 to 59. *Paris, Kentucky, printed by Joel R. Lyle*, 1812. 1439*

The Narrative of Colonel Smith's Captivity had already become scarce, when the patriotic veteran, on the breaking out of the war with Great Britain, fully comprehending the danger of underrating the savage foe, whom that government would make its allies, issued this treatise of military instruction. The work has become even rarer than the first one.

SMITH (Col. James).

An Account of the Remarkable Occurrences in the life and travels of Col. James Smith, during his captivity with the Indians, in the years 1755, 56, 57, 58, & 59. With An Appendix of Illustrative Notes. By Wm. M. Darlington, of Pittsburgh. *Royal 8° Pref. pp.* xii. + *Smith's Account, pp.* 1 *to* 161 + *Appendix, pp.* 163 *to* 190. *Cincinnati, Robert Clarke & Co.*, 1870. 1440

The interesting narrative of Colonel Smith's adventures and captivity, is greatly enriched by the notes of Mr. Darlington, a gentleman whose knowledge of western history and the localities of its historic scenes, is more intimate and accurate than that of any person now living.

SMITH (John).

A True Relation of Virginia by Captain John Smith, with an introduction and notes by Charles Deane. 4° *pp.* xvii. + (vi.) + 88. *Boston, Wiggin & Lunt*, 1866. 1441

This is a reprint of the rare tract, *True Relations of the famous John Smith*, first published in 1608, in which are given some of the earliest relations of the Indians of Virginia. From no other source have we derived so many authentic incidents of the life and customs of the aboriginal tribes of that colony before the advent of the white man.

[SMITH (William).]

An Historical Account | of the expedition | against the Ohio Indians, | in the year MDCCLXIV. | Under the command of | Henry Bouquet, Esq. | Colonel of foot, and now Brigadier General in America. | Including his Transactions with the Indians, | Relative to the Delivery of their Prisoners, | And the Preliminaries of Peace. | With an introductory account of the Preceeding Campaign, | And Battle at Bushy-Run. | To which are annexed | Military Papers, | Containing Reflections on the War with the Savages; a Method of forming Frontier | Settlements; some Account of the Indian Country; with a List of | Nations, Fighting Men, Towns, Distances, and different Routs. | The whole illustrated with a Map and Copper-Plates. | Published from authentic Documents, by a Lover of his Country. | 4° *Title* 1 *leaf* + *prel. pp.* xiii. + *folding map* + *pp.* 71, *plan and two copper plates. Philadelphia, printed:* | *London, Re-printed for T. Jeffries, Geographer to his Majesty,* | *at Charing Cross,* MDCCLXVI. | 1442

For nearly a century this book was attributed to Thomas Hutchings, whose name is found upon the map of Colonel Bouquet's route. Mr. Spofford, the librarian of Congress, first called attention to a letter written by the indefatigable Rev. William Smith of Philadelphia, in which he announces himself as the author. The rarity of the book is not the only quality for which it should be sought, nor the fact that it was embellished by engravings after drawings from the pencil of the eminent painter Benjamin West.

The treatise narrates the details of the first victory, gained over Indian forces by English troops, after the savages had been taught the use of fire-arms. Nearly twenty years elapsed before the whites gained another, during which period they suffered such dreadful defeats in thirteen battles at the hands of the Indians, that the blood thickens with horror at their narration. Colonel Bouquet by his judicious arrangements first laid down the plan, in following which General Wayne secured the same result.

[Smith (William).]

Relation Historique de L' Expedition, contree Les Indiens de L' Ohio en MDCCLXIV. Commandee par le Chevalier Henry Bouquet, Colonel d Infanterie, & ensuite Brigadier-General en Amerique; contenant ses Transactions avec les Indiens, relativement a la deliverance des Prisonniers & aux Preliminaires de la Paix; avec un Recit Introductoire de la Campagne precedente de l'an 1763, & de la Batallle de Bushy-Run. Ou y a joint des Memoires Militaires Contenant des Reflections sur la guerre avec les Sauvages: une Method de former des establissemens sur la Frontierre: quelques details concernant la contree des Indiens; avec une liste de nations, combattons, villes, distances, & diverses routes. Le tout enrichi des Cartes & Taille-douces. Tradiut de l' Anglois, Par C. G. F. Dumas. 8° *A Amsterdam, Chez Mar-Michael Rey*, MDCCLXIX. 1443

Half title 1 leaf, title 1 leaf, preface pp. vii. to xvi. + 147 pp. + (ix.) 4 folding plans and two copperplates The Preface is a sketch of the life of Colonel Bouquet, written by the French translator, Mons. Dumas, and adds some very desirable information to our previous knowledge of the skillful officer and wise negotiator, whose last peaceful campaign was not excelled in military sagacity by his former bloody one.

[Smith (William).]

An Account of the Proceedings of the Illinois and Oubache land companies, In pursuance of their purchases made of the Independent Natives, July 5th, 1773, and 18th October, 1775. 8° *Title*, 1 *leaf; introduction*, 7 *leaves; Indian Deeds*, 55 *pp.; Memorial, pp.* 1 *to* 8. *No. I. To the Committee, pp.* 1 *to* 8. *No. II. Ad' Statements, pp.* 1 *to* 7. *No. III. To the Hon. Committee, pp.* 1 *to* 7. *total number of pages* 101. *Philadelphia: printed by William Young, No.* 52 *Second Street, the corner of Chestnut Street*, 1796. 1444

Smith (William).

A Discourse Concerning the Conversion of the Heathen Americans, and The final Propagation of Christianity and the Sciences to the Ends of the Earth, in Two Parts [*etc.*, 9 *lines*]. By William Smith, D. D. 12° *pp.* 65. *Philadelphia, printed by W. Dunlap*, 1760. 1445

[Smith (William).]

A | Brief View | Of the Conduct of | Pennsylvania, | For the Year 1755; | So far as it affected the General Service of the | British Colonies, particularly the Expedition | under the late General Braddock. | With an Account of the shocking Inhumanities, | committed by Incursions of the Indians upon the | Province in October and November, [*etc.*, 5 *lines.*] Interspersed with several Interesting Anecdotes and original | Papers, relating to the Politics and Principles of | the People called Quakers: Being a Sequel to | a late well known Pamphlet, | intitled, | A Brief State of Pennsylvania. | In a Second Letter to a Friend in London. | 8° *pp.* 88. *London*: | 1756. | 1446

SMYTH (J. F. D.).

A Tour in the United States of America: containing An Account of the Present Situation of that Country; The Population, Agriculture, Commerce, Customs, and Manners of the Inhabitants; Anecdotes of Several Members of the Congress, and General Officers in the American Army; and Many other very singular and interesting Occurrences. With A Description of the Indian Nations [*etc.*, 7 *lines*]. By J. F. D. Smyth. 8° 2 vols. Vol. I. *Pref. pp.* (xii.) + 400. Vol. II. *Pref. pp.* (x.) + 455. *London*, 1784. 1447

The Tory scout and spy, who was the author of these volumes, narrowly escaped hanging by the Whigs on more than one occasion, but lived to record many interesting particulars of the first days of the Revolution, and some incidents and statistics, regarding the Indians, of no great consequence. Chapters xxiv. and xxv. record the particulars of a visit to the Catawba Indians, and chapters xxxv., xxxvi., and xxxvii. his rencontre with the Indians, beleaguering a frontier block-house, and the incidents within the fort. Chapters xliii. and xliv. are devoted to a general account of the Indians, and a list of the different Indian nations.

SMITH (Seba).

Powhatan a metrical romance in Seven Cantos by Seba Smith. (With notes on Indian History). 12° *New York, Harper & Brothers*, 1841. 1448

SMITH (Edmund R.).

The Araucanians; or, notes of a tour among the Indian Tribes of southern Chili. By Edmund Reuel Smith, of the U. S. N. Astronomical expedition in Chili. 12° *pp.* 335 + 7 *full page plates and* 10 *woodcuts in the text. New York*, 1855. 1449

The author affords us in this work almost the only authentic narrative of personal intercourse, with a nation of savages, which had defied the Spaniards for three hundred years, and defeated them in more battles than all the other aboriginal warriors of America. Everything relating to their characteristics, manners, and customs, receives his attention.

SMITH (T. Marshall).

Legends of the War of Independence, and of the earlier settlements in the West. By T. Marshall Smith. 8° *pp.* 397. *Louisville, Ky.: J. F. Brennan, publisher*, 1855. 1450

The author professed to have derived his narratives of scouts, border warriors, Indian skirmishes, etc., from the lips of the actors, or their comrades and children. Relating, as he does, the adventures of Tories, Whigs, and frontiersmen, a considerable portion of his volume is devoted to biographical sketches of Indian fighters and their rencontres with the savages.

SMITH (Joshua Toulmin).

The Discovery of America by the Northmen in the Tenth Century. By Joshua Toulmin Smith. With maps and plates. *Post* 8° *pp.* 344 + *two folding maps and two plates. London: Charles Tilt, Fleet Street*, 1839. 1451

All the arguments in favor of the author's hypothesis, are derived from the ancient sagas, Indian traditions, and inscriptions on the rocks. They are most clearly cited, and logically enforced, but the colloquial style adopted by him gives his work a puerile character, which the learning and ability of the author and his work do not deserve.

SMITH (Ethan).

View of the Hebrews; or the Tribes of Israel in America. Exhibiting [*Table of Contents*, 5 *lines*]. By Ethan Smith, Pastor of a church in Poultney (Vt.). Second edition, improved and enlarged. 12° *pp.* 285. *Poultney* (*Vt.*), 1825. 1452

The pastor of a church at Poultney, Vt., struck with those points of resemblance between the Jews and Indians, which have startled so many before him, adduces several hundreds of curious incidents from Adair, Hunter, Bartram, and many other writers, principally on the habits of the Northern Indians. He insists most strenuously upon the similarity of certain Hebrew words to synonymous terms in Indian languages.

SMITH (John).

Narrative of the Shipwreck and Sufferings of the crew and passengers of the English brig Neptune [*etc.*, 5 *lines*]. Of seventeen souls on board but six succeeded in reaching the shore [*etc.*, 5 *lines*], were fortunately discovered and conducted to an English settlement by a friendly Indian. 12° *pp.* 36. *New York*, 1830. 1453

SMITH (M.).

A Narrative of the Sufferings in, and Journey from Upper Canada to Virginia and Kentucky, Of M. Smith, minister of the Gospel. (A narrative of the treatment of American residents of Canada by the British and Indians during the War of 1812 to 1814). *Second Title and pp.* 229 *to* 287 *of* "*A Complete History of the Late American War,*" *etc.* 18° *Lexington, Ky.*, 1816. 1454

This book, which contains some interesting particulars of the Indian allies of Great Britain, has a curious bibliographical history. After making his escape from Canada, the author sold the right to print a certain number of copies of the MS. work he had brought away with him, in each of the large cities through which he passed; his compensation being a fixed proportion of the number of copies. Editions were therefore printed at Hartford, of 13,000 copies, in New York of 3,000. Another large edition was printed in Trenton, another in Philadelphia, and one in Baltimore of 2,500, with the addition of an appendix, and nearly 1,000 names of subscribers, residents of Maryland and Virginia. The edition printed at Lexington alone contains the personal narrative. Of the various editions, not less than 26,000 copies have been printed, and the book is now scarce.

SMYTH (W.), and Mr. F. LOWE.

Narrative of a Journey from Lima to Para, across the Andes and down the Amazon: undertaken with a view of ascertaining the practicability of a navigable communication with the Atlantic, by the rivers Pachitea, Ucayali, and Amazon. By Lieutenant W. Smyth, and Mr. F. Lowe. 8° *pp.* 305 + 13 *plates and maps. London*: 1836. 1455

Chapters x., xi., and xii., pp. 189 to 249, are devoted to a minute description of several Indian tribes, not hitherto noticed.

SMITH (Mary).

An affecting narrative of the Captivity and Sufferings of Mrs. Mary Smith, Who with her Husband and three daughters, were taken prisoners by the Indians, in August last (1814) and after enduring the most cruel hardships and torture of mind for sixty days (in which time she witnessed the tragical death of her husband and helpless Children) was fortuna-tely rescued from the merciless hands of the Savages by a detached party from the army of the brave General Jackson. Now commanding at New-Orleans. *Providence (R. I.)*: (1817), *printed by L. Scott.* 12° *pp.* 24 + *folding plate.* 1456

The narrative of Mrs. Scott's captivity fills the first eighteen pages, and following that is an account of "The Indians Killing and Scalping Thirty Persons." The folding-plate is the most astonishing piece of wood engraving.

SMITH (Mary).

[*Title as above with the addition of:*]

☞ As the preceding pages will be found to con | tain a particular account of the engagement | between the handful of Jackson's brave boys | , and the party of Savages above alluded to | the reader may judge of what materials | the hardy sons of Tennessee & Ohio | are composed. | *Providence (R. I.)*: *Printed for L. Scott* (1818). 12° *pp.* 24. 1457

In this edition, the narrative of Mary Smith's captivity occupies the whole of the twenty-four pages, instead of, as in the other edition, filling only the first eighteen pages," and the relation of "The Indians Killing & Scalping Thirty Persons," is wholly omitted.

SMITHSONIAN INSTITUTION CONTRIBUTIONS. 1458

See Squire & Davis, Mon. Miss. Valley; Riggs' Dakota Dictionary; Lapham, Antiquities of Wisconsin; Whittlesey, Ancient Mining on L. Superior; Mayer, Obs. on Mexican Archæology; Haven, Archæology of U. S.; Squier, Aboriginal Mon. of N. York.

SMITHSONIAN INSTITUTION.

Annual Report of the Board of Regents of the Smithsonian Institution showing the operations, expenditures and condition of the institution for the year. 25 *vols.* *Washington*, 1847 *to* 1871. 1459

A large amount of material relating to the history, character, and antiquities of the American Indians, as well as treatises on the structure of their languages, all of which were prepared by the most intelligent and thoroughly prepared writers.

Vol. for 1854 contains Carleton's Diary of an Excursion to the ruins of Cities in New Mexico, pp. 296 to 316.
Vol. for 1855 has Letherman's Sketch of the Navajo Tribe of Indians, pp. 280 to 297.
Vol. for 1856. Guest. Ancient Indian remains near Prescott, pp. 271 to 276.
Vol. for 1862. North Am. Archæology, by Sir J. Lubbock, and Account of human remains and mummies from Patagonia.
Vol. for 1863. Peale. Ancient mounds at St. Louis, pp. 386 to 396.
Vol. for 1863. Account of Aboriginal Inhabitants of California, by Baegert, pp. 352 to 384, and continued in Vol. 1864 on pp. 378 to 400.
Vol. for 1866. Gibbs' Notes on the Chippewyan Indians: pp. 303 to 327. Hellwald. The American Migration, pp. 328 to 345. Rau, Indian Pottery,

pp. 346 to 355. Brinton. Shell Deposits by the Indians, pp. 356 to 358. Dille. Sketch of Ancient earthworks in Ohio, pp. 359 to 365.
Vol. for 1867. Gunn. Indian remains near Red River, and other articles on the Indians, pp. 399 to 432.

SNELLING (Mrs. Anna L.).
Kabaosa; or, the Warriors of the West. A tale of the last war. By Mrs. Anna L. Snelling. 12° *New York:* 1842. 1460

SNOWDEN (James Ross).
The Cornplanter Memorial. An Historical Sketch of Gyantwachia — The Cornplanter, and of the Six Nations of Indians. By James Ross Snowden. And the report of Samuel P. Johnson, on the erection of the monument at Jennesadaga, to the memory of Cornplanter. 8° *pp.* 115. *Harrisburg, Pa.:* 1867. 1461

This volume is the testimony of the descendants of the whites who murdered his countrymen, to the virtues and talents of an Indian chief. A small number of copies were printed, by the direction of the Legislature of Pennsylvania.

SOCIETY.
Charlestown, May 27, 1789.
To the Members of the Society for propagating the Gospel among the Indians and others in North-America. 4° *pp.* 9. *Printed by S. Hall in Cornhill, Boston, n. d.* (1789). 1462

SOCIETY
For propagating the Gospel among the Indians and others in North America. Reports of the Select Committee. 8° *pp.* 28. *Cambridge:* 1819. *Do.* 8° *pp.* 24. *Cambridge:* 1824. 1463

SOLIS (Antonio de).
The History of the Conquest of Mexico by the Spaniards. Done into English from the Original Spanish of Don Antonio de Solis, Secretary and Historiographer to His Majesty. By Thomas Townsend. *London:* MDCCXXIV. 1464

Folio. Five books, separately paged, and seven plates and maps.

SOLIS (Antonio de).
The History of the Conquest of Mexico by the Spaniards. Translated in English from the Original Spanish of Don Antonio de Solis, Secretary and Historiographer to His Catholick Majesty, By Thomas Townshend, Esq.; The whole Translation Revised and Corrected By Nathanael Hooke, Esq. *Two vols.* 8° *London: Printed for John Osborn, at the Golden Ball in Pater-noster Row,* 1738. Vol. I. *pp.* 479 *and* 6 *plates and maps.* Vol. II. *pp.* 475 *and* 2 *plates.* 1465

This work affords the most minute narration of the slaughter of the Indians of Mexico by the Spaniards, and the prodigies of valor exhibited by iron-mailed warriors in fighting naked savages.

SOME
Account of the conduct of the Religious Society of Friends

towards the Indian Tribes in the Settlement of the Colonies of East and West Jersey and Pennsylvania: with a Brief Narrative of their Labours for the Civilization and Christian Instruction of the Indians, from the time of their settlement in America to the year 1843. 8° *London:* 1844. 1466

SPAULDING (M. J.).
Sketches of the early Catholic Missions of Kentucky: from their commencement in 1787, to the Jubilee of 1826–7: embracing a summary of the early history of the state; the adventures of the first Catholic emigrants; biographical notices of the early missionaries; [*etc., 5 lines*] compiled from authentic sources, with the assistance of the very Rev. Stephen Theodore Badin, the first priest ordained in the United States. By M. J. Spaulding, D. D. *Louisville: B. J. Webb & Brother. John Murphy, Baltimore, n. d.* 12° *pp.* 308. 1467

The first three chapters are full of interesting particulars of the sufferings of the early settlers from the Indians, most of them written by the good bishop, from the lips of the survivors. The remarkable narrative of the captivity of John Lancaster is here printed for the first time.

SPEECHES
On the Passage of the Bill for the Removal of the Indians, made in the Congress of the United States, April and May, 1830. 8° *pp.* 304. *Boston:* 1830. 1468

The history of the forced emigration of a sovereign people is given in these speeches. The most remarkable of them all is that of David Crockett; for the highest qualities of oratory, clear, logical deductions, enforced with great eloquence, impelled by honest convictions. Aware that probably not a single individual, within a hundred miles of the frontier of which he was a representative, but would be outraged by his opinions, he fearlessly avowed himself the champion of the rights of the Indian. On a later invasion of them by the government, another noble frontiersman, General Samuel Houston, took the same intrepid course.

SPEECHES
delivered by several Indian Chiefs and an extract of a letter from an Indian Chief. *New York: printed by Samuel Wood.* (.) *Reprinted at Ipswich by J. Bush,* 1812. 16° *pp.* 23. 1469

SPENCER (O. M.).
Narrative of Oliver M. Spencer; comprising An Account of his Captivity among the Mohawk Indians, in North America. Revised from the Original Papers. 12° *London:* 1842. 1470

SPENCER (Rev. O. M.).
Indian Captivity: A True Narrative of the Capture of Rev. O. M. Spencer, by the Indians, in the neighborhood of Cincinnati. Written by himself. *New York: published by Carlton & Lanahan.* 16° *pp.* 160. *Plates.* (1854.) 1471

SPIX (Dr. Joh. Bapt. Von) and MARTIUS (Dr. C. F. Phil Von).
Travels in Brazil, in the years 1817–1820. Undertaken by command of His Majesty the King of Bavaria. By Dr. Joh.

Bapt. Von Spix, and Dr. C. F. Phil. Von Martius. *London: printed for Longman & Co.*, 1824. *Two vols.* 8° *pp.* xxii. + 327 + 4 *plates.* Vol. II. *pp.* viii. + 298 + 5 *plates.* 1472

Much of the space of this very interesting work of two German savans is occupied with minute and, we may be certain, accurate descriptions of the Indians of the pampas and mountains, of whose physique and customs the plates are illustrative.

Spizelius (T.).

Theophili Spizelli elevatio Relationis Montezinianae de repertis in America tribubus Israeliticis; et discussio Argumentorum Pro Origine Gentium Americanarum Israelitica a Menasse Ben Israel in מִקְוֵה יִשְׂרָאֵל seu spe Israelis Conquisitorum. Cum celeberrimi viri Johannis Buxtorfie de Judaico isto conatu ad Theophilum Spizelium Epistola. Basileae, 1661. Joannem Konig, 1661. 8° *Pref. pp.* (24) + 1 *to* 128. 1473

[Strictures of Theo. Spizelius on the account of Montesinos concerning the Israelitish tribes found in America; and discussion of the arguments for the Israelitish origin of the American people, by Manasse Ben Israel, in the hope of the triumph of Israel.]

Sprague (Mr.).

Speech of Mr. Sprague of Maine delivered in the Senate of the United States 16th April 1830 in reply to Messrs. White, McKinley and Forsyth upon the subject of the Removal of the Indians. 8° *pp.* 36. *Washington:* 1830. 1474

Sprague (J. T.).

The Origin, Progress, and Conclusion of the Florida War; to which is appended a record of officers, non-commissioned officers, musicians, and privates of the U. S. army and marine corps, who were killed in battle, or died of disease. [*etc.*, 7 *lines.*] By John T. Sprague, Brevet Capt. 8th Reg. U. S. Infantry. 8° *pp.* 557 + *map* + 10 *plates. New York: D. Appleton & Co.*, 1848. 1475

Of the ten plates, seven are portraits of Indian chiefs. The story of the wonderful contests of a savage tribe of less than four thousand, of all ages, in 1822, and less than one thousand in 1845, with the disciplined forces of the United States, for nearly a quarter of a century, is here told with all its minutest relations. It is a sad story of heroism, gallantry, and patriotism on the side of the Aborigines, and of treachery, unscrupulous covetousness, and barefaced lying on the part of the government and its officials; including the President, the Senate, and the generals in command. The great republic was only victor at last, by inveigling the Indian chiefs, under the most sacred promises of safe conduct, into imprisonment and chains; and after losing one hundred soldiers for every Indian taken or slain, forty-five millions of treasure were expended in reducing these seven hundred patriots.

Spring (Samuel).

A Sermon delivered before the Massachusetts Missionary Society at their annual meeting May 25 1802. The Annual report also of the trustees and several interesting matters relative to missions. 8° *Newburyport:* 1802. 1476

SPROAT (G. M.).

Scenes and Studies of Savage Life. By Gilbert Malcolm Sproat. 12° *pp.* xii. + 317. 1 *Plate. London: Smith, Elder, & Co.*, 1868. 1477

This little volume contains the records of seven years' experience of the peculiarities of life on the extremest frontier of Western America, and is devoted entirely to that phase of it which the savages of Vancouver presented. This vast island has hitherto been a terra incognita, at least so far as the striking characteristics of its savage inhabitants are concerned. Mr. Sproat exercised the functions of a local magistrate at the settlements among them, and studied their peculiarities with great curiosity and diligence. Speaking their difficult and almost unpronounceable language with facility, he was able to obtain so many particulars of their life and customs, as to add largely to our sources of knowledge of aboriginal manners. A vocabulary of the Aht language, spoken universally by the twenty tribes inhabiting Vancouver, occupies fourteen pages, in double columns, and affords us the meaning of nearly one thousand Aht words.

SQUIER (E. G.).

Observations on the Aboriginal Monuments of the Mississippi valley; the character of the ancient Earth-works, and the structure, contents, and purposes of the Mounds: with notices of the minor remains of ancient art. With Illustrations by E. G. Squier. From the second volume of the Transactions of the American Ethnological Society. 8° *pp.* 79 + 2 *folding plans, and many cuts in the text. New York: Bartlett & Welford*, 1847. 1478

SQUIER (E. G.).

Observations on the uses of the Mounds of the West, with an attempt at their classification. By E. G. Squier, Chilicothe, Ohio. 8° *pp.* 14. *New Haven:* 1847. 1479

SQUIER and DAVIS.

Ancient Monuments of the Mississippi Valley: comprising the results of extensive original surveys and explorations. By E. G. Squier, A. M., and E. H. Davis, M. D. Accepted for publication by the Smithsonian Institution, June, 1847. 4° *pp.* 306 + 48 *plates.* [*Washington:* 1848.] 1480

SQUIER (E. G.).

New Mexico and California. The Ancient Monuments, and the Aboriginal, Semi-Civilized Nations of New Mexico and California; With an abstract of the early Spanish Explorations and Conquests in those regions, particularly those now falling within the territory of the United States. By E. G. Squier, A. M. [From the *American Review* for November 1848.] 8° *pp.* 1 *to* 26. *Map and illustrations. New York:* 1848. 1481

SQUIER (E. G.).

Aboriginal Monuments of the State of New York. Comprising the results of original Surveys and Explorations; with an Illustrative appendix, by E. G. Squier, A. M. Accepted for publication by the Smithsonian Institution, October 20th, 1849. 4° *pp.* 188 *and* 14 *plates.* *n. d.* (*Washington*). 1482

Squier (E. G.).
American Archaelogical Researches, No. 1, The Serpent Symbol, and the Worship of the reciprocal principles of Nature in America. By E. G. Squier. 8° *pp.* xvi. + 11 *to* 254 + 4 *plates.* *New York:* 1851. 1483

The plates on separate leaves, and sixty-four wood-cuts in the text, are representations of some of the ancient temples, idols, or structures in serpentine form, which have been found in North America. These are compared with correspondent symbols discovered in Egypt, India, and other parts of Asia.

Squier (E. G.).
Nicaragua; its People, Scenery, Monuments, and the proposed Interoceanic Canal. With numerous Illustrations and original Maps. By E. G. Squier. *Two vols.* 8° *New York:* 1856. 1484

Vol. I. pp. xxii. + 424 + 2 maps, folding plate, 8 octavo plates, and 35 wood-cuts in the text. Vol. II. pp. iv. + 452 + 7 maps, 12 octavo plates, and 25 wood-cuts in the text.

Mr. Squier's explorations form a fitting sequel to those of Mr. Stephens, extending as they did over an adjacent territory, equally rich in the relics of the ingenious and civilized race of aborigines which once peopled it. Almost every article of their manufacture, which was not readily perishable, is represented in the excellent engravings. Their idols, temples, columns, sculptures, utensils, and architecture are most copiously illustrated, and clearly described. A division of the second volume, entitled "Aborigines of Nicaragua," pp. 303 to 362, treats of the Indians now resident in that portion of the peninsula.

Squier (E. G.).
Waikna; or Adventures on the Mosquito Shore. By Samuel A. Bard. With sixty illustrations. 12° *pp.* 365. *New York: Harper & Brothers,* 1855. 1485

Although written in no very serious vein of research, indeed a scoffing book; there are some illustrations of the character of the aborigines which afford the reader an insight into their mode of life and peculiarities not elsewhere shown. In the appendix will be found a short vocabulary of the Mosquito dialect.

Squier (E. G.).
Collection of Rare and Original Documents and Relations, concerning The Discovery and Conquest of America. Chiefly from the Spanish Archives. No. [*engraving*] 1. Published in the Original, with translations, illustrative notes, maps, and Biographical sketches, By E. G. Squier. 4° *Map and pp.* 129, *with* 2 *pp. errata.* *New York: Charles B. Norton,* 1860. 1486

This is the first volume of an intended series, which has so far been followed by no other. The second title announces the subject of the work: *Being a Description of the Ancient Provinces of Guazacapan, Izalco, Cuscatlan, and Chiquimula, in the Audiencia of Guatemala: With An Account of the Languages, Customs and Religion of their Aboriginal Inhabitants and a Description of the Ruins of Copan.* Mr. Ternaux printed a French translation of the MS. from which this edition is published in his Collection of Memoires. Mr. Squier says, Herrera drew the whole of Chaps. viii., ix., and x. of the Eighth

Book of the Fourth Decade from this *Relacion*, by Don Palacio. As shown by the sub-title, Palacio's work is almost wholly devoted to a description of the characteristics of the Indians of the provinces of Guatemala, in 1676.

SQUIER (E. G.).

Historical and Mythological Traditions of the Algonquins; With a translation of the "Walum-Olum," or bark-record of the Lenni-Lenape. By E. G. Squier. 8° *pp.* 28. *n. d. s. l.* 1487

SQUIER (E. G.).

American Ethnology: Being a summary of some of the Results which have followed the Investigation of this subject. By E. G. Squier. *pp.* 14. *n. d.* 1488

STADEN (Hans).

Véritable Histoire et description d'un pays habité par des Hommes Sauvages nus, féroces et Anthropohagu situé dans le Nouveau Monde Nomme Amerique, inconnu dans le pays de Hesse, avant et depuis la naissance de Jésus-Christ, jusqu' a l' annee dernière. Hans Staden de Homberg, en Hesse, L' a' connu par sa propre experience et le fait connaître actuellement par le moyen de l' impression. *Marbourg*, 1557. 8° *pp.* 885. *Paris: Arthus Bertrand*, 1837. 1489

[True History and description of a country inhabited by savage men, naked, ferocious and cannibals, situated in the New World, called America, unknown in the country of Hesse; before and after the birth of Jesus Christ until the last year. By Hans Staden de Homberg, en Hesse, who knew it by his own personal experience, and has made it known actually by his own handwriting.]

This work forms the third of Ternaux-Compans' series of *Voyages et Relations.*

Honest Hans Staden's book is the most valuable and interesting of all the relations of his time, as he narrates with great minuteness the incidents of his long captivity among the Carios Indians. The whole work is devoted to descriptions of his intercourse and battles with the natives; but Chapters xviii. to li., pp. 85 to 216, are entirely occupied with the narrative of his captivity, his sufferings, and final escape. At page 265, a division of the work entitled, "*True and Precise Relation of the Manners and Customs of the Tuppinambas, among whom I was prisoner,*" occupies the remainder of the book. Hans Staden's Relation was first printed in Germany, at Marbourg, in 1557, in small 4°. De Bry translated it into Latin, and inserted it in his *Grand Voyages.* Levy made use of it in his work, *Voyage to Brazil.* He confirms Staden's account of the savages, and vouches for the correctness of his statements from his own experience.

STANSBURY (Howard).

Exploration and Survey of the Valley of the Great Salt Lake of Utah, including a Reconnoissance of a New Route through the Rocky Mountains. By Howard Stansbury. Captain Corps Topographical Engineers, U. S. Army. 8° *pp.* 487 + 45 *plates. Philadelphia:* 1852. 1490

STANLEY (J. M.).

Portraits of North American Indians, with Sketches of Scenery, etc., painted by J. M. Stanley, deposited with the Smithsonian Institute. 8° *pp.* 76. *Washington:* 1852. 1491

STARK (Caleb).

Memoir and official correspondence of Gen. John Stark, with notices of several other Officers of the revolution. Also, a biography of Capt. Phineas Stevens, and of Col. Robert Rogers, with an account of his services in America during the "seven years' war." By Caleb Stark. 8° *Portrait, and pp.* 495. *Concord*: 1860. 1492

STATEMENT

of the Indian Relations, with a reply to the article in the sixty-sixth number of the North-American Review on the Removal of the Indians. 8° *pp.* 21. *New York*: *Clayton and Van Norden, printers*, 1830. 1493

STEDMAN (Capt. J. G.).

Narrative, of a five years' Expedition, against the Revolted Negroes of Surinam, in Guiana, on the Wild Coast of South America; from the year 1772 to 1777: elucidating the History of that Country, and describing its Productions, Viz. Quadrupedes, Birds, Fishes, Reptiles, Trees, Shrubs, Fruits, & Roots: with an account of the Indians of Guiana, & Negroes of Guinea. By Captn J. G. Stedman, illustrated with 80 elegant Engravings, from drawings made by the Author. *London*: *Printed for J. Johnson, St. Pauls Church Yard*, 1796. 1494

Two Volumes, 4°. Vol. I. pp. xviii. + 407 + vii. and 40 plates. Vol. II. pp. vi. + 404 + vi. and 40 plates. If there is a spot on earth, within which the horrors of the infernal regions are anticipated, it must be Surinam. The moment that civilized man sets his foot upon the soil he becomes a fiend, and the atrocities which he perpetrates upon his kind would shame his brother devils. Stedman's work is a record of such horrors, that few will brave the appalling category of bloodshed and murders, to reach the chapter or two descriptive of the Indians of Guiana. The intercourse of Stedman with the aborigines was very limited, yet he gives some new and interesting particulars regarding them.

STEELE (Zadoc).

The Indian Captive; or a Narrative of the Captivity and Sufferings of Zadoc Steele. Related by himself. To which is prefixed an account of the Burning of Royalton [*motto, 3 lines*]. 18° *pp.* 142. *Montpelier, Vt.*: *Published by the Author, E. P. Walton, printer*, 1818. 1495

STEPHENS (J. L.).

Incidents of Travel in Central America, Chiapas, and Yucatan By John L. Stephens. Illustrated by Numerous Engravings. In two volumes. 12th Edition. *New York*: *Harper & Brothers*, 1867. 1496

Large 8° Vol. I. pp. 424 + map, and 21 separate plates, with 10 wood-cuts in the text. Vol. II. pp. 474 + 43 plates on separate leaves. It is difficult to believe that two individuals were capable of such an astonishing amount of labor, as is evidenced in these volumes. The wonderful structures of the race of Indians which once inhabited the peninsula of Central America, are here described by pen and pencil, with great clearness and minuteness. The temples, sculptures, idols, utensils, buildings and architec-

ers, of that active, intelligent, and almost mythical people, are illustrated by more than seventy large engravings, from drawings by Mr. Catherwood. Mr. Stephens did not neglect their modern representatives, as his book is filled with incidents of his associations with them.

Stephens (J. L.).

Incidents of travel in Yucatan. By John L. Stephens. Illustrated by 120 Engravings. In two volumes. 8° *New York: published by Harper & Brothers*, 1858. 1497

Vol. I. pp. xii. + 9 to 459 + map, large folding frontispiece and twenty-three plates on separate sheets. Vol. II. pp. xvi. + 9 to 478 + 51 separate plates. In October, 1841, one year after the termination of his first explorations, the author set out upon the one, the incidents of which are here narrated. So far from exhausting the antiquities of the peninsula in his first two volumes, these add to our astonishment by portraying the gigantic ruins of still more imposing structures, erected by the vanished race of peninsular aborigines.

Stevens (Edward T.).

Flint Chips; a Guide to Pre-historic Archæology, as illustrated by the collection in the Blackmore Museum, Salisbury; by Edward T. Stevens, Hon. Curator of the Blackmore Museum. 8° *pp.* xxvi. + 12 to 593 + xxxviii. + *plates. London*, 1870. 1498

This extraordinary collection of material, representing the labor of aboriginal man in Europe and America, is the result of the munificence and taste of Mr. William Blackmore, who not only provided the very large sum needed for the establishment of the institution, but has made several voyages to America to complete its series. Much the largest portion of the volume is devoted to the description of the utensils, weapons, and ornaments manufactured by the American Indians. Their habitations, mounds, fortifications, and antiquities are described at great length, and with much evident research. The text is accompanied by a large number of wood-cuts, illustrative of the various objects forming the collection.

Stewart (John). 1499

The Missionary Pioneer. See Mitchel.

Steward (James).

History of the Discovery of America, of the Landing of our Forefathers at Plymouth, and of their most remarkable Engagements with the Indians in New England, from their first landing in 1620, until the final subjugation of the Natives, in 1668. To which is annexed the defeat of Generals Braddock, Harmer, and St. Clair by the Indians, at the Westward, &c. By the Rev. James Steward, D. D. 8° *pp.* 176. *Brooklyn* (*L. I.*), *n. d. His. Mag. Vol. I. pp.* 876. 1500

This book must have been a very popular one, as it is announced as having been printed at several places, under various titles, and by almost as many authors. It is usually found entitled, *Indian Wars, by H. Trumbull.* The edition now under our notice, is the first of a score of forms under which this really worthless book appeared. It subsequently issued from the press in almost every town in New England which possessed one. All of these editions, however, claimed for their author, Henry Trumbull, of whom as little is known as of James Steward. The historic value of the work may be ascertained from the testimony of Peter Force, under the title "Trumbull."

STICKNEY (Charles E.).

A History of the Minisink Region: which includes the present towns of Minisink, Deerpark, Mount Hope, Greenville and Wawayanda, in Orange County, New York, from their organization and first settlement to the present time; also, including A general history of the first settlement of the county. By Charles E. Stickney, Middletown, N. Y. 12° *pp.* 211. *Coe Finch & L. F. Guiwits, publishers,* 1867. 1501

This local history of a portion of Orange County, from Chapter v. to ix., pp. 59 to 114, is occupied with "Incidents of the French and Indian War," "Indian Depredations," "Invasion by Brant's Indians and Tories," and "The Battle and Massacre of Minisink." Other portions of the volume are largely devoted to the "Adventures of Tom Quick, the scout, and of the Indian chief, Ben Shanks."

STITH (William).

The | History | of the | First Discovery | and | Settlement | of | Virginia: | Being | an Essay towards a General | History of this Colony. | By William Stith, A. M., | Rector of Henrico Parish, and one of the Governors of | William and Mary College. | [*Motto*], Williamsburg: | 8° *Title and prel. pp.* viii. + 331. *Appendix, title and prel. pp.* v. + 34. *Total pp.* 378. *Printed by William Parks,* M,DCC,XLVII. 1502

Three editions of this work are believed by some bibliographers to have been printed; but as the London edition of 1753 perfectly corresponds with the Williamsburg edition of the same date, it may be true that both of them were printed either in London or in Williamsburg. They differ solely in the substitution of the title-page. Two uniform peculiarities of the edition of 1747 may be noticed: the discoloration of signature x, and the error in numbering the first page of that signature 895, instead of 305. In consequence of this error there are pp. 293 to 304 in duplicate. The style of the writer is rigid and harsh to a degree which renders his work almost unreadable; but the history, which is more strictly the *Annals of the Colony*, is faithfully compiled. In his narration of the aboriginal history, he has added little new material, nor has he brought out what we already knew, in any stronger light, yet we are indebted to him for having printed some documents not easily accessible.

STOBO (Major Robert).

See Craig. 1503

STOCKTON (Mr.).

Remarks of Mr. Stockton of New Jersey, on the Indian appropriation bill, and on the resolution of Mr. Merriwether of Kentucky. Delivered in the Senate of the United States, August 11th & 14th, 1852. 8° *pp.* 16. *Washington,* 1852. 1504

STODDARD (Major Amos).

Sketches, Historical and Descriptive, of Louisiana. By Major Amos Stoddard. 8° *pp.* 488. *Philadelphia, published by Mathew Carey,* 1812. 1505

The relation of the Indians of Louisiana to the Spanish, French, and English conquerors of the territory, occupy the first 73 pages of this volume, while Chapter xiii., pp. 344–351, is devoted to antiquities, Chapter xvi., pp. 409–463, is entitled "The Aborigines," and Chapter xvii., pp. 465–488, "A

Welsh Nation in America," or an investigation of the hypothesis that some of the Indian tribes are descendants of colonists who emigrated from Wales under Prince Madoc in the twelfth century.

STONE (W. L.).
Uncas and Miantonomoh; a Historical Discourse, delivered at Norwich (Conn.), on the fourth day of July, 1842, on the occasion of the erection of a monument to the memory of Uncas, the white man's friend, and first chief of the Mohegans. By William L. Stone. 18° *pp.* 209. *New York*, 1842. 1506

STONE (W. L.).
Border Wars of the American Revolution. By William L. Stone. Two volumes. 16° *New York*, 1864. 1507

This work is composed principally of the narratives and incidents of adventure with the Indians, which are found in the two large volumes of the "Life of Brant."

STONE (W. L.).
The Life and Times of Red-Jacket, or Sa-go-ye-wat-ha; being the Sequel to the History of the Six Nations. By William L. Stone. 8° *pp.* 11 + 484. + *portrait. New York and London*, 1841. 1508

Beside the voluminous life of the pacific Indian orator, the work contains a biography of Farmer's Brother, pp. 407 to 419, and another of Cornplanter, pp. 421 to 462, two celebrated chiefs of the Senecas. A subsequent edition with a memoir of the author, was printed in 1866, but much inferior in typography and paper.

STONE (William L.).
Life of Joseph Brant, (Thayendanegea) including the Border Wars of the American Revolution, and Sketches of the Indian Campaigns, of Generals Harmar, St. Clair, and Wayne, and other matters connected with the Indian Relations of the United States and Great Britain, from the peace of 1783, to the Indian peace of 1795. By William L. Stone. *In Two Volumes. pp.* xxxi. + 500–630 + 4 *portraits and* 3 *plans. Albany:* 1864. 1509

The original edition was printed in 1838; this has the addition of an Index. Fifty copies printed on larger and better paper are distinguished by a rubricated title.

STONE (W. L.).
The Poetry and History of Wyoming; containing Campbell's Gertrude, and the history of Wyoming from its discovery to the beginning of the present century. By William L. Stone. 12° *pp.* xxiii. + 406. *Albany: J. Munsell*, 1864. 1510

A reprint of the edition of 1845, with index and notes. Fifty copies were printed with rubricated titles.

STONE (W. L.).
The Life and Times of Sir William Johnson, Bart., by William L. Stone. Two Vols. 8° Vol. I. *pp.* xv. + 9 *to* 555. Vol. II. *pp.* xv. + 544. *Albany: J. Munsell*, 1865. 1511

The work was commenced by the biographer of Brant, but remained unfin lated at his death, and was completed in its present form by his son. The life of the celebrated royal superintendent of Indian affairs, for a period of forty years, beginning in 1738, is full of material for Indian history. By far the most valuable contributions to it are contained in the Appendix, in which are printed for the first time, and from the original MSS., two Journals, kept by Sir William, of expeditions to Niagara, Oswego, and Detroit, through the cantonments of the Six Nations, and the Ottawa Confederacy. Vol. II. pp. 389 to 476, "An Account of the Language and Customs of the Six Nations," and, "An Account of the Location and Numbers of Indian Tribes," both written by the Baronet, pp. 479 to 490, in the same volume.

STORIES.

150 Stories about Indians. 32° *pp.* 192. *Concord, N. H.: Rufus Merrill,* 1853. 1512

STORRS (Henry).

Speech of Mr. (Henry) Storrs, of New York, in Committee of the whole House on the Bill for the Removal of the Indians West of the Mississippi. 8° *pp.* 53. *Utica,* 1830. 1513

STRACHEY (William).

The Historie of Travaile into Virginia Britannia; expressing the Cosmographie and Comodities of the Country, togither with the Manners and Customes of the people. Gathered and observed as well by those who went first thither as collected by William Strachey, Gent., the first secretary of the colony, now first edited from the original manuscript, in the British Museum. By R. H. Major, Esq., of the British Museum. 8° *Preliminary pp.* viii., *introduction* i. *to* xxxvi., *and pp.* 1 *to* 203, *map and six plates. London: Printed for the Hakluyt Society.* 1849. 1514

The author, of whom almost nothing is certainly known, was evidently a person of some importance in Virginia during the period of which he writes,—from 1610 to 1612. Book I., pp. 23 to 133, is almost wholly occupied with a description of the Indians of Virginia, their customs and peculiarities. It was written probably some years before Captain John Smith's *General History of Virginia,* and is more especially remarkable as having afforded Mr. Deane and Mr. Neil the data to charge the name of Pocahontas with infamy.

The following passage will scarcely be considered sufficient evidence to convict the Indian maiden: "Their younger women goe not shadowed amongest *their owne companie,* until they be nigh eleaven, or twelve returnes of the leafe old, nor are they very much ashamed thereof, and therefore would the before remembered Pochahontas, a well featured, but *wanton* yong girle, Powhatans daughter, sometymes resorting to our fort, of the age then of eleven or twelve yeares, get the boys forth with her into the markett place, and make them wheele falling on their hands turning up their heeles upwards, whome she would followe and wheele so her self, naked as she was, all the fort over, but being once twelve yeares, they put on a kind of semecinctum lethern apron before their bellies, and *are very shamefact to be seene bare.*" On the modern interpretation of the word wanton, rests almost all the weight of the arguments against Pochahontas' chastity. A word used two centuries ago, like "wench," "quean," and many other terms, since degraded by use to reproach, is here in the sense of saucy, hoydenish, reckless, and other kindred terms indicating boldness and want of propriety. Like other native girls she was incapable of viewing her nudity with shame, because her youth forbid the association of sexual indulgence, or even desire, with it.

STRATTON (R. B.).
Captivity of the Oatman Girls: being an Interesting Narrative of Life among the Apache and Mohave Indians. Containing an interesting account of the massacre of the Oatman family, by the Apache Indians in 1851; the narrow escape of Lorenzo D. Oatman; the Capture of Olive A. and Mary A. Oatman; the death, by starvation, of the latter; the five years suffering and captivity of Olive A. Oatman; also her singular recapture in 1856; as given by Lorenzo D. and Olive A. Oatman, the only surviving members of the family, to the author, R. B. Stratton. Twenty-seventh thousand. 12° *portrait, pp.* 292 + 2 + 3 *plates and nine wood-cuts in the text. Published for the author, by Carlton & Porter. New York:* 1867. 1515

STREET (Alfred B.).
Frontenac: or The Atotarho of the Iriquois. A metrical romance by Alfred B. Street. From Bentley's London edition. 12° *portrait, pp.* xii. + 324. *New York: Baker & Scribner,* 1849 1516

An historical preface occupies pp. v. to x., and notes historical, descriptive, and philological, fill pages 261 to 324.

STREET (Alfred B.).
The Burning of Schenectady and other poems by Alfred B. Street. 12° *pp.* 63. *Albany.* 1517

A string of verse on the massacre at Schenectady, with two pages of descriptive prose.

STRENGTH | out of | Weaknesse; | Or a Glorious | MANIFESTATION | Of the further Progresse of | the Gospel among the *Indians* | in NEVV-ENGLAND. | Held forth in Sundry Letters | from divers Ministers and others to the | Corporation established by Parliament for | promoting the Gospel among the Hea | then in New-England; and to particular | Members thereof since the last Trea | tise to that effect, formerly set | forth by Mr. Henry Whitfield | late Pastor of Gilford in | New England. | Published by the aforesaid Corporation. | [*Motto, 3 lines.*] *Small* 4° *London;* | *Printed by M. Simmons for John Blague and* | *Samuel Howes, and are to be sold at their* | *Shop in Popes-Head-Alley,* 1652. 1518

(Title — reverse blank.) To the Supreame Authoritie of this Nation, *The Parliament of the Common Wealth* of ENGLAND. (Running title.) *Epistle, Dedicatoria,* 4 pp. (Signed) John (Owen and eleven others.) To the Reader 5 pp. (Signed) W. Gouge and thirteen others. (Reverse of 5th p. blank.) To the Christian Reader, 3 pp. (Reverse of 3d p. blank.) and pp. 1 to 40. Reprinted pp. 146 to 196, Vol. 4, 3d Series, Mass. H. S. Col. (—) Sabin's Reprints, Large and Small 4°. New York, 1865. Three editions are said by Mr. Sabin to have been issued in the same year. Variation 1st as in Mr. Sabin's Reprint, *Dedication to Parliament,* signed by *William Steele, President.* *William* Gouge. | Variation 2d, *Published by Henry Whitfield. Dedication* signed *John Owen.* "W." Gouge. | Variation 3d. Dedication, signed *William Steele, President.* "*Wiliam*" Gouge. Published by the aforesaid

Corporation. | The title of the copy given, now in my possession, indicates that there was a fourth edition, as the Dedication is signed John Owen and 11 others, and W. Gouge and 13 others, published by the aforesaid Corporation." It is the sixth of the Eliot tracts, or Reports of Missions among the Indians.

STRENGTH out of Weakness; Or a Glorious Manifestation of the further Progresse of the Gospel amongst the Indians in New England. *Small* 4° *New York*, 1865. 1519

Reprint of above.

STRICKLAND (W. P.).

Old Mackinaw; or the Fortress of the Lake and its surroundings. By W. P. Strickland. 12° *pp.* 404. *Map and 2 plates. Philadelphia*, 1860. 1520

Local Indian legends, and sketches of Indian life, fill the greater part of pp. 1 to 106, quoted in great part from other publications.

STRICKLAND (W. P.).

Autobiography of Rev. James B. Finley; or pioneer life in the West. Edited by W. P. Strickland, D. D. 8° *pp.* 543. *Portrait. Cincinnati, printed at the Methodist Book Concern for the Author. R. P. Thompson, printer*, 1867. 1521

STRICKLAND (W. P.).

The Pioneers of the West; or, life in the woods. By W. P. Strickland. 12° *pp.* 403 + 7 *plates. New York*, 1856. 1522

A compilation of narratives of Indian wars, captivities, and border life, some of them apparently from original sources.

STROCK (Dl.).

Pictorial History of King Philip's War; comprising a full and minute account of all the massacres, battles, conflagrations, and other thrilling incidents of that tragic passage in American History. With an Introduction; containing an account of the Indian Tribes, their manners and customs. By Daniel Strock, Jr. With 100 Engravings, from Original Designs. By W. Croome. 8° *pp.* 448. *Boston*, 1853. 1523

STRONG (Nathaniel T.).

Appeal to the christian community on the condition and prospects of the New-York Indians, in answer to a book entitled, The Case of the New-York Indians and other publications, of the Society of Friends. By Nathaniel T. Strong, a Chief of the Seneca Tribe. 8° *pp.* 63. *New York*, 1841. 1524

This is the first replication, in a long series of statements and rejoinders, between the Society of Friends, the Seneca Indians, the Commonwealth of Mass., and the agents of the U. S. Government. There was, undoubtedly, some collusion between some of the chiefs and the agents of Mass., whose consent was necessary to perfect the sale of the Seneca lands, by which a small number of the tribe were made to appear to be the majority. The inevitable, unvarying result followed, and the Indians were cheated and driven from their homes. See SENECA INDIANS.

STUART (Col. John).

Memoir of Indian Wars and other Occurrences in the early

History of Western Virginia, particularly of the battle of Point Pleasant, by Col. John Stuart of Greenbriar, Va., an officer of provincial troops on that occasion. 8° *Printed by the Virginia Historical and Philosophical Society from the MS. presented by Chas. A. Stuart, son of the narrator. Richmond*, 1833. 1525

This very interesting narrative contains an account of the battle of Point Pleasant, one of the few contests between the Indians and the frontiersmen of Penn. and Va., in which the whites were successful. The narrator was also present at the massacre of Cornstalk and his son by the dastardly border whites, while the chiefs were voluntary hostages for the execution of a treaty. This Memoir of Indian wars has been printed only in the Virginia Historical Collection, of the first and only volume of which it forms pp. 35 to 68.

Swan (James G.).

The Northwest Coast; or, Three years residence in Washington Territory. By James G. Swan. With numerous illustrations. 12° *pp.* 435. *Map and 27 plates. New York*, 1857. 1526

The author's sojourn in the territory of three years, commencing in 1853, afforded few incidents not connected with the Indians, then in undisturbed possession of almost the whole country. Everything relating to their mode of life, habits, ceremonies, and condition, receives minute record from this intelligent observer. Twelve of the engravings also illustrate these features of the aborigines of the territory. Pages 412 to 422 contain "A Vocabulary of the Chelalis and Chenook, or Jargon Language."

Symmes (Thomas).

The Original Account of Capt. John Lovewell's "Great Fight" with the Indians at Pequawket, May 8, 1725. By Rev. Thomas Symmes, of Bradford, Mass. A new edition with notes, by Nathaniel Bouton, Corresponding Secretary of the N. H. Historical Society. *Small* 4° *pp.* 48 + *map. Concord, N. H.: P. B. Cogswell, printer*, 1861. 1527

The very rare tract of which this is a reprint, entitled, "Lovewell Lamented; or a Sermon occasioned by the fall of the brave Capt. John Lovewell," is a favorite object of competition among book collectors. Only one perfect copy, and that of the second edition, has been sold at public auction for many years, and this one has been three times offered in that manner. At the last public bidding it was bought for $175. The second edition appearing with the same date is entitled, "Historical Memoirs of the Late Fight at Piggwacket," etc. Boston, 1725. 12°, half-title, title, pp. xii. + 32.

Tales of the Northwest; or, sketches of Indian life and character. By a resident beyond the frontier. (W. J. Snelling.) 12° *pp.* viii. + 288. *Boston: Hilliard, Gray, Little, & Wilkins*, MDCCCXXX. 1528

The author asserts, that after seven years intimate acquaintance with Indian and border life, he chose the narrative form, as a medium for exhibiting the traits of aboriginal character he had observed.

Talmadge (James).

Speech of the Honorable James Talmadge, Jr., of Duchess County, New York, in the House of Representatives of the

United States on the Seminole War. 8° *pp.* 31. *New York, printed by E. Conrad, No. 4, Frankfort Street,* 1819. 1579

TANNER (R. P. Matthias).

Die Gesselschaft Jesu bisz zur vergiess ung ihres Blutes wider den Gotzendeenst Unglauben, und laster, fur Gott, den Wahren Glauben und Tugevedten in allen vier Theilen der Welt streitend: Dasist: Lebens-Wandel. und Todtes-Begebenheit der Jenigen, die ausz der Gesellschaft Jesu umb verthatigung Gottes des Wahren Glaubens und der Tugenden, gewalthatiger Welsahingerichtel Worden: Dorbero Lateinisch beschreiben, Von R. P. Mathia Tanner. *S. J. Theologe, Gebruckt in Prag,* 1683. 1580

Folio. Engraved title 1 leaf, title 1 leaf, and 8 prel. leaves + pp. 1 to 738 + iv. pp.

[The Society of Jesus fighting till the bitter End, against religious Unbelief and Vice, and for God's Glory, and the true Faith and Virtue, in all the four parts of the World: that is, the Life and Death of those Members of the Society of Jesus, who were violently killed, in the defence of true Belief and Virtue. Originally written in Latin. *Prague,* 1683.]

A rare and very important historical work. It contains the lives and martyrdoms of the Jesuit missionaries, in the four parts of the globe. Part IV. is devoted entirely to America, comprising pages 563 to 738, and contains biographies (some of them very full) of fifty-eight missionaries, all of whom were put to death by the Indians. These terrible deaths are represented by thirty-nine copper-plates in the text, representing a sickening variety of tortures, each more frightful than the last, almost equaling in refinement of cruelty that of the Spanish (Christian) savages who first explored and devastated the New World. Nine perished in Florida, several in Peru, Brazil, Paraguay, Mexico, and California. But perhaps the most interesting part of the volume to us, is included in pp. 647 to 694, wherein is narrated the martyrdom of the French Jesuits among the Hurons, the Iroquois, and other nations of New France (part of which is now the State of New York). This part of the work comprises the biographies of Fathers Jogues, Daniel, Brebeuf, Lallemant, Garnier, Chabanel, Reudin, Basil, and Vhoerax. The life of Father Jogues alone fills twenty-seven pages He is represented as being tortured by the Iroquois on the 18th of July, 1643, first by three Indians pulling out the nails of his fingers and toes with pincers. It was however not at this infliction of torments that Father Jogues received his martyrdom, as Mr. Stevens seems to suppose. The deformed and mutilated missionary so far recovered as to be rescued by minister Megapolensis, of Albany; returned to France, and unable to resist the demands of his conscience, to preach the gospel to the Indians, returned to the country of the Iroquois, and by them was slain at Caunawagha in 1647, four years subsequently to his torture.

Tanner was also the author of a work on the same subject entitled, *Confessore,* etc., which contains the life of Father White, the first priest in Maryland. Much of the work whose title is given, is taken from that of Alegrambe, entitled *Mortes Illustres Soc. Jesu. Roma.* Folio, by Alegambe and Nadasi. The German edition of Tanner is translated from the Latin, but contains forty pages of additional matter.

TANNER (Mathio).

Societas Jesu, etc. [Latin original of above]. 1581

TAPIA (Zenteno).

Arte Novissima de Lengua Mexicana, Que dicto D. Carlos de Tapia Zenteno [*Official Titles and Dedication* 19 *lines*]. Con licencia de los superiores. En Mexico por la Viuda de D. Joseph Bernardo de Hogal. 4° 11 *prel. leaves* + 58 *pp.* *Ano de* 1753. 1532

The tenth leaf has an engraved diagram on the recto, forming a series of Elogia on the author.

[New Grammar of the Mexican Language, dictated by Don Carlos de Tapia Zenteno].

TAYLOR (G.).

A Voyage to North America, Perform'd by G. Taylor, of Sheffield, In the Years 1768, and 1769; With an Account of his tedious Passage [*etc.*, 6 *lines*]. The Authors Manner of trading with the Indians; a concise History of their Manners, Diversions and barborous Customs [*etc.*, 28 *lines*]. 18° *pp.* viii. + 248. *Nottingham:* 1771. 1533

TAYLOR (N. G.).

Remarks of Hon. N. G. Taylor, President Indian Peace Commission and Commissioner of Indian Affairs, on the question of the Transfer of the Indian Bureau from the Interior to the War Department. *n. d. n. l.* 8° *pp.* 6. 1534

TAYLOR (James W.).

History of the State of Ohio. By James W. Taylor. First Period, 1650–1787. 12° *pp.* 557. *Cincinnati: H. W. Derby & Co., publishers. Sandusky: C. L. Derby & Co.*, 1854. 1535

As will be seen by the announcement on the title-page, of the period which these annals of Ohio is intended to cover, it is devoted almost entirely to its aboriginal history. The early Jesuit Missions, the wars of the Eries and the Iroquois, the border warfare which was waging for nearly a quarter of a century, between the Scotch-Irish inhabitants of Pennsylvania and the Delawares, Shawanese, and Wyandots, are the subjects which nearly fill the volume. The Appendix contains other and more minute particulars of the various Indian tribes which once inhabited the State, and of the white borderers and Indian chiefs who were noted in their warfare with each other. The work is a very judicious and interesting collection of material already printed in one form or another, not always accessible to the student, even in great libraries.

TAYLOR (R.).

Historical Memoir, of the past and present condition, of the Indian Tribes of the two Californias. [*Principal title:*] "Bancroft's Hand-Book Almanack Official Register & Business Directory for the Pacific States, for 1864." 8° *San Francisco*, 1864. 1536

TAYLOR (James W.).

The Sioux War: what shall we do with it? The Sioux Indians: what shall we do with them? A reprint of papers communicated to the St. Paul daily Press, in October, 1862. By James W. Taylor. 8° *pp.* 16. *Saint Paul: Office of the Press Printing Company*, 1862. 1537

TAYLOR (James W.).

The Sioux War: What has been done by the Minnesota Campaign of 1863: What should be done during a Dakota Campaign of 1864. With some general remarks upon the Indian policy, past and future, of the United States. By James W. Taylor. 8° *pp.* 16. *Saint Paul:* 1863. 1538

Taylor (Alfred B.).

Golden Relics from Chiriqui. A paper read before The Numismatic and Antiquarian Society of Philadelphia, On Thursday Evening; October 5, 1865. By Alfred B. Taylor. 8° *pp.* 8. *Philadelphia:* 1867. 1539

Ternaux-Compans (H.).

Voyages, Relations et Memoires originaux pour servir a l' histoire de la decouverte de l' Amerique, publies pour le premiere fois en Francais par H. Ternaux-Compans. 8° *First & Second Series of* 10 *volumes each.* *Paris* 1837 *&* 1840. 1540

This noble collection has rendered accessible, in a familiar language, many of the rarest and most valuable narratives of conquests and adventure among the Indians of America. Some were indeed to be found alone in manuscripts jealously guarded, and all were, beside rarity, almost as obscure by reason of their Gothic print, equally antique Spanish, or barbarous Latin, as the pictographs of the Aztecs, or the quipus of the Peruvians whose stories they recounted. Their value can best be estimated by the titles of the several volumes.

First Series.

I. Federman's *Narrative of his voyage and travels, in the West Indies,* 1557.
II. Magalhane's *History of Brazil*, 1576.
III. Staden's *History of a country inhabited by naked and cannibal Savages,* 1577.
IV. Pizarro (Pedro) *History of the Conquest of Peru*, 1547.
V. Schmidel's *History of a Voyage to Brazil*, 1550.
VI. Cabeza de Vaca, *Commentaries*, 1555.
VII. Cabeza de Vaca, *Relations of Shipwreck & Travels*, 1555.
VIII. Ixtlilxochitl, *Horrible Cruelties Committed by the Conquerors of Mexico*, 1826.
IX. Casteneda de Nagera, *Relation du Voyage de Cibola*, 1540.
X. Collection of pieces relative to the history of Mexico, 1837.

Second Series.

XI. Zurita, *Description of the chiefs of Mexico*, 1840.
XII, XIII. Ixtilxochitl *History of the ancient kings of Tezcuco.*
XIV. Obiedo y Valdes, *History of Nicaragua.*
XV. Balboa, *History of Peru.*
XVI. Second collection of documents on Mexico.
XVII. Montesinos, *Memoirs on ancient Peru.*
XVIII. XIX. Velasco *History of Quito.*
XX. Collection of documents on Florida.

Ternaux-Compans (Henri).

Recueil de pieces relatives a la conquete du Mexique, inedit. 8° *pp.* 472. *Paris*, 1837. 1541

[Collection of papers, relating to the Conquest of Mexico, not before printed.] Vol. X. of Ternaux-Compans' *Voyages, Relations, et Memoires*, 1st Series. All the pieces are illustrative of the conquest of the Aztecs, and are copies of the original relations of the conquerors themselves; but some are more particularly descriptive of the characteristics of the various tribes of the conquered people. The third Relation is entitled, "Of the order of succession observ'ed by the Indians, relative to their lands." The 4th article, "Of the Ceremonies observed by the Indians, when they make a *Tesle*." The other papers contain a large amount of similar material.

TERNAUX-COMPANS.

Recueil de Pieces sur La Floride. Inedit. [*With the general title:*] Voyages, Relations et Memoires Originaux pour servir a l'histoire de la decouverte de la Amerique. 8° *Prel. pp.* 7 + 368. *Paris*, 1841. 1542

This twentieth volume of Ternaux' collection of voyages, relations, and memoirs, entitled, *Collection of Pieces on the History of Florida never before printed*, contains some very valuable material for the student of aboriginal history. The first narrative is that of Hernando d' Escalente Fontanedo, written about 1527, entitled "Memoir on Florida, its Coasts and its Inhabitants." It is followed by a "Letter written by De Soto," Biedma's "Relation of what happened during the Expedition of Ferd. de Soto," and Betem's "Relation of Florida." In all these pieces, the first attention of the narrators is given to the peculiarities of the Indian natives, and meagre as we feel them to be, for the purpose of satisfying our curiosity, they are with those of Cabeca de Vaca, and the Gentleman of Elvas, the sole means we have of gratifying it, even in part. The Relation of Biedma adds some curious details, to those we already possessed, relating to the fatal expedition of De Soto. Among others he narrates: "One day the Indians killed more than twenty of our men, and wounded more than two hundred, which last received six hundred and sixty flesh wounds. During the night we dressed their wounds with grease (obtained by roasting) the Indians we had killed. We had no other medicament, everything in our possession had been burned during the battle." The remaining papers do not possess less interest. Mendoza's report of the expedition and massacre by the bloody Menendez; the history of the last voyage by Jean Ribaut to Florida; and last the glorious expedition of Gourges, the hero who had the skill and good fortune to unite all the Indian tribes of the coast of Florida, with his little band of Frenchmen, to punish with swift destruction the Spanish monsters who had participated in the massacre. This document is here printed for the first time, from the MS. in the Bibliotheque Royale.

TERNAUX-COMPANS.

Archives des voyages ou collection d' auciennes relations inedites ou tres-rares de lettres, memoires, itineraires, et autres documents relatifs a la geographie et aux voyages, suivies d' analyses d' anciens voyages et d' anecdotes relatives aux voyageurs tirees des memoires du temps. Ouvrage destine a servir de complement a tous les recueils de voyages Francais et etrangers. Par H. Ternaux-Compans. 8° *2 vols. each two parts, pp.* 479 *and* 480. *Arthus Bertrand, Paris*, 1840. 1543

[Archives of Voyages, or Collection of ancient relations unedited or very rare. Of letters, memoirs, journals, and other documents, relative to geography or travels.]

The Archives contain exact reprints of Cartier's Relations of his two voyages to Canada, copies of some letters written by Villegaignon, containing some account of the natives of South America, one from the celebrated Claude Abbeville, and a relation of some affairs with the aborigines, in Canada. The four parts form a complement to the series of Voyages and Relations.

THACHER (James).

History of the Town of Plymouth, from its first settlement in 1620, to the present time: with a concise history of the aborigines of New England, and their wars with the English, &c. By

James Thacher. Second edition, enlarged and corrected. 12° *pp.* 401. *Boston: Marsh, Capen, & Lyon,* 1835. 1544

On p. 351 is a half title: "The Aborigines or Indian Natives of New England," which subject occupies fifty pages, being the remainder of the volume.

THATCHER (B. B.).

Indian Biography; or, an historical account of those individuals who have been distinguished among the North American Natives as orators, warriors, statesmen, and other remarkable characters. By B. B. Thatcher. In two volumes. 24° *pp.* 324 & 320. *New York: Harper & Brothers,* 1858. 1545

THATCHER (B. B.).

Indian Traits: being Sketches of the Manners, Customs, and Character of the North American Natives. By B. B. Thatcher, author of "Lives of the Indians." In two volumes. 24° *pp.* 234 *and* 216. *New York: Harper & Brothers, publishers,* 1865. 1546

THEVET (Andrea).

Historia | dell' India America | detta altramente | Francia Antartica, | di M. Andrea Tevet: | Tradotta di Francese in | Lingua Italiana, da | M. Giuseppe Horologgi. | Con privilegio. In Vinezia appresso Gabriel | Giolito de' Ferrai. | *Small* 12° *pp.* (xvi.) + 364 + 1 *plate.* MDLXI. | 1547

[History of the American Indies, otherwise called France Antarctic. By M. Andre Thevet. Translated from the French, into the Italian language, by Guiseppe Horologgi. Venice 1561.]

Thevet's *Singularites de la France Antarctique,* was first printed in French at Paris, 1558, in 4° with wood engravings. It subsequently in the same year appeared with the imprint of Christopher Plantin, Anvers, also with wood-cuts. An English paraphrase, entitled *The Newfound worlde,* was printed in London, 1568, in 4°. Although all the editions are somewhat rare, the Italian is least esteemed of the four. The English edition has sold at as high a price as ten guineas; both French editions at seven, and the Italian at four to five guineas. This last has a leaf at the end, with an engraving of the arms of the printer on the recto, reverse blank, which is usually missing.

THOMSON (Charles).

An Enquiry into the Causes of the Alienation of the Delaware and Shawanese Indians from the British Interest, And into the Measures taken for recovering their Friendship. Extracted from the Public Treaties, and other Authentic Papers relating to the Transactions of the Government of Pennsilvania and the said Indians, for near Forty Years; and explained by a Map of the Country. Together with the remarkable Journal of Christian Frederick Post, by whose Negotiations, among the Indians on the Ohio, they were withdrawn from the Interest of the French, who thereupon abandoned the Fort and Country. With Notes by the Editor explaining sundry Indian Customs, &c. Written in Pennsylvania. 8° *Map* + *pp.* 184. *London: Printed for J. Wilkie, at the Bible, in St. Paul's Churchyard,* MDCCLIX. 1548

One of the principal causes of the hostility of the Pennsylvania Indians, was the wicked craft practiced upon them by Governor Thomas Penn, and other proprietors in 1737. Certain chiefs having been called together by the speculators, two persons were found to testify that they were present at a council fifty years before, at which as much land was ceded to William Penn, as a man could walk around in a day and a half. There was a chief living who could have proved this testimony false, but he was carefully kept in ignorance of the council, and by mean fraud, endless perjury, and tempting but specious gifts, the surreptitious deed was ratified. To locate as large a territory as possible, a trained pedestrian was employed, who was met at appointed stations by refreshments, and thus was enabled to traverse a route which cut off a million acres from the Indian territory. Less than one third that quantity of land was the amount which the Indians had been led to expect would be ceded. Endless conferences, and numerous councils, were followed by bloody massacres, that devastated the border settlements of Pennsylvania and Virginia, for twenty years. Mr. Thomson's work fully analyses the cause of the *alienation*, which the heroic Quaker, Christian Post, hazarded his life to overcome.

THOMAS (David).

The Western Country in the Summer of 1816: including notices of the natural history; topography, Commerce and Antiquities, agriculture and manufactures. With a map of the Wabash Country now settling, by David Thomas. 12° *pp.* 320. *Auburn (N. Y.): Printed by David Rumsey*, 1819. 1549

Pages 285 to 305 are devoted to notes on "The Ancient Inhabitants." Mr. Thomas was one of the first to draw attention to the aboriginal monuments of central New York.

THORNTON (J. Quinn).

Oregon and California in 1848: By J. Quinn Thornton, late Judge of the Supreme Court of Oregon. With an appendix, including recent and authentic information on the subject of the gold mines of California, and other valuable matters of interest to the emigrant, etc. With Illustrations and a Map. In two volumes. Vol. I. *pp.* 393 + 5 *plates & map.* Vol. II. *pp.* 379 + 6 *plates. New York: Harper & Brothers, publishers*, 1864. 1550

THOROVVGOOD (Thos.).

Iews in America, | or, | PROBABILITIES That the Americans are of | that Race. | With the removall of some | contrary reasoning, and earnest de | sires for effectuall endeavours to | make them Christian. | Proposed by Tho: Thorovvgood, B. D. one of the | Assembly of Divines. | [*Motto* 5 *lines* + *do.* 3 *lines.*] *London: Printed by W. H. for Tho. Slater, and are to be sold | at his shop at the signe of the Angel in Duck-Lane*, 1650. 1551

4° 1 leaf + Epistle 14 pp. + Preface 8 pp. + Epistolical Discourse, 16 pp. + Jews in America, on verso of a leaf with recto blank + Iewes in America. pp. 1 to 138, and 3 unnumbered pp. Total pp. 181.

This is the first dissertation in English, on that fertile subject of controversy and hypothesis, the origin of the American Indians. The Puritans of New England awoke to it with a zeal, untempered by the knowledge that keener intellects and higher scholarship, had been stimulated by its attractive mystery a century before. They seem to have been unaware that Las Casas,

Torquemada, Garcia, and Herrera, Grotius, Horn, and De Laet, had wrought the vein until all the metal was exhausted. But a new cycle of disputation now commenced, and in 1652, Thorowgood's treatise was answered by Hamon L' Estrange, in a tract entitled *Americans no Jews*. London, 1652. Thorowgood made his replication in a second work, *Iewes in America, or Probabilities that those Indians are Judaical*. Lond. 1660. Thorowgood reproduced his work in 1652 with the following title: —

Digitus Dei: | New Discoveryes; | with | Sure Arguments to prove that the Jews (a Na | tion) or People lost in the world for the space of near | 200 Years, inhabite now in *America*; How they came thi- | ther; Their Manners, Customs, Rites and Ceremonies; The | unparallel'd cruelty of the Spaniard to them; And | that the *Americans* are of that Race. | Manifested by Reason and Scripture, which Foretell the | Calling of the Iewes; and the Restitution of them into their | own Land, and the bringing back of the Ten Tribes from all | the ends and corners of the Earth, and that great | Battell to be fought. | With the Removall of some contrary Reasonings, and an earnest | desire for effectual endeavours to make them Christians. | *Whereunto is added* | An Epistolicall Discourse of Mr. Iohn Dury, with the History of | *Ant: Montezinus*, attested by Manasseh Ben Israell, chief Rabby. | By Tho: Thorowgood, D. D. [*Same matters as edition of* 1650.] *Prel. leaves* 21 + 139 *pp. London: Printed for Thomas Slater, and are to be sold at his shop* | *at the signe of the angell in Duck-Lane*, 1652.

THOROWGOOD (Thos.).

Iewes in America or Probabilities that those Indians are Judaical, made more probable by some Additionals to the former Conjectures, an Accurate Discourse is premised of Mr. John Eliot, (who first preached the Gospel to the Natives in their own language) touching their Origination, and his Vindication of the Planters. 4° *London: Henry Brome*, 1660. 1552*

Five prel. leaves namely: Title, reverse blank + "To the Kings most excellent Majesty," 8 pp. "To the Noble Knights, Ladies and Gentlemen of Norfolk," 33 pp. "Summe of the first Treatise," 2 pp. Half title, "Conjectures of Eliot," 28 pp. "Discourse concerning Am.," 67 pp. The first work of Thorowgood printed in 1650, was sharply answered by Harmon Lestrange. To recover the ground from which he had been driven, Thorowgood brought to his aid the Indian apostle Eliot, and their essays are joined in this replication. It was reproduced with the following title: —

Vindiciae | Judaeorum, | or | A true Account | of the | Jews. | Being more Accurately Illustrated | then heretofore. | By T. T. B. D. | Ezekiel 34. 6. | [*Motto, 2 lines*]. *London*, | *Printed for Henry Brome at the Gun* | in *Ivy Lane*, 1660. |

Collation: 4° title, 1 leaf + To the Kings most Excellent Majesty, 4 leaves + To the Noble Knights, &c.; 30 numbered pp. + 8 unnumbered do. + 1 leaf, half title + The learned conjectures of Rev. Mr. John Eliot, pp. 1 to 32 + A Short Discourse, pp. 1 to 67. Total pp., 147.

TIMBERLAKE (Lieut. Henry).

The Memoirs of Lieut. Henry Timberlake, (Who accompanied the Three Cherokee Indians to England in the Year 1762) containing Whatever he observed remarkable, or worthy of public Notice, during his Travels to and from that Nation; wherein the Country, Government, Genius, and Customs of the Inhabitants, are authentically described. Also the Principal Occurrences during their Residence in London. Illustrated with An Accurate Map of their Over-hill Settlement, and a curious Secret Journal, taken by the Indians out of the Pocket of a Frenchman they had killed. 12° *pp.* viii. + 160 + *Map.* *London: Printed for the Author*, 1765. 1553

TIPTON (John).

Speech of the Hon. John Tipton, of Indiana, on the bill for the Protection of the Aborigines. Delivered in the Senate of the United States, April 18, 1838. 8° *pp.* 15. *Washington*, 1838. 1554

TODD (Rev. John).

The Lost Sister of Wyoming. An authentic narrative. By Rev. John Todd. 18° *pp.* 160. *Northampton*: 1842. 1555

TOMO Chachi.

Georgia, a poem. Tomo Chachi, an ode. A Copy of Verses on Mr. Oglethorpe's Second Voyage to Georgia. [*Motto, 2 lines.*] *Folio, pp.* 19. *London: Printed and sold by J. Roberts, in Warwick-Lane*, MDCCXXXVI. [Price one shilling]. 1556

TORQUEMADA (F. Juan de).

Primera (Secunda) (Tercera) Parte De Los veinte ivn libros ritnales I monarchia Indiana, con el origen y guerras, de los Indios Occidentales de sus poblaciones, descubrimiento, conquista, conuersion, y otras cosas marauillosas de la mesma tierra distribidos en tres tomos. Compuesto por F. Juan de Torquemada Ministro provincial de la Orden de Nuestro Serafico Padre, San Francisco En la Prouincia del Santo Evangelio de Mexico en la Nueva Espana. Con privilegeio. *En Madrid en la officena y acosta de Nicolas Rodriguez Franco.* *Ano de* 1723. 1557

Three vols. folio. Vol. I. Engraved title + (6) prel. leaves + pp. 623 + (lvii.) Vol. II. (xix.) prel. leaves + pp. 768 + (lxx.) + colored map. Vol. III. (9) prel. leaves + pp. 634 + (42).

[First (second) (third) Part, of the twenty-one books of ceremonies, and the Indian monarchy, with the origin and wars of the West Indies, of their peoples, discovery, conquest, conversion and other marvelous matters of the same land, distributed in three volumes. Composed by Fray Juan de Torquemada, provincial minister of the order of our Seraphic Father, Saint Francisco, in the Province of the Holy Evangel of Mexico in New Spain. With permission. In Madrid in the (printing) office and at the cost of Nicolas Rodriguez Franco. The year 1723.]

Juan de Torquemada, whom Alaman calls in his *Disertaciones*, the "Livy of New Spain," studied in Mexico, where he took the habit of St. Francis, and became the Provincial of the order for that country. He wrote his *Indian Monarchy*, after having collected everything which he could find that related to the history of the country, and the customs, manners, laws, &c., of its aboriginal inhabitants. This work forms a collection, indispensable to all who desire to know much of the ancient history of Mexico, and its inhabitants, as well as to all those writers who expect to borrow their material from the stores of others.

The edition of 1723 is the most complete, having been edited by the indefatigable Barcia, and is preferred by scholars to the first edition, printed in three volumes at Madrid in 1613. Ternaux says, "Although I find no other notice of the author than what is conveyed on the title, that he was a Franciscan monk, this work is, nevertheless, the most complete we possess on the ancient history of Mexico." A great part of the first volume is devoted to the history of the country, before its discovery, and the whole of the second, to the religion and the laws, manners, and customs of the Mexicans, and a comparison of these peculiarities, with those of the ancient nations of Europe.

Ternaux could hardly have consulted Clavigero, who says, that "Torquemada knew the Mexican language well, conversed with the Mexicans in their own tongue, for upwards of fifty years, and labored at his history for more than twenty. In spite, however, of his diligence and advantages, he frequently betrays want of memory, critical skill, and good taste; many gross contradictions also appear, particularly in chronology, several childish details; and a great deal of superfluous learning. Nevertheless there are many things of curiosity and value in it." This is a very harsh judgment, which one may hope was, even in the learned Clavigero, inspired somewhat by jealousy. Clavigero asserts that Torquemada received some assistance from *The Historical Memoirs of the Kingdom of Acolhuacan* written by the Indian, Antonio Pimentel Ixtlilxochitl, a grandson of the last Indian king of that country. Diego Mugnoz Camargo, a noble half-blood native of Tlascala, wrote a history of the city and republic of Tlascala, which Torquemada found of much use, as he did *The Historical Memoirs of the Kingdom of Cholula*, by Juan Batista Pomar, a descendant of the Royal House of Tezcuco. The MSS. of these valuable works by native historians, Torquemada found deposited in the libraries of the colleges in Mexico.

Rich says, "Some curious chapters of the original MSS. were omitted by order of the Inquisition, of which one was entitled, 'How the Devil wished to imitate the Almighty, by choosing a favorite people.' It is probable that it offended, by comparing the migration of the Toltecs to that of the Israelites."

TOWNSEND (John K.).

Narrative of a Journey across the Rocky Mountains, to the Columbia River, and a visit to the Sandwich Islands, Chili, &c. With a scientific appendix. 8° *pp.* 352. *Philadelphia:* 1839. 1558

TO THE

Members of the Society for propagating the Gospel among the Indians and others in North America. Incorporated by an Act of this Commonwealth. [*Address on first line.*] 4° *pp.* 9. *Charlestown, May* 27, 1789. 1559

TRACTS

Relative to the Aborigines. Published by direction of the meeting for sufferings. From 1838 to 1842. 8° *London:* 1843. 1560

Contains the following tracts, for which see the titles.

No. 1. "Information respecting Aborigines in British Colonies," 1838.
No. 2. "Effects of Ardent Spirits & Implements of War." 1839.
No. 3. "Further Information respecting Aborigines & Seminole War," 1839.
No. 4. "Facts relative to the Canada Indians," 1839.
No. 5. "Report of the Aborigines Com' for 1840," 1840.
No. 6. "An Address of Christian Counsel to Emigrants," 1841.
No. 7. "The Report of the Meeting for Sufferings resp't Aborigines," 1841.
No. 8. "Further Information respecting the Aborigines," 1842.

TRACY (William).

Notices of Men and Events connected with the Early History of Oneida County. Two lectures, delivered before the young

men's association of the City of Utica, by William Tracy. 8° *pp.* 45. *Utica:* 1838. 1561

A biography of Mr. Kirkland, the Indian missionary, and sketches of Oneida chiefs, with incidents of border warfare, form a principal part of this tract.

TRAITS

Of American-Indian Life and Character. By a fur trader. 8° *pp.* xv. + 218. *London:* 1853. 1562

TRANCHEPAIN (St. Augustin de).

Relation Du Voyage des premieres Ursclines a la Nouvelle Orleans et de leur etablissement en cette ville. Par la Rev. Mere St. Augustin de Tranchepain, Superieure. Avec les lettres circulaires de quelques unes de ses Sœurs, et de la dite Mere. Nouvelle York, Isle de Manate, de la Presse Cramoisy de Jean-Marie Shea. 4° *pp.* 62. 1859. 1563

[Relation of the voyage of the first Ursulines to New Orleans, and of their establishment in that city.]

TRANSACTIONS

Of the American Ethnological Society. *New York: Bartlett & Welford.* 1845–1848. 1564

The complete series consists of two volumes, and Part I. of volume three. Vol. I. pp. xiv. + 491 + 3 folding plans and 2 pl. Vol. II. pp. clxxxviii. + 298, and map. Vol. III., Part I., pp. 202. Part II. will probably never be published, as the society has been formally dissolved.

This collection preserves a large amount of material, illustrating the history, antiquities, languages, and origin of the American Indians. In volume first, we find, Albert Gallatin's "Notes on the Semi-Civilized Nations of Mexico and Central Am.," pp. 1 to 305. Prof. Troost's "Acc't. of Ancient Remains in Tenn., with traces of Phallic Worship," pp. 355 to 369. Schoolcraft's "Obs. on Grave Creek Mound," pp. 369 to 424. Vol. II. contains "Hale's Indians of N. W. Am., and Vocabularies of N. A.," xxiii. to clxxxviii. + 1 to 130. Squier's "Obs. on Aboriginal Monuments of Miss.," pp. 131 to 208. Morton's "Acc't. of a Craniological Collection." Cotheal's "Gram. Sketch of Mosquito Language," pp. 224 to 235. Vol. III. part I. contains Bartram's "Obs. on Creek and Cherokee Indians, 1789," pp. 1 to 81. Squier's "Obs. on the Archæology and Ethnology of Nicaragua," pp. 83 to 158. Turner's "Aborigines of New Mexico," "Choctaw Tradition," "Aborigines of Panama, and Cuban Antiquities," pp. 160 to 202.

TREATIES

with certain Indian Tribes, ratified by the President, with the advice and consent of the Senate, In December 1817. 8° *pp.* 19. *Washington: Printed for the Department of War,* 1818. 1565

TREATIES

between the United States of America and the several Indian tribes, from 1778 to 1837: with a copious table of contents. Compiled and printed by the direction, and under the supervision of the commissioner of Indian affairs. 8° *pp.* 699. *Washington:* 1837. 1566

TREATY WITH THE FLORIDA INDIANS.

Letter from the Secretary of War, transmitting the Information required by a Resolution of the House of Representatives, of the 5th ultimo, in relation to the instructions given to the commissioners for negotiating with the Florida Indians, &c., &c., February 6, 1826. Read, and referred to the Committee on Indian Affairs. 8° *pp.* 109. *Washington:* 1826. 1567

The letters and documents forming this report give a very full detail of the steps which led to a second Seminole war.

TRIAL (The)

of Alpheus Livermore and Samuel Angier, before the Supreme Judicial Court of the Commonwealth of Massachusetts, upon an Indictment for the Murder of Nicholas John Crevay, an Indian, committed November 23, 1813. Containing the Evidence at large, the Arguments of the Solicitor General, and of the Counsel for the Prisoners, the Charge of the Hon. Judge Sewall to the Traverse Jury, and his Address on pronouncing Sentence of Death. (From minutes taken at the trial.) 8° *pp.* 50. *Boston: Published by Watson & Bangs,* 1813. 1568

TRUMBULL (Henry).

History of the Discovery of America; of the landing of our forefathers at Plymouth, and of their most remarkable engagements with the Indians in New-England, from their first landing in 1620, until the final subjugation of the natives in 1679. To which is annexed, the particulars of almost every important engagement with the savages at the westward to the present day. Including the defeat of generals Braddock, Harmar and St. Clair, by the Indians at the Westward; The Creek and Seminole War, &c. By Henry Trumbull. *Folding plate, pp.* 256. *Boston:* 1828. 1569

TRUMBULL (Henry.)

History of the Indian Wars: to which is prefixed a short account of the Discovery of America by Columbus, and of the landing of our forefathers at Plymouth, with their most remarkable engagements with the Indians in New-England, from their first landing in 1620, until the death of King Philip, in 1679. By Henry Trumbull. To which is now added a historical account of the sufferings of the inhabitants of the frontier settlements by the savages, during the French and Revolutionary wars; and also the particulars of every important engagement with the Indians, in the Southern and Western States and Territories, to the present time. A new edition, with an entire new arrangement, essential corrections, and large additions. 8° *pp.* 320, *plates* 3. *Boston: Philips & Sampson.* 1846. 1570

This work, under all its Protean forms, bears evidence that it was written for a comparatively unlettered public: as, according to the testimony of Col. Peter Force, there is not a page which is not crowded with errors. He stated to Mr. Henry C. Murphy that he believed there was scarcely a date correctly given in the whole book, having discovered twenty-two chronological errors on a single page. Many editions, with varying titles, were published for the purpose of being hawked through the country. The first purports to have been printed at Brooklyn, L. I., in which edition the author's name is announced as James Steward. Another is entitled, *History of America.* Under all forms there is only a variation of worthlessness.

TRUMBULL (J. Hammond). 1571

A Key into the Language of America, edited by J. Hammond Trumbull. Vol. I. 4° *pp.* 1 *to* 222 *of Publications of the Narraganset Club (First Series). Providence, R. I.:* 1866.

A biographical memoir of Roger Williams, of 60 pp., precedes this new edition of his work upon the language of the Narraganset Indians. Following the memoir, Mr. Trumbull's preface occupies pp. 1 to 16. The Key fills pp. 18 to 220, in the lower margins of which the editor has placed three hundred and eighty-six explanatory notes. Many of these are of great length; and all are characterized by the learning and ability, which are the fruit of his long study of the Indian languages of America. Nothing is settled by hypothesis, and little left to conjecture, while incidentally many characteristics of aboriginal life are woven into his analyses.

TRUMBULL (J. Hammond).

On some mistaken notions of Algonkin grammar, and on mistranslations of words from Eliot's Bible, &c. By J. Hammond Trumbull. (From the Transactions of the American Philological Association, 1869–70.) 8° *pp.* 1 to 19. 1871. 1572

Among other heresies which Mr. Trumbull exterminates is that bewildering one of which Mr. Duponceau was the apostle, that the (Mass.) Natick language could be demonstrated from Eliot's Bible, to possess an infinitive mood. As this would unsettle the belief, authorized by the best scholars, in the incapability of the expression of abstract action or being, and almost of abstract substantives, by most, if not all, Indian languages, it is a good service to philology to sweep it away. Another error in the opposite direction, originated by Mr. Edwards and sustained by Mr. Bancroft, General Cass, and others, that verbs had no expression unless associated with both actor and subject, is completely refuted. Some amusing stories regarding the whimsical modes of expression Eliot is said to have adopted, which have obtained so much authenticity as constant repetition and universal belief can give, are shown by translations of the paragraphs in question to be untrue.

TRUMBULL (J. Hammond.) 1573

On the best method of studying the American languages. By J. Hammond Trumbull. (From the Transactions of the Am. Phil. Association, 1869–70.) 8° *pp.* 1 *to* 25. 1871. 1574

Mr. Trumbull writes upon a subject which he more fully comprehends, and can better illustrate, than any other scholar — perhaps in the world. The polysyllabic, or synthetic structure of the words, of all Indian languages, is most clearly exhibited and demonstrated in this essay. Their agglutinative formation has struck every student upon the most superficial examination, but it remained for Mr. Trumbull to suggest that the readiest and most scientific mode of learning them was to reverse the order of composition. "*The aim of the student should be, the resolution of synthesis by analysis.*"

TSCHUDI (Dr. J. J. Von).

Travels in Peru, during the years 1838–1842, on the coast, in the Sierra, across the Cordilleras and the Andes, into the primeval forests. By Dr. J. J. Von Tschudi. Translated from the German by Thomasina Ross. *Large* 8°. *Plate, pp.* 506. *London: David Bogue,* 1847. 1575

TSCHUDI.

Travels in Peru. 12° *pp.* 354. *New York,* 1865. 1576

Any work by Dr. Von Tschudi — one of the authors of *Peruvian Antiquities*

— upon a country so full of the material which excited his interest, could not fail to contain much relating to the living representatives of a race, whose ruined monuments he labored with such zeal to rescue from oblivion. Throughout the whole work, interesting details of the life and habits of the modern Peruvian Aborigines occur on almost every page; but the last three chapters are almost entirely devoted to new, and doubtless authentic information regarding them.

TSCHUDI (John James).
PERUVIAN ANTIQUITIES, by Marino Edward Rivero and John James Tschudi. (Translated into English by Francis L. Hawks, D. D.) 8° *pp.* 306. *New York*, 1853. 1577

See Riviero.

TSCHOOP,
The converted Indian Chief. Written for the American Sunday School Union, and revised by the committee of publication. 18° *pp.* 36. *Philadelphia, n. d.* 1578

TUBBEE (L. C. M. E.).
A Sketch of the Life of Okah Tubbee, *alias*, William Chubbee, Son of the Head Chief, Mosholeh Tubbee, of the Choctaw Nation of Indians. By Laah Ceil Manatoi Elaah Tubbee, his wife. *pp.* 84 *and printed covers. Springfield, Mass. Printed for Okah Tubbee. By H. S. Taylor.* 1848. 1579

TURNER (G.).
Traits of Indian character; as generally applicable to the aborigines of North America. Drawn from various sources; partly from personal observation of the author. By G. Turner. In two vols. 12° *pp.* 207 *and* 196. *Philadelphia: Key & Biddle.* 1836. 1580

TYSON (Job R.).
Discourse on the surviving remnant of the Indian Race in the United States. Delivered on the 24th October, 1836, before the Society for commemorating the landing of William Penn. By Job R. Tyson. 8° *pp.* 36. *Philadelphia: printed by A. Waldie, 46 Carpenter Street*, 1836. 1581

TYLOR (Edward B.).
Anahuac: or Mexico and the Mexicans, Ancient and Modern. By Edward B. Tylor. 8° *pp.* xi. + 1 *to* 344 + *map* + 4 *plates and* 26 *wood-cuts in the text, mostly illustrative of the antiquities of the Aboriginal Mexicans. London: Longman, Green, Longman, & Roberts.* 1861. 1582

Beside the interesting personal narration of intercourse with the Indians of Mexico, this work treats, in a pleasant, unscientific manner, of the ancient history of the Mexicans. Such of the antiquities as fell in his way he describes, and of some he gives illustrative engravings.

TYTLER (Patrick Fraser).
The Northern Coasts of America, and the Hudson's Bay Territories. By Patrick Fraser Tytler. With continuation, by R. N. Ballantyne, author of "Hudson's Bay; or Every-day life in

the Wilds of North America." 12° pp. 409. *London: T Nelson & Sons, Paternoster Row; and Edinburgh.* 1854. 1583

This book is an excellent *resumé* of the most remarkable incidents of Indian life and habits, narrated by the Arctic explorers and Northwest voyageurs.

ULLOA (Don Antonio de).

Noticias Americanas: entretenimentos fisico historicos, sobre La America Meridional, y la Septentrional Oriental. Comparacion general De los Territorios, Climas, y Producciones en las tres especies, Vegetales, Animales, y Minerales: Con relacion particular De las Petrificaciones de Cuerpos Marinos de los Indios naturales de aquellos Paises, sus costumbres y usos: De las Antiquedades: Discurso sobre la Lengua, y sobre el modo en que pasaron los primeros Pobladores. Su Autor Don Antonio de Ulloa, Comendador de Ocana, etc. 4° 12 *prel. leaves, pp.* 407 + *Table Errata,* 1 *p. En Madrid: En la Imprenta de Don Francisco Manuel de Mena, Calle de las Carretas.* M.DCC.LXXII. 1584

The last six chapters, pp. 305 to 407, are devoted to a description "Of the Customs and Manners of the Native Indians;" "A Comparison of their peculiar Traits with those of other Nations;" "A Treatise on the Religion of the Aborigines;" "A Notice of the Antiquities discovered in the Country;" "An Account of some of the Writings of the Indians; and of some Figures in the Form of Idols; of the Language of the Indians, and the Manner in which these countries were peopled."

ULLOA (Don Antonio de).

Noticias Americanas: entretenimientos Fisico-Historicos sobre La America Meridional, y la Septentrional Oriental: comparacion general de los territorios; climas y produciones en las tres especies: vegetal, animal y mineral; con una relacion particular de los Indios de aquellos paises, sus costumbres y usos, de las petrificaciones de cuerpos Marinos, y de las Antiquedades. Con un discurso sobre el Idioma, y conjeturas sobre el modo, con que pasaron los primeros pobladores. Su Autor El Exc. Sr. Don Antonio de Ulloa. Con Licencia. *Madrid: en la Imprenta Real. Año* 1792. 4° 8 *prel. leaves* + 1 *to* 342. 1585

[American Notices. Historical and physical conversations upon the southern part of North America and the Eastern portions of South America. A general view of its Territories, Climates, and the three Classes of Productions, Vegetable, Animal, and Mineral. With a Particular Relation of the Petrifactions of some marine bodies; of the Indians, natives of these countries; of their customs, habits, and of their antiquities. With a Discourse upon their Language and upon the manner in which the country was first peopled.]

ULLOA (Don Antonio).

Memoires Philosophiques, historiques, physiques, Concernant la decouverte de l'Amerique, ses anciens Habitans, leurs mœurs, leurs usages, leur connexion avec les nouveaux Habitans, leur religion ancienne & moderne, les produits des trois regnes de la

Nature, & en particulier les mines, leur exploitation, leur Immense produit ignorè jusqu ici. Par Don Ulloa, Lieut. General &c. Avec des Observations & Additions sur toutes les matiers dont il est parle dans l'ouvrage. Tradult par M.—— 2 vols. 8° *pp.* viii. + 386. Vol. II. *pp.* ii. + 499. *A Paris:* 1787. 1586

[Philosophic and Historic Memoirs, Concerning the discovery of America. Its ancient Inhabitants, their manners, their habits, and their connexion with the Europeans and their descendants. The ancient and modern religion of the Natives. The products of the three kingdoms of Nature, & in particular the mines, their examination, and their immense product hitherto unknown. With Observations & Additions on all matters spoken of in the work.]

This work is a first translation of the work of Don Ulloa printed at Madrid in 1747. Although apparently occupying a much greater bulk, it seems to be a faithful translation of the work of Ulloa, to which the translator has added his own *Observations*, which occupy all after page 134 of volume two. So close is the reproduction of the original, that the division into chapters is identical. The subjects of Chapters xvii. to xxii., pp. 1 to 134, of volume two, as indicated by their headings, are: "Of the Native Indians in the two Americas: their Manners, Customs and Habits; of the Religion of the Indians: their tombs, their diminution, and of their castes of half-breeds, of the antiquity of the Indians; of different works constructed or invented by them, and of many figures of idols and amulets; of the language of the Indians, and the conclusion we can arrive at regarding the first population of America."

ULLOA (Don George).

A Voyage to South America. Describing at large, the Spanish Cities, Towns, Provinces, &c. on that extensive Continent. Undertaken by Command of the King of Spain, By Don George Juan, and Don Antonio de Ulloa, Both Captains of the Spanish Navy; [*etc.*, 2 *lines*]. Translated from the original Spanish. The Third Edition. To which are added, By Mr. John Adams, of Waltham-Abbey, who resided several Years in those parts, Occasional Notes and Observations; an Account of some Parts of the Brazils, hitherto unknown to the English Nation; and a Map of South America, corrected. (*Two volumes.*) 8° *pp.* 479, 419 *and seven leaves Index. Map and* 4 *folding plates. London,* 1772. 1587

ULLOA (Don Antonio de).

Noticias Secretas de America, sobre el estado naval, militar, y politico de los reynos del Peru y provincias de Quito, Costas de nueva Granada y Chile: gobierno y regimen particular de los Pueblos de Indios: Cruel opresion y extorsiones de sus corregidores y curas: abusos escandalosos intruducidos entre estos habitantes por los misioneros: causas de su origen y motivos de su continuacion por el espacio de tres siglos. Escritas fielmente segun las instrucciones del excelentisimo Senor Marques de la Ensenada, primer Secretario de Estado. Y presentadas en informe secreto á S. M. C. el Senor don Fernando VI. Por Don Jeorge Juan, y don Antonio de Ulloa. [*etc.*, 4 *lines.*] Por

Don David Barry en dos partes. *Londres:* 1826. *Folio two partes, pp.* xiii. *and* 707. 1588

[Secret Notices of America, upon the naval, military, and political condition of the kingdom of Peru, the provinces of Quito, New Granada, and Chili. The expense of their government, and particularly of the management and care of the Indian Tribes. The cruel oppression and extortions of the officials and curates of the Indians; and the scandalous abuses introduced among the inhabitants, by the Missionaries. Examination of their origin, and cause of their continuation for three centuries. Written faithfully from the information of his Excellency the Marquis de la Ensenada, first Secretary of State, and presented as secret reports, to his Majesty the King, Ferdinand VI.]

This work is an expose of the secrets of the Spanish Colonial Government, and is divided into two parts: Parte II. On the government, administration of Justice, and state of the clergy, among the Indians of the interior: with descriptions of their customs. Chapters I. to ix., pp. 229 to 614. "The benevolent and virtuous Las Casas has been accused of exaggeration and falsehood in his account of the cruelties of the Spaniards to the Indians, exercised upon them soon after the discovery of their country, up to the middle of the sixteenth century. But although his accounts were denied and declared to be calumnious, we find the Indians of Peru treated with the same cruelty two hundred years afterward." — *Rich.*

The learned author has brought abundant testimony to prove that the oppression and tyranny described by Las Casas as exercised upon the Aborigines was scarcely less atrocious during the closing years of the Spanish dominion. "These secret memoirs are written with that truth, impartiality, and good judgment which distinguished the informants, — the brothers Ulloa." — *Salvi.*

The book was printed in London, because its publication in Spain would have been prohibited. It had remained in MS. for more than fifty years.

UPHAM (C. W.).

Life, explorations and public services of John Charles Fremont. By Charles Wentworth Upham. With Illustrations. 12° pp. 365 + 12 *plates.* *Boston: Ticknor & Fields,* 1856. 1589

To the frequently reprinted details of Fremont's explorations and adventures among the Indians, this volume adds a number of portraits of the savages of different tribes, and illustrations of their warfare and councils.

URICOCHEA (Ezequiel).

Memoria sobre las Antiquedades Neo-Granadinas por Ezequiel Uricochea. 4° *pp.* viii. + 76 + 5 *pp. of plates.* *Berlin: Libreria de F. Schneider I Cie,* 1854. 1590

[Memoir upon the Antiquities of New Grenada.]

The scope of the author's investigations is well expressed in a paragraph of his introduction: "The social and private life, the rites and ceremonies, the commerce, and in one word, the usages and customs, are the indices by which we mark the state of civilization." These characteristics of the Chibchas and Armas, Indian nations inhabiting New Grenada, form the entire material of his work. The plates are representations of their idols, weapons, utensils, and craniology.

UTAH EXPEDITION.

The Utah Expedition; containing a General Account of the Mormon Campaign, With Incidents of Travel on the Plains; Account of Indian Tribes, &c., From its Commencement to Present Time. By a Wagon-master of the Expedition. 8° *pp.* 48. *Cincinnati:* 1858. 1591

VAIL (Eugene A.).
Notice sur les Indiens de l'Amerique du Nord, ornée de quatre portraits coloriés, desinés d' apres nature, et d' une carte, par Eugene A. Vail. 8° *pp.* 244 + 4 *plates and one map. Paris: Arthus Bertrand, editeur,* 1840. 1599
[Notice of the Indians of North America, Illustrated with four portraits drawn from life, and a map.]

VANDELEUR (John) and VANLEASON (James).
A Narrative of a voyage, taken by Capt. James Vanleason, from Amsterdam to China: and from there to the Western Continent of North-America; Where he found a Vast number of Indians, and one of the largest Rivers in the World, lying in the lat. of 53° 30^m north. The owner of the ship, Mr. John Vandeleur, went in her as Supercargo, and bought a great quantity of fur of the natives. Also, an Account of Mr. Vandeleur's being left behind on the Continent, by the misconduct of the ships company, where he lived almost seven years. Likewise, An Account of his Marriage, With a Sachem's or Kings Daughter, one of the Indian Nation; by whom he had a Son and a Daughter. With an account of his conversion in that Western World; And the Conversion of the King, or Sachem, the Queen, and the Sachems family, with abundance of others. Together [*etc., five lines*]. A Religious Tale. 12° *pp.* 45. *Ballston Spa: printed for the purchaser.* 1816. 1598

There is little in the course of literary pursuits more vexatious, than to chronicle the existence of a wretched performance like this, unless it be that of having paid an extravagant price for it, only to find it utterly worthless in every view, except its extreme rarity.

VAN DER DONCK (Adriaen).
Beschryvinge | Van | Nieuw-Nederlant, | (Gelijck het tegenwoordigh in Staet is) Begrijpende de Nature, Aert, gelegentheyt en vruchtbaerheyt | van het selve Landt; mitsgaders de proffijtelijcke ende gewenste toevallen, die | aldaer tot onderhoudt der Menschen, (soo uyt haer selven als van buyten inge | bracht) gevonden worden. Als mede de maniere en ongemeyne Eygenschap- | pen vande Wilden oste Naturellen vanden Lande. Ende een byfonder verhael | vanden wonderlijcken Aert ende het Weesen der Bevers. | Daer noch by-gevoeght is | Een Discours over de gelentheyt van Nieuw-Nederlandt, | tusschen een Nederlandts Patriot, ende een Nieuw-Nederlander. | Beschreven door | Adriaen Vander Donck, | Beyder Rechten Doctoor, die tegenwoordigh | noch in Niew-Nederlandt is. | En hier achter ly gevoeght | Het voordeeligh Reglement vande Ed: Hoog. Achtbare | Heeren de Heeren Burgermeesteren deser Stede, | betressende de saken van Nieuw Nederlandt. | Den tweeden Druck. | Met een pertinent Kaertje van' tzelve Landt verciert, | en vanveel druck-fouten gesuyvert. | [*Coat of arms.*] *t'Aemstaldam, | By Evert Nieuwenhof, Boeckverkooper woonende*

op | *t Ruslands in t Schrijf-boeck, Anno* 1656. | *Met Priviligie voor* 15 *Jaren.* 1594

[Description of New Netherland, (such as it now is,) including the Nature, Character, Situation and Fruitfulness of that land, together with the profitable and happy accidents there found, for the support of man (whether natives or foreigners). As also the manners and uncommon qualities of the savages, or aborigines of the country, and a particular account of the wonderful nature and habits of the Beaver. To which is also added, a discourse on the situation of New Netherland, between a Netherland Patriot, and a New Netherlander. Described by Adriaen Van der Donck, Doctor of Laws, who is still in New Netherland. And to this is appended: The advantageous regulations, of the Most Worshipful, the Burgomasters of this City, regarding the affairs of New Netherland. The second edition, ornamented with a pertinent map of that land, and cleared of many printing faults.]

4° Four preliminary leaves, namely, 1st, containing title, reverse privilege; 2d, with four coats of arms above the word Opdracht; 3d, Aan de Leeser, 1 p. + A poem of 3 stanzas, 1 p. + the text, pp. 1 to 100, succeeded by 12 unnumbered pp., namely, Register, 3 pp. reverse of 3d blank + Condition (title of 14 lines, coat of arms Amsterdam, etc., 3 lines, 1656), 7 pp., and Lyste, 1 p. Total, 120 pp., with folding map of Nova Belgica.

A large part of this very rare work is devoted to a description of the natives of the New Netherlands. Van der Donck arrived in New Amsterdam in 1642. He served as the sheriff of the colony of Rensselaerwyck, and purchased an estate on the Hudson, near the site of the village of Yonkers. Before this work was published, he had printed *An Exposition of the New Netherlands* (Hage, 1650,) in which the administrations of Kieft and Stuyvesant were vigorously assailed. A division of the work before us, found on page 52, is entitled, "Of the Manners and peculiar Custom of the Natives of the New-Netherlands." This is subdivided into twenty-two sections, each treating of some of the peculiarities of the savages of the State of New York. The whole covering pp. 52 to 81. The treatise possesses an interest beyond its rarity, in being the relation of an educated man, regarding the Indians of the island and neighborhood of New York. The work was translated by Gen. J. Johnson, and printed in the sixth volume of the New York Historical Society.

The second edition of this work is a reprint of the first from the 1st to the 16th pages. The remainder is so exact a reproduction, page for page, of the first edition, as to favor the hypothesis, that the sheets from signature C to to N 3 were never reprinted. There would have apparently been no difference discoverable, had the plate of New Amsterdam been retained in the second edition. The map and Condition properly belong only to this edition, but are wanting in several of the copies known to be in existence. A very high authority in bibliography, Mr. Henry Stevens, is of the opinion that a copy of Van der Donck with the date of 1656, and view of New Amsterdam on the 9th page, must be made up of the two editions, by prefixing a title of the second to the text of the first. I have lately found three copies, with exactly the same collation, and although this is merely negative evidence, the correspondence of so many copies authorizes at least the fair presumption, that three editions may have been printed. We must otherwise suppose, that three copies of an exceedingly rare book have been mutilated to form a hybrid of two editions.

Van Heuvel (J. A.).

El Dorado; being a narrative of the circumstances which gave rise to reports in the sixteenth century, of the existence of a rich and splended city in South America, to which that name was given, and which led to many enterprises in search of it; including a Defence of Sir Walter Raleigh, in regard to the relations made by him respecting it, and a nation of female warriors, in the vicinity of the Amazon, in the narrative of his expedition to the Oronoke in 1595. With a map. By J. A. Van Heuvel. 8° *pp.* viii. + 166 + *map* + *vocabularies of five Indian Nations in Guiana. New York: J. Winchester, New World Press* (1844). 1595

VAN TRAMP (John C.).
Prairie and Rocky Mountain Adventures, or, Life in the West. To which will be added a view of the states and territorial regions of our Western Empire: embracing history, statistics and geography, and descriptions of the chief cities of the West. By John C. Van Tramp. 8° *pp.* 649. *Columbus: Gilmore & Segner*, 1866. 1596

VEGA (Garcilasso de la Vega).
See Garcilasso. 1597

VELASQUEZ (Pedro).
Memoir of an Eventful Expedition in Central America, resulting in the discovery of the idolatrous city of Iximaya, in an unexplored region, and the possession of two Remarkable Aztec Children, Descendants and Specimens of the Sacerdotal Caste (now nearly extinct) of the Ancient Aztec Founders of the ruined Temples of that Country, described by John L. Stevens Esq., and other Travellers. Translated from the Spanish of Pedro Velasquez of San Salvador. 8° *pp.* 35. *New York: E. F. Applegate, printer*, 1850. 1598

This purports to be transcripts of the journal of Velasquez describing the adventures of the writer and two young Americans in an expedition among the Indians of the Maya race, which resulted fatally to the latter adventurers. It is the most circumstantial fiction which the brain of an advertising agent ever conceived.

VENEGAS (Padre Miguel).
Noticia de la California, Y de su conquista temporal y espiritual, hasta el tiempo presente. Sacada de la Historia Manuscrita, Formada en Mexico año de 1739, por el Padre Miguel Venegas, de la Compania de Jesus; y de otras Noticias, y Relaciones antiguas, y modernas. Añadida de algunas mapas particulares, y uno de la America Septentrional, Asia Oriental, y Mar del Sur intermedio, formados sobre las Memorias mas recientes, y exactas, que se publican juntamente. Dedicada Al Rey N.tro Señor por la Provincia de Nueva-España de la Compania de Jesus. Con licencia. *Three Vols. small 4° Map bordered with plates of Indians, and the Massacres of the Jesuit Missionaries, by them.* Vol. I. *pp.* 24 + 240. Vol. II. *pp.* 564. Vol. III. *pp.* 436 + 3 *maps. En Madrid*, M.D.CCLVII. 1599

VENEGAS (Miguel).
A natural and civil history of California. Containing An accurate Description of that Country, [*etc.*, 3 *lines.*] The Customs

of the Inhabitants, Their Religion, Government, and Manner of Living, before their Conversion to the Christian Religion by the missionary Jesuits [4 *lines*]. Illustrated with 4 Copper Plates, and an accurate Map of the Country and the adjacent Seas. Translated from the original Spanish of Michael Venegas, a Mexican Jesuit. Published at Madrid, 1778. In Two Volumes. 8° Vol. I. *pp.* xviii. + 455. Vol. II. *pp.* v. + 387. *London*: 1759. 1600

[Noticia of California: of its conquest, temporal and spiritual, from that time to the present. From the Manuscript History of that province, composed in Mexico, in the year 1739, by Father Venegas, of the order of Jesuits, with other Sketches and Relations, both ancient and modern.]

The history of Father Venegas was edited by Father Andro Buriel, who died in the city of Mexico in 1762. He found the MS. of Father Venegas' work at Madrid in 1749, it having been finished ten years previously. The sources from which Venegas derived his history are a number of relations composed by the missionaries in California, and sent to the Provincial at Mexico, where they are still preserved in the libraries of two colleges. The work of Father Venegas is undoubtedly the most faithful narration we possess, regarding the original condition of the Indians of any part of North America, connected with the history of their gradual progress towards civilization and Christianity.

With the habitual contempt for accuracy which distinguishes English editors of the last century, this translator of Venegas has constructed a title for the good Father's work to suit his own whimsical taste. It is, however, a fair synopsis of the contents of the work, though much extended, in comparison with the original.

VETROMILE (Eugene).
Indian Good Book, made by Eugene Vetromile, S. J., Indian Patriarch, for the benefit of the Penobscot, Passamaquoddy, St. Johns, Micmac, and other tribes of Abnaki Indians. This year, One Thousand Eight Hundred and Fifty-Seven. Old-Town Indian Village, and Bangor. Second edition. 12° *English title*, 1 *leaf*; *Indian title*, 1 *leaf*; *and pp.* 3 *to* 450 + 10 *plates*. *New York*: *Edward Dunigan & brother* (*James B. Kirker*) 1857. 1601

VETROMILE (Eugene).
The Abnakis and their history. Or Historical Notices of the Aborigines of Acadia. By Rev. Eugene Vetromile, missionary of the Etchemins, etc. 12° *pp.* 171. *New York*: *James B. Kirker*, 1866. *Sold for the benefit of the Indians.* 1602

VICTOR (Mrs. Frances F.)
The River of the West. Life and adventure in the Rocky Mountains and Oregon; embracing events in the lifetime of a Mountain-Man and Pioneer: with the Early History of the North-Western Slope, including An account of the Fur Traders, The Indian Tribes, the Overland Immigration, the Oregon Missions, and the tragic fate of Rev. Dr. Whitman and family. Also, a description of the country, its condition, prospects, and resources; its soil, climate, and scenery; its mountains, rivers, valleys, deserts, and plains; its inland waters, and natural wonders. With numerous engravings. By Mrs. Frances Fuller

Victor. Published by subscription only. 8° *pp.* 602 + 13 *plates and* 18 *woodcuts in the text. Hartford, Conn., and Toledo, Ohio: R. W. Bliss & Company,* 1870. 1603

VIDE (V. V.).

American Tableaux. No. 1. Sketches of Aboriginal Life. By V. V. Vide. 12° *New York:* 1846. 1604

VILLAGVTIERRE (Don Juan).

Historia. | de la Conquista | de la provincia de el Itza, | redvcion, y progressos | de la de el Lacandon, | y otras naciones de Indios barbaros, | de la mediacion de la reyno de Guatimala, | a las provincias de Yucatan, | en la America | Septentrional. | Primera Parte. | Escrivela | Don Juan de Villagvtierre | Soto-Mayor. | Abogado, y relator, qve ha sido | de la Real Chancelleria de Valladolid: | y aora relator | en el real, y | supremo consejo de las Indias. | Y la dedica a el mismo real, y supremo consejo. | (*s. p. n. d.*) *Folio. Privilege dated Madrid,* 1701, *title, and engraved title, each* 1 *leaf* + *prel. leaves, unnumbered,* 31 + *text, pp.* 660 + *Tabla,* 17 *leaves.* 1605

[History of the Conquest of the Province of Itza, the reduction and growth of that of the Lacandons, and other savage Indians, of the annexation of the kingdom of Guatemala to the provinces of Yucatan, in North America.]

Villagutierre's relation of the wars, by which the Spaniards conquered the Indians of Yucatan and Guatemala, has from its extreme rarity remained almost unknown. Like most of the Spanish histories of affairs in America, it is more largely devoted to the spiritual than the military conquest of the Indians; yet it is a valuable repertory of facts, relating to the Savages of the peninsula.

Only this *Primera Parte* was ever printed.

VINCENT (P.).

A | True Relation of | the Late Battell fought | in New England, between | the English, and the Pequet | Salvages: | In which was slaine and taken pri- | soners about 700 of the Salvages; | and those who escaped, had their | heads cut off by the Mohocks: | VVith the present state of | things there. | *London,* | *Printed by M. P. for Nathaniel Butter,* | *and Iohn Bellamie,* 1638. 1606

4° Title, reverse blank. 1 leaf. Ad Lectorem, signed P. Vincentius, 1 leaf, reverse blank. A true Relation, 22 pp. The first 10 are unnumbered, and with a running title; the last 12 without running title, and numbered from 11 to 22. The authorship of this exceedingly rare pamphlet, has been attributed to the personage, whose name is signed to the poem addressed to the Reader, with no authority I think beyond that of conjecture. The publishing Committee of the Massachusetts Historical Society thus ascribed it, in their note to the reprint of the Relation, in the Third Volume of their Collections. It is a narrative of the battle with the Pequods, fought by Captains Mason and Underhill, an account of which was written by the last doughty commander, and printed in 1638, under the title of *News from America.* Vincent's Relation is of even greater rarity than Underhill's. This is attested by the fact that the reprint named was made from a mutilated copy, the imperfections of which were uncorrected in the reprint: from the impossibility of finding a perfect one for comparison. The tract was considered of sufficient consequence to induce the printing of another edition with the title: *A True*

Relation of the Late Battle, etc. *Printed by Thomas Harper for Nathaniel Butler and John Bellamie.* 1638, 12° 2 prel. leaves + 8 unnumbered leaves, and 14 lines on the 17th page.

The principal features of difference between the two editions, are summed up as follows: The 4° edition has a total of 26 pp.; the 12° 21 pp. The 4° is printed by M. P.; the 12° by Thomas Harper. The 4° is printed in large, fair-face type; the 12° in small, rude letters.

VINTON (Francis).

Louis XVII. and Eleazer Williams. Were they the same Person. By Francis Vinton, STD. Reprinted from Putnam's Magazine for the Long Island Historical Society. 8° *Two photographs, and pp.* 331 *to* 340. 1868. 1607

Portraits of Williams, and of Shenandoah, an Oneida chief.

VIRGINIA.

The Virginia Historical Register and Literary Advertiser. Edited by William Maxwell. *Richmond, Printed for the proprietor. Six vols.* 8° *Printed* 1848 *to* 1853, *inclusive.* Vol. I. *pp.* 200. II. to VI. 238 *&* 240. 1608

The work was issued as a serial, published quarterly, and complete in 24 Nos. "The Narrative of the Destruction and Captivity of James Moore's Family," occupies pp. 90 to 98, and 147 to 156 of Vol. IV. "The Expedition against the Shawnee Indians," pp. 20 to 34, and 61 to 76, of Vol. V. "Braddock's Defeat," pp. 121 to 141, Vol. V. "The Battle of Point Pleasant, and Capt. Stobo's Narrative of Captivity," pp. 181 to 207, same volume.

VIRGINIA.

Collections of the Virginia Historical & Philosophical Society, [*etc.*, 14 *lines.*] 8° *pp.* 67. *Richmond:* 1833.

[*Sub-title:*] — Memoir of Indian Wars, and other Occurrences; By the late Colonel Stuart, of Greenbrier. Presented to the Virginia Historical and Philosophical Society, By Charles H. Stuart, of Augusta, Son of the narrator. *pp.* 35 *to* 68. 1609

This is the only form in which Col. John Stuart's narrative of the Battle of Point Pleasant ever appeared in print.

VOLNEY (C. F.).

View of the climate and soil of the United States of America: to which are annexed some accounts of Florida, the French colony on the Scioto, certain Canadian colonies, and the savages or natives. Translated from the French of C. F. Volney, with maps and plates. 8° *pp.* xxiv. + iv. + 503 + *two maps and two plates. London: Printed for J. Johnson.* 1804. 1610

Appendix V. is entitled, "General Observations on the Indians or Savages of North America," to which is added, a "Vocabulary of the Language of the Miamis, a tribe settled on the Wabash." This portion of the work extends over pages 383 to 503. The author spent three years in the United States, ardently engaged in collecting facts for his work, principally relating to the state and manners of the Indians, and the climate.

VOLNEY (C. F.).

A view of the soil and climate of the United States of America: with supplementary remarks upon Florida; on the French colonies on the Mississippi and Ohio, and in Canada; and on the aboriginal tribes of America, by C. F. Volney. Translated with occasional remarks, by C. B. Brown. With maps and plates. 8° *pp.* xxviii. + 446 + *two maps and two plates. Philadelphia,* 1804. 1611

The author's interest was particularly excited as a savant, by coming in contact with an aboriginal race in America. Accordingly, his work teems with the most interesting particulars, which he observed or learned, regarding the Indians. He has occupied the whole of Appendix VI. pp. 352 to 429, with observations on the condition, numbers, and characteristics of the Indians, while No. VII., pp. 429 to 446, is devoted to an examination of the structure of the language of the Miami tribes, with a copious vocabulary. The work was the result of three years' residence and travel in the United States.

Von Tempsky (G. F.).

Mitla. A Narrative of Incidents and Personal Adventures on a Journey in Mexico, Gautemala, and Salvador, in the years 1853 to 1855. With observations on the modes of life in those countries. By G. F. Von Tempsky. Edited by J. S. Bell. 8° *Plates and map. pp.* 430. *London:* 1858. 1612

This description of the antiquities of Mitla, and of the savage and unconquered tribes of Indians inhabiting Central America, possesses much to elicit our interest. Yet he is accused by the authors of other works on Central America, with supplying by invention what his investigations failed to discover.

Voyage

A la Guinne et a Cayenne, Fait en 1789 et Annees suivantes. [*etc.,* 13 *lines.*] Suivi d un Vocabulaire Français et Galibi des Noms, Verbes et Adjectivs les plus usites dans notre Langue, comparee a celle des Indiens de la Guiane, pour se faire entendre relativement aux objects les plus necessaires aux besoins, de la vie. Par L . . . M . B . . . . Armateur ouvrage orne de cartes de gravures. 8° *pp.* x. + 400 + *map and* 8 *plates. A Paris. An vi. de la Republique.* 1613

[Voyage to Guiana and Cayenne, made in 1789, and following years: accompanied by a Vocabulary of French and Galibi Nouns, Verbs and Adjectives: most commonly used in our language, compared with those of the Indians of Guiana.]

Chapter vii., pp. 127 to 166, is entitled, "Manners, Usages, and Customs of the Indians of Oronoque." Chap. xviii., "Of the Indians of French Guiana;" and pp. 369 to 400, "Of the Language of the Indians."

Mr. Ludewig says this work is not the account of an actual voyage, but a superficial compilation, made by Louis Prudhomme, from other writers.

Vries (David Pietersz.).

Korte historiael, | ende | Journaels aenteyckeninge, | vom verscheyden voyagiens in de vier | deelen des Wereldts-Ronde, als Europa, | Africa, Asia, ende Amerika gedaen, | Door D. | David Pietersz. | de Vries, Artillerij-Meester Vande Ed: M: | Heeren Gecommitteerde Raden van Staten vau West— | Vrieslandt ende 't Noorder-quartier | Waerin verhaelt werd wat Batailjes by te Water | gedaenheeft: yder Landtschap zijn Gedierte, Gevogelt, | wat soort van Vissen ende wat wilde

Menschen naer 't leven | geconterfaeyt, ende vande Boomchen ende Ravieren | met haer Vruchten. | t' Hoorn. | Voor David Pietersz. de Vries, Artillerij-Meester van't Noorder— | quartier. Tot Alckmaer, by Symon Cornelisz. *Brekegeest.* *Anno* 1655. | 1614

Portrait + Title, one leaf, with coat of arms engraved on reverse + 6 prel. pp. + pp. 1 to 190; copperplate engravings in the text of pp. 9, 15, 60, 74, 76, 79, 125, 131, 139, 154, 156, 159, 168, 170, 174, 175, 177, 186. The last twelve are illustrative of some of the peculiarities of form, habits, or life, of the natives of New Netherlands.

VRIES (David Petersen).

Voyages from Holland to America, A. D. 1632 to 1644. By David Petersen de Vries. Translated from the Dutch, by Henry C. Murphy. 4° *pp.* 199 *and portrait.* *New York:* 1853. 1615

This translation of that portion of De Vries' Journal relating to America, was performed at the suggestion, and printed at the cost, of Mr. James Lenox. Mr. Murphy has also furnished us with a biographical sketch of De Vries, in the Introduction, pp. 5 to 14. Page 15 is a translation of the full title of the original: [Short historical and Journal notes of several Voyages made in the four parts of the World, namely, Europe, Africa, Asia, and America, By D. David Pietersz. de Vries, Ordinance-Master of the Most Noble Lords, the Committed Council of the States of West Friesland and the North Quarter. Wherein are described what Battles he has had by Water: Each Country, its Animals, Birds, kind of Fishes and Savage Men — Counterfeited to the Life, — and the Woods and Rivers, with their Products. Hoorn. Anno 1655.]

In it the infamous treachery of Kieft, the unresisted massacre of the too confiding Indians at Hoboken, the horrible revenge taken by their countrymen, and the consequent desolation of the Dutch Colony, with the cowardice of the miserable governor, are all candidly and lucidly narrated.

De Vries was a witness of the terrible atrocities perpetrated by the Dutch under Governor Kieft upon the Indians, which caused them to become such cruel avengers of their wrongs. Mr. Murphy concludes his excellent preface, with this enunciation of the value of De Vries' Journal: —

"His narratives, where he speaks from personal knowledge, are entitled to the highest credit, for not only do they bear internal evidence of truth, but they are corroborated in many instances by other evidence, and by the records which we have. His relation of the disgraceful and disastrous Indian war, in which he was an actor and friend of the Indians, is the only authentic one extant, of any completeness, except that of the government, and is therefore of great interest and value."

Of its rarity, Mr. Murphy says (in 1853): "The book is one of the rarest to be found, — no printed copy being known to have been extant in this country before the one from which the following translation has been made, and which was obtained by James Lenox, Esq. Twenty years has enabled the bibliopoles of America to gather at least six copies in this country. Mr. Lenox, Mr. Murphy, Mr. Brown, have each a copy, beside the one of which I give the title. Another was sold by Mr. Muller, in 1872, for one hundred and twenty-five dollars. For the one I possess Mr. Lenox paid three hundred dollars.

VANCOUVER (Capt. George).

A Voyage of Discovery to the North Pacific Ocean, and round

the world; in which the Coast of North-West America has been carefully examined and accurately surveyed. Undertaken by his Majesty's Command, principally with a view to ascertain the existance of any navigable communication between the North Pacific and North Atlantic Oceans; and performed in the years 1790, 1791, 1792, 1793, 1794, and 1795, in the Discovery Sloop of War, and Armed Tender Chatham, under the Command of Captain George Vancouver. In Three Volumes. *Large* 4° *London:* 1798. 1616

Although Vancouver lost the opportunity of recording himself as the discoverer of the Columbia, the merit of which fell to the lot of the American Captain Gray, he was the first to inform the public of the peculiarities of some of the Indian Tribes inhabiting the shores of the North Pacific, and the Islands that form the Aleutian Archipelago. But a small portion of these great volumes is, however, devoted to aboriginal affairs, and that is only the baldest narration of incidents; but as they contain the earliest notices of the natives of the countries visited, and several plates illustrative of their life and appearance, they are placed in this catalogue.

WAFER (Lionel).

A New Voyage and Description of the Isthmus of America, Giving an Account of the Author's Abode there, The Form and Make of the Country, [*etc.*, 3 *lines.*] The Indian Inhabitants, Their Features, Complexion, &c., their Manners, Customs, Employments, Marriages, Feasts, Hunting, Computation, Language, &c., With Remarkable Occurrences in the South Sea, and elsewhere. By Lionel Wafer. Illustrated with Several Copper Plates. 12° *pp.* (viii.) + 224 + (xvi.) + *map and* 13 *plates. London: Printed for James Knapton, at the Crown in St. Pauls Churchyard*, 1699. 1617

Title, 1 leaf; dedication, 1 leaf; To the Reader, 3 leaves; map and pp. 1 to 224; Index 7 leaves; Advertisements, 1 leaf. Plates at pp. 28, 102, 140.

WALCOT (James).

The | New Pilgrim's Progress; | or, the | Pious Indian Convert. | Containing | A faithful Account of Hattalo Gelash | min, a Heathen, who was baptis'd into | the Christian Faith by the Name of | George James, and by that means | brought from the Darkness of Paganism, | to the Light of the Gospel, of which he | afterwards became an able and worthy | Minister. | Together with | A Narrative of his laborious and dangerous | Travels among the Savage Indians for their | Conversion; his many Sufferings and miracu | lous Deliverances, and the wonderful Things | which he Saw in a Vision. | Published for the Instruction of Mankind in general, | but more particularly for the Impenitent and Un | reformed. | By James Walcot, A. M. | [*motto*, 1 *line.*] 16° *pp.* 316. *London:* [3 *lines*] MDCCXLVIII. 1618

The Journal of George James, late Hatto Gelashmin, on his pilgrimage among the Natives of South Carolina, and the account of his vision, occupy pp. 253 to 316. The remainder of the volume seems to be the record of the life of the author in South Carolina and Jamaica. Its readers will continue to remain, as in the past, in bewildering uncertainty, whether imagination or experience had most hand in its composition.

WALKER (Adam).

A | Journal | of two campaigns of the fourth regiment of | U. S. Infantry, | in the | Michigan and Indiano Territories, | under the Command of | Col. John P. Boyd, and Lt. Col. James Miller | during the years 1811 & 12. | By Adam Walker, | late a Soldier of the 4th regiment. | 8° *pp.* 143. *Keene, N. H.:* | *Printed at the Sentinel Press,* | *By the Author,* | 1816. 1619

This Journal of a campaign against the Indians and their British allies, although of comparatively late publication, is much rarer than many of the New England imprints of a century and a half earlier. It is the only copy I have met with, either in public or private libraries.

WALKER (C. I.).

The North West during the Revolution. Annual Address before the State Historical Society of Wisconsin. Tuesday Evening, Jan. 31, 1871. By Hon. Charles I. Walker of Detroit. 8° *pp.* 46 + *printed cover. Published by order of the Legislature. Madison, Wis.:* 1871. 1620

Mr. Lyman C. Draper says of this pamphlet: "This Address contains much new matter relative to the British and Indian forays having their origin at Detroit, the headquarters of British influence."

WALLACE (Alfred R.).

A Narrative of Travels on the Amazon and Rio Negro, With an account of the Native Tribes, and observations on the climate, Geology, and natural history of the Amazon valley. By Alfred R. Wallace. With a Map and Illustrations. 8° *pp.* viii. + *map* + 541 + *folding sheet of table of Comparative Indian Vocabularies, and 7 plates and plans. London: Reeve & Co., Henrietta Street, Covent Garden,* 1853. 1621

Beside many incidental notices of personal intercourse with the Native Tribes of the Amazon, the author has given a very complete account of their life and customs in Chapter xvii. pp. 476 to 519, entitled "On the Aborigines of the Amazon." Following this is a folding table of a comparative vocabulary of eleven Indian languages. The Appendix, pp. 521 to 541, is entitled "Vocabularies of the Amazonian Languages," to which subject the author had evidently devoted not a little attention, aided by very respectable learning.

WASHBURNE (Rev. Cephas).

Reminiscences of the Indians. By the Rev. Cephas Washburne, A. M.; many years superintendent of the Dwight Mission among the Cherokees of the Arkansas. With a biography of the author. By Rev. J. W. Moore of Arkansas. And an Introduction by Rev. J. L. Wilson, secretary of foreign Missions. 12° *pp.* 236. *Richmond: Presbyterian Committee of Publication* (1869). 1622

The narration of this devoted missionary to the Indians, reminds us in its details of the most wonderful self sacrifices, told with the utmost self abnegation, and with an utter unconsciousness of their heroism, of the kindred relations of the early Jesuits in America. Like them, he left but the unalternative of martyrdom to success. Like them, the salvation of an abandoned and outcast tribe was his only aim, but unlike them he lived to see its realization. A pioneer of civilization, hundreds of miles beyond its farthest reach, a missionary of the gospel thirty years before the formation of Christian churches, he saw populous cities rise where morasses and forest only spread when he first saw them.

WASHINGTON (Major George).

The | Journal | of | Major George Washington, | Sent by the | Hon. Robert Dinwiddie, Esq; | His Majesty's Lieutenant-Governor, and | Commander in Chief of Virginia, | to the | Commandant of the French Forces | on | Ohio. | To which are added, the | Governors Letter: | and a | Translation of the French Officer's Answer. | With | A New Map of the Country as far as the | Missisippi. | 8° *Map* + *pp.* 32. *Williamsburgh Printed,* | *London, Reprinted for T. Jeffreys, the corner* | *of St. Martins Lane,* | MDCCLIV. [*Price one Shilling*]. 1623

The original edition printed at Williamsburgh, Va., in the same year, is so rare that but two copies are known to exist. This with the London imprint, is only less rare than the other; and is sufficiently curious, as being the first of Washington's official actions recorded in print. It is principally occupied with a relation of his councils with the Indians, west of the Alleghanies.

WASHINGTON (George).

The Journal of Major George Washington, sent by the Hon. Robert Dinwiddie to the commandant of the French forces on Ohio. With a map. *Large* 8° *pp.* 46 + *map. New York: Reprinted for Joseph Sabin,* 1868. 1624

A reprint of the preceding. Of this edition a large and small octavo also were printed.

WASHINGTON (Major).

Major Washington's Journal (of his Mission to the Indians of Western Penn.) 1754. See Livingston Wm., Review of Military Operations in N. A. 1625

WASHINGTON (Capt. John).

Esquimaux and English Vocabulary, for the use of the Artic Expeditions. Published by order of the Lords Commissioners of the Admirality. *Oblong* 12° *pp.* xvi. + 160. *London: John Murray, Albemarle Street,* 1850. 1626

This vocabulary, drawn up in three parallel columns, consists of the dialects of Esquimaux, as spoken at Kotzebue Sound, Melville Peninsula, and in Labrador. It was collected by Captain John Washington from Fabricius' *Dictionary*, Parry's second voyage, Beech and Ross's voyages, with some aid from MS. vocabularies, for the use of the Arctic Expedition, in search of Sir John Franklin.

WA-O-WA-WA-NA-ONK.

Speech of Wa-o-wa-wa-na-onk, an Indian Chief. 12° *pp.* 12. *n. d. n. p.* 1627

The second page announces the place and purport of the speech in these terms: "Speech of Peter Wilson, an educated Indian Chief, to the committee of Friends on Indian Concerns at Baltimore, 10th month, 26, 1848."

WAR (The)

In Florida: being an exposition of its causes, and an accurate history of the campaigns of Generals Clinch, Gaines, and Scott. By a late staff officer. 12° *Map and plan of battle with the Indians. Baltimore: Lewis & Coleman,* 1836. 1628

WARDEN (M.).

(D'une) Dissertation sur l' Origine de l' Ancienne population des deux Ameriques et sur les diverses Antiquites de ce Continent par M. Warden. (*Part of Antiquites Mexicaines.*) See Dupaix. 1629

WARREN (G. K.).

Explorations in the Dakota Country, in the Year 1855. By Lieut. G. K. Warren, Topographical engineer of the "Sioux Expedition." *Washington:* 1856. 1630

8° pp. 79 + vi. + 3 folding maps, one of which is folded in pocket. On pp. 15 to 19 is a category of the Indian tribes occupying the territory explored, with the number of lodges, inmates, and warriors.

WAYNE (James M.)

Speech of James M. Wayne, of Georgia, on the bill to provide for the removal of the Indians West of the Mississippi. Delivered in the house of representatives of the United States, May 24, 1830. 8° *pp.* 16. *Washington:* 1830. 1631

WEBB (J. Watson).

Altowan; or Incidents of life and adventure in the Rocky Mountains. By An amateur traveler. Edited by J. Watson Webb. In two volumes. 12° *pp.* 255 *and* 240. *New York:* 1846. 1632

An English officer, who subsequently became a lord, fell, on his arrival in this country, into the hands of that eminent taft-hunter James Watson Webb. The Englishman, an ardent sportsman, spent five years, from 1832 to 1837, in the wilds between the Mississippi and the Pacific. The journal of his adventures among, and residence with the Indians, was, together with his verbal narrations, edited by his American friend, and these two volumes are the product. Indian life, character, and legends form the staple of their composition.

WEISER (Conrad).

Narrative of a journey, made in the year 1737, by Conrad Weiser, Indian Agent and Provincial Interpreter, from Tulpehocken in the Province of Pennsylvania to Onondago, the head quarters of the allied Six Nations, in the province of New York. Translated from the German by Hiester H. Muhlenberg, M. D., of Reading, Pa. 8° *pp.* 33. *Philadelphia:* 1833. 1633

Number one of the Collections of the Pennsylvania Historical Society.

WEST (John).

The substance of A Journal during a residence at the Red River Colony, British North America; and frequent excursions among the North-West American Indians, in the years 1820, 1821, 1822, 1823. By John West late Chaplain to the Hon. the Hudson's Bay Company. 8° *pp.* viii. + 209. *London:* MDCCCXXIV. 1634

WEST (John).

The substance of a journal, during a residence at the Red River Colony British North America: and frequent excursions among the northwest American Indians, in the years 1820, 1821, 1822, and 1823. Second edition enlarged with a journal of a mission to the Indians of New Brunswick, and Nova Scotia, and the Mohawks on the Ouse, or Grand River, Upper Canada, 1825–1826. By John West, late Chaplain to the Hon. the Hudson's Bay Company. 8° *pp.* xvi. + 326 + *map and 4 plates. Published by L. B. Lesley & Son, London:* MDCCCXXVII. 1635

WESTERN

Scenes and Reminiscences: together with thrilling Legends and Traditions of the Red-Men of the Forest. To which is added several narratives of adventures among the Indians. 8° *pp.* 495 + 6 *plates. Auburn:* 1853. 1636

Another form in which the Protean Schoolcraft manifested himself and his works, with additions by an unknown hand.

WETMORE (Alphonso).

Gazeteer of the State of Missouri. With a map of the State from the office of the Surveyor-general, including the latest additions and surveys: To which is added An Appendix, containing frontier sketches, and illustrations of Indian Character. Compiled by Alphonso Wetmore, of Missouri. 8° *pp.* 382, *plate. St. Louis: Published by C. Keemle,* 1837. 1637

The appendix, pages 281 to 350, is a collection of incidents of border life and Indian biography.

WHEELOCK (Eleazer).

A plain and faithful NARRATIVE of the Original Design, Rise, Progress and present State of the *Indian* Charity-School At Lebanon, in Connecticut. By Eleazer Wheelock, A. M., Pastor of a Church in Lebanon. 8° *pp.* 55. *Boston: Printed by Richard & Samuel Draper, in Newberry Street,* M.DCC.LXIII. 1638

WHEELOCK (Eleazer).

A Continuation of the Narrative Of the State, &c., of the Indian Charity School, At Lebanon, Connecticut; From Nov. 27th, 1762, — to Sept. 3d, 1765. By Eleazer Wheelock, A. M., Pastor of a Church in Lebanon. 8° *pp.* 23. *Boston: Printed by Richard & Samuel Draper, in Newberry Street,* 1765. 1639

In some copies an appendix of one page numbered 25 follows after Finis on p. 23 and the blank 24th page (Dr. O'Callaghan).

WHEELOCK (Eleazer).

A brief Narrative of the Indian Charity-School, In Lebanon in Connecticut, New England. Founded and Carried on by That Faithful Servant of God, The Rev. Mr. Eleazer Wheelock. 8° *pp.* 64. *London: Printed by J. & W. Oliver, in Bartholomew Close, near West-Smithfield,* MDCCLXVI. 1640

Dr. O'Callaghan is disposed to believe that his own copy and that of Mr. J.

C. Brown are perfect with only forty-eight pages, as the word Finis is printed near the middle of the 48th page, on which only eight lines of text appear. There succeeds in mine, however, an appendix paged continuously to the 64th page. The assumption that there was a second edition does not account for the discrepancy in pagination, as No. 4 is that second edition, being an exact reprint in every particular, except the omission of the last eight lines forming the 64th page of the first edition; omitted for no reason, I can conceive, except to prevent the overrunning of the composition, of eight lines beyond upon the 63d page.

WHEELOCK (Eleazer).
A brief Narrative of the Indian Charity-School, In Lebanon in Connecticut, New England: Founded and Carried on by That Faithful Servant of God, The Rev. Mr. Eleazer Wheelock. The Second Edition, With an Appendix. 8° *pp.* 63. *London: Printed by J. & W. Oliver, in Bartholomew-Close near West Smithfield*, MDCCLXVII. 1641

A reprint of No. 3 (issued the year before), in every particular, except that the eight lines forming the 64th page of No. 3 are omitted. (Number 5 of this series, is entitled "Continuation of the Narrative," &c. 8° pp. 145. London: 1769).

WHEELOCK (Eleazer).
A Continuation of the Narrative of the Indian Charity-School, in Lebanon, in Connecticut; From the Year 1768, to the Incorporation of it with *Dartmouth* College, And Removal and Settlement of it in Hanover, In the Province of New Hampshire, 1771. By Eleazer Wheelock, D.D. President of Dartmouth College. Printed in the Year 1771. *n. p.* 8° *pp.* 61. 1642

No. 6 of the Reports of Wheelock's Indian Charity School.

WHEELOCK (Eleazer).
A Continuation of the Narrative of the Indian Charity-School begun in Lebanon, in Connecticut, now Incorporated with Dartmouth College in Hanover in the Province of New Hampshire, (from May 6, 1771 to Sept. 1772). 8° *pp.* 40. *n. p.* 1773. 1643

No. 7 of Wheelock's Reports of the Indian Charity School.

WHEELOCK (Eleazer).
A Continuation of the Narrative of the Indian Charity-School, begun in Lebanon, in Connecticut; now Incorporated with Dartmouth College, in Hanover, in the Province of New Hampshire. By Eleazar Wheelock, D.D., President of Dartmouth College. 8° *pp.* 68. *Hartford: Printed in the year* 1773. 1644

No. 8 of Wheelock's Reports of the Indian Charity School, from September 1772, to September 1773.

WHEELOCK (Eleazer).
A continuation of the Narrative of the Indian Charity-School, begun in Lebanon, in Connecticut; now Incorporated with Dartmouth College, in Hanover, in the Province of New Hampshire. With a Dedication to the Honorable Trust in

London. To which is added An Account of Missions the last year, in an Abstract from the Journal of the Rev^d Mr. Frisbie, Missionary. By Eleazer Wheelock, D.D., President of Dartmouth College. 4° pp. 54. *Hartford: Printed by Ebenezer Watson near the Great Bridge*, MDCCLXXV. 1645

This is the ninth, and last, of the Reports of the Indian Charity School, established by Mr. Wheelock. It was originally termed the Moors Charity School, commencing in 1754, at Lebanon, and in 1771 transferred to Hanover, where it formed the germ of the institution, known as Dartmouth College. Among the first pupils came young Brant, the Mohawk warrior, who afterwards desolated the Wyoming Valley, and sat beside the Mohegan Indian, Samson Occum, who preached the gospel of peace to the same bloody savages. The fruits of the noble and disinterested labors of Mr. Wheelock, were visible among the aborigines for many years after the date of this report. At one time twenty-five Indians were receiving instruction in his school. Honored be the name of Eleazer Wheelock during all time, as one of the wisest and noblest friends of the red man.

WHEELER (Thos. Capt.).

An Historical Discourse, delivered at West Brookfield, Mass., Nov. 27, 1828, on the day of the annual thanksgiving. By Joseph I. Foot. With Capt. Thomas Wheeler's Narrative, now annexed, and additional notices of occurrences in the town, since the first publication of the discourse. 8° pp. 96. *West Brookfield: Published by Merriam & Cooke*, 1843. 1646

This is the second edition of "Captain Wheeler's narrative of an expedition with Captain Edward Hutchinson into the Nipmuck Country, and to Quaboag, now Brookfield, Mass. First published in 1675." The first edition of this narrative of an expedition against the Indians has become so rare that a copy sold in the Boon collection for $175.

WHIPPLE (Lieut. A. W.).

Report upon The Indian Tribes, by Lieut. A. W. Whipple, Thomas Ewbank, Esq. and Pro. Wm. W. Turner. *Washington, D. C.*, 1855. 1647

4° pp. 127 + 41 Illustrations, eight of which are full-page and colored. All of these were drawn by Mollhausen, who subsequently published two volumes of travels, containing much of the matter of Whipple's Report, with, however, great additions of his own personal experience among the Indian tribes of the Plains and Rocky Mountains.

WHITE (Samuel).

History of the American Troops during the Late War under the command of Colonels Fenton and Campbell [*etc.*, 4 *lines*]. The taking of Fort Erie, the battle of Chippewa, the imprisonment of Col. Bull, Major Galloway and the author (then a Captain) and their treatment. Together with a historical account of the Canadas. 12° pp. 107. *Baltimore:* 1830. 1648

The author and his comrades were made prisoners by the Indians. Of their captivity the book gives us a brief account.

WHITE (Elijah).

A concise view of Oregon Territory, its colonial, and Indian relations; compiled from official letters and reports, together with the organic laws of the Colony. By Elijah White, late

Sub-Indian agent, of Oregon (with minute accounts of Indian affairs). 8° *pp.* 72. *Washington:* 1846. 1649

This pamphlet is the record of the first establishment of organized society in Oregon and of the association in that task of the remarkable man who accomplished it. It also contains an account of the establishment of the mission among the Nez Perces and Walla-Wallas, by Mr. and Mrs. Whitman, subsequently so barbarously murdered, and many incidents of the author's association with the Indians.

WHITE (Henry).

The Early History of New England, illustrated by numerous interesting incidents. By Rev. Henry White. 12° *pp.* 428. *Concord, N. H.: Published by I. S. Boyd,* 1845. 1650

This work is a collection of incidents of Indian warfare, captivities of the early colonists, and anecdotes and incidents of their association in peace and war with the aborigines. It was subsequently issued with additional matter under the following title: —

WHITE (Rev. Henry).

Indian Battles: with incidents of the Early History of New England. By Rev. Henry White. Containing thrilling and stirring narratives of battles, captivities, escapes, ambuscades, assaults, massacres, and depredations of the Indians. The habits, customs, and traits of character peculiar to the Indian race. The life and exploits of Capt. Miles Standish. The history of King Philip's war, and personal and historical incidents of the revolutionary war. 12° *pp.* 412. *New York: D. W. Evans & Co., 677 Broadway* (1859). 1651

WHITFIELD (Henry).

The Light appearing more and more to | wards the perfect Day. | OR, A farther Discovery of the present State | of the INDIANS | in | New England, | Concerning the Progresse of the Gospel | amongst them. | Manifested by Letters from such as preacht | to them there. | Published by Henry Whitfield, late Pastor to the | Church of Christ at Gilford in New England, | who came late thence. *London, Printed by T. R. & E. M. for John Bartlett, and are to be | sold at the Gilt Cup, near St. Austins gate in Pauls Church-yard,* 1651. 1652

Small 4° 1 leaf with text on verso signed Joseph Caryl + Title, 1 leaf, reverse blank + 2 leaves Epistle Dedicatory + pp. 1 to 46. Total pp. 54.

This is the fifth in order of publication of the Eliot Tracts. It was reprinted, pp. 100 to 147, vol. 4, 3d series, *Mass. Historical Society Collections.* It also forms No. 3 of Sabin's Reprints, large and small 4° New York, 1865. In this last form, the title has been changed to the following: —

WHITFIELD (Henry).

A farther discovery of the Present State of the Indians in New England, concerning the Progress of the Gospel among them, manifested by letters from such as preached to them then. By Henry Whitfield. 4° *six prel. leaves* + *pp.* 1 *to* 46. *New York: Printed for J. Sabin,* 1865. 1653

This is a reprint of the fifth of the Eliot Tracts known as *Light Appearing.* Some embarrassment has been thrown in the way of the collector and the student, by the change of titles, or rather by the invention of new ones, which is however in some measure remedied by the addition of the original on the fourth page.

WHITTLESEY (Charles).

A Discourse relating to the Expedition of Lord Dunmore, of Virginia, against the Indian Towns upon the Scioto in 1774. Delivered before the Historical and Philosophical Society of Ohio. By Charles Whittlesey, of Cleveland. 8° *pp.* 32. *Cleveland: Printed by Sanford & Co.*, 1842. 1654

WHITTLESEY (Charles).

Fugitive essays, upon interesting and useful subjects, relating to The Early History of Ohio, its Geology and Agriculture, with a biography of the first successful constructor of Steamboats; a dissertation upon the Antiquity of the material universe and other articles, being a reprint from various periodicals of the day. By Charles Whittlesey. 12° *pp.* 397. *Hudson, Ohio: Sawyer, Ingersoll, & Co.*, 1852. 1655

Article vii., pp. 128 to 154, is entitled "Lord Dunmore's Expedition to the Scioto Towns." Article viii., pp. 155 to 179, "Antiquities of America." Article xvi., pp. 377 to 384, "Relation of the Indian Tribes in 1776." Article xvii. "Indian Tribes in Ohio."

WHITTLESEY (Charles).

(Smithsonian Contributions to Knowledge.) Ancient Mining on the Shores of Lake Superior. By Charles Whittlesey. *Washington City: Published by the Smithsonian Institution, April*, 1863. 4° *pp.* 29 + *map, illustrations in the text. New York: D. Appleton & Co.* 1656

WHYMPER (Frederick).

Travel and Adventure in the Territory of Alaska, formerly Russian America, now ceded to the United States, and in various other parts of the North Pacific. By Frederick Whymper. With Map and Illustrations. 8° *pp.* xxx. + 331 + *map and* 37 *plates and cuts. London: John Murray*, 1868. 1657

WILDE (Mr.).

Speech of Mr. Wilde, of Georgia, on the bill for removing the Indians from the east to the west side of the Mississippi. Delivered in the house of representatives, on the 20th of May, 1830. 8° *pp.* 64. *Washington:* 1830. 1658

WILLETT (Colonel Marinus).

A narrative of the military actions of Colonel Marinus Willett, taken chiefly from his own manuscript. Prepared by his son, William M. Willett. 8° *pp.* 162 & *portrait. New York: Published by G. & C. & H. Carvill*, 1831. 1659

Colonel Willett was an eminent partisan officer during the Revolution, serving principally on the frontiers of New York, in campaigns against the Six Nations. The narrative is therefore in great part composed of incidents connected with Indian warfare.

WILLETT (William M.).

Scenes in the wilderness: an authentic narrative of the labours and sufferings of the Moravian Missionaries among the American Indians. By Rev. William Willet. 16° pp. 208. *New York: Published by G. Lane & P. P. Sandford*, 1842. 1660

WILLEY (Benj. G.).
Incidents in White Mountain History: containing facts relating to the discovery and settlement of the mountains, Indian history and traditions, [*etc.*, 3 *lines*,] together with Numerous Anecdotes Illustrating Life in the Back Woods. By Benjamin G. Willey. [*etc.*, 7 *lines*.] 12° pp. 322 + 8 *plates*. *Boston & New York*: 1856. 1661

The author has, with creditable assiduity, collected much of that perishable historical material, which only tradition and family manuscripts preserve even the traces of. Chapters iii., xiv., xv., and xvii., are wholly devoted to the incidents of Indian history and border warfare.

WILLIAMS (Roger).
A Key into the | Language | of | America: | or, | An help to the *Language* of the *Natives* | in that part of America, called | New-England. | Together, with briefe observations of the Cu | stomes, Manners and Worships, &c. of the | aforesaid *Natives*, | in Peace and Warre, | in Life and Death. | On all which are added Spiritual *Observations*, | General and Particular by the *Author*, of | chiefe and Speciall use (upon all occasions) to | all the *English* Inhabiting those parts; | yet pleasant and profitable to | the view of all men: | By Roger Williams | of *Providence* in *New-England*. | *London*, | *Printed by Gregory Dexter*: 1643. 1662

16° Title, reverse blank + To my Deare &c., pp. (xii.) + Directions, (8.) + An Helpe &c., pp. 1 to 197 + The Table, 2 pp. + Licence, signed John Langley, 1 p. (Total pp. 216). This very rare work by the celebrated founder of Rhode Island and Providence Plantations, is not only the first book printed relating to the Indians of New England, but it is the first of a philological character, on the Aboriginal languages north of Mexico except that of Father Sagard. It has been reprinted by the Massachusetts and Rhode Island Historical Societies, and by the Narragansett Club, with notes by J. H. Trumbull. This copy has a note written on a fly leaf: "I had this book from Benjamin Franklin of Philadelphia, minister from the United States of America at the court of Versailles. E. Poor."

WILLIAMS (Roger).
A key into the language of America, or an help to the language of the natives in that part of America called New-England. [*etc.*, *as above*.] 8° pp. 166. *Providence*: 1829. 1663

Vol. 1 of the Collections of the Rhode Island Historical Society.

WILLIAMS (John).
An Enquiry into the truth of the tradition, concerning the Discovery of America, By Prince Madog ab Owen Gwynedd, about the year, 1170. By John Williams. [*Motto*.] 8° *Half title*, 1 *leaf*; *title*, 1 *leaf*; *preface*, *pp*. v. *to* viii.; *An Enquiry*, *pp*. 1 *to* 82; *Appendix*, 2 *leaves*; *advertisement*, 1 *leaf*. *London: Printed by J. Brown, at the Printing Office, Fair Street Horsly-down, &c. Entered at Stationers Hall*, MDCCXCI. 1664

WILLIAMS (John).

Farther observations on the Discovery of America, By Prince Madog ab Owen Gwynedd, about the year 1170. Containing the account given by General Bowles, the Creek or Cherokee Indian, lately in London, and by several others, of a Welsh Tribe or Tribes of Indians, now living in the Western parts of North-America. By John Williams LL. D. [*motto, 6 lines.*] 8° *Half title* + *prel. pp.* ix. + 52. *London: Printed by J. Brown at the Printing-Office.* [*etc., 3 lines.*] MDCCXCII. *Entered at Stationers Hall.* 1665

The propositions of the learned author in favor of the existence of a tribe of Welsh Indians, are so well sustained by veritable evidence, and yet so positively known to be untrue, that it makes us doubt the value of all ratiocination. He adduces the positive testimony of more than twenty persons who had visited, or spoken with them in that language. Of all the conjectures regarding the origin of the Indians, not one has been fortified by a tithe of the absolute evidence of respectable authorities and witnesses Mr. Williams obtained, and yet not a single scholar has been convinced. If such a cordon of impregnable proofs can be thrown around a totally improbable hypothesis, there will be little we cannot doubt and nothing we may not believe.

WILLIAMS (John Lee).

The Territory of Florida: or sketches of the topography, civil and natural history, of the country, the climate, and the Indian Tribes, from the first discovery to the present time, with a map, views, &c. By John Lee Williams. 8° *pp.* 300 + *map and 3 plates. New York: A. T. Goodrich*, 1837. 1666

Pages 152 to 209 are entitled "History," and pages 209 to 300 "Indians." In these divisions will be found a very full account of the wars with the Seminoles.

WILLIAMS (Eleazer).

Good News to the Iroquois Nation. A Tract, on Man's primitive rectitude, his fall, and his recovery through Jesus Christ. By Eleazer Williams. 16° *pp.* 12. *Burlington Vt.: Printed by Samuel Mills, January*, 1813. 1667

This tract in the Mohawk language was written by the suppositious Bourbon prince.

WILLIAMS (Rev. Eleazer).

The Book of Common Prayer, according to the use of the Protestant Episcopal Church in the United States of America. Translated into the Mohawk or Iroquois Language, by the request of the domestic committee of the board of missions of the Protestant Episcopal Church. By the Rev. Eleazer Williams. Revised edition of his former translation. 12° *pp.* 101. *New York: H. B. Durand*, 1867. 1668

This translation is made by the noted Indian missionary, son of a chief of the Caughnawaga Tribe, and a descendant of one of the daughters of the Rev. John Williams of Deerfield, who had been carried away into captivity with her father, and became the wife of an Indian who assumed her name. The missionary Williams became famous from a claim made for him by Mr. Hanson, that he was the son of the unfortunate Louis XVI. who was believed to have perished under the cruel treatment of Simon the Jacobin shoemaker. Many extraordinary coincidences were educed in favor of this hypothesis by Mr. Hanson, and subsequently by the Rev. Dr. Vinton.

WILLIAMS (Rev. Eleazer).

Selection of Psalms and Hymns, according to the use of the Protestant Episcopal Church in the United States of America. Translated into the Mohawk or Iroquois Language, by the request of the domestic committee of the board of Missions of the Protestant Episcopal Church, by the Rev. Eleazer Williams. Revised edition of his former translation. 12° *pp.* 38. *New York: H. B. Durand*, 1867. 1669

This translation of psalms and hymns is usually to be found at the end of the prayers.

WILLIAMS (Eleazer).

Life of Te-ho-ra-gua-ne-gen, alias Thomas Williams, a Chief of the Caughnawaga tribe of Indians, in Canada. By the Rev. Eleazer Williams, Reputed son of Thomas Williams, and by many believed to be Louis XII. son of the last reigning monarch of France, previous to the Revolution of 1789. 8° *pp.* 91. *Albany: J. Munsell*, 1859. 1670

WILLIAMS (John).

See American Pioneer. 1671

WILLIAMS (John).

The Redeemed Captive returning to Zion: or, a faithful history of Remarkable Occurrences in the captivity and deliverance of Mr. John Williams, Minister of the Gospel in Deerfield; who, in the Desolation which befell that Plantation, by an Incursion of French and Indians, was by them carried away, with his family and his Neighborhood, into Canada. Drawn up by himself. Annexed to which, is a sermon, preached by him upon his return. Also, an appendix, By the Rev. Mr. Williams, of Springfield. Likewise, an appendix, By the Rev. Mr. Taylor, of Deerfield. With a conclusion to the whole, By the Rev. Mr. Prince, of Boston. The Sixth Edition. 12° *pp.* 132. *Boston: Printed by Samuel Hall, No. 53, Cornhill*, 1795. 1672

WILLIAMS (John and Mary Rowlandson).

The captivity and deliverance of Mr. John Williams, pastor of the church in Deerfield, and Mrs. Mary Rowlandson, of Lancaster, who were taken, together with their families and neighbors, by the French and Indians, and carried into Canada. Written by themselves. 12° *pp.* 116 *and* 80. *Brookfield: Printed by Hori Brown, from the press of E. Merriam & Co. September*, 1811. 1673

Williams' captivity and deliverance occupy pages 1 to 116, and the captivity of Mary Rowlandson succeeds with a full title and pages 1 to 80, each a complete work of itself, except that the first title announces both works.

WILLIAMS (Stephen W.).

A biographical memoir of the Rev. John Williams, first minister of Deerfield, Massachusetts, with a slight sketch of ancient Deerfield, and an account of the Indian Wars in that place and vicinity. With an Appendix, containing the Journal of the Rev. Doctor Stephen Williams, of Longmeadow during his Captivity, and other papers relating to the early Indian Wars in Deerfield. By Stephen W. Williams. 12° *pp.* 127. *Greenfield, Mass.: Published and printed by C. J. J. Ingersoll,* 1837. 1674

WILLIAMS (John).

The redeemed captive returning to Zion: or, a faithful history of remarkable occurrences in the Captivity and deliverance of Mr. John Williams, minister of the gospel in Deerfield, who in the desolation which befell that plantation by an incursion of the French and Indians, was by them carried away, with his family and his neighborhood, into Canada, drawn up by himself. To which is added, a biographical memoir of the reverend author, with an appendix and notes, by Stephen W. Williams. 12° *pp.* 192. *Northampton:* 1853. 1675

WILLIAMSON (Peter).

French & Indian Cruelty; Exemplified in Life And various vicissitudes of Fortune of Peter Williamson; Who was carried off from Aberdeen in his infancy, and Sold as a Slave in Pennsylvania. Containing The History of the Author's Adventures in N. America; his Captivity among the Indians, and manner of his escape; the customs, dress, &c. of the Savages; military operations in that quarter; with a description of the British Settlements, &c. &c. [*etc., 5 lines.*] The Fifth Edition with large Improvements. 12° *pp.* vi. + 147 + *portrait and map. Edinburgh: Printed for the Author, and sold by him at his shop in the Parliament House,* MDCCLXII. 1676

WILLIAMSON (Peter).

French and Indian Cruelty exemplified, in the Life, and various vicissitudes of fortune, of Peter Williamson, who was carried off from Aberdeen in his infancy, and Sold for a Slave in Pennsylvania. Containing The History of the Author's surprising Adventures in North America; his Captivity among the Indians, and Manner of his Escape; the Customs, Dress, &c. of the Savages; Military Operations in that Quarter; with a Description of the British Settlements, &c. &c. [*etc., 6 lines*]. 12° *pp.* vi. + 150 + *portrait. Edinburgh:* 1787. 1677

WILLIAMSON (Hugh).

Observations on the Climate in different parts of America, compared with the climate in corresponding parts of the other continent. To which is added remarks on the different complexions of the human race; with some account of the Aborigines of America. Being an introductory discourse to the history of North Carolina. By Hugh Williamson. 8° *pp.* viii. + 199 + 2 *plates of Aboriginal fortifications. New York: Printed & sold by T. & J. Swords,* 1811. 1678

WILKIE (Franc B.).
Davenport Past and Present; including the early history, and Personal and Anecdotal Reminiscences of Davenport; together with biographies, likenesses of its prominent men, compendious articles upon the physical, industrial, social and political characteristics of the City; full statistics of every department of note or interest. By Franc B. Wilkie. 8° *pp.* 333. *Davenport:* 1858. 1679

Chapters two, three, and five are entirely devoted to details of the Indian history of the country.

WILSON (Thomas).
The knowledge and practice of Christianity made easy to the meanest capacities or an essay towards an Instruction for the Indians. [*etc.* 12 *lines*]. The fifth edition. By the Right Reverend Father in God Thomas Lord Bishop of Sodor and Man. 18° *pp.* 270. *London;* 1743. 1680

This book, which was written for the Indians of Georgia, has been many times reprinted.

WILSON (Thomas).
Same title, printed for F. & C. Rivington. *London:* 1806.
The eighteenth edition. 1681

WILSON (Marcius).
American History: Comprising historical sketches of the Indian Tribes; a description of America antiquities, with an inquiry into their origin, and the origin of the Indian Tribes: History of the United States, with appendices showing its connection with European History; history of Mexico and history of Texas, brought down to the time of its admission into the American Union. By Marcius Wilson. 8° *pp.* 672. *New York:* 1847. 1682

Pages 16 to 94 are devoted to American antiquities and the Indian tribes.

WILSON (D.).
The life of Jane McCrea, with an account of Burgoyne's Expedition in 1777. By D. Wilson. 12° *pp.* 155. *New York; Baker, Godwin, & Co., printers,* 1853. 1683

In this volume are collected the traditional and historical versions of the massacre of the Allen family, and of Miss McCrea, with little addition of new evidence. Not a little doubt, however, has been thrown upon their correctness by some investigations of Mr. Wm. Stone, the results of which were printed in the *New York Galaxy.*

WILSON (R. A.).
A new history of the Conquest of Mexico. In which Las Casas' denunciations of the popular historians of that war, are fully vindicated. By Robert Anderson Wilson. 8° *pp.* 539. *Frontispiece. London: Trubner & Company,* 1859. 1684

This work, written with a zeal which often degenerates into vehemence, is an arraignment of the Spanish historians, from whom all the current notions of the Spanish invaders have been acquired. With much show of reason, he maintains the unworthiness of their accounts on the following grounds: —

1st. Cortes was an adventurer, a buccaneer, who found his interest in assuming the role of a zealot, to impose upon the Inquisition and the emperor.

2d. The historians from Bernal Dias to Botturino, including Sahagun, Torquemada, and Ixtlilxochitl, being all monks, were all liars, for neither the Inquisition nor the court would permit the unadulterated truth to appear.

3d. The Aztec civilization was a myth, in which the Moorish tinge of its inventor's intellect is clearly apparent, the story of the burning of the historic paintings a necessary falsehood to account for their absence, and those still extant only daubs to impose upon a credulity, which had greedily swallowed the clumsy tale of the miraculous apron of our lady of Guadaloup.

4th. The remains of temples, pyramids, and other structures, convince the author that their builders were Phœnicians and not Aztecs, the latter being a race of savages, and incapable of such monuments of skill and industry.

WILMER (Lambert A.).

The life, travels and adventures of Ferdinand de Soto, Discoverer of the Mississippi. By Lambert A. Wilmer. Steel engravings. 8° *pp.* 532. *Philadelphia: J. T. Loyd*, 1859. 1685

Twelve full-page engravings and fifty wood-cuts inserted in the text, are nearly all designed to illustrate battles with the Indians, or the terrible cruelties inflicted upon them.

This well printed and beautifully illustrated book is written in a style worthy of its subject. The story of De Soto's life is told with a vigor and nervous energy, characteristic of his restless and ambitious career. The great cavalier, chivalrous gentleman, and splendid adventurer, was the only one of the type of courtly and Christian knights who sought for gold and renown on the continent of North America. His wonderful story of great resolve and terrible misfortune, is interwoven with the threads of that ever melancholy history of Indian massacre and defeat. Although scores of Spaniards fall in the wild rush of battle, or in the dense thickets and swamps, it is by thousands that the savages are trampled down before the charge of the Spanish horse, or perish by the murderous culverin and matchlock.

WINNEBAGO INDIANS

From Document No. 229 of the House of Representatives, containing Allegations of Fraud in relation to the settlement of the claims of the Half-Breed relatives of the Winnebagoe Indians, in which case the commission of General Simon Cameron was set aside. The original paper being now on file in the War Department in the City of Washington. 8° *pp.* 88. *Harrisburg, Pa.:* 1839. 1686

This is a record of the evidence of the conversion of the funds, appropriated for the sustenance of an Indian tribe, by a present Senator of the United States.

WINTHROP (Theodore).

The Canoe and the Saddle, adventures among the northwestern rivers and forests; and Isthmiana. By Theodore Winthrop. 12° *pp.* 302. *Boston: Ticknor & Fields*, 1863. 1687

Four pages are devoted to a vocabulary of the Chinook Jargon. The first three hundred pages contain many interesting details of personal observations of Indian life and manners.

WISCONSIN

Historical Society. Collections of the State Historical Society of Wisconsin. 8° *First to fifth annual reports*, 1854 to 1859. *Madison.* 1688

This is one of the noblest collections ever made by any historical society. It is a vast mass of original material, written mostly by border warriors, pioneers, voyageurs, and others who saw the events of which they wrote. By far the largest portion relates to the Aborigines who once occupied the territory. It is to the intelligence and zeal of the learned antiquary, Lyman C. Draper, that the public are indebted for this model of historical collections. It is only to be regretted that the typographical and mechanical labor is so far below the merit of the work.

Vol. I. Contains Lieutenant Gorrel's journal of a mission to the Indians near Detroit in 1761; Haskin's "Legend of the Winnebagoes"; "Early Times in Wisconsin"; "Indian Names of localities in Wisconsin."

Vol. II. Lockwood's "Early Times and Events in Wisconsin, with an account of Wars with the Indians, and descriptions of their customs," pages 98 to 232. "Pioneer Life in Wisconsin, and Petonica Battle Controversy, with account of Skirmishes with the Indians, and strictures on Ford's acct. of Black Hawk War," pages 326 to 414, by Parkison. "Some Account of the Advent of the N. Y. Indians into Wisconsin," by Ellis, pages 415 to 450.

Vol. III. "Early Jesuit Missionaries (among the Indians), and The Indian Tribes of Wisconsin," pages 87 to 138; "The Cass MSS. Abstract of the life and customs of the Indians of Canada, 1723," pages 139 to 177; "Ancient Mounds in Crawford County — Antiquities of Wisconsin," pages 178 to 196. Grignon, "An Indian Trader's Seventy-two Years Recollections of Wisconsin, containing a minute account of the Indians and Traders," pages 195 to 295; "Witherl's Reminiscences of Gen. Wayne, Tecumseh, Capture of Detroit, Battle of the Thames, Death of Tecumseh" etc., pages 297 to 337; "The Chippewas of Lake Superior," pages 338 to 369.

Vol. IV. "Origin of the American Indians," by J. Y. Smith, pages 117 to 151; "Recollections of Wisconsin by Colonel Childs, one of the hardiest frontiersmen who ever lived — whose adventures with the Indians are almost incredible," pages 153 to 196; "The Stockbridge Indians and memoir of John Quincy, Chief of the Tribe," pages 298 to 333. Besides the articles noted, a great amount of incident and short relations and sketches of Indians is given in the volumes.

Wisner (Benjamin B.).

A Sermon delivered before the Society for Propagating the Gospel among the Indians and others in North America, November 5, 1829. By Benjamin B. Wisner. 8° *pp.* 44. — *Report on the Missions among the Indians, pp.* 23 *to* 44. *Boston.* 1289. 1689

Withers (Alexander S.).

Chronicles | of | Border Warfare, | or | a History | of the | settlement by the Whites, | of North-Western Virginia: | and | of the Indian Wars and Massacres, | In that section of the State; | with | reflections, anecdotes, &c. | By Alexander S. Withers. | 12° *pp.* 319 + *Advertisement, one leaf; Contents, four pages unnumbered. Clarksburg, Va.:* | *Published by Joseph Israel,* | 1831. 1690

Of this scarce book, very few copies are complete or in good condition. Having been issued in a remote corner of Northwestern Virginia, and designed principally for a local circulation, almost every copy was read by a country fire-side until scarcely legible. Most of the copies lack the table of contents. The author took much pains to be authentic, and his chronicles are considered by Western antiquarians, to form the best collection of frontier life and Indian warfare, that has been printed.

[Wood (Silas).]

Thoughts on the state of the American Indians. By a Citizen of the United States. 16° *pp.* 36. *New York:* 1794. 1691

WOOD (George W.).

Report of Mr. Wood's visit to the Choctaw and Cherokee Missions, 1855. 12° *pp.* 24. *Boston:* 1855. 1692

WOOD (J. G.).

The Natural History of Man; being an Account of the Manners and Customs of the uncivilised Races of men. By the Rev. J. G. Wood, with new designs by Zwecker Angas, Danby, Handley, etc., etc. Engraved by the brothers Dalziel. Australia, New Zealand, Polynesia, America, Asia, and Ancient Europe. 8° *pp.* 864. *London: George Rutledge & Sons, the Broadway, Ludgate. New York:* 416, *Broome Street.* 1870. 1693

The author of this voluminous treatise upon the customs of Aboriginal Nations has made a copious and generally a judicious selection from works treating upon the peculiar rites, manners, and modes of life of the American Indians. Of the eight hundred and sixty-four pages which comprise the volume, two hundred and thirty-seven pages (513 to 750) are devoted to descriptions and illustrations of the savages of the Western continent and islands. One hundred and twelve engravings of their ceremonies, warfare, weapons, utensils, and dwellings accompany the text.

WOODRUFF (H. N.).

A Sermon, preached at Scipio, N. Y. at the Execution of John Delaware, a native; for the Murder of Ezekiel Crane. August 17, 1804. By the Rev. Hez^h N. Woodruff. Preached and published by request. 8° *pp.* 22. *Albany:* 1804. 1694

The only scrap of historical information this pamphlet vouchsafes, is the statement that John Delaware did not repent the murder of Ezekiel Crane, but "expected to meet and hold a parley with the victim of his wrath, and wants his powder-horn on which his name is graven, as a passport to the World of Spirits."

WORCESTER and BOUDINOT.

The Gospel according to Mathew Translated into the Cherokee language and compared with the translation of George Lowrey and David Brown: By S. A. Worcester and E. Boudinot. [5 *lines in Cherokee Character*]. Printed for the American Board of Commissioners for Foreign Missions. Second Edition. 24° *pp.* 124. *New Echota: John F. Wheeler, printer,* 1832. 1695

WORCESTER and BOUDINOT.

The Acts of the Apostles translated into the Cherokee Language. By S. A. Worcester & E. Boudinot. [2 *lines in Cherokee Character*]. Printed for the American Board of Commissioners for Foreign Missions. 24° *pp.* 127. *New Echota: John F. Wheeler and John Candy, printers,* 1833. 1696

WORCESTER and BOUDINOT.

Cherokee Hymns compiled from several authors and revised. By S. A. Worcester and E. Boudinot. [5 *lines in Cherokee Character*]. Fourth Edition. 24° *pp.* 48. *New Echota: J. F. Wheeler and J. Candy, printers,* 1833. 1697

WORSLEY (Israel).

A view of the American Indians, their general character, customs, language, public festivals, religious rites, and traditions: showing them to be the descendants of the Ten Tribes of Israel. The Language of Prophecy concerning them, and the course by which they traveled from Media into America. By Israel Worsley. 12° *boards, pp.* xii. + 185. *London: Printed for the author, and sold by R. Hunter, St. Paul's Churchyard, and the author at Plymouth, June,* MDCCCXVIII. 1698

WRAXALL (Sir C. F. Lascelles).

The Backwoodsman; or Life on the Indian Frontier. Edited by Sir C. F. Lascelles Wraxall, Bart. With illustrations by Louis Guard, engraved by John Andrew. 12° *pp.* 302, *and* 8 *plates. Boston: Published by T. O. H. P. Burnham. New York: Oliver S. Felt,* 1866. 1699

There is not a word of preface or self-assertion in this book, to indicate that the numerous incidents of border warfare with the Comanches, Wiecos, and other Indian tribes, are only imaginative, but they are told with a freedom from colloquial dramatizing, that gives an air of verity to them. They are perhaps personal experiences, with more or less picturesque coloring.

WRIGHT (Robert).

A Memoir of General James Oglethorpe, one of the earliest reformers of prison discipline in England, and the founder of Georgia in America. 8° *pp.* 414. *London:* 1867. 1700

Much the largest portion of this volume is occupied with a narrative of Oglethorpe's association with the settlement of Georgia, his wise treatment of the Indians, their fidelity and attachment to him, and sketches of their chiefs. It is the record of the means by which one of the most sagacious English governors attached the Indian chiefs and people to his person and interests, by just and considerate dealings.

WYTH (John). (The Natives of Virginia).

Graphic sketches from old and authentic works, illustrating the Costume, Habits, and Character of the Aborigines of America; together with rare and curious fragments relating to the discovery and settlement of the country. 8° 24 *plates from De Bry, with alternate pages of text. New York:* 1841. 1701

XERES (F.).

Relation veridique de la conquete du Perou de la Province de Cuzco nomme Nouvelle-Castile, subjugeê par François Pizarre, Captain de sa majeste l' Empereur, notre maitre. Dédiée a sa majesté l' empereur, par F. Xeres, natif de la tres-noble et tres-loyale ville de Séville; Secretaire du suadit Captaine dans toutes les provinces et les pays conquis de la nouvelle-Castile, et l'un des premiers conquerants de cette Contree. Ouvrage revu et examinee par ordre de Messieurs les inquisiteurs Salamanque 1547. 8° *pp.* 198. *Arthus Bertrand, Paris:* M.DCCC.XXXVII. 1702

[True Relation of the Conquest of Peru, and of the Province of Cusco called

New-Castle; subjugated by Francisco Pizarro, Captain of his majesty the emperor our master. Dedicated to his majesty the emperor by F. Xeres, secretary of one of the first conquerors of that country.]

This very rare work was reprinted by Barcia in his *Historiadores Primitivos.* It was written by one who knew personally the actors in the conquest of the Incas, and witnessed many of the great and sanguinary events which attended that wonderful change of dynasty. He becomes of course the apologist of the invaders, and endeavors to extenuate their deeds of rapine, destruction, and massacre. This edition forms one of the first series of Ternaux-Compans' *Voyages, Relations, et Memoires.*

XIMENES (Francisco).

Las Historias del origen de los Indios de sta provincia de Guatemala, traducidas de la lengua Quiche al Castellano para mas comodidad de los ministros del S. Evangelio. Por el R. P. F. Francisco Ximenez, cura doctrinero por el real patronato del pueblo de S. Thomas Chuila. Exactamento segun el texto Espagnol del Manuscrito original que se halla en la biblioteca de la universad de Guatemala, publicado por la primera vez, y aumentado con una introducion y anotaciones por el Dr. C. Scherzer. A expensas de la Imperial Academia de la Crencias. 8° *pp.* xvi. + 216. *Viena:* 1857. 1703

[The History of the Origin of the Indians of the Province of Guatemala, translated into Spanish, from the Quiche language, as it was communicated to the missionaries. By the Rev. Father Francisco Ximenes. Exactly copied from the text of the Spanish Manuscript, now published for the first time, augmented with an Introduction and Notes by Dr. Scherzer].

The work of Father Ximenes on the Origin of the American Indians, was published by Dr. Scherzer from a copy of the original MS. which he found in the library of the university of Guatemala.

YATES (J. V. N.) and MOULTON (J. W.).

History of the State of New York, including its Aboriginal and Colonial Annals. By John V. N. Yates, and Joseph W. Moulton. Vol. I. Part I. 8° *pp.* xi. + 325. *New York: Published by A. T. Goodrich,* 1824. 1704

The work consists of four parts. History of the State of New York: Part II. Novem Belgam, by J. W. Moulton. New York; 1824. 8° pp. vii. + 330 to 428 + Map. Part III. View of the City of New Orange (now New York), as it was in the year 1673. With explanatory notes. By Joseph W. Moulton. New York: 1825. 8° Folding plate, pp. 40. Part IV. New York one hundred and seventy years ago: with a view, and explanatory notes. By Joseph W. Moulton. New York: December, 1843. Folding plate + pp. 24. Pages i. to xi. are occupied with notes and authorities relating to the aboriginal history of New York. Pages 12 to 101, are included under the running title, "Origin of the Aborigines and ancient ruins," and pages 102 to 125, are devoted to an examination of the question, "Was America known to Europe before Columbus," and pp. 214 to 239 to the history of the New York Bay and River Indians. Nearly the whole volume, parts I. and II., is occupied with a very careful and scholarly resumé of all that is known regarding the Indians of New York prior to 1633.

YOUNG (Thomas).

Narrative of a residence on the Mosquito Shore, during the Years 1839, 1840, & 1841: with an account of Truxillo, and the adjacent Islands of Bonacca and Roatan. By Thomas Young 8° 3 *plates and pp.* iv. + 172. *London:* 1842. 1705

An intimate acquaintance of three years with that queer commonwealth, the Mosquito Kingdom, invented and fostered by the tortuous and incomprehensible motive called British policy, enables the author to give us some new and very interesting views of savage life. The whole volume is occupied with scenes and incidents which strongly portray that of the Caribs, the Poya, the Tronchs and Albatoinasian tribes of Indians. The author has also confined himself to a narration of what he saw, except in one or two interesting relations of Catholic missions among the interior savage tribes, and the martyrdom of the evangelists by them. A vocabulary of the Mosquito jargon fills the last three pages of the book.

ZARATE (D' Augustin de).

Histoire de la De' couverte et de la conquête du Perou. Traduite de l' Espagnol D' Augustin de Zarate, Par S. D. C. *Two Vols.* Vol. I. 24° *pp.* (xl.) + 360 + 14 *plates and* 1 *map.* Vol. II. *pp.* (vi.) + 470. *A Paris, Rue S. Jacques,* MDCCXVI. 1706

A French translation of the history of Zarate, whose early narrative of the Spanish Conquest fully confirms the terrible story of Las Casas. The prints are principally descriptive of the horrible cruelties perpetrated by the Spanish monsters on the Indians.

ZARATE (Don Augustin de).

Histoire de la decouverte et de la Conquete du Pérou, traduite de l' espagnol d' Augustin de Zarate. Par S. D. C. 8° *Two Vols.* Vol. I. *pp.* xxxi. + 317. Vol. II. *pp.* 443. *Paris, imprimé aux frais du gouvernement pour procurer du travail aux ouvriers typograpes. Aout* 1830. 1707

[History of the discovery and Conquest of Peru, translated from the Spanish of Zarate. Printed by the government to furnish employment to the printer.] Zarate filled the office of treasurer general in Peru, from 1543 to 1548. Having noted carefully in his journal, the incidents which occurred within the range of his own observation, he was enabled after his return to Spain, to write his history of the Conquest of the Incas, with great fidelity and clearness. The first volume is divided into four books, of which the first is devoted to descriptions of the natives of Peru, with some brief discussion regarding their origin. The remaining books are occupied with the relations of their conquest.

These volumes form a part of the series of historical works printed by the government of France, during one of her revolutionary paroxysms, to placate the most dreaded class of her citizens.

ZEISBERGER (Rev. David).

The History of our Lord and Saviour Jesus Christ: comprehending all that the Four Evangelists have recorded concerning him; all their relations being brought together in one narration, so that no circumstance is omitted, but that inestimable history is continued in one series, in the very words of Scripture. By the Rev. Samuel Lieberkuhn. Translated into the Deleware Indian Language. By the Rev. David Zeisberger, Missionary of the United Brethren. 12° *pp.* 222. *New York: Printed by Daniel Fanshaw, No.* 20. *Slate-Lane.* 1821. 1706

www.ingramcontent.com/pod-product-compliance
Lightning Source LLC
Chambersburg PA
CBHW032311280326
41932CB00009B/778

9783741197789